AMERICAN ZIONISM
FROM HERZL TO THE HOLOCAUST

AMERICAN ZIONISM FROM HERZL TO THE HOLOCAUST

Melvin I. Urofsky

ANCHOR PRESS/DOUBLEDAY
GARDEN CITY, NEW YORK
1975

Library of Congress Cataloging in Publication Data

Urofsky, Melvin I
   American Zionism from Herzl to the holocaust.

   Bibliography: p. 497
   Includes index.
   1. Zionism—United States. I. Title.
DS149.U76   956.94'001
ISBN 0-385-03639-6
Library of Congress Catalog Card Number 74–19757

For Susan
an ever-changing delight

ACKNOWLEDGMENTS

It is a truism of historical research that while the author alone bears the burden for the shortcomings of his work, many people contribute to its merits, and that is especially true in this instance. The kindnesses shown to me by librarians, scholars, and former Zionist officials not only has put me into their debt; it would have been impossible to explore the multitudinous resources available or begin to understand the labyrinthine convolutions of Zionist history without the assistance they so generously offered.

Mr. Benjamin V. Cohen, Rabbi Israel Goldstein, Mrs. Rose Halprin, Mrs. Charlotte Jacobson, the Honorable Louis Levinthal, Dr. Jacob R. Marcus, Mr. Robert Szold, and the late Bernard G. Richards all took time from their busy schedules to talk to me about their involvement, past and present, in the Zionist movement, and to answer numerous questions about people and events of long ago. A very special debt of gratitude is owed to Dr. Emanuel Neumann, who has been a constant source of encouragement in this study. He spent many hours with me recalling and explaining Zionist events over the past seventy years; he also allowed me to examine his memoirs, and his generosity permitted me to return to Israel in 1972 for further research.

My work in various libraries and archives was greatly facilitated by the co-operation and knowledge of curators and librarians both in the United States and in Israel. I wish to thank particularly Sylvia Landress and her staff at the Zionist Archives and Library in New York, Esther Togman, Rebeccah Zapinsky and Leah Novogrodsky, who made my numerous visits to the Library both profitable and enjoyable. Thanks are also due Helen Goldenberg and Charity Roth of the Interlibrary Loan division of the SUNY-Albany library; Louise Calef of the Weizmann Library in Rehovot; Michael Heymann, director of the Central Zionist Archives in Jersualem, and his associate, Dr. I. Philipp; Miriam Leikind, curator of the Silver Papers at The Temple in Cleveland; Fannie Zelcer of the American Jewish Archives in Cincinnati; Pearl von Allmen, an old friend who for many years now has facilitated my work in the Brandeis Collection at the University of Louisville Law Library; and the staffs of the Library of Congress, the National Archives, the Franklin D. Roosevelt Library in Hyde Park, the New York Public Library, the New York State Library, and the library of the State University of New York at Albany. Dr. Geoffrey Wigoder, director of the Oral History Project at the Hebrew University in Jerusalem, made transcripts of several interviews available, while Rabbi Daniel Jeremy Silver allowed me to read the manuscript memoirs of his father. Travel and photocopying expenses were underwritten by grants from the American Council of Learned Societies and the Research Foundation of the State University of New York, and I am grateful to them for their support. Much of the work done on the *Brandeis Letters* proved valuable to this study, and for its generous support of that project I am grateful to the National Endowment for the Humanities.

A number of friends and colleagues read all or part of this work in earlier drafts, and their comments and criticisms were invaluable in helping me to rethink and rewrite my original work. My longtime friend and colleague on the *Brandeis Letters,* Professor David W. Levy of the University of Oklahoma, provided me with a careful and searching critique of the kind I have come to expect of him. The dean of American Jewish historians, Dr. Jacob Rader Marcus of the American Jewish Archives, helped me avoid numerous mistakes, and to his reputation for kindness to younger historians I can gladly attest. My good friend Jerome Eckstein, chairman of the Judaic Studies Department at SUNY-Albany, provided a commentary that was as enlightening and entertaining as it was thorough, and I am forever in his debt.

In addition, I received helpful comments from Ben Halpern of

Brandeis University, Robert D. Cuff of York University (Toronto), Monty Penkower of Touro College, Henry Feingold of Baruch College, Evyatar Friesel of Hebrew University, Sefton D. Temkin of State University of New York at Albany, Victor R. Greene of the University of Wisconsin—Milwaukee, Marc Lee Raphael of the Ohio State University, and Stephen Berk of Union College. To all of them I am most appreciative for their time and patience. A special note of thanks goes to Loretta A. Barrett, my friend and editor at Anchor Books, whose original interest, encouragement and editorial suggestions contributed so much to this book.

While we were in Israel, my two sons, Philip and Robert, not only made me explain Zionism to them, but constantly delighted and educated us with their comments and perceptions. My wife Susan has been such an integral part of this work from the beginning—questioning my ideas, encouraging my work, and reading the manuscript—that no words could begin to repay her. The dedication is a small token of my love and appreciation for all she has been.

Richmond, Virginia
August, 1974

CONTENTS

AMERICAN ZIONISM
FROM HERZL TO THE HOLOCAUST

PREFACE

To even the most casual observer of the news, recent events in the Middle East have pointed to a special relationship involving the state of Israel, American Jewry, and the United States Government. It is a situation that influences the domestic and foreign policies of two sovereign states, and has created a unique status for the more than six million Jews of this country who comprise the world's largest and most powerful Jewish community. No other ethnic group in American history has had so extensive an involvement with a foreign nation; no other nation relies upon a body of private individuals who are neither residents nor citizens of their land to underwrite a major portion of their budget. American Jews buy Israel bonds, give generously to the United Israel Appeal, lobby their governmental representatives to pursue a pro-Israel policy, travel extensively to Israel (where they are greeted by "Welcome Home" signs), respond immediately to every crisis in that part of the world, and yet maintain passionately that they are Americans first and Jews afterward. It is a curious, puzzling, and yet totally logical arrangement, and this book is an attempt to explore the beginnings of that relationship in the growth and development of the Zionist movement in this country.

Zionism as a modern movement began early in the nineteenth century, but its most modern expression, the idea of re-establishing a Jewish state in Palestine, dates from the publication of Theodore Herzl's *Der Judenstaat* in 1896 and the convening of the First Zionist Congress at Basle the following year. In Europe, where messianic hopes for redemption had always existed in the midst of Jewish misery, the movement soon gained a large following. But until 1914, Zionism in America was a moribund affair, totally shunned by the wealthy, assimilated Jewish community and deriving what little support it had from the Yiddish intellectuals among the recently arrived Russian immigrants. The lack of an anti-Semitic tradition in this country, the economic opportunities available, made many of the newcomers look on the United States as their new Zion, and those with brains and skills and ambitions soon reaped the rewards of their labor. For others, the hardships of life in the urban ghettos left little time or money for a chimerical dream. America offered Jews freedom and opportunity, but in a land built by immigrants, it also demanded their full loyalties. Many Americans, Jew and non-Jew, saw Zionism as some sort of foreign ideology, inimical to true Americanism.

The outbreak of war in Europe in 1914 led many American Jews to the realization that while they had reached a safe and open life, their brethren in Europe were still ravaged by every misery and catastrophe that came along. A new group of men and women assumed the leadership of the Zionist movement, and building upon their experience in progressive reforms, reshaped and redefined American Zionism so that it now spoke and acted in terms that would be effective in the context of this country's social and political requirements. Louis D. Brandeis, Stephen S. Wise, Julian W. Mack, and others legitimized Zionism by Americanizing it. It is the argument of this book that Zionism in America has not been limited to a narrow Jewish experience, but has been part of and reflective of larger trends in the over-all society; that in the United States, the movement has not only been Zionist, but American as well; and that it has enjoyed its greatest successes precisely when its goals and methods have coincided with the dominant trends in the broader society.

I have tried to write an account of how that happened, looking primarily at the history of the movement—its leaders, its successes and failures, its philosophy—but at all times trying to place American Zionism in the one and only context in which these developments make sense, American society in the early decades of the twentieth century. The frame of reference is American history, and the focus is the Jewish experience in this country. If that experience is unique, it is because American history itself is unique, and differed sharply during these years from that of Europe. The balance is not an easy one to strike, but unless we attempt to find it, the richness and variety of American Zionism are lost. Once found, then some of the more recent developments involving Israel, American Jewry, and the United States become more understandable.

This account ends with the Biltmore Conference of 1942, and not with the establishment of the state of Israel in 1948. While 1948 is the logical terminus of the movement in terms of its worldwide experience, 1942 marks a significant cleavage in time for American Zionism. All that happened before—the Americanization of the movement, the struggle with the world organization, the growing anti-Semitism in this country, and the reaction to the rise of Hitler— all this appears, to me at least, of a piece whole unto itself, while the problems and achievements of American Zionism since 1942, and the relation of American Jewry to Israel, form a separate and unified story, but one that must be told at another time. This early period may well be considered the apprentice years of American Zionism, in which it came to grips with the problems posed on the one hand by the need to rebuild Palestine, and on the other by the need to live and function as American citizens. Suffice it to say here that in the later period, a greatly transformed movement, one that had adjusted itself to these needs, became even more intertwined and reflective of the massive changes and events that overtook the United States as a whole, both domestically and in foreign affairs.

As a final note *pro liber sua,* the infinite variety of the Zionist movement, and my own interests, have imposed a certain selectivity on the events and people examined. The left-wing labor Zionists, the religiously orthodox Mizrachi, the Revisionists, and fraternal groups have all played important roles in the movement, but their significance has been more in the development of worldwide ideological positions than on events in the United States. American society has always eschewed the fringes and avoided overly specific ideological positions. Political and social change have reflected the consensus in the middle, and in Zionism as well, the general momentum has been found in the centrist groups that ultimately coalesced as the Zionist Organization of America. Its leaders have been the ones recognized by the American public as the heads of the movement, and its policies have been the ones that determined whether Zionism in the United States prospered or withered. It is here, in the center, that the various trends both of twentieth-century American society and the ages-old longing for redemption came together, and where, I believe, we can best find the clues for understanding that interaction and the legacy it has left us for today.

CHAPTER ONE

"IF I FORGET THEE, O JERUSALEM"

Rising from the desert floor, the mountain, sheared level at the top, dominates the area. To the east the Dead Sea lies shrouded in mist, and beyond that the route Moses and Joshua took in their forty-year march from slavery. To the south, the shimmering sands of the Negev change from purple to gold in the morning sun. Westward and stretching to the north are the Judean hills, in the heart of which stands Jerusalem, the city of David, holy to three of the world's great religions. This is Masada, once the fortress of Herod, and in the year 73 C.E. the last stronghold of Zealot Jews trying to break away from Roman domination. As the 10th Legion tightened its seven-year siege and inexorably threw a rampart up the rear of the mountain, the 960 Jews under Eliezar ben Ya'ir reached a decision. Rather than surrender and be taken into slavery, they would die. Lots were chosen, and those selected began to kill their comrades, their wives, and their children, after which they fell on their own swords. When the Romans reached the plateau, they found only seven survivors: two women and five children.

Not for another nineteen centuries would there be a self-governing Jewish state in Palestine, yet during all those years a dream stayed alive. Although dispersed and crowded into the ghettos of Europe, traditional Jews continued to regulate their lives by the ancient laws of a country they had never seen and did not possess. Their major holidays marked the planting and harvest times, and the more learned among them studied regulations about which seeds could or could not be sown side by side, which trees could or could not be grafted. The great medieval poets and liturgists all placed the idea of redemption second only to the glory of God himself.[1] And every spring at the Seder—the ritual remembrance of deliverance from Egyptian bondage—after the last cup of wine had been drunk, the whole family would fervently declare *"L'shanah haba'ah b'Yerushalayim!"* ("Next year in Jerusalem!").

During these nineteen centuries, Jewish life took on an ominous and dreadful pattern. Fleeing from persecution, Jews would find haven in some new country, welcomed by the local monarch seeking to build up commerce. After a few generations of relative peace and prosperity, the passions and prejudices of Jew hatred would rise again, fed by the jealousy of the poor and the ignorant, and fanned by the ambitions of new groups of would-be merchants or the enmity of the church. Eventually the inevitable edict came: "The Jews must leave—now" or "The Jews must convert—or die." The story was similar in England, in Italy, in Spain. The late seventeenth century found Jews throughout Europe and North Africa, some living in relatively large groups, but many the shadowy remains of once-thriving communities, driven away by implacable Jew-hatred.

It is little wonder that throughout these centuries Jews spoke of themselves as living in *galut,* in exile, and considered their misery and persecution a result of having broken faith with God. After all, God had warned their forefathers that if they defied His will, they would be driven out of the land of Canaan into a life of terror and hardship. They prayed for redemption, but recognized God's justice. Yet they also appealed to His mercy, and turned to the Bible for confirmation of the Lord's promise that some day He would redeem them from their exile. The prophets had pledged that God would not forsake His chosen people, that He would remember the covenant made with Abraham: "I will plant them upon their land, and they shall no more be plucked up out of their land which I have given them, saith the Lord thy God."[2]

It is also not surprising that whenever Jewish fortunes seemed at their lowest, hope for imminent deliverance reached new peaks. Time and again men appeared claiming to be God's messengers, promising to lead the children of Israel back to their ancient land. The most famous of these false messiahs was Shabbetai Zvi. Soon after the Chmielnicki massacres of 1648 and 1649, Zvi heard a "heavenly voice" tell him to lead the Jews back to their own land. Handsome, glib, and princely, he soon ignited the hopes of the masses throughout Europe. A young woman in Hamburg commented in her diary how letters describing Zvi's activities were received in that city: "Most of the letters were received by the Sephardim, who thereupon went to their synagogues and had them read. There they were joined by the Ashkenazim, young and old. The young Portuguese would dress themselves in their best garments. Each one wore a wide green band of silk [the livery of Zvi], and dancing and singing as if it were the Feast of the Drawing of the Water, they would go to their synagogue to read those letters. Some of them, unfortunately, sold all they had—house, land and possessions—hoping to be redeemed any day."[3] In 1666, Zvi went to Constantinople to depose the Sultan, and soon landed in jail. There, to escape death, he converted to Islam, but his followers claimed that the mystical Book of the Zohar required the Messiah to descend to the depths of depravity in order to save the souls of the people. The Zvi movement died almost as quickly as it had appeared, although remnants of it surfaced again in the eighteenth century, led by another would-be savior, Jacob Frank.

Well before the French Revolution, Jewish life had settled into a fairly well-recognized pattern. Prejudicial laws forced Jews to live in restricted sections, the ghettos of the cities or the "pales of settlement" in the country. Depending on the whims of the local rulers, Jews could engage in a variety of occupations, and although there were doctors, lawyers, and other professionals among them, most Jews were small merchants or artisans, trying to eke out a meager livelihood. Salo Baron has pointed out that discriminatory laws did not necessarily make Jews a pariah people, but that in many ways the social and legal arrangements of the premodern state enabled the Jews to exercise a large measure of legally secured autonomy. In religion, education, and judicial and fiscal matters, Jews for the most part governed themselves. They created a society within and apart from the larger Gentile society, one in which they could carry out the precepts of Torah and Talmud, and govern themselves on most matters free from the arbitrary interference of state officials.[4]

Life in the *shtetls* was not easy, and there was always the fear of a *pogrom* or some official decree raising taxes or imposing some new restriction. But within the ghetto, a thriving Jewish communal structure existed, with its own social strictures, its own schools and courts, its own devices for helping one another. The Jew knew who he was and where he stood in relation to his fellow Jews and the Gentile society. Even as he prayed for a return to Zion, he could count on the everyday stability of a life governed by Jewish custom and authority.[5]

The rationalist enlightenment of the eighteenth century and the nationalist movements of the nineteenth destroyed much of this stability and unleashed the forces that ultimately emerged as modern Zionism. The secularist drive to establish a Jewish state resulted from the grafting of these two forces onto the ages-old religious yearning for Zion. Yet Jews also suffered from the contradictions inherent within these two movements. The rationalist force that released Jews from second-class status also destroyed the stability and security of a separate communal life, at least in western Europe, while the nationalist impulse also gave rise to the irrationality that in the twentieth century exterminated six million human beings.

The Enlightenment, with its commitment to reason and its abhorrence of prejudice, found discrimination against the Jews senseless. Anticlerical on the one hand and self-consciously tolerant on the other, the *philosophes* could not justify persecution of a people whose only sin lay in their desire to worship God in a different manner.*

---

* Many of the *philosophes*, notably Voltaire, were anti-Semitic, but on an intellectual plane. They demanded the abolition of all prejudicial legislation. Some hoped that by freeing the Jews, they could ultimately convert them.[6]

Emancipation of Jews from legal and social restrictions was not central to the over-all philosophy of the Enlightenment, but merely one item in the grand social scheme of the *philosophes*. In their assault on the medieval mind and society, however, they determined to free the Jews.

The French Revolution not only overturned the *Ancièn Regime,* it upset all of the social relationships built up in the preceding centuries. It suddenly unlocked the doors that had kept Jews separate from the main society, and invited them to come in. But in doing so, it required that Jews assume the burdens and obligations as well as the rights and opportunities that membership in the state implied. They would have to forsake allegiance to all countries save that of their citizenship, and obey only the laws of that nation. In 1807, Napoleon decided to pose the question to a Sanhedrin (high court) of rabbis and Jewish notables: "Would the Jews, once emancipated, be unreservedly loyal to the state?" The assembly shouted its loyalty to France, and took the fateful step of proclaiming that the civil laws of the state overrode contrary proscriptions of Jewish religious law and ritual. The rabbis did draw the distinction, however, that they were only giving up the political law of Judaism, since religious laws "are, by their nature, absolute and independent of circumstances and time." In the everyday world, however, the Jew would be a loyal citizen of the secular state in which he lived.

After a brief period of hesitation, French Jews rejoiced in their new freedoms and grew zealous in their loyalty to France. As Enlightenment ideas spread, other countries also emancipated their Jews, and by the 1870s anti-Jewish regulations had all but disappeared in Western Europe. The Jews entered into the cultural, political, and economic mainstreams of their countries, founding great merchant and banking houses, entering parliaments and cabinets, writing concertos and secular poetry. But as Robert Alter has pointed out, the freedom from the restrictive practices of the inbred ghetto and from the state were offset by a partial loss of self-identity and protection within the *kehillah,* the Jewish community.[7] The social structure based on strict adherence to Torah had protected Jewish life through the centuries, but it had also insulated Judaism from external developments. Now that Jews moved outside the ghetto walls, they perceived a disparity between a religion tied to an ancient society and the need to function in a modern state. For some this trauma led to a rejection of Judaism entirely, while others, overwhelmed by the demands of their new status, retreated in panic into an even more isolated existence.

Most Western Jews, however, tried to find a midpoint between the needs of their religion and their civic obligations and duties. In the late eighteenth century, a Jewish Enlightenment, the *Haskalah,* developed. The *Maskilim,* the scholars who led this movement, hoped to win full civic rights for Jews, to raise their standard of living, and most importantly, to bring about a Hebraic renaissance that would insure Judaism a full place among the enlightened peoples of the world. The *Maskilim* undertook to write, both in Hebrew and in secular languages, books on religious as well as nonreligious topics. They tried to make their fellow Jews aware of the intellectual currents of the times, and they wanted Jewish children to study things other than the Bible and Talmud. While the very traditional considered these ideas heretical, those Jews trying to find their place in a new world supported their efforts.[8]

While the *Maskilim* labored to modernize secular learning, a number of German rabbis began working to change Judaism's ritualistic and theological trappings. For Abraham Geiger and the other founders of the Reform movement the vitality that had marked ancient Judaism had atrophied during the rabbinic age and petrified in Talmudic dictates. In order for their religion to cope with the modern world, for it to have real meaning to current generations, Judaism needed to recapture the spirit of change that it had lost. To save Judaism it would be necessary to modernize it, to tear it away from what they considered the dead hand of an outmoded theology. Reform Judaism, as it came to be called, sought to make religion relevant to the modern world, to make Jewish practices seem less bizarre compared to Christian worship. Gradually they introduced the vernacular into services and modified or abolished some ritual laws covering daily practices. The German reformers denied especially the idea of exile; rather they interpreted the dispersion from Palestine as part of a mission to teach the ethical principles of Judaism and the knowledge of God to other nations. Again, the freedom that

Haskalah and Reform brought to newly emancipated Jews was purchased at the expense of the security and stability of the old ways.

The nineteenth century also gave birth to nationalism, the most powerful of modern political movements, and saw the map of Europe rearranged as small principalities gave way to large nation-states. But the growth of nationalism also saw the romanticist retreat from the nationalism and universalism of the Enlightenment. Proponents of nationalism began to appeal to an alleged "national soul," one that bound past, present, and future generations together. Heinrich von Treitschke's statement that "the evolution of the State is, broadly speaking, nothing but the necessary outward form which the inner life of a people bestows upon itself" required an almost mystical worship of the state.[9]

Under the emancipation Jews had been encouraged to be part of the larger society. Nationalism, on the other hand, said that Jews could never be part of society. "True patriotism," according to the historian Fustel de Coulange, "is not love of the soil, but love of the past, reverence for the generations which have preceded us."[10] Jews had been excluded from those past generations, and therefore could not be part of the present society. At the very time that Jews were taking full advantage of their new-found freedom and opportunity, nationalist writers castigated them as a people who would never be real citizens of any state. Goethe wrote that Jews could not be part of a civilization whose origins they negated, while Fichte argued against allowing Jews full citizenship because they would always be a state within a state. One radical solution, proposed by Hundt-Radowski, was to eliminate the Jews, and in order not to disturb public order, he proposed the castration of all Jewish males, the sale of females to bordellos, and the disposal of children to the British for slaves in their overseas plantations.[11] Since much of the nineteenth century was in reaction to the Enlightenment, so the emancipation of the Jews became identified with everything the foes of rationalism despised. "Thus the Jewish Problem," as Ben Halpern concluded, "posed in the clear light of eighteenth-century Enlightenment as an issue requiring rational solution, continued to be kept alive by the anti-Semitic irrationalism of the nineteenth century, which, in the twentieth, sought to bring it to a final inhuman solution."[12]

The last remaining bars to full equality for Jews in England, Germany, and Italy fell in the 1850s and 1860s, and a surge of nationalism soon led to unification of Germany and Italy. Most Jews looked, not for a return to Zion, but toward assimilation or religious reform. Yet within the fragmented Jewish community, torn between the past and the future, a tiny handful of men began to apply the ideas of the *Haskalah* and the emotions of nationalism to the "Jewish Problem," and for them the solution lay in a reconstituted Jewish homeland in Palestine. Yet as Jews, religion and nationality were so welded together that the spiritual and political parts could not be separated. Zionism inevitably developed as a form of religious nationalism.

II

In the eighteen centuries after the Roman destruction of the Second Temple, there had been numerous proposals to resettle the Jews in Palestine. Nearly all of the pseudomessianic movements called for a return to Zion, but many secular schemes were also advanced. Oliger Paulli, a Danish merchant, submitted elaborate plans to William III of England, Louis XIV of France, and other European monarchs in 1695. An anonymous French Jew published a broadside in 1798 pleading for the restoration of a Jewish nation, a document that allegedly prompted Napoleon, in his Syrian campaign, to call for the Jews to rally behind him "in order to re-establish ancient Jerusalem."[13] In the eighteenth and nineteenth centuries, a number of Christian groups advocated the return of Jews to Zion as a precondition for the second coming of Christ, although Jews, for the most part, looked at such would-be allies with more than a modicum of suspicion.

Much of this proto-Zionist agitation centered in England, home to several millenarian societies, and involved leading political figures and novelists. In 1838 and again in 1840, Lord Shaftesbury urged wide-scale Jewish settlement in the Holy Land under protection of the major powers. Benjamin Disraeli, later Lord Beaconsfield, pleaded for restoration in several of his novels. In *David Alroy,* he has the high priest say: "You ask me what I wish: my answer is, the Land of Promise. You ask me what I wish: my answer is, Jerusalem. You ask me what I wish: my answer is, the Temple, all we have forfeited, all we have yearned after, all for which we have fought, our beauteous country, our holy creed, our simple manners, and our ancient customs."[14] An even more passionate plea appeared in George Eliot's *Daniel Deronda.*

By the 1850s, isolated Jewish writers on the Continent also called for redemption in Zion. Although much of their work anticipated more modern Zionist arguments and proposals, their appeals went largely unnoticed until rediscovered decades later. Among these forgotten proto-Zionists were Judah Alcalay (1798–1878), Zvi Hirsch Kalischer (1795–1874), and Moses Hess (1812–75).

Alcalay served as the Sephardic rabbi in Semlin, Serbia, not far from where the Greeks had recently won their independence from Turkey. Other national groups, including the Serbs, had already begun agitating against the Turks, and talk and ideas about freedom and restoration filled the air. In 1834, Alcalay published a small pamphlet proposing creation of Jewish colonies in Palestine. Although this idea contradicted orthodox belief that ultimate redemption would come only through God's miraculous intervention, Alcalay claimed that the holy texts justified self-redemption.

A revival of the Blood Accusation* against the Jews of Damascus in 1840 aroused the indignation of Jews and many Christians all over the world, and propelled Alcalay to the conviction that only in Palestine could his people find security and freedom. From then on, a constant stream of books and articles flowed from his pen urging self-redemption. He thought the Turks might be willing to sell Palestine, and called for a "Great Assembly," the creation of land and donation funds, and the floating of a national loan, all of which would later be realized in the Zionist movement.[15]

---

* In the Middle Ages Jews were accused of killing Christian children prior to Passover, so they could mix their blood into the dough of matzoth, and also drink blood in the traditional four cups of the Seder Service.

Where Alcalay left nothing concrete to show for his efforts, Rabbi Zvi Hirsch Kalischer of Posen did prompt some practical work in the Holy Land. Like Alcalay, the Ashkenazic Kalischer also believed in self-redemption, and as early as 1836, he appealed to the Berlin branch of the Rothschild family for help in reclaiming Palestine. Kalischer's most important work, *Derishat Tzion* (Seeking Zion) appeared in 1862, and proposed a colonization society. This led to the purchase of land on the outskirts of Jaffa in 1866 and the founding of an agricultural school in 1870. Little more was done, however, and Kalischer, despite his reputation as a Talmudic scholar, found his proposals bitterly denounced by pietists who claimed that tilling the soil would lead Jews away from the study of the Torah.

Alcalay and Kalischer spoke primarily to the Jews of eastern Europe, who for the most part remained untouched by either enlightenment or nationalist ideas. In western Europe, however, Moses Hess fared no better. In 1840, commenting on the Damascus affair, he wrote: "We shall always remain strangers among the nations; these, it is true, will grant us rights from feelings of humanity and justice; but they will never respect us so long as we place our great memories in the second rank, but in the first the principle, *ubi bene, ibi patria* (where it is well, there is our country)." His great work, *Rome and Jerusalem* (1862), laid down nearly all of the premises and proposals that Herzl would popularize four decades later. He differed from Alcalay and Kalischer in that where they started from religious motives, Hess, one of the early German socialists, based his proposals on secular arguments. But he too made little impact. Abraham Geiger, the leader of German Reform Judaism, contemptuously referred to Hess as an outsider who "after bankruptcy as a Socialist and all kinds of swindles wants to make a hit with nationalism." Few socialists and liberals knew anything about Hess's book, while those who did read it tended to dismiss it as a romantic chimera.[16]

Most assimilationist Jews believed that a cosmopolitan rationalism would be the best guarantee of Jewish welfare. Only by escaping from the past would Jews gain the rights and opportunities that the new society had to offer. This rosy view of man's progress was cruelly shattered in 1881 when a vicious wave of violence swept across Russia, followed by a series of harsh anti-Semitic laws. Under the relatively enlightened policy of Czar Alexander II, anti-Jewish restrictions had been loosened; his death, falsely attributed to Jewish revolutionaries, brought to power his reactionary son, Alexander III. With official encouragement, *pogroms* broke out in Odessa in the spring, and quickly spread across Russia in the next two years. High Russian officials openly proclaimed the goal of ridding Russia of its Jews: one third by conversion, one third by emigration, and the rest by starvation. For a while, it seemed as if the new policy would be successful, as hundreds were killed and thousands fled their homes.

At a terrible cost, Russian-Jewish intellectuals learned that rationalism by itself would not relieve the plight of their people. More and more they turned to the idea that the best thing they could hope for in strange lands was toleration. Many turned to socialism, but others began to proclaim true freedom for Jews would require a homeland of their own. The most important statement of this new attitude, and in a sense the beginning of modern Zionism, can be found in the writings of an assimilated Russian physician, Leo Pinsker (1821–91), stunned out of his complacency by the brutality and mindlessness of the *pogroms*. Even as the violence raged, Pinsker began to analyze the Judeophobia he saw all around him. He considered it a psychic aberration, one passed down from generation to generation for two thousand years. But where Jewish intellectuals had agreed that enlightened rationalism would break this chain, Pinsker condemned such efforts as futile: "Against superstition even the gods fight in vain."[17] Painfully, Pinsker turned his back on assimilation, and in a pamphlet tellingly entitled *Auto-Emancipation* (1882), he called upon his fellow Jews to liberate themselves.

Pinsker asserted that Jews could not then be considered a nation. The Jewish people "lacks most of those attributes which are the hallmark of a nation. It lacks that characteristic national life which is inconceivable without a common language, common customs, and a common land. The Jewish people has no fatherland of its own, though many motherlands; it has no rallying point, no center of gravity, no government of its own, no accredited representatives. It is everywhere a guest, and nowhere at home." Under such conditions, the emancipation offered by the Gentile nations would never raise their real status. True equality would come only when the Jews had a land of their own, only when they became a real nation living on their own soil. To achieve this end, Pinsker proposed a congress of Jewish notables, who would define common goals for the attainment of a Jewish homeland,* raise money, and take the necessary practical steps toward those goals.[18]

Pinsker's thesis was indeed revolutionary. He raised a strong voice against several generations of assimilationist argument, and declared that anti-Semitism would never be erased by reason, no matter what liberties were accorded them, Jews would never be fully accepted, equal citizens. His pamphlet touched an immediate chord of response among Russian Jewry, where traditionalist resistance to Enlightenment ideas had always been strong. By declaring emancipation bankrupt, and urging Jews to look to themselves for redemption, he made possible the connection between proto-Zionist nationalism and the traditionalism of eastern European Jewry.[19]

Pinsker's appeal fell on fertile ground. In the 1860s and 1870s several Hebrew periodicals had gained a substantial circulation in eastern Europe. Peretz Smolenskin (1842–85) had already begun to espouse resettlement of Palestine in the pages of his influential monthly, *Ha-Shahar* (The Dawn). One of its regular contributors, Moshe Leib Lilienbaum (1843–1910), like Pinsker, had been an assimilationist until the shock of the *pogroms* led him back to his people. After one of the riots he wrote in his diary: "I am glad I have suffered. At least once in my life I have had the opportunity of feeling what my ancestors felt every day of their lives. Their lives were one long terror, so why should I experience nothing of that fright which they felt all their lives? I am their son, their sufferings are dear to me, and I am exalted by their glory."[20] Among cultured Jewish families the talk of Palestine was constant. Chaim Weizmann recalled that as far back

---

* Pinsker never used the word "state," but spoke of a "home" or a "colonist-community" (*Kolonistengemeinwesed*).

as he could remember, his father's household "was steeped in rich Jewish tradition, and Palestine was the center of the ritual, a longing for it implicit in our lives. Practical nationalism did not assume form until some years later, but the 'Return' was in the air."[21]

Representatives of several Palestinian societies met in Kattowitz, Prussia (now Poland), in November 1884, under the chairmanship of Pinsker. While he himself had never mentioned Palestine specifically as the Jewish homeland, the delegates, who reflected the mood of the common people more accurately than did the assimilated doctor, insisted on a return to the ancient land, and to stress this point adopted the name Hoveve Zion (Lovers of Zion). In the next dozen years, the Hibbat Zion (Love of Zion) movement spread throughout Europe, with societies established as far away as the United States. Pinsker chaired the Odessa Committee, as the governing body became known, until his death in 1891. The various groups established a few colonies and helped to popularize the idea of settlement in the Holy Land. Under their influence, the first group of European colonists moved to Palestine.

Led primarily by intellectuals who opposed the way of life spawned in Western Europe by the emancipation, Hibbat Zion sought to restate the older Jewish messianic idea in a form compatible with modern needs. Men like Rabbi Samuel Mohilever (1824–98) worked diligently to persuade the orthodox that self-redemption did not conflict with pietist principles, and to convince the agnostic intellectuals that greater sensitivity to the Jewish heritage would make their task easier.

The Hoveve Zion, however, were not Zionists. They sought to establish colonies, and did not consider themselves a movement to redeem all Israel. Hesitant as to goals and methods, they never articulated a consistent philosophy, and later drew back in confusion from the political implications of Herzl. Nahum Sokolow, who moved from Hibbat Zion to leadership in the Zionist organization, admitted that had it not been for the Hoveve Zion, there would have been no place for the new Zionism. "They were our teachers, and we owe them thanks. They showed us ways which we never knew before—the ways to settle Eretz Yisroel."[22]

Nevertheless, the Hoveve Zion did launch the first *aliyah,* the first wave of modern immigration from Europe to Palestine. Between 1882 and 1903, almost twenty-five thousand Jews made their way to the Holy Land. Inspired by Pinsker, a group of Jewish students at Kharkov University formed a society dedicated to going to Palestine as *chalutzim* (pioneers). They adopted as their motto the call of the prophet Isaiah: *"Bet Ya'akov L'chu V'nelcha"* ("O House of Jacob, come ye and let us go forth"), and took the name BILU, made up of the first letters of the verse. The Biluim formed the cutting edge of Hibbat Zion, the young men and women who translated into action the lofty ideals of the movement.[23] The initial group of fourteen landed in Jaffa in June 1882, and labored in the first modern Jewish settlement in Palestine, Rishon L'Tziyon (First in Zion).

The Biluim ran into numerous obstacles. Farming in hot, arid Palestine was quite different from tilling the soil in the fertile Ukraine. Moreover, most of the *chalutzim* had been clerks and students before emigrating, and they found the adjustment to continuous hard physical labor extremely difficult. One of the settlers at Rishon L'Tziyon kept a diary, and his entry for August 21, 1882, is revealing: "It is already ten days that I have not written a word. It has been physically impossible to do so. My hands are covered with blisters and bruises. I cannot straighten out my fingers. And in Russia I used to dream that I would be able to work eight hours a day and devote the rest of the time to intellectual pursuits! How can the mind entertain any thoughts here when your back is broken, when you are so dreadfully tired, and when upon your return from work you have but one desire, to eat your supper hastily and throw yourself upon your bed and go to sleep."[24]

They also faced hostility from the Jews of Jerusalem, who saw the Biluim as contenders for the charity monies (*Halukkah*) sent each year from abroad to support the religious communities in Palestine. They also feared the newcomers as subversive of orthodox principles. There was not a single pair of *Tefilin* (phylacteries) in all Rishon L'Tziyon, the rabbis complained; worse yet, young men and women danced together. "It would be preferable that the land of our forefathers should be again an abode of jackals than become a den of iniquity." It would be many years before the ultra-orthodox thought any more kindly about the "Russian anarchists."[25]

Somehow, the Biluim managed to hold on, to learn the proper farming techniques, and to protect their meager holdings against the petty thievery of neighboring Bedouins. In 1884 they founded a second settlement at G'dera, and with continued help from Hibbat Zion societies, as well as a timely grant from Baron Edmond de Rothschild, they managed to succeed. Although few in number and their concrete achievements limited, the Biluim had enormous historical impact. They proved that Jews from European ghettos could once again be farmers in the land of their ancestors.

III

Just as the shock of *pogroms* turned Russian Jews toward the idea of self-redemption in Palestine, so in 1895 another great trauma undermined the confidence of many Western Jews in the progress of rationalism. Alfred Dreyfus, a Jewish captain assigned to the French General Staff, was accused of spying for Germany. Found guilty by a military court, he was publicly degraded and sentenced to life imprisonment on Devil's Island. In 1896, the military tried to suppress evidence which identified the real culprit as Major Ferdinand-Walsin Esterhazy. The pro-Dreyfusards forced the General Staff to try Esterhazy, but despite overwhelming evidence of his guilt, the military tribunal quickly acquitted him. The travesty of this "trial" stirred up a storm throughout France. Emile Zola penned his famous *J'accuse* in 1898, charging the military with anti-Semitism, and had to flee to England to avoid incarceration for libel. Anti-Jewish riots erupted across the country, and the Army moved to purge Dreyfus defenders from its ranks. A second trial led to a reduced sentence for Dreyfus, but in 1899 he received a pardon from the President of the Republic, and seven years later a final military hearing completely exonerated him.

The fact that such blatant anti-Semitism existed in Republican

France, home of the Enlightenment and Emancipation, shook the faith of many Jews in assimilation. For one reporter covering the trial, the public humiliation of Dreyfus at the École Militaire—stripped of his epaulets and drummed out of the gate while a howling mob screamed *"à bas les Juifs!"*—marked a turning point not only in his life but in the course of Jewish history. At the end of the degrading ceremony, Theodore Herzl turned to one of his colleagues and asked: "Why are they [the crowd] so delighted? The traitor deserved his fate, and he received no more punishment than he merited. But how can they find such intense joy in the suffering of a human being? Granted he is a traitor—but a traitor is still a man." His fellow reporter replied: "No, the French do not feel he is a man. They see him not as a human being but as a Jew. Christian compassion ends before it reaches the Jew. It is unjust—but we cannot change it. It has always been so, and it will be so for ever."[26] Herzl had come to Paris as a highly successful journalist and assimilated Jew; he left the trial to become the founder of modern Zionism and of the Jewish state.

Born in Pest, Hungary, in 1860, Herzl had attended a Jewish elementary school, but for the most part, his education reflected the ideas of emancipated, assimilated German Jewry. He completed law studies in Vienna, but found his calling as a journalist, writing short stories and *feuilletons* on the nature of modern man; he also wrote several successful plays. From 1891 to 1895 he served as Paris correspondent of the Vienna *Neue Freie Presse,* one of the most influential liberal papers in Europe. An astute reporter, he early noticed the rising tide of anti-Semitism, and beginning in 1892 wrote occasional essays on the subject; but the Dreyfus trial left Herzl convinced that the problem would not be solved through assimilation.

In the summer of 1895 Herzl began devoting more and more of his time and energy to a study of the Jewish problem. He wrote, and then rewrote, an "address to the Rothschilds," in which he hoped to enlist their support. He read these drafts to Jewish leaders in Vienna, Paris, and London, but only convinced one, Max Nordau (1849–1923), who became Herzl's right-hand man for the next eight years. Finally, after being rebuffed by the Rothschilds, Herzl decided to present his ideas to the public. He expanded his "address," and in February 1896, he published a thin volume entitled *Der Judenstaat* (The Jewish State). An immediate sensation, the book was quickly translated into dozens of languages; from its publication can be dated the rise of modern Zionism.

The tone of *The Jewish State* is strikingly detached and modern. This is no ghetto Jew talking, but a man of the world, and his ideas owed more to the writings of Hegel than to the books of the Bible. The main theses can be summarized as follows: While the Jews culturally and psychologically constitute a people, they lack the physical attributes of nationhood. This abnormality—statelessness—is the root cause of Jewish suffering and anti-Semitism. Unless the Jews could defend themselves and find expression for their inner nature, Jewish civilization and culture would be in danger of destruction. The logical means to achieve this would be a national state for the Jews, one that would guarantee Jewish survival and a continuing Jewish contribution to the world's culture.

Herzl dismissed emancipation as foredoomed to failure because of the unique nature of Judaism. "The Jewish question still exists. It would be useless to deny it. It is a remnant of the Middle Ages, which civilized nations do not even yet seem able to shake off, try as they will. They certainly showed a generous desire to do so when they emancipated us. The Jewish question exists wherever Jews live in perceptible numbers. Where it does not exist, it is carried by Jews in the course of their migrations. We naturally move to those places where we are not persecuted, and there our presence produces persecution. This is the case in every country, and will remain so . . . till the Jewish question finds a solution on a political basis."[27] Yet this very misery could be harnessed to achieve the end of a Jewish state, if only the Jews themselves would recognize the need for it. "The Jews have dreamt this princely dream throughout the long night of their history. 'Next year in Jerusalem' is our ancient watchword. It is now a matter of showing that the vague dream can be transformed into a clear and glowing idea."[28]

Despite this reference to Jerusalem, there is no clear identification of any country in Herzl's description of his would-be state. In the beginning he stood quite as ready to accept Argentina as Palestine, and although eventually won over by the attachment of the Russian Jews to Eretz Yisroel, his basic argument had nothing in it that required Zion as the place for the solution.[29] In fact, except for his analysis of anti-Semitism, there is very little "Jewish" in *The Jewish State*.

Herzl's book caught the Jewish imagination less for what it said than for the way he said it. Herzl was totally unaware that many of his ideas had already been advocated by the Hoveve Zion or discussed in the Hebrew press. "Yet the effect produced by *The Jewish State* was profound," wrote Chaim Weizmann. "Not the ideas, but the personality which stood behind them appealed to us. Here was daring, clarity and energy. The very fact that this Westerner came to us unencumbered by our own preconceptions had its appeal. We of the Russian group in Berlin were not alone in our response. The Zionist student group in Vienna, Kadimah, was perhaps more deeply impressed than we. . . . It was from these sources that Herzl drew much of his early support."[30]

Although much of what Herzl said had been anticipated by other writers, he differed significantly from them. Moses Hess had based his writings on a firm faith in divine guidance and the goodwill of man; to him, restoration would be the ultimate triumph of humanitarian rationalism. Herzl, on the other hand, in his belief that one man—himself—could affect the restoration of his people, appears as the Nietzschean changing history.[31] The similarity in ideas between Herzl and Pinsker is more striking. Indeed, when Herzl finally read *Auto-Emancipation,* he noted in his diary: "Dumbfounding agreement on the critical side, great similarity on the constructive. A pity I had not read it before my pamphlet was printed. Still, it is a good thing I knew nothing of it—or perhaps I might have abandoned my own undertaking."[32] But Pinsker, writing in the midst of a *pogrom,* could see no help from the Gentile world in saving his people; Herzl, throughout his life, believed the Western nations would help, less for the benefit of the Jews, but on a rational understanding of what it would mean to them.

Herzl's daring conception was that the state could and should come into existence with the help of the great European powers. He believed that countries like France and England, Germany and

Russia, would not be sorry to see their Jews depart. But the Jews should not go until they were assured of a home. Here was a grand vision: no creeping in by the back door of colonization, a few hard-pressed refugees at a time, but the open migration of masses of people, triumphantly moving to a legally secured homeland.[33] Herzl's genius lay in that he took a quietly desperate, impossible scheme held by a few dreamers and raised it to the status of a grand vision held by the masses.

Herzl always thought of his scheme and of himself on a grand scale. His personality, moreover, fit the mythic needs of a new movement. Although a successful journalist, he had no credentials to act as the leader of world Jewry; but in the confused conditions of the European Jewish community at the end of the century, a vacuum of leadership existed, and Herzl claimed the role. From the beginning, he saw himself as a leader. "I shall try to do something *for* the Jews—but not *with* them," he told Baron de Hirsch.[34] Joseph Klausner, still a university student when he first met Herzl, recalled that Herzl "created something that can hardly be expressed in words. A different atmosphere prevailed, something altogether new had come into being. . . . One Hebrew writer was so bold as to apply to him the Biblical verse, 'And he was king in Jeshurun.' It can be said that the whole of Zionism acquired something regal." When Herzl spoke, according to Rabbi Mordecai Braude: "Suddenly a compelling force had arisen, and he dominated us with his extraordinary personality, with his gestures, manner of speech, his ardor and vision."[35]

After his rebuff by the Rothschilds, Herzl despaired of converting the wealthy, assimilated Western Jews to his cause, and turned to the East. He based his right to lead on the will of the people, and brushed aside all class and social distinctions by his assertion that "we are all one people." Among the Russian Jews, however, Herzl's personality inevitably raised messianic hopes. Martin Buber said Herzl had "a countenance lit with the glance of the Messiah," and countless writers and contemporaries have all employed the messianic simile. He fortified his nationalistic appeal with such emotions, that, after accepting the need to locate his state in Palestine, Herzl could direct his people's ancient yearnings toward the creation of a modern nation. By his charisma, Herzl married nationalism to the dream of restoration and created the Zionist movement.

Herzl chose to exercise his leadership through the creation of a Congress. He took the ancient Roman legal device of the *negotiurum gestio* and converted it into a political theory, whereby a minority could speak and act on behalf of all the Jews by assuming that it represented them. The Congress was to become the national assembly of the Jewish people, a forum where the important issues confronting them could be discussed, both now while in exile and later in a state of their own.[36] In response to Herzl's call, 204 men and women from 17 countries met in Basle, Switzerland, from August 29 to 31, 1897. In his opening speech, Herzl set forth the aim of the Congress in one sentence: "We are here to lay the foundation stone of the house which is to shelter the Jewish nation."

Largely preparatory in nature, the main value of the First Congress lay in the symbolic importance attached to it by Jew and non-Jew alike. For the first time in eighteen centuries, a Jewish assembly had gathered to debate the future of the people. In concrete terms, the Congress adopted the "Basle Program," which became the authoritative pronouncement of Zionist aims for the next fifty years:

> Zionism strives to create for the Jewish people a home in Palestine secured by public law.
> The Congress contemplates the following means to the attainment of this end:
> 1. The promotion, on suitable lines, of the colonization of Palestine by Jewish agricultural and industrial workers.
> 2. The organization and bringing together of the whole of Jewry by means of appropriate institutions, local and international, in accordance with the laws of each country.
> 3. The strengthening and fostering of Jewish national sentiment and consciousness.
> 4. Preparatory steps toward obtaining Government consent, where necessary, to the attainment of the aim of Zionism.

Immediately after the Congress, when he returned to Vienna, Herzl wrote in his diary: "At Basle I founded the Jewish State. If I were to say this today, I would be met by universal laughter. In five years, perhaps, and certainly in fifty, every one will see it."*

The Congresses have continued to meet ever since, and until the creation of the State of Israel, served as the main forum for debating Jewish problems and for guiding the growth of the *Yishuv,* the Jewish settlement in Palestine. Herzl lived to attend five more Congresses, and saw the creation of the institutions mentioned in the Basle Program. The Second Congress (1898) established the Jewish Colonial Trust, the Zionist financial agency to aid in the development of Palestine, and also set up the General Hebrew Language Society to promote Hebraica. The Fifth Congress (1901) approved the formation of the Jewish National Fund, which became the chief instrument in securing funds for the purchase of land in Palestine. The Zionist Organization also introduced the *Shekel* (membership fee), which provided basic administrative expenses and determined representation at the Congresses. With one exception (Keren Hayesod, the Foundation Fund), all of the essential institutions and forms of the movement, as they exist to this day, were established by the first six Congresses.

At the same time, Herzl pursued the chimera of a charter from Turkey that would give the Jews their legally secured homeland. Above all, Herzl wanted Zionism to move on a lofty and noble plane. He opposed the Hoveve Zion's colonization as a mere smuggling operation, a plan unworthy of a great people and a great cause. Before anything else could be done, political rights had to be secured. This view often brought Herzl into sharp conflict with those who believed in immediate colonization, with or without a charter, as the first step toward reclaiming Palestine. This struggle between the "political Zionists" and the "practical Zionists" continued long after Herzl's death, but eventually Zionism shifted most of its resources and energies into colonization.

Negotiations with Turkey had begun even before the First Con-

---

* At the Jubilee Celebration of the Congress in 1947, David Ben-Gurion (who would become Prime Minister of Israel seven months later) quoted this entry, and then commented: "This was no outburst of enthusiasm on the part of a dreamer, but the expression of a profound historical intuition. On that day the Jewish State was indeed founded, for a state is founded first in the hearts of the people."[37]

gress. In May 1896, according to one source, the Sultan had sent a secret emissary to Herzl with the offer of a Palestinian charter if he could get the European press to stop its vilification of Turkey because of the Armenian massacres.[38] Neither Herzl nor the Jews had the power to do this, even if they had wanted to. Herzl later conceived of a plan to get rich Jews like the Rothschilds and the Montefiores to offer Turkey a loan; the bait led Abdul Hamid II to grant Herzl and David Wolffsohn an interview. Jewish bankers told Herzl they might be able to raise money once the charter was in hand; the Sultan promised to grant the charter once the money had been raised. Herzl and Wolffsohn found themselves running around in circles, constantly paying out *baksheesh* (bribes) to secure interviews with highly placed Turkish officials.*

In 1902, after months of negotiation, Turkey seemed ready to act. The Sultan awarded Herzl the Grand Cordon of the Mejidieh Order, and Zionist executives were openly optimistic. The Turkish offer dashed their hopes. The Sultan would allow Jews to settle in any of his Asian provinces except Palestine, and they could not settle in concentrations of more than a few families.[39] Actually, Herzl's dream of a Turkish charter had been doomed from the start, as some of his advisers had tried to tell him. Turkish law did not permit the Sultan to cede land except that lost through battle; no matter what Herzl might have offered, the Sultan would have been unable to deliver.[40]

His diplomatic efforts with Turkey frustrated, a saddened Herzl was suddenly revivified by hope from an unexpected quarter. The Zionists had approached Great Britain to see if a Jewish settlement could be established in the Sinai at El Arish, just outside Ottoman Palestine. Joseph Chamberlain, the Colonial Secretary, in turn offered Uganda in East Africa as a site suitable for colonization, and Sir Clement Hill, superintendent of African Protectorates, confirmed the willingness of England to have Jews settle there, with eventual

---

* In November 1898 Herzl went to visit Palestine, and while there managed to secure an audience with German Emperor Wilhelm in Jerusalem. Herzl hoped to get the German Chancellory to persuade the Sultan to grant a charter, but the Kaiser, much more sensitive than Herzl to the realities of international relations, knew better than to interfere in Turkey's domestic policies.

political autonomy.[41] A formal offer reached Herzl just as the Sixth Congress opened at Basle on August 23, 1903. When he presented the proposal to the delegates, the meeting erupted in bitter controversy. Herzl emphasized that he did not consider Uganda as an alternative to Palestine; those favoring the British plan explained, in Max Nordau's phrase, that the territory would serve as a *Nachtasyl* (temporary refuge) until Palestine could be secured. The horrors of a new *pogrom* in Russia made the need for such an asylum imperative. The Russian delegates would have none of it, however, and their political instincts saw the acceptance of the British offer as the death knell of any restoration in Palestine. Once the Jews had some refuge, the great powers would have no incentive to help them attain a homeland in Eretz Yisroel. Menahem Ussischkin declared: "If we have to do without Eretz Yisroel or without Herzl —then we will do without Herzl. Herzl is part of us only to the degree that he gives us Eretz Yisroel."[42]

The only way out without insulting Great Britain lay in appointing a commission to study the suitability of the area. A motion to this effect carried 295 to 178, upon which the Russian delegates, including young Chaim Weizmann, walked out. They returned only after Herzl pleaded with them to retain the unity of Zionism. At the closing session, Herzl reaffirmed his faith in a Palestinian homeland, and read from Psalm 137, "If I forget thee, O Jerusalem, let my right hand forget her cunning." It was his last speech to the Congress he had created. Worn out by his exertions, he died on July 3, 1904, at the age of forty-four.

After his death, the Herzl legend continued to grow in the Jewish world. His analysis of the Jewish dilemma would be tragically confirmed in the Holocaust, while his plans for the Zionist movement bore fruit, as he had predicted, fifty years after the First Congress. Herzl's devotion to Palestine was sincere; a great power had, in its offer of territory, granted the Zionists status and legitimacy, and so the offer could not be summarily dismissed. But, as he wrote to Sir Francis Montefiore: "I am a Zionist convinced that the settlement of our people's question can only be effected in that country, Palestine, with which are indelibly associated the historic and sentimental bias of its national existence. No place on earth could, therefore, in my mind, supplant or take the place which Palestine holds as the object for which we are striving."[43]

In his will, he asked to be buried near his father in Vienna, until such time as the Jewish people had a home of their own. In August 1949, an Israeli Air Force plane carried his body to the newborn Jewish State he had conceived, and his remains were reinterred, with full ceremony, in a tomb hewn from the rock atop Mount Herzl in Jerusalem.

IV

The East African dispute did not die with Herzl, but became the central issue at the Seventh Congress, which met in Basle in late July 1905. The special commission reported the Guas Ngishu plateau in East Africa unsuited for large-scale Jewish settlement, much to the satisfaction of the Russian delegates, who also pushed through several measures aimed at greater practical work in Palestine. But Israel Zangwill (1864–1926), the noted English author, refused to accept the commission's findings, or be bound by a resolution rejecting any settlement scheme outside of Palestine. Zangwill led forty dissidents out of the Congress to form the Jewish Territorial Organization (ITO), devoted to establishing a homeland, and one not bound by religious ties to the past. As Ben Halpern notes, the renunciation of Zion was not a very great ideological sacrifice as much as an attack on the past and on sentimental, irrational links to Palestine. The many socialists who joined ITO considered Palestine a historical anomaly, one totally unsuited for the demands of a modern nation-state.[44] The ITO controversy sharply divided the Zionists, with many of the "politicals," who agreed with the socialists that a Jewish state was then unrealistic, following Zangwill. This left the World Zionist Organization pretty much in the hands of the "practicals," the advocates of cultural work in the Diaspora and greater colonization in the Holy Land.

The country the practical Zionists wanted to build up had changed greatly from the land flowing with milk and honey that God had promised to Moses. Centuries of warfare and neglect had denuded it of the protective cover of trees and stripped off the topsoil; ancient water sources had either dried up or fallen into disuse. Mark Twain, visiting Palestine in 1868, reported: "Palestine sits in sackcloth and ashes. Over it broods the spell of a curse that has withered its fields and fettered its energies. . . . The hallowed spot where the shepherds watched their flocks by night, and where the angels sang Peace on earth, good will to men, is untenanted by any living creature, and unblessed by any feature that is pleasant to the eye. Renowned Jerusalem itself, the stateliest name in history, has lost all of its ancient grandeur, and is becoming a pauper village. . . . The noted Sea of Galilee, where Roman fleets once rode at anchor and the disciples of the Savior sailed in their ships, was long ago deserted by the devotees of war and commerce, and its borders are a silent wilderness; Capernaum is a shapeless ruin; Magdala is the home of beggared Arabs; Bethsaida and Chorazin have vanished from the earth, and the 'desert places' round about them where thousands of men once listened to the Savior's voice and ate the miraculous bread sleep in the hush of a solitude that is inhabited only by birds of prey and skulking foxes. Palestine is desolate and unlovely."[45] A dozen years later the American consul in Jerusalem confirmed Twain's description: "For centuries the country has been declining and it is still declining. The population and the wealth of Palestine has not increased during the last forty years."[46]

Although the Romans under Hadrian had exiled nearly all of the Jews in Palestine after the Bar Kochba revolt in 135 C.E., small communities managed to survive. In 1840, Sir Moses Montefiore received an estimate of the Jewish population in the Holy Land as sixty-five hundred; on the eve of the First Aliyah forty years later, this figure stood at around twenty-five thousand. Most of these Jews lived in the four "holy" cities of Jerusalem, Safed, Tiberias, and Hebron, their sole activity the study of sacred literature. Historically, these communities of scholars constituted a link with ancient Judea, a living witness to the undying attachment of Jews to Eretz Yisroel. For their witness and study, *meshullachim* (messengers) collected alms in Europe, and later also in America, and the Jews of Palestine lived off this charity. For those concerned with creating a modern nation-state, *Halukkah* represented not a sacred charity, but the dead hand of the past holding back the future. The scholars contributed nothing to the reclamation of the land or the growth of industry, and in turn, despised and feared those who hoped to build a new nation.

Not all of these native Jews studied Bible and Talmud, though, and as early as 1839, a group from Jerusalem had petitioned Montefiore to help them establish a farm colony. In 1855 a group actually bought some land, but no real effort took place until 1878, when Joshua Stampfer led a small coterie of would-be farmers to a malarial area just north of Jaffa. They called their settlement Petach Tikva (Gate of Hope), but the mosquitoes and Arab hostility soon dashed their optimism, and the colony failed.* The growth of Hibbat Zion, and later the encouragement of the Zionist Organization, led to the establishment of fifty-nine colonies, with holdings of one hundred thousand acres, by the eve of the First World War. Many of these colonists owed their continued existence to the generosity of Jewish philanthropies established by Edmond de Rothschild and Maurice de Hirsch, which sent money and agronomists, established vineyards, wine cellars, and even an agricultural school, although usually through bureaucratic administrators who neither understood nor sympathized with the aims of the *chalutzim*. The growing support of the colonies by the Zionists led to the greater emphasis on the upbuilding of the land as preparation for an ultimate Jewish homeland in Palestine, a task facilitated by such brilliant Zionist officials as Arthur Ruppin, who directed land activities in Palestine for four decades.[47]

The departure of the Territorialists and the triumph of the "practicals" did not mean that the Zionist Organization faced no problems. On the contrary: The prewar years saw challenges to Zionist ideology and organization from both within and without the movement. Though the Sixth Congress could report the growth in the number of societies to 1,572, opposition to the movement had also

---

* Five years later a second group began anew, this time successfully, and Petach Tikva is now a thriving city of eighty thousand. Stampfer had literally walked from Russia to Palestine, and David Ben-Gurion was fond of using him as an example of the courage and devotion of the early settlers.

increased perceptibly, and the bulk of the criticism came primarily from the Western, assimilated communities who still believed in the promise of the emancipation.

Reform Jews had long forsaken the idea of return to Zion. They had taken the concept of the Dispersion as Exile (a punishment for sins) and converted it into the ideal of Mission, with Israel chosen to spread the knowledge of God among the nations. The loss of homeland had not been a calamity, but an opportunity, and allowed the Jewish people to spiritually break out of the confines of a nation-state.[48] This view made prayers for a return to Zion incongruous within the Reform theology, and in 1845 the Frankfurt Rabbinical Conference voted that "all petitions for the return to the land of our fathers, and for the restoration of a Jewish state, should be eliminated from the prayers."[49] By the 1880s, the bulk of the Reform movement had adopted this attitude.

Herzl originally had wanted to hold the First Congress in Munich, but a formidable outcry arose against the proposal. The executive committee of the Association of Rabbis in Germany issued a statement condemning the idea. Their arguments soon became a classic formulation of the anti-Zionist position[50]:

1. The efforts of the so-called Zionists to found a Jewish national state in Palestine contradicts the Messianic promises of Judaism as contained in the Holy Writ and in later religious sources.
2. Judaism obligates its adherents to serve with all devotion the Fatherland to which they belong, and to further its national interest with all their heart and with all their strength.
3. However, those noble aims directed toward the colonization of Palestine by Jewish peasants and farmers are not in contradiction to these obligations, because they have no relation whatsoever to the founding of a national state.

Outside of Germany there was also strong opposition to the Congress. Hermann Adler, chief Ashkenazic rabbi of England, called Zionism an "egregious blunder," while the chief rabbi of Vienna, Moritz Gudemann, railed against the "Kuckucksei of Jewish nationalism." Even sympathetic Hoveve Zion began to question the wisdom of the Congress, fearful that the uproar might alienate the support of the Rothschilds for the Palestinian colonies.[51]

The real nub of the anti-Zionist protest lay not in theological interpretation but in political policy. Despite the Dreyfus affair, many Western Jews considered their religious beliefs irrelevant to their national identity. They saw themselves as citizens of France, Germany, or England who happened to be Jewish. Their national loyalties belonged to the country of their citizenship. As early as 1792 Samuel Halevi had written: "France, who first wiped out the disgrace of Judah and broke the shackles of all captives, she is our land of Israel; her mountains—our Zion; her rivers—our Jordan."[52]

To those who believed in assimilation, Zionism represented a threat to their recently won status. Herzl implied that despite emancipation, Jews could never really be at home in any country; their ultimate allegiance had to be to a Jewish state. If this were true, then Jews could never be patriotic to the lands of their citizenship; they would always be seen as temporary dwellers, as disloyal. When Herzl read *The Jewish State* to Zadok Kahn, the chief rabbi of France murmured partial agreement, but suggested that France also claimed his loyalty. In his diary, Herzl noted: "Yes, a man has to choose between Zion and France."[53]

Those who rejected Herzl's view vehemently attacked Zionism, as if the heat of their passion proved their patriotism. The English journalist Laurie Magnes charged the Zionists with being partially responsible for the current anti-Semitism. How could the European countries, which the Zionists now proposed to abandon, justify their retention of the Jews? Why should civil equality be extended to them if, since they would soon depart, they were merely temporary visitors? One of the most sustained attacks, and in the light of later history one of the most ironic, came from the pen of Professor Ludwig Geiger, son of one of the founders of the Reform movement: "Zionism is as dangerous to the German spirit as are social democracy and ultramontanism. . . . The German Jew who has a voice in German literature must, as he has been accustomed to for the last century and a half, look upon Germany alone as his fatherland, upon the German language as his mother tongue, and the future of the German nation must remain the only one upon which he bases his hopes. Any desire to form together with his co-religionists as a people outside Germany is, not to speak of its impracticability, downright thanklessness towards the nation in whose midst he lives—a chimera; for the German Jew is a German in his national peculiarities, and Zion is for him the land only of the past, not of the future."[54]

Herzl valiantly attempted to answer these objections that Zionism threatened the status of emancipated Jewry. If French Jews had been fully assimilated into the French nation, with no ethnic bonds to other Jews, then the establishment of a Jewish state would not harm them. In fact, it would help them by drawing off Jews who were unable to assimilate; those who chose to stay would then no longer be embarrassed by those incapable of fitting in. At heart, though, Herzl did not really believe that Jews would ever be at home anywhere except in a Jewish state. When an American delegate argued that Zionism should only mean providing a home for such Jews who were homeless, Herzl patted him on the head and said: "All Jews have homes, and yet they are all homeless."[55]

Despite Herzl's call at the Second Congress to "capture the communities," Western Jewry remained aloof from the movement. Unlike the Eastern European Jews (other than the Marxists) who saw themselves as a distinct ethnic group, Western Jews—especially those gaining some measure of success—remained untouched by Zionism. Chaim Weizmann, after moving to England, noted a typical attitude among the Jewish communities there: "A handful of devotees to the cause among the lower middle classes, indifference or hostility among the upper classes."[56] While many willingly supported the Palestinian settlements (perhaps as modernized form of *Halukkah*), they shied away from any suggestion of common ethnic or national ties to a Jewish homeland there. If most Jews were aware of Zionism, it is fair to say that only a small minority—less than 1 per cent—openly supported its goals.

V

Within the movement, the decade after Herzl's death saw a number of reorientations and critiques of the founder's philosophy. The "practical" group, influenced by the Russian Hoveve Zion, considered the political goals of an internationally guaranteed charter unattainable, and wanted the organization to support colonization. As Chaim Weizmann, a leader of this group, put it: "Zionist progress could be directed only through Palestine, through tedious labor, every step won by sweat and blood."[57] At the Seventh Congress (1905), the "practicals" pushed through a resolution endorsing colonization; by the Tenth Congress (1911), they had won control of the movement. But two other philosophies, both originating in the Russian experience, strongly affected the course of the movement, and ultimately determined the political and social nature of the future Jewish state.

If Hibbat Zion excited the Jewish nationalists, socialism stirred the blood of all who wanted to create a better society. Throughout Russia, reformers rallied to Marxist ideas, and Jews took prominent roles in the battles against Czarist autocracy. Young Jewish intellectuals found themselves caught between seemingly opposite attractions: the renascence of Jewish nationalism and the call to destroy a corrupt society and build a classless utopia. Insofar as socialism considered nationalism a vestige of outmoded capitalism, it condemned Zionism as an irrelevant effort to solve the Jewish problem. Capitalism had created anti-Semitism, and the triumph of the classless society would eradicate this evil; Jews who supported Zionism, therefore, only prolonged their own oppression.

The same year that Herzl convened the First Congress saw the formation of the General Jewish Workers' Union in Russia and Poland—the Bund—which in the next three decades became the most powerful Jewish mass movement in Europe. The socialist Bund appealed to the lowest strata among the Jews, the common workers and peasants, and popularized for them the theory of the class struggle. It taught young tailors and farmers the ideas of Marx and Engels, that labor was paramount in the economic system, and by its power could transform mankind into a classless society.[58] Negating the need for a national homeland, the Bund advanced the idea of "national cultural autonomy." Jewish peoplehood and culture, and pride in them, made a particular geographic center unnecessary. "Historic destiny," according to one of the Bundist leaders, "has made the Jewish people into a stateless nation and—whether we like it or not—it is bound to remain so."[59] The separate

Jewish culture that the Bundists applauded was not, however, the Hebraic learning of the Orthodox, but the common Yiddish culture of the masses. As the socialists saw it, Jewish identity could be maintained, even in the classless society, by the institutional right of Jews to run their own social and cultural affairs.*

Inevitably efforts were made to bridge the gap between Zionism and socialism, and as early as the 1860s Moses Hess had attempted a fusion of the two philosophies. But as long as orthodox Marxists declared the nation-state an outmoded relic of capitalistic oppression, there would be little room for Zionists and socialists to coexist peacefully until Ber Borochov (1881–1917) and Nachman Syrkin (1867–1924) laid the ideological bases for socialist Zionism.

Of the two, Borochov was the more orthodox Marxist in defining a nation as a sociological entity created by common economic conditions and united by a common past, a definition that did not necessarily follow geopolitical considerations. The nationalism of the proletariat—a true nationalism—aimed at the ultimate liberation of the people from the chains of capitalism, through the reform of the modes of production. The Jewish people, however, lacked the economic base to join in the revolution, because it lived and worked in "extraterritorial" conditions, and this in turn forced them into the lowest ranks of society. To join in the class struggle, therefore, the

* This doctrine led directly to the concept of "Diaspora nationalism," the idea that Jews—despite the lack of geopolitical homeland—still constituted a distinct nationality. In Europe at that time, other recognized nationalities such as the Czechs and Hungarians lacked independence, and the Bund argued that all of them should have cultural autonomy and civil and political rights as separate groups within the countries where they lived. Originally, Zionist philosophy held that Jews would never enjoy full freedom until they moved to Palestine, but by the turn of the century many Zionists, especially in the Austro-Hungarian and Russian empires, recognized that a distinct Jewish homeland would not be established in the near future. They then called for *Gegenwartsarbeit* (work for the present) to improve the civic position in 1905, as did the Russian Federation a year later. For the Zionists, Diaspora nationalism was a temporary measure to secure better status for Jews in alien lands until the establishment of a Jewish state. While it made much sense in prewar Europe, where differences often existed between citizenship and nationality, it created distinct problems for the Zionists in America, where nationality and citizenship were the same. See Chapter Three.

Jews had to overcome their humiliation. "We must understand once and for all," he asserted, "that one who has no national dignity has no class dignity." Rejecting the Bundist arguments, Borochov argued that the Jewish people would find no help in exile; they needed a home of their own, where a Jewish proletariat could gain a role in the class struggle at the same time they achieved national dignity.[60]

Borochov identified the land where this nationalizing process would take place as Palestine, not for historic or religious reasons, but because it lay undeveloped, with a native population that had not yet crystallized into a socio-economic organism. The task of Jewish socialists now became not only the furthering of the proletarian revolution, but also to aid the bourgeois in securing a Jewish homeland where Jews could gain the dignity to join in the class struggle.

While Borochov framed his arguments within the complex strictures of orthodox Marxist dogma, Nachman Syrkin had earlier developed his socialist Zionism along broader and more humanitarian lines. He published the major statement of his ideas in 1898, only two years after Herzl's *Judenstaat,* and in it he challenged both the Zionists and the socialists. Syrkin drew much of his inspiration from traditional Jewish sources, and from socialism took primarily its idealism and some of its practical conclusions; unlike Borochov, he had little use for a materialistic philosophy of history. To Syrkin, the Jewish problem lay rooted in Jewish homelessness, and it would only be solved by the creation of a state. He condemned assimilation as an invention of the Jewish bourgeoisie, designed to extend their exploitation of the poor. Socialism provided the remedy for economic abuse, but only through Zionism could the Jew achieve spiritual redemption. "A classless society and national sovereignty are the only means of completely solving the Jewish problem."[61] Syrkin castigated those Jewish socialists who ignored Jewish suffering in the vain belief that the revolution would, overnight, erase centuries of persecution; moreover, he pointed out that save for Jewish intellectuals, the socialist leaders of other minority groups all opposed assimilation with the dominant majority. On the other side, Syrkin berated the Zionists who wanted to base their Jewish state on the rights of private property, thus building in a basis of social inequality. A Jewish state would be of little value if it kept the Jewish worker in bondage.

At the time he published "The Jewish Question and the Socialist Jewish State," Syrkin had no intention of starting a separate movement. His essay was a theoretical statement, designed to demonstrate that Zionism and socialism were not incompatible, but in fact were organically whole. He and a few other socialists attended the First Congress in the hope there would be room for them within the general framework of the movement. Herzl, who earlier in his life had been sympathetic to socialist doctrines, had become increasingly hostile over the years, and by 1895 saw Zionism as a means of preventing socialist inroads among the Jewish masses. By the Second Congress there seemed no way to bridge the gap between the orthodox economic views of the leadership and the radical proposals of the socialists.[62] Within the Russian-led "Democratic Faction," Chaim Weizmann and Leo Motzkin gathered around them a group of liberals who stopped short of social revolution. Syrkin sneeringly dismissed them as social hypocrites: "When they called for a constitution, they meant not a democratic constitution for Russia but a democratic constitution for the Zionist Congress."[63] By 1907, there were enough socialist Zionist—or Poale Zion—groups in Europe and the United States to form the World Socialist Union of Jewish Laborers. Despite numerous schisms over territorialism, social action, and participation in the general class struggle, eventually the major factions identified Palestinian work as the prime focus of their efforts. In Russia, Poale Zion followed Borochov's analysis of why resettlement had to be in Palestine, but Syrkin's social democratic views, as well as his synthesis of Jewish ethics and social-economic justice, ultimately shaped both socialist Zionism and the Jewish state of Israel.

Of equal if not greater impact on the course of Zionism were the ideas of Asher Ginsberg (1856–1927) better known by his pen name of Ahad Ha'am (one of the people). For him, the establishment of a Jewish homeland in Palestine had to be preceded by the spiritual regeneration of the people. Commenting on the First Congress, he asked if the Jews, even if given a charter, were morally fit to accept it. As early as 1889, he had declared that "so long as the

Hibbat Zion is not a living and burning passion in the heart of the people we lack the only basis on which the land could be regenerated."[64]

Ahad Ha'am stood apart from other Zionists, and even from some of the Hoveve Zion, because he conceived of the homeland as a spiritual center. He never believed that all Jews would go to Palestine, and in fact opposed the suggestion that they should. The Jewish homeland had to be "a fixed center for our national spirit and culture, which will be a new spiritual bond between the scattered sections of the people, and by its mystical influence will stimulate them all to a new national life."[65] If this center were to fulfill these functions, then a proper foundation had to precede its establishment, and preparatory work for this had to take place in the Diaspora. The spiritual redemption of those Jews who would live in Palestine had to occur before they were fit to enter into the rebuilding of Eretz Yisroel. Time and again he warned: "Do not attempt to reach the goal before the conditions necessary to its attainment have been created."

Ahad Ha'am criticized the Herzlian program from the beginning. For the Western Herzl, the problem could be stated in straightforward political terms: A homeland would provide a refuge for persecuted Jews. Ahad Ha'am saw the problem not as one of *Jews,* but of *Judaism,* not the dilemma of individuals, but the future of a nation.[66] Herzl's emphasis on diplomatic maneuvering distressed him as premature and representing misplaced values. What good would the homeland be if it failed to incorporate the spiritual and cultural heritage of the people, if it were not Jewish through and through? In one of his most quoted sayings, he declared that "the salvation of Israel will be achieved by *prophets,* not by *diplomats."*

Because they viewed the redemption of their people so differently, it is understandable why Herzl and Ahad Ha'am, when they met at the First Congress, could not communicate in any meaningful way. Ginsberg dismissed most of the delegates as ignorant of Jewish culture and lacking in real Jewish feeling. Max Nordau, confused by the Russian's attitude, at one point asked him: "But are you a Zionist?" Ginsberg replied, *"I* am a Zionist," implying that his was the true philosophy of Jewish redemption. Herzl, to his credit, recognized that many Eastern European Jews shared Ginsberg's views, and their inner unity and thorough commitment to Judaism moved him deeply. Yet he, because of his background, could not remake his own views, and before his death the gap between him and the Russians widened, coming to a head over the East Africa offer, when they rebelled over even considering a Zionism without Zion. Never committed to the Zionism created by Herzl, Ahad Ha'am at one point proposed establishing a separate organization whose sole function would be the furtherance of Jewish culture, not only in Palestine but in the Diaspora as well. Political Zionism, and even colonization, robbed the Jewish people of their heritage unless it went hand in hand with a commitment to the spiritual needs of the people. While Judaism had survived two thousand years without Zionism, Zionism could not survive without the faith and teachings of the prophets.

Fortunately for the movement, most of those who shared Ahad Ha'am's views also believed in the necessity for political and practical work, and chose to remain within the Zionist framework. Led by Chaim Weizmann, Bertol Feiwal, and Martin Buber, the so-called "Democratic Faction" worked to incorporate cultural Zionism into the program. "We fought these problems out internally," recalled Weizmann, "for we always recognized that the Congress had come to stay; we, not less than Herzl, regarded it as the Jewish State in the making. . . . The Democratic Faction sought to strengthen and deepen the spiritual significance of the movement, and to make the Organization the reflection of the forces of national Jewry."[67] At the Tenth Congress (1911), the Zionists added cultural work, especially the fostering of Hebrew, to their political and colonization programs, much to the distress of many Westerners, who still placed their faith in political action.[68]

Although Ahad Ha'am spoke of the need for preserving the cultural and spiritual heritage of Israel, he did not mean that the Zionists should adopt the beliefs and practices of Orthodox Jewry. Ultrareligious Jews had from the start opposed Zionism as a contravention of divine will; Israel would be redeemed by God when

He so chose, through the sending of the Messiah. The majority of the orthodox saw no necessary conflict between the establishment of a national homeland through man's own efforts and the ultimate spiritual salvation of the people by God. However, they viewed the success of the Ahad Ha'amists, with their emphasis on secular culture, as a distinct threat to orthodox religious practices, and just as the cultural Zionists saw political work as ignoring the nature of the people, so traditional Jews felt a need for more religion in the movement.

The commanding figures among religious Zionists were three rabbis, Isaac Jacob Reines (1839–1915), Abraham Isaac Kook (1865–1935), and Meyer Berlin (1880–1949), who later Hebraicized his name to Meir Bar-Ilan. Reines, longtime rabbi of Lida, Russia, was an early adherent of Hibbat Zion, and with the advent of Herzl joined in enthusiastically in promoting Zionism. In 1902, seeking to increase the influence of traditional Jews in the movement, he convened a conference of rabbis and laymen in Vilna at which the Mizrachi movement was founded. During the Uganda crisis, Reines and other religious Zionists voted to support the East Africa scheme, agreeing with Herzl that the suffering Jews of Eastern Europe needed immediate relief. Kook, like Reines, especially worked to resolve differences between Zionism and messianic expectation, between nationalism and religion. He saw nationalism, not in the secular mode of the nineteenth century, but as part of the spiritual heritage of Israel. "The national sentiment is holy and exalted in itself," he wrote, and part of "the very foundation of Judaism and essential to it." Nationhood had played an integral role in religion, helping to maintain Jewish loyalties through centuries of exile. By reinforcing nationalism, Zionism would contribute to spiritual progress.[69]

Berlin, one of the founders of Mizrachi, spent nearly all of his life attempting to fuse piety and modernity in Jewish self-redemption, and constantly fought what he saw as a lack of religious commitment in Zionism. To those who relegated religion to a private matter for individual conscience, he answered that the issue of religion in Jewish life could not be treated as a question of church and state. Judaism as a people and as a religion was unique; the people could not exist without its religion, and Zionism could not ignore spiritual demands.[70]

The early Congresses had carefully avoided cultural and religious matters, and Herzl hoped to unite the various factions through a commitment to political work. The demand for cultural programs could not be stilled, however, and while religious Zionists favored the promotion of Hebrew,* they rebelled at the seeming godlessness of the socialist and liberal reformers, and at the emphasis on secular culture of the Ahad Ha'amists. When the Democratic Faction came to power at the Tenth Congress, it precipitated the formation of an anti-Zionist orthodox movement, and in 1912 a number of pietists met in Kattowitz to form Agudat Israel. Anti-Zionist in orientation, Agudat Israel exerted a large influence in Eastern Europe for many years. It adopted an extensive educational and economic program that also included work in Palestine, but its members fought Zionism at every opportunity.[72]

Most of the religious Zionists did not leave the world organization, but instead diverted their energies and resources into Mizrachi, which soon gained recognition as the distinct party of religious Zionism within the movement. Originally founded in Russia in 1903, the Mizrachi successfully fought for the right of orthodox Jews to autonomy in cultural and religious activities of their own, and secured resolutions at the early Congresses emphasizing that the Zionist Organization should do nothing to offend religious scruples. The religious Zionists also embarked upon an educational program of their own to balance off the "irreligious" cultural Zionists, and established model schools in Jerusalem and Jaffa, which combined modern educational techniques with strict religious practices.[73] While Mizrachi proved unable to inject more traditional religious

* According to Raphael Patai: "Religious Jews, even those who were not Zionists, recognized the promotion of Hebrew by the Zionists as a positive Jewish value. Only the ultra-orthodox fringe, represented by some of the Hasidic rabbis and their followers, opposed Hebrew. In 1930, I heard the Rabbi of Munkac, in a Sabbath morning sermon in Marienbad, execrate the Zionists who spoke 'b'loshn hebraish, Rahmone litz'lon' ('in the Hebrew language, God preserve us'). And in the 1950s, the rabbi of the Satmarer Hasidim, Joel Teitelbaum, issued from Brooklyn a *ukaze* prohibiting his followers from learning and speaking Hebrew."[71]

traits into the movement, it did influence the over-all program and made many Zionists more sensitive to the ideals and needs of their traditionalist brethren, a sensitivity sorely needed by those who scorned the so-called "ghetto Jews."

VI

On the eve of the First World War, Zionism as a movement had changed radically since Theodore Herzl published *Der Judenstaat*. Membership in the organization stood at 130,000, certainly a minute percentage of world Jewry, yet Zionist ideas extended far beyond those on the rosters. In Russia, which officially prohibited many Jews from joining, Zionism enjoyed large popular sympathy. A fund for land purchase and a bank for development had been established, as well as organs for the dissemination of propaganda.

The rather narrow and rigid political approach of Herzl had given way to a variegated mélange of philosophies, including the socialism of Poale Zion, the religiosity of Mizrachi, and the culturalism of Ahad Ha'am. Undoubtedly, the most important shift had occurred with the triumph of the "practicals," with the resulting emphasis on Palestinian colonization. As Otto Warburg told the Seventh Congress, the Jews' "right to the land by reason of their having possessed it two thousand years ago is not a sufficient claim; they must create a modern title, which would consist in the fact that Palestine depended economically upon the Jews, owing its progress to Jewish initiative and resources."[74] By 1914, that "modern claim" had begun to materialize in the form of eighty-five thousand people in the Yishuv, and fifty-nine settlements supported by the Zionist organization.

Zionism had also had its setbacks as well. The pietists on the one side and the assimilationists on the other both opposed Jewish nationalism. No tangible gains had resulted from Herzl's extensive diplomatic maneuvering, and Turkey still would not allow large-scale Jewish immigration into Palestine. While the British offer of land in East Africa had given the movement a greater measure of legitimacy in the eyes of the world, it had also created a schism, with thousands of Zionists joining the Jewish Territorial Organization. A smaller fissure followed the adoption of a cultural program, with many pietists flocking to Agudat Israel. Yet for all this, a functioning organization committed to Jewish self-redemption in Palestine had developed, with branches all over the world.

At the Twelfth Congress in 1921, the first to meet after the war, Chaim Weizmann, by then president of the World Zionist Organization, recalled the situation seven years earlier: "After many years of striving the conviction was forced upon us that we stood before a blank wall, which it was impossible for us to surmount by ordinary political means. But the strength of the national will forged for itself two main roads towards its goal—the gradual extension and strengthening of the Yishuv in Palestine and the spreading of the Zionist idea throughout the length and breadth of Jewry. Our colonization work . . . could look forward to a period of steady growth. . . . In the Diaspora we saw our national idea gaining ground and we were justified in hoping that by steady work we should succeed in winning for it its rightful place in the life of the Jewish people."[75]

As the guns began to thunder in Europe in August 1914, the center of influence in world Jewry and in the Zionist movement shifted across the ocean to America, the "golden land" to which millions of Jews had fled from persecution and in search of a better life.

CHAPTER TWO

THE
GOLDENAH MEDINAH

I n the United States as in Europe, various precursors including a
Hibbat Zion movement predated nationalistic Zionism. From the
beginning, however, the free status of American Jewry and the nature of American society made Zionism and its forerunners much
different from their European counterparts.

Perhaps the heady atmosphere of liberty, so strange to Jews after
centuries of persecution, accounted for the bizarre nature of some of
the early proto-Zionist ventures in America. Certainly Mordechai
Manuel Noah's grandiose scheme of establishing a Jewish colony in
the New World was far stranger than any of the European proposals
prior to Herzl's *Judenstaat*. In 1818, he predicted the imminent
breakup of the Turkish Empire and the collaboration of the European powers to re-establish the Jews in their ancient homeland.
When Noah realized that the Sultan was not about to be dispossessed,
he hit upon the idea of creating a refuge for Jews of all nations in
America. Inducing some friends to purchase land on Grand Island
in the Niagara River near Buffalo, New York, he proclaimed the

founding of a new city to be called "Ararat." On September 2, 1825, a variety of governmental leaders, Christian clergymen, Masonic officers, and even some Indians (whom Noah thought were the Ten Lost Tribes of Israel) gathered for the cornerstone ceremonies. As it turned out, there were too many invited guests and insufficient transportation to get them to Ararat, so the proceedings took place in an Episcopalian church in Buffalo.[1]

In his dedicatory address, Noah made clear that he had not abandoned Palestine; Ararat would be a temporary refuge until the Jews regained Zion. "It is proper for me to state," he declared, "that this asylum is temporary and provisionary. The Jews never should and never will relinquish the just hope of regaining possession of their ancient heritage." Then, "by the grace of God, Governor and Judge of Israel," Mordechai Noah issued a proclamation commanding that a worldwide census of Jews be taken; that all Jews pay a tax to Ararat of three silver shekels annually; that Jewish soldiers in European armies stay at their posts until they received further orders from him; and finally that those Jews who did not want to settle in Ararat could remain in their adopted homes. He then offered the title of "Commissioner" to a number of important European Jews, and enjoined upon "all our pious and venerable rabbis, our presidents and elders of the synagogue . . . to circulate and make known this my proclamation and give it full publicity, credence and effect."[2]

Although a few Americans took Noah seriously (the Buffalo *Emporium,* for example, took pride in "this great work" by "a fellow citizen"), most people both in Europe and America dismissed the scheme as the work of a lunatic.[3] The chief rabbis of London and Paris immediately declined the proferred titles, and found the whole plan sacrilegious. Anticipating later Orthodox opposition to Zionism, Abraham de Cologne, Grand Rabbi of Paris, informed Noah that "God alone knows the epoch of Israelitish restoration; that He alone will make it known to the whole universe by signs entirely unequivocal; and that every attempt on our part to re-assemble with any political-national design, is forbidden as an act of high treason against Divine Majesty." Among other Jewish leaders, especially in Germany, the plan elicited nothing but contempt for the fancies of an addle-brained visionary. Discouraged by this reception, Noah eventually abandoned Ararat, but until the end of his life continued to urge the establishment of a Jewish state in America.[4]

A more practical project came forth from a character only slightly less original than Noah, Warder Cresson, or as he chose to call himself, Michael Boaz Israel. A convert to Judaism, Cresson came from a well-to-do family that tried to have him declared insane. He served briefly as United States consul in Jerusalem, and in the 1840s proposed agricultural rebuilding of Palestine as a prelude to full restoration. After unsuccessfully attempting to secure a governmental appointment as minister plenipotentiary to Tunis (a title he claimed had in fact been granted), he moved to Palestine in 1850 and founded a colony in the valley of Raphaim near Jerusalem. Cresson, whatever his delusions, knew how to farm, and his work proved useful in convincing a number of wealthy patrons to subsidize later colonization schemes.[5]

Many non-Jews were attracted by the idea of Jewish restoration, although Cresson alone converted and moved to Palestine. William E. Blackstone, a Chicago businessman and lay preacher who affected the title "Reverend," had seen the miserable condition of the Jews in Europe and had also visited the Holy Land. In what can only be described as a truly Christian gesture, he decided to mobilize public opinion in favor of re-creating a Jewish homeland in Palestine. In early 1891 he drafted a petition calling upon the President of the United States to influence the European powers "to secure the holding, at an early date, of an international conference to consider the condition of the Israelites and their claims to Palestine as their ancient home." Blackstone gathered the signatures of 413 of the country's leading citizens, including Chief Justice Melville W. Fuller, Senator Chauncey M. Depew of New York, Speaker of the House Thomas B. Reed, and numerous congressmen, governors, judges, mayors, and other officials. The list also included the names of eight rabbis and seven Jewish laymen.

The memorial, which was personally received by President Benjamin Harrison and Security of State James G. Blaine (and then completely ignored), evoked widespread comment since it had also been endorsed by such giants of industry as J. P. Morgan, John D. Rockefeller, Cyrus W. Field, William E. Dodge, and others. In the Jewish press, it predictably received a cool reception from Reform leaders. Supporters of restoration at first applauded Blackstone, but then discovered that while he undoubtedly sympathized with the plight of Russian Jewry, he—like many others—believed that Jewish redemption would precede the second coming of Christ. The Hebrew periodical *Ha-Pisgah* noted that Christians did not want to convert the Jews now, but in some utopian future. "Let the Christians do whatever they can to help us in the resettlement in Palestine. As to the question of our faith, let that rest until Elijah returns and then we shall see whether or not their dream materializes." Just as in Europe, Zionism would often find strange allies among Gentiles seeking the millennium.[6]

Ideas closer to modern Zionism could be found in the writings of Rabbi Isaac Leeser in the mid-nineteenth century. Although he never used the term "Jewish state," the Philadelphia rabbi wanted the Jews to be "a nation, a unit, a people having a government and home of our own" and "in no other country than the land of Palestine." From his pulpit, Lesser urged that Judea "is the land which is the Israelite's home and he should always regard himself as having an interest in its soil, although he has been born in exile, in the country of the stranger." Despite this last comment, Lesser did not suggest that American Jews go to Palestine; rather they should help make it a refuge for European Jews escaping persecution.[7]

As editor of the influential periodical *Occident,* Lesser helped to keep American Jews aware of developments in Palestine, and reported regularly on Cresson's colony. There were other, more traditional means of spreading such news, however, and as early as the 1830s *meshullachim* (messengers) came to America to collect *Halukkah* for the support of religious communities in the Holy Land. The earliest known Hevrah Terumat ha-Kodesh (Society for Offerings for the Sanctuary) was formed in 1832, and in 1853 Samuel Myer Isaacs established a fund to support Orthodox scholars in Jerusalem. Isaacs also edited *The Jewish Messenger* and saw that its readers had the latest news from Palestine. Orthodox Jews nonetheless preferred to hear the stories directly from the mouths of the traveling fund raisers and this assured the *meshullachim* a rapt audience as they went from synagogue to synagogue.[8]

Perhaps the best known of the proto-Zionists is the poetess whose words adorn the Statue of Liberty. Emma Lazarus arrived at her nationalism through both pity and scorn—pity for the victims of persecution and *pogroms,* scorn for Jews still tied by custom and superstition to the Middle Ages. Repelled by the waves of Eastern European Jews then coming to the United States, she wrote: "What they need is Education, Enlightenment, Reformation; a sweeping out of the accumulated cobwebs and rubbish of Kabbalah and Talmud, darkening their very windows against the day, and encrusting their altars and their hearths with the gathered dust of the ages."[9] Together with this education, she urged the revival of a nationalist spirit, one that would unite Jews all over the world. "I do not hesitate to say that our national defect is that we are not 'tribal' enough," she wrote, "we have not sufficient solidarity to perceive that when the life and property of a Jew in the uttermost provinces of the Caucasus are attacked, the dignity of a free Jew in America is humiliated. . . . Until we are free, we are none of us free."[10] For those Jews who turned their backs on other Jews, even on the poor benighted Talmudists, she had nothing but contempt. When she heard that almost four hundred poor Jewish families in Jaffa and Jerusalem were being taken care of by a Christian missionary society that hoped to convert them, she publicly reproved the American Jewish community for failing to take care of its own, for ignoring the ancient commands of charity and justice.[11]

In that same year, 1883, Emma Lazarus published her "Songs of a Semite," in which she lashed out at both the savage and the civilized enemies of her people, those who slaughtered them and those who turned their backs on Jewish plights. In militant tones she called for a revival of the spirit of ancient Israel, of heroes like Joshua and Bar Kochba:

> O for Jerusalem's trumpet now
> To blow a blast of shattering power,
> To wake the sleepers high and low

And rouse them to the urgent hour!
No hand for vengeance—but to save
A million naked swords should wave.
O deem not dead that martial fire,
Say not the mystic flame is spent:
With Moses' law and David's lyre
Your ancient strength remains unbent.
Let but an Ezra rise anew
To lift the banner of the Jew!

If Emma Lazarus hoped in some way to sound the opening note
to a nationalistic Jewish revival in America, her vision remained
constricted by a romanticized ideal of the past. Ancient Israel provided her model, while the mood of nineteenth-century nationalism
aroused her passions. But she failed to take into account the fact
that the Jewish experience in America had been far different from
that of Europe. Even when the wave of immigrants from Eastern
Europe brought Hibbat Zion to the United States in the 1880s and
1890s, the nature of American society, and its treatment of Jews,
quickly transformed the urge to restoration.

II

Jewish history in America began in 1654, the same year that the
Spanish Inquisition burned ten Jews to death in Cuenca and twelve
in Granada. On September 1, the ship *Saint Charles* sailed into New
Amsterdam Harbor, carrying twenty-three Jews fleeing Portuguese
persecution in Brazil. Most of their possessions had been lost during
the stormy voyage, and what little they had left went to pay the
captain. They came seeking refuge, and hoped to find in the Dutch
colony the same tolerance Jews enjoyed in Holland.

New Amsterdam's governor, the legendary Peter Stuyvesant,
wanted to expel them at once, but mindful of the Jewish investors
in the Dutch West India Company, decided to seek permission from
the directors. Stuyvesant's letter reached Amsterdam in early 1655

and immediately drew forth a sharp protest from the city's Jews. On April 26, 1655, the West India Company reluctantly ordered their governor to allow the Jews to stay. While the directors would have liked to accede to his request, a large amount of Jewish money was invested in the company's shares, and they could not afford to affront their own stockholders. "Therefore after many deliberations we have finally decided and resolved . . . that these people may travel and trade to and in New Netherland and live and remain there, provided the poor among them shall not become a burden to the company or to the community, but be supported by their own nation. You will now govern yourself accordingly." Stuyvesant grudgingly acquiesced, but continuing to harass the newcomers, he tried to prevent them from serving in the militia, a responsibility open only to citizens. The Jews refused to give in, insisting on their right to stand the watch and to engage in trade. In the face of such obstinacy, the peg-legged governor soon surrendered, probably muttering about the burdens of his office.

Jewish immigration trickled into the American colonies before the War for Independence, and by 1776 the Jewish population on the Atlantic seaboard totaled about two thousand. The smallness in number of those who left Europe did not reflect satisfaction with Old World conditions; rather, relatively few Jews had the means to undertake the costly and dangerous voyage. To most of them, America meant nothing as yet, and no Jewish West India Company encouraged them with grants or promises. Of those who did come, a number were Sephardim, the descendants of Portuguese and Spanish Marranos dwelling in Holland, France, or England, people involved in sea commerce who were not terrified of the ocean voyage.

Politically, the situation of the Jews varied from colony to colony. They had had to fight for their rights in New Amsterdam, and were never openly welcomed anywhere. But the frontier conditions that made European social attitudes and structures irrelevant in America also broke down the remnants of medieval anti-Semitism. The idea of a ghetto section of a city made no sense in a country where nine out of ten people lived on farms. Economic restrictions would have been futile where unlimited opportunity and land beckoned to all. In 1740, Parliament authorized the naturalization of Jews in the colonies, and thereafter "Jews enjoyed more freedom, legally and in fact, in the British colonies in America than anywhere else in the world."[12]

Most Jews supported the Revolutionary cause. Jewish soldiers fought in the Continental Army, while Jewish merchants and financiers, most notably Haym Salomon, gave financial aid to the rebels. The leaders of the new nation promised that Jews would always enjoy full freedom and equality in the United States. Both John Adams and Thomas Jefferson predicted a bright future for the children of Israel in America, while George Washington, in response to inaugural greetings from the Hebrew Congregation of Newport, Rhode Island, penned an oft-quoted reply: "It is now no more that toleration is spoken of as if it was by the indulgence of one class of people that another enjoyed the exercise of their inherent natural rights. For happily the Government of the United States, which gives to bigotry no sanction, to persecution no assistance, requires only that those who live under its protection should demean themselves as good citizens, in giving it on all occasions their effectual support. . . . May the Children of the Stock of Abraham, who dwell in this land, continue to merit and enjoy the good will of the other inhabitants, while every one shall sit in safety under his own vine and fig tree."[13]

Following the adoption of the Federal Constitution, Jews and other groups—most notably Catholics—fought to wipe out discriminatory clauses that still existed in all of the state constitutions with the exception of Virginia and New York. Georgia abolished religious discrimination in 1789, and Pennsylvania and South Carolina followed suit a year later, thus guaranteeing full freedom in those states with vigorous Jewish communities. Although Delaware wiped out its legal restrictions in 1792, other states moved much more slowly. Rhode Island abandoned Roger Williams' legacy of tolerance, and with the Jewish community in Newport nearly obliterated by the war, did not establish full equality until 1842. North Carolina kept restrictive practices on its statute books until 1868, and New Hampshire until 1876. Despite these anachronistic laws, more honored in the breach than in practice, American Jews took full advantage of the opportunities open to them in the young nation.

Despite the legal equality and the commitment of most American leaders to tolerance and freedom, there were occasional examples of anti-Semitism. Uriah Levy had to fight his way through layers of entrenched prejudice in the Navy, and when he tried to institute much-needed reforms—such as eliminating flogging—he was consistently hauled up before courts-martial, where time and again the blatant biases of his accusers were exposed.[14] In 1861, Congress established the office of chaplain for the Union Army, but required that anyone appointed to this position "must be a regular ordained minister of some Christian denomination." On December 11, Abraham Lincoln received Rabbi Arnold Fischel of New York, who had been disqualified as chaplain of "Cameron's Dragoons." Speaking for the Board of Delegates of American Israelites, Fischel presented a memorial that claimed that the chaplaincy acts "are oppressive in as much as they establish a prejudicial discrimination against a particular class of citizens on account of their religious beliefs," and they violated the Constitution "inasmuch as they establish a religious test as a qualification for office under the United States." Lincoln promised to help, and in July 1862 Congress changed the offensive phrase to read "some religious denomination."[15]

Six months after this affirmation of Jewish equality came the single most blatant act of anti-Semitism that occurred in nineteenth-century America. On December 17, 1862, General Ulysses S. Grant, in command of the Department of the Tennessee, issued General Order No. 11, expelling all Jews from the area within twenty-four hours. Grant declared that Jews violated every regulation of trade, and as such undermined the war effort. All Jews not leaving would be arrested as prisoners. In Holly Springs, Mississippi (Grant's headquarters), and in a few other towns, Order No. 11 was actually carried out. But in Paducah, Kentucky, Cesar Kaskel sent Lincoln a telegram and then went to Washington to plead his people's cause with the President. Lincoln saw Kaskel on January 3, 1863—just two days after the Emancipation Proclamation went into effect—and immediately directed Army Chief of Staff Henry W. Halleck to have Grant's order rescinded. A few weeks later, Halleck privately explained to Grant that Lincoln had "no objections to your expelling traitors and Jew peddlers, which I suppose, was the object of your order; but as in terms proscribing an entire religious class, some of whom are fighting in our ranks, the President deemed it necessary to revoke it."[16]

Most Americans applauded Lincoln's actions regarding both the chaplaincy acts and Order No. 11,* and indeed, the actions did reaffirm a basic faith in equality and freedom. The incidents catch our eye because anti-Semitism in early and mid-nineteenth-century America seems to have been the exception and not the rule. The unlimited possibilities of a frontier society affected all Americans, but to those who for centuries had seen their aspirations thwarted and their opportunities restricted, the United States offered a welcome arena in which they could, for the first time, openly test their talents and abilities. Of all the groups who came to America seeking a better life, none took greater advantage of this challenge than those Jews who migrated from Germany starting in the 1830s and 1840s.

III

The condition of the Jews in the German states in the early nineteenth century made then ripe for emigration to the New World. Mainly artisans and small merchants, they labored under heavy taxes and humiliating restrictions that subverted their chances of business success and even personal fulfillment; Bavaria, for example, limited the number of Jewish marriages. Although emancipation ideas had begun to filter into the German states, the fall of Napoleon reversed the trends, and it would be decades before Jews finally broke free of anti-Semitic regulations. In the late 1830s

---

* The New York *Times,* however, on January 18, 1863, expressed distaste not only for Grant's order but for Lincoln's handling of it and the allegedly "sycophantic" Jewish delegation: "The order to be sure, was promptly set aside by the President but the affront to the Jews conveyed by its issue, was not so easily effaced. A committee of Jews took it upon themselves to thank President Lincoln at Washington for so promptly annuling the odious order. Against the conduct of the committee the bulk of the Jews vehemently protest. They say they have no thanks for an act of simple and imperative justice, but grounds for deep and just complaint against the Government, that General Grant has not been dismissed from the service."

a sharp slump in trade provided still another impetus to emigration, and a steady flow of Jews from Germany, Austria, Bohemia, Hungary, and western Poland—all of whom spoke German and shared basic German cultural values—moved westward to America. Between 1840 and 1880 nearly two hundred thousand of them came, and they reshaped the contours of the American Jewish community.

Many of the early American Jewish settlers had been Sephardic in ritual, that branch of Judaism dominant in Spain, Portugal, and North Africa, which traced its practices back to the Babylonian exiles. The Sephardim preserved a relatively pure Hebrew dialect, and for everyday purposes used Ladino, a mixture of Spanish, Hebrew, and some Portuguese. Numbering about fifteen thousand in 1840, American Jews stayed pretty much to themselves, and through trade and commerce built a small but prosperous communal life. The German immigrants amazed them, not only because the newcomers were poor, but they were also a different type of Jew. In northern Europe, Jews followed Ashkenazic rites derived from the Palestinian ritual; their Hebrew acquired some of the guttural characteristics of the North, while their everyday language, spoken from France across the Continent to eastern Russia, was Yiddish, a polyglot mixture based on Hebrew, German, and several other dialects.

Because many of them had been traders in the old country, they soon strapped packs on their shoulders and set out across the land, selling and trading. Levi Strauss headed for the California gold rush with a roll of heavy denim on his back; when a miner complained that his pants wore out too quickly, Strauss fashioned him a new pair, using copper rivets to reinforce the pockets. The miner was soon boasting of his new pants "from Levi's," and Strauss jeans rapidly became an integral part of the American sartorial and cultural landscape. Others also went West, and South, lugging on their shoulders the goods needed by a frontier society—needles, thread, pots and pans, ribbons and tools; in the cities as well, Jewish peddlers went from door to door selling clothes, food, and household utensils. Peddling proved but the first step for many who soon expanded to open warehouses from which they stocked other peddlers. In the cities they founded the great department stores that still bear their names—Altman's, Thalheimer's, Abraham & Straus, Gimbel's, and Lazarus. Others saw opportunities in industry, and went into manufacturing, as did Meyer Guggenheim, who established a copper kingdom, while Jacob Schiff and others became financiers of expansion.[17]

The success of the German Jews, a success story almost unparalleled in American history, can be seen in the special report John S. Billings compiled as part of the 1890 Census, the only survey of social statistics on Jews ever collected by the government. Ten thousand Jewish families, comprising sixty thousand individuals, most of whom had arrived between 1850 and 1880, provided information. Of the ten thousand families, nearly four thousand had one servant, two thousand had two servants, and one thousand had three or more. Half the men were in business, either as wholesale or retail merchants. One out of twenty was in the professions, and America now had Jewish professors, judges, congressmen, doctors, and lawyers. While one out of eight reportedly engaged in manual labor, they were for the most part skilled craftsmen, such as printers or watchmakers, and many of them owned their own shops. Only one Jew out of a hundred was still an unskilled workman or domestic servant.[18]

At first little distinguished Jews from other German immigrants. Both groups clung tenaciously to the German language; rabbis in the predominantly German-Jewish Reform temples gave their sermons in the old tongue. In 1845, a Jewish elementary school in New York provided all-German instruction, and one of the trustees defended the policy, saying: "I fail to see why the teacher, a native of Germany, should force himself, or be forced to teach the children the elementary subjects in English. Why should the German language in general be ignored or thrust aside?"[19] For him, the community had merely been transplanted from one country to another with all its cultural values intact.

The forces of acculturation soon led to an abandonment of German, just as two generations before upper-class Jews in Germany had dropped Yiddish. America was now their home, and even as they lay the foundations of the great Jewish philanthropic agencies, using their wealth to help their less fortunate brethren, they deliberately downplayed any tendencies that might set them apart from their fellow Americans. In matters of language, dress, and manners, one could discern little difference between the Jewish businessman and his Gentile counterpart. By the 1880s, the prosperous Jewish community, more than 250,000 strong, could bask contentedly in the glow of an open and tolerant society, and confidently claim that in America one could not tell the Jew from the non-Jew.

Even as the great Jewish-American fortunes were amassed, events were afoot in Europe that would soon transform the peaceful world of "our crowd" even more drastically than they had upset the quietude of the earlier Sephardim. The same *pogroms* that had inspired Leo Pinsker and the Hoveve Zion with a desire to have their own homeland had a far different effect on other Russian Jews. The Czar's chief adviser, Constantine Pobyedonostzev, devised a simple formula for ridding Mother Russia of its Jews: one third would accept baptism, one third would starve to death, and the remaining third would leave. Soon the government promulgated dozens of laws to make this harsh policy a reality, and Pobyedonostzev saw at least part of his dream fulfilled. Between 1880 and the closing of free immigration in 1925, over 2.5 million Jews, about one third of the Jewish population of Eastern Europe, came to America.

Packing their few household possessions—bedding, pots, and the ubiquitous samovar—they left thousands of small towns and villages, walking, or when they could afford it, riding to the port cities of Western Europe. At Hamburg or Bremen, they paid dearly for the right to sail three weeks in the steerage holds, jammed into inadequate space that soon stank from a lack of fresh air and from insufficient sanitary facilities. Their diet inevitably consisted of herring, black bread, and tea, so that they could keep the dietary laws of their faith. The passage constituted "a kind of hell that cleanses a man of his sins before coming to Columbus' land," according to one of the popular immigrant guidebooks of the day. Whatever its spiritual values, few who made the crossing would ever forget its horrors.[20]

Their initial reception in America must have made many of them wonder if the traumatic trip had been worth it. At Ellis Island, the main clearing point for most of America's immigrants, inspectors pushed, prodded, examined, and questioned them, often in a language they barely understood.[21] The lucky ones were met by relatives who had come a few months or years earlier, and who now guided the "greenhorns" through the intricacies of bureaucracy. But the gap between this wave of immigrants and contemporary American culture was much greater than that faced by the German Jews a half century earlier. Forced by centuries of restrictive laws into ghettos, practically untouched by Enlightenment ideas, these Jews had turned inward to their religion to find the inspiration and the steadfastness to survive. Western European Jews found them difficult to comprehend, and to the average American they appeared strange indeed. Impoverished, undernourished, wearing long black coats and straggly beards, speaking a Yiddish punctuated by emphatic gestures, and, as a result of overcrowding in the tenements, often dirty, they bore little resemblance to the earlier immigrant groups. In 1882, at the beginning of this tidal flow of humanity, the New York *Tribune* editorialized: "Numerous complaints have been made in regard to the Hebrew immigrants who lounge about Battery Park, obstructing the walks and sitting on the chains. Their filthy condition has caused many of the people who are accustomed to go to the park to seek a little recreation and fresh air to give up this practice."[22]

Once in America the newcomers labored to earn a living and to save enough money to bring over their wives, children, parents, and other relatives. The railroads and mail-order houses by this time had begun to deprive peddlers of their role in the rural distribution of goods, thus closing the avenue followed so successfully by the Germans. New factories catering to urban markets needed workers, so the immigrants crowded into the eastern cities, especially the Lower East Side of New York, and soon made the garment industry their particular province. They worked at sewing machines and at cutting tables not only in the numerous sweatshops and lofts, but in their own homes as well. The bright "greenhorn," taken by a *landsman* (a fellow from the same town or part of the old country) into a sweatshop soon realized that he could enlarge his meager earnings by becoming a contractor, by specializing in one of the many single operations involved in clothes-making, such as the raw cutting, the basting, or the sewing of button holes. His whole family now worked with him, as well as the inevitable boarder—the single man just over from the old country saving to bring his family to America—all of them crowded into the ill-lit, poorly ventilated front room of a tenement flat.

Difficult as these conditions were, they represented a small but significant step upward from working in the hated sweatshop. There the newcomer might work fifteen hours a day, subject to all sorts of petty regulations and harassments, for between six and ten dollars a week, or only three to five dollars if one were a woman. Sanitary conditions were appalling, and tuberculosis became as much the mark of the garment worker as black lung for the coal miner. Some had their lives snuffed out even more quickly in the frequent fires that raged in the ghetto. Only after a conflagration at the Triangle Waist Company in March 1911 claimed 146 lives, nearly all of them young women, did the state legislature finally enact minimal safety standards.[23]

Life in these new ghettos was not easy. Industrialization and technological advances had dried up many of the opportunities available to the earlier German migrants, and their fight for survival often assumed Darwinian overtones. Even as perceptive an observer as Jacob Riis misunderstood the driving forces of the ghetto, mistook the need to survive with greed, and helped perpetuate the myth that Jews hungered only after money. "Thrift is the watchword of Jew-town," he wrote, "as of its people the world over. It is at once its strength and its fatal weakness, its cardinal virtue and its foul disgrace, become an over mastering passion with these people who come here in droves from Eastern Europe to escape persecution, from which freedom could be bought only with gold; it has enslaved them in a bondage worse than that from which they fled. Money is their God. Life itself is of little value compared with even the leanest bank account. . . . Over and over I have met with instances of these Polish or Russian Jews deliberately starving themselves to the point of physical exhaustion, while working night and day at a tremendous pressure to save a little money." Riis failed to understand that the chase was not so much after gold as after opportunity and survival.[24]

And survive they did. Out of one thousand people who applied to the United Hebrew Charities in New York for assistance in 1894, only sixty-seven still required help five years later, and in 1904 only twenty-three remained on the charity rolls. Where nearly one third of the immigrants who arrived between 1908 and 1914 left the United States to return to their native lands, only one out of fourteen Jews did so. While many other migrants came to work for a while, save money, and then return to home and family, the Jews came to stay. The proportion of women among immigrants was twice as high for the Jews as for other groups, and of children under fourteen, two and a half times as many.[25] And as the earlier Russian Jews settled, they helped to bring over their relatives and friends, finding them jobs and spouses. They built up a vibrant culture, Yiddish-speaking with many echoes of the Old World, but peculiarly American in its exuberance and vitality. Theaters and newspapers, social clubs and coffee houses flourished on the Lower East Side of New York and in the other urban centers of Jewish life. Within a single generation, these heirs of centuries of persecution would be moving out of the ghettos; their lofts and sweatshops would be transformed into small factories; and their children, thanks to public education and family thrift, would become a generation of doctors and lawyers, dentists and accountants, teachers and small business-men.[26]

To the German Jewish aristocracy, however, the idea that this human flood would ever amount to anything must have seemed chimerical. From the very beginning, they had been unhappy about this new immigration, seeing it as a threat to their own acceptance into American society. "Those people" seemed barbaric vestiges of the Middle Ages, unsuited for American society. "The thoroughly acclimated American Jew," according to the *Hebrew Standard,* "has no religious, social or intellectual sympathies with them. He is closer to the Christian sentiment around him than to the Judaism of these miserable darkened Hebrews."[27] The New York correspondent of the *American Israelite,* after a visit to Ward's Island, reported: "They looked exactly like the Polish riff-raff of which most European cities are only too familiar. . . . And what is said by those who know of their personal characteristics is not calculated to increase the sympathy which we are all bound to feel for them."[28]

For those already established in America, the influx of Russian Jews presented a dilemma. They recognized a Jewish kinship with the newcomers, however distant it might be, and thousands of the new immigrants benefited from the various philanthropic agencies established by the wealthy German-American Jews or by rich Europeans like the Baron de Hirsch. Moreover, the forces of persecution in Russia that had triggered this new migration bore more than a faint resemblance to the anti-Semitism that had propelled them and their parents to leave Germany.

But why did they have to come at such an inopportune time? Why did they have to come at all? Just when the German Jews believed that a full integration of Judaism into American life was at hand, here came these dirty, vulgar, poor—and worst of all— *unassimilable* Orientals! Led by Isaac Mayer Wise, the Americanized Reform Jews preferred to call themselves "Israelites" or "Hebrews," and they worshiped decorously in temples; now came this cultural shock of meeting their past. It was not a case of confused identity; each group knew who it was and who the others were. "They are Jews," declared Dr. Wise, "and we are Israelites." In response, the Russians proudly answered, "We are Jews, and they are *goyim* (Gentiles)." The general prejudice of the Germans manifested itself at a dance of Russian Jewish immigrants. The guest of honor, an American Jewish lawyer of German origin, began his speech with the comment, "Who would believe this is a gathering of Russian Jews. Everyone looks handsome."[29]

From the 1870s on, spokesmen for America's established Jewry had constantly tried to limit Jewish immigration from Eastern Europe. Although they established a Hebrew Emigrant Aid Society, its secretary took the attitude that "as American Israelites we have a duty to the community in which we live, which forbids us to become parties to the infliction of permanent paupers upon our already overburdened city."[30] The HEAS repeatedly wired its European counterparts to stop sending more Jews. Before a United States commission on immigration in 1901, Simon Wolf testified that there had never been any desire by American Jews to encourage this influx from Russia. "We naturally preferred that they should remain in the countries in which they had been born."

In an effort to stem the tide, Jacob Schiff, Oscar Straus, and Jesse Seligman met with President Benjamin Harrison in 1891. They urged the United States to protest to Russia about the anti-Semitic laws that "forced groups of its people to seek refuge in another country and that country our own." The three men were as much concerned about the suffering of Jews in Russia as that Russian Jews flooded into the United States. Harrison sent two special investigators to Russia, Colonel John B. Weber, the immigration commissioner at Ellis Island, and Dr. Walter Kempster, a specialist in the pathology of insanity and a man also knowledgeable about immigration. In their report, issued the following year, they documented the misery and poverty of Russian Jewry, conditions, they declared flatly, the likes of which they had never seen before and prayed never to see again. The majority of Russian Jews lived in worse conditions than even the poorest Russian peasants or workers, crammed into small hovels, denied basic rights, and restricted in their chances to earn a living. The two men confirmed that death through slow starvation confronted the bulk of them, and urged the President to protest against the Czar's policy, despite the established American aversion to interfering in the internal matters of another country. Harrison, however, refused to depart from what he considered established rules of foreign policy, and lodged no protest.[31]

The aristocracy, unable to stop the flow at its source, then turned to ameliorating some of the worst traits (as they saw them) of the newcomers, and making them fit to be Americans. The various charitable groups all helped the Russians, not only with basic needs, but through a variety of educational projects where the immigrants could learn to speak English and understand the workings of American democracy. The basic insecurity that motivated this drive for uplift can be seen in the remarks of Rabbi William Friedman of Denver to a meeting of the Council of Jewish Women in 1903. "We, who are the cultured and refined, constitute the minority," he said, but we "shall be judged by the majority, by the Russian Jews, by the children of the Ghetto. What a powerful weapon your influence can become in a Jewish community, in lifting up and educating and civilizing the Russian Jews. Their children will far outnumber your children, and your children, though educated, cultured, refined, wealthy, will find themselves in the minority and judged by the Russian Jews."[32] At all times the desire to help, the recognition of other Jews suffering, was tempered by a fear that their own newly won position in society was not yet safe, that they too could be toppled down into the depths.*

More than just wealth and culture separated the older German Jewish immigrants from the Russian newcomers, for there were some less than wealthy or cultured Germans, and many of the Russians soon became quite well-to-do. The Reform movement had already begun to affect German Jewry during the migration of the 1840s and 1850s, and these ideas quickly took root in the New World. When the American Jewish aristocracy said it was Jewish, its members meant they were Reform. Despite the *Haskalah*—the Jewish Enlightenment—Reform doctrine never gained large numbers of adherents in Eastern Europe, where Jews clung to their Orthodoxy. When the Russians came to America, they brought their religion along intact, and, as much as anything else, this loyalty to the rituals and dogmas of their forefathers set these new arrivals apart from their already established coreligionists.

The rise of Reform Judaism in America paralleled its growth in Europe. As emancipation freed Jews from legal restrictions, a need arose to bring the religious aspects of their lives into accord with their new-found social status. The old rituals had reflected their lives —lives of despair and humiliation, in which one importuned God to redeem His people. Now that the way appeared open to Jews to take their rightful places in society, they wanted a worship that (as they saw it) would be more dignified, more tasteful, more modern, and, as some were willing to admit, more Christian. For so many centuries

---

* The Germans also sponsored a number of projects to divert the immigrants from settling in the eastern cities. By reducing the size of the ghettos and dispersing small groups around the country, the immigrants would, hopefully, be Americanized faster, and their lessened visibility would reduce anti-Semitism. Despite much energy and large sums of money, this attempt to make farmers out of Russian townspeople failed; by 1912, less than four thousand Jewish families were settled on the land. The policy did succeed to a degree, though, in that it created numerous Jewish communities in the smaller cities of the South and Midwest.

the Jews had been a people set apart; now Reform leaders worked to minimize the differences between Jewish and non-Jewish practices.

Among the leaders of Reform Judaism in America, David Einhorn and Samuel Hirsch worked out the main theological tenets, while Isaac Mayer Wise and, to a lesser extent, Max Lilienthal effected the changes in ritual and practice. All of them drew upon the German rabbis who had founded the Reform movement, and especially on the writings of Abraham Geiger. The two major theoretical issues concerned the status of the traditional law (*Halakah*) and the status of the Jewish people. Orthodox Jews held *Halakah* to be permanent and immutable, decreed by God through the Torah, and developed by the rabbis in the Talmud, that great compendium of legal, religious, and social commentary dating from the Babylonian exile. *Halakah* demanded that Jews follow certain dietary laws, that they conduct their public and private lives according to certain ethical and ritualistic codes, that men and women assume different social and religious roles, and much more—most of which enlightened Jews found unsuited to the world of the nineteenth century. Reform, on sound historical grounds, pointed out that the law need not be considered unchangeable—the Bible and the Talmud both contained many examples of how the law had changed, and even during the Middle Ages, rituals and practices had been transformed. For Judaism to remain a living and vital force, they argued, its practices must change, its law must be progressive, even at the same time that its basic ethical concepts rooted in the unity of God and the dignity of man were preserved.

The status of the Jews constituted a much thornier issue. If they were a people, did this mean that they would always be a group apart, expecting some day to return to Palestine? Or were they merely men and women who shared common religious principles, and, as such, made no claim to the organic unity of nationhood? This need not have been an issue in nineteenth-century America, since all sorts of groups came to these shores, bringing their religious and ideological baggage with them. As long as no one group tried to impose its views on others, the country officially adopted a live-and-let-live doctrine. In the exuberance of youth and growth, the United States had no time to waste trying to define itself. Like a nation of Whitmans, it could call out:

> Do I contradict myself?
> Very well then I contradict myself,
> (I am large, I contain multitudes).

But the issue was at that time very much alive in Europe, thanks to the rise of nationalism and romanticism, and when Samuel Hirsch came to America in 1866 he brought the latest German Reform thinking with him. Three years later Einhorn and a number of other liberal rabbis met in Philadelphia, with David Einhorn the intellectual leader of the group. The meeting took a significant step toward denying a peoplehood for the Jews. Jews were not in exile, as the Orthodox maintained, but had been chosen by God to disperse the knowledge and worship of God throughout the world. The Diaspora, therefore, could not be interpreted as a punishment, but as a mission. The rabbinical statement (issued in German, of course) declared in part that "the messianic aim of Israel is not the restoration of the old Jewish state . . . but the union of all the children of God."[33] Sixteen years later, organized American Reform met in Pittsburgh to draw up a more comprehensive theological statement, and the platform the assembled rabbis adopted marked a high point in Reform universalism. Self-consciously a product of its age, the Pittsburgh Platform reflected the general belief that reason and science would ultimately triumph over evil in the world, leading to a new (messianic) stage marked by both spiritual and material progress. Not only did the rabbis reject the dietary laws and the concept of priestly purity, they also firmly put aside any hope of a return to Palestine. Jews henceforth, at least in the Reform view, would be citizens of their countries who accepted a certain ethical and spiritual attitude.[34]

While Einhorn and Hirsch developed a modernistic, Kantean theology, Isaac Mayer Wise took the lead in erecting the institutional forms and practices of American Reform. Wise put into effect Abraham Geiger's radical proposals emancipating women from Orthodox restrictions and encouraged mixed choirs and family pews in temples. In the *Minhag America,* Wise rigorously excised all references to the

Diaspora as exile, to the restoration of the Temple, or to a return to Zion. Finally, Wise almost single-handedly created the great lay and rabbinic organizations that unified American Reform, the Union of American Hebrew Congregations and the Central Conference of American Rabbis. In Cincinnati he founded the Hebrew Union College, and since Lilienthal headed the large and influential Bene Israel congregation there, that city soon became the center of Liberal Judaism in America.

Yet, as Nathan Glazer maintains, underneath all of the rationalist ideology and rhetoric, there remained a basic attachment to a Jewish people that allegedly no longer existed. Only such a feeling could have led to the retention of circumcision and the continuing ban on intermarriage, two of the tenets that had symbolized the separateness of the Jewish people for so many centuries. "And it was this loyalty to the Jewish people, which they had formally declared no longer existed, that led them to accept responsibility for the masses of Eastern European Jews who began to come into the country around 1880."[35] This may be true, but the Germans feared and resented the Russians and their Orthodox ways, and not until both groups became more secure in their status as Americans would this hostility wane.

Occupying the religious middle ground between Reform and Orthodoxy was the Conservative movement, which sympathized with many of the modernistic ideas of Reform, but reacted against the alleged "excesses" in its innovations. Conservatism did not have a national spokesman until the famed English scholar Solomon Schechter came to the United States in 1901 to head the newly established Jewish Theological Seminary in New York; in 1913 Schechter founded the United Synagogue of America, the Conservative equivalent of the Reform Union of American Hebrew Congregations. While some adopted mixed choirs and family pews and even the use of the organ, Conservative Jews upheld much of the *Halakah* and maintained the primacy of Hebrew in Jewish life. A most important difference lay in the Conservative belief in a return to Palestine, and when Zionism arose in America, two branches of American Jewry squarely opposed the third.

IV

While prejudice against Jews would never reach the levels found in European countries, after the Civil War quantitative and qualitative changes took place in American biases against Jews. Whether it was the strange behavior and dress of the Russian Jewish immigrants, the remembrance of centuries-old animosities, or the development of a large exploited and frustrated body of industrial workers, the German aristocracy's fears about anti-Semitism seemed to come true toward the end of the century.

Most Americans from the time of the Founding Fathers had prided themselves on the lack of anti-Semitism in the United States. "In all the various intercourse of social life," declared one writer in 1833, "we know of no uncharitable barriers between Jews and Christians in our happy community." While many immigrant groups undoubtedly brought racial stereotypes and prejudices with them, the climate of the frontier allowed little room for such hatreds to grow, and there seems to have been no identifiable biases against Jews as a people. "Here you stand," one Christian told American Jews, "on the same level with your fellow citizens of other sentiments; and if, in some cases, prejudices are still entertained against you, they are not stronger certainly than those which many denominations of Christians entertain against others."[36]

Undoubtedly the smallness of the early Sephardic community mitigated against the buildup of resentments, especially in a society composed of many immigrant groups. The arrival of the German Jews in the 1840s and 1850s coincided with the first major outbreak of nativism in America, the Know-Nothing movement, which opposed all foreigners, but primarily the Irish Catholics. Yet although the Jewish population expanded from 15,000 in 1840 to 250,000 in 1880, it still accounted for little more than 0.5 per cent in the total population of 50 million. Within a short period, most of these newcomers appeared to have assimilated themselves into American society.

Even social anti-Semitism showed little strength in the United States before the 1870s. Jews in the larger cities moved freely among the social, economic, and intellectual elites. In the 1850s, the president of the outstanding men's club in Philadelphia was Jewish and president of his synagogue; in New York, the distinguished Knickerbocker Club counted Moses Lazarus among its founders, while the equally prestigious Union League Club had Joseph Seligman as a charter member. Society magazines carried Jewish weddings, and the most patrician clubs welcomed Jewish applicants. Even Brahmin Boston encouraged Jews to take leading places in the city, and elected Leopold Morse as their representative in Congress.[37]

All this began to change after the Civil War, and according to John Higham, as the German peddlers spread out across the nation, the same peddlers who within a generation would be successful and wealthy merchants and bankers, the European stereotype of the Jew as Shylock appeared in the New World. As the German Jews climbed the economic and social ladder—as did far more numerous Gentiles—some of the unease at the excesses of the Gilded Age focused on the Jews, and the resentments against the times became an indictment of Jewish manners. Jews were now characterized as mercenary, unscrupulous, and self-assertive, barbarians attempting to elbow their way into polite society—charges that applied equally as well to nearly all of the Gentile robber barons of the times. Vulgarity and ostentation marked the era and rapidly upset the previous simplicity of American life. But where the Gentile *nouveaux riches* were able to buy their way or marry into accepted society, Jews could not. "In an age of parvenues, the Jews provided an all too visible symbol of the parvenue spirit."[38]

Patterns of social exclusion thus developed in the last two decades of the nineteenth century that would not change significantly until after the Second World War. In 1877 the Grand Hotel in Saratoga turned away the eminent banker Joseph Seligman, a policy soon adopted by other fashionable hotels, resorts, clubs, and schools. The *Social Register* closed its list to Jews, and in 1892 the Union League Club blackballed Theodore Seligman, son of one of its founders. Within a decade, Jews found themselves excluded from all of New York's important clubs with the exceptions of the Lotos, patronized by intellectuals, and the Knickerbocker, haven for many Democratic politicians. In the nation's colleges, anti-Semitism became a common feature of campus life. The honor societies and eating clubs at Yale and Princeton normally turned down Jews, and one of the dormitories at Harvard acquired the reputation of "Little Jerusalem" because of the supposedly large number of Jewish students living there. In 1913, a national fraternity suspended the charter of its chapter at the City College of New York because "the Hebraic element is greatly in excess." Before long, the nation's best private colleges instituted subtle and not-so-subtle quota policies limiting the number of Jewish students, and the better residential areas in many cities openly posted signs indicating that Jews would not be welcome.[39]

For the most part, the German Jews did not fight back against this sustained policy of social prejudice. Clannish to begin with, they recognized the right of people to associate with whom they chose, although they deplored the reasons behind this snobbery. Moreover, while it may have been unfair and unethical, it was certainly not illegal to limit Jewish access to basically private facilities. The most frequent response seems to have been the creation of equivalent social institutions and country clubs, catering to predominantly Jewish memberships, and oftentimes ostentatiously more luxurious than their Gentile counterparts. When a Lakewood, New Jersey, resort turned away Nathan Straus, the head of Macy's, he immediately bought the land next door and built a far more sumptuous hotel for Jews, a policy John Slawson later termed "separate and superior facilities." Having emerged so recently from centuries of legalized restrictions, Jews did not yet feel so sure of themselves—or of American society—to make a fuss over social ostracism as long as their economic and civil opportunities went unhindered. Admittedly well off by European standards, "still our equivalence is not established. We realize, smouldering under our apparently calm surfaces, a general antagonism to our race."[40] They retreated into their own version of the closed society, one that mimicked most of the social forms of the outer society, and they limited their contacts with non-Jews primarily to business dealings.

When the German Jews said they feared increased anti-Semitism because of the Russian immigrants, they downplayed the social dis-

crimination they already faced. Their worries centered on the possibility of European-type legislation or even *pogroms* appearing in
America. Ironically, those who condemned the Russian Jews as unsuited and ill-equipped to understand American democracy themselves lacked a deep and abiding faith in the country. Despite their
outward acculturation, they remained inwardly uncomfortable and
unsure of their new status. And in the 1890s, another form of anti-
Semitism did flourish briefly, primarily in the writings of some
Populists who blamed the monetary crisis on the control of international banks by Jews. In comic magazines, the grasping Jewish
moneylender joined the drunken Irishman, sinister priest, gaudy
black, stupid German, and avaricious Yankee as stock stereotypes.[41]
The general anti-urban attitude of the Populists and many other
agrarian and small-town Americans contributed to this anti-Jewishness, for the cities, after all, were where the Jews lived. And if some
of the rantings of a Tom Watson could be dismissed, the sophisticated
and pseudoscientific anti-Semitism of Houston Stuart Chamberlain,
which anticipated Nazi doctrines, received wide attention among the
"better" classes.

Although the tone and the volume of anti-Semitism jumped sharply
toward the end of the nineteenth century, by continental European
standards the United States still seemed a haven, a land of opportunity, and there were many Jews who would later be unable to recall
overt anti-Semitism in their youth. Throughout this time the Jews had
numerous defenders, many of them Gentiles. Zebulon B. Vance, the
distinguished senator from North Carolina, delivered a speech in
defense of the Jews that was repeated and widely distributed under
the title *The Scattered Nation*. In 1895, Pastor Hermann Ahlwardt,
a disciple of Adolph Stoecker, came to the United States to preach
his message of virulent Jew-hatred. Fearful of trouble at a mass meeting in New York that he planned to address, he requested special
police protection, and the commissioner promptly dispatched a number of big, strong, healthy patrolmen to guard the German. The next
day, after Ahlwardt had characterized the Jew as puny, sickly, and
racially unfit for modern life, he went over personally to thank the
police commissioner for the special detail, and complimented the
men on their good looks and fine physiques. When he had finished,

Theodore Roosevelt took him over to meet the men, and then informed Ahlwardt that every one of them was Jewish. According to one historian, these years saw as much philo-Semitism as anti-Semitism. Americans were "horrified by the Dreyfus case, condemned *pogroms* in Russia, ritual murder charges in Hungary and the distorted propaganda of the Stoeckers and Drumonts in France and Germany."[42]

American anti-Semitism differed significantly from European hatred, and while Americans recognized this, they did not understand how or why. Ideological and nationalistic anti-Semitism never developed in the all-encompassing manner it had in continental Europe, and never insinuated itself into the social and emotional fabric of the nation.[43] Religious motifs constituted a minor theme in American prejudice, except among later Fundamentalist-minded groups such as those led by Gerald B. Winrod and Gerald L. K. Smith. Although one could always find isolated references to a Judas nature, the charges of Christ-killer gained little acceptance in nineteenth-century America.[44] As a whole, America and American Jews never faced the trauma of emancipation, and nationalism in the United States carried few of the psychological tensions and frustrations so common in nineteenth-century Europe. In this country, the great historic upheaval is not the emancipation and assimilation of Jews but of blacks. Nationalistic anti-Semitism has just not appeared in the United States because the historic conditions for it were lacking. There were no medieval walled ghettos to leave, no long chain of legal restrictions to break.[45]

Economics provided the most common basis of American prejudice against Jews, and here again, while never attaining European dimensions, the Jew as Shylock became a staple theme in American nativism. In the Populist diatribes as well as in the later hate literature distributed by Henry Ford, Jews were linked to an international conspiracy to rule the world through control of the banking and money structures, a stereotype derived directly from Europe, but one that also reflected the peculiar tensions of American industrialization. Fortunately, the openness of American society acted as a limit upon the growth of such biases, and concentrated them mainly in the social sphere. Jews enjoyed full civil and economic equality, and took full advantage of opportunities there. As they gained wealth and success, however, continuing social discrimination became more annoying.

V

To guard against the possibility of social pettiness becoming something more widespread and ugly, American Jewry made several attempts to organize so that it could speak as one voice, efforts for the most part frustrated by religious and social differences. Whenever proposals appeared calling for unity, it signaled instant attack by loud voices in opposition. Indeed, a common saying in Jewish folklore is that where you have two Jews, you have three opinions and four organizations.

The first effort to unify American Jewry set the pattern for many attempts to follow. In 1841 Rabbi Isaac Leeser of Philadelphia, a noted Orthodox scholar and community leader, proposed uniting the country's synagogues so they could co-operate in meeting religious and educational needs, such as the baking of matzoth, supervision of kosher slaughtering, and the training and examination of cantors and teachers. The Sephardim rejected the plan, fearing domination by the Ashkenazim, while the latter objected to the possibility of yielding to certain Sephardic customs. Leeser tried again, also unsuccessfully, in 1845, 1849, and 1855, the last two times in co-operation with Isaac Mayer Wise, who hoped that a common prayerbook might be adopted.

Efforts to join Jews together to protest foreign outrages met with as much success as Leeser's campaign to secure religious co-operation. In 1840, the revival of the blood libel in Damascus led to a call for a protest meeting in New York. Originally, the committee wanted the gathering to convene in Shearith Israel, the most prestigious Sephardic congregation in America, but the trustees refused permission on the grounds that "no benefit can arise from such a course." Here indeed was a portent of things to come, for whenever public action was urged on behalf of Jewish interests, there would be those who objected to any public airing of Jewish issues.[46]

In the late 1850s a series of outrages in Europe led to the establishment of an agency that might have become a national spokesman for American Jewry. A number of Jews traveling in Switzerland were denied the right to do business in certain cantons. Protests made to the State Department and transmitted to the Swiss Government elicited the reply that under the country's constitution, the cantons retained all powers over their domestic affairs, and while the federal government regretted the anti-Jewish nature of the local laws, it had no power to annul or modify them.* In 1858, Jews all over the world were shocked and incensed by the "Mortara Case." A Catholic nurse in Bologna baptized a Jewish child, Edgar Mortara. Priests later kidnapped the boy, and the Church refused to return the child to his parents, claiming that the baptism made it mandatory that he now be raised by Catholics. Protest meetings took place all over Europe and America, resolutions flooded in on the Vatican, but the Pope refused to order the child sent back to his family.

The Mortara case led many Jewish communities to put aside, at least temporarily, their internal squabbling and organize effective national organizations. In France, the Alliance Israélite Universelle was formed in 1860, while English Jews created the Anglo-Jewish Association (1871), and the Israelitische Allianz zu Wien (1873) spoke for Austrian Jews. In America, despite continuous bickering and sectional jealousies, a number of congregations managed to reach agreement to form the Board of Delegates of American Israelites.

Rabbi Samuel Isaacs of Shaaray Tefilla in New York sent out requests to all the congregations in the country to send two representatives to a convention in New York on November 27, 1859. Isaac Mayer Wise at first offered to join, but then withdrew because he had not been invited to issue the call. He refused to co-operate with the Eastern rabbis because he could not dominate them. David Einhorn, speaking for the more radical reformers, attacked Isaacs, arguing that American Jews should act as American citizens and

* In 1874 a new Swiss Constitution established religious liberty and made the treatment of aliens a federal matter. American protests undoubtedly played some role in this, but constitutional revision reflected many internal pressures.

not as Jews. In the end, most Reform congregations boycotted the meeting. At the convention, attended by twenty-four synagogues, the debate centered not on the need, but on the nature of the proposed organization. Isaac Leeser, elected as one of the vice presidents, fought for an activist agency, but caution (or timidity) prevailed, and the Board's mandate limited it primarily to information gathering and relief work, although it would also serve as a watchdog, alert to any infringement of Jewish rights.

The Board lasted nineteen years, and in that time proved the need for a national Jewish organization. It led the fight to amend the chaplaincy acts and to rescind Grant's Order No. 11. As states revised their constitutions after the Civil War, the Board worked to eliminate any vestigial religious restrictions, and in 1866 persuaded Congress to delete a Christian oath from the Reconstruction Act. Educationally, it established the first free Hebrew School in New York, and in 1872 founded a Jewish Publication Society. Overseas, the Board worked with the State Department to ease anti-Jewish regulations, and contributed liberally to various relief and charitable projects. Considering the refusal of large segments of American Jewry to commit themselves to any national organization, the Board's achievements were impressive. In the 1870s the Board established closer ties with Reform groups, and in 1878 became a standing committee of the Union of American Hebrew Congregations, designated as the Board of Delegates on Civil and Religious Rights.[47]

Despite Wise's hope that the UAHC could speak for lay Jewry, non-Reform congregations refused to join, and in 1891 another effort was launched to establish a nationwide Jewish organization. This time a number of the new Russian immigrants became involved, as did the French Alliance Israélite Universelle, which had visions of becoming a spokesman for world Jewry. Representatives from nineteen cities met in Philadelphia and created the Jewish Alliance of America, with the aim of uniting "Israelites in a common bond for the purpose of more effectually coping with the grave problems presented by enforced emigration." The Alliance quickly formed thirty-one branches, but fell apart within a year. The wealthy Jews as well as the Reform leaders boycotted it, while the fumbling interference of the French agency alienated others.[48]

During the 1880s and 1890s, as the German-Jewish immigrants and their children came to prominence, they revived an old European institution, the *shtadlan* (back-stairs petitioner). In every *shtetl* and ghetto of Europe, there would be one or two men who had access to the Gentile authorities. They interceded for their fellow Jews to avert trouble, reduce taxes, and, in general, to mediate between Jew and non-Jew. Normally they were the richest men in the community, and because of their business connections, knew which officials to bribe, and with how much.[49] In America, of course, the German Jews reached positions of power and wealth far beyond anything imagined by the ghetto merchant, and they chose to deal in terms of personal influence and reason rather than with bribes. Simon Wolf, a prominent Washington attorney, became the chief *shtadlan* during this time. His contacts with both the Board and the large Jewish fraternal group, B'nai Brith, as well as with numerous federal officials on up to the President, made him the prime conduit for communications of matters affecting Jewish interests. In the late 1890s, Wolf was joined by a number of other German Jewish Americans, and when a new series of *pogroms* broke out in Russia in 1903, these *shtadlanim* took the next step in organizing American Jewry.

On February 6, 1903, a Gentile youth named Michael Ribalenko was murdered at Dubossary, a small village near the Bessarabian town of Kishineff. The murderer, as it later turned out, was a relative who hoped to gain a greater part of a joint inheritance, but the charges of blood being needed for Passover matzoth soon led to the accusation that Jews had murdered Ribalenko. A number of secret anti-Jewish societies sprang up, while various newspapers fanned the flames of anti-Semitism. On April 19, three days of rioting broke out in Kishineff, and the wave of *pogroms* spread across Russia. Forty-seven Jews were killed, hundreds more injured and assaulted, and thousands made homeless. This new *pogrom* shook American Jews out of their parochialism again, and the National Committee for the Relief of Sufferers by Russian Massacres soon dispatched $1,250,000 to aid the Russian victims, while many more thousands of dollars aided refugees to settle elsewhere. Protest meetings took place in 50 cities across the country, and a petition against *pogroms* gathered 12,544 signatures from Jews and non-Jews alike. But despite the efforts of President Theodore Roosevelt and Secretary of State John Hay, Russian authorities refused to accept the petition or even discuss what they considered internal Russian matters. The next three years saw more than three hundred outbreaks of anti-Semitic violence in Russia, frequently with the sanction and co-operation of local police and officials. In 1906, Congress adopted a joint resolution expressing its horror over the outrages and extending its sympathies, but seemingly nothing could be done to stop the massacres.[50]

By 1906, many of the leading Jews in America felt frustrated. They had raised money, giving generously from their own pockets, they had circulated petitions, they had spoken to the President—and still the Russians murdered and raped Jews. Recognizing that something more permanent and influential than *ad hoc* committees was needed, the leaders of the German Jewish aristocracy held a series of informal meetings in the spring of 1906. This time the idea of organization had the backing of the nation's most prominent and influential Jews—Louis Marshall, Jacob Schiff, Julius Rosenwald, Cyrus Adler, Simon Wolf, Oscar Straus, and Judge Mayer Sulzberger, to name a few. They faced the problem, not of creating an agency, but of deciding which type of organization would be most effective. One faction, led by Louis Marshall, proposed a democratically elected group, representing all of the country's congregations.

The bulk of the *shtadlanim,* however, resisted Marshall's proposal, afraid that open elections would hand over control to the Russian immigrants, who far outnumbered them. Adolf Kraus, president of B'nai Brith, bluntly asked: "Is it necessary that this Committee represents the riff raff and everybody? If the Committee represents the representative and high class Jews of America, that is enough."[51] Kraus and Simon Wolf candidly expressed their fears to Mayer Sulzberger, who presided over the early meetings: "The danger must be clear to any unbiased observer of the situation that unless this proposed new corporation . . . be composed of the most conservative men, the standing of the Jews in the American nation will be seriously affected for the worse. With the machinery for election as outlined, the probabilities are that the conservative elements . . . will be crowded to the rear, and the new organization will fall into the hands of radical theorists whose vagaries will then be accepted by the American nation as expressive of the views and intentions of the whole Jewish community."[52]

The natural conservatism of the group, their patrician outlook, and their experience led to the adoption of a plan vesting power in a small executive committee of fifteen, which would then co-opt another thirty-five men. Self-perpetuating and responsible only to themselves and their consciences, the most powerful Jews in America thus founded the American Jewish Committee in 1906. On its first seal they inscribed the Hebrew words *Chazak V'nitchazeka Be'ad Ameinu* (Be of good courage and let us prove strong for our people [I Chron. 19:13]). For the next decade, this self-appointed closed committee assumed the task of speaking for the American Jewish community. Americanized and assimilated, they worked to Americanize the hordes of Russian immigrants pouring into the country. Lest their own patriotism be questioned, they rejected the idea that Jews constituted a separate group within the United States. They were merely American citizens who subscribed to the Jewish religion, and insisted their actions to protect Jewish interests were secondary to their desire to promote American ideals. The Committee led the drive to revoke the Russo-American Treaty of 1832, under which Russia claimed the right to apply domestic law to American citizens; as a result of that agreement American Jews traveling in Russia were subject to a whole variety of humiliating restrictions. The Committee argued that these regulations were offensive to the United States, since an insult to any American citizen was an affront to all of them. The Committee's activities on the treaty revocation set the tone for most of its future campaigns: quiet contact with influential politicians, co-operation with Gentile groups, and lack of publicity about its own actions.[53]

While this approach worked regarding the treaty, it evoked bitter complaints from Russian Jews when New York Police Commissioner Theodore Bingham charged them with comprising the bulk of the city's criminals.* Marshall and the AJC were incensed at the charge,

* Bingham charged that although Hebrews made up 25 per cent of the city's population, they accounted for half of its criminals. An examination

and they quickly and quietly began their work, which ultimately led to an apology and retraction by Bingham. But they refused to speak out openly, believing more could be accomplished without inflamed rhetoric or sensational publicity. As the days passed and no apology came forth, the Yiddish newspapers on the Lower East Side screamed for action. In response, the *American Hebrew,* which often spoke for the German community, deplored this "excessive sensitiveness of the Jews," and suggested that the Yiddish press practice moderation. The *Tageblatt* quickly responded: "The American Hebrew, organ of the Jewish four hundred, attacked the hotheads of the East Side and soft-pedaled Bingham. Is this the Torah of Americanism which you teach us? Instead of teaching us to be proud citizens . . . of the land of freedom, you preach the Old Torah of fawning, to bend the back quietly and be still." If the Jews should win the struggle with Bingham, the editorial concluded, the credit would not be due to the Jewish "magnates," but to the protest of the East Side.[54]

Although in fact the American Jewish Committee did secure a retraction, the *Tageblatt* had identified a basic problem with the whole concept of the Committee. While in Europe, the Jews had been dependent on the *shtadlanim;* in America, the very idea of a backstairs petitioner offended the ideals of democracy. Many of the newcomers brought socialist ideas with them, and they were not about to substitute a self-appointed aristocracy—even a Jewish one—for the despotism they had fled. In many ways, the American Jewish Committee contradicted itself. It preached Americanism, yet practiced an old European elitism; it proclaimed that American Jews had to be American citizens first and not act as Jews, yet in fact its rhetoric only thinly disguised an acute sensitivity to any slight, real or imagined, against Jews. It deprecated the masses of Russians with their strange ideas and manners, yet it worked long and hard to help and protect them. The American Jewish Committee could claim

---

of the record indicated that of 175,370 people arraigned in police courts in 1908, only 12,192, or 7 per cent, were "Russian," and presumably Jewish. Most of these, it can also be assumed, were charged with infractions of city ordinances on peddling or Sunday law violations, hardly the type of "crime" suitable to the wholesale indictment of a people.

much credit for combating anti-Semitism, yet its refusal to become a truly representative—and therefore truly American—organization left American Jewry still bereft of a single, strong, unified voice.

VI

On the two hundred fiftieth anniversary of the arrival of the first Jews in America, Louis Marshall declared: "May we never prove recreant to this holy obligation, to this tremendous trust, and may our descendants never forget the debt of gratitude that we owe to the God of our fathers, Who has led us out of Egypt into this land of freedom."[55] For all the problems faced by successive generations of Jewish immigrants, to nearly all of them America was a *goldenah medinah,* a golden land of opportunity and freedom. Even before they left Europe, they saw America as a promised land. The European Hebrew papers continuously equated the United States and Palestine as the only two places where Jews could live freely, and preference often went to the United States.[56]

A general compatibility between Jewish and American values had existed from the start. The Puritans in New England studied Hebrew and saw themselves as the spiritual descendants of the ancient Israelites, now starting a new Zion in the wilderness. Thomas Jefferson, in designing a seal for the United States, proposed a picture of the Jews fleeing Egypt.[57] The commitment to freedom, and especially freedom of religion, made Americans sympathetic to those escaping persecution, and in return made Jews all the more appreciative of American liberties. For the first time in nearly two millennia, Jews could worship as Jews and still feel they were part of the secular society. "It has always been my conviction," wrote Louis Marshall, "that the glory of our country was that every citizen worshipped God according to his own conscience, and that there was no occasion for him to make any concessions to government by way of subordinating his religious beliefs."[58]

Once here even the newest immigrant perceived the differences between America and Europe. Ephraim Wagner recalled the last stage of his voyage to his new home in 1888: "Already on the [ship], when I could clearly see New York City, I fell in love with America. My heart told me that this is the greatest, the freest and the best country in the world. . . . It reminded me on [*sic*] the Garden of Eden, and I began to perceive that here the Tree of Life and the Tree of Knowledge are still in existence."[59] The newcomers were greenhorns, and they knew it, but like green apples, they too would ripen in time, and despite an occasional twinge of nostalgia for the old *shtetl,* they set about the work of learning English and becoming Americans. When a former *yeshiva* student came into a tenement to teach a child Hebrew, he asked the mother to "open the *fenster.*" She objected strongly: "Look at you, an educated young man and you say *fenster.* You're in America now, say 'vinda.' "[60]

For all of the hardships, there were opportunities as well as freedom. After pressing coats all day, Ephraim Wagner attended free public school at night, as did tens of thousands of other immigrants. And if the demands of a livelihood precluded too great a pursuit of education, their children would reap the benefits. "The Jew undergoes privation, spills blood to educate his child," boasted a Yiddish daily in 1902. "In [this] is reflected one of the finest qualities of the Jewish people. It shows our capacity to make sacrifices for our children . . . as well as our love for education, for intellectual effort."[61] While this passion can easily be romanticized, the facts confirm that a higher percentage of Jewish children attended college than that of any other immigrant group, and in America education was one of the keys to social mobility and success.

Not all of the voices agreed that America was the new promised land, however, and chief among the objectors were those who feared a loss of Jewish feeling and devotion to the ancestral faith and homeland. Recently many Jewish intellectuals have claimed that the processes of Americanization homogenized the immigrants and made Judaism a pale reflection of the prevailing Christian ethos. America offered not to treat Jews as Jews, runs this argument, if Jews promised not to behave like Jews. As early as 1885, the Russian Hebrew journal *Ha-Melitz* wrote: "This new land is not prepared to receive the old Jewish religion. This agreement does America make with each new immigrant: 'Give me your soul and you may take the material possessions.' "[62]

Whether the immigrant would, in fact, lose his "Jewish soul" was a question that troubled many American Jews, especially those who nurtured the fledgling Zionist movement here.

CHAPTER THREE

ZIONISM
COMES TO AMERICA

The expansive nature of American society, the numerous opportunities available to Jews, the tolerant nature of the political system—all stood in glaring contrast to Eastern Europe. There,
Zionism implied a basic societal anti-Semitism, and incorporated it
both ideologically and tactically. In the United States, a Zionism
directed at anti-Semitism seemed pointless, and both Jews and non-
Jews refused to take it seriously. More important, Jewish energy, so
long confined by ghetto restrictions, burst forth in the New World.
American Jews were too busy being successful to worry much
about a pie-in-the-sky plan for restoration.

Some of the early European Hoveve Zion found the slow growth
of the movement in America particularly puzzling. In November
1883, David Gordon, editor of a Hebrew journal in Germany, wrote
a friend in San Francisco, urging him to form Hibbat Zion societies.
The answer came back several months later. The portrait of American Jewry as drawn by Zvi Falk Widawer-Halevi would have discouraged the most ardent Lover of Zion. The Jews who had come

to America, he claimed, did so only to make money and had no interest in religion. "They are now living in comfort, enjoying the bounty of this land, giving no thought to Eretz Yisroel. Every spark of love and holy feeling for the land of our fathers, for God and His Torah, has been extinguished in them, destroyed to the very foundations—all this, because they worship the Golden Calf." He would not even approach them about colonization, because he knew in advance what their answer would be: "What have we to do with Palestine? America is our Palestine and our Synagogue is our Temple. We don't believe in the coming of the Messiah."[1] All in all, he saw no hope for establishing Hoveve Zion groups in America. Although Widawer-Halevi correctly assessed the attitude of the German American Jewish community, and despite the economic depression of the mid-1880s, his prediction proved false within a year.

On the Fourth of July 1882, as a matter of fact, the first concrete step had been taken to organize a Lovers of Zion society. Dr. Joseph Isaac Bluestone, an Orthodox Jew touched by the Enlightenment and a recent emigrant from Lithuania, had spoken to an Eastern European cultural society about the Hibbat Zion movement then spreading across Russia. As a refugee from cruelty and oppression, Palestine undoubtedly appealed to European Jewry; in America, however, where Jews already enjoyed freedom, a love of Zion would serve a spiritual purpose as a safeguard against assimilation.[2] It is striking that almost from the very start, American Zionists recognized that the conditions that had brought the movement into being in Europe did not apply in the United States, and began to look for alternative justifications that would fit the American scene. Both those who favored restoration and those who opposed it always cast their arguments in terms of the American experience; agreement would not come until events in Europe made both sides come to terms with both Americanism and Zionism.

It would be nearly two years after Bluestone's speech before he could organize the first Hoveve Zion society in New York, with Aaron Simcha Bernstein as president and himself as vice president. Over the next few years Bluestone devoted much of his time to the movement. In 1886 he edited a regular supplement to the New York

Yiddisher Zeitung, and in 1889 issued *Shulamith,* a Yiddish journal devoted to Hibbat Zion and to Palestinian colonization. Many of the members Bluestone recruited were traditional Jews who had either come into contact with the movement before they had left Europe or had read about it in one of the various Hebrew journals. A fairly large number of rabbis were counted among them.

Troubles beset the movement from the start. Ultra-Orthodox Jews denounced it as contrary to the will of God, the socialists ridiculed it as reactionary, and the Reform leaders would have nothing to do with it. For a while, a rival society sprang up, claiming to be the only true Hibbat Zion group. Bluestone characterized the opposition in *Shulamith:* "The very religious consider us heretics, who wish to bring on the redemption before its time. The liberals look upon us as fanatics, who obscure the light of civilization with this new-fangled idea. The 'know-nothings' are against us from sheer inertia. And there are the critics . . . who are not in favor of this nor of that, but nevertheless think it necessary to find fault with anything and everything."[3]

The Hibbat Zion movement grew, but very slowly, and it never achieved the strength it did in Eastern Europe. A variety of societies and discussion groups could be found in almost any city where large numbers of Jews lived. Many devoted themselves primarily to the study of Hebrew or of Jewish culture. Adam Rosenberg and the ubiquitous Bluestone initiated *Shave Zion* societies in 1891 to buy land in Palestine for Jewish resettlement there, and the idea of a limited membership land company soon found adherents in New York, Boston, and several other urban centers. In the early 1890s the Baltimore Hoveve Zion society became one of the most active in the country, transmitting money to Palestine for a land bank, and supporting schools and libraries. Much of its vigor resulted from the addition of two members thoroughly opposed to assimilation, Harry Friedenwald and Henrietta Szold.

This theme, which would recur constantly in American Zionist literature, had been ably expressed by Friedenwald's father, Dr. Aaron Friedenwald, one of the outstanding leaders of the Baltimore Jewish community. On December 23, 1894, he delivered an address,

"Lovers of Zion," before the Mikve Israel Society of Philadelphia, a talk that summed up the essential ideas of Hibbat Zion in America. He rejected the notion that the Jews had to suffer patiently in silence until the coming of the Messiah. Man must live in the here and now, not in expectation of some utopian future. The Hoveve Zion offered a solution to the Jewish problem, and by reviving the national idea, Jewish dignity would be preserved and enhanced. To do less than this would be suicidal. "The Jew is confronted by the alternative," he declared, "either to make a brave resistance against the modern influences which conspire to bring about his disintegration, and to come out of the fight with a new victory to add to his glorious record; or, misled by the false meaning of assimilation, to surrender to what he is made to believe is inevitable, and to suffer the ignominious doom of the forgotten. But Israel will not surrender." Zionism, which would mean refuge and salvation to persecuted Jews, would mean identification and cultural survival in a land of freedom.[4]

The most enduring legacy of the American Lovers of Zion consisted of the large number of its members who eventually found their way into the Zionist movement. Of concrete accomplishments, it had little to show. The Shave Zion did raise enough money to send Adam Rosenberg to Palestine to purchase land. Unfortunately, he bought acreage east of the Jordan far from existing Jewish settlements, and the whole project eventually had to be abandoned. Those who hoped to create a Hebraic culture found general apathy among the Yiddish-speaking masses; Wolf Schur's efforts to publish Ha-Pisgah, a Hebrew journal, met constant frustration. Am Olam, groups of Russian immigrants who had come to America to start life anew tilling the soil in preparation for ultimate removal to Palestine soon fell apart or became discussion circles of young intellectuals and semi-intellectuals. Sincere differences of opinion, petty rivalries, jealous leaders, and inept management—all hurt the movement and retarded its growth. Turkish restrictions on immigration and land purchase dimmed the hope of restoration in Palestine, while the flames of liberty and opportunity leaped high in America. While Hibbat Zion in this country may not have been dead by 1896, as one historian claims,[5] by comparison with its European counterpart it certainly appeared moribund.

II

The publication of *Der Judenstaat* and Herzl's call for a Jewish Congress brought the Hoveve Zion back to life; indeed, all of American Jewry closely followed news of the First Congress, and within a few years Zionist societies, inspired by the world movement but American in outlook, flourished across the land.

In Chicago, a reading of *The Jewish State* led attorney Harris Hourwich to convene a meeting for the purpose of forming a Zionist club in February 1897. Hourwich excitedly read parts of Herzl's pamphlet to the fifty people in attendance, and urged them to join together in support of Jewish nationalism. Despite Hourwich's enthusiasm, the opposition of both Orthodox and Reform proved too strong; a motion to form a Zionist society lost by a vote of better than five to one. A few weeks later, Hourwich tried again, and this time took pains to see that those attending were more sympathetic to Zionist goals. This second meeting led to the founding of the "Chicago Zionist Organization No. 1," with Harris's brother Bernard as president. The numeral, they later explained, was hopefully a portent of many other groups to follow.[6]

In Philadelphia, the excitement engendered by Herzl's publication led some of the Hoveve Zion to band together in June 1897—two months before the Congress—as the Philadelphia Zionist Organization. Like their counterparts in Chicago, the Philadelphians found themselves caught between Reform and Orthodox, assimilationists and new immigrants. On their first anniversary in 1898, they reported how brotherly love functioned among the city's Jews: "We have much to contend with uptown and downtown, with Yehudim [rich, assimilated Jews] and Yidden. The uptowners have dubbed us Russians, and in the eyes of the downtowners we are Germans. But we are neither Germans nor Russians. We are Jews and Zionists."[7]

Within the American Jewish press, Herzl and the forthcoming Congress dominated the news. For the most part, the various journals regarded him as a fantastic figure, but one lacking the expected qualities of either a redeemer or an emancipator. The *American*

Hebrew wondered which way he would turn, either into another pseudomessiah like Shabbetai Zvi, or just into an out-and-out impostor. The Orthodox denounced his secular approach to Jewish problems, afraid that religion would be subordinated to nationalism.[8] Since nearly all of the Jewish periodicals published in English reflected Reform sentiment, they unfailingly ridiculed both Herzl and the Congress. Faced by this solid wall of journalistic opposition, Herzl's supporters organized a series of mass meetings at which they explained Zionism and challenged the anti-Zionists to debates. Joseph Parvein brought out the short-lived *Star of Israel* in order to provide the Zionists with an editorial outlet.

Perhaps one sign of the weakness of Hoveve Zion and the general confusion among American Zionists was that only the strong Baltimore society sent an official delegate, Dr. Shepsal Schaeffer, to Basle. In New York, which had the country's largest Jewish population as well as several Hibbat Zion societies, the clubs between them could not raise the one hundred dollars needed to cover the expenses of sending a delegate. As it turned out, however, three other Americans joined Schaeffer at Basle, and the Congress officials decided to list all of them as participants. Mrs. Rosa Sonnenschein, the publisher and editor of the *American Jewess* (Chicago), attended as a reporter; Davis Trietsch came independently to promote a project for settling Jews on Cyprus; and Adam Rosenberg was there to confer with European Hoveve Zion about Palestinian land purchases. Only Rosenberg spoke to the Congress, giving them an overview of Jewish life in America as well as discussing some of the problems faced by the colonization societies.[9]

Excited by Herzls' charisma and the dream of a Jewish state, Zionist and Hoveve Zion societies suddenly sprouted in numerous American cities in the summer and fall of 1897. It soon became evident that the enthusiasm and energy generated by the Congress would quickly dissipate unless unity and direction could be instilled. In November, thirteen New York societies joined together in a Federation of New York Zionists, and elected as chairman thirty-five-year-old Richard Gottheil, professor of Semitic languages at Columbia University and son of Rabbi Gustav Gottheil, one of the few Reform rabbis sympathetic to Zionism. Soon Gottheil contacted similar groups in other cities, but plans to call a national meeting in May 1898 had to be canceled when the Spanish-American War broke out.

In the meantime, however, internal strife and petty bickering erupted, a condition that would plague American Zionism for the better part of the next two decades. Joseph Bluestone and Rabbi Philip Klein, both of whom had been active in Hibbat Zion for many years, resented Gottheil's assumption of leadership and his disregard, indeed ignorance, of the work done by the Lovers of Zion. Moreover, where most of the Hoveve Zion societies had been dominated by traditional Jews, the new Zionist Federation showed indifference to religious concerns, a reflection of Herzlian secularism. One month after the formation of the New York Federation, Bluestone, Klein, and Michael Singer convened a meeting of Orthodox-leaning Zionist groups, who then united as the Federation of Zionist Organizations in the United States, with Rabbi Klein as president. Like the earlier group, the Klein-Bluestone federation established a Central Bureau to co-ordinate Zionist efforts in the New York area.

Bluestone and Gottheil recognized that local harmony would have to be achieved before any national organization could take place. Sometime in early February 1898 the two men met to discuss their differences, and Bluestone bluntly stated that the Orthodox feared the movement would be led into secular, antireligious directions. Gottheil promised that religious interests, insofar as they did not impinge upon the consciences of non-traditional Jews, would be respected, and on February 28, representatives of both federations met to formally unite as the Federation of Zionist Societies of Greater New York and Vicinity, with Gottheil as president and Bluestone as treasurer. The group immediately ratified the Basle program, and pledged itself to work for colonization in Palestine and the promotion of the Hebrew language and literature. To placate the Orthodox, the group's constitution noted that all efforts "shall be made to foster the Jewish spirit." Klein, however, refused to join and led a splinter party of Hoveve Zionists out of the coalition.

While Gottheil and Bluestone worked to organize the New York area, Leon Zolotkoff proceeded with work in the Midwest, and by March a Western Zion Alliance united twelve organizations ranging from Indianapolis to St. Paul. In Boston, where the level of infighting seemed lowest, the nine largest societies formed the Zionist Council of Greater Boston, representing about fourteen hundred people. Finally, one hundred delegates representing nearly as many groups met in New York on July 4 and 5, 1898, at the Bne Zion Club on Henry Street. This founding convention of the Federation of American Zionists (FAZ) naturally endorsed the Basle program; affiliated itself with the World Zionist Organization, which had recently opened offices in Vienna; and elected as its first officers Richard Gottheil as president, Joseph Bluestone and Herman Rosenthal as vice presidents, and a young Reform rabbi, Stephen S. Wise, as secretary. It also nominated Gottheil, Wise, and William Cowen as delegates to the Second Congress, and each of the men agreed to pay his own expenses to Basle.[10]

Despite the spirit of unity that prevailed at the meeting, signs of future difficulties could already be discerned. Leon Zolotkoff reported on the weakness of Zionism in the Chicago area, then lectured the New Yorkers on their feuding, which he claimed was setting a bad example for the rest of the country. A provision that religious views would not be considered in choosing leaders of the FAZ antagonized many of the Orthodox. Most important of all, the organizational structure of the FAZ made it impossible from the start for it ever to exercise any strong leadership in American Zionist affairs. The Federation joined together societies, and not individuals, in a loose coalition; the individual Zionist belonged to a local society, paid his dues to a local society, worked for that local society, and owed his loyalty to the local society and not to the national Federation. There were no sanctions the FAZ could impose upon either societies or individuals, nor did it ever have the financial resources to undertake the educational and organizational work that would have made for a strong union. The constituent societies were Zionist only in the broadest terms. In addition to the newly established Zionist clubs and older Hoveve Zion groups, member societies included Hebrew clubs, fraternal lodges, educational groups, and even synagogues; the total commitment to a strong nationalistic program implied in the acceptance of the Basle program was lacking, and only that commitment could have welded the Federation into a powerful Jewish group.

This failure of commitment reflected the fact that American Jews still straddled several stages of acculturation into American society. At one end stood the most recent immigrants, Yiddish in language and culture, and still imbued with the European spirit of Hibbat Zion as well as a strong adherence to traditional Judaism. For them America was still an unfamiliar experience, and while they had come to the United States seeking freedom, they still had the mentality of ghetto Jews afraid of anti-Semitism. For this group, Zionism had personal meaning, either as a potential refuge or as a reinforcement of traditional Jewish values. At the other end stood the Americanized Jews, many of them Reform but a number Orthodox, who saw Zionism in secular and nationalistic terms. For them, Palestine would be a refuge for the persecuted Jewry of Europe, especially of Russia; their home was now and would remain the United States. Between these two extremes stood those in transition from being European to being American, and the societies they belonged to reflected the interests peculiar to their different stages of acculturation. Not until 1918, after the trauma of a world war, another two decades of Americanization, and the emergence of a new leadership would many of the problems of organization and purpose be resolved.

Little of this was apparent at the time, and the FAZ leaders set about fulfilling Herzl's task of "winning the communities." Herzl and Max Nordau from the beginning had recognized great possibilities, especially in financial help, from the New World's Jewry. In an open letter to the American community, Herzl declared that: "A crucial moment has arrived in the history of the Jews. Shall they miss this unprecedented opportunity of laying the ghost of the Jewish question, of ending the tragedy of the wandering Jew? Will the Jews of America, in particular, forget in their own happiness in the glorious land of freedom, how heavy is the bondage of their brethren?"[11] At first, despite internal division and external opposition, it seemed that Zionism in America would become a strong partner in the world movement. Within a year, the Federation grew from 25 to 125 societies, and 10,000 men and women purchased the $.50 shekel of membership.[12] In Chicago, the "Zionist Organization No. 1" re-constituted itself as the Knights of Zion, patterned after the numerous fraternal lodges then enjoying a vogue of popularity. They called the individual units "Gates," after the words of the Psalmist: "This is the gate of the Lord; the righteous may enter it" (Ps. 118:20). Within a few years ten new chapters had opened, pulling in thousands of members. In Chicago especially, under the leadership of Max Shulman, the Knights of Zion attracted dozens of men who would later play important roles in American Zionism. At the Third Congress, eleven delegates represented the United States, and Got-theil, who was elected second vice president of the WZO, could report that Zionism was now receiving serious consideration in Amer-ica. While most of this growth took place on the local level, much of the credit for any success claimed by the Federation had to go to Gottheil and to Stephen Wise, who, after being called to an Oregon congregation, directed Zionist activities on the West Coast. The two men wrote reams of Zionist propaganda and traveled extensively to support local organizing efforts.

In March 1899 Gottheil informed Herzl that his work at Columbia University had been seriously neglected as a result of his Zionist ac-tivities. Elected to the council of the Jewish Colonial Trust, he also assumed the thankless task of trying to sell shares in the Zionist bank. Gottheil also wrote *The Aims of Zionism,* the first pamphlet issued by the Federation, in which he explored the relation of Zionism and a Jewish state to those Jews who had chosen to settle in America. "What becomes of the Englishman in every corner of the globe; what becomes of the German?" he asked. "Does the fact that the great mass of their people live in their own land prevent them from doing their duty toward the land in which they happen to live? Is the German-American considered less of an American because he cultivates the German language and is interested in the fate of his fellow Germans at home? Is the Irish-American less of an American because he gathers money to help his struggling brethren in the Green Isle? Or are the Scandinavian-Americans less worthy of the title Americans because they consider precious the bonds which bind them to the land of their birth, as well as those which bind them to the land of their adoption?"[13]

Although this became the standard reply to critics who charged Zionism with fostering mixed allegiances, Gottheil himself seemed to have subscribed to a more traditional view of the relationship of Jews to Zion. In a talk to a young people's group at Shaar Tephilla in New York, he said: "Palestine is the place where we can live that Jewish life we are called upon to live, and only there can we take up the greater work of preparing for the Messianic time."[14] This confusion as to the relation of Jews to Palestine, the inadequate analogies between English colonials and American Jews, would continue to haunt the movement for many years. On the one hand, their ancient heritage did make Jews different, and this lay at the heart of the Zionist idea. Yet at the same time, Zionists tried to assure those Jews who wanted to eliminate ancient prejudices and differences that their status would not be affected. Although the early leaders of the Federation anticipated the later synthesis of Zionism and Americanism, they were still too tied to the European past to pull it all together.

Wise's life was, if possible, even more frenetic than Gottheil's. Upon his return from the Second Congress he embarked on several speaking tours recruiting new members. For a while, he edited a section in the *American Hebrew,* inserting Zionist news in the basically anti-Zionist paper, and was also the American correspondent of the London *Jewish World* and *Die Welt,* the official publication of the Zionist movement. In letters to Herzl he detailed an exhausting travel schedule, designed to bring the Zionist message to Jewish groups everywhere.[15]

The work of winning the communities had begun, but was far from successful either in America or in Europe, when Theodore Herzl died on July 3, 1904. Jewish newspapers, including many that opposed Zionism, carried black headlines. In Zionist clubrooms across the land, men and women wept openly, while mass meetings as well as eulogies in synagogues marked the passing of the leader.* Even the *Forwards,* whose socialist leanings had made it decidedly cool toward Zionism, noted that "the Zionists do not overestimate Herzl.

---

* Not all mourned his passing. At a meeting of rabbis in a small East Side synagogue, Rabbi Samuel Jaffe, leader of an ultra-Orthodox group, prayed: "Blessed is the Lord who struck him down."

He was a prominent leader in the Zionist movement, no matter what we Jewish Socialists think about it." In the *Maccabean,* the official journal of the Federation of American Zionists, Lewis N. Dembitz sounded the call to move forward: "The news of Herzl's death, instead of being an occasion for bowed heads, for a craven flight from his ideals, for a breakup in the Zionist camp, should be sounded as a trumpet call to redouble efforts to a closer union, to harder work. Let us form new societies; let us bring new members into the old ones; let us buy shares in the Colonial Trust, and make our neighbors buy shares; let us remove all causes of quarrel and dissension, not only among the Zionists, but among Jews in general; let us be worthy of restoration—and we will be restored to our ancient greatness."[16]

III

In June 1900, Gustav Gottheil, a Reform rabbi who had emigrated from Germany via England three decades earlier, declared: "There is no such thing as an anti-Zionist. A man need not be a supporter of our ethics, but how can anyone in whose veins flows Jewish blood oppose the movement? Every true Jewish heart is naturally Zionistic."[17] Gottheil's statement must have come as something of a shock to the large number of American Jews who most decidedly opposed Zionism, and chief among the detractors of the movement were Gottheil's own colleagues, the Reform rabbis.

Just as Reform in Europe had identified its future with the secular state, so in the United States Reform Jews saw themselves as primarily American. Biblical Israel represented only a historical part of Judaism, whose mission now lay in spreading the idea of God throughout the world. As if to emphasize their allegiance, Reform throughout the nineteenth and early twentieth centuries went out of its way to negate any ties to Palestine. When Charleston Jews dedicated the first Reform temple in America in 1841, Rabbi Gustav Poznanski had proudly proclaimed: "This country is our Palestine, this city our Jerusalem, this house of God our Temple." Time and again over the next hundred years Reform leaders would solemnly intone this formula. Reform Judaism, they argued, lived in the here and now, not in some half-forgotten idealized past. On the whole, said Isaac Mayer Wise, "we think it about as well to let the old Jerusalem rest under the accretion of ages as it is described in the Bible and Josephus. The consequence to mankind cannot be found under the rubbish of 2,000 years." David Philipson, a member of Hebrew Union College's first graduating class and a lifelong opponent of Zionism, declined to join in the reading of Lamentations on the Ninth of Ab, the traditional date of the destruction of the Temple, explaining that as far as he was concerned, the day should be one of rejoicing, not of sorrow, since the dispersion of the Jews led them on to a greater mission.[18]

One of the leading popularizers of this view of modern Judaism preached innumerable sermons to both Jewish and Gentile audiences in Boston. As rabbi of Temple Israel, Solomon Schindler hoped to win the respect and understanding of non-Jews for Reform emphasizing its modern, enlightened, democratic nature and its rejection of traditional messianic beliefs. While antagonizing many traditional Jews, Schindler won plaudits from the Harvard Divinity School, whose faculty praised Reform for its "intellectual clearness and its ethical activity." His insistence that a man cannot have two countries at the same time led him to charge that no Jew who dreamed of returning to Palestine could be a good American. The Boston *Transcript,* spokesman for the city's ruling elite, heartily approved; it reprinted many of Schindler's sermons, and commented that in turning their backs on Palestine, Jews would be "as American as any of us can be."[19]

Schindler, Isaac Mayer Wise, and other Reform Jews were caught in a dilemma of their own making, a result of attempting to transplant European ideas and experiences to American soil. Inspired by the dream of emancipation, they devised new versions of Judaism that excised all national claims, denied any desires for Palestine, transformed the concept of exile into mission, and limited itself to ethical considerations. They failed to recognize that the emancipation represented not the beginning of a new Age of Reason, but the last gesture, almost an afterthought, of the Enlightenment. Even while Reform Jews tried to prove their loyalty as citizens in terms of

eighteenth-century rationalism, modern anti-Semitism developed in
the context of irrational nineteenth-century nationalism, which so
defined race and nationality that assimilation could only come
through total denial of Jewishness—through conversion—and this
step Reform could not and would not take.

While the fear of conflicting loyalties made some historic sense in
the European experience, it made little sense in American society.
The United States from the start had been a nation of immigrants,
and while isolated castes like the Boston Brahmins, the New York
Knickerbockers, and the First Families of Virginia claimed a certain
aristocracy based on blood, they were about the only people to take
such claims seriously. Societies like the Daughters of the American
Revolution and the Order of Cincinnatus have, outside their own
membership, never commanded much respect. Blood lines for most
Americans have been mixed, and three centuries of open immigration
prevented the growth of those fantasies of blood and race common
to European nationalists. Not until the twentieth century did the
concept of "true Americanism" arise, and even then, with the exception of a few extremists, it emphasized ideals and customs rather
than lineage. But the German migrants, insecure in their new home,
clung to the ideas they had brought with them. Recognizing that
America was different, they nonetheless determined to prove their
loyalty within the framework of European emancipation. Hibbat
Zion and later political Zionism threatened, at least in their minds,
to raise the same charges of divided loyalty from which they had
fled in Germany.

As a result of these fears, Reform leaders attacked any Zionist
proposals as indicative of divided loyalty or of raising prejudices by
setting Jews apart. They condemned Emma Lazarus as trying to create
barriers between Jews and their Christian neighbors, and when she
advocated Jewish colonization in Palestine, they accused her of taking
the same approach as Stoecker and the other anti-Semites.[20] Even
Halukkah for the Jews of Palestine raised objections by some that
this charity kept alive distasteful differences between Jew and
non-Jew, and they suggested that if the pietists spent the same energy
migrating to places where they could find decent jobs as they had in
getting to Jerusalem, it would be better both for them and for Juda-

ism.[21] Since most of the supporters of Hibbat Zion and of Herzl could be found among the Russian immigrants, the dislike the Germans felt for them amplified the charges that they were unfit to be Americans, and of Zionism as an "alien" philosophy. Kaufman Kohler, rabbi of Beth-El in New York and later head of the Hebrew Union College, identified Zionism as one of the "oriental" aspects of the new immigrants, and called their prayers for a return to Jerusalem "a blasphemy and lie upon the lips of every American Jew." Indeed, the bulk of the Zionists were characterized as "recent immigrants who are illiterate and utterly ignorant of American society," and to point out the differences between them, the *American Israelite,* chief organ of German Reform, noted that "not one solitary prominent native Jewish American is an advocate of 'Zionism.'"[22] The strongest statement had come when Reform rabbis assembled in Pittsburgh in 1885 to draw up a creed for American Jewry: "We consider ourselves no longer a nation, but a religious community, and therefore expect neither a return to Palestine, nor a sacrificial worship under the sons of Aaron, nor the restoration of any of the laws concerning the Jewish state." At the founding session of the Central Conference of American Rabbis (CCAR), Isaac Mayer Wise demanded a Judaism liberated from "all antiquated, meaningless, tribal, merely national and merely local paraphernalia, which impress it with the appearance of one-sidedness and awkwardness, as a stranger in the land of the living, a foreigner in its own home."[23]

The calling of the Basle Congress in 1897 provoked a flurry of denunciation from the Reform rabbinate. Both the CCAR and the Union of American Hebrew Congregations (UAHC), the lay organization, officially went on record as totally in opposition to Zionism, and resolutions condemning the movement would be passed frequently at these meetings for many years to come. Here again Isaac Mayer Wise took the lead in delineating true Judaism and Americanism from "that crazy scheme," "that new messianic movement over the ocean."[24] Reform rabbis around the country quickly took up the cudgels alongside the elderly Wise. Samuel Sale of St. Louis and Henry Berkowitz of Philadelphia termed Zionism "the besetting sin and evil of this age." Kaufman Kohler announced that "our Zion is humanity religionized, not Judaism nationalized," and he carried

out Wise's policy by forcing the resignation of three HUC professors
—Henry Malter, Max L. Margolies, and Max Schloessinger—because of their alleged Zionist sympathies. When the students petitioned
for the reinstatement of the three men, the trustees overwhelmingly
supported Kohler.[25] Even the Kishineff massacre, which led Rabbi
Emil Hirsch of Chicago to see the need for a refuge, failed to budge
most of the rabbinate. Kohler, alarmed by the rise in Zionist
sentiment after Kishineff, warned that "the Zionist who clamors for
a specific Jewish land does not understand the design of God and
the nature of Judaism."[26] In their dread of secular nationalism, in
their fear that their Americanism might be doubted, in their belief
that Judaism had a universal rather than a particularistic message,
the rabbinate of American Reform united to fight Zionism.

There were, however, a few chinks in an otherwise solid wall of
Reform opposition. From the beginning, men like Gustav Gottheil
and Bernhard Felsenthal, the famed anti-slavery advocate, supported the primacy of Palestine in Jewish thinking; Gotthard Deutsch
attacked as Philistine the contention that Jerusalem had no meaning
for modern Jewry, and Stephen S. Wise played an active role in the
FAZ. While opposing the idea of a nationalist state, many of the
rabbis favored colonization. In his presidential address to the CCAR,
Joseph Silverman of New York's cathedral Temple Emanu-El
praised Herzl's project to raise money for colonization, and called
on his colleagues to support this approach even as they opposed
political Zionism.[27] By 1904, a small number of rabbis were suggesting that Zionism and Reform need not be incompatible. Caspar
Levias and Max Schloessinger urged their colleagues to recognize
that Zionism had strong spiritual as well as secular features, and
Schloessinger prophesied that "Reform Judaism will be *Zionistic* or it
will *not be at all!*" In 1906, Maximillian Heller of New Orleans, the
most outspoken of the Zionists, led a successful fight to tone down
anti-Zionist resolutions at the CCAR meeting; he could not, however,
convince the assembly to acknowledge a basic harmony between
Reform and Zionism.[28] Heller's personal reputation and integrity
earned him the respect of his peers despite his Zionism (which many
of them undoubtedly considered an aberration in an otherwise admirable mind), and in 1909 they elected him president of the Con-

ference. But Hebrew Union College, which normally awarded honorary doctorates on such occasions, refused to do so for Heller. The New Orleans rabbi, never one to mince words, noted that "as a Zionist, you suppose you are an outlaw and like the ex-professors, must be disciplined." HUC continued to fight Zionism, and although it relaxed its militancy enough to allow intellectual discussion of the movement, the climate at the seminary remained unfriendly to Zionism until the 1940s.[29]

From the German American aristocracy, of course, came near unanimous rejection, similar to the attitude of the Reform rabbis in whose temples they worshiped. Some proved more open to Zionist ideas than others, and a number even helped support various undertakings in Palestine. But they all agreed that Zionism raised the threat of dual loyalties, and with that they would have nothing to do.

Just before the First Congress, Cyrus Adler wrote Herzl about a plan for finding a refuge for Jewry in Mesopotamia. Adler, who had visited the Middle East and Palestine in 1891, had from the start disparaged the idea of a Jewish state in the Holy Land, but recognized the need for some haven from persecution. Like other German American Jews, he feared the results of too great an influx of Eastern Europeans to America, and Herzl's initial proposal, which did not mention Palestine as the site of the homeland, attracted him. Unfortunately, Adler's letter failed to reach Herzl, and by 1899 Adler had rejected the Basle Program. A scholar and president of Dropsie College, Adler admitted that one had to take Zionism seriously, even if one disagreed, as he did, with Herzl's plans, and his criticism of the movement never reached the level of bitterness and hostility of the rabbinate.[30]

The leaders of the aristocracy, Jacob Schiff and Louis Marshall, had no reservations about the potential danger inherent in Zionism. Political Zionism, according to Schiff, "places a lien upon citizenship" and would create "a separateness which is fatal." If American Jews were ever to be free from prejudice, there could be no claim upon loyalty but that of the United States. There should be no strings on one's allegiance.[31] Herzl, recognizing Schiff's influence in America as well as the wealth he commanded, had tried to see Schiff when the latter toured Europe in 1904. Schiff, after an initial reluctance, agreed to meet, but Herzl's final illness set in, and a close friend of the ailing Zionist came to explain the movement to the American. After Herzl's death, Schiff confided that as far as he could tell, all of Herzl's grandiose schemes had come to naught. Although Schiff generously gave to a number of Palestinian projects, and after the war even offered to co-operate with the Zionists in rebuilding the Haifa Technicum, he insisted that he was no Zionist and condemned the secularists for undermining Jewish spirit.

Marshall, about whom much will be said later, agreed with Schiff regarding the indivisibility of allegiance, and also considered the idea of a Jewish state an impossible scheme. But he saw the pride engendered by Zionism among the poor Jews, and shared to some extent the belief that Palestine could serve as a spiritual center. He read widely on the subject, and seemed to have an open mind; moreover, his close contact with the Russian Jews of the East Side (he even learned to speak Yiddish so as to better communicate with them) tempered the disdain most of his class felt for the newcomers.[32] But he too considered Zionism an impracticable solution to the Jewish problem, and although the Zionists would mourn at his death, in these years they considered him an enemy.

As with Schiff and Marshall, so it was with the lesser personalities among the German Jews. Publisher Adolph Ochs constantly disparaged Zionism, and ordered that the movement should receive little space and no support in the pages of the New York *Times*. When some students at Columbia joined together to form a Zionist club, Felix Adler, professor of ethics and morals as well as the founder of the Ethical Culture Society, and Edwin R. A. Seligman, president of the American Economic Association, both hastened to persuade the students to drop the plan, lest they introduce a "divisive force" among the students.[33] As for the *shtadlanim* on the American Jewish Committee, needless to say they had no sympathy at all for Zionism, especially when it claimed a share in the leadership of American Jewry.*

In his memoirs, Chaim Weizmann tells the story of a visit he

* See Chapter Five.

made in Kiev to Brodsky, the sugar king. Brodsky opposed Zionism, but he promised to support Weizmann's project for a university in Palestine. Weizmann writes: "Then, as later, those wealthy Jews who could not divorce themselves from a feeling of responsibility toward their people, but at the same time could not identify themselves with the hopes of the masses [i.e., Zionism], were prepared with a sort of left-handed generosity."[34] So too with the wealthy Americans. They opposed Zionism, but still, deep in their souls, they felt some attachment to Jerusalem and to Palestine, no matter what their Reform rabbis might say. They did not believe in Jewish nationalism, and fought it when they could. In their minds, they failed to see that the upbuilding of Palestine also meant the strengthening of Zionism. As Stephen Wise wrote to a friend in 1898, the rich Jews would have to be won over by stages. Zionism would have to infiltrate their consciousness by what he feared would be "a slow and tedious process."[35] While correct in his general prediction, Wise could not see that some of the *shtadlanim* would never come to terms with Jewish nationalism.

IV

The German aristocracy and its Reform rabbis might not have worried so much about the "threat" of Zionism had they known more about the numerous internal difficulties the Federation faced. Indeed, Reform leaders far overestimated Zionist strength. In the years before the First World War, the FAZ led a precarious existence, time and again nearly torn apart by tensions between it and its constituent societies, or undermined by a vacillating policy on the part of the world organization. The handful of men and women trying to hold it together almost failed for lack of leadership, and its operations were constantly disrupted by administrative chaos. Membership in the Federation never extended to more than a minute fraction of American Jewry, and even the masses of Yiddish-speaking Russian immigrants, whom the *shtadlanim* saw as overwhelmingly Zionistic, remained largely indifferent to the movement.

The very nature of the Federation almost proved its undoing, since as a coalition of constituent societies (much like the United States during the Confederation period), it could only function to the extent that its member groups would allow. The FAZ did set up local chapters, but these proved largely unsuccessful in attracting members. During these early years, the different Zionist groups had their own views on what Zionism should and should not be, as well as on who should lead it, resulting in unending bickering between the Federation and the societies, withdrawals and reaffiliations, and a constant lack of money to underwrite projects.

Trouble existed right from the start with the Hoveve Zion, who refused to give up their identity and saw the FAZ as too secular in its approach. After a brief rapprochement with Richard Gottheil, Dr. Joseph Bluestone opened a new schism by organizing the Free Sons of Zion, modeled on the successful Knights of Zion in Chicago, which he hoped would attract East Side Jews looking for fraternal association. Gottheil and Stephen Wise protested that all Zionists should be members of FAZ chapters, thus uniting their strength, but Bluestone argued that the movement needed a variety of forms appealing to different interests. Bluestone left the Federation in 1901, and together with Rabbi Philip Klein (who had never come to terms with the FAZ), set up a rival organization, the United Zionists, with Klein as president. Most of the Hibbat Zion groups, who resented Gottheil, followed Bluestone and Klein, and over the next few years, other independent clubs of Hoveve Zion also withdrew from the Federation. The United Zionists sent Bluestone as their delegate to the Sixth Congress in Basle in 1903, where the Federation tried unsuccessfully to have his credentials disqualified.[36] Herzl then stepped in to try to make peace, but found his efforts futile. Interestingly, Bluestone explained to him that the split represented differences between the Yiddish-speaking new immigrants, who were more traditional in their outlook, and the Americanized secularists of the Federation. This analysis, however, ignored the jealousy of the older Hoveve Zion leaders, who felt they had not received sufficient recognition for their early labors in Zion. The United Zionists, although initially causing the FAZ a good deal of trouble, fell apart within a few years when Bluestone's failing health led to his retirement.

Without ambitious leaders, the United Zionists did not stand philosophically far enough from the Federation to support a separate membership.

The alleged secularism of the Federation also upset many Orthodox Jews, who held themselves aloof from the movement on the traditional religious grounds that restoration could not be man's work, but God's alone. When Julius Haber tried to talk Zionism and raise money for Palestine in a small East Side synagogue, an elderly man told him: "Young man, you are going against God's will. If He wanted us to have Zion again, He would restore it without the help of the so-called Zionists. God doesn't need apprentices, believe me. Please go *schnorr* [beg money] somewhere else and let us lament in peace, like good Jews."[37] The many Orthodox Jews who felt this way were as vehement in their denunciations of Zionism as the Reform rabbis; but where Reform counted many leading assimilated Jews in its ranks, pietistic opposition to Zionism was limited to small, albeit vocal, groups.

Many Orthodox Jews, in fact, did not object to man's efforts to save himself, but only to the secular emphasis of Herzlian Zionism. The *Hebrew Standard,* which reflected Orthodox sentiment in America, pointed this out when it condemned those who fasted on the Ninth of Ab for the fall of Jerusalem, but ignored the spiritually more important fast of Yom Kippur, the Day of Atonement.[38] Unlike neo-Orthodoxy in Germany, which like Reform adopted an anti-Zionist stance, American Orthodoxy, with the exception of the ultra-religious fringes, favored restoration. At its first convention in 1898, the Orthodox Jewish Congregational Union of America affirmed that Zionism conflicted neither with religious injunctions nor with the demands of loyalty to the United States.

For these Jews, the Mizrachi organization, founded in Lithuania in 1902, provided an outlet for Zionist energies. *Mizrachi,* which literally means "eastern" (the direction of Eretz Yisroel), is also a contraction for *merkaz ruhani* ("spiritual center"), and Mizrachi has attempted to force Zionism to take greater account of the spiritual nature of Judaism. At first the American Mizrachi chapters affiliated with the Federation, which in turn made significant concessions to demands regarding educational work in Hebrew. But even then the Orthodox found the FAZ too secular for them, and continuously harassed its leaders for their supposed lack of Jewish feeling and their failure to promote Judaism.[39] When Rabbi Meyer Berlin arrived in the United States to assume command of the Mizrachi, he found his followers disenchanted with the Federation, and in 1914 Mizrachi severed its ties to the FAZ and established closer relations with the parent body in Europe.

Between Orthodox and Reform stood the then numerically small group of Conservative Jews, who tried to retain much of the ritual and theology of traditional Judaism, but adapt it to modern needs. In 1906, Solomon Schechter, the famed rabbinic scholar and president of the Jewish Theological Seminary, announced his endorsement of Zionism, and published a lengthy defense of the movement on both religious and national grounds. The Seminary became a veritable bastion of Zionism with scholars like Schechter, Israel Friedlaender (who translated Ahad Ha'am into English), Mordechai M. Kaplan, and Louis Ginsberg all defending Jewish nationalism against both sides. Eventually, as the number of Conservative Jews increased, this group became an important source of Zionist support.[40]

The Federation leaders also found themselves badgered by the socialists for their alleged indifference to secular problems. Orthodox socialist thought had no room for nationalism, but conceived of a universal unification of the working class. Anti-Semitism was but another of the evils of oppressive capitalism and, theoretically, would disappear with the overthrow of the system. When Zionism first arose in Europe, Jewish socialists had denounced it as subversive and divisive, and these same anti-Zionist, antinationalist views traveled to America with the great migrations from Eastern Europe after 1880. Since many of the sweatshops in which the Jewish immigrants worked were also owned by Jews, the socialists argued that worker and capitalist—even if both Jewish—could not share the same secular ideology. They portrayed Zionism as an attempt to postpone the inevitable, an antilabor device of the capitalists and a hobby of the bourgeoisie. In 1890, the first conference of Jewish working groups declared: "We have no Jewish problem in America. The only question is . . . how to prevent the emergence of 'Jewish questions' here." As to secular and religious goals, the socialists dismissed both Zionism and Judaism—"The world is our fatherland, socialism our religion."[41] Since socialism saw anti-Semitism as a reflection of capitalist evils and Zionism conceived of it as a problem in national identity, for many years a large chasm yawned between the two groups. But again, as in Europe, the attachment of Jews to their cultural and religious identity, and the failure of many Gentile socialists to drop their anti-Semitic attitudes, led to the bridging of the gap.

The first Zionist Socialist group formed in New York in March 1903, under the name of National Radical Verein Poale Zion, with Abraham Goldberg, later a pillar of American Zionism, as one of the founders. At first, most socialists ignored the group, too absorbed in their own ideological quarrels. But Zionist sentiment shot upward after the Kishineff massacre, especially among the recent Russian emigrés, and interest in the group increased. Socialist purists like Benjamin Feigenbaum continued to denounce the Zionists, maintaining that true believers "without exception are opponents of nationalism," but abhorrence of continuing anti-Semitism often outweighed ideological purity.[42] In December 1905, despite the split caused by the Uganda offer within the over-all Zionist movement, Poale Zion held its first national convention in Philadelphia. In its program, the Socialist Zionists declared that normal social, political, and economic development of Jews could not take place without a land of their own, and that land should be Palestine. However, they demanded that any Jewish state should be based on socialist principles, with the workers owning the land and the means of production.[43]

Labor Zionists would continuously face hostility from both sides —the middle-class Jews objected to their socialism, while the socialists objected to their nationalism. Moreover, the identification of a number of Jews with radicalism in general led to animosity from both embarrassed Jews and non-Jews who feared the spread of communism. Eventually, Poale Zion gained a fair amount of strength among the Jewish workers, although it never became the force it did in Europe or in Palestine. While its leaders constantly called for greater attention to social and economic problems, Poale

Zion nonetheless affiliated with the FAZ since, unlike the Mizrachi, they did not consider the Federation's basic outlook hostile to their own interests.[44]

The Mizrachi and Poale Zion drew nearly all of their members from the new immigrants who crowded into New York's Lower East Side, the West Side of Chicago, and other urban ghettos. To both Zionist and non-Zionist, it seemed a truism that practically the entire movement came from the Yiddish-speaking masses. To be a Zionist at the turn of the century, recalled Stephen Wise, meant being from the Eastern European immigration. According to the *American Israelite,* the Zionists were "recruited entirely from the ranks of the newly-arrived immigrants, and these know little of its political significance, and care less."[45] Later historians have also placed the source of Zionist strength in the Russian refugees who streamed into America.

While it is true that most of these early Zionists came from the immigrant ghettos, the fact is that Zionism made very little headway among the Yiddish-speaking masses prior to 1914. There undoubtedly existed a reservoir of Zionist sympathy, as the outpouring of emotion on Herzl's death indicated. Moreover, once the war broke out, the upsurge in Zionist membership came mainly from the urban Jewish areas. But as a whole, Zionism had too many obstacles to overcome to reach more than a handful of intellectuals. Out of 1.5 million American Jews, combined membership in all Zionist groups totaled less than 20,000.

Zionism, even among its most devoted followers, stood for a dream of the future. Palestine might be redeemed for a Jewish homeland, but few expected it to come in their lifetimes or even in those of their children. For hundreds of thousands of ghetto dwellers, earning their daily bread took precedence over dreaming about a utopian future. Working six days a week, ten to fourteen hours a day, for barely enough to pay for food and shelter, the average Jew had no time and no money to give to Zionism. If he subscribed to any ideology, he supported socialism, with its concern over bread-and-butter issues, and he would spend whatever spare time he had discussing various ways to improve the economic system so that all men and women could live decently. Among the

Yiddish papers, only one—the *Jewish World* edited by Zvi Hirsch Masliansky—featured Zionist news; the rest either opposed Zionism or ignored it. In 1910, the FAZ began publishing its own Yiddish circulars in a vain attempt to reach the masses.[46] But it was socialism, not Zionism that mattered, and especially the Bundist variety, which emphasized Yiddish culture. Moreover, the constant barrage of propaganda from the *shtadlanim* and from non-Jews about the need to Americanize also retarded the growth of a movement many condemned as creating divided loyalties. Ultimately, the masses did respond to an invigorated Zionism after 1914, but by then both American Zionism and the immigrants themselves had changed.

V

The worst problems facing the Federation involved its own dysfunctional organization and its relations with the European leadership. For all the long hours put in by Gottheil, Wise, and other dedicated leaders of the FAZ, they lacked the administrative talent to shape the Federation into an efficient, smoothly functioning operation. Because of its minuscule budget, the FAZ relied on one or two paid clerks and various volunteers to take care of day-to-day details. Their handling of the bank shares typified their procedures.

One of the first agencies Herzl had established had been the Jewish Colonial Trust, an English-chartered bank that would help finance colonization and developmental work in Palestine. To raise money, the World Zionist Organization called on local affiliates and individuals to purchase shares in the JCT. Gottheil, who had been elected to the governing council of the bank, assumed responsibility for the sale of shares in the United States. He first ran into problems when he unsuccessfully tried to find a bank to act as agent for the shares, a difficulty due primarily to the failure of the FAZ to establish contacts with financial institutions. He finally gave up and opened a temporary office, naming himself as agent.[47]

In response to Herzl's appeal, a number of local Zionist societies agreed either to subscribe or to sell JCT shares. In Chicago, Bernard Hourwich, president of the Knights of Zion, ordered three thousand shares to sell, and personally guaranteed payment. The certificates should have arrived within a few weeks, but three months went by without delivery. Hourwich sent cables demanding the shares, and answers came back that they had been sent weeks before. Since he had not only guaranteed payment, but had also widely advertised the sale in the Jewish press, his anxiety increased daily. One afternoon Hourwich stopped by to visit Leon Zolotkoff in the office of the *Jewish Daily Courier*. Zolotkoff was not in, and Hourwich decided to wait. "My attention was attracted to a big bundle lying in the corner, half covered with torn and old papers. Upon investigating I found that there were the shares for which we had been waiting so long." Administrative mixups constantly retarded the sale of certificates, and in the end, only twelve thousand shares were sold in the United States, less than the number taken in the city of Odessa alone. Similar mixups occurred in the issuance of golden book certificates for the Jewish National Fund, with some delays running upward of two years.[48]

None of the early leaders seemed to have had the administrative capacity to overcome such problems. Gottheil, tired and dispirited, refused to accept another term in 1904, and the Federation elected Dr. Harry Friedenwald of Baltimore as president. A kindly man, Friedenwald's commitment to Jewish restoration traced back to the days of Hibbat Zion; his charm, as well as a firm Jewish background, made him more attractive to the Orthodox and Hoveve Zion groups, who had always resented Gottheil's authoritarian manners and Reform convictions. But Friedenwald, despite his charm and learning, lacked aggressiveness, the one trait absolutely necessary in those days to have built up American Zionism. Moreover, because he lived and worked in Baltimore, he had very little time to pay attention to the administrative work of the New York office. During his tenure, the FAZ experienced little growth, and the membership in 1914 stood at about the same level it had a decade earlier.

Undoubtedly lack of money and the instability of constituent societies compounded the problems faced by the leaders. During 1902–3, for example, the number of societies affiliated with the Federation increased from 174 to 183, but 63 groups—more than one third of the total—withdrew and disbanded. In New York alone, over three fourths of the societies established between 1898 and 1914 fell apart in less than two years.[49] The large number of Zionist clubs indicated weakness rather than strength in the movement, since nearly all of them had small memberships, some of not more than 25 or 30, of whom only a handful actively participated. The marriage of several members of one Daughters of Zion club, for example, led the group to fold, while other societies disbanded after petty quarrels among the members. One correspondent noted that he always saw the same few dozen people at all the Zionist meetings in New York, and from what he could tell, even among the shekel payers, apathy far outweighed interest. In order to insure a decent turnout at the annual conventions, the Federation regularly scheduled these meetings in resort towns like Tannersville, New York, or Atlantic City, New Jersey, hoping that the excuse of a vacation would attract delegates. When the FAZ met in Cleveland in 1912, and in Cincinnati the following year, the sparseness of audience and program was apparent.[50]

The leadership recognized the need for better organization, and intermittently tried to do something about it. In 1907, Judah Magnes reported to the Actions Comité (the executive board) of the world organization that the Federation's main endeavor in the coming years would be building up a proper organization, both internally through administration and externally by new members. The following year, Friedenwald sent out a circular to the societies noting that lack of proper organization had not allowed the Federation to exploit the vast Zionist sympathy in the country.[51] Not until 1910 did the Federation finally secure the services of someone with a natural talent for organization and administration, but Henrietta Szold found the office in a shambles. Elected as honorary secretary, she was soon working day and night but, as she felt, in vain. After six months on the job, she wrote: "The affairs of the Federation were in a hopeless muddle when I took hold of them; I can say that the muddle has been cleared, but the hopelessness remains. So, you see, there is endless work, and no gratification. I cannot flatter myself that I am doing Zionist work; cleaning up other people's Augean stables is far too removed from Jewish ideal hopes."[52] Yet it was just this type of work that the Zionists needed more than anything else, a painstaking attention to details, and a follow-up on all problems. But Miss Szold could only do so much, and the passive attitude of her friend Harry Friedenwald prevented her from pushing too far for an overhaul of the total structure.

Finally, the organization never had enough money. Dues and the shekel tax were always in arrears, and much of the secretarial work consisted of sending out dunning letters to the societies begging for back payments. In its best years, the annual budget rarely exceeded twelve thousand dollars, including collections for the world organization funds. And as Louis Lipsky pointed out, as long as the constituent societies insisted on a stubborn independence, they had no one but themselves to blame if the Federation did not provide sufficient educational and propaganda services.[53]

Certainly the blame for much of the inefficiency and lethargy of the Federation should be placed on the recalcitrance of the affiliates, who stubbornly refused to yield any of their independence to the national body. The Order Knights of Zion, the largest Zionist group outside New York, consistently refused to co-operate with the Federation, and insisted upon direct relations with the WZO. In 1907, the Eighth Congress legislated that any group that purchased three thousand shekels on a worldwide basis would be recognized as an independent party, which immediately gave the American Mizrachi and Poale Zion their freedom from the FAZ. The Knights also applied for independent status, which the Actions Comité, over the objections of the Federation, approved. The Knights left the FAZ and did not reaffiliate until 1913, and then only as a semi-autonomous "district."[54] The Federation did make periodic but futile attempts to gain greater control over the member societies. In 1902, after a particularly bitter fight, the convention voted seventy-four to forty-eight to require all societies to seek subsidiary charters from the Federation. The delegates, however, refused a companion motion that would have required financial statements from the societies.[55] Most affiliates simply ignored the new requirement, and the FAZ had neither the will nor the means to enforce it.

The American leaders found little help with their problems when they turned to Europe. From the beginning, the European Zionists had seen America as a land of wealth, and assumed that all its Jews had fortunes. The failure of the Federation to raise large sums of money confused the members of the Actions Comité, and they persisted in dunning the Americans for amounts that had not been and could not be raised. In turn, they excluded the Americans from the important councils and committees, and undermined the Federation in its efforts to organize and unite American Zionists.

Despite Herzl's various appeals to American Jews, and Nordau's contention that the United States would be the salvation of the movement, the Europeans from the start treated the American Zionists contemptuously. Without consulting Gottheil, Herzl dispatched a number of private missionaries to the United States to spread Zionist propaganda. Both Michael Singer and Joseph Zeff proved singularly slow to recognize that the separatist rhetoric used in Europe would not work in the United States. American Zionists as well as non-Zionists believed the condition of the Jews here to be different than it had been in the old country. To have zealots now tell them that they were still enslaved did nothing to enlarge their Zionist ardor, while it seemingly confirmed the worst accusations of the anti-Zionists. Increasingly concerned over Gottheil's leadership, Herzl, in 1900, proposed sending his English secretary, Jacob deHaas, to America to help Gottheil. The American strongly resented this, suspecting that deHaas was being sent to spy on him. "To send a second- or third-rate man like Mr. deHaas," wrote Gottheil, "would be regarded here as a slap in the face of all of us who have been trying to lead the Movement."[56] Despite such protests, Herzl insisted on deHaas joining the Federation, but relations between deHaas and Gottheil remained cool.*

* In fairness to deHaas, he quickly spotted the weakness of the FAZ, and became an ardent advocate of the AC giving it greater autonomy. DeHaas was far from being a "second- or third-rate man" and had already won a reputation as a prominent Zionist in Europe. He would go on to become Louis D. Brandeis's most trusted Zionist confidant, and hold a variety of offices in American Zionism. As Marnin Feinstein suggests, the real reason Gottheil may have disliked deHaas lay in the latter's reputation as an excellent English-speaking orator, which would have made him a rival of the Columbia professor, who was one of the few early Zionists with a proper command of the language.

The problem of authority over the affiliates and finances provide a leitmotiv in the relations between the FAZ, the other national affiliates, and the Actions Comité in the years before 1914. At the Third Congress in 1899, Gottheil was already complaining that a number of societies refused to join the Federation and had instead entered into direct relations with the main office in Vienna. American Zionism, he warned, would be strengthened "only if the Actions Committee makes it clear that all Zionist organizations must keep in touch with the FAZ." Gottheil continued to insist that the AC endorse the Federation's exclusive right to represent the world movement in America. In 1902, Herzl rejected the idea of a single national organization, and said the AC believed that different forms of Zionist groups, reflecting various interests, should be encouraged. While this attitude may have made sense in Europe, with its larger Zionist membership and its factions so heavily committed to ideology, it ignored the conditions in the New World. The United Zionists, a number of Hoveve Zion clubs as well as the Knights of Zion, emboldened by Herzl's attitude, openly bypassed the Federation, thus insuring the continued weakness of all American Zionist societies.[57]

Gottheil's frustration increased as he saw his efforts to unify American Zionists undermined from abroad. Finally in 1904 both he and Stephen Wise, the only American member of the Greater Actions Comité (the advisory council of the WZO), resigned. Wise exploded right after a meeting of the GAC following the East Africa offer, and his letter indicates plainly the resentment Americans felt about their treatment. "I cannot and will not work with men who refuse to place me in their fullest confidence," he declared. "That Herzl and his colleagues fail to take counsel with the only American member of the GAC then present in Vienna, touching the status of affairs in America, constitutes an indignity to which no gentleman can submit with honor. . . . I am as much a member of the GAC as Herzl or any man. It was and is his duty to deal with me, with us, frankly and honestly—I am not a Russian underling nor yet a Turkish landowner who must be kept in the dark as to the real purposes of things."[58]

Two months earlier, Gottheil had sent an even stronger letter to the Actions Comité accusing the world body of breaking every promise made to the Federation, and working to subvert not only the American organization but the aims of Zionism as well. "You are giving our enemies just the support that they need and are thus playing . . . a 'double game.' " Requests for information had gone unanswered, and regular notices of WZO activities had not been sent to the Federation. Because of these actions, as well as the detrimental effect they had had on his health, he was resigning from the Federation presidency and from his positions within the world body.[59]

When Friedenwald took over the reins of the Federation, he had made several efforts to improve relations between the American branch and the world headquarters. While "the relationship between the Federation and the Actions Comité has not been as close as it might have been," the Americans promised they would co-operate if only the world leaders did the same. The letter, the third in a series, elicited no response, and before long Friedenwald's communications to Vienna and Cologne took on a familiar plaintive tone. When the Congress recognized the Knights of Zion as an independent body, the Federation officials felt completely humiliated, and in November 1908, the FAZ Executive Committee nearly voted to sever ties with the world organization.[60] This seemed to have shocked the AC into finally beginning to deal more seriously with the Americans, although relations improved only slightly over the next few years.

The Actions Comité refused to grant the Federation sole representation in the United States for a very simple reason: money. As long as the independent societies paid the shekel dues, contributed to the Jewish National Fund, and purchased shares in the Jewish Colonial Trust, the central administration was not going to jeopardize these sources of revenue in order to impose a unified authority that, whatever might be its ultimate merits, would reduce immediate income. At no time in its history would the World Zionist Organization be able to count on sufficient resources to fund its various projects, and while some of the officials saw the long-term benefits of better organization and clearer lines of authority, the current cash needs made it imperative to bring in every dollar. Herzl justified his refusal to designate the FAZ as sole representative of the movement in America on the grounds that it might choke off the development of new societies that would bring in desperately needed funds.

Had the Federation been able to show that unity would have yielded more revenue, it might have presented a stronger case. As it was, the FAZ could not meet regular payments on its own shekel tax. Toward the end of 1902, the Federation asked permission to submit the tax in installments. Although it did not spell out the reasons for this request (which Herzl refused), precarious finances had forced it to use the shekel money to pay for local projects, especially the publication of the *Maccabean*. Of the $1,500 collected in the preceding year, only $250 had been transmitted to Vienna, and despite pledges that the arrears would be paid in monthly installments, no further amounts were sent. Moreover, of all the national federations, only the FAZ failed to submit regular financial reports to the world body. It is little wonder that Herzl favored recognizing rival organizations, if they could produce cash. An indication of the financial state both of the FAZ and the Actions Comité can be seen in a letter from Herzl to Gottheil, asking him to put extra stamps on his letters, since the AC had had to pay postage due on nearly all of his communications.[61]

Throughout these prewar years, money—not organization—dominated the thinking of the European leaders, and they never understood that without proper organization, the money would never come in. They dunned Federation officials to raise more cash, to contact the rich Jews, to make a greater effort. Even in the few instances when the AC tried to mediate between rival factions, it did so only in the hope of increasing contributions. As Joseph Jaison sarcastically noted, "we are being constantly reminded how much more we ought to do."[62] The Europeans seemed to think that Jews in America had enormous amounts of money to give, and would gladly give it if only the Federation or some other Zionist society properly asked for it. In fact, with the exception of a small upper stratum of the well-to-do, most Jews had little money, and Zionism had little or no priority on what few extra dollars they might have. This attitude of the Europeans would never be dispelled, and would continue to create ill will on the part of American Jews, who believed that all the world organization wanted was their money. In time, American Jews did become the financial backbone of Zionism and gave heavily to create and maintain a Jewish state, but European and Palestinian Zionists could never admit that their brethren in the United States had other things to offer besides cash.

VI

With all the problems it faced—internal jealousies and quarreling, attacks from both Reform and Orthodox Jewries, lack of money, poor administration, jurisdictional rivalries, and conflict with the world organization—prewar Zionism in America could hardly claim to have been a success. Yet it could point to some achievements, and just as Hibbat Zion paved the way for Herzlian Zionism, so the Federation and other groups laid the groundwork for the new leadership that took command in 1914. In these years, a corps of men and women joined the movement who provided the nucleus for later growth and expansion; enterprises and activities began that could involve Jews of all interests and ages; the basic responses to Reform and Orthodox critics was formulated, and merely awaited final revision and synthesis; and although the movement in America failed to draw a large membership, it did develop sufficient resiliency to survive the territorialist crisis far better than did many of the European national groups.

The offer by Great Britain to provide an area of settlement in East Africa initially split American Jews much as it did those in other countries. At the Congress, six of the eight delegates voted to establish the Commission of Inquiry. The more secular-minded, who primarily wanted a refuge for those fleeing persecution, favored the proposal, while the more traditional Jews would not forsake their ties to Palestine. But even anti-Zionist journals admitted that the Zionists had called attention to the plight of Russian Jews as no one else had done, and the British offer indicated that the movement had gained greater influence than many had believed. On the whole, however, the Jewish press in America showed little enthusiasm for Uganda; if there was to be a Jewish homeland, a true Zion could only be found in Palestine. The Federation, while noting the graciousness of the offer, reaffirmed its own adherence to a Palestinian homeland, declaring that to be the only arena in which the Jewish people could carve out its destiny.[63]

After Israel Zangwill founded the Jewish Territorial Organization, he came to the United States to explain the purpose of his group. With Palestine closed, the Jews needed some place to start relearning the art of self-government, something they had not practiced for two thousand years. For the most part, the new homeland would attract Russian Jews, but he also mentioned the possibility of future anti-Semitism in the United States, an offhand remark that immediately earned him the denunciation of all sections of American Jewry. The ITO attracted a number of Jews, ranging from Nachman Syrkin (of Poale Zion) to Oscar Straus and Mayer Sulzberger (who had earlier supported a settlement scheme in Mesopotamia) to Daniel Guggenheim (who explained that the ITO supplemented the basic aims of restoration). Zangwill even received an offer of $100,000 from Joseph Fels, the soap king, if Zangwill would promise that the new homeland would adopt a single-tax system. Within two years, territorialism in the United States had died away, leaving few if any scars. Most of those who joined felt, like Bernard G. Richards, that ITO offered a good way to get something done quickly.[64] When the ITO failed to get an offer from the British Government, the bulk of the Zionists found confirmation that they had been right not to forsake Palestine. The FAZ, which took a strong stand against the ITO, suffered practically no losses to territorialism.

During these years, various spokesmen began responding to the charges that Zionism conflicted with traditional Jewish injunctions or with the demands of American loyalty. Harry Friedenwald denied that Zionism was overemphasizing the secular at the expense of the religious. Zionism does not stand for irreligion, he declared at the 1908 convention; to the contrary, "the religious spirit which has dropped to so lamentable an ebb in western lands will flourish anew in a Jewish center." By building a Jewish homeland, Zionists sought to create a climate where Jewish life and learning could grow freely. The revered Bernhard Felsenthal tore into those who claimed traditional Judaism incompatible with nationalism. "The ancient prophets of Israel were all and every one, without exception, outspoken Jewish nationalists," he declared, and even in messianic times it was expected that Israel would remain a nation apart.[65]

To those who charged Zionism with fostering dual loyalty, Zionists began fashioning a response that emphasized the responsibility of Jews to aid their less-fortunate brethren as well as the fact that American Jews need not leave the United States. Leon Zolotkoff, in a debate with Rabbi Emil Hirsch, denied that the Zionists wanted to force all Jews to go to Palestine. But since the United States could not indefinitely absorb all those fleeing persecution in Europe, some refuge had to be found for them, sentiments echoed by Rabbis Samuel Schaffer and Stephen S. Wise. At the sixth convention of the FAZ, Gottheil proclaimed that an obligation rested upon those "living under the benign sun of freedom" to help "those that still sit in darkness." As to charges of divided loyalty, Friedenwald declared that they had responsibilities both as Jews and as Americans, but these need not be contradictory, and at a mass meeting at New York's Cooper Union, the Zionists adopted a resolution denouncing those who charged them with being disloyal, and accused them of promulgating allegations that were themselves un-American.[66] But although Zionists tried to counteract Reform opposition, they could do little more than deny the charges of dual allegiance; they needed, but could not achieve, a positive approach portraying Zionism as a fulfillment of obligations and Zionist work as the natural extension of Jewish and American ideals.

Finally, the Zionists could point with pride to a number of achievements. The FAZ began publishing the *Maccabean* in 1901 under the direction of Louis Lipsky. Despite constant financial pressures and numerous handicaps, it became an outstanding journal, with articles not only on Zionism, but on all aspects of Jewish life in America. Lipsky ran original fiction and drama as well as translations from Yiddish and Hebrew, and together with deHaas carried on a spirited defense of Jewish nationalism. By 1914, the *Maccabean* reached thousands of readers and enjoyed a reputation of being a serious literary periodical as well as the chief English advocate of the movement. While *Dos Yiddishe Folk,* the Federation's Yiddish journal, faced much stiffer competition from an established Yiddish press, it too ran quality pieces and raised a Zionist voice to counter the socialist dailies. To reach different interest groups, the FAZ sponsored fraternal orders like the Sons of Zion, and at the 1909 convention established Young Judea to reach boys and girls aged ten to eighteen. Within five years, Young Judea had 175 clubs with over 5,000 members, many of whom went on to become leaders in the movement. In 1912, several chapters of the Daughters of Zion united to form Hadassah, the women's Zionist organization, which ultimately affected and involved hundreds of thousands of American women in providing medical and social services in the Holy Land.

Adolph Böhm, the great German historian of Zionism, adjudged that Zionism proved unable to gain a foothold in the United States before 1914.[67] Despite numerous problems and failures, these early American Zionists could not have been all that unsuccessful. Without their work, the great and sudden emergence of the American movement on the world stage, to which we now turn, would never have occurred.

CHAPTER FOUR

"MEN!
MONEY! DISCIPLINE!"

From 1911 until the beginning of the war in August 1914, the practical work of the Federation of American Zionists lay in the hands of a few dedicated souls whom the annual convention elected —and re-elected—annually. Bernard Rosenblatt recalled that the administrative committee, on which he sat, met each week in a cafe on New York's Lower East Side. There he, Louis Lipsky, Abraham Goldberg, and Senior Abel would attempt to plot new ways to spread the Zionist idea on a budget that any other national organization would have been ashamed to mention. The meetings were lively and talkative, lasting over many glasses of tea, and despite the emptiness of the treasury, not without their redeeming moments of insight and humor. One of the group, probably Senior Abel, would invariably object to each new plan with the cry, "The masses are opposed!" until one night journalist Bernard Richards, who often joined the group, burst out in exasperation, "Why do you always object that the masses are opposed? I met the masses last night in Sachs' Cafe on Grand Street and he was not against this proposal."[1]

Moments like this undoubtedly helped the administrative committee keep its perspective on Zionist life in America, because it must have been obvious to them that "the masses" had not yet swung over to Zionism. At the Rochester convention in June 1914, the secretary reported that a little over 12,000 members had paid the shekel tax, and the delegates groaned when they realized that the proposed budget of $12,150 exceeded estimated income by more than $2,600. The friendly gesture of a nearby church in playing "Hatikvah" ("The Hope," the Zionist anthem) on its carillon appeared to many a mockery of the movement in the United States. Ten years after Herzl's death, American Zionism still had not "captured the communities."[2]

Had the assembled delegates been given a glimpse into the near future, none of them would have believed the changes that would take place in the movement in the next few years. A totally new group of men would assume control of Zionist destinies in America, and within five years would transform American Zionism from a backwash of the world movement into its strongest and most aggressive part. In so doing, this leadership would create new philosophical and organizational structures, so that the emphasis on the phrase "American Zionism" would be evenly distributed. By making the movement part of the flow of progressive reform, Louis Dembitz Brandeis and his associates cleared away the last barriers preventing American Jewry from endorsing the goal of a Jewish homeland in Palestine.

I

The war that broke out in Europe in the summer of 1914 came as a shock to most people, both in Europe and in America. It had been exactly a century since the end of the Napoleonic wars, and the hundred years between had been marked by only limited conflicts. The peace movement, which hoped to substitute negotiation and arbitration for guns and soldiers, had won many adherents, a number of countries signed arbitration treaties with one another, and people began to think in terms of abolishing war altogether. A few observers interpreted the growing commercial rivalry between Great Britain and Germany as a possible source of conflict, but most people assumed that both sides had too much to lose by going to war. The June 28 assassination of Archduke Francis Ferdinand, heir to the throne of Austria-Hungary, by a Serbian nationalist hardly seemed the type of event that could plunge all of Europe into a nightmare of bloodletting and destruction, yet within five weeks the major powers on the Continent had mobilized and begun to fight.

For the Jews of Europe, the conflict proved a double curse. Many of the men were immediately conscripted to fight a war that had little or no meaning for them. In Russia and Eastern Europe especially, anti-Jewish measures remained harsh, but ghetto and *shtetl* residents now had to bear arms in defense of countries that had persecuted and vilified their people for centuries. On the eastern front, the battle lines between the German and Russian armies ran through the heavily Jewish areas of Poland, and each shift of the fortunes of war destroyed homes and property, making women, children, and old men destitute and homeless. As for the Zionists, the exigencies of war forced the world organization practically to cease functioning. While Berlin housed the main headquarters, the Jewish Colonial Trust operated out of London; Palestinian colonies lay under Turkish rule, but many of the settlers still retained Russian citizenship. Members of the Actions Comité were, of course, scattered across the Continent and could not get together. In this chaos, the Jews and Zionists of Europe turned to the only major Jewish community in the world untouched by the conflagration, and sought not only material relief, but guidance and leadership as well.

One member of the Actions Comité, Shmaryahu Levin, had just sailed for Europe after a speaking tour of the United States when war broke out. Rather than face British warships, the *Kronprinzessin Cecelie* turned back to port, and Levin found himself in the United States for the duration of the hostilities. His presence would soon lend an aura of legitimacy to American Zionist activities. Upon receiving news of the collapse of the Berlin office, Levin met with Louis Lipsky and other Federation officials to see what the American Zionists could do. As they wrestled with that problem, word came of the crisis facing the Palestinian colonies. Dr. Arthur Ruppin, chief Zionist official in the Holy Land, had contacted the American ambassador to Turkey, Henry Morgenthau, with a plea for help. Normal payments from Jewish agencies in the belligerent countries had been cut off, and the maritime blockades now threatened to strangle the citrus and wine trades that were the economic mainstays of many of the settlements. As in Europe, many of the able-bodied men had been dragged off into the army, leaving no one to tend the soil. Morgenthau had cabled that fifty thousand dollars would be needed immediately.[3] To raise relief money for European and Palestinian Jewry, and to breathe new life and purpose into American Zionism, Levin sent out a call for an emergency meeting to take place in New York on August 30, 1914.

Among those receiving urgent invitations to attend the conference was Louis D. Brandeis. An assimilated Jew and a highly successful Boston attorney, he had won a reputation as a brilliant and determined reformer, and also enjoyed the confidence of Woodrow Wilson, the President of the United States. Brandeis' association with Zionism dated back little more than two years, and he had so far avoided any entanglement with either the leadership or the projects of the FAZ. Jacob deHaas, who had been patiently tutoring Brandeis about Zionism, proposed that the Bostonian be elected chairman of the temporary conference, not in recognition of his Zionist loyalties (of which there had so far been little evidence) but because of his national reputation as a reformer. Of all those who gathered at the Hotel Marseilles that day, only Brandeis' name would have been recognized by a majority of Americans. If the conference wanted to raise money, it needed a leader who was himself rich and who had access (hopefully) to the wealth of other men. As deHaas later noted, no one really expected Brandeis to take his leadership seriously.[4]

Brandeis accepted the nomination of what would be called the Provisional Executive Committee for General Zionist Affairs,[5] and in a brief speech talked about the serious plight of Jews in the war-afflicted areas. He then announced the establishment of an Emergency Fund and began the subscription with a donation of one thousand dollars, to which Nathan Straus added another five thousand dollars.

So far everything had gone according to expectations: a relief fund inaugurated, a well-known personality to head it, and now they would let him get some of his rich friends to give more. Then the script suddenly changed. Brandeis, pleading his ignorance of the many organizations represented, asked the assembly to stay on and meet with him that evening and the following day. He needed to know more about them, their leaders, their memberships, their administrative arrangements. For the next day and a half, Brandeis sat patiently in a crowded hotel suite, absorbing fact after fact about Zionism and Jewish life in America, occasionally asking a question or repeating a strange-sounding Hebrew or Yiddish name. When he finally adjourned the meeting late on August 31, his orderly mind might well have been reeling from the realization that nearly all of the groups present had poor organization, modest enrollments, minuscule financial resources, and very, very few people ready to do real work. But the shock to the men and women representing American Zionism was immeasurably greater; rather than a figurehead, the extraordinary conference had brought them a man who had the ability, determination, and reputation to be their leader, and who intended to be just that. The Hotel Marseilles meeting marked a turning point not only in the life of Louis Brandeis, but more importantly, in the fortunes of American Zionism.

Little can be found in Brandeis' family background, nor even in the first five decades of his life, to explain his relatively sudden interest and passionate involvement in Zionism. In Europe, his great-grandparents had adhered to traditional Jewish practices, but his maternal grandparents had joined a messianic sect that followed the teachings of Jacob Frank, whose star had briefly shone in Central Europe in the middle of the eighteenth century. The Frankists discarded much of the ritual and dogma of Orthodoxy, and many of them ultimately converted to Christianity. In the Dembitz family, the rejection of traditional Judaism led not to conversion but to a form of deism.[6] Frederika Dembitz Brandeis, at her son's request, wrote a brief memoir recalling her youth, and in it she spoke warmly of the Friday night dinners at her grandmother's. Of her beliefs and those of her parents she wrote: "I do not know what they believed and what Jewish doctrines they discarded, but I do know that they believed in goodness for its own sake and they had a lofty conception of morality with which they imbued us and which I developed further for myself. I do not believe that sins can be expiated by going to divine service and observing this or that formula; I believe that only goodness and truth and conduct that is humane and self-sacrificing towards those who need us can bring God nearer to us, and that our errors can only be atoned for by our acting in a more kindly spirit." She resolved to raise her own children without religious affiliations, since "I wanted to give them something that neither could be argued away nor would have to be given up as untenable, namely, a pure spirit and the highest ideals as to morals and love." Brandeis explained that his early training had not been Jewish, nor had it been Christian: "My people were not so narrow as to allow their religious belief to overshadow their interest in the broader aspects of humanity."[7]

The Brandeis family lived comfortably in Louisville, Kentucky, where Louis was born on November 13, 1856. At the age of nineteen, without any collegiate training, he enrolled directly in Harvard Law School, then in the initial stages of revitalization under C. C. Langdell. The years at Harvard were exciting ones, and Brandeis drank deeply of the intellectual currents then at full flood. He met Emerson, Longfellow, and the elder Holmes, and upon graduation, after a short apprenticeship in St. Louis, opened his own law practice in Boston. His brilliant mind, keen perception, and natural empathy for the intellectual and moral traits peculiar to New England, as well as his partnership with Brahmin scion Samuel D. Warren, soon made him a most successful and sought-after attorney. He moved in the best of circles, and numbered among his friends and clients members of the finest families in town. In practically all respects, he had become a Brahmin.

During these years, his association with Judaism remained tenuous. He never joined a synagogue or any of the fraternal groups, and while never denying his Jewish ancestry, neither did he advertise it. He made a number of donations to various Jewish charities, evidently had numerous Jewish clients, and in 1903 he shared a platform with Rabbi Charles Fleischer at the dedication ceremonies for Mt. Sinai Hospital. But Brandeis gave equal or greater amounts to non-Jewish civic causes, and his presence at the dedication perhaps attested more to his reputation as a lawyer than to his involvement as a Jew. He is not even mentioned in the *Jewish Encyclopedia,* and those who knew him well in those days later reported that they could not recall any evidence of Jewish identification. His letters and speeches rarely mentioned religion, and when he sprinkled quotations among his writings, he invariably went to Shakespeare, Goethe, and the Greeks, hardly ever to the Bible.[8]

By the end of the century Brandeis had achieved considerable success as a lawyer. In an age when 75 per cent of the country's attorneys earned less than five thousand dollars annually, his yearly income exceeded fifty thousand dollars. Important railroads and corporations clamored for his services, and young law school graduates vied to be chosen by his firm. But the moral strictures both of Puritanism and of his family's deism would not allow him to be satisfied with being just another successful counsel. He became aware of the social and moral havoc created by industrialization, and of the growing threat to fundamental liberties inherent in the large concentration of money and power. Like so many others who believed the country to be in a state of danger, he turned to reform, first on a local and state level, and then as his fame spread, on a national scale. He took on corrupt street franchises and fought for licenses that would force public utilities to serve and not dominate the public. He secured acceptance of a sliding-scale gas rate fair to both consumer and investor, and when the great insurance scandals erupted in 1906, he devised a plan for savings bank life insurance that would provide workingmen with an alternative to the rapacious schemes then in effect. In his fights, he developed to a fine art the massing of large citizen groups into effective political organizations. The Public Franchise, the Savings Bank Life Insurance and Anti-Merger Leagues were the forerunners of the citizen lobbies of the 1960s and 1970s, and his skill in arousing and demonstrating public opinion proved successful in securing many of the desired reforms.

Brandeis stood head and shoulders above other reformers of his time. He not only knew what he opposed—the corrupt and brutalizing forces of large industry—but he also developed a cohesive social philosophy. America had become a great nation because it gave to each man unlimited opportunity to develop his ability, to enter the marketplace and strive with others for success. Like other Progressives, Brandeis endowed economic competition with moral overtones. Free enterprise allowed the best to triumph with success marking personal achievement over great odds. When the robber barons entered the marketplace and gigantic monopolies arose, they crowded out the individual entrepreneur and cut off the opportunity for the common man. Democracy, however, depended on the individual being able to prove his abilities in whatever field he chose, to shape his destiny himself provided his ability measured up to his dreams. Monopolies, by curtailing opportunity, threatened not only economic but civil and political liberties as well.

To counter this, Brandeis proposed—and the Wilson administration tried to enact—a series of measures that would restore competition in place of economic oligopoly, and would regulate that competition to prevent rapacious industrialists and enormous firms from dominating not only the economy but the political system as well. Brandeis' economic theory, however it may have flown in the face of irreversible historic trends, tied together the social and political problems as well as the economic difficulties facing America. His solution, a regulated competition under limited government, attempted to retain the essential features of Jeffersonian democracy. His methods relied on a basic faith in the democratic process by which the people would defend their own interests once they recognized the problems.[9]

In 1910 a Brandeis client, department store owner A. Lincoln Filene, appealed to him to mediate the great garment workers' strike that had paralyzed the industry, thrown thousands of people out of work, and tied up millions of dollars of materials and partly finished goods. Filene and other retailers feared that their shelves would soon be emptied unless the predominantly Jewish workers and their employers settled quickly. Brandeis reluctantly agreed after both sides indicated their faith in his fairness, and within a relatively brief time devised a "protocol" that brought peace and stability to the industry for the next five years. This was his first real encounter with the immigrant Jews from Russia,* and the experience moved him deeply. He had never realized that workingmen and -women could be so

* The Brandeis family had come over in the great German migration of the mid-nineteenth century, and most of the Jews he knew or with whom he associated were of German origin.

interested in intellectual and social problems, nor have so great a sense of pride and self-worth in the midst of such degrading conditions. While going through the lofts, he heard numerous quarrels between workers and their bosses, and was amazed that they treated each other more like equals than as inferiors and superiors. In one argument an employee shouted at the owner, *"Ihr darft sich shemen! Past dos far a Yid?"* ("You should be ashamed! Is this worthy of a Jew?"), while at another time a machine operator lectured his employer with a quotation in Hebrew from Isaiah[10]:

> "It is you who have devoured the vineyard, the spoil of the poor
>   is in your houses.
> What do you mean by crushing My people, by grinding the face
>   of the poor? says the Lord God of hosts.

Later that year, Jacob deHaas interviewed Brandeis about savings banks life insurance for the Boston *Jewish Advocate*. As deHaas rose to leave, he asked if Brandeis were related to Lewis N. Dembitz, and upon receiving an affirmative reply, said that "Dembitz was a noble Jew." Asked to explain what he meant, the Jewish editor spent the next two hours telling Brandeis about Herzl, about his uncle's involvement in Zionism, and what the movement hoped to accomplish in order to save the Jews. When deHaas finally left, Brandeis asked him to send over any materials he had on Zionism, and promised to discuss the matter with him further. Over the next few years, as was his custom whenever confronted with a new problem, Brandeis read widely on the subject, while periodic meetings with deHaas filled in the gaps and clarified obscure points. In 1912 he formally joined the Federation.[11]

Brandeis' growing commitment to Zionism did not become publicly known until 1913, when he chaired a Boston meeting in honor of Nahum Sokolow, a member of the Actions Comité then in America on a speaking tour. Bernard Rosenblatt, traveling with Sokolow, asked Brandeis if he cared to make any introductory remarks; the Boston lawyer demurred, saying he would provide a brief introduction and then wait to hear what the visitor had to say. Sokolow described the pitiable conditions of Eastern European Jewry, and then launched into a visionary description of how a Jewish homeland would solve the Jewish problem. As he finished, according to Rosenblatt, Brandeis jumped to his feet and exclaimed: "Thank you, Mr. Sokolow, you have brought me back to my people." He then turned to the audience and told them that Sokolow's great vision might yet become a reality, and it was their task, and that of all the Jewish people, to help realize the dream. Paraphrasing Herzl's famous aphorism, he declared, "If you wish it, you can by service bring it about."[12]

Despite Rosenblatt's story, Brandeis publicly moved very slowly toward "his people" in the next year and a half. He joined the Boston Zion Association, and even consented to become honorary president after turning down the active leadership. He accepted nomination to the Associate Executive Committee of the FAZ, but whenever Louis Lipsky asked him to attend meetings or undertake projects, he evaded the offers, apologetically claiming that his other commitments precluded his taking a more active role in Zionism. When the Federation nominated him as a delegate to the Eleventh Congress, he declined election.[13] So it went until August 1914, when deHaas persuaded him that the urgency of the situation demanded that he take on the work.

There have been many theories advanced about Brandeis' conversion to Zionism, ranging from a revival of a sense of blood kinship with fellow Jews to the accusation that he became a Zionist to further his political ambitions.[14] The why can probably never be answered, but we can certainly look at the how. Louis Brandeis came to Zionism, as he himself said many times, through Americanism, and his American experiences and attitudes, rather than his marginal Jewishness, reshaped Zionism in America. A careful examination of Brandeis' writings and his activities as head of the movement clearly reveal that his approach to the Jewish problem remarkably resembled his approach to the secular problems confronting industrial America. Brandeis and the men and women he attracted to the movement had a clear and firm commitment to American ideals and democratic principles. They objected to anti-Semitism not from personal suffering but because it offended their sense of decency. Zionism, which reflected so many of the Progressive ideals, became for many of them a reform movement, akin to women's suffrage or factory legislation.

This outlook on Zionism, as a reform to solve the Jewish problem, provided the strength—and the weakness—of their leadership.

Brandeis faced three great tasks on assuming the Zionist leadership, and his success or failure in handling them would determine whether Zionism emerged as a potent force in American Jewish life or continued an anemic existence, of consequence to none but the devoted few. He had to reorganize Zionist forces into an effective form; he had to identify specific projects that would attract those who shared only a marginal interest in Zionism; and finally, and most importantly, he had to redefine Zionist assumptions to fit the needs of American as well as Jewish society.

II

As late as 1910, Brandeis shared the concern of many Americans who feared that the masses of new immigrants, Jewish as well as non-Jewish, would cling too tenaciously to their Old World loyalties. In 1905, at ceremonies marking the two hundred fiftieth anniversary of the Jewish presence in America, Brandeis anticipated Theodore Roosevelt's dictum that America had no room for "hyphenated" Americans. "There is room here for men of any race, of any creed, of any condition in life," he declared, "but not for Protestant-Americans, or Catholic-Americans, or Jewish-Americans, not for German-Americans, Irish-Americans, or Russian-Americans. This country demands that its sons and daughters whatever their race—however intense or diverse their religious connections—be politically merely American citizens." Five years later he repeated these comments in an interview with the *Jewish Advocate,* and added that "habits of living or of thought which tend to keep alive differences of origin or classify men according to their religious beliefs are inconsistent with the American ideal of brotherhood, and are disloyal."[15] At this time, nothing that Brandeis said would have differentiated him from men like Jacob Schiff or Louis Marshall, who condemned Zionism as antithetical to true Americanism.

Undoubtedly Brandeis' involvement in the New York garment strike altered his attitudes toward the Russian immigrants, a group he admittedly knew little about. They impressed him with their learning, with their spirit, and with their pride. This contact, as he testified, led him to understand for the first time the Jewish experience and culture. But he saw, not the religious ritual and dogma, but a reflection of those very traits that his New England experience had made dear—democracy, social justice, and individuality tempered by group responsibility. "I now saw the true democracy of my people, their idealistic inclinations and their love of liberty and freedom."[16] Brandeis had discovered, as would many Progressives, that diversity need not be detrimental in a democratic society, provided that different groups subscribed to a common set of ethical and social principles. In his speeches, Brandeis began to develop those ideas that Horace Kallen later termed "cultural pluralism."

By interpreting Jewish-Zionist idealism as complementary and supportive of American democracy, Brandeis undercut the claim that Zionism was inconsistent with or antithetical to Americanism. "America's fundamental law seeks to make real the brotherhood of man. That brotherhood became the Jews' fundamental law more than twenty-five hundred years ago. America's twentieth-century demand is for social justice. That has been the Jews' striving ages-long." Addressing the 1915 Zionist convention in Boston, he proclaimed: "The highest Jewish ideals are essentially American in a very important particular. It is Democracy that Zionism represents. It is Social Justice which Zionism represents, and every bit of that is the American ideals of the twentieth century."* Time and again he declared that "Zionism is the Pilgrim inspiration and impulse over again."[17] The ideals and desire for liberty that had characterized the earliest Americans and had shaped the nation's destiny now stood reborn in a movement to allow the Jews to live in freedom. How much more American could a movement be?

---

* Brandeis, either consciously or unconsciously, used "Jewish" and "Zionist" interchangeably. While nearly all Zionists were Jewish, the obverse was far from true. This juxtaposition endowed Zionism with all the traits he found so admirable in Jewish culture and ethics, and forced anti-Zionist Jews into the awkward position of trying to explain how a Jewish movement was not really Jewish.

This perception of Zionism as reflective of fundamental American ideals attracted Brandeis, and throughout the rest of 1914 and 1915 he told numerous audiences that his approach to Zionism had been through Americanism, that the two shared common principles of democracy and decency. He fully admitted his lack of a Jewish background, but proudly declared that as he learned about the Jewish heritage, he saw that "Jews were by reason of their traditions and their character peculiarly fitted for the attainment of American ideals." This observation led him to make the ultimate link, not only bridging Zionism and Americanism, but welding the two together: *"To be good Americans, we must be better Jews, and to be better Jews, we must become Zionists."*[18]

Decades of anti-Zionist argument could not, of course, be swept away with the assertion that America demanded its Jews to become Zionists, even when it came from such an eminent personality, so Brandeis carefully responded to the main concerns of dual loyalty and the relation of American Jews to a Palestinian homeland. But he went beyond just denying charges, and rather than merely defending Zionism, he called for Jews to be openly proud of its goals and accomplishments.

From the start, anti-Zionists had attacked the movement as fostering divided loyalties. One could not be fully patriotic, they asserted, if one supported a Jewish homeland somewhere else. Such statements on the surface seemed reasonable enough, and Brandeis himself had often argued that one could not serve two masters at the same time. Such logic, however, seemed to assume that the two goals had to be in conflict, that one could not support Zionism because it would weaken one's Americanism. Brandeis seized upon this assumption and labeled it as false. "Multiple loyalties are objectionable only if they are inconsistent," he maintained, but the American political system clearly proved that such need not be the case. "A man is a better citizen of the United States for being also a loyal citizen of his state, and of his city; for being loyal to his family, and to his profession or trade; for being loyal to his college or lodge."[19] The true loyalty of an American lay not in a superficial allegiance to the symbols of a country, but in a deeper, heartfelt commitment to the principles that the nation represented. One believed in freedom, justice, and democracy not just in one place or for one group, but everywhere and for all people, and in working for these goals, one demonstrated a greater depth of feeling. "Every Irish-American who contributed toward advancing home rule was a better man and a better American for the sacrifices he made," Brandeis asserted, and the same would be said of the Jews. By supporting a free and democratic homeland for their brethren in Palestine, they would be giving the best possible proof of their loyalty to America.

That an established member of the Boston bar, a progressive reformer of the first order, and a confidant of the President of the United States said these things undoubtedly gave them a sanction hitherto lacking among Zionist spokesmen. Moreover, his personal career, now that he had assumed the mantle of Zionist leadership, confirmed his faith that Zionism and Americanism did not preclude each other. In 1915 he became the first Jew to give the Fourth of July oration in historic Faneuil Hall, an honor by which Boston put its seal of approval on the impeccable character of Brandeis' patriotism. And on January 28, 1916, Woodrow Wilson nominated him to be an Associate Justice of the Supreme Court of the United States. With some satisfaction, Brandeis wrote that "in the opinion of the President there is no conflict between Zionism and loyalty to America."[20]

Brandeis undoubtedly perceived the changes then taking place in ideas about what constituted patriotism. There were some—there would always be some—who never saw beyond the surface symbols, who believed that outward shows of devotion were all that mattered. But for those Progressives who worked with the immigrants, who agonized over the meaning of "Americanization," there emerged a philosophy that emphasized strength in diversity. They looked back and saw that immigrants from many lands had come to these shores, and while submerging their most blatant differences and assuming outward uniformity, the Germans, Irish, Italians and others still cherished memories and values they had brought from the old country. These values, however, did not conflict with the basic premises of American society, but augmented and strengthened them. By emphasizing such characteristics in Zionism (which aimed to reconstitute a Palestinian homeland), Brandeis placed it on the same level as the love other immigrant groups felt for their already existent homelands. Far from trying to assimilate, Brandeis in effect told American Jews that they should work to preserve their own group identity, that they owed this both to the country and to themselves. He termed assimilation "national suicide" and said that only a Jewish homeland would help keep alive the peculiarly Jewish spirit.[21]

In Europe, widespread anti-Semitism had endowed Zionism with a sense of urgency and need; Jews would continue to be discriminated against and so would have to go to the new Jewish homeland. In America, however, the overwhelming majority of Jews did not face outrageous prejudice and did not want to move to Palestine. To these people Brandeis spoke words of comfort and assurance. "Zionism is not a movement to transport compulsorily to Palestine all the Jews in the world." Indeed, it would be impossible to relocate more than a fraction of the world's fourteen million Jews. Those living in freedom would stay where they wanted, but those suffering oppression had to have a refuge to which they could flee, a land where they too would enjoy liberty. Zionism, he said, "is essentially a movement of freedom, a movement to give the Jew more freedom, not less, to give to him the same freedom which the other peoples enjoy, the freedom to go to the land of his fathers or to remain or go to some land as he may choose, the freedom which is enjoyed by every people and nation practically in all the world, be that nation small or large." American Jews living in a land of freedom had the responsibility to help in the creation of a homeland where their oppressed brethren could also be free.[22]

Political Zionism actually made a great deal of sense within the context of the American experience. Since the United States had become a homeland for millions of Europeans, many ethnic groups, such as Irish-Americans and Serbian-Americans had long supported movements to free their native lands, without wanting to go there themselves. Only if one adopted the European blood-notion of nationalism did interest in and support of Zionism become subversive. Europeans termed those who lived outside their own homeland "exiles" or "expatriates"; in America they became immigrants. The United States cut the Gordian knot of Diaspora nationalism by the simple expedient of ignoring it. Today, when nearly all American

Jews strongly support Israel, the charge of divided loyalty is rarely mentioned; endorsement of freedom and independence for other countries has become part of the American ethos.[23]

A Palestinian homeland, moreover, would help Jews achieve the sense of pride and identification that other national groups enjoyed, and that enlarged their contribution to American society. As important as proving that Palestine was capable of becoming a Jewish homeland was the need to prove "that the modern Jew is fit for Palestine." After centuries of impoverished city-dwelling, the *Yishuv* now stood as testimony to the courage of the Jewish people. Moreover, the Holy Land would serve as a spiritual center to inspire Jews everywhere. Time and again Brandeis referred to the *idealism* of Zionism, to its tone of moral uplift. He reminded his audiences that even though Palestine would always be a tiny country, it had already inspired three of the world's great religions. "The only thing of real value in life is the ideal," he asserted, and the Zionist movement brought out the best in the Jewish people.[24] Striving for an ideal made people better than they thought they were, and he frequently quoted Herzl, *"Wenn ihr es wollt, ist es Kein Maer schen."* ("If you will it, it is not a dream.")

As Louis Levinthal has pointed out, neither Brandeis' Zionist ideology nor his concept of Americanism were new, but his unique contribution to Jewish life in America lay in his synthesis of the two.[25] Thoroughly American in spirit, his imagination was captured by a vision of a homeland where a people he hardly knew could live freely, a vision popularized by another assimilated Jew, Theodore Herzl, who had also discovered his Jewishness late in life. Brandeis gave liberally, not only of his time and energy, but of his fortune as well, and even those who broke with him later, such as Louis Lipsky, acknowledged the depth and sincerity of his commitment.[26]

This profound hold that Zionism exercised on him, however, must be seen in terms of his ideals as a reformer of the prewar era, years in which human optimism rode high. Brandeis saw Palestine as a small country free from the "curse of bigness," one that could experiment in enlarging the bounds of freedom and social justice, much as a state within the United States could serve as a laboratory for legislative experimentation. He assumed from the start that the Jewish homeland would be a democracy, with men and women equal partners in building up a free society, and four decades of Jewish pioneering gave him ample grounds to believe in the ultimate growth of a good society. Revealingly, he once wrote that the ideals he had for America "should also prevail in the Jewish State." He recognized that the United States could not continue to accept unlimited immigration indefinitely, so Palestine became necessary as a land where Jews could be free to be different, to be themselves. A people, like a nation, had the right to shape its own destiny, and a Jewish homeland would give Jews that right. In all this he paid little or no attention to religious injunctions and ritual; he cared for people, not for dogmas.[27]

III

In essence, Zionism represented a reawakening of the Jewish spirit, a revival of a long-dormant nationalism. It also marked the beginning of a rebellion in which Jews for the first time in eighteen centuries refused to knuckle under to repression. This pride, this idealism, this effort to shape one's own destiny appealed not only to Brandeis but to other Progressives as well. The element of protest fit into the over-all reform temperament, and won Zionism a sympathetic response in the progressive ranks. This sentiment brought into the movement Jewish men and women who, with few exceptions, had had little contact with either Zionism or even Jewish communal life. When Shmaryahu Levin joyously reported to the Actions Comité in 1915 that a "new Zionism" had developed in the United States, he termed its leaders "men of earnestness and of character, who demand logical completeness in the movements with which they affiliate, who devote themselves full-heartedly to the movement of which they are part."[28] This new leadership dominated American Zionism from 1914 to 1921, and it would later return to power in the 1930s. Like Brandeis, who personally recruited many of them, they all shared a fundamental commitment to American ideals, and they had often won their reputation in fields extraneous to Judaism.

The most important figure, next to Brandeis himself, would be United States Circuit Court Judge Julian William Mack. Educated at Harvard, Mack had practiced law in Chicago, where he also taught at Northwestern and the University of Chicago law schools. Mack was heavily involved with Jewish communal life in Chicago, and had joined the fraternal Order Knights of Zion, but his main interests prior to 1914 lay in social work rather than in Zionism. He pioneered in the concept of a juvenile court system, in which youthful offenders were treated as errant children rather than as hardened criminal adults, and he presided over one of the first such courts in the country from 1903 to 1906. Together with Jane Addams, Julia C. Lathrop, Graham Taylor, and Florence Kelley, he founded the Juvenile Protective Association to advance the ideas of child correction. In the Chicago area he served on numerous charitable boards, both of Jewish and non-Jewish agencies, and fellow social workers elected him president of their national conference in 1912.

During the world war, the Council on National Defense's Labor Committee requested Mack to serve as chairman of the Section on Compensation and Insurance for Soldiers, Sailors and their Dependents. The plan he devised, which is still in effect today, called on the federal government to establish a low-cost life insurance plan for servicemen, thus providing protection for their families, a protection unavailable through the private, commercial companies. Woodrow Wilson, recognizing Mack's long experience in the area of community relations, asked him to undertake the difficult and sensitive task of reviewing conscientious objector cases appealed from local draft boards.[29]

Mack came to Zionism because of his growing convictions on cultural pluralism as well as through his contacts with Brandeis. He embraced the movement, not for religious reasons, but because of what he saw as the inherent justness of the cause. At the Paris Peace Conference in 1919 he told the peacemakers that the Zionists "ask no more for the Jews than we do for anyone else." Within the American Jewish Committee (of which he was a charter member), he was one of the few who supported Zionism, and in Brandeisian tones lectured the *shtadlanim* on the relationship of Zionism to Americanism: "I have not, I never had, the slightest fear that any of those ideas will make the Jews of this country any less good Americans or that there is such a conception as a political nation within the American nation. The only conception of nationality that I can see is that of the Jews as a people. There is no difference in my mind between the nationality of the Germans and the Irish of this country, and the fact that we claim that we belong to a people is exactly the claim of the Germans that they belong to the German people and makes them none the less American."[30]

After Brandeis went on the Court in 1916, Mack became head of the Zionist organization, and although it often seemed that he still served merely as Brandeis' lieutenant, he was very much his own man. Mack carried out the reorganization of American Zionism in 1918, and three years later led the fight against Weizmann. At the Paris Peace Conference, he represented not only the Zionists, but together with Louis Marshall spoke for the Jews of the world.

Next to Brandeis and Mack, the most dominant voice in Zionist affairs during these years belonged to Rabbi Stephen Samuel Wise of New York. Although ordained as a Reform rabbi, Wise's interests centered on ethical issues rather than theological problems, and he conceived of religion as valid only insofar as it addressed itself to daily problems. Although his education had included some Hebrew and Talmud, he was much more conversant with the New England Transcendentalists and their ideas on social involvement greatly affected his ministry.

Wise had begun his career in New York, but then had gone to Portland, Oregon, where his talents as a rabbi, preacher, and social worker matured. He soon knew most of the labor leaders and social agitators on the West Coast, and unlike most rabbis of that day, devoted his sermons to current issues. His involvement, however, went far beyond polite or academic interest; Wise practiced what he preached and threw himself headlong into battles for municipal reform and effective labor laws.

In 1905, Temple Emanu-El in New York, the great cathedral temple of American Reform, offered Wise its pulpit, but its directors, who included some of the most prominent Jewish laymen in the country, made it clear that while they would never question the rabbi's judgment on religious and ritual matters, they would retain the final say on secular issues, including sermon topics. Although all young Reform rabbis dreamed of securing the Emanu-El appointment, Wise rejected the offer, and in a famous letter to Louis Marshall spelled out his views on the role of the rabbi: "The chief office of the minister, I take it, is not to represent the views of the congregation, but to proclaim the truth as he sees it. How can he serve a congregation as a teacher save as he quickens the minds of his hearers by the vitality and independence of his utterances? How can a man be vital and independent and helpful, if he be tethered and muzzled? A free pulpit, worthily filled, must command respect and influence; a pulpit that is not free, howsoever filled, is sure to be without potency and honor. A free pulpit will sometimes stumble into error; a pulpit that is not free can never powerfully plead for truth and righteousness."[31]

This view, while it undoubtedly had the support of some Reform leaders, had its basis not only in Jewish tradition, but even more so in the Social Gospel movement of the late nineteenth century, as expounded by Protestant ministers like Walter Rauschenbusch. For these men, the living church could be found only where people needed it—in the slums and stockyards, not in the plush and manicured enclaves of the well-to-do. A religion thrived only as it tackled the social problems of the day, and the job of the minister consisted in telling his congregants about these problems and what their responses in the light of moral and ethical teachings should be. In 1907, Wise founded the Free Synagogue in New York so he could have a pulpit from which to preach on the social responsibility of men and women in the twentieth century. Nominally Reform in ritual, the Free Synagogue emphasized the ethical and moral teachings of Judaism and how they applied to contemporary social conditions.[32]

Herzl's appeal had originally captured Wise's imagination in the 1890s, and Wise had joined Richard Gottheil in trying to build an effective Zionist organization in the United States. His disgust with the European leaders' treatment of the FAZ led him to drop out of the movement, but Brandeis' appeal to him could not be denied, and in 1914 he again enlisted his great oratorical talents in the service of Jewish nationalism.

Wise's Zionism reflected his deep emotional attachment to the Jewish people as well as his faith in American democracy. In 1900, walking near the Lower East Side, he wondered "whether a people can ever be helped and lifted up save from within. They look and seem so wretched, yet they have something of a soul life —witness the preparation for the Sabbath. They must in the end save themselves, but the way must be shown."[33] Wise's love for his people came pouring out of him unabashedly, and of all the Brandeis group, none was more beloved by the masses than he. Nahum Goldman wrote: "Not only did he love the Jewish people; he loved every individual Jew. He would turn his hand to finding help for a poor refugee, arranging for the adoption of an orphan, or providing for a destitute widow as willingly as solving a great social problem. This explains his unsurpassed popularity with the Jewish masses of America. Other Jewish leaders may have been more revered, feared or admired than he, but none was so beloved."[34]

Equaling Wise's love for his people was his love for his country. To his son he once wrote that he continuously thanked God for his family's decision to come to the United States. "I thank God for America—my parents' and ours and yours! And I have tried to repay my debt to America in part. Anything you and Justine [his daughter] will in the future do is to be a further installment of my indebtedness to America." Like Brandeis, Wise too had been deeply involved in social reform, and thus had little in common with the rich Jews. When Brandeis asked him to raise funds, Wise replied: "There is no man in New York who would be less likely to succeed in interesting rich New York Jews in the cause than would I. Access to them is denied me not because of the heterodoxy of my pulpit, but because of the social, economic, and ethical heterodoxies of my teaching, which I am happy, if not proud, to say have made me wholly unacceptable to the rich Jews." At another time, he declared simply, "They do not like me or the things for which I stand."[35] For him, Zionism represented the ideal, and he foresaw a Jewish people regenerated by having a home of their own, one in which Jewish ethics and American social democracy would reign. The overtly religious aspects of the movement held little appeal for him, and according to Louis Lipsky, Wise considered the spiritual Zionism of Ahad Ha'am as "a form of opiate for the Jewish masses, which would keep them in the bondage of a culture that never could lead to political rebirth."[36]

Many commentators have noted that Wise was one of the great speakers of his time, and his very presence guaranteed enormous turnouts at rallies or protest meetings. An imposing man, his speeches lacked deep intellectual content, but his personal commitment invested his talks with an appeal that loftier speakers never achieved. In the 1930s he was one of the few American-Jewish leaders to see the threat of Hitlerism, and unsuccessfully tried to alert the United States to the peril. He never became the leader many thought he would because he lacked the subtlety and temperament of the politician. He wore his emotions—loyalties and prejudices—too openly, and at the same time he aroused the passions of a crowd he alienated the more circumspect, and influential, members of the Jewish community.

Although he avoided the limelight surrounding many of his colleagues, and even refused to hold formal office, Felix Frankfurter must be counted among the members of the Brandeis group. Born in Vienna in 1882, he was brought to the United States while still a child. After graduation from Harvard Law School, he became an assistant United States attorney under Henry L. Stimson, and when the latter went to Washington as Secretary of War in 1911, Frankfurter joined him as an aide. In 1914 Brandeis (with whom Frankfurter had become close friends) played an instrumental role in bringing Frankfurter to Harvard Law School as a faculty member, where he taught until another friend, Franklin Roosevelt, nominated him to the U. S. Supreme Court in 1939. During his years at Harvard he earned a reputation as a brilliant teacher and scholar, and annually supplied clerks to Justices Holmes and Brandeis.

But like them, he believed the life of the law lay in action, in making the law conform to societal needs. When Brandeis went on the bench in 1916, Frankfurter assumed the load of fighting for wages and hours legislation through court cases. During the 1920s, when fear and reaction threatened to erode civil liberties, Frankfurter actively defended those rights, helping to found the American Civil Liberties Union and playing a central role in the Sacco and Vanzetti case. Essentially, he shared Brandeis' economic and social as well as legal views, and during the 1930s counseled Roosevelt to limit bigness in industry and to encourage the growth of a small-unit economy.

While his parents had observed traditional rites, Frankfurter recalled that the rituals and dogmas of Judaism held little meaning for him. "I remember leaving the synagogue in the middle of a service saying to myself, 'It's a wrong thing for me to be present in a room in a holy service, to share these ceremonies, these prayers, these chants, with people for whom they have inner meaning as against me for whom they have ceased to have inner meaning.' I left the service in the middle of it, never to return to this day. By leaving the synagogue I did not, of course, cease to be a Jew." He frequently referred to himself as "a reverent agnostic" or "a believing unbeliever." He entered the Zionist movement at Brandeis' request, and his counsel commanded respect. In 1919 he served as the legal adviser to the Zionist delegation at the Paris Peace Conference, and his direct access to President Wilson proved valuable. On the whole, Frankfurter's devotion to the movement could be considered less than wholehearted, and while he took an interest in Zionist affairs, the secular problems of the day occupied the bulk of his time and energy.[37]

Jacob deHaas played a central, though at times shadowy, role in the new leadership. He had brought Brandeis into the movement, hailing him as a "second Herzl," and he exploited this relationship to enlarge his own power and influence. He had served as Herzl's English secretary, and at the leader's request had moved to the United States in 1902 to try to instill some order in the FAZ. For a while he had edited the *Maccabean,* but after continued hostility from Gottheil as well as frustration in trying to improve the organization, he moved to Boston, where he edited the *Jewish Advocate* for many years.

DeHaas had a clear grasp of Zionist policies and politics, and

proved an invaluable guide to Brandeis in these years. The two
men saw each other almost daily, and Brandeis consulted him on
matters both great and small. DeHaas' pen proved a powerful
instrument of propaganda for Zionism, and his administrative skills
served the organization well during his years as executive secretary.
He held a deep commitment to Zionism, dating back to his youth
in London. His father had taken him to see the arrival of Russian
refugees at a London dock, and enjoined him: "Never forget Russia made the Jews suffer. When you grow up, remember you saw
them; pity them; respect them; if you can, help them." Zionism was
deHaas' way of helping them, and years later he would say that he
had never forgotten them.

His devotion to Brandeis brooked no criticism, and he quickly
lashed out at real or imagined slights against his idol. Brandeis in
turn so trusted him that he ignored complaints about deHaas' blun-
ders. Felix Frankfurter recalled that deHaas always seemed to ir-
ritate other people, that he lacked subtlety and tact: "He didn't
realize that there are various ways of skinning a cat, and he would
skin the cat the hard way, the insensitive way. Instead of saying,
'Well, I hadn't thought of it that way,' he'd say, 'You're wrong!'"
After the break between Brandeis and Weizmann in 1921, deHaas
never forgave the latter nor his American lieutenants. He worked
with Mack and Robert Szold to oust the Lipsky faction, but unlike
many of the Brandeis group who wanted peace and reconciliation,
deHaas seemed to go out of his way to insult old enemies and
reopen old wounds.[38]

Judaism does not canonize, but if it did, nearly everyone would
demand sainthood for Henrietta Szold. A gentle woman, she devoted her life to securing justice for her people. Her dedication to
save her fellow human beings—from the scourge of disease or
from the gaping jaws of Hitler's death camps—overrode the petty
politics that so often incapacitated the Zionist movement. She came
from a traditional Jewish background, and religious commitment
remained steadfast throughout her life, but for her the most important part of Judaism was its ethics and not its ritual, and her
methods and activities reflected the reformist trends that swept the
country at the turn of the century.

The Szold family of Baltimore, where Henrietta was born in 1860, occupied a prominent position in that city's large German-Jewish community. But her father, unlike many of his contemporaries, sympathized with the plight of the Russian refugees and with their Zionist ideals. Her father's house served as a meeting place for many of the Russian intellectuals, and here she came into contact with the *Haskalah,* the Jewish Enlightenment, learning about the latest works in Hebrew and Jewish literature. But she also saw the problems confronting the newcomers, the difficulties they faced in surviving in a foreign land. With a group of friends she founded what may have been the first night school in the country dealing specifically with immigrant problems. They began by teaching just English classes, but soon realized that these men and women also needed training in job skills. Sewing, carpentry, plumbing, and other crafts soon found their way into the curriculum. Here Henrietta Szold, while responding primarily to the needs of Jewish immigrants, found herself in the forefront of the progressive education movement, with its faith in the school as the ultimate instrument for solving industrial America's social problems. She founded the school in opposition to official opinion that such agencies were unnecessary; she proved their worth by showing that they worked, and then forced Baltimore's city fathers to assume the burden of continuing the program.[39] These tactics would prove successful time and again in forcing the Zionist bureaucracy into assuming the various social welfare projects she established in Palestine.

Neither the plight of the Russians nor even anti-Semitism can be credited with her lifelong devotion to Zion. "I became converted to Zionism," she said in one of her early propaganda talks, "the very moment I realized that it supplied my bruised, torn, and bloody nation, my distracted nation, with an ideal—an ideal that is balm to the self-inflicted wounds and to the wounds inflicted by others—an ideal that can be embraced by all, no matter what their attitude may be to other Jewish questions." Over twenty years later she again asserted that for her Palestine was not just a refuge for the Jew, but for Judaism, a place where the whole Jewish people could be rehabilitated and regain its self-respect.[40]

She joined the FAZ and helped to organize study groups, but while subscribing to its Zionist goals, she found the Federation's methods desultory and self-defeating, while the discussion sessions lacked real purpose. Then in 1909 she visited Palestine with her mother, and there found her life's work. In Jaffa they saw little Arab children with flies buzzing around their eyes, many of them half blind. Inside the Jewish Girls School all of the students seemed healthy, and upon inquiring why, the principal explained that the school provided regular health care. As they left, her mother turned to her and said, "This is what your group ought to do. What is the use of reading papers and arranging festivals? You should do practical work in Palestine."[41]

On her return from the Holy Land, the Federation elected Henrietta Szold honorary secretary, and she set about the thankless task of bringing order out of the chaos then rampant in the FAZ administration. But she did not forget her mother's comment, and early in 1912 she helped found the New York chapter of a new national women's group, the Daughters of Zion, with the biblical motto *aruchath bat ami* ("the healing of the daughter of my people" [Jer. 8:22]). She spoke on the need for a definite project, and Hadassah, as the group soon called itself (after the Hebrew name of Queen Esther), elected her president and told her to find a project. By the end of the year, they had a project, but only $283 in their treasury.

"Then Mr. and Mrs. Nathan Straus appeared on the scene and asked me to visit them," she later recalled. "They told me they had heard our purpose was to introduce visiting nurses in Jerusalem; they wanted to know why we didn't do it. I said we had only $283 in the treasury. They said, that doesn't matter—start! I said there was no money; and Mr. Straus repeated, that has nothing to do with it. Mrs. Straus kept nodding her head behind his back as if to say, 'The Lord will provide.'" The Straus family agreed to pay the passage of the two nurses to Palestine, and Eva Leon (Richard Gottheil's sister-in-law) found backers in Chicago to guarantee annual expenses of $2,000 for five years. In January 1913, Hadassah began its medical work in Palestine with the dispatch of Rose Kaplan and Rachel D. Landy to Jerusalem.[42]

Within a short time, the idea caught on, and Hadassah elected Miss Szold national president. When Brandeis came on the scene, he not only recognized her organizational ability but also shared her intuitive beliefs about organizing American Jewry, and he backed her efforts not only to enlarge Hadassah projects but to make Hadassah an independent force. On her part, she saw him as the leader that American Zionism needed, and she held this view until the end of her life.[43]

In Hadassah one can see the fullest development of the new leadership's philosophy. On the cultural level, it has sponsored Hebrew study groups, youth camps, and the like, all designed to emphasize the unity of the Jewish people through a common ethical and cultural heritage. With the obvious change, Hadassah subscribed to the Brandeis dictum of "Men! Money! Organization!" In nearly every Jewish community in the country, Hadassah chapters sprang up and tens—ultimately hundreds—of thousands of Jewish women joined, not out of religious convictions, but because they found an area in which they could work for well-defined goals.

Henrietta Szold's master stroke was her identification of health care as Hadassah's special medium. In the early twentieth century, women played key roles in expanding health and social services in American cities; somehow it was thought that—aside from doctors—this was a particularly appropriate area for engaging women's interests. Rather than talk about vague abstractions like self-emancipation or spiritual centers, the Hadassah leaders have always emphasized specific, concrete tasks. So many dollars were needed to send nurses, to build hospitals and clinics and medical schools, to save German-Jewish children. And the results could be seen, in the now-clear eyes of small children, in the number of mothers and infants who no longer died at childbirth, in the men and women who had adequate medical care for the first time in their lives, and in the boys and girls plucked from the flames of Hitler's crematoria.[44]

This emphasis on the practical, on the identifiable project, as opposed to vague generalizations or philosophical abstractions, is a peculiarly American trait. Americans have never had much to do with philosophizing, but always concentrated on the practical. One might philosophically agree with the abstraction of a "Jewish home-land," but one could work for and identify with Hadassah programs. Moreover, American women did not have to worry about the charges of dual loyalty. Hadassah did not make *aliyah* (immigration) to Palestine central to its programs, but emphasized the humani-tarian aspects of its work. Who could object to providing decent health care, building hospitals, or saving children from brutal ex-termination?

For Henrietta Szold, like Louis Brandeis, Zionism drew much from her American experiences and from her commitment to Western culture. (During the 1930s, meeting a group of children Hadassah had just brought in from Nazi Germany, she urged them: "Do not forget your Goethe or your Schiller. They are German too."[45]) She wanted to introduce into Palestine a whole range of social services of the type then being advocated by progressive reformers. She learned the techniques of setting up a small but successful pilot project, drawing attention to it, and then by withdrawing support, forcing the public officials to assume responsibility. Despite all the years she spent in Palestine, many of them as a member of the Jew-ish Agency, she always considered herself an American, and saw her various trips to the United States—usually for the purpose of urging new projects on Hadassah—as "going home." But she was more than an American in Jerusalem. She epitomized Brandeis' hope of bringing America to Zion, of investing American ideals and prac-tices in the Jewish homeland. And because she had so much more of a Jewish background than he did, she was able to bridge the two, to join them together, as Brandeis hoped they might be but which, in the end, he could not do himself.

IV

Brandeis' call for members brought in more than the leaders and those willing to lend their name to a cause; it also led to the enroll-ment of tens of thousands of American Jews who had previously ignored Zionism. At the 1914 convention, the FAZ claimed a membership of little more than 12,000; by 1919 the figure stood at over 176,000, with thousands of others associated with the Mizrachi or various labor-Zionist groups. This huge jump growing out of the war crisis, made possible the increased growth in budget as well as the reorganization of the Federation of American Zionists into the Zionist Organization of America. In all his work, Brandeis stood by the motto: "Men! Money! Discipline!"

But nothing could be done without members, and Brandeis hammered home this demand wherever he went. "Organize! Organize! Organize! until every Jew in American must stand up and be counted—counted with us—or prove himself, wittingly or unwittingly, of the few who are against their own people." Members provided muscle with which to persuade governments. Members provided workers who would spread Zionist propaganda. Members provided fund raisers to get money for Palestinian colonies. Members provided the one essential resource that made possible the assumption of new projects and responsibilities.[46]

To secure these members, the Provisional Committee adopted a number of stratagems. Brandeis and others who went on speaking tours appealed for new members. Whenever people asked how they could help, the answer invariably came back to enroll as a member and then bring in others. "Every one of you should consider himself an organizer, and no day should elapse without some addition to the number of members in the local organization." Brandeis, never content with merely preaching to others, rigorously followed his own orders, and "talked Zionism" to nearly all of the Jewish reformers he knew. After several weeks of importuning by Brandeis and Frankfurter, Eugene Meyer, Jr. finally threw up hands and "consented" to head the newly formed University Zionist Association. Mary Fels, Louis Kirstein, Nathan Straus, and others also acceded to such personal suasion.[47]

While the leadership had access to "names," real growth in membership had to occur on the local level. Here the oganizational methods of the Brandeis group contrasted vividly with the haphazard and random recruitment of the FAZ. In addition to constant encouragement, the leadership instituted procedures to promote orderly yet rapid growth, and also established new organizations appealing to groups previously untouched by Zionism.

At the lowest level, members received instructions on private gatherings and home parties, with local organizations responsible for providing speakers or demonstrations. At these gatherings, non-Zionists would be told about the aims of the movement and about the need to save the Palestinian colonies. Then within a few days, there would be a follow-up, inviting them to pay the shekel and join the Federation. Those still in doubt would be contacted again, until they decided definitely either to join or stay out. In mid-February 1915, the FAZ officially endorsed this approach, the first time in its history that it had adopted any organized means of securing members.[48]

At the next level, local groups were assigned specific quotas, with target dates by which these goals should be met. A speakers bureau, set up by the Provisional Committee, supplied Zionist orators, both in English and in Yiddish, to the mass rallies run by the local societies, with immediate follow-ups to see how effective their efforts had been. Sometimes the targets appeared unrealistic. When the Zionists held their 1915 convention in Boston, Brandeis appealed to the Chelsea Zionist Society to "set an example of Jewish unity, not only to America but to the whole world . . . by enrolling as a member of the Chelsea Zionist Society every adult male Jew in the city, and by enrolling every member of his family as a shekel payer." Where existing societies were weak, or where no organized Zionist groups existed at all, the Provisional Committee co-opted local Zionists to start new groups. In a typical letter establishing such a committee, the PC enclosed a model set of by-laws, suggested annual dues, fixed quotas for growth, and requested weekly reports on progress.[49]

The weekly and monthly reports by the constituent societies were not just for show, or to make local committees believe that someone back at headquarters was watching. Under the direction of Jacob deHaas, the office committee had begun accumulating a master card index. Every Jew in America who paid the shekel had his name on a card, as did those who contributed to any of the Zionist affiliated funds. This index became the starting point for intensive recruiting campaigns, and ultimately consisted of over one-half million names.

For the first time, the Zionists had reliable information on membership, and realistic data from which to seek new shekel payers. The method, of course, had been utilized by many progressive groups, and reflected the impulse for orderliness that characterized much of the reform mood at this time. That the FAZ had made practically no efforts to organize its recruitment into some manageable form indicated how far it had stood from the mainstream of American life.

The new leadership took a special interest in recruiting college students and graduates, a group that had hitherto been ignored by the FAZ. "It is from those still young to whom we must look in Jewish affairs, as in others, for progressive work," wrote Brandeis.[50] To gain this membership, the Provisional Committee subsidized the work of Henry Hurwitz's Menorah Society, and Brandeis and his friends personally undertook the sponsorship of the University Zionist Association, a federation of Zionist clubs at different schools. Brandeis spoke a number of times to the Harvard group, and underwrote the club's expenses in bringing in speakers.* Interestingly, the European Zionists had always been well represented at the universities, and many of the movement's leaders first came to prominence in student groups. The prestige of Brandeis, Mack, and Frankfurter, and their standing as reformers, appealed strongly to idealistic college students. Even some papers unfriendly to the movement admitted that the Zionists had done much to reclaim Jewish youth alienated from their people.[51] The search for membership among "the intellectuals and men of leadership" reflected more than the obvious need to swing this influential group's support behind Zionism. The PC had to offset the hostility of the established German-Reform Jews, but it also wanted to balance the huge influx of Eastern European Jews who made up the overwhelming bulk of the Zionist membership.

The majority of American Jews in 1914 claimed Eastern European origin, with many of them but recently arrived from Russia, Poland, or parts of the Austro-Hungarian Empire. They spoke Yiddish, and

* Looking even more to the future, the PC endorsed the Young Judea program, which Brandeis termed "the apprenticeship school of the Zionist movement, from which the younger generation is to graduate into active membership in our various organizations."

had created a theater, a press, and a literature in that language. They still worked in factories or small shops, and until the war, socialist ideology concerned them far more than Zionism. A number of historians note that the Yiddish-speaking masses cared practically nothing for Zionism prior to 1914, yet they also claim that these same East Side Jews provided the bulk of the movement's membership after 1915. Moreover, these Eastern European immigrants came into the movement at the behest of an assimilated, English-speaking leadership.[52] With a few years, moreover, these immigrants would overthrow the Brandeis regime and follow one of their own, Russian-born Chaim Weizmann.

This seemingly contradictory situation makes more sense if we look at the Eastern Europeans not just vis-à-vis Zionism, but more importantly, as aliens seeking a new home. In coming to America, hundreds of thousands of Jews, like other millions who came in three centuries of open immigration, chose America as their Zion. They came seeking freedom from religious or ethnic persecution, or in search of a better economic life for themselves and their families. While Palestine undoubtedly exerted an emotional appeal for Jews, only the United States could offer the freedom and opportunity they desperately sought. Once here, the immigrant had to adjust to life in America, be it on the western plains or in the eastern cities. They had to learn a new language and new customs. They looked on helplessly at the rapid acculturation of their children who, in the process, often rejected old customs and manners. For Jews as well as other groups, the demands of everyday life far outweighed utopian wishes. Socialism appealed to the urban proletariat because it addressed itself to the problems of the here and now.[53]

They did not forget Zion, of course, nor could they have done so even if they had wished. The entire Jewish milieu of Eastern Europe, with Hibbat Zion, the messianic fervor, and the strong ties of traditional Judaism, could not be thrown off on a boat trip. But once here, they realized that America would keep them and give them freedom and opportunity only if they gave unstintingly of their loyalty to this country. The warnings that the German aristocracy gave them that they could not be loyal to both Zionism and the United States, warnings repeated by Theodore Roosevelt in his polemics against hyphenated Americans, did not go unheeded. They wanted to outgrow their greenhorn status, they wanted to become Americans. In this, they were no different from other immigrant groups, and studies of the Irish and Slavs show that these groups also submerged their feelings for ethnic nationalism in the desire to become Americans.

Given this attitude, only a thoroughly assimilated leadership like the Brandeis-Mack group could exploit their latent Zionism. They all had relatives in Europe affected by the war, and even those with small means wanted to help as much as they could. When Brandeis called on them to help the Zionists help their European brethren and when he declared Zionism and Americanism compatible, he unleashed long-buried emotions. Now they could be both Zionists and Americans, and Brandeis' example gave the lie to charges that "real" Americans did not belong to the movement. Here again, the experience of other immigrant groups is instructive. The Slavs who came to America also had dreamed of a free country of their own that would be free from the domination of Austria-Hungary. Yet once in the United States, they ignored pleas from revolutionary groups seeking independence. Not until the war, when Woodrow Wilson announced the concept of self-determination and declared himself in favor of a free and independent Czechoslovakia, did American Slavic groups begin to support the independence movement at home. Those who came had not forgotten the old country, but they had made a choice; they would do nothing to jeopardize their new status as American citizens.[54]

Another factor, less obvious but more personal, lay in the anti-Semitism faced by the new immigrants. They learned English, shaved off their beards, threw away their *yarmulkes,* and turned their backs on the old ways, just as the Schiffs and Marshalls had urged them to do. But one cannot become an American overnight, and they soon ran into prejudice which, while not as pervasive nor anywhere as brutal as in Europe, still reminded them that they were Jews. They found their opportunities restricted, and their liberty less than total. No longer able to escape into the security of the *kehillah,* many turned toward a Zionism that urged them to be proud of their Jewishness, and that claimed that their Americanism need not drown out their hopes and dreams of Zion.

Although in 1921 a number of them would turn against the Brandeis group, it would be a mistake to equate the Zionism of New

York's East Side with that of Eastern Europe. In the old country, Zionism had strong messianic overtones, a movement to save people from the hellish existence of Czarist Russia or Poland; in America, day-to-day life might be harsh, but the constant fear of hostile edict or *pogrom* was blessedly absent. Zionism became a means of saving others, not themselves, and as much as those already acculturated, the recent immigrants also wanted assurances that Zionism did not mean they would actually have to go to Zion. At first, only a small number of intellectuals supported the movement, since as an ideology it did not satisfy the daily needs of the masses. Only when Zionism assumed the burden of saving their European relatives did it directly affect the masses.

To these immigrants, Brandeis served as a bridge between two cultures, that of the assimilated American society and that of the Yiddish-speaking East Side, even though he had practically no roots among the latter. But he had not forsaken his people, and like the prodigal son, they saw his return through Zionism as a sign. Abe Goldberg, the editor of *Dos Yiddishe Folk,* wrote him a moving note that bespoke the thought of many of the recent immigrants: "I am myself mystically and religiously inclined, although I usually appear very rationalistic. And believe me, that since the Boston convention [1915], never yet a day passed that I did not think of you, and I never went to bed without praying for your health."[55] Even when they disagreed with his policies, they did not criticize him. He had legitimized Zionism, both for them and for America. By the end of the war, with thanks in large measure to the Balfour Declaration, the East Side had become enthusiastically Zionistic, and in just the reverse of the prewar situation, practically every Yiddish newspaper supported the cause.[56] The Zionism latent among the immigrants had been awakened, but only after they had been convinced that it would not affect their status in the new Zion.

V

Prior to the war, the World Zionist Organization's support of Palestinian colonies relied almost entirely on contributions from

European Jewry. Within a matter of days after fighting broke out, the movement's leaders recognized that European Jews would no longer be able to give much to the cause. Shmaryahu Levin urged American Jews to rise to the challenge: "We in America now have the good fortune to show our manhood in this emergency, and it is our duty to meet it with earnestness, willingness and optimism. No sacrifice of time or energy or means should appear to us too heavy to make. Upon us, and our handling of the situation depends, perhaps, the future of our organization for which we have struggled these many years."[57] Although no one recognized it at the time, the war marked a turning point in Zionist finances; after 1914, American Jewry provided the bulk of the money for the movement. As Weizmann prophesied in 1918, "the burden will not be lifted from your shoulders, I am afraid, for a long time to come. . . . We shall all turn to you and to your great country for help, advice and guidance —for help in men and money."[58]

Considering the inability of the FAZ ever to raise more than twelve thousand dollars annually before the war, Zionist leaders both in Europe and America appealed more from despair than from any realistic belief that they would get the sorely needed funds. As late as July 23, 1914, Lipsky had advised the central office that the rich Jews, "the leading philanthropists," would not give to Zionism. When Brandeis announced that the Provisional Committee would establish a relief fund of one hundred thousand dollars, the old-timers at the emergency meeting gasped in disbelief, and doubted whether, without the help of the Schiffs and the Guggenheims, they could ever raise that amount.[59] In some ways the dissenters were right; not until the Second World War would the Zionists have access to the really wealthy Jews. But hundreds of thousands could and would be raised by appealing to those of limited and moderate means, and to this well the new leadership went.

It has been said that guilt is the great motive force of charity, that people give money to assuage subconscious anxieties when others are suffering while they have been spared. Certainly the Progressives, who organized charitable giving to the level of a fine art, played numerous changes on this theme. Those who had been materially blessed owed it to society to use their money for the benefit of others. Andrew Carnegie's "Gospel of Wealth" applied not only to millionaires but to those in the prosperous middle class as well. Fortune's blessings carried responsibilities, and a generation of progressive reformers had carried this message to the general public.

Simplicity itself underlay both the theme and the method of the Brandeisian approach. "The Jews in America, most fortunately placed, can and must work out the gigantic problem that now confronts our people. And in American Israel—we, the Zionists, must bear the brunt of effort and sacrifice. We are that 'saving remnant' which our traditions tell us have always escaped the holocaust and saved our people." Not since the exile of the Jews from Spain in 1492 had such suffering been seen, and both Jewish and American traditions demanded that brother help brother. "The more fortunate Jews in America must give quickly and liberally, not from their income merely but from their capital also," Brandeis urged, and he gave generously from his own pocket as an example.[60] But now he, Stephen Wise, Horace Kallen, and others went on speaking tours raising funds, first for the PC's Emergency Fund and later for the American Jewish Relief Committee (predecessor of the Joint Distribution Committee). Their appeal everywhere followed the same pattern: European Jewry stood devastated; funds were needed to help them and to support the Palestinian colonies; everyone should give according to his ability; each city had a quota; and the New York office dunned local leaders to follow up mass rallies until the goals had been met.

The Provisional Committee utilized several approaches in its fund raising. At first, in the flush of excitement, mass rallies with collections brought in much of the money. Louis Kirstein reported women giving their jewelry and young boys turning in their Bar Mitzvah rings in lieu of cash.[61] Although mass rallies continued throughout the war, the Committee gradually shifted its emphasis toward ongoing pledges for the duration of the war, and to a lesser degree, personal appeals to the wealthier Jews. In this latter area, however, the Zionists quickly realized that they could reach only limited funds. Of all the really wealthy Jews, only Nathan Straus of Macy's actively supported the Zionist cause. He not only gave over fifty thousand dollars for Palestinian relief, but also sold his yacht, the *Sisilina,* with the proceeds going to the PC. Samuel Untermyer,

Eugene Meyer, and Brandeis all gave liberally for their means, but they obviously did not have anywhere near the great wealth of a Schiff or a Guggenheim. Aside from the *shtadlanim's* anti-Zionism, the new leadership had antagonized them in other areas. Brandeis, Wise, and Frankfurter had been in the forefront of the attack on concentrated wealth. Brandeis' exposé of the great banking and finance houses, *Other People's Money* (1914), included attacks on Schiff and other magnates, who now funneled their substantial contributions for European relief through agencies run by their own people.

With the great fortunes closed to them, the Provisional Committee concentrated on securing pledges from those of more modest means. At the numerous rallies and dinners at which they spoke, Zionist leaders asked not for one-time donations, but for continuing pledges that would last until the emergency ended. The amount mattered less than the commitment. Brandeis pledged $1,000 monthly to the general fund, and committed himself for lesser amounts to local Boston campaigns; he then urged his colleagues also to set an example for the rank and file. Form letters asked every Zionist to give at least $10 a month during the war, with special requests going to those who could afford larger amounts. The efforts paid off on a scale much larger than the Zionists had expected. In the nine months following the Hotel Marseilles meeting, the Zionists raised $170,000 for Palestinian relief, a sum nearly equal to all the FAZ had raised in its previous fifteen years of existence.[62]

The Provisional Committee also inaugurated a transfer operation by which individuals could send money directly to relatives or friends in Europe and Palestine. Because of American neutrality in the first two and a half years of the war, both the Allies and the Central Powers allowed various relief and charitable groups to distribute food, money, and clothing in the war zones. Jacob deHaas suggested that if the belligerent governments would allow it, much more could be sent on an individual basis. It was one thing to give $25 to a general relief fund, but if one knew that the money would go directly to an aunt or cousin, more people would give larger amounts. Brandeis contacted the State Department to see if there would be any objection from the government, and after receiving assurances that this would not violate American neutrality, the Provisional Committee established its Transfer Department. At first it handled only a few dollars a day, but within weeks the volume had swollen to thousands, and by the end of the war, millions had been handled. While the Zionists originally hoped to aid suffering Jewish families, they agreed to distribute money for non-Jews as well. The sender paid nothing for the service, and the Provisional Committee bore the charges of transmittal and exchange. Even the State Department utilized its service to send monies and private messages, while large companies like Standard Oil, which had many overseas offices, facilitated the work. In a perfect operation involving tens of thousands of people and millions of dollars, the Zionists generated a great deal of goodwill.

But even beyond this, the Zionists saw their chance to build for the future. Through fund raising, Brandeis explained, "we must unite the Jews and make clear to them also that it is through the establishment of a publicly recognized, legally secured home for the Jews in Palestine that our unity must find expression." Although the Brandeis leadership has often been accused of diverting Zionist interest into mere money-grubbing, the fact is that Brandeis saw fund raising as a first step on the road to awakening a Jewish consciousness and a Zionist interest. Money had to be given, because only money could buy clothes and food and medicine, but one also had to understand that the Jewish situation made them suffer more than other victims of war, and only a homeland would alleviate that problem. "If there can be awakened in America a desire to tackle the problem of the Jew fundamentally and see it through to a successful end," he said, "we shall have passed on one stage further in our struggle for complete and universal rights." Brandeis had once described money as important to him only insofar as it made him free; now money, in the long run, would only be important to American Jews if it freed their minds to see the ultimate need of a Jewish homeland.[63]

Within limits the Zionists did well. Several hundred thousands of dollars poured in for relief, and the Provisional Committees' Transfer Department handled millions more. Through the good offices of the Wilson administration, the U.S.S. *Vulcan* carried sorely needed foodstuffs and medicines to Palestine, the bulk of which the PC collected. Hadassah dispatched a medical unit to Palestine, and steadily augmented its scope of operations through the war. Membership also rose dramatically, with the number of shekel payers doubling, and then doubling twice again. In the long run, however, the Zionists yielded their relief activities to the Joint Distribution Committee, and concentrated their energies and resources on Palestine and on building up their own organization. The fund raising did, however, blunt the differences between "political Zionism" and "philanthropic humanitarianism," and blurred over ideological problems. Old-line and labor Zionists later attacked the Brandeis leadership for abandoning ideology, for taking Jewish identity out of Zionism. In fact, only by this deliberate blurring did they make possible the ultimate pragmatic union of Zionists and non-Zionists working together for a Jewish homeland.

VI

Shortly after Brandeis accepted the chairmanship of the Provisional Committee, Horace Kallen reported on a lengthy meeting the two men had. "Mr. Brandeis is ready to do whatever is necessary to realize our plans," noted Kallen, "but he points out that at present there is nothing more important to do than to strengthen the organization, and to establish it as a body of men and women whose voice will be heeded."[64] As in no other aspect of his work in the movement, Brandeis' emphasis on effective organization reflected his experience as a reformer. In his campaigns to establish savings bank life insurance and in his fight against J. P. Morgan's attempt to monopolize the New England railroads, he had come to realize that in American politics, the voice of any individual, no matter how articulate, carried little influence compared to the power of an organized citizenry. Indeed, this emphasis on organization and rationalization characterized the entire Progressive movement.[65] In Zionism, there had been only a few articulate voices, and no effort to shape even a limited membership into an effective whole. Now, with a swelling in the ranks, the potential influence of thousands of new members would be lost unless the organization itself could be restructured.

The mark of a good organizer is the ability to take a complex problem and dissect it into identifiable and manageable chores. The mark of a leader is the ability to keep the strands of these chores discrete and yet weave them together into a strong braid. The Zionist situation in 1914 required even more than this. The pressure of the hour required that new tasks be undertaken even before old problems had been sorted out. Thousands of men and women joined the movement, clamoring for work to do and for leadership to tell them what had to be done. Between 1914 and 1921, it is fair to say that the new leadership solved most of the organizational problems that had befuddled the Federation, and that it provided a sense of direction as well as a spirit of purpose in the American movement. Yet so overwhelming were the contradictions within the American membership and the conflicts with the European organization that in the end much of the work came undone.

The first tasks, obviously, involved sorting out the tangled skein, and giving eager workers a sense of direction. Louis Lipsky has given us a portrait of Brandeis at work: "He would come to the Zionist offices in New York early in the morning and remain for hours, receiving visitors, questioning them and assigning tasks. He presided at the frequent meetings of the committee and won general admiration for the cogency and subtlety of his questions and the sagacity of his conclusions. He was innocent of vanity or conceit and unconventional in his behavior. He had a cordiality that won confidence. He was seldom direct in attack, but with rare subtlety insinuated the trend of his thinking into the discussion. But he could be merciless in judgment too, and his indignation could be devastating. You did not feel that he was forcing his views; he drove them home by logic and dominated the situation with tact and reason. He would take his coat off, loosen his tie, ruffle his hair, use his hands actively and twist his body in the chair as he carried on a hearty discussion with infinite patience."[66]

He appointed numerous committees to deal with specific problems, such as politics or propaganda, and demanded regular reports on their progress. He bombarded the office committee in New York with directives and questions, and insisted that they report to him weekly with details of their progress. To Benjamin Perlstein, who as administrative secretary had charge of the daily affairs of the Committee, he sent as many as five or six letters a day seeking data, offering suggestions, demanding action. Field offices in Boston and other cities received similar attention. "I hope very much that you and our friends in Pittsburgh will undertake, particularly for the next two months, to push in every way the development of the Zionist organization," he wrote. "Upon the size, strength and efficiency of the Zionist organization will depend the accomplishments not only of what may be done for Palestine, but what may be done for the Jews elsewhere."[67] He had a mania for details, and by constantly prodding his associates, he forced them to reorganize their particular tasks to yield these data. In doing so, they simultaneously improved the efficiency of their own operations.

Of all Zionist functions, none had been so sloppily handled as finance, and nothing irritated Brandeis more than financial mismanagement. Felix Frankfurter recalled that Brandeis wanted the Zionists to handle their money as conservatively as a bank, accounting for every penny collected and expended. Soon after Brandeis took over, he installed Robert D. Kesselman, a certified public accountant, in charge of the Provisional Committee's finances. Kesselman had a most difficult time getting the old-line Zionist workers to accept the need for proper money handling and record keeping.[68] They had always been rather casual about it, collecting when they could, keeping donations in their coat pockets or in paper bags, and turning it in whenever they happened to stroll by the office. The old *pushke* (tin box) gatherers never reconciled themselves to the need for such efficiency, but by mid-1916, Kesselman was satisfying the chief's demands for daily financial reports.

Part of the reason for Brandeis' insistence on such stringent accounting procedures derived from the huge demand by Palestinian institutions for help. With the normal sources of revenue in Eastern and Central Europe suddenly cut off, the *Yishuv* turned to the United States, with the assumption that all of the monies being raised for relief from American Jewry would be for their use. They failed to realize that most of these funds were earmarked for European relief, and that non-Zionist, and in some cases anti-Zionist, officials controlled their disbursement. The Provisional Committee did assume the responsibility for the maintenance of the Zionist offices in Palestine, arranged for a loan to the orange planters, and responded to numerous requests to keep schools and hospitals open. But despite the quantum jump in revenues, it still could not cover all of the demands, and even though the Zionists could now secure credit, Brandeis refused to expend more than could be collected. Time and again the Committee had to inform Arthur Ruppin, the chief Zionist official in Palestine, that it had no more money for that month or that quarter. While the Europeans may have considered this a niggardly approach, the fiscal conservatism that Brandeis demanded in Zionist operations undoubtedly had a salutary effect on the organization and made its approach to handling emergency funding much more realistic and effective.

The Federation's major organizational problem involved its dependent relations with the affiliated societies. Individual Zionists belonged to different lodges, benevolent associations, and clubs rather than to the FAZ. Moreover, since the Federation had no real coercive power over the societies, it could only act through moral suasion. The Provisional Committee, in fact, had been created to bypass the organizational weaknesses of the Federation. The Committee took over nearly all of the records and staff of the FAZ, but purposely emphasized its distinctness from the older organization. For all practical purposes, the Federation of American Zionists existed in name only after 1914.

The new leadership recognized that the answer lay in a reorganization that would bypass the local societies and tie in each individual member to the national body. Practical considerations dictated that the local clubs could not be abolished, but their powers had to be lessened and made subordinate to the parent group. Ideally, there would be one organization speaking and acting for all of American Zionism and claiming the loyalty of each individual member. In addition, for social, educational, and political work, local clubs would act as agents for the national executive. The needs created by the war clearly demonstrated the weaknesses of the old Federation; the war also created the opportunity in which an effective reorganization could occur.

The problem of reorganization engaged Brandeis' interests from the start, and by early 1915 a plan emerged that ultimately led to the creation of the Zionist Organization of America in 1918. The plan the leadership adopted involved the identification of the Provisional Committee as *the* national spokesman for American Zionism; creating services to attract the interests and loyalties of the local clubs and members; securing the co-operation of the affiliates in acting together; and finally, a formal reorganization that established a single national organization.

By itself, an affiliation of such nationally known figures as Louis Brandeis, Julian Mack, and Felix Frankfurter focused attention on the Provisional Committee immediately. The publicity given the relief funds, the transfer operation, and the supply ship added to the prestige of the Committee. In addition, spokesmen for the movement constantly emphasized the national scope of the problems confronting American Zionism. A great opportunity awaited the American movement, an opportunity and a responsibility to fill the vacuum of leadership created by the war; but only through unified action could they assume that leadership. On a quieter and more subtle basis, the new leadership initiated a voluminous correspondence with local Zionist leaders and sent out numerous bulletins to all shekel payers keeping them informed of the Committee's activities.[69] Through these letters, the Provisional Committee established that direct contact with individual members that had been so notably lacking during the Federation period.

While the FAZ had always supplied propaganda for local societies, it had provided little else to the affiliates, and in fact had known very little about what they did. The Provisional Committee stepped up the propaganda drive, tying it into the relief campaign, and offering name speakers to local communities upon guarantee of a minimum amount to be raised. But the Committee also established regional bureaus across the country to provide information on political activities, fund raising, organizational techniques, propaganda, and other services. Ultimately, the PC hoped to establish a bureau in every major city to carry out directives, as well as to shift loyalties and attention away from the local societies to the Committee.[70] At the same time, the bureaus kept the national executive up to date on what local Zionist groups were doing, information that hitherto had not been available.

All this, of course, could not be done behind the backs of the local affiliates, and the leadership openly explained that a reorganization would serve the best interests not only of the movement, but of the affiliates as well. As Brandeis explained to Nathan Kaplan of the Chicago-based Knights of Zion, by centralizing those activities that required national direction in the Provisional Committee, the Knights and other Zionist groups would be relieved of an onerous burden, and could then concentrate on those tasks and social functions that they did best. Rather than view this as a weakening of the Knights, Brandeis suggested that it would strengthen the group in those areas where special opportunities for service were now lost because the organization spread itself too thin.[71]

The Provisional Committee consistently urged the different groups to work together in their fund-raising and propaganda efforts. It would not do to show a divided front, or have potential donors alienated because they were approached by competing societies. In 1915, Brandeis convinced the ten largest Zionist affiliates to hold their annual meetings jointly in Boston at the end of June. The Provisional Committee dominated the convention, and Brandeis' personal prestige led the city fathers to prepare a near-royal welcome for the delegates. Special floral arrangements, featuring the Star of David, decorated the Public Gardens, local groups held numerous receptions for the Zionists, and the Boston newspapers gave extensive coverage to the convention. As Brandeis had hoped, the delegates realized that at their independent meetings they had hitherto gone practically unnoticed, but acting—indeed, just meeting—together had created the impression of size and influence. After mid-1915, the initiative in Zionist affairs passed completely into the hands of the Provisional Committee, and a noticeable momentum had been created for a reorganization to capitalize on the joint strengths of the affiliates.

Final merger came in 1918, when the Provisional Committee, the Federation of American Zionists, and other units joined to form the Zionist Organization of America, based on individual membership and organized in geographical units. Within the ZOA certain groups, such as Hadassah and Young Judea, maintained their separate identities, since they appealed to specific interests. The Poale Zion stayed outside the ZOA, but continued to co-operate closely. The Mizrachi also stayed aloof for similar reasons as well as for the fact that it alone of all the Zionist groups had refused to subordinate its American activities to the PC.[72] With the creation of the ZOA the new leadership wiped away the most serious of the organizational weaknesses that had plagued the Federation, and converted American Zionism into an effective instrument for the dissemination of Zionist ideas, the raising of funds, and the wielding of political influence. The lessons learned by the Progressives in their reform activities proved equally valuable in the pursuit of Zionist goals.

At the same time they established hegemony over the American Zionist movement, the Brandeis group tackled another problem that had weakened the Federation: relations with the world organization. The FAZ had been trapped in that as long as it could not demonstrate dominance in American Zionism, the Actions Comité would not give sanction to its claim of primacy; but as long as the WZO refused to grant that recognition, the Federation could not gain ascendancy. The needs of war and the creation of the Provisional Committee quickly established the leadership of the Brandeis group. The problem of relations with the parent body now took on different dimensions.

The international makeup of the Actions Comité condemned it to fragmentation with the outbreak of war. They could no longer meet in Berlin, headquarters of the movement, and many of the members, caught up in war fever, joined some form of government service. Those like Shmaryahu Levin and Nahum Sokolow, caught away from the Continent, tried to work for the cause through national bodies like the Provisional Committee or the English Zionist Federation. The central committee set up a temporary office in Copenhagen under Victor Jacobson, but in the absence of any forceful leadership, it never amounted to much. Indeed, since the death of Herzl, leadership had resided in the AC more through institutional loyalty than from force of personality. With the institution itself now partially crippled, its normal sources of revenue closed off, and the sudden emergence of the Brandeis faction in America, pressure arose on both sides of the Atlantic to shift direction of the world movement to the United States.

In calling the emergency meeting at the Hotel Marseilles at the end of August 1914, both Shmaryahu Levin and Louis Lipsky took for granted that the Actions Comité no longer functioned, its members having scattered to the winds. At the meeting itself, and in the hectic weeks following, Brandeis also assumed that the world movement had lost its rudder.[73] To Chaim Weizmann, who had his own differences with the AC, and who now wanted to disassociate the movement from anything and anybody German, it seemed imperative that the conduct of Zionist affairs during the war should be entrusted to the Provisional Committee. "I do not doubt that by this way only the Organization could be saved from falling to pieces. In view of the tensions now prevailing, I consider the activities of the old Actions Committee impossible and even dangerous for the future of our cause. . . . The American Provisional Committee should be given full power to deal with all Zionist matters until better times come."[74]

The Provisional Committee showed no hesitation in wanting to fill the vacuum of leadership. Jacob deHaas, who thought he had discovered a second Herzl in Brandeis, urged the Boston attorney from the start to push for full and complete autonomy in world Zionist affairs. In October, the PC informed Weizmann that it stood ready to act "on behalf of the whole Zionist Organization at such times when action is necessary. We wish to send money direct to Palestine. This permission had been granted already by the Actions Comité in Berlin. We wish, if necessary, to communicate with Canada and other English-speaking countries. We wish to take political action when necessary, on behalf of the Zionist organization and we wish, in general, to act on behalf of the Actions Comité over the whole organization, whenever, after due deliberation and careful consideration we find this necessary." By November, a steady stream of telegrams reached the Copenhagen office urging transfer of all powers to America.[75]

Despite the seeming chaos of those first few months of war, however, the Actions Comité had not disintegrated. Enough members remained in Berlin to carry on essential tasks, and gradually they began reasserting their authority. Nahum Sokolow, who remained in England during the war, urged the Americans to do their utmost for the cause, but not to push too far for control. They were all members of the same organization, he reminded them, and had to hold together, each doing his own share. Soon Weizmann also urged the

Provisional Committee to avoid assuming too many tasks.[76] By the spring of 1915, the Americans accepted the fact that the AC had not gone under. The Provisional Committee's efforts to achieve control of the world movement had only been half-hearted at best, primarily because the leaders had their hands full at home.

The Provisional Committee did, however, manage to impress upon the Actions Comité that it, and it alone, now spoke and acted for American Zionists. It demanded, and received, authority to collect and disburse all Zionist monies gathered in the United States, although the issue of handling funds in other English-speaking countries was never fully resolved. For funds being channeled to Palestine, Brandeis demanded centralized authority in the Holy Land, a request that Arthur Ruppin, who received the assignment, had long supported. Brandeis also demanded that the members of the AC cease sending confidential information to local officials. All information should be sent to the PC, which would then determine its distribution. Although minutes of the Committee's meetings were regularly sent to Copenhagen, the flow of information from Europe to America seemed too disjointed to be blamed on the war alone. Time and again the Provisional Committee, like the Federation before it, complained that while the Europeans were quick to ask for more money, they failed to keep the Americans informed about important issues.[77]

* * * *

The Brandeis leadership summed up its three major goals in the often-repeated motto of "Men! Money! Discipline!," and worked diligently after 1914 to bring in new members, raise money, and restructure the Zionist movement. The conversion from a moribund fringe group into a prime focus of American Jewish energies, however, faced formidable obstacles, and while successful, the drive took its toll. Many of the damages would not be apparent until later, but few people failed to understand that as the Provisional Committee reached for leadership in American Jewry, it would have to confront the power of the *shtadlanim* in the American Jewish Committee.

CHAPTER FIVE

THE
CONGRESS FIGHT

The rapid growth of Zionism during the war years did not sit well with all segments of American Jewry. Despite the Brandeisian synthesis emphasizing the American aspects of the movement, a number of Reform rabbis still condemned Zionism as subversive of true patriotism. For the most part, the Zionist leadership avoided open conflict whenever possible, and tried to isolate its anti-Zionist critics. But a much more serious challenge came from the aristocracy of the American Jewish Committee. At first, both sides tried to work together in raising relief money, but the AJC clearly had far greater access to monied contributors than did the Provisional Committee, and eventually gained control of the relief program. The crucial fight came over a proposal to call a Jewish congress. Here both sides saw the issue as one not only of principle but of power, believing that the winner would have the dominant voice in American Jewish affairs.

I

Officially, the attitude toward Zionism of Hebrew Union College and the other Reform organizations had not changed since the days of Isaac Mayer Wise: Jews no longer believed in or expected restoration in Palestine; they owed their loyalty to the country in which they lived; and Zionism, because it created a divided loyalty, was condemned. Although Reform Jews joined in efforts to raise funds for relief in Europe, they diverted their funds to non-Zionist agencies. Toward the end of 1914, the seminary authorities forced the students to cancel a lecture by Horace Kallen because of his Zionist affiliation, although Kallen was to have spoken on "The Meaning of Hebraism." In 1917 the Central Conference of American Rabbis reaffirmed Reform's opposition to "the new doctrine of political Jewish nationalism, which finds the criterion of Jewish loyalty in anything other than loyalty to Israel's God and Israel's religious mission."[1] Despite the adherence to the cause of men like Maximillian Heller and Stephen Wise, the Reform rabbinate staunchly opposed Zionism, and nowhere could stronger opposition be found than in Cincinnati, home of Hebrew Union and of several of the most important Reform congregations in the country. Kaufman Kohler, president of the seminary, and David Philipson, rabbi of the Rockdale Avenue Temple, led the opposition, and so great was their influence in the Jewish community that they silenced local Zionists practically by force of their personalities.

The temptation to stand and do battle in Cincinnati appealed strongly to many of the Zionists. Wise, Heller, and other Reform rabbis who supported Zionism rankled over the abuse they received from the Reform institutions, while local Zionists wanted to end the dominance of Philipson and the "Hill crowd" over communal affairs. Brandeis, a native of nearby Louisville, had extensive contacts in the city, and the desire to do battle sorely tempted him. By winning over the Jews of Cincinnati to Zionism, not only would a severe blow have been dealt to the prestige of Kohler and Philipson, but other Reform opponents would be muted as well. All this should have made an all-out fight in Cincinnati inevitable, and indeed many people sought one. Brandeis, however, recognized that, personal satisfaction aside, the Zionists were not yet strong enough to take on the powerful Reform leadership, and he chose instead a policy of isolating them. The Zionists would avoid a head-on battle in Cincinnati until their numbers and prestige gave them an incontestable superiority.

This strategy got off to a shaky start when Louis Lipsky, overeager to take the Zionist cause to Cincinnati, agreed to have Brandeis speak there in October 1914 on terms dictated by Philipson. The Zionists could explain the need for relief funds, but the meeting would be held under non-Zionist auspices, and the speakers could appeal neither for aid nor membership in the movement. Upon receiving news of these conditions, Brandeis berated Lipsky for agreeing to such terms, and warned him never to yield to similar conditions in the future. While sensitive to the fact that different approaches would have to be made before different audiences, "a meeting which undertakes to restrict my liberty of speech is not a meeting which I want to address." Since Lipsky had already accepted, however, he saw nothing to do but go ahead with it.[2]

Despite acceptance of his terms, Philipson seemed intent on undermining Brandeis' appearance from the start. The Friday before the scheduled meeting, Philipson devoted his sermon to a slashing attack on the fallacies of Zionism, and when Brandeis arrived in the city, a rabbinical delegation demanded that he not even mention Zionism in his talk. This far Brandeis refused to go, and the anti-Zionist sponsors of the rally withdrew, forcing its cancellation.[3]

Given the scarcity of Zionist resources, the leadership had little choice but to concentrate its energies in those cities where sentiment for the movement ran high. Some of the Provisional Committee members wanted to make a frontal assault on the Philipson clique, and Horace Kallen, still smarting from his own humiliating experiences there, urged Brandeis to go back to Cincinnati, but the chairman demurred. "I feel very strongly that our policy should be to avoid controversy and to win those who at present are indifferent. We can cover but a small part, with our present forces, of the field that is open to us. If we develop Zionism in those communities where our prospects are bright, we shall reap a much larger crop; and if our work is well done, Philipson and the like will be isolated and will shrivel up." When Kallen raised the question of supporting local Zionists like Max Senior (who later became a rabid anti-Zionist), Samuel M. Fechheimer, and other old-line German Jews struggling to break Philipson's power, Brandeis again urged that the struggle in Cincinnati be limited to those on the scene. Reports indicated that a number of congregants in Philipson's temple resented his anti-Zionist stand. Given enough time, they would rebel, but they might also rally to his defense if it looked as if outsiders were trying to interfere.[4] To Fechheimer and Senior, Brandeis offered encouragement, and promised to send speakers as soon as an open forum could be obtained. But, he warned, public discord would only hurt the movement, and open controversy might be disastrous. Zionism now needed unity above all.[5]

Although Stephen Wise and Julian Mack eventually went to Cincinnati, and the local Zionists there grew stronger, the policy of isolation achieved only partial success. Philipson and Kohler continued to dominate Cincinnati Jewry for many more years, and together with other anti-Zionists like Samuel Schulman of New York's Beth-El, contributed numerous articles attacking Jewish nationalism.[6] But by avoiding an open fight, the Zionists did isolate the antinationalist Reform leaders. The Eastern Council of Reform Rabbis, in which Stephen Wise wielded great influence, refused to support the Cincinnati group's extreme position, and Rabbi Maurice Harris, president of the Council, openly declared that he saw no conflict between Zionism and either Judaism or Americanism.[7] In late 1915, when Wise and Mack went to Cincinnati, they received a warm welcome from the community, despite the obvious absence of Kohler and Philipson. The Jewish press, including several non-Zionist periodicals, berated the two rabbis for their lack of openmindedness as well as courtesy.[8] Despite the fact that the Zionists also issued large quantities of propaganda, that they fought back when attacked, their refusal to confront the Reform leadership had the desired effect: The Zionists seemed to be looking for harmony and unity, while the Cincinnati group sought a fight. In the end, the Balfour Declaration closed the argument, with the Zionists decidedly the winners, although to the end of his life, Philipson continued to denounce what he considered the folly of Jewish nationalism.[9]

II

The outbreak of hostilities presented a clear problem to the American Jewish community, the need to raise funds for the relief of their brethren in Europe, and to a lesser extent, for the Palestinian settlements. At the same time that the Provisional Committee established its relief fund, the American Jewish Committee laid plans for a co-ordinated drive. In addition, religious groups set up the Central Relief Committee, while the labor organizations banded together in the People's Relief Committee.

All but the most obstinate individualists recognized the need for co-ordination, since the various relief agencies all competed for essentially the same sources of money. Yet so jealous was each group of its own prerogatives and projects that over a year passed before the four relief committees agreed to pool their efforts. By itself, the relief wrangle would be but another example of the petty bickering that plagued American Jewry at the time. In a larger setting, the fight to control relief represented another facet in the struggle for dominance and leadership between the newly organized Zionists and the established powers of the American Jewish Committee.

At the conclusion of the emergency meeting in August 1914, Brandeis immediately wrote Louis Marshall, informing him that the Zionists stood ready to co-operate with any and all groups in raising funds for the Jews of Europe and Palestine.[10] The letter took Marshall somewhat by surprise, since the AJC assumed that it would take the leadership and initiative in activities involving American Jewry. But the Zionists did have special claim for responsibility for the Palestinian settlements, and while many of the Committee's financial backers concerned themselves primarily with the problems of European Jewry, Marshall also considered the plight of the Palestinian settlers of equal importance. Ambassador Morgenthau had cabled that the Jews in the Holy Land needed one hundred thousand dollars immediately, and had pledged half of it if the balance could be raised in the United States. Even before formal steps to co-ordinate relief occurred, the AJC and the Zionists agreed to raise the other fifty thousand dollars.[11] In these early weeks, neither group recognized relief as part of a power struggle, but merely as an organizational problem, although the AJC undoubtedly saw the Zionists as an upstart group, one with more than its share of *chutzpah* (nerve).

On Sunday, October 25, representatives of the Zionists, the American Jewish Committee, and other Jewish organizations interested in relief met at Temple Emanu-El in New York. Jacob Schiff and Oscar Straus, speaking for the AJC outlined an organization that would have access to the monied Jews, but would be under the near-complete domination of the Committee. Stephen Wise and Judah L. Magnes (who belonged to both the AJC and the PC) opposed Schiff, and demanded that a more representative and democratic agency be created. Brandeis for the most part kept silent, asking occasional questions, but letting Wise put forward the Zionist position. Finally, they all agreed on at least the need for an umbrella organization, and decided to meet again on November 24 to hammer out the details. Again, the power of the Committee dominated the meeting. The name of the new agency, which would co-ordinate all Jewish relief activities in the United States, would be the American Jewish Relief Committee (deliberately designed, many thought, to emphasize the importance of the AJC), and the president, secretary, and treasurer, as well as seventeen of the twenty-five members of the Executive Committee, belonged to the AJC.[12]

Beginning with these two meetings, Brandeis recognized that in the field of relief, the Zionists would find their efforts eclipsed by the AJC. With the exception of Nathan Straus, not a single one of the really wealthy Jews endorsed Zionism, while the AJC had access to the riches of Schiff, Guggenheim, and their friends. It would undoubtedly be organizationally beneficial to receive hundreds, indeed thousands, of small donations and then recruit the donors to the cause, but the plight of war-afflicted Jews demanded money—large quantities of money—immediately. The stark reality of the situation was that Jacob Schiff could give more individually than could thousands of Zionists combined. By December 1914, the basic decision to leave the burden of relief in non-Zionist hands had been made, although its full implementation would be delayed for nearly a year.[13]

During 1914 and 1915, the Zionists worked on their own Emergency Fund for Palestine, establishing the Transfer Department, and in co-operation with the AJRC, securing supplies for a relief ship for Palestine. In addition, they worked wholeheartedly in general fund raising for the AJRC, with Zionists manning many of the field positions, and Brandeis himself heading the New England branch. By late summer, outward signs indicated that the Zionists had been exceedingly successful—over one hundred thousand dollars subscribed to the Emergency Fund, the Transfer Department operating smoothly, the supply ship *Vulcan* dispatched, and funds pouring into the AJRC coffers. Yet inwardly the Zionists were fuming. Organizational mixups by the AJRC staff often had the effect of pitting the Zionists against other groups, while the PC's efforts to recruit members antagonized the non-Zionists. Although nearly all of the foodstuffs collected for the *Vulcan* came from the Zionists, the AJRC's publicity releases ignored the Provisional Committee's efforts. Most importantly, the Zionists believed that the American Jewish Relief Committee shortchanged Palestine in its distribution of monies, since the Zionists raised proportionately more money for the combined relief campaign than the Committee sent to the Holy Land. Time and again Brandeis complained to Louis Marshall and the other executives on the AJRC, but to no avail. Even Nathan Straus, who normally preferred to stay quietly in the background, objected that fifty thousand dollars he had given specifically for Palestinian activities had been diverted to other causes.[14]

By the fall of 1915, the Zionists recognized that despite great efforts, their own drives had failed to yield the amounts needed by Palestine. The failure could not be ascribed to lack of zeal, since nearly all relief officials acknowledged that the Zionists had contributed some of the best workers in communal affairs. Despite a growing membership, the PC still did not have access to the great fortunes. Zionist leaders now began to consider seriously the full centralization of relief operations, with the PC retaining control of disbursements for Palestine. But even this the Marshall group would not concede, nor would Felix Warburg, head of the AJRC, guarantee a fixed percentage of funds for the Holy Land. Although Brandeis recognized the dangers of agreeing to centralization without assurances, the Provisional Committee leadership recognized that only the rich *yahudim* had access to the amounts of money necessary for relief. In the name of the common good, the Provisional Committee decided to turn over control of all relief operations to the AJRC.[15] This agreement led directly to the formation of the Joint Distribution Committee, which over the next thirty-five years would funnel massive amounts of aid to distressed Jews overseas. From the viewpoint of effectiveness, the "Joint" has undoubtedly been successful, much more so than had American Jewry continued to channel their charity through competing agencies.

For the Zionists, the agreement, while necessary, further alienated them from the sources of money and gave the Provisional Committee even less control over disbursements. The anti-Zionist attitude of a number of JDC officials meant that little more than bare relief funds would be allocated for the Palestinian colonies, and over the next two years Zionist officials had to fight, not always successfully, to secure even this minimal amount.[16] Although the Zionists might claim that "relief work is extra work,"[17] the fact of the matter is that had they been able to reach the rich Jews, the Zionists would have made relief work the main focus of their wartime operations. As it was, the Zionists seized upon a far more dramatic issue with which to challenge the supremacy of the American Jewish Committee.

III

Although relief and organizational matters dominated the Hotel Marseilles meeting in August 1914, the delegates did discuss briefly the need for representative agency to defend Jewish interests in any postwar negotiations, and Brandeis solicited Marshall's co-operation in preparing for that time.[18] The Zionists at first sought not to break the power of the Committee, but merely to secure a broader-based group that would be more truly representative of the American Jewish community. In the end, the fight for an American Jewish Congress became, in fact, a power struggle, and to secure a democratically elected organization, the Zionists had to tackle the *shtadlanim* head-on.

Despite numerous attempts in the nineteenth century, American Jewry had been unable to agree on any single body or group as its spokesman. In Europe, the Board of Deputies of British Jews stretched back to 1760, while France, Austria, and Germany also had national Jewish bodies dating back many years. The first modern mention of an American Jewish Congress came in January 1903, when the Union of American Hebrew Congregations had adopted a resolution calling for a Jewish body that would discuss "any and all of those serious problems which are arising all the time in connection with Jewish interests and questions," and that would have "as its constituent bodies all national Jewish organizations of a religious, common philanthropic and educational character."[19] In 1909, Nachman Syrkin had begun advocating a "Jewish Parliament," and two years later he and Abraham Shomer, the Yiddish playwright, issued a call for a world Jewish congress. By the time of the Hotel Marseilles meeting, Baruch Zuckerman and other Yiddish-speaking Zionists had been won over to Syrkin's idea, but had been unable to effect any plans of their own.[20] With the arrival of the Brandeis leadership, the supporters of the congress found new allies; by emphasizing the democratic aspects of the proposal, the Zionists not only appealed to the Yiddish-speaking masses, but undercut the American Jewish Committee, making it appear aristocratic and exclusionary, which in fact it was.

The AJC had long recognized that it represented only a portion of American Jewry, and in 1911 had invited representatives of all the major Jewish organizations to serve as members-at-large. Most of the groups failed to respond, but the following year the Federation of American Zionists agreed to elect a delegate, provided "he shall in no wise be bound by any discussion or policy" which ran counter to the program of the international Zionist organization. The Committee, whose charter and by-laws made no provision for special terms, rejected the application. Louis Lipsky, advising the Actions Comité of what had happened, requested advice as to whether the Federation should join without such precautions, and noted what he termed the antidemocratic spirit of the Committee. The Actions Comité suggested that it might be useful to join, but lack of follow-up, and then the war, precluded the alliance.[21]

While many of its members opposed Zionism, the AJC included Zionist leaders Harry Friedenwald, Julian W. Mack, and Felix Frankfurter, as well as Judah L. Magnes. Anti-Zionism clouded the issue, but the fight over the congress was not a fight for or against Zionism. Rather, it marked the coming to maturity of the Russian immigrants, and their desire to have a major say in the American Jewish community. It also denoted the effort of the Zionists to become a leading force among American Jews. Intertwined in the struggle were the fears of Reform Jews that Zionism would stigmatize them as a separate nation, and their dislike for any public airing of Jewish disputes. The fight's leitmotiv proved to be democracy, and the effort to dominate Jewish affairs quickly became a battle between democracy and aristocracy. Once the public accepted this as the heart of the controversy, the AJC arguments, no matter their merits, fell on deaf ears.

The main proponents of the American Jewish Committee included three of the pillars of the community: Jacob Schiff, Cyrus Adler, and Louis Marshall. Of the three, Schiff, one of the wealthiest members of the aristocracy, bluntly opposed Zionism, and considered the congress movement a mere façade for Jewish nationalism. He denounced the Zionists for their blatantly irresponsible actions, which had now called the loyalty of all American Jews into question. "With the actual holding of the proposed Congress," he warned, "the coming of political anti-Semitism into this land will be only a question of time. There is no room in the United States for any other Congress upon national lines, except the American Congress." The machinations of the Zionists would encourage Gentile Americans to look upon the Jews "as an entirely separate class, whose interests are different than those of the gross of the American people."

Should a congress be held, it would proclaim to the world "that we are Jews first and Americans second."[22]

Jews undoubtedly had the right to look after their own interests; that consideration, after all, had prompted the original organization of the American Jewish Committee. But the methods had to be discreet and subtle so as not to call attention to Jews as a group. While supporting some efforts to place Jewish interests before the peacemakers, Schiff bitterly opposed an open convention where fire-eating demagogues could broadcast Jewish business to the world. Let the better men, the more conservative and tested representatives of established groups meet quietly, and they would accomplish more than a Zionist-sponsored congress could ever hope to do.[23]

Adler, who conducted much of the negotiations with Brandeis and Mack, reflected the antinationalist mood of the Committee, as well as its distrust of open and uncontrolled meetings. Abraham Sachar described Adler as "retiring, cautious, conservative, unimpressed by all who believed that public protest or public pressure reflected defense techniques. He preferred personal persuasion, a dignified letter, a solidly documented memorandum, a well-groomed interview."[24] A scholar and administrator, Adler preferred small committees where men of similar background could iron out their differences in a reasonable and honorable way. Like his friend Adolph Kraus, he could dismiss the masses as "riffraff," confident that the "best" people would always act for the benefit of the entire community.

The most imposing leader of the AJC, and the dominant personality in the American Jewish community for over two decades, Louis Marshall, both personally and through different organizations, persistently fought any limitations on freedom or tolerance, especially for Jews, in the United States. A brilliant lawyer and inveterate letter-writer, Marshall's ideas and tactics governed the Committee from its origin in 1906 to well beyond his death in 1929. Like the others, he too opposed the congress movement because of its allegedly uncontrollable nature. It would give "blatant and flamboyant orators an opportunity to make themselves conspicuous for a moment irrespective of the permanent injury which they inflict upon Jewry." Marshall's biographer notes that a theme of moderation governed his life, and that he believed the Jewish position in America would be jeopardized by the indiscretions, intemperateness, and rivalries of the noisier Jewish factions. Great controversies always hurt the Jews, and normally could and should be avoided. The kind of Jewish leadership Marshall exemplified, according to Morton Rosenstock, "was symbolic of the self-designated elite whose claim to prominence was based on economic, social and political influence."[25]

Unlike the others, however, Marshall had a much more sympathetic attitude toward the Russian masses and even toward Zionism, although he opposed the idea of an autonomous Jewish state. He learned Yiddish so he could talk with the new immigrants, and subsidized a Yiddish newspaper so that he and his associates could more effectively reach the newcomers and help them to become good Americans.[26] He supported Palestinian settlement as an honorable and worthy endeavor, and after the Balfour Declaration in 1917, he demanded that non-Zionists be allowed to help in the upbuilding of the homeland. He led many of his wealthy friends into a working alliance with Chaim Weizmann and the Zionist Organization in the 1920s, an alliance whose full fruition was cut short by Marshall's untimely death.*

Nearly all of the opponents of the congress constantly held up the specter of dual loyalty, and warned that a congress would raise doubts about the role of Jews in America. Nearly all of them had also worked or contributed to the Americanization of the Russian immigrants, warning that they should not remain alien and bizarre, but should be integrated into American life as soon as possible. Yet for all their oratory about Americanism, all their worries about the Russian Jews failing to understand American institutions and processes, in the fight over the congress they proved themselves to be the ones who failed to comprehend the nature of a democratic society, they who clung to the outmoded ghetto concept of the *shtadlan,* they who did not trust the openness and tolerance and opportunity of American life. Horace Kallen, who worked closely with Brandeis and Mack, wrote: "The members of the [American Jewish] Committee distrusted the rank and file. They were afraid of the publicity. They were afraid of having their 'Americanism' impugned. One of them . . . stated that the Congress must not be held because

* See Chapter Eight.

some poor, anonymous devil of a radical might say something about the Tsarist Government which would then have a very bad effect upon the fate of the Jews in Russia. Others brought analogous objections. The class as a whole . . . showed distrust of democracy, fear of frankness, a consciousness of moral and social insecurity; showed themselves living under the dread of anti-Semitism. They insisted that whatever could be done, could be done quietly, by wire pulling, by use of the influence of individuals, by the backstairs method of the Sh'tadlan of the Middle Ages and of the Russian Ghetto."[27]

The Zionists, led by Brandeis and backed by the Yiddish-speaking intellectuals, fought the battle for the congress along lines designed to point out this aristocratic, antidemocratic nature of the AJC, and to emphasize the American nature of their own plan. By seizing upon the congress issue, the Brandeis group could reinforce their own arguments regarding the legitimacy of the movement in the United States, and they undercut the anti-Zionist position by alleging that they—the Zionists—represented the real spirit of democracy. The masses, previously awed by the *yahudim* and sensitive to the need to become "Amerikaners," supported the congress movement, recognizing it would give them a vehicle to exercise their power and influence in American Jewish affairs. They could strike out at the aristocracy, and at the same time justify their fight in terms of democracy. And with the mood of the country at large supporting the "democratic" Allies against the Kaiser's gang, one could hardly defend aristocratic action as "more American" than an open and freely elected congress.

IV

Aware ahead of time that the Hotel Marseilles meeting was going to consider some form of national Jewish organization, the AJC reacted quickly to Brandeis' letter soliciting co-operation. Marshall and Schiff were concerned not only with protecting their primacy in Jewish affairs, but also that the Provisional Committee might issue rash and embarrassing statements. Since the AJC also was in session on August 31, Marshall immediately answered that his group had already recognized the need to consider the condition of the Jews after the war, and stood prepared to co-operate with any organizations desirous of the same ends. A special committee of Cyrus Adler, Judah Magnes, and Marshall would be glad to meet with a similar group appointed by the Zionists.[28] At first reading, the Committee's response seemed to indicate complete agreement with the PC. In fact, by accepting the invitation, the AJC blocked the Zionists from any further activity until the two groups conferred. Temporarily, at least, the AJC had silenced an upstart group that gave every appearance of being vocal, volatile, and disturbing. The Marshall group had bought time until, as they saw it, clearer heads might prevail.

Despite Marshall's acceptance, when the two committees met, it became clear that they did not agree. But throughout the fall of 1914, urgent relief work occupied nearly the full attention of all the Jewish leaders, and despite occasional promptings from the Zionists, the Committee continuously postponed following through on the suggestion. In the meantime, pressure built within the American Jewish community to have all Jews unite in order to secure full and equal rights for European Jewry after the war. Both the *American Hebrew* and the *American Israelite* urged that internal bickering and past feuds be forgotten so that the community could act together. Various lodges of B'nai Brith passed resolutions in favor of a congress, and called on the national leadership to take the initiative. At its convention in December, Poale Zion called for a congress to work for the emancipation of Eastern European Jews, while the *Jewish Daily News, Warheit,* and the *Jewish Leader* all lent editorial support to the congress proposal.[29]

Despite this growing pressure, the American Jewish Committee gave no indication that it would move. Marshall had no intention of giving in to a mere clamor by groups "who do not hesitate to pass judgment on the most delicate questions of diplomacy without a moment's thought."[30] The Zionists, although strongly in support of the congress, hesitated to act. Brandeis now realized the trap he had fallen into, but questioned whether the Zionists had enough strength yet to challenge the AJC openly. As the demand for a congress grew, however, the Zionists realized that further inaction would be seen as a sign of impotence. Finally the issue was forced on March 21, 1915, when Gedalia Bublick, editor of the *Yiddisher Tagblat,* announced the formation of the Jewish Congress Organization Committee (COC) whose membership included many of the Eastern European nationalists and Yiddish journalists. The same day, the Federation of Bessarabian Jews, with a membership of ten thousand, adopted a resolution in favor of a congress. In April a number of Jewish labor groups formed the National Workmen's Committee on Jewish Rights to agitate for equal rights for Eastern European Jews. On May 9, 1915, the Provisional Committee decided to wait no longer for Marshall, and announced itself in favor of a congress.

Although Brandeis and a large number of Zionists took active roles in the congress movement, and while many of those who supported a congress showed sympathy to Zionist aims, the congress movement embraced far more than just Zionism. Brandeis and Stephen Wise provided a leadership and prestige that, in the eyes of the immigrant masses, balanced that of Marshall and Schiff. Bernard Richards, who saw the battle primarily in terms of "uptown, aristocratic *yahudim*" vs. "downtown democracy," declared that the East Siders might never "have gone against the power, the influence and the wealth that surrounded Mr. Marshall if it were not for the balancing influence and prestige of Brandeis."[31] But while Brandeis interpreted the congress fight primarily in terms of democratic principle, the Russian immigrants saw it as a matter of independence and maturity as well as of right and justice. Even those who did not share Zionist beliefs worked with them in this fight, and the Zionists took care to emphasize that this was a democratic movement, one that transcended even their own program.

Not all Zionists favored the congress, and of the leadership, only Wise, Kallen, and Frankfurter energetically worked with Brandeis to support the movement. Undoubtedly some of the members of the PC saw the congress fight solely in terms of increasing their own membership. Julian Mack and Harry Friedenwald were initially cool to the idea, while Judah Magnes, after a futile attempt to reconcile the two groups, angrily resigned from the Provisional Committee, accusing the Zionists of fomenting disunity among American Jews and of endangering the Palestinian settlements.[32] But as long as the newly awakened Yiddish-speaking masses supported him,* Brandeis carried on the fight, even over the objections of some of his closest associates among the leadership.[33]

As the battle heated up, calmer heads on both sides urged moderation and compromise. Julian Mack, a member of both the Provisional Committee and the AJC, tried to assure the old leadership that a congress would not mark the Jews as a separate group; at the same time, he urged Brandeis to control some of the downtown hotheads, whose intemperate remarks merely aggravated the situation. Cyrus Adler by his own lights also sought an acceptable middle ground, but insisted that the Zionists would have to yield in order to maintain peace.[34] Unfortunately, both sides now saw the controversy in terms of principles of such magnitude that, as honorable men, they could not yield. Marshall labeled the congress "positively detrimental to all that we hold dear," while Schiff feared that the congress would undermine the position of Jews in America.[35] For Brandeis and his associates, the questions of power and influence boiled down simply to democracy vs. aristocracy.[36]

By June 1915, a number of Jewish organizations had declared themselves one way or the other on the congress issue. The fraternal societies of Free Sons of Israel, Sons of Israel, and Brith Shalom, and the federations of Galician, Bukowinian, and Russian-Polish Jews, representing some 125,000 members, all called for a congress. The New York and Philadelphia Kehillahs and the Order of Brith Abraham backed the AJC. Nearly the entire Yiddish press backed the congress, while the leading Reform journals opposed it. Realizing that sentiment was running strongly against it, the American Jewish Committee took a first step toward securing a more representative association. On June 20, 1915, it issued a call for a conference

---

* Although the AJC membership consisted mainly of German-American Jews, not all the members of that community supported the Committee in this fight. A number of them sided with Brandeis, not in support of Zionism, but because they agreed in principle with the need for greater democracy in Jewish affairs.

in Washington that fall, limited to 150 delegates from the largest Jewish organizations, and a few days later invited the Federation of American Zionists to attend.[37]

The Zionists met in convention late that June, and at the annual business meeting, Louis Lipsky read the AJC invitation to the delegates. As soon as he finished, chaos broke loose as dozens of men and women began to attack the *shtadlanim*. Throughout these denunciations, delivered in both English and Yiddish, ran the charge that the AJC opposed democracy for American Jews and that it would pack the October conference roster in order to control the meeting. After an emotion-charged debate, the convention overwhelmingly voted to authorize the Provisional Committee to unite with other groups in calling a congress. In the face of such a response, the AJC, at Mack's insistence, asked Brandeis to meet privately with Cyrus Adler and with one of the six men who belonged to both groups; Brandeis chose Felix Frankfurter.[38]

Adler, Brandeis, and Frankfurter met at the Hotel Astor in New York on July 12, and their sparring indicated that although both sides talked about compromise and negotiation, the Zionists and the American Jewish Committee now realized that the outcome could determine who exercised dominance in American Jewish affairs. Throughout the meeting, Adler spoke only of a "conference," while Brandeis would talk only of a "congress." Brandeis indicated that the total number of delegates, even the size of the congress, mattered far less than the manner in which the representatives were selected. He then proposed that the three of them choose a nuclear list of twelve to twenty-four organizations to be invited to a preliminary conference, which would compile a list of all Jewish organizations in the United States, decide on a method of selecting delegates, and then on a basis of membership, allocate delegation sizes. This last point obviously threw the majority of seats into the hands of the large *landsmanschaft* organizations to which hundreds of thousands of Yiddish-speaking Jews belonged. Unbelievably, Adler came back with a proposal for a *prepreliminary* committee, which would decide which organizations should be represented at the preliminary conference, which in turn would decide all questions for the final conference, or, as Brandeis insisted on calling it, congress. The

Zionist leader, astonished by this suggestion, demurred that he would have to consult with his colleagues. Adler urged him to act quickly, since the AJC Executive Committee had scheduled a meeting the following day.[39]

Brandeis had no need to rush. The Executive Committee endorsed Adler's prepreliminary proposal, but then declared that under no circumstances could it alter the original plan, purpose, and scope of the October conference. The only change would be that the AJC would now invite eight other groups, including the FAZ, to act as cosponsors. Brandeis indignantly rejected the idea, and proceeded to spell out the Zionists' reasons for insisting on a congress, less for Adler's sake than for the public. The congress advocates considered the AJC plan undemocratic in its mode of selection, repressive in the arbitrary limits placed on debate,* and unrepresentative in that it did not accurately reflect the makeup of the American Jewish community. In the distribution of delegates, the AJC had alloted one organization with eighty-four thousand members five seats, another with four thousand members two seats, and a third with forty thousand only one place. Adler's lengthy response (by now both men were writing for public consumption, and the COC published the correspondence) attempted to refute the Zionist charges, and defended and renewed the call for a conference in which the Zionists would participate. To this late request, Brandeis again said "No."[40]

To the Zionists, the Brandeis-Adler negotiations reaffirmed their faith that they were fighting for democracy; the Committee, on the other hand, saw the Zionists as shrill, irresponsible upstarts who did not have the good sense to leave important matters in the hands of those who understood them. Solomon Solis-Cohen of Philadelphia took another view: "The Adler-Brandeis letters exhibit two pig-headed and prejudiced antagonists instead of two statesmen endeavoring to reach a common basis for action."[41] Yet the whole nit-picking affair marked a turning point in the congress fight. The

---

* The AJC, fearful of any issues that might mark Jews as separate, wanted to limit discussion to questions of relief and protection of civil liberties after the war. It wanted to avoid any mention of nationalism or of national rights for Jews as a group.

AJC, by its stubborn refusal to make any concessions had maneuvered itself into a corner from which it could not escape. The obvious intent to run a controlled meeting, the ludicrous allotment of delegates, confirmed the popular image of the Committee as authoritarian. The Zionists now realized that they had the upper hand, and so did the Committee; even the letter Adler sent to important Jews in America and Europe soliciting their views had a hollow ring.[42]

On August 16, the momentum definitely shifted into Zionist hands with the reorganization of the Jewish Congress Organizing Committee headed by Louis Brandeis, and three days later, at a mass rally at Cooper Union, East Side Jews roared their approval of the congress. Despite futile attempts by Adolph Kraus of B'nai Brith to mediate the dispute, the Zionists now began to lobby those organizations that had previously indicated their willingness to attend the AJC-sponsored October conference. The Order of Brith Shalom withdrew on August 16, and declared in favor of a congress, as did the Order of Western Star a few days later. After Adler and Brandeis had publicly debated the issue before the New England convention of the Young Men's Hebrew Association, the delegates voted overwhelmingly in favor of a congress. Wherever Committee spokesmen went, they found audiences continuously objecting to the arbitrary allocation of seats and the limits on discussion. By October 10, 1915—the deadline set by the AJC for selection of delegates to the Washington conference—only sixteen organizations had accepted invitations, and only seventeen representatives had been named. Five groups had refused to attend, nine others gave vague answers or demanded that the Committee accede to COC demands, and twelve national organizations did not even bother to respond. Given this situation, the American Jewish Committee had little choice but to cancel the meeting.[43]

V

In the face of seemingly overwhelming support for the congress, the AJC and the National Workmen's Committee, which had supported the conference, now offered to co-operate with the COC, provided details could be worked out that would meet some of their main objections. The American Jewish Committee in particular wanted to delay the congress until after the war so as to avoid any hint that Jews had other loyalties; and in November its Executive Committee voted to sponsor a postwar congress. The arrangement did not sit well with some of the congress advocates. "Such a proposal would seem to be a concession on the principle," Horace Kallen argued, "but it is to my mind a complete perversion of it. I believe that we must hold the congress *before the war ends* and as soon as possible," and Pinchas Rutenberg, Bernard Richards, and most of the Eastern European leaders agreed with him. Stephen Wise, on the other hand, felt the timing of the congress to be a secondary issue to breaking the power of the aristocracy. Julian Mack and Harry Friedenwald pleaded with Brandeis not to force the issue. The Committee had yielded much, and unaccustomed defeat tasted bitter in their mouths. If pushed on the question of timing, chaos instead of unity would result, to the detriment of European Jewry.[44]

Brandeis now found himself tugged from both sides. He had met privately with Marshall, and the two men found themselves in general agreement on the program that American Jewry should pursue in order to secure equal rights for their European brethren. If he declared for an immediate congress, he would alienate the Marshall group which, despite the congress fight, still remained the most prestigious Jewish body in the country. Moreover, Mack and Friedenwald insisted that since the AJC had gone so far, the congress people had to make some concessions as well. Still, a third consideration involved the enormous task of arranging a congress. Although the Zionists had taken great pains to point out that they were but one agency working for a congress, and though they claimed that they did not control the COC, in fact the Zionists constituted the backbone of the movement. Brandeis headed the COC, Stephen Wise was its most vocal champion, Bernard G. Richards served as secretary, and the Zionist rank and file (including several Palestinians temporarily in exile) made up the bulk of the organizing teams. To move ahead on the congress would mean a drain on the Zionists' own work, and Brandeis feared that either the

Provisional Committee's program would suffer, or the congress would be poorly handled, if this small body of men and women tried to do too much.[45]

On the other hand, the congress drive now had momentum, and the dominance of the AJC could be broken. Privately, Brandeis distrusted the Committee's "compromise" and motives. He urged Richards to have the COC and the Yiddish press point out, but without quoting him, that the Committee had adopted an absurd position. "A congress after the termination of hostilities may mean a congress after the time has passed when Jews could accomplish something by participating in a [peace] conference. It is perfectly clear that there might be peace conferences while hostilities were still underway." The AJC demand would so abridge the discretion of a congress as to make it useless.[46] With the Yiddish masses eager for action, Brandeis also realized that hesitation might lose the Zionists a large base of support. There had already been grumblings about too much caution by the leaders.

To avoid the dilemma, Brandeis urged that the congress agitation be kept up so that the AJC would realize that its proposal had little popular or organizational support. Together with Lipsky and de-Haas, he worked out a proposal that would push ahead with plans for a congress, gradually building up local branches, educating American Jewry as to the issues, yet not going so far as to alienate the *yahudim*. The essential purpose, as he saw it, "has been throughout of making the Congress movement truly what it purported to be—a democratic movement." In doing this, he hoped that non-Zionists, uncomfortable with the aristocracy, would emerge as leaders of the congress, and they would, in the future, be willing to work with the Zionists on a mutually beneficial basis.[47]

Although they did not realize it, control of the situation had already slipped out of the hands of both the American Jewish Committee and the Zionists. Neither side had realized the emotional impact that the congress movement had exerted on the Yiddish-speaking masses, nor how they saw the congress as their opportunity to express their own beliefs and exercise their own influence. On December 23, the Congress Organizing Committee issued an ultimatum to both the AJC and the National Workmen's Committee.

Either they agreed on a conference that would have full power to decide all issues that might come before the congress, as well as on the date the body would convene, or the COC would independently call the congress. The two organizations had until January 15, 1916, to reply. This move caught Brandeis completely off guard, and he denounced the ultimatum to Lipsky as "likely to prove disastrous to the Congress movement. . . . Its only effect can be to throw the onus of the break on us, and the onus of a Congress on us, under conditions which we are not able to bear." A few days later, Lipsky hesitantly replied that the COC did not agree, and its mood was more militant than ever.[48]

Brandeis—indeed, nearly all of the Americanized Jewish leaders on both sides of the argument—failed to understand the depth of feeling in the Eastern European community on the congress issue. Leadership of nearly all the communal and philanthropic agencies and disbursement of monies had been tightly controlled by the *yahudim*. Despite Brandeis' constant pleas to view the fight as one for a democratic principle, the Eastern European leaders and the AJC saw it in terms of power. The fact that a high moral principle could be involved gave the downtowners a sense of legitimacy and respectability, a feeling reinforced by the presence of Brandeis, Wise, and other assimilated Jews. Brandeis hoped to use the congress fight not only to establish a new partnership of power in the Jewish community, but to exploit the latent nationalistic feeling among the Yiddish masses. That he partly accomplished this second aim is indisputable, and tens of thousands of Jews, excited by the congress fight, did join the Zionist ranks. But instead of creating a new balance of power, the destruction of the American Jewish Committee's hegemony left merely a handful of organizations squabbling among themselves with no single group—Committee, Congress, or Zionists—able to claim leadership.

Unable to control the demand for the congress, Brandeis had little choice but to try to channel it along constructive lines. On January 24, 1916, the Congress Organizing Committee staged a monster rally at Carnegie Hall, and Brandeis, who in just four days would be nominated to the United States Supreme Court, gave the main address on "Jewish Rights and the Congress." In a masterly summation of the main arguments that had fostered the drive for a Congress, Brandeis emphasized that only if the Jews of America united in a democratic and representative alliance could they hope to demand and achieve equal rights and opportunities for their brethren in Europe.[49] Obviously riding the crest of victory, the congress backers gave no indication that they felt any pressure to yield on even minor procedural matters to the AJC.

In a last-ditch effort to preserve at least some of the AJC's influence, Marshall met with Brandeis, Baruch Zuckerman, Bernard Rosenblatt, and Abe Goldberg to see if any means could be found for the Committee to participate without losing face. A far cry from the AJC's original intransigence, Marshall now said he would agree to a planning conference of national organizations that would establish the machinery for a congress, and that while a congress could be elected during the war, it should not meet until immediately after the cessation of hostilities. While Zuckerman, undoubtedly one of the most volatile of the Yiddish intellectuals, objected strongly, the others appeared to be willing to make some concessions for the sake of peace. Brandeis admitted that in all probability the congress would not meet—indeed, should not meet—until after the war, but in case circumstances changed, he did not want the executive committee's freedom circumscribed.[50]

Again, the leaders failed to appreciate the build-up of emotions. Even while Brandeis and Marshall tried to reach agreement, the Congress Organizing Committee issued a call for a preliminary conference in Philadelphia for March 26 and 27, 1916. Marshall angrily denounced the move, intimating that he considered it near-treacherous when he and Brandeis seemed to have been moving so close to agreement. Jacob Schiff pleaded with Brandeis to use his influence to annul the decision, and to allow men of goodwill, both Zionists and non-Zionists, to find some platform on which they could both stand.[51] The AJC refused to participate in the conference, as did the National Workmen's Committee, and Marshall charged the conference organizers with hand-picking the delegations to assure the outcome. In another gloomy jeremiad, Schiff predicted that should the congress be held, "it will not be long before political anti-Semitism will rear its ugly head in these United States of America."[52]

A total of 367 delegates from 83 cities and 28 states attended the Philadelphia meeting, representing 33 national organizations with a combined membership of more than 1 million Jews. In a rousing keynote address, Stephen Wise declared that the creation of an American Jewish Congress marked a new day for American Jews, one characterized by democracy and equality. Criticizing those who would deny to the Jewish community the "substance of democracy," he asserted that the people "are resolved to be free of their masters whether these be malevolent tyrants without, or benevolent despots within the life of Israel. . . . Let it be said that whatever may have been the necessities of the past, the time is come for a leadership by us to be chosen, a leadership that shall democratically and wisely lead rather than autocratically command."[53]

Despite the absence of the AJC and several of its affiliated organizations, the success of the Philadelphia conference in laying the procedural groundwork for a congress was too plain to ignore. Even the *American Israelite* conceded that the movement had gathered more popular support from among American Jews than had ever been seen before.[54] The AJC acknowledged defeat among themselves, and set about salvaging what they could of their leadership in the Jewish community. While democratic elections, as the Congress proposed, would surely mean they no longer controlled events, even worse was the possibility of their becoming leaders of a minority faction. Disregarding Judah Magnes' plan for an energetic counterattack, Schiff and Marshall decided to emphasize "unity" among American Jews. They recognized, as did the Zionists, that the AJC represented a powerful segment of the community, a segment that could not be ignored by a democratic, representative Congress. Indeed, throughout the fight, no one had ever suggested that the uptowners should be excluded from Jewish affairs, but merely that they would have to share power with the others. The Committee would go along with the Congress, and try to use its influence to moderate the fire-eaters and prevent harm from coming to the community.[55]

A warning as to how far the Committee stood from popular opinion came in early June when Dr. Harry Friedenwald, a charter member of the American Jewish Committee and longtime president of the Federation of American Zionists, resigned from the Committee. In a bitter letter, he lamented that "a class of Jewry is arranged against the overwhelming masses—the unorganized masses which have so long been silent." Those Jews "who feel that their life is part of the throbbing, anxious, suffering Jewish life, belong to that body which is now seeking self-expression in the Congress movement," and he chose to stand with that group.[56] Together with Israel Friedlaender, who had also recently resigned, Friedenwald had been among those who had worked diligently, but in vain, to reconcile the Committee and Congress groups. Their resignations, followed by that of Felix Frankfurter, clearly indicated that moderate opinion in the Jewish community had swung in favor of the congress. On June 16, the Committee invited a number of organizations to a meeting at the Hotel Astor in New York to discuss the congress. At that gathering on July 16, the *shtadlanim* not only salvaged their defeat, but achieved a certain victory.

VI

On June 1, after a four month battle, the United States Senate confirmed Louis D. Brandeis as an Associate Justice of the U. S. Supreme Court. As early as February, Jacob Schiff had tried to get the nominee to resign from Zionist and congress affairs, since his new status would preclude such partisan activities.[57] Despite the attack launched against his nomination, and although he withdrew from nearly all of his reform activities, Brandeis continued his leadership of Zionist affairs, much to the relief of his associates. Given the circumstances, it was, as Yonathan Shapiro notes, an exceptionally courageous act. With Brandeis now on the bench, however, the AJC began plans that would either force him to resign his Zionist leadership, modify his stance on the congress, or both. Had he suspected this, Brandeis might not have agreed so readily to attend the July 16 conference. But the Committee had been defeated, and the now inevitable meeting of the American Jewish Congress would seal that defeat. The East Siders agreed with the leadership that instead of excluding the *yahudim,* some way should be found to bring them back into the community. They still controlled much wealth and enjoyed great prestige; to freeze them out would only hurt the Jewish cause.

The Hotel Astor meeting took place in a strained atmosphere, to say the least. The representatives of the American Jewish Committee resented the defeat they had suffered in the congress fight, while the Eastern Europeans, smug in their victory, realized that the situation was still quite fluid. Brandeis, who attended the gathering as head of the Congress delegation, had been under great pressure to make peace in the community.[58] When twenty-three organizations that had not joined the Congress agreed to come to the Astor conference, with the AJC indicating its willingness to find a solution, the opportunity for peace seemed at hand.

To show their willingness to reach a concord, the Congress sent in addition to Mr. Justice Brandeis, Judge Hugo Pam of the Chicago appellate court and ex-judge Leon Sanders of New York. Prior to hearing the three men, the other delegates adopted a resolution favoring a congress that would seek full religious, civil, and political freedom for Jews, but that limited the congress to this one area. In addition, most of the men attending indicated their preference that the congress not meet before the end of the war.

The question of date, which had long been a sticking point in the struggle, opened this debate as well. Oscar Straus wanted to know if there was any way possible of postponing the congress. Brandeis explained that at Philadelphia, the Executive Committee of the Congress had been charged to convene a full session between September 1 and December 31, 1916, and the only way this could be changed would be by a three-fourths vote of the whole membership. Straus indignantly charged that compromise was obviously impossible, since it appeared that the assembled groups had no power either to change the date or to convince the Congress of the recklessness of the decision. Brandeis repeated that only the Congress could change the terms of the mandate laid upon its Executive Committee, and that, in effect, the groups represented at the Astor would have to join the Congress on those terms, and then if they still wanted change, would have to work from within as members of the organization. At this point, Judah Magnes, still bitter at Brandeis over his leadership of both the Zionists and the congress movement, charged the Congress delegation with autocracy. "If Mr. Justice Brandeis goes before the Jews of this country on such an issue," Magnes yelled angrily, "I predict for him as great a defeat as his reception this afternoon was overwhelming. To come before this conference and to tell it: 'Either you come into our organization on our terms or you cannot come in at all' is no way to promote peace and harmony."

Brandeis retorted that this was hardly a tone to promote good feeling, but immediately several other men joined in the attack. In the middle, Judge Mayer Sulzberger stood up and announced that he had not come to this meeting to listen to "fancy speeches." "Five millions of our brothers are bleeding to death, and here we are talking about organizations and procedures," he said, and walked out. During all this time, as the crescendo of attacks on Brandeis and the Congress mounted, Louis Marshall, chairing the meeting, deliberately kept his silence until one of the delegates objected to the rudeness to which Brandeis was being subjected. Then, and only then, did Marshall suggest that personalities be left out of the debate. Soon thereafter, the congress delegation left.[59]

The indignities to which Brandeis had been subjected immediately aroused the ire of the Yiddish press, but the New York *Times,* whose owners closely associated with the AJC, suggested that it had been Brandeis who had been out of place. The paper took him to task for violating the custom "faithfully honored by observance, for the Justices of the Supreme Court of the United States, upon taking office, to withdraw from many activities of a political or social nature, in which as private citizens they were free to engage, in order . . . to avoid all controversies which might seem in any degree to affect their judicial impartiality of mind." The editors commended Brandeis for his courage and ability, but "it was evident that a good deal of feeling was aroused, and . . . Justice Brandeis might with very great propriety have avoided taking part in such a controversy. Now that he has discharged his duties to the Congress committee, he ought to withdraw from all extra-judicial activities."[60]

What had been one of the worst fears of the Zionists now came to pass. Since the time of his nomination, the Zionists had worried whether confirmation would require Brandeis to step down from the leadership.[61] Now, even though he recognized that the *Times* editorial and letters sent in support of it were premeditated, and that the Astor meeting had been a trap, he also realized that as a Supreme Court justice, he could no longer afford to participate in such controversial matters. On July 21, without consulting any of his associates, he resigned all of his offices in the American Jewish Congress, the Joint Distribution Committee, the American Jewish Relief Committee, and the Provisional Executive Committee. He acknowledged that the Hotel Astor incident, even though deliberately provoked, had shown him that he could no longer act as if he were a private citizen. "There is at least this compensation," he noted. "My enforced withdrawal did not come until after the triumph of the Congress movement has been assured, and the desired unity of the Jews of America has been made possible."[62] Despite impassioned pleas from his followers, Brandeis, having reached his decision, refused to budge.

At first glance, Brandeis' resignation seems indeed precipitate. Yet in examining both the man and the situation, it becomes obvious that even without the instigation of the Hotel Astor incident and the *Times* editorial, Brandeis' withdrawal from official leadership could not have been long delayed after he took his seat on the Court in June. Brandeis had always had more than the lawyer's traditional respect and love for the law. To him, law allowed men to act in a civilized manner, and the proper function of law was to permit men to improve their society in an orderly way. In a society governed by laws, the courts and judges especially had to be beyond reproach. Even before going on the bench, Brandeis had divorced himself from all of his reform activities; in later years he would not even accept honorary degrees. Even in his private letters he refused to comment about cases before the Court.[63] It is a mark of his devotion to Zionism that he had not resigned earlier. Yonathan Shapiro also suggests that Brandeis' continued involvement in Jewish affairs had already begun to create an awkward situation. Brandeis told deHaas that although non-Jews did not seem to object to his retaining leadership in the Zionist movement, many Jews did, and this created obstacles in his relations with other members of the Court. According to Shapiro, his roles as a "representative Jew," Zionist leader, and Justice came into conflict; given Brandeis' background, it was inevitable which ones would be sacrificed.[64]

While resigning his official position, Brandeis did not sever his relations with Zionism. In fact, for the next five years he exercised *de facto* leadership in the movement, while Stephen Wise and Julian Mack occupied the formal positions. Through daily memoranda and letters to Wise, Mack, deHaas, and Lipsky, as well as frequent meetings in Washington, New York, and Boston, Brandeis became the "chief." He made no secret of his continued interest in Zionism, and the public, both Jewish and non-Jewish, knew and accepted this as legitimate. But his deep involvement and the extent of his control remained hidden from all but his closest associates and lieutenants.

Within two months after the Hotel Astor meeting and Brandeis' resignation, the American Jewish Committee and the American Jewish Congress reached agreement. Some commentators have mistakenly assumed that Brandeis' insistence on the AJC meeting the terms of the Congress Executive Committee had run counter to the wishes of his associates, and that his resignation cleared the way for compromise.[65] In fact, Brandeis himself engineered the agreement, against the desire, not only of the Eastern Europeans, but of people like Wise and Lipsky.

The bitterness generated by the Astor incident brought home to both Brandeis and Louis Marshall the need for reaching agreement quickly. One week after the meeting, Marshall sent a long letter to the Justice formally apologizing for the rudeness of the attack and for his own failure to prevent it. But, as he noted, he himself had been subjected to similar attacks over the preceding two years, and he hoped that both of them could put aside their grievances for the sake of the Jewish people.[66] Despite the continued objections of Jacob Schiff and others to the Congress, Marshall stood prepared to accept it, and he hoped that those issues that seemed so dangerous to his colleagues might be, at least temporarily, removed from the Congress agenda. In a series of closed meetings, the leadership of the two sides reached agreement. The AJC conceded the name "congress," but the Zionists agreed that it would be only a temporary body with a limited program. Democratic elections would take place, but recognized national bodies would be alloted 25 per cent of the seats. Relief measures could be considered (this over the objections of the JDC), as well as the nature of the rights Jews should strive for after the war. But the term "group rights for Jews" was eliminated, and the Zionists also agreed to change the phrase "Palestine as the Jewish National Home" to "a Jewish National Home."[67]

The Committee had conceded much, but it had also won much. The important concession, limiting the congress to a temporary body dealing only with war-related issues, seemingly would leave the powers of the AJC intact after the war. Here Brandeis had great difficulty in forcing his followers to accept the agreement, for they also recognized the political implications of the compromise. The Yiddish press damned the arrangement, and many of the Zionist leaders lost heart. Stephen Wise refused to participate in the negotiations for implementing the decision, and Horace Kallen lamented that "our people have sold our birthright for a mess of pottage."[68] Only after two meetings of the Executive Committee and over the vociferous objections of the Yiddish intellectuals could the agreement be ratified, and then it left a bitter taste that would have serious implications for the future.

Brandeis' decision and his concessions to the AJC can only be explained in terms of the crisis gripping American Jewry. By mid-1916 the immigrant masses had in effect won their demand for a voice in American Jewish affairs, yet a large number of organizations, representing the older, established communities, could not be denied their legitimate role either. By forcing the issue, the congress supporters would have had a congress free of restrictions, but without the voluntary participation of the American Jewish Committee and its associates, that congress could not have claimed to speak for all of American Jewry. Unless concessions were made, warfare and not unity would have prevailed, and the more important issues of help and rights for European Jewry would have been ignored. Marshall and the Committee had come a long way from their initial position in 1914; they now agreed to a democratically elected congress that would meet before the war and have an agenda that included discussion of Jewish national rights. As for limiting the congress program to war-related issues, and its tenure to the war, it is possible that Brandeis, and perhaps Marshall, realized that this concession involved form rather than substance. Could either man really believe that the hundreds of thousands of congress supporters would willingly give up their power and influence so readily after the war? Given the political sophistication of the two men, it seems unlikely.

In late December 1916, 140 delegates representing a real cross section of American Jewry met to work out the administrative and procedural methods for electing an American Jewish Congress to convene the following spring. As it turned out, the United States entered the war in April 1917, and at the Wilson administration's request, the Congress was delayed until the end of hostilities. The December gathering elected Nathan Straus as chairman, and Zionists controlled most of the major offices and committees.[69] Since the American Jewish Committee voluntarily participated in the Congress, it had now bound itself to follow the rule of the majority. Despite the pessimism of Wise and others, the situation in American Jewry had radically changed in little more than two years. The bitterness of rabid pro- and anticongress advocates, however, and the continuing controversy over Jewish nationalism, would continue to preclude any true unity in American Jewry for many years to come.

CHAPTER SIX

WAR AND PEACE

Although I am always trying not to exaggerate in depicting the situation, still I must tell you that the misery of our Jewish population has reached a most fearful degree in the last months. A large part of them is no longer able to procure the necessary means of subsistence and as a consequence cases of illness and death from underfeeding and starvation occur now in numbers which were unseen up till now and they show a constant increase." So wrote Arthur Ruppin, head of the Zionist office in Palestine to the American ambassador to Turkey, Henry Morgenthau, a year and a half after the outbreak of hostilities. The Jews in the Holy Land, Zionist and non-Zionist alike, looked to Morgenthau as a providentially inspired protector. He had arranged for relief funds within days after the onset of the war, and had intervened on several occasions to soften the anti-Jewish decrees of Djemal Pasha, the governor of Syria. Yet even American pressure had been unable to prevent the expulsion of six thousand Jews to Egypt, mainly Russian immigrants, as "enemy aliens." When the U.S.S. *Tennessee* visited Palestine in early 1915, its captain, after extensive interviews with Zionist and Turkish officials, reported that the entire Zionist work there stood in real danger of destruction.[1]

The delicate state of Palestinian affairs had a significant effect on American Zionist policies. Only the fact that the United States remained neutral before 1917 made it possible to raise and transmit hundreds of thousands of dollars in relief funds, or send the U.S.S. *Vulcan* with food and medical supplies. Yet behind the strenuous endeavors to raise money and save the settlements loomed the ominous realities that Turkey was a belligerent, that the Ottomans completely controlled Palestine, and that any missteps on the part of the Zionists, especially in America, could spell doom for the Yishuv. Given these conditions, the Provisional Committee declared itself neutral regarding the conflict.

It was one thing, however, for a politically sophisticated leadership to assert neutrality, and another to impose that policy upon thousands of members, especially the Eastern European immigrants, who strongly hated Russia. The efforts of both Germany and Great Britain to win over American Jewish support to their respective sides made it extremely difficult for Zionist leaders to pursue their goals. After the United States entered the war on the side of the Allies, the Provisional Committee found itself hampered in efforts to help Chaim Weizmann and the British Zionists secure issuance of a declaration promising to establish a Jewish homeland in Palestine after the war, since neither Col. Edward House, Wilson's closest adviser, nor Secretary of State Robert Lansing wanted to entangle Zionist interests in American foreign policy. Even after the promulgation of the Balfour Declaration in November 1917, the State Department wanted to avoid unnecessary provocation of Turkey, with which the United States was not at war. At the peace negotiations, Wilson's overt sympathy for Zionist aspirations proved embarrassing to his fervant demands for self-determination, and a variety of anti-Zionist groups worked to thwart the conversion of the British promise into the reality of a protectorate over Palestine. Along all of these tangled paths, the American Zionists had to tread carefully, pulled on the one side by their European counterparts demanding greater and more open support by the Provisional Committee, and on the other by their loyalties to the United States, which had legitimate reasons to downplay the Zionist program.

I

With the Actions Comité barely functioning,* the Americans assumed the task of speaking and acting for the world movement, and emphasized that Zionists did not challenge Turkish rule in Palestine. Within days after the Hotel Marseilles conference which reorganized American Zionism, members of the leadership both publicly and privately affirmed Zionist neutrality. Louis Lipsky cautioned local affiliates to employ great care in their actions and statements, while Judah L. Magnes urged his coreligionists to heed President Wilson's plea for neutrality: "We are neutral as Americans and as Jews."[2] Stephen S. Wise, who knew Morgenthau intimately, asked him to inform the Turks that the Zionists wished no harm to the Ottoman Empire, and desired nothing more than for the settlements to exist peacefully under Turkish rule. The official word came from Brandeis, who made sure that both sides understood the Provisional Committee's position: "Zionism is not a movement to wrest from the Turks the sovereignty of Palestine. Zionism seeks merely to establish for such Jews as choose to go and remain there, a legally secured home."[3]

The logic for such a policy was overwhelmingly clear, as Magnes explained. If at the end of the war, Turkey retained control of Palestine and the Zionist organization had been loyal, then the Yishuv would have legitimate claims upon Turkish friendship. Should the Allies win the war, no one could blame the Zionists for their loyalty, since Jews in every country were rallying to defend their respective

---

* The international makeup of the Executive assured both sides that as a movement, Zionism stood unaligned. Of the six members, two were German (Otto Warburg and Arthur Hantke), three Russian (Yeechial Tschlenow, Nahum Sokolow, and Victor Jacobson), and Shmaryahu Levin, although Russian-born, had recently acquired Austrian citizenship. The General Council included twelve men from Germany or Austria-Hungary, seven from Russia, two from England, and one each from Belgium, France, Holland, and Romania.

governments. But more than this had to be done, Magnes insisted. Those Zionists who occupied important positions in government-sponsored activities should resign from the Zionist movement; like Caesar's wife, the Zionists not only had to *be* neutral, they also had to *appear* so. Max Bodenheimer, for example, gave up the chairmanship of the Jewish National Fund when he joined one of the German war committees.[4] From August 1914 until early 1917, the American Zionists labored diligently to demonstrate their professed neutrality. At the 1915 convention, the leadership formally declared that it would not and could not take sides, and the *Maccabean* went out of its way to delete any article or statement that might be interpreted as favoring one belligerent camp or the other.

With but a few exceptions, the members of the PC, whatever their own private view may have been, hewed strictly to the official policy of neutrality. Richard Gottheil, a former president of the Federation of American Zionists, gave an interview in late November 1914 in which he expressed support for the Allies, and immediately drew down the wrath of Rabbi Magnes.[5] Like Shmaryahu Levin, Magnes distrusted the Allies because of Russia, and although he properly chastised Gottheil for his breach of neutrality, his own activities would soon cause the Zionists a great deal of embarrassment. Of all the members of the PC, Magnes held the most uncompromising anti-imperialist beliefs, and he thought Great Britain had gone to war primarily to extend its empire. He would later oppose American entry in the war on the side of England, and he became a leading spokesman for the pacifists. Unfortunately, his pacifism often assumed shades of pro-German sentiment, and he was too quick to belabor Zionists whose "impartiality" did not measure up to his own. He found the declaration of neutrality issued by the 1915 convention unsatisfactory, since "not one syllable was uttered manifesting the Zionist loyalty to the government which is sovereign in Palestine." His brother-in-law, Louis Marshall, pleaded with him in vain to at least keep quiet, since his statements reflected badly upon American Jewry. When Magnes finally quit the Provisional Committee in mid-1915, the other members breathed a long sigh of relief.[6]

The funneling of relief monies into devastated areas of Europe also required the most delicate maneuvering. If either side felt the Zionists or the American Jewish Relief Committee favored the other, the entire relief program would be jeopardized. Yet a number of the large donors came from German ancestry, and openly supported the Central Powers. Stephen Wise, who prior to the war managed to keep his pro-Allied bias to himself, rejoiced that men like Jacob Schiff were not identified with the Zionists, since they would have hurt the movement's standing in France and England.[7] When the AJRC chose as its agent in Palestine Ephraim Cohn-Reiss, the outspokenly pro-German director of the Hilfsverein schools, Brandeis lodged a strong protest with Felix M. Warburg, and with Marshall's backing, succeeded in having a more neutral committee nominated. Within occupied territories, the two men agreed that whenever possible, American agents would handle the distribution of funds.[8]

If the leadership recognized the necessity for neutrality, the bulk of American Jewry, at least prior to 1917, passionately hoped the Central Powers would triumph. Those of German origin had obvious blood and cultural ties, but the Eastern European immigrants also shared such sentiments, not out of love for Germany but out of hatred for Russia. Vladimir Jabotinsky summed up this attitude: "From the first moment I hoped and prayed with all my heart and soul for the defeat of Russia. If the fate of the war had depended on me in those weeks, I would have decided: Quick peace in the West, without victors or vanquished—but first of all, Russia's defeat."[9] On the East Side, imperial rivalries among the major powers meant nothing, but hatred of Russia, which had so cruelly persecuted its Jews, meant everything. France and Great Britain supported Russia, and were thus tainted by association; Germany, whatever its faults, was at war with the Czar. "The Jews support Germany because Russia bathes in Jewish blood," ran one editorial, and the theme repeated itself time and time again.[10]

For some reason, the belligerents believed that Jewish loyalties to their faith transcended national ties, and that by appealing to American Jewry, all of the world's Jews could be won over to one side or the other. The Germans, cognizant of the emotional value of Palestine, interceded with their Turkish ally to soften anti-Jewish restrictions, and propagandists in the United States emphasized that the Germans were the true friends of the Jews. One of the chief German agents in this country, Isaac Strauss, faithfully attended numerous Zionist functions, repeating over and over how much the Fatherland supported their cause. During most of 1915, German military success on the battlefield bolstered the propaganda drive, and Sir Cecil Spring-Rice, the British ambassador to the United States, reported despondently that American Jews persisted in their strong attachment to the Emperor. Israel Zangwill, the great English Jewish writer, bitterly resented American Jewry's seeming one-sided attitude regarding the war, and even the London *Times* denounced the American Yiddish press for its single-minded hatred of Russia, which blinded its readers to the real issues of the conflict.[11]

The Allies, of course, also tried to win over the American Jewish community, and despite Spring-Rice's pessimism, most of the leadership privately favored the Allied cause. Like their British counterparts, they found the presence of Russia in the Triple Entente an embarrassment, but their own sympathies with France and England, based on cultural and political ties, made no impression on those Jews whose hatred of Russia stemmed from bitter personal experience. Every Russian retreat left horrible evidence of atrocities against the Jews; every German advance into Poland was accompanied by exemplary regulations regarding treatment of Jewish civilians in occupied territories.[12] Marshall, Brandeis, and others publicly proclaimed their neutrality while privately endorsing the Allies; but as long as the war continued, Marshall informed the British Conjoint Committee, there could be no question of any open demonstration of sympathy. Brandeis utilized his Yiddish-speaking associates on the PC, especially Abe Goldberg, to try to influence some of the Yiddish editors to tone down their anti-Allied polemics. Even a minor pro-Allied statement, however, could be blown out of all proportion by the Turks, and Henry Morgenthau reminded the Zionists that the Ottomans kept a close eye on American affairs, and could vent their dissatisfaction on the Yishuv with no one to stop them. Until the end of 1916, American Zionists found neutrality difficult, but necessary.[13]

Events in early 1917 radically altered the perspective through which the PC viewed world affairs. The resumption of German U-boat warfare, especially against neutral shipping, swung American opinion behind the Allies, and on April 2, Woodrow Wilson asked Congress for a declaration of war against Germany. At the same time, the Provisional Committee learned of Chaim Weizmann's secret negotiations with the British Government that would eventually lead to the Balfour Declaration. Both patriotism and self-interest now dictated that American Zionists endorse the Allies, yet they still had to treat Turkey very carefully, since the American declaration of war did not include the Ottoman Empire. The Zionists could, and did, cajole the Wilson administration to approve Allied statements regarding the future of Palestine, but these endeavors by necessity were circumscribed owing to the supposed neutrality of the United States regarding Turkey.

Predominantly an immigrant group, American Jews had never been neutral in their emotions, despite the leadership's claims of impartiality. After the 1915 Zionist convention, while the *Maccabean* carried the official statement of neutrality, *Dos Yiddishe Folk,* the official Yiddish publication of the Federation, declared: "Nobody has implied that the word 'neutrality' means that one should remain unmoved by the blood of innocent people." The masses favored Germany and opposed Russia, a situation decidedly uncomfortable not only for the pro-British leadership, but for the socialist Zionists as well. As late as February 1917, the Central Committee of the Poale Zion was still denouncing the "imperialist" war and calling for the brotherhood of man; two weeks after the American declaration of war, the *Yiddisher Kemfer* condemned "Wall Street's war" in traditional socialist fashion. In July, a majority of Poale Zion still opposed conscription.[14]

The realities of an American society at war forced German sympathizers, socialists, and pacifists to re-examine their views. Stephen S. Wise, an avowed pacifist, announced that the American flag would drape his pulpit until the "morning of the dawn of peace for humanity." At the annual convention of the FAZ in June 1917, Harry Friedenwald called on American Zionists to rally to their country's cause, and the delegates pledged the wholehearted support of the movement to the war effort. Nachman Syrkin resigned from Poale Zion in October, announcing his support of the Allied war program, and Baruch Zuckerman and Ber Borochov supported his stand.

When the American Federation of Labor and the Jewish Socialist League came out in support of United States entry into the war, the militant socialists among the Poale Zion found themselves in an increasingly untenable position.[15]

The Russian revolution of February 1917 solved the dilemma of those who could not support the Allies as long as a Czarist Russia fought in the Triple Entente. The abdication of Nicholas and the bright promise of democratic reform under Kerensky removed many of the objections of the Eastern European immigrants to the Allied cause. On May 3, speaking before the Jewish League of American Patriots, Jacob Schiff summed up the feelings of many American Jews: "Six or eight weeks ago the Jews [of the United States] would have heeded the call to arms as a duty but with heavy hearts, as they would have known they would be fighting to perpetuate Russian autocracy. But now all that has been changed. Russian democracy has become victorious, and thanks are due to the Jew that the Russian revolution succeeded. If we want to help the Russian people, we must do our duty to assist the land of our adoption." Even more importantly, on November 2, 1917, His Majesty's Government announced its approval of the establishment of a Jewish homeland in Palestine after the war. Confronted by the overthrow of the Czar and the British endorsement of Zionist aims, even the most fervent Jewish socialist found it impossible to remain neutral.[16]

II

In the halcyon days immediately following the war, Great Britain's espousal of the Zionist cause seemed the logical culmination of a manifest historical destiny. After all, Englishmen had long been interested in the idea of restoration. Lord Palmerston had tried to persuade the Turks to allow large-scale Jewish settlement in Palestine, and in 1839 had instructed British representatives in the Holy Land to use their good offices to assist the Jewish community there. It had been England that gave Zionism its first measure of legitimacy by offering East Africa, and despite the internal scars left by that episode, it had remained a mark of British goodwill. Even before the East Africa offer, Theodore Herzl had written: "From the first moment I entered the Zionist Movement, my eyes were directed toward England, because I saw that by reason of the general situation it was the Archimedean point where the lever could be applied."[17]

When war broke out in the summer of 1914, however, the British Cabinet considered Zionist aspirations in Palestine of little importance. While a number of government members privately understood and sympathized with the movement, the war priorities required an official coolness, especially in the Foreign Office, which politely but firmly told Nahum Sokolow that it did not wish to discuss Zionism with him. By November, though, a few people both within and outside the government recognized that a historic opportunity might be at hand. In the House of Commons, Prime Minister Herbert Asquith announced: "It is the Ottoman Government and not we who have rung the death-knell of Ottoman Dominion, not only in Europe but in Asia," and by these words declared the empire of the "sick man of Europe" to be up for grabs. H. G. Wells, in an open letter to Israel Zangwill, asked: "And now, what is to prevent Jews having Palestine and restoring a real Judea?" English Zionists had already begun thinking along similar lines. Chaim Weizmann predicted that Palestine would fall within the British sphere of influence after the war, and England's best hope of creating a buffer east of Suez would be a Jewish Palestine: "We—given more or less good conditions—could easily move a million Jews into Palestine within the next fifty to sixty years, and England would have an effective barrier and we would have a country." For the next three years, Weizmann, whose chemical research for the Admiralty gave him access to high-ranking officials, labored to convince them that it was in England's own self-interest to further the aims of Zionism.[18]

Within the government Herbert Samuel, president of the Local Government Board and later to be the first British high commissioner in Palestine, approached Sir Edward Grey, the Foreign Secretary, about restoring a Jewish state in Palestine after the collapse of Turkish rule. Grey expressed not only a sentimental sympathy for the plan, but aware of France's designs upon Syria, saw the need of expanding British influence in the Middle East. With Grey's encouragement, Samuel submitted a memorandum, "The Future of Palestine," to the Prime Minister. Asquith reacted coolly, and in his diary guessed that Samuel's Jewishness had disturbed his otherwise "well-ordered and methodical brain." Yet other members of the War Cabinet found themselves more and more attracted to the idea. David Lloyd George, a Welsh Nonconformist brought up on the Bible, wanted to liberate Palestine from the heathen, and considered it Britain's destiny to plant a Jewish home there. For Winston Churchill, the main consideration was imperial security, and he saw that Jewish claims in Palestine could be used not only to protect Suez, but as a convenient moral justification to limit French ambitions in the area.[19]

During 1915, Weizmann and his colleagues lobbied incessantly to cultivate latent sympathy, endlessly explaining Zionism and justifying their claims not only in the light of Jewish history but of British self-interest. By early 1916, the idea of establishing a Jewish home in the Holy Land had gained sufficient currency within the government that Sir Edward Grey decided to test the reaction of Russia.[20] The proposal, however, excited the fears of a number of prominent English Jews, who worried that a Jewish home in Palestine would endanger their rights as British citizens. As the government moved closer to promulgating a concrete statement, the tempo of Jewish anti-Zionist opposition increased. Sir Edwin S. Montagu, Minister for Munitions and then Secretary of State for India, in particular opposed a Jewish state, and at one point in the Cabinet discussion, submitted a memorandum accusing the government of anti-Semitism for even thinking of creating one. More than any other person, Montagu delayed action and toned down the nationalistic drafts submitted by Weizmann, and caused the final statement to be so vague that it immediately triggered a debate as to just what His Majesty's Government really had in mind.[21]

With the entry of the United States into the war in April 1917, the proposed statement assumed greater importance, since from the beginning, British leaders saw in it the possibility of winning over Jewish support to the Allied cause.[22] But with the moralistic Wilson frowning upon imperialistic war aims, it would now be necessary to gain American approval, a goal complicated by the absence of a state of war between Turkey and the United States. To secure American acceptance, Weizmann turned to Brandeis.

Good relations between the Provisional Committee and the Administration had undoubtedly been facilitated by the close personal ties between Brandeis and Wilson. In more than thirty months of neutrality, the State Department and the White House frequently utilized the foreign contacts of the PC, and little bits of information that could not be obtained through formal requests could often be secured quietly and quickly by a call to deHaas. Several Cabinet members, who knew Brandeis personally and sympathized with Zionist aspirations, proved willing to help the cause on humanitarian grounds. While William Jennings Bryan served as Secretary of State, he pressed Morgenthau to do all he could to mitigate repressive Turkish measures against Jews in Palestine, and saw to it that the Provisional Committee received copies of departmental communications bearing on Palestine.[23] When the AJRC could not find commercial ships to carry food and medical supplies to Palestine, Secretary of the Navy Josephus Daniels suggested to Wilson that a Navy collier, due to sail with fuel for American ships in the Mediterranean, could make room for the supplies; the President declared that he was delighted "to find that one of our ships was bound in that direction." Through the State Department, the Zionists prevailed upon the Allies to lift the blockade off Turkish waters so that the *Vulcan* could land. According to Frank Manuel, hundreds of instructions and dispatches were handled by the State Department dealing with Zionist relief activities, and the Department allowed the PC to use its cipher facilities when necessary.[24]

Yet the overt friendship of Wilson and a number of his Cabinet members was misleading. The State Department was cool toward Zionism, especially the Near Eastern Division, where career officers expressed their annoyance at the intrusion of narrow Jewish interests in the conduct of foreign policy. The hostility of wealthier Jews toward Zionism, and the fear that American business interests in Turkey would suffer accounted for part of the opposition, and undoubtedly anti-Semitism played its part as well. But considerations of policy, of the fact that American endorsement of Zionist goals would have constituted interference with the internal governance of a country with which the United States was not at war—such considerations could not safely be ignored by the President no matter where his personal sympathies lay, and Robert Lansing, who became Secretary of State in June 1915, consistently represented the Department's interests to Wilson. While Brandeis could—and did—plead the Zionist case in the White House, he recognized that as an American citizen and as a Supreme Court Justice, he had to respect these limits on American foreign policy. Chaim Weizmann, whose loyalty to Zionism outweighed even his great love of England, constantly importuned Brandeis to act, and could not understand the restraints that bound him.

Brandeis had vague intimations about Weizmann's negotiations with the British Government as early as December 1915,[25] but not until January 1917 did the Americans first discuss a British declaration with Colonel Edward M. House, Wilson's shadowy confidant and closest adviser on foreign affairs. This initial contact set the pattern that followed. Wilson considered the creation of foreign policy his own prerogative, with the Secretary of State carrying it out and the Department responsible for information gathering, analysis, and handling of routine matters. The members of the Provisional Committee who dealt with foreign affairs—Wise, Brandeis, and Frankfurter—habitually dealt with either Colonel House or with the President himself, usually without Lansing's knowledge. Wilson frequently bypassed his Secretary of State, but Lansing focused his resentment on the Zionists, and his hostility toward them proved a serious handicap in the postwar negotiations.[26]

Less than a week after the United States entered the war, Weizmann wrote Brandeis on the status of the proposed declaration, and noted that "an expression of an opinion coming from yourself and perhaps from other gentlemen connected with the government in favor of a Jewish Palestine under a British protectorate would greatly strengthen our hands." It was an awkward position for the American. It was one thing to talk to House or Wilson, and indeed, while Weizmann's letter had been in transit, Stephen Wise had concluded a long interview with House, and had confidently reported that the Texan believed the Jews would get Palestine after the war.[27] Yet for

Brandeis to publicly approve the activities of a foreign country, even an ally, could prove embarrassing not only to the American Government but to Zionism as well. Moreover Weizmann's letter asked not only for his approval of a Jewish Palestine, but one under a British protectorate, and Brandeis, aware of the friction between Great Britain and France, knew that to get involved in that area would only harm Zionism.

In January 1916, Sir Mark Sykes had concluded negotiations with François-Georges Picot over the disposition of Ottoman territories in the Mideast after the war. The two men, diplomats who knew the area well, agreed that France should have the dominant role in Syria and Lebanon, while England would assert its power over that part of Palestine west of the river Jordan and south of a line running from the middle of the Dead Sea to the Mediterranean below Gaza, but which would also include a port area around Haifa. The balance of Palestine would be in a special international zone, including Jerusalem. As the British Government began to give serious consideration to a Jewish center in Palestine, second thoughts arose on the Sykes-Picot agreement. Recognizing that the French might fear too large a British influence in the area, Balfour began to float the idea of an American protectorate over the Holy Land. He sent Sykes, by now an impassioned Zionist, to France and Italy to sound out the Allies on the idea, and also to see if the proposed boundaries could be changed. France soon agreed to establish a Jewish homeland, thanks in part to the efforts of Nahum Sokolow, but remained silent on just who would have the protectorate; the Vatican, through Monsignor Eugenio Pacelli, later Pope Pius XII, also expressed approval of the homeland, but made it quite clear it did not want the French in charge of the holy places.[28]

When Balfour came to the United States in late April, one of the first people he met with was Brandeis. The two men took an immediate liking to each other, especially after Balfour pledged his own personal support of Zionism. At a White House reception on April 23, and in several private interviews, they explored the problems of a declaration, the need for American endorsement of it, and the intricacies of Anglo-French rivalry. When the British Foreign Secretary suggested that perhaps the United States might assume a protectorate over the Holy Land, Brandeis quickly informed him that it was out of the question. The Wilson administration, as the Justice knew, had no interest in territorial expansion on the other side of the globe, and American Zionists, therefore, wanted British control.[29] Balfour probably had been hoping to hear this, since dominion over Palestine would make Great Britain the dominant power in the eastern Mediterranean, and he pressed the Justice to secure American endorsement of a British declaration.[30] Meanwhile, Weizmann and Baron James de Rothschild also urged Brandeis to gain American approval. The Foreign Office, which still kept the terms of the Sykes-Picot agreement secret from the Zionists, now saw the possibility of utilizing Jewish pressure to change the boundary lines. If the United States endorsed a British protectorate, France would have no choice but to accede.[31]

Brandeis held off replying to this last stream of cables until he had a copy of the draft declaration in hand, and then on May 6 spent nearly an hour with Wilson discussing Anglo-French friction and the aspirations of Jews to re-establish a homeland in Palestine. The President gave his blessing to a British protectorate, and also approved the Zionist formula of "a publicly assured, legally secured homeland for the Jewish people in Palestine." Wilson cautioned, however, that because of France he would not be able to give immediate assent to a British declaration, but he would do his best to calm the French. Then, and only then, would he feel free to endorse publicly a Jewish homeland.[32] That same day, Brandeis cabled Weizmann: "We approve your program and will do all we can to advance it. Not prudent for me to say anything for publication now. Keep us advised." Over the next few weeks, the Justice met again with Balfour, and sent several encouraging notes to the British Zionists. On May 20, Weizmann openly informed the English Zionist Federation that a British declaration on Palestine would soon be forthcoming.[33]

The failure of the American Zionist leadership to speak out openly at this point has been roundly criticized. Jacob Rubin declared that the Brandeis group could not deliver when most needed, while Herbert Parzen and Ben Halpern have also belittled the American role.[34] Yet on balance, American involvement turned out to be important, although not as crucial as some of Brandeis' admirers have claimed. In England, Chaim Weizmann, Nahum Sokolow, and other Jewish leaders constituted a form of Zionist government-in-exile; whatever their passports may have read, they already saw themselves as citizens of the Jewish state. Fortunately for them and for the Jewish people, British and Zionist aims dovetailed during the war. They could push His Majesty's Government, they could complain, they could wheedle, they could issue statements, less because the Lloyd George administration favored Zionism than because it benefited imperial interests. Had the British not wanted Palestine, all of the Zionist noise would have been in vain.[35]

The United States, which had no territorial ambitions in the Mideast, proved a different story. Weizmann expected the American Zionists to create the same kind of pressure that he did, without ever realizing that it would have done no good at all. Wilson could be moved, by reason and by appeal to moralistic, humanitarian causes. He sympathized with the Zionists and trusted Brandeis, but he also had the responsibility to pursue American interests, and in early 1917 these did not necessarily coincide with the wishes of either the Zionists or the British. America was not at war with the Ottomans, as Robert Lansing repeatedly stressed, although diplomatic relations had been severed by the Turks. Perhaps Turkey could be lured away from the Central Powers by a separate peace, a hope that Wilson and House long entertained.* For the United States to

* Undoubtedly the most bizarre attempt to reach a separate peace with Turkey involved former ambassador Henry Morgenthau, who fancied that he knew the Byzantine mind. In 1916, he had publicly proposed that the Jews buy Palestine, which brought immediate outrage from the Sultan and pleas from European Zionists to have the PC shut him up. In the summer of 1917, Morgenthau went to Europe, and with the blessing of Wilson and Lansing, planned to go on to Constantinople if there seemed even a remote chance of negotiating a peace agreement. At Brandeis' request, Felix Frankfurter was assigned to travel with Morgenthau, as he soon learned, to try to control him. The British Government, also worried, sent Weizmann to meet the Morgenthau party at Gibraltar, while the French also sent an observer. Within a short period of time, it became evident to everyone that Morgenthau's idea of Turkish conditions was far removed from reality, and that his overactive imagination and enthusiasm had carried the President and Lansing too far. Weizmann

approve the dismemberment of Turkey would have doomed any chance of a separate peace. Brandeis well understood both the man and the situation. In time, he expected Wilson to endorse the British plan, but not until every path toward a separate peace with Turkey had been explored. His own ties to the Administration prevented him from speaking, since Turkish officials might interpret his remarks as reflecting Wilsonian policy. Given this dilemma, Brandeis left Weizmann and the British to work out a plan, while the Americans built up organization and resources—men, money, and discipline—and, at the proper time, would back their colleagues overseas.

Interestingly, the British themselves did not raise the issue of American endorsement, but hoped to achieve it through private contacts. The State Department did not even see a draft copy of the declaration until June, and then it was submitted not by the Foreign Office, but by Mr. Justice Brandeis. Not until September 1917, after the British had thrashed out the problem and conceded several points to English anti-Zionists, did they formally submit a proposed declaration to Wilson. Lansing immediately objected, noting that the United States was not at war with Turkey. Stressing the viewpoint of department professionals, Lansing argued that the nation had enough on its hands already, and would gain nothing by a gratuitous involvement in a rather hare-brained scheme of an ally. Wilson reluctantly acceded to Lansing's legal argument, although he had previously assured Stephen Wise that when necessary, he would act.[37]

At its meeting on September 3, the British War Cabinet decided that Wilson's views should be obtained before issuing any statement, and to inform him that the government was being pressed to declare its sympathy with Zionist aims. The following day, Lord Robert Cecil cabled House that he "should be very grateful if you felt able to ascertain unofficially if the President favors such a declaration."

---

said the Zionists would have nothing to do with the idea, and Frankfurter wired Washington to get Morgenthau back home before he made a further fool of himself. "Get him away from Europe," warned Frankfurter. "He is dealing with Europe the way he dealt with parcels of real estate in Brooklyn and the Bronx." Finally, after a press conference in Paris, the whole mission petered out, and the State Department requested him to return home.[36]

Three days later Wilson, preoccupied with the nation's lagging war production, still had given no indication of his opinion. House, who had always seemed so sympathetic to Zionist representations,[38] confided that "there are many dangers lurking in it," and wondered why the British wanted to get involved. On the tenth, House informed the Foreign Office that Wilson considered it inopportune to issue anything more than a vague statement of sympathy, and one that made no real commitment.[39]

The cable stunned Whitehall. The assimilationist anti-Zionists, who had fought bitterly to prevent any statement, now hoped the government would drop the crazy scheme entirely. The stunned War Cabinet, which had devoted an inordinate amount of time to the wording, had expected American approval in the light of earlier contacts. Despair is the only word that can describe the Zionist mood. Weizmann, angry that he had heard nothing from Brandeis, began firing off cables to American Zionists in Washington and New York. Two weeks after House had informed Cecil of Wilson's negative response, Brandeis suddenly cabled Weizmann informing him of a complete reversal in the President's attitude.

Although the documentary evidence is sparse, it seems possible to reconstruct most of the events in those hectic weeks. Problems of war production and organization stood foremost in Wilson's mind, as they did for most Americans. The rather casual tone of Lord Robert's cable to House provided little evidence for either House or the President to guess that the British considered a statement important, and it is certain that Wilson did not bother to consult with either Brandeis or Wise on his response. When Weizmann cabled him regarding the consternation created by House's message, and sent him a copy of the revised declaration on the nineteenth, Brandeis arranged to see Colonel House on September 23. At that meeting, he evidently convinced him that the American Government should endorse the British proposal, for soon after he cabled Weizmann: "From talks I have had with President and from expressions of opinion given to closest advisers, I feel that I can answer you that he is in entire sympathy with declaration quoted in yours of the nineteenth, as approved by Foreign Office and Prime Minister. I of course heartily agree."[40] It is impossible to determine if Brandeis saw Wilson personally, or referred to earlier conversations with the President. Leonard Stein suggests that House, having been convinced by the Justice that the declaration would command American support, had checked with Wilson and secured his approval of the Brandeis cable to Weizmann. Balfour, informed of the American change of heart, sent a formal request for clarification on October 6, noting reports "that the German government are [sic] making great efforts to capture the Zionist movement."[41]

From the Zionist viewpoint, the situation still remained critical. The anti-Zionist forces, led by Edwin Montagu, mounted a last-ditch fight either to kill the declaration or to so water down its wording as to render it meaningless. Weizmann called upon Brandeis to secure open public support by American Jewry (something that Brandeis could not do) and endorsement by Wilson (which Brandeis had already done). When Wilson received the final draft of the British statement, this time from the Foreign Office, he passed it on to Brandeis, Wise, and deHaas, and they suggested some changes in wording.[42] Wilson evidently still considered the whole affair of minor import, for on the thirteenth he breezily wrote House: "I find in my pocket the memorandum you gave me about the Zionist Movement. I am afraid I did not say that I concurred in the formula suggested from the other side. I do, and would be obliged if you would let them know it." This House did on October 16, but with the request that news of Wilson's approval be withheld until he could announce it in the United States at an appropriate time.[43] With Wilson's blessing in hand, the dam broke, and the last vestige of opposition collapsed. On November 2, 1917, Arthur James Balfour wrote to James Lord Rothschild:

Dear Lord Rothschild:

I have much pleasure in conveying to you on behalf of His Majesty's Government the following declaration of sympathy with Jewish Zionist aspirations, which has been submitted to and approved by the Cabinet:

"His Majesty's Government view with favour the establishment in Palestine of a national home for the Jewish people, and will use their best efforts to facilitate the achievement of this object, it being clearly understood that nothing shall be done which may prejudice the civil and religious rights of existing non-Jewish communities in Palestine or the rights and political status enjoyed by Jews in any other country."

I should be grateful if you would bring this Declaration to the knowledge of the Zionist Federation.

Yours sincerely,

The Balfour Declaration, followed by General Allenby's dramatic capture of Jerusalem a few weeks later, seemed to signal a new era in Jewish history. "I felt as if a sun-ray had struck me," said Weizmann, "and I thought I heard the steps of the Messiah."[44] News of the Declaration appeared in the British press on November 8, alongside dispatches from Petrograd about the Bolshevik Revolution, and the papers took it for granted that the Jews would have a state after the war. Indeed, before a wildly cheering crowd at the London Opera House on December 2, Lord Robert Cecil, whose ancestors had served the Crown since the days of Elizabeth, declared that "Arabia was for the Arabs, Armenia for the Armenians, and Judea for the Jews." At the same rally, Israel Zangwill led the territorialists back into the Zionist camp, declaring any opposition to a Jewish home in Palestine would be "treason to the Jewish people."[45]

News of the Declaration stunned most American Jews, who had received few hints in advance. At first, no one seemed able to believe it, perhaps because, as deHaas noted, "the sort of feeling that the bear's skin was being divided before the bear was caught." As the realization sank in, expressions of joy and approval abounded in the Jewish press: "The daily prayers of Israel for the restoration of Zion have at last been answered." . . . "The greatest occurrence in modern Jewish history." . . . "There is joy this day in Israel. Shout it in the ear of every fellow Jew." Among the Yiddish papers only *Der Morgen-Journal,* reflecting ultra-Orthodox opinion, expressed reservations. *Dos Yiddishe Folk* declared that: "For the first time in 2,000 years, we again enter the arena of world history as a nation."[46]

While most American Jews applauded the news, die-hard anti-Zionists, especially in the Reform camp, were outraged. Despite a growing tolerance and even acceptance of Zionism in the Reform organization, the Central Conference condemned the idea that "Pal-

estine should be considered the homeland of the Jews." The Conference passed a similar resolution in 1920 after a mandate for
Palestine included the declaration's wording; both times CCAR
officials ignored the fact that no one claimed Palestine as the only
homeland for the Jews.[47] David Philipson, who would remain a
bitter foe of Zionism until his death, tried to rally sentiment for
anti-Zionist action, but lay leaders like Jacob Schiff and Oscar Straus
refused to co-operate with him. Straus reflected the attitude of most
American Jews who had previously ignored Zionism. "I am not a
Zionist," he told Max Kohler, "but I will co-operate with them
knowing that what will be accorded to them under the Balfour
Declaration will be no more than what they should have, equality
for all in Palestine—just as they and we have in free America." As
to the old bugaboo of a Jewish state, Straus philosophically left
that point to the future: "We need not quarrel now before we have
anything."[48]

The American Jewish Committee, which had neither been informed nor consulted about the Balfour Declaration, took its time in
issuing a statement, due to the deep divisions within its Executive
Committee. Jacob Schiff and Louis Marshall, both of whom had been
privately wooed by the Zionist leadership, had already begun to
retreat from a strong anti-Zionist stand to the point where they favored Jewish development in Palestine, provided it did not threaten
the political status of Jews in other countries. In late November,
Marshall, Schiff, and Julian Mack, together with Eugene Meyer, met
to explore areas of agreement; to their surprise, they found much they
could agree on. The *yahudim* were relieved when they discovered
that the Zionists had no desire to push for an immediate state, while
Mack and Meyer welcomed the interest shown by these two influential men in building up a Jewish center in Palestine.[49] At a
special meeting of the AJC on February 2, 1918, Marshall and
Cyrus Adler[50] urged that all Jews, not only Zionists, had the right
and the duty to work for Palestine. Despite unanimity of sentiment
that Palestine should be a haven for oppressed Jews, the Zionist
program still alienated many people, and a statement by Harvard
historian Albert Bushnell Hart that American Jews had to choose
between America and Palestine only increased this anxiety. Judah

Magnes opposed any statement at all, but the Committee felt it had to say something, and it finally appointed Marshall and Adler to draft a document that could be "endorsed by the great majority of American Jews, irrespective of their previous attitude toward the subject."[51]

On April 28, 1918, nearly six months after the Balfour Declaration, the American Jewish Committee issued a qualified endorsement. It recognized that the dream of restoration had been cherished for centuries, and applauded the aims of the British. The Committee pledged to co-operate in establishing in the Holy Land "a center for Judaism, for the stimulation of our faith, for the pursuit and development of literature, science, and art in a Jewish environment." The Committee reaffirmed, however, as "axiomatic" that Jews in this country gave their full allegiance to the United States, and would continue to enjoy the rights of citizenship, as would Jews in other countries continue to be loyal to their governments.[52] With this statement, the hard-core opposition to Zionism by the American Jewish Committee practically ceased. Although the Committee to this day has concerned itself with the relation of a Jewish state to Jews living in other lands, the *fait accompli* of the Balfour Declaration led its members to seek areas of co-operation with the Zionists. Undoubtedly the fact that Great Britain sponsored the Jewish home calmed many of their fears, since English Jews had achieved prominent places in society, and the various English associations emphasized their full rights as British subjects. But, as Cyrus Adler asserted, Eretz Yisroel belonged to all Jews, even those who would never go there, and all Jews had the responsibility and the privilege to share in its upbuilding. Not even the most assimilationist Reform rabbi had ever denied that Palestine played a major role in Jewish history. Now, with the dream of restoration suddenly become a real possibility, the ages-old yearning for "next year in Jerusalem" affected even those who thought such sentiments out of date and irrelevant.

If the AJC waited six months before commenting on the Declaration, it would be another four months before Woodrow Wilson made his long-awaited public pronouncement. House's note to the British had indicated that Wilson would issue a statement in response to requests from American Jews. However, events following the Balfour Declaration pushed that "appropriate time" farther and farther away. The State Department vehemently opposed American endorsement, and Wilson's action, bypassing the career experts, rankled the bureaucracy. In fact, the Department knew so little about the background of the British move that it requested its embassy staff in London to investigate. Within the Department, there was an extreme reluctance to get involved in what appeared to many officials a poor policy. Samuel Edelman, who had served as vice consul in Jerusalem, summed up this attitude: "From an American viewpoint, therefore, our interests in Palestine, aside from a sentimental reverence for its sacred memorials, are of a negligible quality. It is only the virulent and incessant demands of the American Zionistic faction, who are heading the entire government, which must be reckoned with. If they have succeeded in influencing the British government for a partial declaration in their favor—and it is very doubtful if British support for the scheme will continue once the war is over—it imposes no condition upon our government to follow in these footsteps. On the contrary, everything possible should be done to lead Zionistic aspirations into proper channels—the fruition of British occupation in Palestine should assure the Jewish population of equal political rights with the rest of the population; the theater of Bible history should receive world respect from Jew, Christian or Mohammedan alike; but a Jewish state should never be tolerated."[53]

Lansing shared these views, and on December 13, 1917, cautioned the President to avoid endorsing the British position. In addition to the fact that the United States and Turkey were not at war, the Secretary of State pointed out that not all Jews favored restoration, while "many Christian sects and individuals would undoubtedly resent turning the Holy Land over to the absolute control of the race credited with the death of Christ." After Wilson reluctantly acceded to Lansing's advice, the Secretary suggested to Sir Cecil Spring-Rice, the British ambassador, that it would be advisable not to speak at any Zionist-sponsored affair, lest the wrong impression be made.[54]

The President himself placed a further obstacle in his path toward endorsement when he delivered his famous "Fourteen Points" speech in early January. The pledge of no annexation of territory and the principle of national self-determination placed the Zionists on the defensive, since in essence the Balfour Declaration, with its intimation of a British protectorate, violated both concepts. Despite a growing Jewish settlement in Palestine, the overwhelming majority of residents were Arab, and even the most optimistic Zionist conceded that it would be decades before the Jews achieved majority status. It is difficult to determine to what extent Wilson recognized the inherent contradiction between support of the British pledge and self-determination in Palestine, either in 1917 or at the Peace Conference in 1919. On the one hand, he shared the belief common among many Christian groups at this time that the Jews should be restored to their ancient land, and Louis Brandeis and Stephen Wise presented the Zionist case in terms of the morality and social justice which appealed to the President. At the same time, it was quite obvious that the Jews constituted a very small percentage of the Palestinian population. While Arab opposition to Zionist claims may not have been heard in 1917, spokesmen for emerging Arab nationalism would make a strong presentation to the peacemakers at Paris. Wilson hesitated in 1917 and 1918 primarily for political reasons, with both Lansing and House urging him to be cautious. Herbert Parzen believes that Brandeis was frankly informed that despite the President's private sympathies, Wilson would not issue a public statement. When Weizmann pleaded for an open avowal of support, Brandeis had to warn him to keep Wilson's views confidential.

For reasons that are unclear, the President finally decided to express his approval. Perhaps repeated requests from Zionist leaders, especially Stephen Wise, convinced him. Perhaps by the summer of 1918, rapidly deteriorating conditions within the Ottoman Empire persuaded him to ignore the State Department's advice. It is certain that he did not consult either with Lansing or with career officials when he drafted a New Year's greeting to the Jewish people, addressed to Wise. In it Wilson openly approved the Zionist program, the Balfour Declaration, and the work of the Weizmann Commission* in Palestine, which had just laid the cornerstone of a Hebrew

* See below, pp. 224ff.

university in Jerusalem. The Zionists responded to this long-awaited pronouncement ecstatically, and the White House and the State Department received numerous letters praising the President's stand. Nahum Sokolow expressed the appreciation of the World Zionist Organization for "the recognition by you of the justice of our claim," while Brandeis, in a rare moment of abandon, declared that opposition to Zionism could henceforth be considered disloyalty to the United States.[55]

Despite the passage of time and the establishment of the State of Israel, controversy still swirls over the meaning of the Balfour Declaration, and to a lesser extent, the role Wilson and the American Zionists played in its enactment. British policy, epecially after 1930, when England seemingly repudiated its pledge, aroused many charges of perfidy, and the vacillating role of American governments led many people to question our sincerity or interest in a Jewish homeland. One has to distinguish between what the Balfour Declaration actually said, and what people thought it said; similarly, in evaluating the American role, there is a vast difference between what people would have liked to do and what they could do.

To begin with, the Balfour Declaration was a wartime measure, and its final wording reflected the numerous compromises that had been necessary to placate British Jews and officials opposed to a Jewish homeland in Palestine. Max Nordau and Ahad Ha'am both thought the document should have said more, and blamed Weizmann for failing to insist on stronger language; but as Sokolow noted: "None of us were satisfied, and we did and still do demand more; but that formulation was the maximum that could be obtained."[56] The imprecision of the wording resulted from the contradictory demands made upon the Cabinet. The Zionists hesitated to ask for a Jewish state, recognizing their own real weakness,* and thus fell back on the Basle formula of *a* national home, a phrase that anti-Zionists accepted on the understanding that it did not mean

---

* In 1927, Chaim Weizmann, speaking at a banquet in Czernowits, said: "The Balfour Declaration of 1917 was built on air, and . . . every hour of these last ten years, when opening the newspapers, I thought: Whence will the next blow come? I trembled lest the British Government would call me to ask, 'Tell us, what is this Zionist Organization? Where are they, your Zionists?' "[59]

that Palestine would become *the* Jewish state. Even those who had a major hand in drafting it differed on its precise meaning. Sir Mark Sykes believed it did not mean a Jewish state, and Lord Robert Cecil, despite his "Judea for the Jews" speech, told the American ambassador that the British Government had merely pledged to put the Jews in Palestine on an equal footing with other groups. In the House of Commons, in answer to a direct question as to whether the Declaration meant an independent state or not, Balfour replied: "It is not possible at this date to forecast the future constitution of Palestine."[57]

On a more cynical level, the Declaration can be seen as simply a war measure, as Winston Churchill later told the Commons, designed to secure Jewish support in other parts of the world, especially in Russia and the United States. A similar situation can be seen in the correspondence between Sir Henry McMahon and Sherif Hussein of Arabia, promising the Arabs independence from the Turks after the war. Both documents were war measures, but at that time few people realized that they might be in conflict. As Disraeli once said, "It is the general impression which counts."[58] The general impression in late 1917, however, depended on one's outlook. For the Zionists, the Balfour Declaration meant the realization of the Basle program, the securement of Herzl's long-sought-for political guarantee. To those who considered it only "a scrap of paper," Stephen Wise responded that it had been signed by His Majesty's Government, "and therefore it is sacred and inviolable." The English Zionist Federation termed it "the beginning of the Fulfillment."[60] To neutralists like the American Jewish Committee, it meant cultural renascence and not political independence, while to the military officers fighting under Allenby, it meant nothing. Like most political documents, it could be interpreted in different ways. In the long run, the ambiguity dictated by expediency played no small part in the tragedy of the 1930s.

Perhaps viewing the Balfour Declaration as a war measure makes the American role more understandable. From Wilson's viewpoint, domestic production of war materials had reached a critical stage in late 1917, requiring the President's near-constant attention.[61] The rather casual interest he showed in the British statement certainly indicates that, at best, the only credit he is due is allowing it to happen. Yet the British thought his hesitation an act of considered diplomacy, and were prepared to scrap the idea completely unless he assented; his acquiescence, therefore, was indispensable. That Brandeis secured that assent made his own contribution more than negligible, and Chaim Weizmann himself acknowledged it as "one of the most important individual factors in breaking the deadlock." Similarly, Wise's prodding finally led to Wilson's New Year's message which, unfortunately, also lacked precision; and in bypassing the State Department, the President failed to clothe his letter in the full authority of the government. In later years the Department studiously ignored this letter, although at the time most observers considered it an official statement of policy, which Wilson undoubtedly meant it to be. The career bureaucrats, however, insisted on interpreting it as a private expression of sentiment, and in numerous memoranda would ingenuously ask whether the United States had ever formally approved of the Balfour Declaration.[62]

III

For the most part, the Zionists enjoyed full co-operation from the Wilson administration, although there were times when the State Department seemed less than enthusiastic. In such cases, the President usually supported the Zionists. One of the major undertakings of Hadassah, for example, involved dispatching a medical unit to Palestine. The idea, first broached in 1916, languished for more than eighteen months because the belligerents would not agree on licenses for transport of medical supplies. With the British capture of Palestine, these difficulties vanished, and the Provisional Committee applied to the State Department for passports and for formal recognition of the unit. Lansing, exceedingly reluctant to grant this approval, outlined his objections to Wilson: First, the United States had never recognized British plans for Palestine; second, the United States was not at war with Turkey; and third, "a possible embarrassment may arise on account of the presence in Palestine of individuals, even though their errand is one of mercy, sponsored by an organization having distinctly political aims." Wilson nonetheless authorized the mission, and the government accorded the unit and its insignia, the Mogen David, an equal status with the Red Cross.[63]

On the same day that Wilson overrode Lansing on the medical unit, he concurred with the Secretary's opinion that America should not be represented on the Zionist Commission that Weizmann, with British approval, was leading to Palestine. As Allenby's army swept into the Holy Land, they found a country exhausted by war, its population depleted, its lands untilled, its livestock nearly gone, and the remaining settlers reduced to poverty levels. With its commitment to re-establishing a Jewish homeland there, the Cabinet welcomed Weizmann's proposal to go to Palestine, assess the problems, and start the process of rebuilding with Zionist capital. Weizmann wanted a strong American contingent to go, possibly including Brandeis or Felix Frankfurter, but the Justice, sensitive to American diplomatic needs, realized that the State Department would not approve. Instead, the Provisional Committee transmitted large sums of money for Weizmann to use in Palestine, and sent detailed suggestions on procedure. In the end, either with or without Lansing's approval, New York lawyer Walter Meyer accompanied the Commission, but without official status.[64]

Brandeis' letter to Weizmann is interesting, not only in the light of later charges that he wanted Palestine developed only by private capital, but because it reflects so intensely his deeply rooted Jeffersonian faith. "The utmost vigilance should be exercised," wrote Brandeis, "to prevent the acquisition by private persons of land, water rights or other national resources or any concessions for public utilities. These must all be secured for the whole Jewish people. In other ways, as well as this, the possibility of capitalistic exploitation must be guarded against. A high development of the Anglo-Palestine Company will doubtless prove one of the most effective means of protection. And the encouragement of all kinds of co-operative enterprise will be indispensable. Our pursuit must be primarily of agriculture in all its branches. The industries and commerce must be incidental merely—and such as may be required to insure independence and natural development."[65]

Weizmann, informed through a personal message of the reasons the Americans could not participate, sailed for Palestine, but once there and confronted by the sheer magnitude of reconstruction, renewed his plea for American membership. Appealing directly to Brandeis, and indirectly through the Foreign Office, he vainly tried to get the American Government to change its mind.[66] The key to Weizmann's desperate desire for American representation can be found in a thirteen-page report he sent to the PC, detailing the misery he had seen in Palestine and the difficulties he faced with the British military bureaucracy. "I need hardly add that the attitude of your Organization is deeply appreciated by everybody in the towns and in the colonies, and they are all united in their deep gratitude to you and to your committee. . . . But in view of the situation in Russia, and the chaotic state of Russian Jewry, the burden will not be lifted from your shoulders, I am afraid, for a long time to come. For some years to come, until Russia has settled down, we shall all still turn to you and to your great country for help, advice and guidance—help in men and money." A similar message went from Weizmann to the annual ZOA convention, and he suggested that at the least, there would be needed a long-term loan of several million dollars.[67]

The failure of the Americans to respond promptly to these letters, or to reverse the State Department ruling, soon had Weizmann suspecting nefarious plots to cut the ground out from under Zionist work. To Sokolow he poured out a tale of Byzantine intrigue on the part of "Turcophile anti-Zionist elements, chiefly Morgenthau and his group." In Washington, forces "were at work to frustrate and counteract Anglo-Zionist plans, and I am afraid our friends are not in a position to counteract in their activity." The Americans who might have helped had been strangely silent, and Wilson (at that point) had still not approved the Balfour Declaration.[68] In a bid to get Brandeis to act publicly, Weizmann dispatched Aaron Aaronson to the United States to explain the full dimensions of the danger.

Aaronson, whom Brandeis had first met in 1912 and who would die in a plane crash in the English Channel in 1919, arrived in America in August 1918, and immediately went to see members of the Provisional Committee. While he explained Weizmann's difficulties, he also learned of the delicate situation limiting their own activities. Aaronson also discerned, as he later reported, that the Americans had raised large sums of money, and hoped to build up a permanent organization that could meet the needs of the Yishuv. In the meantime, however, they had grown rather nervous about the seemingly endless demands for money made upon them. He did secure their agreement that Weizmann should stay on in Palestine, and that the scope of the Commission's work should be expanded. In their turn, the Americans would try to press the British to be more co-operative, and they also promised to supply the Commission with all the technical and financial resources possible.[69] This minor rift between Brandeis and Weizmann had been easily mended by Aaronson, but the conditions that caused it—great pressure on Weizmann, a belief on the part of the Europeans that the Americans had unlimited money, the feeling by the Americans that the Europeans wanted nothing but money, the difficulties in long-distance communication—would crop up again after the war, leading to the calamitous schism at Cleveland in 1921.

This lingering friction not only presaged future conflict, but also reflected some of the inner tensions in the movement. Prior to the war, the Americans had been shut out of the Executive, despite the fact that in total numbers they constituted the second-largest federation in the world. The emergence of the Provisional Committee as the single most potent Zionist agency, and the constant exhortations for unity by the leadership, did not prevent old animosities and new ambitions from cropping up. Before the war ended, a number of cracks marred the Zionist façade. From the outset, Louis Lipsky and Jacob deHaas had pushed Brandeis to assert American primacy in the movement. Weizmann had originally concurred in this sentiment, but a rump meeting of the General Council in Copenhagen in December 1914 decided to leave central headquarters in Berlin. As late as 1916, however, there were still a number of voices urging the transfer of authority to the United States.[70] Although the PC kept in touch with the Berlin office until early 1917 and sent lengthy reports of its activities, misunderstandings kept cropping up. In England, Weizmann would have nothing to do with the Copenhagen office, and until late 1915 avoided keeping the Americans as informed of his activities as they kept him up to date on theirs, since, he claimed, "the general attitude of the Provisional Committee is not clear to me."[71] When several members of the Actions Comité wanted to come to the United States, presumably to take a greater hand in running Zionist affairs, the Americans consistently demurred, discovering one reason after another why it would be undesirable for them to do so. Not until after the war did any of the major European leaders visit the United States.

At home, the PC never did make peace with the Mizrachi, and on June 28, 1917, both the Mizrachi and the Poale Zion withdrew from the Committee. Brandeis had tried numerous stratagems to secure co-operation with Rabbi Meyer Berlin, but the religious Zionists seemed determined to go their separate way. Recommendations for compromise by the WZO resulted in the Mizrachi temporarily rejoining the united front. Ideology, however, not independence, marked the attitude of the socialist Poale Zion. The PC had only one socialist Zionist on it, Nachman Syrkin, and by the lights of some of the younger and more radical socialists, he seemed too willing to work with the capitalistic establishment. David Ben-Gurion, then living in New York while in exile from Palestine, joined the Poale Zion leadership and demanded a stronger stand on socialist principles. At a stormy meeting in which the Poale Zion presented its case, Horace Kallen accused them of being "hyphenated Zionists," implying that their socialism made them less than loyal to Zionism, and with accusations and countercharges in the air, the Poale Zion walked out.[72] When the war ended, most American Zionists stood behind the leadership of the Provisional Committee, however, and despite minor schisms and tensions, looked forward with confidence and strength to the peace conference.

IV

The convolutions of two years of negotiations that finally incorporated the Balfour Declaration into a British mandate over Palestine illustrate dramatically the dangers of viewing history through a single lens. The Wilson administration, the French and British governments, the European and American Zionists, the State Department careerists, the Protestant missionary groups, the anti-Zionists, and the Arabs all had interests at stake, and every event, every statement stood open to numerous interpretations and misinterpretations. No one group controlled events at the conference, and the final disposition of Palestine reflected endless compromises and an ultimate weariness. Lurking behind the seeming Zionist triumph of the mandate, disagreements over means and meaning already pointed to future tragedy.

The end of the war found American Jewry more united than ever, and the Zionists at a peak of their strength, with nearly two hundred thousand members. The American Jewish Congress, dominated by Zionists and Zionist sympathizers, would soon meet, and would legitimately claim that it spoke for a large section of the three million Jews in America. While there still existed a substantial number of bitter anti-Zionists, the influential magnates of the American Jewish Committee adopted a policy of co-operation with the Zionists, a change of heart engendered not only by the Balfour Declaration but by the realization that the days of open immigration into the United States were near an end. Palestine, now in British hands, could provide a haven for their oppressed brethren.

The most dramatic about-face involved Jacob Schiff, the foremost figure in the German-Jewish community, who had staunchly opposed Zionism before the war, although his wide-ranging philanthropy supported several Palestinian agencies. Schiff's conversion began during the war, when he saw a need "to turn Palestine into a Jewish homeland where our people can have the opportunity to develop their own life and culture." Although the question of dual allegiance continued to bother him, he publicly admitted that many of the objections he had previously had against Zionism no longer existed, and he wanted his people to have Palestine again. By mid-September 1917 he had begun a dialogue with the Brandeis group through Elisha Friedman, in which he sought to delineate areas of agreement, and to distinguish between those who, like himself, supported a cultural homeland and the extreme nationalists who wanted a state.[73] A satisfactory definition of nationalism eluded him, but by 1918 the old antagonisms were gone. Schiff donated large sums for support of the Palestinian colonies, and when Rabbi David Philipson tried to secure his aid in denouncing the Balfour Declaration, Schiff cut him cold.

Louis Marshall proved even more sympathetic to Zionism, although he too remained upset by what he considered the extreme position of the nationalists. Like Schiff, he declared his sympathy and support for a Jewish homeland, and tried to differentiate among the Zionists. Relations with the Brandeis group grew more cordial once Marshall determined that they had no immediate aspirations for a state, and afterward he defended them from charges of extremism.[74] While undoubtedly differences existed among the Zionists as to the need for a state, or when it should come into being, this effort by Marshall and Schiff to distinguish the nationalists from the moderates had more than a touch of self-delusion. Zionism meant statehood eventually, and while Brandeis and Mack were willing to achieve that goal more gradually than were some of the over-excited Eastern Europeans, both groups agreed that there had to be a state. The Zionists, much as they wanted Schiff and Marshall to join them, could not disguise this fact.

Ironically, in the light of his earlier opposition, it was Marshall to whom the American Jewish Congress turned to head its delegation to the Paris peace conference. During the war, the whole question of a congress had lain dormant at Wilson's request. Marshall still believed that a conference would have been a better idea, yet once embarked on this path, it would have been fatal to Jewish unity to have tried to subvert the congress. Moreover, Marshall began to disassociate himself from the anti-Zionists, declaring: "Not only am I not opposed to the Zionist idea, but in a certain sense I am for it. I too favor the creation of a Jewish Center in Palestine."[75] When the congress met at the Lee-Lu Temple in Philadelphia on December 15, 1918, Marshall told the cheering delegates: "We here in America sympathize with every Jewish aspiration. Many of us who have in the past been disconnected with the Zionist organization, have nevertheless felt that it would be a privilege to assist in the rehabilitation of the land of our fathers. This is not on my part an eleventh-hour recantation or acceptance of principles. There are some of us who have in the past been classified as anti-Zionist—which we never were—who have gladly inaugurated work in the Holy Land for the purpose of developing it agriculturally and educationally."[76]

The delegates, many of them ardent Zionists as well as representative of the downtown Yiddish-speaking masses, recognized and accepted the conciliatory attitude of the *yahudim,* and, in turn, not only reciprocated but indicated the respect they had always held for these men. They chose Marshall and Harry Cutler of the AJC as vice presidents, Jacob Schiff as treasurer, and named Marshall and Cutler to the congress delegation to the peace conference. The AJC Executive Committee undoubtedly winced at some of the resolutions passed at the congress, and its instructions to its own representatives, Marshall and Cyrus Adler, explicitly repudiated the idea of special "national" claims for European Jewry. But, as the peacemakers assembled, American Jews presented a relatively united front, with basic agreement on the desirability of a Jewish center in Palestine, as promised in the Balfour Declaration, and the need to protect Jewish rights in Europe; at the same time, they tacitly agreed to ignore, as much as possible, those points of disagreement that could destroy the façade of unity.[77]

The desire for unity reflected a pervasive feeling that at this peace conference, something could and would be accomplished for the Jews. That the Jewish question should be on the agenda of an international conference was, by itself, no novelty; it had been discussed at every important international gathering since the Congress of Vienna in 1815. The London Congress of 1830, which had recognized an independent Greece, guaranteed equal treatment for all minority groups in its constitution. Meetings in Paris in 1856 and 1858, and in Berlin in 1878 failed to secure Jewish rights in the Balkans, as did the Bucharest Conference in 1913.[78] But this time the major powers had all endorsed the idea of a Jewish home in Palestine, while the Allied rhetoric clearly embraced the principle of equal treatment for Jews in all lands. Moreover, the recognition accorded the Zionists by the British, and the close ties between Wilson and American Jewry, meant that for the first time a powerful Jewish voice would be heard in the councils of the mighty. In January 1918, the Jewish position at the peace conference seemed the strongest of any of the petitioning groups.

Yet the conflicting claims and interests of the big powers, their drive to expand their areas of influence, the contradictory motives of different interest groups (through many of which ran a common thread of anti-Semitism)—all worked to undermine the Jewish position. And if the pressures of external, uncontrollable forces were not enough, the tensions between the nervous Europeans and the confident American delegation contributed to the weakening of Jewish strength. Given the seemingly strong position of the Jews at the start of the negotiations, they should have gotten more than the imprecisely worded British mandate over Palestine; given the real weaknesses of the Jewish forces, it is amazing that they got even that.

The first indication of that weakness came even before the silence of the Armistice settled across Europe. On the same day as they congratulated Wilson on the peace, Julian Mack and Louis Marshall alerted the President to the outbreak of a wave of *pogroms* in Poland and Romania, and the evidence that further bursts of violence against Jews could be expected in Germany and Austria-Hungary. They appealed to Wilson to do something about it, and the President told his secretary to see if they had any practicable measures to suggest. When Marshall urged Wilson to issue a public announcement condemning the outrages, the President drew back. "I think you can hardly realize all the reaction to my attempting leadership in too many ways," he wrote, but there would be many opportunities to express his opinion at the peace tables, and there he "would deem it a privilege to exercise what influence I can." A few weeks later, Wilson discussed the problem at length with Cyrus Adler, and again he expressed his determination to do what he could at the right time; but while hundreds died, the Western powers did nothing. Between 1918 and 1920, about fifteen thousand Jews were killed in Eastern Europe, and many more wounded, while much Jewish property was destroyed. But after the bloodletting of the great war, these numbers aroused little interest.[79]

Zionist hopes at the conference rested on two main supports: the

British declaration and the expressed endorsement of Zionist aims by the Wilson administration. Certainly there had been enough statements and promises to encourage these hopes, but neither country could afford a foreign policy in which Jewish aspirations played a dominant role. As the Zionists would discover time after bitter time, dreams of restoration, when weighed against considerations of power, counted for little.

Certainly the statesmen responsible for the Balfour Declaration knew what it meant, and they publicly interpreted it as a prelude to an independent Jewish state. David Lloyd George, Arthur Balfour, Lord Robert Cecil, Winston Churchill, and Jan Smuts all attested to that, and Lloyd George in particular read the Declaration as a promise of a future Jewish state. By the time the power brokers met in Paris, France, Italy, China, and Japan had endorsed the Declaration, as had the United States. But while the statesmen spoke in Whitehall, the career diplomats and military officials in the field studiously ignored the import of the British promise. When Weizmann reached Palestine with the Zionist Commission, he quickly discovered the rampant anti-Semitism among the military. Both during and after the war, British officials in the Mideast regarded the Balfour pledge as a mistake, and one that should not be considered binding. Especially among the Arabists, hope glimmered that a pan-Arabic union might be effected under British sponsorship, excluding the French and the Zionists from the former Turkish Empire.[80] Even while the Lloyd George Government reaffirmed its sincerity regarding a Jewish homeland, British officers did all they could to delay its implementation. Nearly eighteen months after the war ended, the Foreign Office continued to receive reports that Lord Allenby wanted to drop the whole Zionist policy, while his chief aides displayed a marked anti-Semitism.[81] The longer negotiations dragged on in Paris, the more influence lower-echelon staff could exert to reverse the earlier policy.

The Zionists had even more reason to rely on Woodrow Wilson's goodwill and support. He had, after an initial hesitation, endorsed the Balfour Declaration, and in January 1919 told Stephen Wise that the Zionists could count on his full support. On March 2, after returning from his first trip abroad, the President met with the

American Jewish Congress delegation before it left for Paris. "I am persuaded," he told them, "that the Allied nations with the fullest concurrence of our own Government and people are agreed that in Palestine there shall be laid the foundation of a Jewish commonwealth." As the meeting broke up, Wilson called Rabbi Wise to a corner and spoke with him for a few minutes, reaffirming his support. As they shook hands, Wilson told him: "Don't worry, Dr. Wise, Palestine is yours."[82]

But Wilson the diplomat had a world to save, and despite his best intention, Palestine occupied but a small corner of it. Once the American delegation reached Paris, Wilson found himself in a quagmire of claims and counterclaims, and the decidedly more hostile "experts" began to question the American commitment to a Jewish homeland. Even before the conference began, the four American commissioners expressed their doubts. Colonel House, despite his show of friendship to Brandeis and Wise, had been very skeptical and cautious in advising Wilson about the British declaration, while Secretary of State Lansing made no bones about his opposition to American involvement in Zionist affairs. Henry White privately opposed a Jewish homeland, while General Tasker Bliss, who thought the whole problem irrelevant, seems to have accepted some of the anti-Zionist propaganda current in Paris. Before long, the entire delegation found itself swayed by petitions from those who opposed Zionist plans for Palestine.

Jewish anti-Zionists in the United States more than made up in activity for their lack of numbers. They commissioned Professor Morris Jastrow of the University of Pennsylvania to write a "scholarly" critique of Zionism, and they also gave wide publicity to former ambassador Henry Morgenthau's opinions on the fallacy of resettlement. From the Central Conference of American Rabbis came a long appeal begging the peacemakers to do no more than assure equal rights to all Jews wherever they might live, and not to create a separate Jewish home. Congressman Julius Kahn gathered the signatures of nearly three hundred anti-Zionist Jews in a petition opposing a Jewish homeland, and although the President ignored it, his advisers considered it indicative of the majority of Jewish thinking in America.[83]

While intrigue certainly abounded at the peace conference, the erosion of Zionist strength cannot be attributed alone to nefarious, anti-Semitic plots among inferiors working to undermine the noble sentiments of Big Four statements. In fact, the Zionist position lost ground precisely because the American staff took Wilson's Fourteen Points seriously. Two millennia of Jewish suffering and the idealism of the Zionist dream undoubtedly appealed to the nobler sentiments of the American President, but restoration in Palestine ran directly counter to one of Wilson's most cherished principles, that of self-determination. For the Jews to receive Palestine, the peacemakers would have had to ignore the wishes of the seven hundred thousand Arabs living there, who for the most part wanted nothing at all to do with the Zionists. It is in the light of these dichotomies between principle and practice—indeed, between principle and principle—that we can look at Zionist activities, especially those of the Americans, at the Paris Peace Conference.

V

The American staff to the conference arrived early in December 1918, and by mid-January had prepared the first concrete proposals on Palestine. Its "Outline of Recommendations" incorporated nearly all of the Zionist requests, paraphrased the Balfour Declaration, provided for generous boundaries, and downplayed Arab claims to the area; it expressed the maximum, but logical, implications of the Declaration, and fully satisfied the Zionist goals.[84] Yet anti-Zionist reports coming from Arabist-leaning British field officers, as well as petitions from American Jews opposed to a Palestinian homeland, began to weigh upon William L. Westermann, the Cornell professor of ancient history who headed the Western Asia Division. Over the next several months, Westermann wrote a series of memoranda analyzing American interests, Wilsonian principles, and the Zionist program, and came to the conclusion that the United States could not afford to support the Balfour Declaration. The most valid argument against it, he wrote, "is that it impinges upon the rights and desires of most of the Arab population of Palestine, numbering five to every Jew in the land, who do not want their country to be made into a 'homeland' for the Jews." For Westermann and others, the claims of the Arabs made much more sense in Wilson's own terms, and they sympathetically circulated Arab material. And, without exaggerating it, a number of the American staff found the idea of a Jewish homeland repugnant for other reasons as well. One memorandum in particular objected to placing "the tomb of the Founder of Christianity under the domination of his murderers."[85]

Following Westermann's barrage came the single most concerted force for whittling down the Zionist demands: the Protestant missionary groups who operated colleges and churches in the Mideast. Dr. Howard Bliss, president of the Syrian Protestant College at Beirut, appeared in Paris and began lobbying for a commission to determine what kind of destiny the native population wanted for itself, an idea eagerly accepted by the American staff and which Wilson could hardly oppose. From Cairo, Professor Philip Marshall Brown of Princeton, on a mission for the YMCA, at Lansing's request, had been sending the Secretary of State reports since mid-1918 to the effect that Zionism would be disastrous not only for the Arabs, but for the Jews as well. Brown also showed up in Paris, and persistently fought the Zionist plans as well as any American involvement to implement them.[86]

To some extent, the missionary attack blunted itself on the apparent cordiality between Arab and Jew in Paris. Weizmann and Emir Feisal of the Hedjaz, had met in January and reached a formal agreement, which posited a Jewish state in Palestine and co-operation between the two peoples to develop the area. The loophole, however, consisted of a postscript by Feisal, tying the Arab-Jewish agreement to the British carrying out their wartime promises to the Arabs. This postscript was not a mark of Arab duplicity, however, for on March 1 Feisal sent a similar letter of understanding to Felix Frankfurter, and allowed it to be published.[87] Despite this, there were a number of officials who persisted in calling for Arab self-determination in Palestine, and who correctly noted that Feisal's assumed leadership in the Arab world rested more upon the machinations of T. E. Lawrence than upon a real following.

Throughout January and February, while plans and counterplans sprang up regarding the future of Palestine, Zionist policy lay mainly in the hands of Chaim Weizmann and Nahum Sokolow, and with one significant exception, the American Zionists were notably absent. Felix Frankfurter, at Brandeis' request, had arrived in Paris in early January to hold a "watching brief," and for two months would be the only important American Zionist there. While Frankfurter and Weizmann admired each other, an implicit tension began to develop between the Americans and the Europeans. Weizmann, after all, had engineered the British declaration, while Sokolow, an experienced diplomat, had secured its approval by the Vatican and the French. Although the United States, in Weizmann's words, had become the great reservoir of Zionist strength, the Europeans were loath to admit them into the leadership as equals. American economic proposals for Palestine and the treaty were ignored, and when the Zionists appeared before the Council of Ten on February 27, Frankfurter did not go with them. Lansing even offered to make more time available for him to appear, but Weizmann politely, but firmly, told him it was unnecessary.[88]

Yet it was Frankfurter, at that time passionately devoted to Zionism, who carried on the crucial drafting of Zionist memoranda and proposals. Acquainted with many of the academics on the American staff, he mingled with them easily, and undoubtedly counterbalanced some of the pro-Arabic and anti-Zionist material reaching them. Had Nahum Sokolow trusted Frankfurter more, much of the internal friction among the Zionists might have been avoided. A legal craftsman whose work won even Brandeis' approval, Frankfurter had also served as head of the War Labor Policies Board and understood the nature and requirements of governmental documentation. Many of the Europeans had a less than perfect knowledge of English, yet they insisted on amending Frankfurter's drafts; moreover, their idea of compromise seemed often to take the form of adding various proposals together without regard for internal consistency. The resulting papers, although they bore Frankfurter's name, were poorly drawn, and hostile critics, such as Captain William Yale, found little problem in tearing them apart.

Zionist plans received a further jolt when Wilson returned to the peace table on March 20 and told the other Allies that he did not consider any of their wartime agreements on the division of Turkey to be binding at the conference. Although the President only a few days earlier had again endorsed the idea of a Jewish homeland in Palestine, he now seemingly committed himself to a full and rigorous application of self-determination in the Middle East. The Council of Four agreed on a commission to investigate the wills of the inhabitants of the former Ottoman territories. Wilson immediately named two American representatives, Henry C. King, president of a Protestant college in Ohio and former religious director for the Allied Expeditionary Force, and Charles Crane, a Chicago businessman. Although Crane had previously worked closely with Brandeis on a number of reform projects, in later years he became a hysterical anti-Semite. To the missionary forces, the appointment of the King-Crane group provided a new chance to upset Zionist plans.

If this turn of events had not been worrisome enough, the Jewish delegation seemed unable to work together. The Congress representatives arrived, and received what they considered a sympathetic hearing from the American commissioners. A few days later, Henry Morgenthau appeared in Paris bearing anti-Zionist petitions, and he immediately set to work attacking Zionist claims and plans. The French Alliance Israélite Universelle opposed a British mandate, while the English Board of Deputies and the Anglo-Jewish Association presented competing plans. Although endorsing the Balfour Declaration, they opposed any special recognition of the Zionists through a Jewish agency. Finally, the Orthodox rabbis from Jerusalem, speaking for the bitterly anti-Zionist Agudath Israel, condemned all of the other Jewish delegations. Louis Marshall, more than anyone, labored mightily to achieve unity, but the best he could do—and this by itself was a significant achievement—was to avert an open break.[89]

The American commissioners, by now thoroughly confused, decided to ask Wilson just what he had meant in his statement on a

Jewish commonwealth. While refusing to deny that he had indeed made such a comment, the President realized that it now presented an embarrassing contradiction to his avowals of self-determination. Rather lamely he told the commissioners that he had only meant to reiterate his support of the Balfour Declaration, although he recognized that he had spoken more strongly than necessary. Since no one had ever explicitly defined just what the Declaration meant, Wilson's explanation still left matters up in the air. But the seemingly powerful position of the Zionists in January had definitely been eroded by the missionary attack, by Wilson's ambivalence, and not least of all by the Jewish delegations squabbling among themselves.

This air of foreboding led Felix Frankfurter to write to the President at length: "You are familiar with the problems and have stated their solution. The controlling Jewish hope has been—and is—your approval of the Balfour Declaration and your sponsorship of the establishment of Palestine as the Jewish National Home. The appointment of the Inter-allied Syrian Commission and the assumed postponement for months, but particularly beyond the time of your stay here, of the disposition of the Near Eastern questions, have brought the deepest disquietude to the representatives of the Jewry of the world. As a passionate American I am, of course, most eager that the Jew should be a reconstructive not a disruptive force in the new world order. I have assured their leaders, with the conviction born of knowledge of your purposes. They have faith; I venture to think no people in Paris have more faith—the faith of two thousand years. But they also have the knowledge of the suffering of millions of Jews, and the hopes of Jews the world over, which nothing will assuage except the re-dedication, at last, of Palestine as a Jewish Homeland. . . . You will forgive me for writing, but circumstances have made me the trustee of a situation that affects the hopes and the very life of a whole people. Therefore I cannot forebear to say that not a little of the peace of the world depends upon the disposal before you return to America of the destiny of the people released from Turkish rule."[90]

Wilson, evidently unaware of the anxieties prevalent in the Zionist camp, acknowledged the letter with a perfunctory note on the thirteenth of May, and immediately threw the Zionist camp into despair. Frankfurter, guessing that the President had not known of all the intrigue and counterproposals that so worried the Zionists, immediately wrote back a dramatic and eloquent note, informing Wilson that his cool response "had occasioned almost despair to the Jewish representatives now assembled in Paris, who speak not only for the Jews of Europe but also for the American Jewish Congress, the democratic voice of three million American Jews." He begged Wilson to reaffirm his policy of securing justice for the Jews, lest world Jewry feel that it had been betrayed and forgotten. Wilson, surprised at the forcefulness of Frankfurter's letter, immediately wrote back that "I never dreamed that it was necessary to give you any renewed assurance of my adhesion to the Balfour Declaration, and so far I have found no one who is seriously opposing the purpose which it embodies. . . . I see no ground for discouragement and every reason to hope that satisfactory guarantees can be secured."[91]

While the Zionists rejoiced in these comforting words, the anti-Zionists had their day as well. After months of delay, the French managed to torpedo an Allied Commission to the Middle East, aware of the large-scale anti-French sentiment there. Secretary Lansing, Colonel House, and Professor Westermann convinced Wilson that the Americans should go by themselves, and at the end of May, the King-Crane Commission departed for a six-week whirlwind inquiry in the Middle East.[92] Frankfurter immediately recognized the dangers, and began sending Brandeis desperate cables imploring him to go to Palestine. The Justice, who had planned only to visit Paris after the Supreme Court adjourned, agreed, and after a brief meeting with Weizmann in London and the Allied leaders in Paris, he sailed for Palestine via Egypt. While there, he confirmed Weizmann's earlier analysis of the reluctance of field officers to carry out Foreign Office instructions, and when he returned to Paris in August, he conveyed his concern to Balfour and other British officials.[93]

Although Brandeis met with the King-Crane Commission and made a strong case for Jewish settlement in Palestine, even his formidable persuasive talents failed to budge those who had apparently made up their minds even before they left Paris. From the time the Commission arrived in Jaffa on June 10, they had provided a sounding board for Arab nationalist sentiment, which they eagerly reported to the American delegation in Paris. In Jerusalem they found a "united and most hostile attitude towards any extent of Jewish immigration," and declared it would take an army to carry out the Zionist program. When the group reached Syria, it deliberately sought out Arab spokesmen who claimed Palestine was part of Syria, and in their reports King and Crane endorsed the major planks of a Syrian Congress platform. After spending forty days in Syria and Palestine, the Americans returned to tell everyone who would listen that the Arab Muslims stood unanimously for a united Syria, and only Jews favored the Zionist plan. In a private addendum, they also urged a major reduction in Zionist claims, and predicted trouble from both Arabs and Muslims at the prospect of a Jewish state in the Holy Land.[94]

The King-Crane report reached the White House a day before Wilson's collapse, and fortunately for all concerned, its recommendations were kept secret until 1922. The blatant anti-Zionist bias would have been politically embarrassing to the Administration and to the British, while its recommendations for a united Syria would have been acceptable only to the French. Both the British and American leaders had gone too far in their support of Zionist aspirations to back down. With the burial of the King-Crane report, a major obstacle in the Zionist path disappeared.

It must be remembered that although the disposition of Palestine occupied all of the Zionists' attention, it was but a minor problem in the over-all concerns of the peacemakers. Wilson had come to Paris to bring peace to the world, and he envisioned his Fourteen Points as a new decalogue, the key to a millennium. Instead of war, there would be legal and nonviolent means of resolving disputes; instead of colonial competition, economic co-operation would prevail. At Paris, he found a Europe unprepared and unwilling to enter this new Eden, and by the time the Big Four signed the German treaty in June, Wilson had surrendered on most of his "nonnegotiable" points. He sailed home to salvage what he could, and left his allies to carve up the former Ottoman possessions pretty much as they pleased. While the Wilsonian spirit may have hovered around the conference table, the voices of European imperialism dominated the discussion.

The French made one more effort to get Syria and Palestine together, along the lines of the old Sykes-Picot agreement, and failed. Feisal was expelled from Syria, demonstrating his lack of broad Arab support. American missionaries continued their lobbying, but with the failure of the King-Crane Commission and the declining fortunes of Robert Lansing, no one really listened to them. Wilson lay partially paralyzed, humiliated and defeated, and refused to make any statement on a Jewish homeland, petulantly claiming that the Zionists wanted constant reassurances.[95] Having lost the major battle for American involvement in world affairs, Wilson had no time for minor skirmishes. The last stages of the treaty scenario, awarding the mandates and fixing the boundaries, had to be played by the Zionists with only limited assistance from the White House.

The boundary issue came before the big powers in February 1920, a year after they had first assembled to begin negotiations. Although the American Zionists had no specific knowledge of proposals, they knew the French hoped to expand their Syrian influence at the expense of Palestine, and Great Britain, eager to secure Palestine, might concede northern boundaries to avoid a struggle. During the late fall of 1919, the Zionists had dispatched a team of English engineers to identify land and water areas that would be essential to developing an economically viable homeland. The Americans began the campaign for maximal boundary lines with telegrams to the leaders of the Big Four, recalling to them their support of the Balfour principle. Brandeis wrote a personal note to the ailing President, pointing out the necessity for broad boundaries, and suggesting that a denial of viable borders would be a betrayal of Christian promises. "I venture to suggest," said Brandeis, "that it may be given to you at this time to move the statesmen of Christian nations to keep their solemn promise to Israel. Your word to Millerand and Lloyd George at this hour may be decisive." Wilson, obviously touched, awoke from his lethargy and instructed Lansing to forward instructions to Paris in support of the Zionist claims. "All the Great Powers are committed to the Balfour Declaration," wrote Wilson, "and I agree with Mr. Justice Brandeis regarding it as a solemn promise which in no circumstances can we afford to break or alter."[96]

The presidential note met with little approval in the State Department; because the United States had practically withdrawn from the negotiations, career officers felt such intrusion unwarranted. Sheldon Whitehouse, a Department staff member, analyzed Brandeis' letter, and concluded that it would only further antagonize already inflamed Arab opinion. Whitehouse recited several cables received from Near Eastern consular officers testifying to Arab resentment over Zionist plans, and concluded that "if the territory claimed by Justice Brandeis should be given to Palestine the interests of the Jews themselves might be the first to suffer." Lansing, although sympathetic to this analysis, nonetheless carried out the President's directive, and after toning it down considerably, directed ambassador Hugh C. Wallace to deliver the message orally and informally.[97]

In Paris, Wallace called on both Sir George Graham, counselor to the British embassy, and on Millerand. The French in particular, while asserting their sympathy with Zionist hopes, nonetheless held their land claims to be excessive. After the conference of ambassadors moved to London, Brandeis appealed again, this time directly to Lloyd George, to secure boundaries that would make sense both in historic terms and in making Palestine economically self-sustaining. The American Zionists wanted land up to the river Litany and the Mount Hermon watershed, and in the east to the plains of Jordan. Julian Mack and Frankfurter urged Frank Polk, then acting as Secretary of State, to send similar instructions to the American ambassador in London, John W. Davis, as had gone to Wallace, and to communicate to Lord Curzon, the new Foreign Secretary, Wilson's wishes in the matter.[98]

As weeks of negotiation stretched into months, the boundary dispute became inextricably tangled with the question of who would get the Holy Land mandate. As the Europeans settled into their traditional postures of jealousy and secrecy, the isolationist mood in the United States deepened. Wilson, despairing because of pub-

lic apathy, could think of little besides his fight for the League of
Nations. Finally, much to the Zionists' satisfaction, the Supreme
Council of European Powers, meeting at San Remo, awarded the
mandate to Great Britain on April 24, 1920, with the American
Government's participation limited to the ambassador to Rome,
Robert Underwood Johnson, sitting as an observer. The final boundaries, not reached until December 1920, did not include the Litany
Valley, but on the whole met Zionist demands.[99] Not until July
1922 would the League of Nations confirm the mandate, but by
then the pattern of British rule, for better or for worse, had been
established, as indeed had relations with the Arab population.

Even before the San Remo conference awarded the Palestinian
mandate to Great Britain, the first signs of tragedy appeared. On
February 27, 1920, the Arab population of Jerusalem rioted in protest
against Zionist plans for a Jewish homeland. A few days later, another outbreak occurred, and in April during the Muslim Nebi
Musa festivities, further violence erupted. Despite the historic belief, acknowledged on both sides, that Jews and Arabs are branches
of the same Semitic family, this past half century has seen nothing
but hatred and bloodshed between them.

The Arabs claimed later that they too had been promised Palestine,
and a wearisome spate of diatribes have been published on the so-
called "twice promised land." During the war, Colonel T. E. Lawrence, Sir Henry McMahon, and Sir Gilbert Clayton attempted to
win over Arab support to the Allies, and held out the lure of an
Arab empire after the war. The British hoped, of course, that this
empire would place itself under their friendly protection. In April
1915, the governor general of Sudan, speaking for the Foreign
Office, had announced that an essential condition of peace would
be that the Arabian peninsula and those cities holy to Islam would
be under the control of an independent Muslim state. English military
officers, especially Allenby and Kitchener, soon became champions
of Arab nationalism, as did many of the career officers in Whitehall.[100]

Much of the wartime Arab claim to Palestine rested on an exchange of letters between Sir Henry McMahon and Sherif Hussein
in 1915, which attempted to delineate the boundaries of the proposed

kingdom of Hedjaz. The stipulations made by McMahon were vague; they excluded those territories in which the French had an interest, and this would have meant, among others, the Vilayet of Beirut, which comprised the greater part of Palestine west of the river Jordan. Both McMahon and Clayton, who took part in the negotiations, later stated explicitly that they always intended to exclude Palestine from Arab dominion.[101]

After the publication of the Balfour Declaration D. G. Hogarth saw Hussein and reaffirmed Allied support of Arab unity. He made clear, however, that the British considered Palestine within the area excluded from the McMahon pledge. There are conflicting reports on how the Arab monarch accepted the news, but all agreed that Hussein was not enthusiastic. However, at the peace conference itself, both in his agreement with Weizmann and in his letter to Frankfurter, Hussein's son Feisal pledged his support of a Jewish homeland, although in later years he lamely attempted to dismiss the two documents as forgeries.

The Jews, for their part, really had given very little thought to the Palestinian Arabs. In 1931, Weizmann noted that the prewar Zionist literature had hardly mentioned the Arabs. Although Ahad Ha'am as early as 1891 foresaw that the native population would strongly object if the Jews tried to take over their land, most Zionists did not take the more than half million Arabs who lived there seriously. The Americans were as guilty of this as anyone else, and in the general celebrating over the Balfour Declaration, made only passing reference to the non-Jews in Palestine, glibly predicting future co-operation between Arab and Jew. At the peace conference, Felix Frankfurter, recognizing the potential danger, made it a point to see Feisal and to stress to him the American tradition opposing colonialism. The last thing the Jews wanted, declared Frankfurter, was to triumph at the expense of the Arab people and Arab civilization.[102]

It is unfortunate, indeed tragic, that at the very moment when the two-thousand-year-old dream of Jewish restoration was on the verge of realization, it ran into the hopes of another people struggling to escape subjugation and enter into the modern world. A number of Arab scholars have recently maintained that Arab nationalism long pre-dated the first world war, that in fact it began with the prophet Muhammed, and that Islam was the prime creator of the national life and political unity of the Muslim Arabs.[103] Be that as it may, between the first *aliyah* and the world war, Palestine was a quiet backwater of the Ottoman Empire, and Jewish settlers there, like most occidentals, looked on the Arabs as poor, benighted natives. Unlike the American pioneers, who saw the Indians as a group blocking progress—and therefore to be eliminated—the *chalutzim* at all times recognized the biblical kinship between Jew and Arab, and hoped that in the rebuilding of Palestine, both peoples could work and prosper together.

But the Zionists failed to take into account the hope that arose among Arab groups with the breakup of the Turkish Empire, or that Palestinian Arabs would harbor as much love and devotion to the Holy Land as the Jews did. Most Zionists dismissed Arab claims to Palestine, since in the long and troubled history of that area, many peoples had possessed the land; the Arabs were but the last in line. Centuries of Jewish rule in Biblical times, as well as God's promise of redemption, seemed to count for more than a few hundred years of recent occupation, especially one that had done nothing to reclaim the land. In the beginning, the Zionists hoped they could live peacefully alongside their Arabic cousins. Sadly, the Arab expressions of goodwill and the pledges of co-operation at Paris proved shallow and transitory, and the resultant tensions between Jew and Arab in the following decades would bring bloodshed and agony to both peoples.

VI

The war and the ensuing peace conference marked a major shift in Zionist strengths. After 1914, as Weizmann had predicted, the United States became the great financial reservoir of the movement, and has remained so until this day. The ZOA reached a peak of influence in 1918 and 1919, with nearly two hundred thousand members, a budget in the millions, and leaders wielding power among the world's statesmen. Domestically, the opposition to the idea of a

Jewish homeland had been muted, and while the Hebrew Union College Board of Governors condemned the San Remo declaration, pro-Zionist ranks within Reform organizations continued to swell dramatically. Despite efforts of the American Jewish Committee to limit the congress to its original single session, the Eastern Europeans reconvened and declared themselves a permanent organization, and no one could doubt their strong Zionist sympathies.[104] Yet even this could not retard the growing friendliness of the *yahudim,* and contacts between the Brandeis leadership and the Schiff-Marshall group continued, with the latter donating heavily to support Palestinian projects.

Undoubtedly Brandeis' close relationship with Woodrow Wilson accounted for much of the Zionist influence during this era. As a crusading attorney, he had been one of the President's closest advisers, and even after Brandeis had gone onto the bench, Wilson had continued to consult him.* Unlike some of the Zionists who constantly importuned Wilson to aid the cause, Brandeis sensed that by limiting his requests to important questions, he could best utilize Wilson's faith in him. Brandeis also recognized that no matter how friendly Wilson might be to Zionist hopes, a President of the United States had to take into account all considerations. At no time could Wilson be asked to give undue precedence to the dreams of Jewish nationalism. Indeed, Wilson often gave signs that he thought the Zionists too pushy, too demanding.[105]

While Wilson personally aided the cause, he failed to create a

* The events of recent years, in which distinctions between the branches of government have either been overstepped or distorted, may raise questions in some minds about the propriety of Brandeis' role in Zionism and his continuing role as adviser to the President. Both men understood the proprieties and demands of their respective offices, and the high regard each held for those positions prevented their relationship from deteriorating into cronyism. But one must be careful to avoid imposing contemporary moral outrage upon differing conditions in earlier times. Both Wilson and Brandeis lived up to the highest moral responsibilities expected of either a president or a judge, even considering that the boundaries between the various governmental branches were less distinct than now. Had the times been such that a stricter separation of powers would have been necessary, I believe that neither man would have transgressed that line.[106]

permanent policy that would sustain the Zionists. Secretary of State Robert Lansing strenuously objected to what he considered an unwarranted intrusion in the conduct of American foreign affairs, and his attitude, not the President's, dominated State Department thinking and the action of field representatives. With the incapacitation of Wilson, there was little to restrain the anti-Zionist careerists in the Department, and after Warren G. Harding's election, they openly proclaimed that the country had made no commitments to a Jewish homeland in Palestine. Much of the problem lay in the absence of a clear-cut policy for dealing with the postwar situation. The Allies went to Paris prepared to carve up the Central Power empires, and to take the choice pieces for themselves. Questions of security and economic self-interest, which should have been given deep consideration by the United States, were sidelined by Wilson's commitment to an idealized peace; the wolves of Europe easily frustrated Wilsonian innocence. Of all the Allies, only the United States refused to join in the wholesale division of the spoils, taking only a few Pacific island chains under trusteeship.* In this context, Wilson proved friendly to Zionist claims because they appealed to his moralistic sense of history; he once explained how fitting it was that a son of the manse would help restore Israel.[107] Yet Zionism ran head-on into the Wilsonian principle of self-determination, and this awkwardly

---

* If the United States had been more willing to assume a role in world politics, the whole history of the Middle East might have been changed Britain, aware that France resented its aspiration to dominance in the eastern Mediterranean, evidently was willing to let the United States have Palestine. This would have created a buffer between British and French spheres, yet one that the British would have considered friendly to their interests. Given the American experience in the Philippines, Puerto Rico, Hawaii, and its other possessions, the Jews might have enjoyed a much better government in Palestine than they did under the British, who were constantly trying to placate the Arabs. As early as 1915, Cecil Spring-Rice wanted the American Zionists to lobby for an American role in Palestine, and shortly after the British had captured Palestine, they approached the State Department to see if the United States "would take a hand there." These suggestions met no encouragement from either Wilson, who opposed them on principle, or from Lansing, whose views of American self-interest dictated that the United States should either stay out of the Mideast or placate Arab potentates, as Great Britain would later do.[108]

limited the President's ability to support fully a plan that disregarded the wishes of an overwhelming majority of the country's inhabitants, a fact easily exploited by anti-Zionists within and without the government.

A final condition limiting Zionist effectiveness reflected the lack of a strong political base. Congressmen and senators now support the State of Israel, and American Jewry provides a strong lobby for Israel in this country, but in 1920 American Jews did not present a united front regarding Zionism; they had not yet come into their own as a political force in the United States. Aside from local urban machine connections, Jews represented a negligible entity in American politics. Not until the 1930s would large numbers of Jews enter the federal government both as elected and appointed officials. Robert Lansing correctly divined that the Zionists by themselves counted little politically, and that politicians could safely avoid paying them more than lip service. While some Christians may have sympathized with the idea of restoration, the overwhelming majority did not care one way or the other. The moral fervor after 1945, which enlisted so many non-Jews in the drive to create the State of Israel, just did not exist in 1919.

This is not to say that American Zionists counted for nothing during the war and its aftermath, for on the stage of world Zionism and of international politics, they represented the most unified and powerful Zionist group, one whose leaders were respected by and had access to great and influential statesmen. At key points during the negotiations over the Balfour Declaration and the disposition of Palestine, they exerted decisive pressure. Yet this marked the limit of their influence. For one brief moment in history, the rulers of great powers stood in agreement on a question that flew in the face of logic—the restoration of the Jewish people to their ancestral homeland in Palestine. Given this abnormal situation, Jewish strength assumed the illusion of a potency far beyond reality. Once that moment passed, once men began to consider the normal realities of domestic politics and international relations, Zionist influence quickly diminished. The disillusionment and apathy that followed the Peace Conference permeated the Zionist ranks as well, and hard on the heels of Paris came disaster.

CHAPTER SEVEN

SCHISM!

The end of the war found American Zionism greatly changed from the puny movement it had been only five years earlier. Its membership stood at nearly two hundred thousand, its budget involved millions, and its leaders dealt with the world's statesmen on the establishment of a Jewish homeland. After the bitterness engendered by the Congress fight, both the Brandeis leadership and the *yahudim* recognized that they would have to co-operate with one another, especially in the upbuilding of Palestine. Yet within the Zionist Organization of America serious divisions that had been submerged during the war crisis now surfaced, and a bitter struggle between American and European leaders over questions of power and principle threatened to tear the movement apart.

I

Despite their previous opposition to Zionism, the leaders of the American Jewish Committee recognized that the Balfour Declaration had drastically changed circumstances. The more religious-minded among them, including Jacob Schiff and Louis Marshall, had never subscribed to the anti-Palestine views of the extreme Reform leaders, but had acknowledged and even shared the special attraction Eretz Yisroel had for Jews. The Declaration made clear that the British did not perceive of Palestine as *the* Jewish homeland, and the carefully worded phrases delineated the rights not only of non-Jews in Palestine but of Jewish communities elsewhere. Thanks to the Brandeisian synthesis, the European notion of personal immigration to the Holy Land had been muted, while Jewish suffering in Europe and newly passed restrictive immigration measures clearly indicated the need to provide a refuge for their persecuted brethren. Even the crude manipulation of the Congress leaders in transforming the temporary gathering into a permanent organizaton could not deflect the Marshall group from seeking a *rapprochement* with the American Zionists.

Brandeis' standing with the *shtadlanim* had increased considerably after his elevation to the Supreme Court. While they might differ with him politically, it had now become, as William Howard Taft shrewdly noted, very difficult for them to oppose him publicly. Even Jacob Schiff nearly crowed in his satisfaction that a Jew had received such high honors.[1] There could be little doubt that Brandeis was now a recognized Jewish leader, and his appointment to the Court conferred prestige on all of American Jewry. But Brandeis had also won them over by his willingness to meet them part way on the congress issue. The AJC had been soundly defeated, yet the Justice's compromise allowed them to emerge from the struggle with their pride relatively intact.

Moreover, when they stopped to examine it, Brandeis' explanation of what Zionism meant in the United States did not violate their strongly held beliefs in the primacy of their loyalty to America. With the victory of the Allies and the Balfour Declaration, Brandeis turned to the problems of developing Palestine, and here he touched a responsive chord among the German-American Jews. Felix Warburg saw the Brandeisian emphasis on practical work as putting an end to the Zionist nonsense of a Jewish state with all its implied political problems. In September 1919, Louis Marshall and the Justice spent several days analyzing Palestinian affairs, a continuation of a series of meetings begun in late 1917, and Marshall happily reported that on the major issues no serious problems separated the two. Brandeis agreed that all Jews had the right to help in the reconstructive work at hand, while Marshall concurred in his analysis of the practical steps necessary before the Holy Land could support a large Jewish population. Brandeis' willingness to accept suggestions regarding political and economic aspects of immigration also pleased Marshall.[2]

On the other side, Marshall's standing with the Zionists had also risen markedly, as had that of Jacob Schiff. Despite his bitterness over Zionism during the war, Schiff had long supported a number of projects in Palestine, and insisted that all Jews had to be given the right and the obligation to share in its rebuilding. In 1919 he offered to buy back the Haifa Technikon from the German Hilfsverein, which had seized it during the war, and indicated his further willingness to co-operate with the Brandeis group. But while Schiff gave generously of his money, he hung back from a full endorsement of a Jewish homeland, and this prevented a complete reconciliation between him and the Zionist leaders.[3]

Marshall, whom the Zionists at one time had detested more than any of the other *shtadlanim,* had also been the one who proved to be the most open-minded and sympathetic of the AJC leaders. His contacts with the Russian immigrants had been extensive, and while they disagreed with many of his views, they recognized his basic decency and intellectual integrity. During the war, he came to see that many of the *yahudim's* fears were indeed groundless, and also to understand the reasons for many of the Eastern Europeans' demands.

Marshall had been selected as one of the Congress delegates to the peace conference, and the Congress program emphasized the need for Jewish rights in Europe as well as for a Palestinian homeland. Prior to the war, the AJC had insisted that while Jews should be guaranteed the same rights as all other groups, they should not receive any special benefits. Isolating Jews, even to protect them, implied a demeaning separatism. While Marshall in 1913 or 1914 would have certainly opposed group rights, the man who went to Paris in 1919 now could understand the reasoning behind such demands. "It is their belief," he wrote, "that the welfare of the State and the happiness of its people will be best promoted by the stimulation of the several racial cultures. . . . If any of these groups is accorded national rights in the sense in which I have explained, then every other group shall have an equal claim to have granted to it the same character of national rights. Hence, if the Ruthenians, for instance, were given such rights, then if the Jews desired similar rights they should be accorded them. We must be careful not to permit ourselves to judge what is most desirable for the people who live in Eastern Europe by the standards which prevail on Fifth Avenue or in the states of Maine or Ohio, where a different horizon from that which prevails in Poland, Galicia, Ukrania or Lithuania bounds one's vision."[4] In this last sentence, Marshall evidenced a broader mind and a greater empathy for his coreligionists than did most of his detractors.

In Paris, Marshall had worked diligently to protect Jewish rights, but he resented the failure of the European Jewish delegations to consult with him on the Palestine question. Before he left for home, he finally demanded to know why that subject had not been brought up for discussion, and discovered that they considered him a non-Zionist. Marshall exploded, and declared that regardless of his personal views, he held a mandate from the American Jewish Congress and considered it his duty to carry out its instructions; moreover, he had drafted a memorial to President Wilson, and stood ready to draw up a petition to the peacemakers on the future of the Holy Land. "In a very shame-faced manner my associates expressed their astonishment at the attitude which I took, believed it almost incredible that anybody should entertain such dispassionate views with regard to complying with the mandate which had been issued by the constituency that had sent me to Europe."[5] Marshall drew up his petition, but after he returned home, the other delegates did not de-liver it.

Not all of the German aristocracy followed the example set by Schiff and Marshall. Julius Rosenwald, for example, opposed any plans for a Palestinian homeland, as did Henry Morgenthau.[6] But many of the *yahudim* realized that in the future, Palestine would probably be the only hope for persecuted Jews, and they saw the restoration of the land as a challenge and an opportunity for all Jews. The moderate views and friendly overtures of the Brandeis group made it easy for them to co-operate, and Marshall in turn went out of his way to praise the Zionist leadership and to make peace with them. On the surface, at least, American Jewry seemed nearly united in its desire to work for the reconstruction of their ancient homeland.

II

Beneath the surface, however, discontent had been simmering among the Yiddish-speaking immigrants. Much as they appreciated what the new leadership had done for the movement, they resented what they considered the dictatorial attitudes of the Brandeis/Mack administration, and what they termed a watering-down of Zionist ideology. Throughout all this, Brandeis personally remained remark-ably immune from criticism. Everyone acknowledged his past and continuing work for the movement, and many approved his ideas for revitalizing American Zionism and bringing new people into the fold. In order not to offend him, they directed their salvos against his lieutenants, and they in turn tried to shield him from the growing discontent. Brandeis' position on the Court, his determination not to allow his judicial responsibilities to be affected by non-Court activities, further insulated him from his followers. Since he had formulated most of the policies under attack, it might have been better for all concerned if instead of sparing him, an effort had been made to establish better communications between the leader and his followers.

Almost from the start, old-line Zionists had objected to the pragmatic approach of the new leadership, an attitude that clearly reflected the American reform outlook. A problem existed that had to be solved, and while philosophical principles determined what general paths a solution would require, the work itself became primary. In Europe, however, ideology itself had been all-important. One identified oneself by a particular set of beliefs, and it made a great difference whether one belonged to Poale Zion or Mizrachi, or termed oneself a "practical" or a "political" Zionist. Aside from the funds and the colonies, European Zionism had never been able to deal with major problems, because it lacked the influence to make itself heard in world affairs. As a result, Zionist congresses and meetings became great debating rallies, where ideologues spent hours and days worrying over the fine points of a future Jewish state. In the United States, the Yiddish intellectuals who formed the nucleus of Zionist clubs followed this tradition.

The very pragmatism that made the Provisional Committee effective and that contributed so much to the growth of Zionism in the United States confused the Eastern European membership. At first, badly shaken by the war, they saw the activism of the new leadership as a tonic and a relief, and gloried in the unaccustomed glow of recognition and influence that Zionism now commanded. But as the PC continued to emphasize "Men! Money! Discipline!," they began to chafe at its apparent dismissal of ideology. Many of the Eastern Europeans felt that Brandeis and his lieutenants did not understand the importance of cultural revival, especially the rebirth of Hebrew, while the Mizrachi lamented the failure of the leadership to emphasize the religious element of Zionism.[7] The 1915 Boston convention stressed unity, but at the Philadelphia convention a year later grumblings could be heard that too little time had been devoted to theoretical review and academic formulation of policy. DeHaas, speaking for the administration, called these critics short-sighted. "We are now facing the critical period of Zionist history," he averred. "We shall be judged not by our abilities to formulate theories and accurately analyze conditions, but by the decisions we make and the judgments we employ in meeting the practical features of the Zionist program." The movement had passed its youthful period in romantic discussion and theory; now it had to grow up and deal with specific problems.[8]

The disinterest in doctrinal matters particularly upset the Yiddish journalists, who saw it as a sign of the alienation of the Americanized leaders from the masses. Although at first relations between the Brandeis group and the Yiddish papers had been cordial, by 1916 signs of disenchantment could be seen in some of the East Side dailies, which charged that the administration's failure to pay heed to ideological matters reflected an ignorance of real Zionism. By the end of the war, Brandeis was complaining about the hostility of the Yiddish press, while the journalists in turn charged that Brandeis and Mack refused to deal directly with them. "There will come a time," wrote Bernard Shelvin of the *Jewish Morning Journal,* "and the time is near, when the Yiddish press will pay more attention to its self-respect, and will not let others spit on its face, especially those who have to thank the Yiddish press for their positions, influence and reputation."[9]

A prime focus of this discontent was one of the most important projects of the new leadership: the reorganization of the movement. The structural weaknesses of the FAZ have already been discussed, and Brandeis had decided that as soon as some semblance of unity could be imposed on the movement, administrative reorganization would be necessary to harness Zionist sentiment and to channel it effectively. As early as the 1915 convention, some members called attention to what they considered too great a concentration of power in the Provisional Committee. Ironically, at the same time that the Zionist leadership, in its fight for the congress, attacked the *shtadlanim* for their allegedly dictatorial attitudes, a growing number of their own followers complained about the lack of democracy within the movement.[10] Undoubtedly Brandeis, a firm disciplinarian, struck many of the Zionists as arrogant and authoritarian, and his aloofness did little to establish close relations with the membership. Also, the insensitivity of Jacob deHaas to legitimate demands for explanations of policy exacerbated this friction. Yet a good part of the criticism resulted from the unwillingness of local leaders to give up their autonomy and to submerge their clubs and societies into a larger, all-inclusive organization. The struggle came to a head in 1918 at the Pittsburgh convention, when the administration proposed a platform of Zionist aims and a thoroughgoing reform of the movement's structure.

Brandeis had been concerned with the administrative weaknesses of American Zionism from the time he had assumed its leadership, and in late 1915 had spelled out the basic proposals for its revamping.[11] But he had recognized that the constituent societies would never give up their independence until it could be shown that only through a unified national organization would Zionism exert influence in the United States. By the 1917 convention it had become clear that the old structure would no longer suffice and that factional infighting sapped the movement of strength it could ill afford to lose. The debate that year at Baltimore centered almost entirely on internal administrative problems, and some of the local chieftains at last began to admit that a reorganization would be necessary.[12]

In the spring of 1918, Brandeis put the final touches on his proposals, and on May 25 presented them to the Provisional Committee. Basically, he advanced a five-point plan. First, there should be a single national organization, to which every Zionist in the country would belong directly, and not through membership in any other club or group. Second, this organization would have a new name, the Zionist Organization of America, to distinguish it from other groups. Third, members would belong to local Zionist chapters that would definitely be subservient to the ZOA, and these districts, in the fourth point, would be grouped by regions. Finally, existing clubs and societies would have an opportunity to work out their own problems and goals, but with the definite understanding that the ZOA held responsibility and authority for Zionist policy in the United States. While Brandeis emphasized that the reorganization plan would funnel individual Zionist energy, through district and regional offices, into a single, powerful, national agency, he had no desire to dissolve existing groups, and specifically mentioned the need to continue and strengthen the work of Hadassah and the religious societies. By centering national needs and work in one organization, they would now be free to put all of their energies into their specialized projects.[13]

Despite Brandeis' disclaimer, many of the local leaders feared that the leadership wanted to destroy the societies and enlarge its already bloated power. Again, the differences between American and European politics, both Zionist and secular, could be seen. In Europe, every ideological group has its own party, no matter how small its constituency or how narrow its program; within the Zionist congresses there also existed several recognized factions. In the United States, political parties have traditionally sought to blur ideological lines to appeal to a wide constituency, and base their power on a broad consensus rather than on narrow principle. The district plan that Brandeis presented reflected progressive American thought on popular organization. It assumed a general agreement on over-all policy, and organizationally grouped people by geography rather than ideology. To those who already objected to the disregard of ideological questions, as well as those who had vested interests in maintaining local autonomy, the reorganization plan bolstered their belief that the Brandeis group not only sought dictatorial powers, but that it stood alienated from the masses.

Open and sharp division between supporters of the plan and its detractors marked the opening of the 1918 convention, and numerous parliamentary fights highlighted the debates, as one group after another tried to exempt itself from subordination to the new central organization. But the obvious benefits of the proposal could not be denied, and with Palestine now in British hands, nearly all the delegates acknowledged the necessity for unity of action. One after another, first Hadassah, then the Knights of Zion, then Young Judea and the Order Sons of Zion came in, and on the final tally, the plan carried easily, although many who voted "yes" did so resentfully and with deep misgivings. As the clerk read the results, someone in the audience spied Louis Brandeis sitting alone in the gallery, and jumping to his feet, began to cheer and wave frantically in his direction. Soon the entire convention joined in the spontaneous demonstration, standing on their chairs and shouting *"Hadad."* Emanuel Neumann optimistically concluded that despite the bitterness at its beginning, "there has hardly been a convention that adjourned with such a feeling of solidarity, with such unanimity, with such a common, all-embracing enthusiasm as this one."[14] The unity, however, was illusory. To implement the reorganization plan, even the most tactful of leaders would have ruffled some feathers; deHaas, who as executive secretary oversaw such details, did not count tact among his strong points, and his high-handedness rekindled many of the antagonisms that had been submerged at the convention.

A more muted resentment also surfaced among those who felt uncomfortable with the statement of principles that the leadership had put forth at the convention. In response to those who wanted a clarification of goals and policies, the administration drew up a program summarizing its long-range philosophy. Pragmatic reasons also dictated the need for such a statement. The Pittsburgh meeting marked the first major gathering of Zionists after the Balfour Declaration and the capture of Jerusalem, and the leadership believed it important to proclaim a code of social justice that would guide the future development of the homeland. Brandeis, although consulting with his colleagues, wrote the so-called Pittsburgh Platform mainly by himself, and it revealed, as did few other documents, how he hoped to merge the progressive impulse for social justice into Zionism. On June 25, 1918, the convention unanimously approved the following statement:

> In 1897 the first Zionist Congress at Basle defined the object of Zionism to be "the establishment of a publicly recognized and legally secured homeland for the Jewish people in Palestine." The recent declarations of Great Britain, France, Italy, and others of the allied democratic states have established this public recognition of the Jewish national home as an international fact.
>
> Therefore, we desire to affirm anew the principles which have guided the Zionist Movement since its inception and which were the foundation of the ancient Jewish State and of the living Jewish law embodied in the traditions of two thousand years of exile.
>
> First   We declare for political and civil equality irrespective of race, sex or faith of all the inhabitants of the land.
>
> Second   To insure in the Jewish national home in Palestine equality of opportunity, we favor a policy which, with due regard to existing rights, shall tend to establish the ownership and control by the whole people of the land, of all natural resources and of all public utilities.

Third   All land, owned or controlled by the whole people, should be leased on such conditions as will insure the fullest opportunity for development and continuity of possession.

Fourth The co-operative principle should be applied so far as feasible in the organization of agriculture, industrial, commercial and financial undertakings.

Fifth   The system of free public instruction, which is to be established, should embrace all grades and departments of education.

Sixth   Hebrew, the national language of the Jewish people, shall be the medium of public instruction.

Although nearly all the tenets of the Pittsburgh Platform eventually became accepted policy in Palestinian development, they reflected the social reform concerns of the American leadership much more than the nationalistic sentiments of the European Zionists. The Mizrachi felt religious considerations had been ignored, while the Hebraicists felt that the last item failed to emphasize the cultural importance of the Hebrew language. Of all the old-line groups present, only the Labor Zionists, who also emphasized social justice, fully identified with the program.[15] But the Yiddish-speaking masses found it meaningless insofar as they understood Zionism; it totally lacked any of the mystic nationalism that they saw as part of redemption from exile. The American leaders, intent on avoiding conflict between Zionists and American patriotism, had studiously downplayed the nationalistic aspects of the movement. While the Poale Zion approved, more orthodox Jewish socialists considered the program weak and insipid. The Yiddish press practically ignored it.

Yonathan Shapiro points out that both the reorganization plan and the statement of principles point up the vacillation of the Brandeis group in deciding just which way American Zionism would develop after the war, into a movement led by a middle-class cadre or into a mass party. The former would attract the more affluent, acculturated middle-class Jews, as well as the very wealthy men who now seemed more sympathetic to Zionism. By emphasizing social justice and efficiency, the ZOA could hope to enlist those who would distrust a movement that smacked too much of European nationalism and/or radicalism. But the real power of the Brandeis group lay in its appeal to the masses, the very group alienated from the *shtadlanim*. While the masses did not have the financial resources to support large-scale work in Palestine, giving up a mass base would have left the Brandeis group powerless vis-à-vis the American Jewish Committee. To the Eastern European leaders, only the mass base made sense in their desire to put pressure on the AJC, and to them, the Pittsburgh program appeared not so much wrong as irrelevant, in that it spoke to the wrong people.[16]

The debates at Pittsburgh brought many of the ZOA's internal tensions out in the open, and this in turn temporarily cleared the air. The obvious benefits of reorganization could not be denied, even by those who resented their own loss of local power. The emergency needs of the war continued, and after the peace came, the exhilaration of victory and the legal recognition of a Jewish homeland maintained the pressures on dissident groups to back the Brandeis/Mack administration. The end of the war, however, marked the beginning of serious friction between the American and European leaders of the movement.

III

Despite their earlier indifference toward American Zionism, the disruption of their own organization had forced the European Zionists to re-evaluate their colleagues in the New World. Chaim Weizmann especially wanted to relocate the central agencies of the movement in the United States, and he looked to America for leadership and material help, although as he noted, "we knew that the American Jews were by no means as deeply permeated with the Zionist ideal as the Europeans." This distrust of the Americans led Weizmann to refrain from informing them about his negotiations with the British Government until it became necessary to seek Wilson's endorsement of British policy. The Americans, in turn, while keeping the various European offices posted about their activities, sought little advice

from them, and in fact discouraged several members of the Actions
Comité from coming to the United States. After the Balfour Declaration, the Provisional Committee recognized Weizmann as *de facto*
leader of the movement in Europe and adopted a more cordial tone
toward him. With the end of the war, both sides saw the need for
closer co-operation. Less than forty-eight hours after the Armistice,
Weizmann and Nahum Sokolow pleaded with the Americans to send
a delegation to London, one preferably headed by Justice Brandeis
himself, to begin preparations for the peace conference.[17] It was
hardly a moment too soon, for tensions had already begun to develop
between the Europeans and the Americans.

Chaim Weizmann, who had emerged as the dominant figure in
European Zionism during the war, was almost the antithesis of
Louis Brandeis. Where one was totally committed to the ideals of
American progressivism, the other drew his strength from centuries
of Jewish culture. Brandeis had come to Zionism late in life, while
Weizmann had grown up nurtured on the idea of restoration. The
cool, patrician Brandeis reflected the moral and social provincialism
of Brahmin Boston, while the worldly Weizmann, at home in several languages, remained most comfortable in the atmosphere of a
Yiddish *shtetl*. Despite Brandeis' deep devotion to Zionism, it constituted but one facet of his life; for Weizmann, even his beloved
chemistry could not compete with the single-minded devotion he
lavished, for more than forty years, on the creation of a Jewish
state. Both men were essential to Zionism, but the clash between
them, a clash of personalities and philosophies, nearly tore the
movement apart in 1921.

Weizmann had been a Zionist all of his life, a member of Hibbat
Zion and a close friend of Ahad Ha'am. He had supported Herzl's
move to organize those who yearned for restoration, but had then
fought Herzl for his failure to pay attention to the spiritual needs
of Zionism and for his indifference to Palestine. At the time of the
Uganda crisis, Weizmann had been one of the leaders of the Russian walkout. Following Herzl's death, Weizmann's involvement lessened for a while after he married and moved to England, where he
secured a readership in chemistry at Manchester University. With
the outbreak of war, his work on acetone soon brought him into

the Ministry of Munitions, where he had access to many of the leaders of the British Government. These contacts, plus his role in the Federation of English Zionists, soon made him the leader of Zionism in Great Britain, a position he brilliantly manipulated in securing the Balfour Declaration, his greatest achievement.

Weizmann had scorned Theodore Herzl, as he would later scorn Brandeis, for a lack of Jewish feeling, of *Yiddishkeit*. To him, "Jewish homelessness was not just a physical discomfort; it was also, and perhaps in a larger measure, the malaise of frustrated capacities. If the Jewish people had survived so many centuries of exile, it was not by a biological accident, but because it would not relinquish the creative capacities with which it had been entrusted. For assimilated Jews, all this was a sealed book; in their complete alienation from the masses, the source of inspiration, they had not the slightest concept of the inner significance, the constructive moral-ethical-social character of Zionism." To Weizmann, every Jew was a potential Zionist, and he pitied and despised those who allowed other loyalties to detract from their Jewish patriotism. Every Jew had to be a Zionist, because in every Gentile heart, no matter how seemingly friendly or sympathetic, lay the bacillus of anti-Semitism. He spent his life carrying this message to Jews in Europe and especially in the United States; it became his mission, and he gloried in it. "I have been pitied," he told one American audience, "because I must go around bringing home to Jews their duty. But I need no pity at all. We conceive of our duties in different ways. If this were no splendid hall, and there were no splendid banquet prepared, if there were only nine Jews sitting here and a tenth were needed to make up a *minyan* [quorum for daily prayers], it would be the duty of a Zionist to come and speak to them. If there were only two Jews and a third were needed to make *mezuman* [quorum for grace after meals], it would be the duty of a Zionist to come and speak to them. It does not detract from our dignity or our pride to do this; it is a privilege." As he himself noted, when it came to Zionism, he had blinders on.[18]

But his strengths were also his weaknesses. Weizmann drew his support from the masses, and always stressed that he was a man of the people. Like Ahad Ha'am, he believed that redemption would come only out of the people themselves. Yet he had a curiously contradictory and ambivalent attitude toward the people. "I know the Jewish people only too well," he once said, "and it knows me even better. And therefore I lack the wings which were given to Herzl. . . . Had Herzl been to a *cheder* [Jewish primary school], the Jewish people would never have followed him." His common touch, moreover, often hid a Nietzschean arrogance, especially when those he sought to lead refused to follow unquestioningly. His devotion to Zionism made him blind to anything that could not be related to the goal of restoration, and even when he read newspapers, he ignored articles that he could not connect to the movement. This single-mindedness could also be cruel, and Weizmann, for all his patience in winning over adherents, could be unfeeling in his dealings with those from whom he expected total support. When Felix Warburg lay dying, his son asked him if there was much pain; after a pause, the old man whispered, "This is nothing compared to some of the things I went through with Weizmann."[19] Chaim rarely forgave those who differed with him, and only a deathbed request from Henrietta Szold led to a reconciliation with Judah Magnes. And yet, without this single-minded fanaticism, would there have been a Balfour Declaration, or the money needed to support the Yishuv, or, in the end, a Jewish state? Weizmann was not just a Zionist, he was Zionism, as Maurice Samuel declared, and this tells us much about the obstacles to the movement and the special qualities needed to overcome them.

One blind spot in Weizmann's makeup concerned Great Britain. The relative lack of anti-Semitism he found there after leaving Russia, the fame he won in English laboratories, the promulgation of the Balfour Declaration, and later on, the loss of a son serving in the British forces, all made Weizmann an unabashed Anglophile, and he could never push too hard against the one nation that he felt had made restoration possible. During the Second World War, when Britain refused to open Palestine to Hitler's victims, Weizmann tried to explain the British policy as a result of war pressures, and maintained that in the long run, the English would save Zion. "The English nation does not change its character. It remains the champion of justice," he said, but "we must have confidence. Happy are those who believe. If I were no believer I could not be a Zionist. And I believe in England." Even in 1948, when the State of Israel came into being despite three decades of broken promises and treachery by Great Britain, Weizmann still saw the British as friends. While the Yishuv fought for its life against Arabs who were armed with British weapons, Weizmann planned to leave the United States to go to Israel in order to prevent the new Ben-Gurion administration from adopting any policies that might offend the former mandate power, whom he still considered Israel's one true friend.[20]

Weizmann's softness toward Great Britain had already manifested itself before the end of 1918.* Shortly after the cessation of hostilities, the public learned of promises made to the Arabs that seemed to contradict the Balfour statement. Trying to avert panic, Weizmann soft-pedaled the discrepancies and claimed that Jewish needs would not infringe upon legitimate Arab rights. This "minimalist" approach, as it later became known, would eventually cause his downfall in the WZO in the 1930s, and in 1918 it brought a sharp warning from the PC that no concessions should be made on either boundary lines or internal administration until the peace conference met.[21]

His general behavior, his seeming loss of confidence, also upset the American leadership. In the four weeks following the Armistice, Weizmann bombarded the PC with pleas that they dispatch a delegation to England at once, that the leaders come over, that nothing could be done without them. "We have reached a crucial point in Jewish history," he declared. "It is our sacred duty to leave nothing to chance." The Europeans could not carry the burden alone, and they wanted Brandeis' counsel and authority. "We consider it to be your duty to take your share in national responsibility by your presence here."[22] After his masterful leadership during the war,

---

* He was later critized, especially by Nordau, for having been too soft in his negotiations with the British over the terms and wording of the Balfour Declaration. Most historians consider this unfair, and suggest that given the circumstances and the impotence of the Zionist movement, the Declaration was a masterpiece of diplomacy dealing from weakness.

this seeming panic by Weizmann created much consternation in the
ZOA, and in mid-December Stephen Wise sailed for London, where
Felix Frankfurter, en route to the peace conference, soon joined him.

Wise's first meeting with the man who had engineered the Balfour
Declaration was far from reassuring. Weizmann stated again and
again that he should not bear the responsibility of leadership by
himself; Brandeis should head the Jewish cause, and the Justice
should personally go to the peace table. Weizmann felt he could
be most effective in Palestine, but he could not go there unless
Brandeis himself agreed to come to Europe. When he spoke of the
work in the Holy Land, the chemist intimated that he knew what
to do and would gladly bear the burden there, but Wise, while
assuring him that the Americans had "a hundred confidences" in
him, were nonetheless not willing to give him unlimited power.
Weizmann's continued nervousness, as well as his secretiveness,
soon upset even the generous Wise. Shortly after, Jacob deHaas
arrived in London, and his old antagonisms toward this detractor
of Herzl soon had him convinced that the Englishman was unfit for
any sort of leadership.[23]

Rabbi Wise returned from Europe to report that a great gulf of
misunderstanding separated the two groups. "The Zionist movement
in Europe," he declared, "admits that there is a Zionist movement
in America, because occasionally, much too occasionally, remittances come to hand, but if those remittances for any reason should
cease to float into the coffers of London or Paris, we should speedily
be cut off from London or France. Our friends there do not know
us, do not believe in us, and do not believe in the reality of our
Zionism." Chaim Weizmann stood out among those most guilty of
this, and Wise charged that the English chemist, despite his demands for greater American involvement, did not comprehend that
America had a serious and important part to play in the future
development of the movement and of the homeland, a role other
than mere financing of the *Yishuv*. The cautiousness that Weizmann
displayed toward the British in his demands for Palestine also upset
Wise, as well as the fact that the Europeans had not bothered to
consult their American colleagues on these matters. Pointing to the
future, Wise warned that unless better communication could be

established between London and New York, great damage would occur; indeed, only the acts of a benevolent Providence had prevented such damage before. Finally, Wise cautioned that what normally should be a relatively minor matter, the postwar reorganization of the Actions Comité, had become fraught with all sorts of dangers, reflecting personal rivalries and local jealousies. Both Weizmann and Nahum Sokolow had agreed on the need for a restructuring, especially after the problems encountered in trying to run the movement during the war. But they had disagreed on the method, and Wise seemed particularly upset by Weizmann's insistence that all powers be lodged in the hands of a single executive office. Brandeis and Julian Mack, appalled by this development as well as by Wise's comments on the slipshod administrative arrangements he had seen, agreed to cable deHaas, still in London, urging that all talk of reorganization be deferred until Brandeis and Weizmann could confer personally. Their first prolonged contact with the European leadership left the American Zionists extremely troubled, with ominous portents of future difficulties all too apparent.[24]

As winter wore on into spring, it became obvious on both sides of the Atlantic that only through personal meetings and full discussion could growing tensions between the Americans and the European leaders be eased. The ZOA Executive continued to worry about the seemingly insatiable demands on it for money, and about the inefficient methods involved in expenditures. Weizmann, now joined by Shmaryahu Levin, Nahum Sokolow, and other members of the prewar Actions Comité, vacillated between dismissal of the Americans as naïfs in Zionism, and pleas that they assume a greater share in the management of Zionist affairs. Finally, Brandeis decided to go to Europe during the Court's summer recess, and meet with the AC to agree on some joint program for administrative reorganization and future developmental work in Palestine. Then Wilson appointed the King-Crane Commission, and Frankfurter implored "the chief" to travel to Palestine. When British officials also indicated their eagerness to have Brandeis visit the Holy Land, he reluctantly acceded, and on June 14 he sailed aboard the *Mauritania* for Europe. On his arrival, he plunged into a frenetic week of meetings with British and Zionist officials, and as he reported home, "My coming was very much needed, more than I ever conceived possible, and I feel that I may be of real value all along the lines—with the British quite as much as with our own people."[25]

The Brandeis party, including Jacob deHaas and Harry Friedenwald, stayed in Paris for only a few days, and then left for Palestine. After a delay in Egypt, where the Justice talked at length with Lord Allenby, they arrived in Palestine on July 8. For the next seventeen days, they traveled the length and breadth of the land, visiting all of the cities and twenty-three of the forty-three Jewish setlements. He made no speeches, but asked innumerable questions everywhere he went. By the time he left, he felt he had grasped the main problems that would have to be handled in order to develop the land.[26] Most importantly, the trip gave Louis Brandeis the one essential experience that had been missing from his Zionism, the single quality he could not get from reading all the books and reports given to him by deHaas: He acquired a love for the land and an understanding of what Palestine meant to the Jews. The land "was a joy from the moment we reached it," he wrote home. "The problems are serious and numerous. The way is long, the path difficult and uncertain, but the struggle is worthwhile. It is indeed a Holy Land." Although he tried to travel as unostentatiously as possible, the colonists of the Yishuv insisted on showing their gratitude to the man who had made their survival during the war possible. At every city and settlement, Jews turned out to greet him, and while the children danced and sang for him, the proud settlers served him the fruits of their own fields and vineyards. Exploring the cactus-covered Temple area by moonlight moved him deeply, as did his visit to Rachel's tomb on the Bethlehem road. There, watching the sun set over the Judean hills, he turned to his traveling companions and said, "I know now why all the world wanted this land and why all peoples loved it." For the rest of his life, he would refer to this trip as setting the final seal on his commitment to Zion.[27]

Brandeis' whirlwind tour could by no means yield the total feeling for and knowledge of the land enjoyed by those with close ties or long experience that stretched over many years. Yet he quickly came to grips with the two most important problems facing the Yishuv: the long-term health hazards that would have to be eradicated before the land could absorb new immigration, and the short-term difficulties created by the anti-Zionist attitudes of local British military officials, many of whom had imbibed the romantic pan-Arabism advocated by the legendary T. E. Lawrence, or who, to put it bluntly, were anti-Semitic. Local Zionist representatives and settlers reported high-handedness by the army of occupation, and blatant efforts to ignore Jewish rights in the Yishuv. Brandeis conveyed these charges to General Money, chief administrator for Palestine, and emphasized that he himself had seen evidence to support these accusations. Money, aware of the Justice's connections in Whitehall, quickly fired off a secret dispatch attempting to discredit Brandeis' criticisms before the American jurist could return to Paris: "Mr. Brandeis was of course entirely unable to appreciate that many of the so-called grievances are due to the special characteristics of the Zionist Jews themselves, particularly to their exclusiveness and to the fact that while other communities are ready to act for the common weal, the Jewish view is invariably to their own advantage, and their manner, whenever they are given authority, is often domineering and objectionable to others."[28] The memorandum, obviously a cover-up for the field staff, stood little chance against Brandeis' personal remonstrances with Balfour in Paris that August. The Foreign Secretary, through the War Office, sent copies of the Declaration to ranking army officers in Palestine, pointedly reminding them that this was now official policy. A number of careerists immediately sought "desirable exchanges," and Colonel Richard Meinertzhagen, a Zionist sympathizer, replaced Sir Gilbert Clayton in Jerusalem in charge of the occupation forces. While the immediate benefits to the Yishuv and to British-Zionist relations could be clearly discerned, Brandeis and other Zionist leaders did not yet fully realize that most British officers, especially those who had fought against the Turks, admired the "romantic" Arabs of the desert, and shared the upper-class disdain of Jews as sickly, ghettoized money-lenders.[29]

In Palestine, Brandeis had seen a land ravaged by centuries of neglect and four years of war, yet one that under the settlers'

hands had been made to bloom. In 1919 the Jews constituted a
distinct minority in Palestine, with the eighty thousand members of
the Yishuv far outnumbered by more than six hundred thousand
Arabs. For the Jews ever to develop Palestine into a real homeland, massive immigration would have to redress the population
imbalance. But in 1919, the scourge of malaria made many potentially arable areas unsuitable for agricultural development. To a
mind conditioned to identifying the heart of a problem and its
solution, the logical initial program for developing Palestine lay in
eradicating malaria. Local health officials confirmed Brandeis' view,
as did Hadassah representatives.[30] Until malaria could be con-
quered, the Jewish settlements would continue to suffer enormous
personal and economic losses; at a settlement near Tiberias, seventy-
eight out of eighty workers fell victim to the disease in one summer,
with each person suffering an average of two attacks during the
season.*

To Weizmann and his associates, still worried over the final terms
of the mandate and trying, rather unsuccessfully, to work out administrative problems with the British, the Brandeisian proposal
seemed bizarre and out of place. In a replay of an earlier battle
between "political" and "practical" Zionists, the Americans now
found themselves at odds with those who fifteen years earlier had
attacked Theodore Herzl for his failure to stress the immediate
rebuilding of the homeland. For Brandeis, Zion could only be rebuilt by people, and people could not come until the land had been
made healthy. The administrative disarray, the chaos, the endless
quibbling over seemingly petty issues confused him; he could not
see any relevance or purpose in the Europeans' discussions. The
Pittsburgh program provided a simple philosophical base, and his
experience in Palestine had led him to propose immediate steps
toward implementing the Balfour Declaration. The older Zionists

---

* Brandeis, foiled by the AC in trying to get an antimalarial campaign
mounted in Palestine, donated ten thousand dollars to Hadassah specifically earmarked for malarial control in the Galilee. At this same
farm a year later, only two cases of the sickness were reported, and in
the surrounding area, out of a population of over one thousand, there
were only five cases. Swamp drainage and the planting of eucalyptus
trees proved extremely effective.

seemed obstacles in the way of a new Zionism, one grounded in economic and social realities, cut free from abstract ideological fetters of an earlier time. When the two sides finally sat down for full-scale discussions in London in August 1919, these differences led almost immediately to large cracks in the Zionist coalition.

Although both the European and American leaders proclaimed their respect and admiration for each other, and pledged full cooperation, the public amenities scarcely concealed deep differences in personal outlook as well as policy. For one thing, the Europeans identified their life work much more closely with the movement than did the Americans. In 1918, when the British requested the Zionists to send a commission to Palestine, Weizmann had immediately resigned his position at the University of Manchester to assume the responsibility, and he quickly secured other Europeans to join him. He then asked Brandeis to leave the Supreme Court and join the commission, a path that the American would not even consider. But Brandeis could not get any of the other top ZOA leaders to go either; Stephen Wise, Felix Frankfurter, and Julian Mack all considered their jobs and activities in the United States more important than joining a commission to go to Palestine. For the Europeans, all other considerations had to take a second place to Zionism; for the Americans, no matter how deeply they felt this commitment to the movement, they saw themselves primarily as citizens of the United States, with their major responsibility in this country.

At the Greater Actions Comité meeting, the Europeans wanted the Zionist Commission to take over the leadership of the Yishuv, and assume responsibility for schools, social and political agencies, colonization, and land reclamation, as well as oversee the immigration into the country, and they wanted it done immediately, with the Americans assuming the task of raising the funds. The Americans did not necessarily oppose the ultimate assumption of these operations by the Zionists, and they recognized that, for the immediate future at least, American Jewry would have to provide much of the money for the Yishuv. But Brandeis insisted on an orderly approach, on preparing the land for the immigration, and this meant first of all that sanitary conditions in Palestine would have to be improved, and he pointed to the work of the Hadassah medical unit as an example of the basic steps that should be taken.

In fact, the medical unit, despite its shining record, now proved a sore point between the two groups. Fully financed and controlled by the Americans, it had run into problems with Menachem Ussischkin, the Zionist Commission's representative in Palestine. Dr. Max Rubinow, a noted physician and social worker, headed the medical unit, and as far as he was concerned, he had come to Palestine to treat sickness and establish health facilities, not to make *aliyah* or play politics. Like many of the progressives, he held strong views on efficiency,[31] and the haphazard administrative practices of the Zionists appalled him. Ussischkin insisted that a Zionist medical group should conduct its business in Hebrew, and pointed out that all of the European officials were struggling to master the ancient tongue, since this would contribute to the regeneration of the Yishuv. Rubinow complained about the waste involved and how it detracted from the medical mission they had come on. All of the official letters, for example, that the unit wrote in English had to be sent to Jerusalem to be translated into Hebrew; when they arrived in London, other translaters rewrote them in English. Moreover, as far as learning Hebrew themselves, as Ussischkin urged, they saw no reason to do so. Ben Zion Mossinsohn, head of the first Hebrew-speaking high school in Palestine, later complained: "We had to wage a struggle for every Hebrew word." That fall, the ZOA decided to channel most of its funds into the medical unit, with directions that expenditures be controlled by Dr. Rubinow, and its donations to the other Zionist agencies and funds dropped precipitately.[32]

The two groups also found themselves at loggerheads over the question of the Jewish Agency which the Mandate called for to assist in Palestinian development. Here Weizmann wanted to bring in representatives of the "National Councils" that had sprung up in Eastern Europe after the war to protect Jewish rights. The Zionists would complement their work by the development of Hebrew and Jewish culture in the Diaspora, or *gegenwartsarbeit*. The Americans resolutely opposed such an approach, since it encouraged so-called

Diaspora nationalism, the idea that all Jews, wherever they might be, owed political and national loyalty to a Jewish peoplehood. This philosophy had always been anathema to the Americans, who saw themselves as citizens of the United States, even while recognizing kinship with and a responsibility for fellow Jews. If the National Councils wanted to join in the upbuilding of the homeland, Brandeis argued, then let them pay the shekel and join the WZO. As for the Zionists developing a Jewish consciousness in the Diaspora, the Americans shuddered at the repercussions this would have among their fellow Jews. On this point Brandeis won a temporary victory, but Weizmann remained bitter over it, and began accusing the Brandeis group of lacking a true Jewish national consciousness. American proposals for Palestine, he charged, "were lacking in historic understanding of Jewish life and wanting in Jewish soul."[33]

If these divisions were not enough, the Americans began to suspect that money, which was getting more difficult to raise in the United States, was being wasted by the poor administration of Zionist officials in London and Jerusalem. Jacob deHaas, sent to London to serve as Brandeis' eyes and ears there, began to report his own sense of dismay at the confusion of the London office. Over the next thirty months, these complaints would grow, with the ZOA demanding a strict accounting of funds and a reorganization of the Executive, and the Europeans complaining that their colleagues had no feeling for the people, no real Jewish consciousness, no interest in anything but dollars and cents. When Brandeis sent Robert Kesselman to Palestine to assist in developing sounder administrative practices, the Europeans fought him every step of the way.[34]

With the Americans complaining of their administration and withholding vitally needed funds, the London Executive decided to convene a *Jahreskonferenz,* a meeting of important Zionist officials but a lesser gathering than a full-fledged congress. They wanted to schedule the conference in early 1920, but Brandeis maintained that he would not be able to come until after the Supreme Court adjourned for the summer recess. In private meetings, however, he also indicated that he wanted to replenish the depleted Zionist treasury, so that the American bargaining position at the meeting would be strengthened.[35] Throughout all of this, little of the growing misunderstanding between the Weizmann and Brandeis groups leaked out to the public.[36] Even when the Yiddish press began probing rumors of increasing tension, the American leadership did and said nothing, thus alienating the journalists even more. The American leadership concentrated their efforts on members, money, and administrative reorganization, and on establishing better relations with the Schiff-Marshall forces. Had they done more to explain their position to their own followers, they would have been much stronger at London the following summer, and even the debacle at Cleveland the following year might have been avoided.

IV

In the months preceding the *Jahreskonferenz,* the ZOA threw itself into the task of strengthening its organization and building up its financial resources. Although the 1918 restructuring had solved many problems, the leadership still worried that the ZOA had not yet coalesced into the well-run and efficient agency that would be needed to support Palestinian development in the months and years to come. Moreover, after the high emotional level generated by the war crisis and the peace negotiations, membership and enthusiasm for Zionist work had dropped off sharply. Many who had joined out of momentary concern or to show group loyalty now left the ranks; in this category could be found Alfred Brandeis, the Justice's brother.[37] Zionism, like many other voluntary groups that had benefited from the war hysteria, now found it most difficult to maintain members and enthusiasm in the return to peacetime conditions. Very little attention was paid by the general public to the growing schism in Zionist ranks. For one thing, there was little public evidence of the tension, and much of it was hidden even from ZOA members. For another, the eyes of the country were riveted on Paris to see what sort of peace treaty would emerge from the conference. Also, the emotional highs created by war do not last much past the end of hostilities, and the American public in 1919 was busily trying to pick up the pieces of pre-war life. Moreover, events totally beyond the ZOA's control adversely affected its fortune. A severe postwar depression hit the country in 1920, and those for whom Zionism constituted only a marginal interest found business conditions a convenient excuse for terminating their support. From its high-water mark of 180,000 in the summer of 1919, Zionist membership dropped in less than eighteen months to only 25,000. This continued decline in their ranks steadily eroded the power base that the ZOA needed to successfully challenge the world organization.

But the momentary, and illusory, calm that engulfed the ZOA in early 1920 also allowed the National Executive to begin serious discussion on a plan very close to Brandeis' heart: a limited profit investment corporation. In line with the social democratic principles of the Pittsburgh program, and reflecting his fear of big business duplicating in Palestine the industrial problems of the United States, Brandeis wanted to establish a stock company whose control would be vested in the ZOA, and which would work to build up the homeland. The company would be particularly involved in supporting the export and distribution of Palestinian commodities, and a special effort would be made to secure small investors willing to accept a limited, but fair, return on their capital. Stephen Wise strongly supported this plan as an alternative to giving endless relief, which he felt ultimately degraded the Zionists. The upbuilding of the homeland, and the support America would provide, had to take place in a framework beneficial to both parties, one that would ennoble them.[38] Unfortunately, this desire to provide a constructive alternative to relief later led to charges that the Brandeis leadership wanted to colonize Palestine for small businessmen and wanted to limit all monetary support to business investment; but nothing could have been farther from the truth. The American leadership sought to provide numerous ways in which Jews could support the Yishuv, some through charity, some through investment, but all doing it in a spirit of co-operation rather than as if it were a dole. Ultimately, the Brandeis group did establish a Palestine Economic Corporation in 1926, but it never fulfilled the dreams of its founders.

The opening months of 1920 saw both sides not only maneuvering to strengthen their own positions, but also some individuals attempting to head off a full-scale confrontation at the *Jahreskonferenz.* Felix Frankfurter, who had established mutually respectful if not friendly relations with Weizmann during the peace negotiations, had been trying for nearly two years to impress upon the British chemist that tact and patience would be necessary for the two sides to understand that despite tactical differences, they still agreed on common goals. "You must permit us to discuss things with you," he urged, but "be patient enough to show us we are wrong. . . . It's a simple thing we want—that we be allowed to co-operate with you, in thought and action. And less—on sober thought—you would not want."[39] The Europeans, however, rebuffed such efforts, and on several occasions tried to send their orators to the United States to build up sentiment on their behalf, a strategy that infuriated the ZOA leadership. With the American public already beginning to retreat from Wilsonian internationalism, the Executive Committee felt that both Jews and non-Jews would be antagonized by European Zionists traveling around the country promoting the cause. Bitter at this attempt by the London group to subvert the ZOA's authority, Brandeis sarcastically suggested that the Argentine would be a better place for the WZO to make *stimmung* [sentiment].[40] Communications between London and New York deteriorated in the spring, as the ZOA vainly tried to get the world organization to declare its position on proposals for future action. On the eve of the conference, and after a series of unanswered letters, the ZOA's Palestine secretary, Marvin Lowenthal, condemned the WZO for refusing to divulge what it had done in specific programs, information that should have been available to all Zionists.[41]

Brandeis himself headed the large, twenty-nine-member delegation to the *Jahreskonferenz,* which opened in London on June 22, 1920. The Zionists had not held a major meeting since the 1913 Congress, but despite the massive growth and achievements of the war years, the atmosphere at Memorial Hall was tense and gloomy. The American leadership by this point distrusted Weizmann and his colleagues, and stood more or less committed to the proposition that they would only co-operate with and support the WZO if it agreed to a basic reorganization that would bring efficiency and order out of the administrative chaos that had plagued Zionist work since the end of the war.[42] Brandeis had also won over an important convert in Julius Simon, an economist and member of the WZO Executive who had worked closely with Weizmann for the past four years. Simon had come to the United States in the spring at Brandeis' invitation to work out practical details for Palestinian immigration. There he discovered that one of Brandeis' closest advisers, Jacob deHaas, stood at the center of the anti-Weizmann agitation. But Simon also recognized that much of the Brandeisian criticism of the World Zionist Organization was all too justified, and in conversations with the Justice in Washington, New York, and on the boat over to London, Simon swung over to support the basic principles of reorganization that the Americans wanted. More importantly, Simon decided that only Brandeis could successfully head the world organization in the trying years to come, and upon arrival in London, he went straightaway to see Weizmann, whom he implored to make the final grand gesture: "Chaim, you have rendered an immortal service to the Jewish people and now I want you to crown your work by offering the leadership to Mr. Brandeis." When Felix Frankfurter heard this, he told Simon, "You couldn't have said anything worse." Weizmann's jealousy of the Americans, and his suspicions of them, were now inflamed.[43]

The question of Brandeis' role in the movement occupied the attention of many of the Zionist leaders gathering in London. Nearly all of them wanted him to assume active leadership of the movement, and there is little doubt that the presidency of the WZO could have been his for the asking. The Americans controlled the bulk of the financial resources, and the British Government had great respect for the Justice personally. Although they resented the tone of his criticism, the Europeans had to admit that he was all too right in attacking the slipshod methods of the administration. Although he seriously considered the idea, and rumors flew thick and fast that he would step down from the Supreme Court, in the end, Brandeis chose to remain on the bench. This decision undercut the ZOA's bargaining position at the London conference, but it truly reflected the American nature of the Brandeis leadership. In 1916, Wilson's nomination of him to the Court had precipitated one of the most bitter struggles of the entire progressive era, one in which the alignments of reformers and standpatters could be clearly discerned.

The President had put his prestige, and a good part of his re-election hopes, on the line, and hundreds of progressives had worked energetically to secure confirmation. Brandeis himself had originally been grateful to Wilson for the honor of the nomination, but not particularly eager to leave the battlefield of social reform for the sanctuary of the Court. As the lines had formed, however, he came to recognize that progressives all over the country looked to him, not only as a symbol of reform, but as a hope for introducing a more flexible and humane awareness of social problems into the Court's deliberations. During the war, Wilson had been tempted on several occasions to ask Brandeis to resign to assume a high-level position in the Administration, but he too felt that, in the long run, Brandeis' value to the progressive faith as a jurist far outweighed the temporary needs of war. His loyalty to his fellow reformers by itself would have prevented Brandeis' resignation, but even beyond that lay the whole question of the synthesis he had forged between Zionism and Americanism. For six years now he had argued that one could be a good American and a good Zionist, that the obligations and loyalties of the two did not conflict. For him, the first Jew ever to sit on the Supreme Court, to leave the bench that he considered "the highest tribunal in the world" would give the lie to all that he had said; it would have proved that Zionists placed their first allegiance to the movement.

On board the *Lapland,* however, and several times during the London meeting, Brandeis gave serious consideration to the plea that he assume the leadership. DeHaas and Lipsky, supported by the Eastern Europeans, pushed him vigorously on this point, but Felix Frankfurter kept telling him that he had a higher obligation, both to American Jews and American reformers, to stay on the Court. Brandeis reached his final decision only after he had met with Bernard Rosenblatt, a young American lawyer whom Brandeis had sent on a fact-finding mission to Palestine. At breakfast on July 4, Rosenblatt told the Justice (a man thirty years his senior and whom he revered) that he doubted if Brandeis was temperamentally fit to lead the movement. "As the first Jewish member of the United States Supreme Court you can be a very important figure for us," Rosenblatt argued. "If you become the leader of Zionism, you'll have to go to Palestine; you'll have to meet opposition, difficulties, disputes with Ussischkin, and I don't know whether it wouldn't be a means of breaking you." The Zionist methods were so alien to the efficiency and rationality of American business and adminstrative techniques that it might prove too frustrating to Brandeis.[44] The strangeness of Zionist methods would be borne home to the Justice quite clearly at the *Jahreskonferenz*.

Prior to the formal opening of the meeting in mid-July, members of the Executive gathered in London in the last week of June to confer with the Americans in an effort to work out their differences privately and quietly. These closed sessions got off to a rickety start on June 22, with charges and countercharges about reorganization filling the air. The Americans wanted a total restructuring of the world Executive, with the transfer of operations to Jerusalem and the shift of emphasis from political to practical work.[45] Weizmann and the Europeans agreed that immigration held the key to the future development of Palestine, and demanded to know how much the Americans would give. Here the Europeans touched on a sore point. The ZOA leaders had been stewing for more than a year in their belief that the world organization wanted money, and nothing but money, from the United States. But the fact of the matter was that collections in 1920 had dropped off precipitately. At the moment Weizmann asked how much American Jewry would give, ZOA accounts stood thirty thousand dollars in the red. Julian Mack, who did not attend the conference because of a severe circulatory infection, urged his colleagues to impress "upon everybody in the organization that not one penny is to be wasted. The effort to get it is much too strenuous." Brandeis had little choice but to admit that it would be difficult to predict how much they could raise, but warned that it would be impossible to raise anything unless they eliminated waste and inefficiency in the movement and adopted precise and effective plans to develop the homeland.[46]

The American leaders, often without consulting the other members of the delegation, began pushing for a plan that would vest power in an Executive of seven, three of whom would be English non-Zionists: Lord Reading, Sir Alfred Mond, and Baron James de Rothschild. The four Zionists would be Weizmann and Sokolow for the Europeans, Brandeis and Bernard Flexner for the Americans. Reading, Mond, and the Baron agreed to work for Palestine provided they would not have to stand for election, so Brandeis proposed a plan that would have the four Zionist members elected to the Executive, with power to co-opt three more persons. The European delegates, disgruntled at the idea of giving non-Zionists so much power, nonetheless felt that out of deference to Brandeis, they should speak with the three men and explain to them the functions of the Executive as they would have them executed. At one o'clock in the morning, as deHaas reported, Mond and Rothschild came out of a hotel room "worried about being responsible for Hebrew education in Palestine and other problems which had nothing to do with the work they had been asked to do. Brandeis had talked to them about the economic upbuilding of Palestine, not the cultural program."[47]

It would be unfair to say that Brandeis had no interest in cultural work, in the restoration of Hebrew or the development of arts, since he had often praised the work of Eliezar Ben Yehuda and others. But to his logical mind, the main problem confronting the movement in 1920 was economic: how to build up an economy to support the large numbers of immigrants who would ultimately make Palestine in truth a Jewish homeland. To do this he felt it necessary to bring in wealthy non-Zionist Jews, many of whom, like Schiff and Marshall, had already indicated their willingness to help, and to emphasize economic expertise and ability over oratorical skills or propaganda experience. The old-line Zionists, however, greeted Brandeis' proposal with horror. After they had spent more than two decades of labor and devotion, of traveling into thousands of *shtetls* to preach the doctrine of restoration, who was this American judge with no sense of true Jewishness, no *Yiddishkeit,* to tell them that they should voluntarily withdraw in favor of "experts"? Even for those who agreed that skilled and efficient administrators had to be brought into the movement, this proved too much.

Although Weizmann had initially agreed to the Brandeis proposal, pressure from Ussischkin, Levin, and Sokolow now forced him to change his mind. In place of seats on the Executive, he offered the three outsiders leadership of an advisory council that would deal only with economic problems and policies, a proposal quite attractive to them, and which would leave political and cultural work in the hands of Zionists on the Executive. There also seems to have been agreement among the Europeans that in order to show their good faith in emphasizing economic development, Brandeis would be elected head of the Executive. But the Justice, when informed of this alteration in plans, charged Weizmann with duplicity. The Europeans had agreed to the Brandeis plan, and then, without consulting the Americans, had offered a new proposal to the three non-Zionists. From that moment on, in Brandeis' eyes, Weizmann could no longer be trusted.

At the opening session of the *Jahreskonferenz* on July 7, however, Brandeis did accept the chairmanship of the meeting, symbolically pointing to the shift of power in the movement across the Atlantic. In his speech, the Justice nearly glowed with enthusiasm over the possibilities of work in Palestine, and the great responsibility that now lay upon all Zionists. The nations of the world had done all they could do through the Balfour Declaration and the mandate. "The rest lies with us. The task before us is the Jewish settlement of Palestine. It is the task of reconstruction. We must approve the plans on which the reconstruction shall proceed. We must create the executive and administrative machinery adapted to the work before us. We must select men of the training, the experience and the character fitted to conduct that work. And finally we must devise ways and means to raise the huge sums which the undertaking demands. For without these funds, the best of plans, perfect machinery, the most capable of devoted men, will avail us naught and the noble purpose which we have set ourselves would be defeated."[48]

One week later, a disillusioned Brandeis met with the American delegation. The conference had been a source of constant frustration and disappointment to him. Used to the clear reasoning of the law and the calmer rhetoric of progressive reformers, the babel of voices at London, all yelling and shouting and haggling over minor irrelevant points of doctrine, revolted him. He had come to London to help build a Jewish homeland, not preside over a "talkfest." The Europeans, in turn, had been equally upset over Brandeis' insistence on parliamentary procedures, on his emphasis on economics and his lack of *Yiddishkeit*. He had insulted them when he complained that shekel money should not be used to pay the expenses of old-line Zionists, and it certainly would have been tactful of him not to call men like Yehial Tschlenow and Leo Motzkin "pensioners," men who had devoted their lives to the movement.[49] Worst of all had been Weizmann's double-dealing, his refusal (or, as it turned out, his inability) to keep his word to Brandeis, and even some of Weizmann's friends had berated him for failing to deal honestly with the Americans. In these circumstances, Brandeis told the delegation, it would be impossible for him to go on the Executive, nor did he want any other Americans to join that group. The Europeans would easily outvote any American representatives, and thus without being able to influence policy, their presence would be interpreted as condoning a bad program. The Executive had to be transformed, and men of skill and ability brought into the movement. The time for propaganda had ended, and the time for work begun, whether the Europeans recognized this or not.[50]

Although there had been grumbling about Brandeis' leadership before, the U.S. delegates now grew visibly agitated and almost broke away from his decision not to place any Americans on the Executive. Only the Justice's personal intervention forced the delegates to yield to his motion that no American accept any position other than the honorary presidency, which carried no responsibility.[51] This decision ultimately led to the downfall of the Brandeis/Mack administration. The American delegates did not object to Brandeis' economic plans nor to his charges of inefficiency in the world administration, which were all too true; but they did object to this abdication of both power and responsibility, and those who shared a deep commitment to cultural work resented his apparent denigration of that aspect of Zionism. From this point on, Weizmann would insist that Brandeis could not criticize the Executive since he had refused to assume the responsibility. Rather than defend his policies, he would offer to give up all power to the Brandeis group, if only they would assume the burden that went with it. Brandeis had too long been the "silent leader" of the ZOA, hidden in Washington, sending out directives through his lieutenants. The world movement had no need of silent leaders.

Brandeis left London in August aboard the *Zeeland,* frustrated in his efforts to reform the WZO and embittered by Weizmann's seeming duplicity. While sailing home, Brandeis drafted an eleven-point memorandum summarizing his plans and ideas for the development of Palestine. The objective of all Zionist work should be "to populate Palestine within a comparatively short time with a preponderating body of manly self-supporting Jews who will develop into a homogeneous people with high Jewish ideals; will develop and apply there the Jewish spiritual and intellectual ideals; and will utimately become a self-governing commonwealth." He then reviewed the difficulties attendant to rebuilding a land ravaged by war and centuries of neglect, and proceeded to spell out practical means by which the ZOA could implement the ideas earlier enumerated in the Pittsburgh program. The *"Zeeland* memorandum," as it became known, epitomized Brandeis' insistence on the primacy of economic development and on the need to substitute energy and direction for *stimmung*. It reflected those traits that Robert Wiebe has termed the progressive "search for order," but neglected the cultural and emotional needs so important to the Eastern Europeans. The document also indicated Brandeis' conviction that the political stage of Zionism had come to an end. With the Balfour Declaration and the mandate, the Jews had won international recognition of their right to a homeland in Palestine. Now they should direct all of their energies and resources into making a reality of this opportunity.

From Brandeis' landing in New York in late August until the 1921 convention turned them out of office, the Brandeis/Mack group stood on this platform: the reorganization of the Zionist administration and agencies to bring in experts; the phasing out of political Zionism and the emphasizing of economic work; and fiscal responsibility and prudence in Zionist affairs. If at London the vacillation of the Weizmann group had blurred these issues, by the time the American Zionists met in Cleveland the following June, these differences had been crystallized.

V

Throughout the fall and winter of 1920–21, the Brandeis/Mack leadership tried to bolster its position among American Jews, but the cleavage between leaders and followers widened considerably. A number of the Yiddish journalists, even when they supported Brandeis' plan, objected to the dictatorial manner in which he had forced it upon the American delegation.[52] By the end of September, Horace Kallen felt it necessary to introduce a vote of confidence in the leadership at a meeting of the National Executive Committee, and Julian Mack agreed that the Brandeis platform either had to be endorsed or repudiated. Young Abba Hillel Silver, who two decades later would assume the burden of leadership himself during the fight to create Israel, and who then counted himself a follower of Brandeis, confessed that he had felt humiliated at London by the failure of the leaders even to consult with the delegation over crucial issues. Silver agreed that no one wanted to overthrow Brandeis, but the facts of the matter could not be denied; the "silent leader" had lost touch with his following.

Emanuel Neumann, then only twenty-seven years old but destined to play a crucial role in the birth of Israel, immediately picked up this theme, and charged that an "invisible government" had grown up over the previous few years; he saw a dangerous trend in the desire of Brandeis to have the ZOA go it alone, independent of the world movement. It remained for Louis Lipsky, the faithful workhorse of American Zionism, to put his finger on the point troubling many of the Committee members. He had loyally followed the leadership even when it had adopted policies not in accord with his own personal judgment. But Brandeis had, at least, led them. At London the Justice had been offered full responsibility and authority to direct the movement, and had refused. Now he wanted to call the tune without the responsibility; he declined to lead, yet refused to follow. This lack of focus, this abdication by Brandeis, had made the London conference an exercise in futility, and was now robbing the American movement of any sense of purpose.

Lipsky's speech cut dangerously close to home, for in fact Brandeis had become the victim of a delusion that he could lead *in absentia*. A man of reason, he naively believed that his ideas, and not his personality, had been the unifying force in the ZOA. But the masses had followed *him* with only a few of them paying critical attention to his program. As long as his ideas led toward the creation of a

Jewish homeland, they remained satisfied. But it had been the personal leadership of an Americanized and successful Jew, a confidant of the President of the United States and a Justice of the Supreme Court, that galvanized the transformation of a weak and impotent Federation of American Zionists into the powerful and influential Zionist Organization of America. The program Brandeis put forward had guided that change, but it could not have been executed without him. In fairness to Brandeis, it is obvious that personal vanity played very little part in this. That he could at times be a proud and stubborn man is indisputable, yet he never considered himself a charismatic leader, and probably did not understand the demand for his personal leadership. If at any time before the Cleveland convention he had agreed to assume the mantle, the cries against his policies would have been stilled immediately; without his presence, however, the masses would accept no program handed down as an edict from Washington. This opposition precluded a vote of confidence as early as September 1920, and the National Executive Committee adjourned after naming a special subcommittee to draft a resolution dealing with the problems confronting the ZOA. In it they would try to harmonize loyalty to the world organization and support of the *Zeeland* memorandum, confidence in the Mack/Brandeis leadership and adherence to democracy in the ranks. It was an impossible task.[53]

Throughout that winter, the debate raged in the Yiddish press. Epithets such as "dictator" and "autocrat" were now hurled at Brandeis, and one cartoon showed him placing a crown on his head, declaring, *"Le Zionisme est moi!"* Article after article analyzed the *Zeeland* document as well as Brandeis' proposals to the London conference; some found them wanting, while others declared them just the presciption for Zionist success. But the common thread running throughout this journalistic cacophony was an appeal for Brandeis to come out of his judicial cave and lead them again. His plans would work, more than one editorialist avowed, only if the Justice himself directed them.[54] In London, meanwhile, Benjamin V. Cohen and Vladimir Jabotinsky tried to find some middle ground that would enable Weizmann and Brandeis to make peace, and Brandeis himself urged Weizmann to come to the United States, where they could settle matters.[55] At the annual convention of the ZOA in Buffalo in November, 1920, Stephen Wise spoke for the administration, and declared "there is no such thing as a European Zionist point of view against an American Zionist point of view." He could not help adding, however, that some of the Europeans stood for Zionism first, and Zion second, while Americans placed Zion above Zionism. As a peace-making effort, it was not a success.[56]

And yet, surprisingly, after the emotionalism of the newspaper debate in the preceding two months, the Buffalo convention voted overwhelmingly to support the Brandeis program, and shouted through a thoroughgoing vote of confidence in the administration. In apprising Weizmann of this, one of the delegates warned him not to be misled by the newspaper battle. The convention had endorsed the Brandeisian program, and repudiated the "democratic agitators." A Yiddish reporter, writing in *Der Tag,* asserted: "At the convention it transpired that so-called anti-Brandeis legends about his despotism, separatism and the like, were groundless, and that he is now even more than ever needed by the organization."[57] On the surface, at least, it seemed that the administration had easily weathered the first serious challenge to its leadership.

But appearances could be deceptive, and anyone who thought that the anti-administration faction would now shrivel up and disappear would have been wrong. The Brandeis/Mack group remained in power not because a majority of the delegates approved their behavior, but because they had no other choice. If the American leadership left, who would take its place? Emanuel Neumann and others who opposed the administration, moreover, did not really want to expel the leadership. They wanted more of a say in determining ZOA policies, as well as more communication between the leaders and the lower-echelon officials. The administration still had prestige, and it had a definite program against which the opposition could offer little more than the charges of authoritarianism and separatism. Furthermore, it is likely that many of the delegates still did not understand the issues separating the ZOA from the London Executive, for when the administration called for a resolution against the commingling of donation and investment funds, the issue that would split the ZOA apart in little more than six months, the convention readily approved.

The Buffalo gathering solved nothing. All that was needed was a focus for the discontent, and the following spring, when Chaim Weizmann came to America for the first time, the dissidents found the missing catalyst.

VI

Weizmann had been planning to come to the United States for a long time, but work on the Palestine Commission, at the Peace Conference, and on the Executive had delayed the trip. The Americans also wanted him to visit, the masses to show their gratitude, and the leadership to get him to understand the local conditions they faced. Unfortunately, by the time he arrived in April, the air had been so poisoned that only die-hard optimists still cherished illusory hopes of peace. At the London conference the preceding summer, the Europeans had proposed an annual budget of nearly two million pounds, and admitted that most of it would have to come from the United States. The Americans saw this as an astronomical sum, and protested that they could not realistically expect to raise more than one hundred thousand pounds. Weizmann, defending the need for the larger sum, said that if the Americans did not think they could get it, he would have to come over to try himself, a gratuitous remark that undoubtedly insulted the ZOA officers.

Then in January 1921, the one agency that might have served to smooth over differences between the opposing factions came apart at the seams, when Nehemiah deLieme and Julius Simon resigned from the Reorganization Commission, and charged the Weizmann Executive with deliberately undermining their work.

One of the few practical results of the *Jahreskonferenz* had been the creation of a Reorganization Commission to look into Zionist work in Palestine and to recommend changes in the Executive. For the Commission, the delegates chose Julius Simon and Nehemiah deLieme, the former a close associate of Weizmann and the latter a Dutch businessman, each of whom was acceptable to both sides in the dispute. The two men then co-opted Robert Szold, a young

American lawyer, in order to have American representation. The
Commission arrived in Palestine in November 1920 to find that Zionist work did in fact need restructuring, and despite their dissimilar
backgrounds, all three found themselves in basic agreement on most
of the fundamental questions facing them. They proceeded eagerly
with their work, since Weizmann had promised them before they
left that their recommendations would be supported. But the more
they probed, the more the old-line Zionists grew upset, especially
Menahem Ussischkin, an implacable foe of the Brandeis approach,
who represented the WZO in Jerusalem. The Commission found local
needs enormous, even for food, while resources could most chari-
tably be described as "limited." In going over the budget, Szold
found an item for a music school in Damascus. When he asked Ussischkin about it, the latter declared that not a single Zionist outpost
could be abandoned. Szold pleaded with him to understand that with
restricted funds, a choice had to be made. How could the Zionists
spend scarce dollars on a music school when unemployed immigrants
were starving? Ussischkin exploded. "Mr. Szold, you want that I
should give up my eye or my arm. I give up neither." When
Szold looked on increduously at this response, Ussischkin added,
"The trouble with you, Mr. Szold, is that I am a *kranker yid* [a sick
Jew] and you are a *gezunter goy* [a healthy Gentile]."[58]

The Commission, which some of its sponsors had hoped would
mediate the Brandeis-Weizmann dispute insofar as it regarded administrative matters, was doomed from the start. With the Brandeis
forces in self-imposed exile, no influential group supported the Commission's criticisms and proposals. The mismanagement of the many
Palestinian officials led them, naturally, to be resentful of the Commission's investigation, and since they constituted the heart of the
Weizmann clique, he could hardly be expected to condemn them.
Upon receiving the Commission's report, Weizmann told Simon
that it fell into "two parts—a beautiful part and a new one. The
new part is not beautiful and the beautiful part is not new," and
then proceeded to attack it vehemently. In one speech where he
criticized the Commission's recommendations on temporarily limiting funds for education, Weizmann demagogically exclaimed: "Who
attacks the Hebrew schools attacks the Hebrew God." On January

20, 1912, after the Executive refused to discuss their recommendations, deLieme and Simon formally resigned, and the Americans had
every reason to believe that the Weizmann group had never had any
intention of carrying out meaningful reform. The experience of the
Commission added up to more proof of Weizmann's apparent duplicity and double-dealing, and the Americans accused the London
office of deliberately undermining the Commission's work.[59]

Weizmann himself did little to heal the breach. In a long letter
to Julian Mack, he unburdened himself of his findings regarding the
ZOA, and accused it of trying to set itself up as an opposition
party. Although he said he would do almost anything within reason
to make peace, the tone of his letter could hardly be considered
conciliatory. At a meeting of the Executive just before he left for
the United States, Weizmann charged that the Brandeis policy was
an impossible one, and vowed to eliminate those who would not
follow the WZO in uniting world Jewry behind work in Palestine.[60]

On the American side, a number of dissident groups recognized
that Weizmann's visit would mark a turning point in Zionist affairs.
Baruch Zuckerman openly called for Dr. Weizmann to assume the
leadership of the many American Jews "not mortgaged to the Brandeis
group." Lipsky, Abe Goldberg, Abraham Tulin, Reuben Brainin, Zvi
Masliansky, and Bernard Richards began laying the groundwork for
the Keren Hayesod, the new financial fund created at the *Jahreskonferenz* to which Brandeis strongly objected; they also pleaded openly
with Weizmann to support their efforts. Bernard Rosenblatt, torn
between his personal loyalty to Brandeis and his intellectual sympathy with the Europeans, met with Samuel Untermyer, a successful lawyer previously unidentified with Zionism, and secured his
promise to head a campaign to raise funds for Palestine.[61]

The unwillingness of the ZOA administration to bend, as well as
its failure to be more candid with the leaders of the Yiddish community, also exacerbated feelings. Abe Goldberg, who had adored
Brandeis and defended administration policy in the Yiddish press,
finally felt he had to part company with a leadership that would
not confide in him or grant him responsibility. In the nine months
after the London conference, he told Mack, he had never been consulted on any of the major issues, and had reluctantly come to the

conclusion that "no matter how able and even ingenious one may be, he stands little or no chance to be treated as an equal and accepted in the good company of the leaders if he should happen to be of Russian-Jewish parentage."[62] Those who had fought the American Jewish Committee for democracy in American Jewish affairs had now seemingly become *yahudim* themselves.

Weizmann arrived in New York on April 3, and while his ship waited in quarantine, he received a note from Judge Mack summarizing the ZOA position, which had been approved by the National Executive two weeks earlier. The ZOA set forth six principles it hoped the Weizmann group could accept, and if they did, Mack saw no reason for any further friction between them. The ZOA called for the upbuilding of Palestine as against *gegenwartsarbeit* (cultural work) and Diaspora nationalism, the inclusion of non-Zionists in this work, and the emphasis on the homeland as a cultural center rather than as a state. In administrative matters, the Americans wanted a separation of investment from donation monies in the Keren Hayesod, a proper and efficient budgeting system, and strong national federations rather than one powerful, centralized office. For Weizmann, the memorandum could hardly be interpreted as an olive branch. In his eyes, it made the local branches dominant over the Executive and made efficient economic work in Palestine the *sine qua non* of the movement. Moreover, the Americans obviously seemed willing to sacrifice any sense of the organic or national purpose of the Jewish people.[63] Given the background of the Mack/Brandeis group, it is understandable how and why they reached this position; given Weizmann's origins and experiences, it is clear that he not only had to reject it, but to fight it as well.

The reception he received that day certainly gave him every reason to believe that if he did challenge the American leadership, he would have the support of the masses. They turned out by the thousands to greet him in a mass demonstration organized against the wishes of the leadership. As he came off the boat, tens of thousands of Jews cheered him, including a special delegation of immigrants from his hometown of Motele. They responded to his Yiddish folksiness, for here stood a man who had become a world-famous chemist and had bargained for the Jewish people in the corridors of power, but who had not lost his Jewish heart. In many ways, they saw the honors heaped upon Weizmann—the keys to the city and later a courtesy visit with President Harding—as honors for the entire Jewish people, a feeling that Weizmann supporters did their best to encourage. In the Yiddish press, the editorial and feature writers outdid themselves in their grandiose interpretations of how the United States, by honoring Weizmann, recognized the greatness and glory of the Jewish nation. Moreover, the world's greatest scientist, Dr. Albert Einstein, promulgator of the immensely important (although to them incomprehensible) theory of relativity, had journeyed to the United States with Weizmann to raise funds for the Hebrew university in Jerusalem. A few days after his arrival, Einstein said everything he had to say about the Zionist controversy during a rally at a Park Avenue armory. The great physicist gave one of the shortest speeches on record, and certainly the shortest one that evening. After a grandiose introduction, he stood up and declared: *"Unser und euer führer, Dr. Weizmann, hat geshproken; folgt ihm!"* ("Your leader and ours, Dr. Weizmann, has spoken; heed him!") and sat down.[64]

Weizmann, while aware that he might have to fight in the end, nonetheless wanted to make peace if he could, if for no other reason than that a struggle with the ZOA leadership, no matter what the outcome, would hurt the movement. For five days he met daily with Judge Mack and other members of the National Executive Committee. At first, Weizmann tried to avoid discussing the memorandum Mack had sent him, and insisted that he had come to the United States only to establish the Keren Hayesod. Mack declared that the ZOA did not oppose the new agency as a donation fund, but that it could not approve a commingling of donations with investment money, and suggested that a separate corporation could be created to handle just investments. Stephen Wise tried to explain that unlike Europeans, Americans expected that their contributions to Palestine would be handled in an efficient and businesslike manner; mixing of funds would not create the necessary confidence in the KH. But their guest would not be swayed. Either the ZOA would co-operate with the world organization, said Weizmann, or he would "colonize" the United States with Zionists favorable to his plan. If the Americans insisted on their demands, then they should also be willing to take over the responsibility for the movement. Mack, inwardly fuming, suggested that perhaps another alternative existed, namely cooperation between the two groups. On this futile plea for harmony, the first day's negotiations ended.

The next morning, Wise, Mack, and Frankfurter all appealed to Weizmann to listen to reason, and to assert his own leadership. They reminded him that he had previously agreed that the particular operations and methods for establishing the KH should be determined by the needs and practices of each country; within the ZOA Executive Committee both the leadership and the opposition agreed that there should be no commingling of funds. Pointedly reminding Weizmann of what they had done during the war to serve the Yishuv, they also urged him to remember that they had been among the first to declare their support of his leadership and had never tried to take it away from him. Ussischkin, however, seemed intent on forcing the issue, and pushed Weizmann to hold his ground, to declare that the Americans had to follow the will of the world organization. The American leaders, convinced not only of the rightness of their position but also of its moderateness, said they would leave the final determination to the organization, but they would resign from their own offices before accepting a policy so contrary to basic principles.[65]

It is probable that, with some exceptions, neither side wanted a direct confrontation, since as events ultimately proved, both sides *in practice* agreed more than they disagreed. Between that first conference at the beginning of April and the dénouement at Cleveland two months later, several moderates tried desperately to find a common ground to preserve unity in the ranks. Bernard Rosenblatt suggested joint control of the Keren Hayesod bureau in the United States, with fair representation for both sides. Some of the Yiddish-speaking leaders who had worked in the Congress even brought in Louis Marshall as a peacemaker.[66] Finally, at a meeting of the National Executive on April 16, this pressure led Weizmann to offer a compromise acceptable to Mack. The KH would be immediately established, but for the time being it would be solely a donation fund. The disposition of the monies collected would be left to the discretion of the world Executive, but two men, to be nominated by the ZOA, would join that body. Finally, the entire issue would be submitted to the next Zionist Congress, which would ultimately decide the questions involved.[67] The Americans joyously accepted, and both sides named representatives to draw up a formal agreement for publication. The compromise, on the face of it, served the best interests of all concerned, and most importantly, served the best interests of the Zionist movement. Weizmann would have his Keren Hayesod, with the ZOA conceding the primacy of the world organization; moreover, by co-opting two Americans onto the Executive, the Americans would have to assume some of the responsibility of leadership. For Mack the principle of no commingling would be followed until the congress met, when he felt confident that reason would prevail; the two members of the Executive, while not exercising control, would nonetheless have an important say in policy.

Unfortunately, extremists stepped in to sabotage this agreement. While Leonard Stein, Abraham Tulin, and Bernard Rosenblatt, representing Weizmann, met with Judge Mack's designee, Samuel Rosensohn, at the Yale Club, Weizmann found himself faced with a revolt if he signed the agreement. Shmaryahu Levin threatened to return on the next boat to Europe to break Weizmann politically, while Ussischkin and Ben Zion Mossinsohn promised to do the same thing in Palestine. Emanuel Neumann and Louis Lipsky, who had been among the American leaders supporting Weizmann, declared they would go on the stump to denounce him as a traitor to Zionism. They all demanded that Weizmann break off the talks and establish a KH bureau responsible only to the WZO. Torn between pressure to negotiate and opposition to any concession, Weizmann had finally reached the point of decision. While he might have wanted a compromise, he too had given signs all along that he had come to America ready to fight. On the morning of April 17, he rejected the agreement he had offered less than twenty-four hours before, broke off all talks with Judge Mack, and proclaimed the establishment of the Keren Hayesod in the United States. Mack, informed of this decision, immediately denounced Weizmann's perfidy, and disassociated the ZOA from the Keren Hayesod.[68]

Despite some last-minute efforts to mediate,[69] both sides now began to pick up steam in their careening toward a headlong collision at the ZOA convention in Cleveland at the beginning of June. Mack demanded Lipsky's resignation, and Lipsky in turn accused the Mack group of endangering the entire Zionist movement. Brandeis, upon hearing of Weizmann's action, came up to New York from Washington to rally the troops personally. His suspicions of Weizmann now seemed fully confirmed. At London he had negotiated in good faith with the chemist, only to see him break his word; now the same thing had happened again. For Brandeis, as much the Puritan as the Zionist, the whole matter no longer represented one man's opinion of policy against another, but involved questions of honesty and principle. To his lieutenants he declared: "Our aim is the kingdom of heaven, paraphrasing Cromwell. We take Palestine by the way. But we must take it with clean hands; we must take it in such a way as to ennoble the Jewish people. Otherwise it will not be worth having."[70] *The New Palestine,* a weekly devoted to carrying the administration's views, made its appearance as the leaders began, belatedly, mending their political fences; reason and logic hopefully would bring the masses to their side. Even before the break, Brandeis had advised Mack that if Weizmann persisted in his stubbornness, the ZOA should allow him to establish the Keren Hayesod under protest, and the administration should then declare "a perfectly definite, immovable policy and to have them adjust themselves to our policy." If, in the end, reason did not prevail, Brandeis declared, there would be no choice but to resign.[71]

Weizmann, in turn, barnstormed the country, shouting, "there is no bridge between Pinsk and Washington," while Meyer Weisgal edited the *New Maccabean,* devoted to the support of Weizmann and his policies. Emanuel Neumann took control of the Keren Hayesod, and reported that by the convention they would have raised $250,000, proving that American Jews supported the world organization. The most damaging count against the Brandeis group was that it had become too separated from its followers, too remote from real Zionist work, and Weizmann eloquently and effectively pounded this charge home in speech after speech. The real issue, he averred, was not economic policy but commitment. Those who criticized his leadership refused to assume responsibility; they talked, but would not act. He time and again dramatically declared that if the Brandeis/Mack group would say, "*We* are prepared to go to Palestine. *We* are prepared to endure the same hell which you are enduring. *We* are prepared to fix a definite program for the work in Palestine," that moment he would gladly respond, "Gentlemen, I am not agreed with your program, but if the Jewish people approve of it, I will serve you and you can carry on the work." In the press, his followers stressed this theme that the Americanized leadership no longer represented real Zionism, and that Jews should be grateful to learn that the movement in America could carry on without them. Despite their earlier contributions to the cause, they had never allowed the movement to grow or flourish in the United States; now Weizmann, a real Jew, could show them the true power of Zionism.[72]

VII

When the convention met in Cleveland on June 5, 1921, both groups predicted victory, but in fact the momentum had clearly gone over on the side of the administration's opponents. The Weizmann party dramatically entered the hall shortly after Judge Mack gaveled the meeting to order, and touched off a five-minute demonstration that ended with the singing of the Zionist anthem, "Hatikvah." The leaders lost no time in getting down to business, and forgoing the usual small talk, Julian Mack presented the story of the ZOA's negotiations with the Weizmann group, and how the Europeans had reneged on their word. Despite constant interruptions from the audience, Mack drew the issues in terms that meant a good deal to the leadership—"method, procedure, order, propriety, right, correctness, following all agreements and orders and mandates." To Mack's credit, he did not try to fudge on any of these subjects, nor to blur the sharp divisions among those present. He rejected completely the demand that the Zionists foster Diaspora nationalism, and declared "that there is no political tie binding together the Jews of the world, but that politically the Jewish citizens of the United States are exclusively American citizens. . . . Fellow Zionists, we want no legalized, political Ghetto here or in Palestine. We want a living, breathing Jewish Nation, in Palestine and of Palestine."[73]

The first sign of the final results came in the election for permanent chairman of the convention. Stephen Wise rose to nominate Mack, and as he praised Mack's fairness, Bernard Rosenblatt called out, "He's a good judge, but not in his own case." Wise turned to the heckler, who owed his judgeship in New York to Democratic politics, and scornfully asked, "What do you think this is, a Tammany courthouse?" Rosenblatt, confident that his side had the votes, yelled back, "No, and it isn't a free synagogue either," as the convention roared.[74] When the vote came, the anti-administration forces easily elected Judge Harry Dannenbaum of Texas by 139 to 75. Despite much debate, and still further efforts at eleventh-hour peacemaking, neither side would now back down. The Brandeis/Mack group believed too strongly in the tenets they had enunciated, and bitter experience convinced them that Weizmann's word could not be trusted. The European delegation, framing the issues in terms of unity, could not allow any national federation to dictate terms. Ironically, their arguments for supremacy of the WZO reflected many of the points Brandeis had used in his restructuring of the American movement three years before. Unfortunately, many of the delegates did not realize that in a fight like this, the opposing antagonists had already destroyed any grounds for reconciliation after the decision. They expected a simple vote, with the losers bowing to majority will, and did not realize that to these men, strongly held principles could not be forsaken or compromised.

The crucial vote came on a resolution by Emanuel Neumann to establish a Keren Hayesod in the United States, one that gave control of the fund to the WZO and made no distinction between donation and investment monies. It came after a long day of speeches and accusations, explanations and countercharges, in which tempers had been worn to a fray. At one-thirty in the morning, the motion carried 153 to 71, and a weary Julian Mack asked permission to speak. He thanked the delegates for the great honor that American Zionists had bestowed upon him in electing him president of the Zionist Organization of America. He had faithfully worked to carry out the policies adopted by the conventions, policies he fully endorsed. But he could not agree with the delegates in their decision to establish a major funding agency without proper safeguards, a move he interpreted as a repudiation of all he and his colleagues had labored for. He then submitted his resignation as president of the ZOA, as a member of the National Executive Committee, and as a member of the Greater Actions Comité of the WZO. Reaching into his pocket, he pulled out a letter from Brandeis and read it to the hushed throng: "With the principles and policies adopted by the National Executive Committee under your leadership I am in complete agreement. Strict adherence to those principles is demanded by the high Zionist ideals. Steadfast pursuit of those policies is essential to early and worthy development of Palestine as the Jewish Homeland. We who believe in those principles and policies cannot properly take part in any administration of Zionist affairs which repudiates them. Upon the delegates in convention assembled rests the responsibility of deciding whether those principles and policies shall prevail in the immediate future. If their decision is adverse, you will, I assume, resign, and in that event present also my resignation as Honorary President. Our place will then be as humble soldiers in the ranks to hasten by our struggle the coming of the day when the policies in which we believe will be recognized as the only ones through which our great ends may be achieved."

As the stunned convention sat in silence, Mack read off the roster of those leaving with him: Stephen S. Wise, honorary vice president; Harry Friedenwald, vice president and former president of the FAZ; Nathan Straus, vice president; Jacob deHaas, and Felix Frankfurter. In addition, thirty members of the National Executive Committee in addition to the officers resigned, including Benjamin Cohen, Bernard Flexner, Max Heller, Horace Kallen, Nathan Kaplan, Robert Szold, and Abba Hillel Silver. Moreover, the heart of the administrative staff, Alexander Sachs, Adolph Hubbard, Reuben Horchow, and A. H. Fromenson, resigned. The sounds of weeping could be heard in the hall as Mack concluded that "no action which you have taken, no action that you can take will ever drive me or any of the other gentlemen whose names I have mentioned from the ranks of membership in the Zionist Organization of America, and will never lessen by the slightest degree the intensity of their Zionism, their devotion to Palestine and their continuous zealous work."[75] And so, at 2 A.M. in a hotel ballroom in Cleveland, the era that had begun in another hotel room nearly seven years earlier came to an end.

VIII

The most common explanation for the schism at Cleveland is that the assimilated Americans, led by the Brandeis/Mack faction, ran headlong into the emotional and intellectual needs and desires of the more Jewish-minded Eastern Europeans, led by Chaim Weizmann and his American lieutenants, Lipsky, Rosenblatt, and Neumann. Weizmann in his speeches kept emphasizing the differences between Pinsk and Washington, and at Cleveland the division of the delegates seemed to many observers a fight between native-born and foreign-born Jews. Journalist Shmuel Melamed accused Brandeis of being too far from his Jewish roots: "His entire conception of Zionism was *goyish* [Gentile] and not Jewish, and this *goyish* conception of Zionism he wanted to impose upon American Jewry." Louis Lipsky concurred in this analysis, and suggested that Brandeis had become a Zionist too late in his life, when his mental patterns had already set, and thus stood alienated from the life stream of Judaism, the masses.[76] Indeed, Ahad Ha'am's comments on Herzl, written in 1897, could have been used by the opposition who derided Brandeis' Jewishness: "Almost all of our great men, those, that is, whose education and social position fit them to be at the head of a Jewish State, are spiritually far removed from Judaism, and have no conception of its nature and its value. Such men, however loyal to their [Jewish] State and devoted to its interests, will necessarily regard those interests as bound up with the foreign culture which they themselves have imbibed; and they will endeavor, by moral persuasion or even by force to implant that culture in the Jewish State, so that in the end the Jewish State will be a State of Germans or Frenchmen of the Jewish race."[77]

And such criticism would have been partially right, for Louis Brandeis did see Zionism as an extension of the ideals and principles he found most valuable in the American tradition. But his goals for the Jewish state did not excite his opponents as much as did his means for getting there, and here can be found another piece of the "Pinsk vs. Washington" slogan. Brandeis certainly did not see Zionism as a business, nor did he wish it run as one. But in an era in which American reformers strove for efficiency and rationalization in all aspects of society, it is not surprising that he expected Zionism to be logical and for its leaders to adopt modern, up-to-date methods. Undoubtedly this passion for efficiency and administrative rationalism could be carried too far; Brandeis wanted all of the Zionist funds to be run as conservatively as a bank, and he wanted men to head the movement and its financial affairs who would be above suspicion. He failed to realize at first that the Europeans were serious in proposing a mixed fund, a concept admittedly unsound even to many of Weizmann's supporters, and when he discovered that they considered sound economic principles unimportant compared to emotional and cultural work, he proved unable to accept either their ideology or their practice. In turn, the Europeans had contempt for a man who apparently put accounting over passion. Menahem Ussischkin never tired of telling the Americans that they had *goyish* heads, while the Europeans had Yiddish hearts. This disdain for American society had long been fashionable in European intellectual circles, which equated the United States with business, rudeness, and lack of emotion—with everything, in fact, antithetical to civilized behavior.[78]

Differing interpretations of Zionism and its goals have continued to cause friction between American Zionists and those in Europe, and later in Israel, even until today. Most importantly, the issue of Jewish nationalism and identity separated them, with the Europeans seeing the Jewish people as an organic unity. From their standpoint, work in the Diaspora developing Jewish consciousness ranked as important as work in Palestine, which represented the ultimate form of identification. "The leaders of American Zionism are not nationalist Jews," Weizmann complained. "To them Zionism is not a movement which gives them a definite viewpoint of the world, which gives them a definite outlook on Jewish life." For the Weizmann group, and indeed for some Zionists down to this day, Bran-

deis' great sin lay in his recasting of Zionist thought to emphasize the
rebuilding of Palestine. Those aspects of cultural work in the Diaspora—*gegenwartsarbeit*—that asserted the national unity of the Jewish people repelled him, as it did most assimilated Jews. They saw a
Palestinian homeland as the goal of Zionist work, and all other
questions had to be subordinated to development of that refuge.
This attitude, which did so much to make Zionism respectable in the
United States, seemed like mere colonization to the Europeans.
Weizmann condemned Brandeis as ignorant of "all those questions
in Zionism which have contributed so much towards the real life
of the movement, like the Hebrew revival, like the desire of the
Zionists to 'judaize' the Jewish communities of the world, to make
their consciousness to fight assimilation with all its manifestations,
in short for all those imponderabilia which form a national movement of which Palestine is merely a territorial aspect of a national
political upheaval." By focusing on Palestine, Brandeis had become a
"colonizer," and Maurice Samuel accused him of fomenting a new
form of "Ugandism," in which the idea of a refuge became more
important than the solution of the problems that had created the need
for that refuge. For those who saw Zionism as a program for the
whole Jewish people, who made no distinction among Jews in different countries, this emphasis on Palestine subverted the very basis of
the whole movement.[79]

Indeed, Brandeis did want to change the movement, since he
believed that the era of politics had come to an end, and that the era
of practical work now had to begin; Weizmann, on the other hand,
asserted the need for continued political and cultural work, especially
for the Eastern European Jews. In part, this reflected their differing
views of Zionism and the role of the Jew in the Diaspora, an issue
that is still in dispute. For Brandeis, Zionism prior to 1917 had
perforce to concern itself with political work, since it had not been
granted recognition; the Balfour Declaration and the mandate, however, had given the movement Herzl's desideratum of an international charter, and the creation of a truly Jewish homeland must now
occupy all of the movement's energies and consume all of its resources. Moreover, the American Jews who, Brandeis knew, opposed Zionism in terms of a nationalistic movement had willingly

assumed the obligation to develop Palestine; he failed to see that in areas where Jewish consciousness lay dormant, the lure of Palestine by itself would not work. Zionism had to be not merely an instrument, a means, for national revival; it had to be part of that awakening, part of the end itself. These conflicting views of Zionism—one centered on the homeland, the other on an awakening of the people —divided the two men more than anything else; many of the other charges and countercharges were mere camouflage.

In the end, most of the practical policies that Brandeis fought for prevailed, since his analysis of the economic and fiscal needs of the movement were correct. Both Weizmann and Levin began to downplay the political work and emphasize the practical efforts needed to rebuild Palestine. The Palestine Development Corporation handled funds earmarked for investment, thus converting the Keren Hayesod into a donation fund. The Jewish Agency, which incorporated non-Zionists, became a reality, while simple necessity required sanitary work to precede massive immigration. As Weizmann's travels in the United States familiarized him with its people and society, he soon stopped talking about Jewish nationalism and started preaching the gospel of Palestinian work. By the end of the decade, little could be found to distinguish the practical programs of the two men.

Yet they remained different, and the movement, especially in the United States, needed them both. Brandeis made Zionism acceptable to American Jewry, not only for those already acculturated but to those who hoped to assimilate as well. He calmed the fears of those worried about dual allegiance, and also legitimized the movement in non-Jewish eyes. His emphasis on practical work in the rebuilding of Palestine gave American Jews the concrete task they needed, the one way they could transform a Zionist philosophy into terms relevant to them. These things, and more, remain Louis Brandeis' legacy to Zionism, and after more than five decades, his definition of Zionism and America's role in it remains meaningful to most American Jews.

But Chaim Weizmann tapped an emotional reservoir closed to the rational approach of the American leadership. One can logically explain the need for a refuge, and appeal to history for justification of reclaiming Palestine. Yet, as the last quarter century has demonstrated, the Palestinian homeland goes far beyond the limits of logic. For Jews, there is a common historical and psychological experience, and Weizmann's messianic outlook, his near-mystical approach to restoration, struck a responsive chord in that experience. There is perhaps no better word to use than *Yiddishkeit*—an all-pervading sense of Jewishness—to describe the key to that appeal. Had Brandeis had it, he would not have been able to legitimize Zionism in America; once he had accomplished that task, however, then Weizmann, the Jew from Motele, could exploit the resources—financial and emotional—of American Jewry in order to build Eretz Yisroel.

Unfortunately for the movement, neither man had the temperament nor the wisdom to recognize that Zionism needed both of them, the Americanized Brandeis and the European Weizmann. It needed one to frame the movement in terms acceptable to the American experience, and it needed the other to provide the emotional link to the ages-long yearning for restoration. But Brandeis' Puritan streak made it impossible for him to compromise his principles, while Weizmann's overweening ambition and pride would not allow him to share his power with others. Unable to reach agreement, they tore the movement apart, and for the next two decades American Zionism worked in vain to heal the wounds ripped open at the Hotel Cleveland. It took Arab riots, British treachery, and Hitler's "final solution" to reunite American Jewry.

CHAPTER EIGHT

THE "PACT OF GLORY"

For those who seek the strange twists and ironies of history, the 1920s must certainly prove a source of fascination. A world that had just gone through four years of bloodletting, fighting to "make the world safe for democracy," refused to heed the lessons of that conflict, and so doomed mankind to an even more terrible holocaust in less than a generation. The high-sounding principles of international co-operation turned into sour notes of provincial isolation, while unbounded horizons of prosperity suddenly evaporated into depression and deprivation. For students of Zionism as well, that decade is laden with bizarre reversals and unexpected developments. The Brandeis/Mack group, defeated in 1921, saw all of its policies adopted by the opposition within a few years, and found itself back in power by 1930. The man who had denounced the American leadership's program as timid and un-Jewish soon proclaimed its truth and validity, even while refusing to acknowledge its source, and Chaim Weizmann's greatest achievement in the twenties lay in the creation of an enlarged Jewish Agency, which lured non-Zionists into Palestinian work and gave them potentially greater power than Brandeis had envisioned at the London conference. Stepping back from the debacle at Cleveland, one can see it not only for the tragedy it was by itself, but as part of a barren landscape dotted by other evidence of the sad plight of Zionism and of Jewry at the beginning of the Roaring Twenties.

I

The United States, alone among the major belligerents, escaped from the war relatively unscathed. It had been spared the physical destruction that crippled France and Eastern Europe, while its 112,000 casualties paled beside the 1,700,000 men lost by Russia or the 1,400,000 sacrificed by the French. America's industrial capacity, spurred on by the demands of the conflict, now far outstripped that of its two major rivals, Great Britain and Germany, over whom the new giant exercised financial domination as well. Yet the psychic scars of America's first faltering steps as a world power left a lingering sense of malaise, a feeling alleviated in part by the decade-long binge of prosperity and good times. For, however, the reaction took the form of a heightened nativism in which a virulent anti-Semitism surfaced for a brief but disturbing period.

Examples of anti-Semitism in the United States could be found prior to the 1920s, in the various eighteenth- and nineteenth-century disabling acts, in Grant's Order No. 10, in the populist rhetoric of the 1890s, and in the lynching of Leo Frank in 1913.* Even those ac-

---

* Leo Frank was a factory superintendent in his uncle's pencil plant in Atlanta, Georgia. On April 26, 1913, the body of young Mary Phagan was found in the plant, and it was later determined that Frank had been the last to see her alive. He was accused of the murder and tried under bizarre circumstances, while a crescendo of anti-Semitic propaganda marked the whole episode. His defense attorneys were practically incompetent, and the trial judge did nothing to prevent mobs outside the courthouse from chanting "Hang the Jew." Only after Frank's conviction and sentencing did Northern civil rights lawyers become interested in the case. Governor John Marshall Slaton, recognizing the irregularities in the trial, commuted Frank's sentence from death to life imprison-

culturated Jews who had achieved material prosperity found themselves still surrounded by invisible social barriers. But compared to the Jew-hatred of Europe and the *pogroms* of Mother Russia, the New World provided Jews with one of the safest and most accepting environment they had enjoyed in over nineteen hundred years. The flood of immigrants from Southern and Eastern Europe between 1880 and the war had touched off concern among many Americans about the effects these hordes of unwashed aliens would have on this country's political and social institutions. In 1917, restrictionist forces scored their first victory in their fight to limit immigration, when they secured passage of a literacy test over Woodrow Wilson's veto. In 1921, Congress erected a temporary quota system, which discriminated against those from Eastern and Southern Europe, a system ultimately perfected in the Johnson Act of 1924. While the law did not specifically mention Jews and Catholics, it severely restricted the number of people who could annually enter the United States from those areas heavily populated by these two groups. The fears of Zionist and non-Zionist Jews alike that the United States would no longer be a refuge for the persecuted now had been realized.

Expressions of prejudice in terms any European anti-Semite would have appreciated now began to be heard in a land built up by immigrants from many lands. "For a real American to visit Ellis Island," wrote the Reverend A. E. Patton, "and there look upon the Jewish hordes, ignorant of all true patriotism, filthy, vermin infested, stealthy and furtive in manner, too lazy to enter into real labor, too cowardly to face frontier life, too lazy to work as every American farmer has to work, too filthy to adopt ideals of cleanliness from the start, too bigoted to surrender any racial traditions or to absorb any

---

ment, an act of courage for which he was hounded out of office. While in prison, Frank was almost killed by another inmate; during his recuperation, a mob plucked Frank out of the hospital on August 16, 1915, and lynched him. Although many of the mob members were known, a Georgia grand jury brought in a verdict of "death at the hands of persons unknown." The Frank case was the first serious outburst of anti-Semitism in the United States, and worried many communal leaders. It led directly to the founding of the B'nai Brith Anti-Defamation League, which became a watchdog to prevent similar events from occurring.[1]

true Americanism, for a real American to see those items of a filthy, greedy, never patriotic stream flowing in to pollute all that has made America as good as she is—is to awaken in his thoughtful mind desires to check and lessen this source of pollution." Not content with excluding additional Jews, nativists turned to the "problem" of those already here. Hiram Evans, the Imperial Wizard of the Ku Klux Klan, condemned the Jews as an unassimilable people, "with no deep national attachment, a stranger to the emotion of patriotism as the Anglo-Saxon feels it."[2] The specter of Bolshevism, fanned by the Palmer raids and the Red scare, made some people see a communist behind every Jew, and Henry Ford launched the Dearborn *Independent* on a crusade to rid the country of them both. Every piece of libel against the Jews, every figment of some demented bigot's imagination, including the spurious "Protocols of the Elders of Zion" found its way into the *Independent* until a libel suit forced Ford to recant. But until then, the man who put America on wheels attacked the Jewish power that crippled the economy from above (the Rothschilds) and destroyed the society from below (Marx and Trotsky).

Colleges were not immune from this virus either. Professor Albert Bushnell Hart, a Harvard historian, declared that the Jews had to choose between Zion and America, while Philip Marshall Brown of Princeton, speaking before the American Society of International Law, accused the Jews of refusing their allegiance to any land. Quota systems in better schools became commonplace, and the Gentile elite greeted the entry of these sons of Russian immigrants with scorn and hostility. One writer put it baldly: The upwardly mobile Jew "sends his children to college a generation or two sooner than the other stocks, and as a result there are in fact more dirty Jews and tactless Jews in college than dirty and tactless Italians, Armenians, or Slovac."[3] Yet in the census of 1920, the number of native-born Jews in the United States exceeded the number of foreign-born for the first time since the great migrations had begun. Even as the children of immigrants—American-born and -educated, English-speaking and acculturated—came to prominence in the Jewish community, prejudice against them seemed on the rise. This virulent phase of anti-Semitism did not last long, and the bulk of nativist resentment spent itself on the Catholics, another seemingly unassimilable group owing allegiance elsewhere. The return to prosperity after a short postwar recession, and the demonstrable fact that Russian communists had not rushed out to foment revolutions all over the world, eased the situation considerably.

But if Jews in the United States worried about the establishment of quotas and the rising incidence of prejudicial rhetoric, their brethren in the land of promise had much more serious threats with which to contend. During the first week of May 1921, Arabs launched a series of attacks on the Jewish populations of Jaffa and several nearby settlements, resulting in 95 deaths (47 of them Jewish) and 219 wounded (146 Jewish). A British Commission of Inquiry under Sir Thomas Haycraft found that Arabs had started the disturbance and inflicted most of the casualties and damage, but this basic finding was soon lost in the storm generated by British handling of the violence. In an effort to appear even-handed and fair, the high commissioner, Sir Herbert Samuel, himself a Jew, bent over backward to appease the Arabs. Aware by now that talk of peaceful co-operation between Arab and Jew had been illusory, Samuel attempted to clarify the terms of the British mandate so as to calm the fears of the native Arab population. His Majesty's Government, he said, had never intended that a Jewish government would be set up to rule over a Muslim majority; rather, Palestine would be a refuge for Jews persecuted in other parts of the world, and their numbers would be strictly limited by the economic capacity of the land. Mass immigration, the heart of the Zionist plan, would be prohibited.[4]

The Zionists could not believe what they heard. England, their friend and savior, had promised the Jews a homeland in the Balfour Declaration, and the Zionists had worked to secure the mandate for Britain, a mandate that specifically included promises of restoration. Now the British Government, suddenly aware that it had to rule over seven hundred thousand Arabs as well as a hundred thousand Jews, began hunting for an acceptable middle ground, a search totally incomprehensible to the Zionists. "We thought we held a promissory note in our hands," recalled Nahum Goldmann, "and we were impatient to see it honored. We took the hesitant British policy as a breach of promise and felt it to be anti-Zionist."[5]

But the British had also made promises to the Arabs, and Winston Churchill, then Colonial Secretary, had the task of fulfilling those obligations as well. His solution satisfied everyone temporarily. He cut off all of the land east of the Jordan River, the Transjordan area, and set it up as an autonomous kingdom under British protection and Abdullah's rule. This partially mollified the Hashemite family, but diminished the size of Palestine by 80 per cent. The mandate covered an area of forty-five thousand square miles, about the size of Pennsylvania; the new homeland, now about ten thousand square miles, was scarcely larger than Maryland. Most Jews cared very little about Transjordan—the entire Jewish population of the area was two persons—although a number of Zionists objected to this diminution of the homeland. The British did try to keep the Jews happy by reaffirming the Balfour Declaration, and establishing a principle of "economic absorptive capacity," that is, immigration would be limited to the ability of land and industry to support new comers, which, on the face of it, appeared to be a most reasonable approach. But as events had already made clear, the Jews had no guarantee of reason, and the British seemed intent on appeasing the Arabs.[6]

Within the Yishuv, disillusionment and suspicion abounded. Samuel tried to defend his policy, suggesting that without his assurances to the Arabs there would have been a bloodbath. Yet the behavior of British soldiers had been far from equitable, and in many instances seemed to condone the anti-Jewish violence. Many settlers remembered that in the 1920 riots, a number of Jews had been seized and imprisoned for the "crime" of self-defense. Vladimir Jabotinsky, a former officer in His Majesty's Army, received fifteen years for the possession of firearms, the exact penalty meted out to an Arab rioter convicted of rape. World outcry had led British officials in London to drop the charges and the penalty against Jabotinsky, but the settlers had little reason to believe in British fairness. Moreover, money from the outside communities slowed to a trickle, as membership in the Zionist movement fell off drastically after the war. The two hundred thousand Jews of Berlin gave more to their communal charities than the whole Jewish people gave to Palestine. Worse, what little money that came in seemed to be spent in a planless and inefficient manner, and more than one person had second thoughts about the "inappropriateness" of the Brandeis plan. Only a Henrietta Szold, in the midst of such despair, could write home that the solution lay in a union of the better Arabs and the better Jews, not only for *aruchat bat ami* but also for *aruchat ha-goyim,* the healing not only of the Jews but of the other peoples as well.[7]

Given the short-lived but vociferous campaign of anti-Semitism in the United States, and the evident failure of the British to push ahead in developing a homeland in Palestine, the fight at Cleveland proved much more debilitating than either side had expected. Membership in the ZOA had begun to decline steeply before the 1921 convention. The letdown following the emotional intensity of the war period affected all groups in society, and in the election of Warren G. Harding in November 1920, the American people had expressed their desire for a return to "normalcy." Jews who had joined the movement primarily to help their suffering brethren also wanted a return to more peaceful, less hectic times, and they dropped out of the ZOA, rationalizing that with the Balfour Declaration and the mandate, the British would now take care of everything. The postwar depression, moreover, hit particularly hard at the small businessman, and such marginal members thus found easy justification for not paying the five-dollar annual dues. At the 1922 convention, American Zionists membership rolls stood at 18,481, a sad decline from the nearly 200,000 of three years earlier. Even the Arab riots failed to arouse emotions except among Zionist groups.[8]

The new administration, headed by Louis Lipsky, inherited a movement structurally much stronger than the old FAZ, but their personal leadership harked back to the days of informality, oratory, and *stimmung.* While they could not be blamed for the condition in which they received the ZOA, their leadership during the 1920s did little to advance the cause. Membership did improve somewhat after Lipsky took over, and by 1925 had climbed to over 27,000, but then it slipped rapidly, so that in 1929, the rolls actually stood at a level lower than 1922, with a handful more than 18,000 members paying the shekel. Even among these, committed activists were rare and could be distinguished from those who merely sent in their dues and did nothing else. The executive committee complained that not one tenth of the membership actively worked in the Keren Hayesod campaigns, and not one in twenty did anything for the membership.[9] The attempt to develop a mass organization, with large numbers of devoted workers in the field, came to a grinding halt after the schism at Cleveland.

Morale in the ZOA understandably enough, deteriorated considerably in this climate, and as a result, funds for Zionist projects, already declining before Cleveland, plummeted even farther. The last year of the Mack administration saw the ZOA break even, with a slight surplus of $3,200, and about $200,000 in assets earmarked for specified purposes. In the next three years, Lipsky and his lieutenants not only proved unable to meet expenses, but ran up a deficit of almost $160,000. Despite encouraging reports by Bernard Richards and others that unity prevailed and work was proceeding, Lipsky's assessment of the situation a year after taking office, "that we have managed to keep agoing without going into bankruptcy is a miracle," was much more honest.[10] On the eve of the 1922 convention, Abraham Tulin confided that Lipsky and his colleagues "are fed up with their jobs and prospects of complete failure ahead, and would like to turn the ship over to the old pilots. . . . The situation here is pretty bad. . . . The organization as such is shot to pieces. Many of the substantial men all over the country have left it. Many of those who have worked hard last year will not work in the future unless Brandeis resumes the leadership."[11]

Without detracting from Lipsky's many years of devotion and hard work for the Zionist movement, and that of his associates, it is plain that without the support and leadership of Chaim Weizmann, Nahum Sokolow, Shmaryahu Levin, and Menahem Ussischkin, they never would have been able to oust the Mack administration. Few of them, at least at that time, could be classified as strong leaders, and this became apparent immediately in the changed relationship between the ZOA and the world Executive. The Brandeis/Mack group had been a force to reckon with, and had compelled the WZO to treat American Zionists as full-fledged partners in the great enterprise of restoration. Weizmann treated Lipsky as a vassal—a worthy one, to be sure, devoted to the cause, but a vassal nonetheless. Within a week after taking office, Lipsky began a series of protests to the

London office over the manner in which the WZO treated the Americans, a series that lasted until he left office and that duplicated the earlier complaints of the Federation. The WZO gave serious consideration to recognizing the Sons of Zion as an additional federation in the United States, which would have weakened considerably the already damaged authority of the ZOA. The London office constantly dunned the Americans for money, and for more money, and when it was not forthcoming gave gratuitous and condescending advice to Lipsky on how he could better manage affairs. Communications between the two headquarters broke down, with each side pestering the other for information. In 1923, the Executive even proposed running a separate shekel campaign in America, thus bypassing the ZOA altogether.[12] As if the experience of the war years had never happened, European Zionists again discounted the value of the movement in America except as a source of funding, an attitude quickly recognized and greatly resented by the Americans. The only bright spot in this otherwise bleak survey occurred in 1922, when the U. S. Congress publicly endorsed the concept of a national home for the Jewish people in Palestine. Yet even here, illusion more than substance comprised this Zionist "victory."

Due to the conflicting interests of the State Department and the White House, the Wilson administration had never really established an official American policy toward the Balfour Declaration. After Robert Lansing left the Department, the new Secretary, Bainbridge Colby, while personally friendly toward Louis Brandeis, did not find Palestinian affairs the most pressing of his many obligations, a condition welcomed by the department careerists. But the Department continued to provide the Zionists with information, and during the Easter riots of 1920 requested the consul in Jerusalem to keep it fully informed of what was happening. But even these courtesies disappeared when the Republicans took control of the government in March 1921. Louis Marshall inquired of the new Secretary, Charles Evans Hughes, whether a British mandate would be opposed by the government; he received a curt and noncommittal reply. Nahum Sokolow, the Zionists' roving ambassador-at-large, got an even colder response when he tried to get an "expression of favor" in support of the Balfour Declaration. The Department consistently refused to meet with ZOA delegations at anything higher than a bureau level, and Hughes especially considered their constant importunements a nuisance.[13]

Unable to secure a sympathetic response from the State Department, the Zionists began to lobby for a congressional endorsement of their program. Rabbi Simon Glazer of Kansas City, who knew a number of senators, convinced several of them that it would be politically beneficial to have them support the idea of a Jewish homeland. Senator Henry Cabot Lodge of Massachusetts and Representative Hamilton Fish of New York introduced resolutions of support in the spring of 1922, and both houses began hearings on the subject. In a replay of earlier debates over a homeland, the Zionists paraded their witnesses, while the perennial Rabbi David Philipson opposed them, declaring that he and many other American Jews unalterably opposed political Zionism.[14] The New York *Times,* whose owners also opposed Jewish nationalism, attacked the resolutions, and charged that Lodge's impending re-election campaign had more to do with his sudden interest in Zionism than any altruistic interest in restoration. A number of Jews also wondered why the Lodge-Fish resolutions, while advocating protection of non-Jewish rights in Palestine, unlike the Balfour Declaration did not mention the guarding of Jewish liberties outside the Holy Land.[15]

The members of Congress, moving in a different sphere than the diplomats at the State Department, saw little harm in the resolutions, and much political advantage. They had antagonized a number of ethnic groups in establishing immigration quotas in 1921, and by supporting Zionist demands, they could make at least partial amends to one of these groups, and seemingly at no cost or involvement by the country. Thinking primarily in terms of domestic politics, they gave little consideration to the influence such a statement might have on foreign policy. It is not unlikely that many of them considered Zionism a rather far-fetched idea, and in any event, whatever they said would have little effect. Moreover, the whole problem lay in British hands, and few congressmen in 1922 worried overmuch about what the British thought. But the foreign service careerists, who had fought so hard to prevent American endorsement of the Balfour doctrine during the Wilson years, immediately saw the proposed resolution as an unwarranted intrusion of petty, ethnic politics into the rarefied domain of foreign policy. They did all they could to prevent the resolutions from passing, and having failed at that, succeeded in nullifying any effect it might have had on the actual workings of foreign affairs.

Zionist standing among the careerists in the Department had never been high, even when a President had publicly endorsed their program, and anti-Zionist sentiment built up after the war. During the Arab riots of 1920 and 1921, some of the disturbances had centered around labor problems, and a number of Russian-born socialists had been involved, thus leading to rumors of Bolshevist incitement. While analysts on the staff had to admit that there were not that many proven communists, they emphasized that some did exist; even more damning in their eyes, however, was the—to them —justifiable resentment that the Arabs had against Jewish immigration. All of this added up to undoubted unpleasantness in the future, a situation the United States would do well to avoid.[16] Secretary of State Hughes shared his subordinates' views on this point, and so repeatedly ignored requests for his views on the proposed congressional action. But when it seemed that Congress intended proceeding regardless of the Department's wishes, Allen W. Dulles, the new head of the Near Eastern Division, began circulating a series of memoranda urging that the government refrain from mixing into what would inevitably prove a morass. As to the Zionists, he considered them "an influential and a noisy group, but while their claims undoubtedly have a certain sentimental appeal, the cold fact remains that the Jews in Palestine now constitute about 10 per cent of the population, and that the 90 per cent majority bitterly oppose Zionism."[17]

To some extent, the Department had a legitimate reason for wanting to avoid making a pronouncement on Palestine. The League of Nations was then debating the mandate, and the United States, although not a member of the League, had commercial interests at stake in some of its decisions.* Since the United States had expressed

* In a series of diplomatic notes begun soon after the San Remo conference, the Department had protested that Americans could not be excluded from equality of rights in mandated territories, even though the

no desire to play a role in Middle Eastern affairs, common diplomatic practices dictated that the Department should not interfere. But Dulles was certainly disingenuous when he concluded that the government had never been committed to the idea of a homeland, or when he noted that "Ex-President Wilson is understood to have favored the Balfour Declaration, but I do not know that he ever committed himself to it in an official and public way."[19]

Political expediency and not diplomatic logic ultimately prevailed. Hughes, in answer to a direct inquiry from Senator Lodge, had to admit that the Department could muster no evidence to oppose the *sense* of the resolution, although he urged that legal and tactical difficulties still remained. Both houses, by a joint resolution, unanimously endorsed the idea of a homeland in Palestine for the Jews, and on September 21, 1922, President Harding added his signature.[20] The State Department considered the document distinctly annoying, and only at the last minute decided not to ask Harding to withhold his approval, and then for reasons dealing with congressional relations on another matter. But just as the careerists had refused to recognize Wilson's public endorsement of a Jewish homeland, so now they proceeded to ignore the resolution of 1922. The Zionists, of course, made heavy propaganda out of it, and got additional mileage after the Second World War when they, rather incorrectly, pointed to it as evidence of traditional American support for a Jewish state. When the League of Nations finally approved the British mandate, Lipsky sent Hughes the traditional telegram, "in deep appreciation of service rendered to a just cause by the State Department under your guidance." This apparent ignorance

---

United States had not ratified the Covenant of the League. Ultimately, Great Britain and the United States signed a treaty in 1924 providing for American enjoyment of all the rights and benefits extended to League members in mandate areas. The treaty included the text of the Palestine mandate, which repeated the wording of the Balfour Declaration. As Frank Manuel concludes, the Anglo-American Convention, read together with the Joint Resolution, indicated that many Americans assented to the basic idea of a Jewish homeland, and that their government had endorsed this principle. But the Department's refusal to concede this led to "muddles, evasive, even dishonest policy-making."[18]

on the part of ZOA officials indicated how far removed they now stood from the seats of power.[21]

II

The ZOA failed to recover from the Cleveland schism, and the social tensions and trends of American society during the 1920s were not conducive to the growth of an organization that had now become identified with Jewish nationalism. As immigrant Jews rose from the working class to the middle class, as their sweatshops gave way to small—and some not-so-small—factories, as their children secured an education and became doctors and lawyers and teachers, they found themselves put off by a movement that might cast doubt on their acceptance as Americans. The nativist hysteria of the times, as well as the normal rejection of old ways in the process of acculturation, made Zionism as unacceptable to the assimilating Russian Jews as it had earlier been to the Germans. The Brandeisian synthesis had assuaged these fears, but the ouster of the Americanized leadership had undermined their work. Given the social tensions of the era, the Brandeisian philosophy required the presence of a leadership demonstrably American. Somehow the arguments that had been put forward since 1914 now carried less force when spoken in a Yiddish accent.

After the verbiage and the emotionalism at Cleveland over the need to return to true Zionism, emphasize ideology and Jewish culture, make Diaspora work—*gegenwartsarbeit*—a major focus of Zionist activity, one would have expected the new regime to have begun, as one of its first projects, some sort of educational campaign. Certainly men like Louis Lipsky, Abe Goldberg, Louis Fishman, and Emanuel Neumann believed that Zionism involved much more than fund raising directed toward the support of Palestine. Yet during the 1920s, the ZOA practically abandoned everything else, and concentrated all of its efforts on securing money. By the end of the decade, development of membership and organization had come to a standstill; district chapters did hardly any educational work, and the central office staff directed a year-'round solicitation.

There was very little choice. With the awarding of the mandate to Great Britain, the main practical work of the Zionist movement had to be in the reconstruction of Palestine. The Brandeisian argument, that the Holy Land would not be truly Jewish without a large immigration, quickly became accepted Zionist doctrine. But, while immigrants would eventually build up the land, in the meantime the land had to be built up to support the immigrants, and that took money. For all their talk on Diaspora nationalism, on raising Jewish consciousness, on fostering Hebrew culture, the exigencies of the situation required that money be raised and spent for Palestine. When the ZOA proved unable to secure the necessary sums, the world Executive created a new institution in 1929, the Jewish Agency, and in doing so, undercut the possibility of the ZOA ever regaining the dominant role it had held during the war years, not only vis-à-vis the world organization, but vis-à-vis American Jewry as well. During the 1920s, the Brandeis group may have enjoyed the irony of seeing their programs adopted and implemented by the same men who condemned them, but with results that neither side had anticipated.

Weizmann took the first step in this process in 1921 when he established the Keren Hayesod in the United States. He anticipated that the KH would become the chief financial instrument in the rebuilding of the homeland, and that the bulk of the money would come from American Jewry. In the long run, this did happen, and the KH today remains the umbrella organ for the collection of funds in the Diaspora.* Between 1920 and 1946, it raised over $72,000,-000, which figured in the financing of every important project in Palestine, and of this, $3.00 out of every $5.00 came from the

---

* The other important fund was the older Keren Kayemeth L'Yisroel, the Jewish National Fund, which Herzl had established at the Fifth Congress. On the eve of the creation of the State of Israel, the JNF owned over 235,000 acres, almost half of all land owned by Jews in Palestine, including large tracts in the Galilee, Samaria, Huleh, the Negev, and the Valley of Jezreel. The Fund has also been the chief instrument in the reforestation of the land, and the purchase of tree stamps is a familiar charitable device among Jews all over the world.

United States.[22] But this was far short of what the Keren Hayesod promoters had expected. Weizmann promised to raise $100,000,000 in five years; at the end of that period less than one tenth of that sum had been realized. In the United States alone, Jews give over $7,800,-000, over three fourths of the world total, but only about 30 per cent of what the Executive had expected. In comparison, the Provisional Committee and the ZOA raised $5,739,000 from 1914 until the Cleveland convention, a respectable sum at a time when the bulk of Jewish contributions went to relief funds for European Jewry.[23] When an exhausted Chaim Weizmann returned to Europe to attend the Carlsbad Congress in September of 1921, he had raised about $2,000,000, much less than he wanted and much less than the Yishuv needed, but four times as much as Brandeis had predicted American Jews would give to a mixed fund.

When the Twelfth Congress adopted a budget of $6,000,000, the Executive expected that at least 75 per cent, or $4,500,000, would come from America. Vladimir Jabotinsky figured out that this would come to $3.00 a head for every Jew in the country, and optimistically noted "that the interest shown by the population is very great; the [KH] delegation meets everywhere with enthusiastic reception. The support of the Yiddish and English press is unanimous. . . . There is no trace of a fight against the Keren Hayesod. Under these conditions I feel entitled to say that we are working in a favorable atmosphere." But he objected to the general method of appeal. Until they could develop enough workers, this would have to do since it brought in immediate cash, but ultimately he wanted the Keren Hayesod to conduct a personal canvass, in which the Zionists spoke to every member of the Jewish community.[24] Interestingly enough, this method, which was later so successfully adopted by the United Jewish Appeal and which has recently raised millions of dollars for Israel, would have provided a marvelous opportunity to spread Zionist ideology, to promote Jewish culture, in short, to do that nonfinancial work that the Brandeis group had been accused of neglecting. Yet nowhere did Jabotinsky even suggest that this canvass should deal with anything but raising money for Palestine.

But after the initial enthusiasm for the Keren Hayesod wore off, it became harder and harder each year to meet the movement's needs. On the face of it, Weizmann kept up his optimism, declaring in early 1923 that the fund was "being more and more rooted in the minds of the public and is becoming an institution which is enjoying a certain reputation. Jews of all kinds are gradually coming to the conclusion that they have to give money to this fund."[25] But privately, Weizmann gradually came to the conclusion that the Keren Hayesod not only did not bring in enough money, but that the Zionist movement in the United States gave signs of imminent collapse. Even as he trumpeted the success of the KH, the National Board of Hadassah threatened to denounce him. They had just received a cable from Henrietta Szold in Jerusalem that she had no money with which to buy Passover supplies for the Yishuv. At a private luncheon, Hadassah told Weizmann that unless he sent $100,000 immediately, they would publicly attack his mismanagement and the failure of his supposed leadership. Arthur Ruppin, on a visit to the United States in 1924, could not believe that the only way the American KH bureau had been able to remit its monthly payment had been to borrow that amount from a bank. Moreover, the fund did not have enough money in hand to underwrite the expenses of its New York campaign, which brought in over half of the annual income.[26] By the end of 1923, even Weizmann admitted that the American Zionists, while "very devoted, very friendly, and very loyal," had little power and were "easily discouraged by the 101 difficulties which we encounter." Money had become very difficult to get; the Keren Hayesod campaign in Europe had failed completely, and American Jews resented being asked to pay for everything.[27] But Weizmann thought he saw a glimmer of hope in the negotiations he had begun earlier that year with Louis Marshall, and which, if successful, would attract wealthy donors to support Zionist work in Palestine.

The prominence of Louis Marshall and his associates in the Jewish community had been recognized by Zionist leaders since the days of the Federation, and they had long tried, unsuccessfully, to woo them into the cause. But as long as Zionism meant Jewish nationalism, the *yahudim* shied away. The Brandeisian synthesis, as well as the emphasis on Palestinian work, provided the opening wedge for the non-Zionists* to join in rebuilding the homeland. The series of conferences among Mack, Brandeis, Marshall, and Schiff had done much to foster better relations, and a few of these extremely wealthy men had already begun to donate money to support the Yishuv. The key, of course, lay in the religious and sentimental attraction they had as Jews for the land of their ancestors. They refused to allow that only Zionists could work for the rebuilding; every Jew had the right and the obligation to help. Marshall strongly denied that he had become a Zionist when a Reform rabbi asked the lawyer if his work for Palestine had made him a nationalist. "I am not a Zionist. I am, however, greatly concerned in the rehabilitation of Palestine, and I regard it to be the duty of every Jew to aid in that cause. Political Zionism is a thing of the past. There is nobody now in authority in the Zionist Organization who has the slightest idea of doing anything more than to build up the Holy Land and to give those who desire a home there the opportunity which they cherish."[28] Brandeis himself could not have said it better. Felix Warburg felt even more strongly a need to save Eretz Yisroel from the Zionists, even if he had to work with them to do it. "If Palestine is to be anything but a trash basket to satisfy Jews or Jewish politicians," he declared, "it has to become more than an arrogant, conceited, perhaps Hebrew-talking mob devoid of the humility of the Jewish religion." He gave $10,000 to Weizmann for Hebrew University, and in doing so told him how little he thought of political Zionism.[29] Practical considerations also entered in, since the American Jewish Committee had lost its battle against immigration restriction. If the United States would no longer accept Jews fleeing from persecution, then a haven in Palestine became the only logical alternative.

Not all of the *yahudim* were as willing as Marshall to partake of the work. In the words of one wit, non-Zionists were horrified that Jews had prayed two thousands years for redemption, *and now it*

---

* There was, and is, a big difference in the terms "anti-Zionist" and "non-Zionist." The former opposed all aspects of the program, and maintained that Palestine had no more meaning than as a relic of a long-dead past. The latter differed with the Zionists over the idea of an independent Jewish state, but shared their love of the homeland, and usually supported the regeneration of Jewish culture.

had to happen to them! Adolph Ochs, the influential publisher of the New York *Times,* found little to attract him in a Palestinian restoration, and worried that the economic development of the land would inevitably lead to nationalism, and how that would affect him and other 100 per cent Americans. "The Jews are not a nation," he lectured Arthur Ruppin, "they only share a religion."[30] Warburg himself had originally opposed the rebuilding work, and only a bold gambit by Weizmann led to his conversion. On a trip to the United States in 1923, the Zionist leader met the polished, German-Jewish banker, who was not only related to the great European banking house, but had also married Jacob Schiff's daughter. Warburg denounced the conduct of the Jewish settlers in Palestine, and repeated as if they were true some of the rumors current after the 1920 and 1921 riots that Bolsheviks and free-thinkers dominated the Yishuv. Weizmann dismissed the rumors for what they were, anti-Semitic gossip, and the financier, abashed that he had not bothered to check the validity of the stories, offered a donation to the Keren Hayesod. Weizmann refused, and suggested that if Warburg really wanted to get at the truth in the matter, he should go to Palestine and investigate conditions there himself. To everyone's surprise, Warburg did just that, and sent Weizmann a postcard saying that he had gone up and down the land, and felt like doffing his hat to every man and tree he saw.[31] Yet his conversion, like that of Marshall's, did not go far enough to suit most Zionists. Warburg too became a builder of Zion, but never a Zionist, and Weizmann described Warburg's early work for the homeland as "just one among the fifty-seven varieties of his philanthropic endeavors."[31]

The vehicle by which Weizmann hoped to bring non-Zionists into Palestinian work derived from Article IV of the mandate given to Great Britain: "An appropriate Jewish Agency shall be recognized as a public body for the purpose of advising and co-operating with the Administration of Palestine in such economic, social and other matters as may affect the establishment of the Jewish National Home and the interests of the Jewish population in Palestine, and, subject always to the control of the Administration, to assist and take part in the development of the country. The Zionist Organization, so long as its organization and constitution are in the opinion of the

Mandatory appropriate, shall be recognized as such agency. It shall take steps in consultation with His Britannic Majesty's Government to secure the co-operation of all Jews who are willing to assist in the establishment of the Jewish National Home."[32]

The first step toward implementing Article IV that would include non-Zionists came when the Actions Comité adopted a resolution in September 1922 that the Jewish Agency should represent the whole Jewish people. The decision did not come easily, for the repercussions of the London and Cleveland meetings still reverberated loudly in Zionist circles, with some of the old-line ideologues worried that non-Zionists would enter into Palestinian work only if the movement diluted its nationalistic and cultural philosophies; Ussischkin still preferred *kranker yiddin* to *gezunter goyim*. Weizmann, who had insisted that he be allowed a wide latitude of discretion, recognized that he really only had two options open to him. One was to convene a World Jewish Congress (an idea already proposed by Stephen Wise), with delegates elected from Jewish communities all over the world. However, the attitude of the American *shtadlanim* in the fight for the American Jewish Congress indicated that they and their counterparts in Germany, France, and Great Britain would not look favorably on this approach, and without their co-operation—and money—the Agency would be foredoomed. The other option, and the one he favored all along, involved personal contact with established organizations and leaders, and somehow getting them to agree on a joint approach to rebuilding Palestine.

In the spring of 1923, Israel Cohen, the general secretary of the London Executive, sent out form letters to a number of Jewish groups in England inviting them to meet with the Zionists to discuss an enlarged Agency. Encouraged by the response, the Actions Comité gave Weizmann the go-ahead to negotiate with non-Zionist groups all over the world. The key to success, of course, lay with Louis Marshall and his friends, and Weizmann sailed to America to win them over. First, however, he had to convince the American Zionists that they should co-operate. The Lipsky administration had no qualms, but a number of the rank and file did, wondering aloud why they had ousted Brandeis only to have Weizmann espouse the same program. Polish Zionist leader Yitzchak Gruenbaum, who headed the anti-Agency Radical Zionists, considered the whole Agency proposal a capitulation to "salon" Jews, and urged delegates at the Baltimore convention not to "surrender our national work in the Diaspora"; dissident Zionists found support for this view among some of the Europeans accompanying Weizmann, notably Mena-hem Ussischkin. But after a bitter debate at the 1923 convention, marked by Weizmann personally pleading with the delegates, the ZOA agreed to negotiate.*

By December the groundwork had been laid, and Marshall con-sented to assemble a full-scale conference of non-Zionists to dis-cuss participation in an enlarged Agency and establishing an invest-ment corporation to aid the economic development of Palestine. On February 8, 1924, Marshall, Cyrus Adler, Herbert Lehman, and Judge Horace M. Stern—all pillars of the German-Jewish commu-nity—sent out a circular letter to over 150 prominent Jews not di-rectly affiliated with the ZOA, including Brandeis and Judge Mack. "The time has come," read the invitation, "when we firmly believe that the duty rests upon the Jews of this country who are not mem-bers of or affiliated with the Zionist Organization, to consider seri-ously their relations to the economic problems of Palestine and to its cultural and industrial upbuilding."

Between this invitation and the conference on February 17, the promoters, and especially Weizmann, did their best to lobby those doubtful of the entire enterprise. He particularly worried about the problems of ideology, and how statements on political Zionism might be interpreted by both the non-Zionists at the meeting and by his own supporters back home. In working with Adler and Stern on possible resolutions, he urged them to unite on a program devoted exclusively to work in Palestine. Zionists, he claimed, wanted noth-ing more than what had already been accorded to them in the man-

* Actually, Weizmann had already begun these negotiations, and in a spirit that at times seemed marked more by a desire for revenge than by statesmanship, deliberately excluded those who had sided with Bran-deis at the Cleveland convention. The only exception was Bernard Flex-ner, chairman of the Palestine subcommittee of the Joint Distribution Committee, and as such welcomed by both the *yahudim* and the Zionists. For relations between the Brandeis group, Marshall and his associates, and the Zionists, see Chapter Nine.

date, and in that document "there is, as you know, no mention of a Jewish State or of political Zionism in any shape or form."[33] Weizmann worked assiduously, as he informed the Actions Comité, to avoid all discussion of ideology, and to keep everyone interested only in the practical problems involved in rebuilding the homeland. Noting the reservations some members of the AC still had on including non-Zionists, he promised to make no firm commitment at the conference. Yet, as he had to admit, if the non-Zionists agreed to raise money for the Keren Hayesod, then the Agency, with a large non-Zionist representation, would take over the power to determine the Palestine budget; the Zionist Congress, which until then had been the supreme authority, would be reduced to an advisory role. Weizmann felt that, if the Marshall group agreed to assume responsibility for an investment corporation and for raising money through the KH, he would be willing to see the Agency become the paramount force.[34]

The conference met in New York at the Hotel Astor on the seventeenth, with over one hundred of America's leading Jews in attendance, including Rabbi Abram Simon of the Central Conference of American Rabbis, who had previously opposed any co-operation with the Zionists. Neither Brandeis nor Julian Mack attended, although both sent messages pledging goodwill toward any useful enterprise that would build up the Holy Land. Marshall, elected chairman of the conference, opened with a lengthy speech in which he balanced the place of Palestine in Jewish hearts with the allegiance they all held to the United States. But the debates of a decade earlier no longer held any meaning, since the Balfour Declaration and the mandate had raised the dream of a Jewish homeland to a reality. With the approval by the U. S. Congress of that homeland, they could now move forward to work for Palestine untroubled by spurious charges of dual loyalty. "As loyal American citizens, therefore, we have the right to consider the question as to what, if anything, we shall do with regard to Palestine and its development, and as loyal Jews we have the duty to take action with regard to this all important subject, and to define ourselves, our thoughts, our ideas and our intentions, with regard to Palestine. We have no right to be indifferent." The Jews of America, the richest Jewish community in the world, had an obligation to act; they could not afford, either out of consideration for their suffering coreligionists overseas or for themselves, to sit idly by. *"I am afraid, I am afraid that non-action of that kind, indifference of that character, can do us a thousand times more harm than all the Ku Klux Klans and Henry Fords that you could crowd into this great city."* Those who had differed with the Zionists in the past now had the opportunity to forget old clichés and to unite in a great work. "We who have complained about Zionism have now an opportunity to show what we can do to assist the cause of Palestine. Let us drop old names and slogans. Let us no longer war about words." Rather, they could now transform a Palestine "which has been in a decline for centuries to its former state of prosperity, and to make of it a real center of culture and of thought."

Just as Marshall had carefully avoided the morass of political ideology, so Chaim Weizmann now did also. But while carefully ignoring any questions of statehood, he did emphasize the great yearning of Jewish masses in Europe to be free. Nothing the conference said or did could change that, but that striving for freedom could be immeasurably advanced if those gathered in the room agreed to help prepare the land. He had seen what American Jewry had been able to do during the war. "I am sure that if the same spirit would animate you in the consideration of the problems which are submitted to you today, Palestine will be rebuilt, and rebuilt Palestine will mean a credit to the Jews of the world. It will, I think, cast glory on all Jews, wherever they may be. It will create a center of Jewish learning and Jewish culture in a country where our sacred traditions still exist and will continue to exist. . . . New views and new ideas may come forth once more from Palestine, and the word of God from Jerusalem."

The positive tone of the entire conference showed how far the *yahudim* had traveled in a decade. Men who had vehemently opposed the Zionists before the war now praised their constructive labors in the Holy Land. But despite the best efforts of the organizers, the problem of ideology would not down. Weizmann explained that as far as the Zionists were concerned, they would be happy to work on a nonideological basis alongside those who did not share their particular philosophical views, and he approvingly quoted the late Judge

Mayer Sulzberger's comment that "it is sometimes good to do the right thing even for the wrong reason."* But Lee Frankel, a noted social worker who later headed a 1927 Palestinian survey and ultimately became a member of the Agency council, said that he and a number of other men had no doubt about the practical feasibility of rebuilding Palestine. They wanted to know exactly what they would have to do, and more importantly, what the attitude of the Zionists would be. For if the Zionist Organization persisted in a program that called ultimately for an independent political state, they wanted nothing to do with it. Marshall and Weizmann responded that all they sought was fulfillment of the terms of the mandate, which said nothing about a Jewish state. With these assurances, the conference overwhelmingly passed two resolutions, one creating a committee to organize an investment corporation to aid in the economic reconstruction of Palestine, and the other establishing a committee to study the subject of the Agency and to devise means by which American Jews could work with the World Zionist Organization for the development of the homeland.[35]

The Zionists, or at least most of them, seemed ecstatic over the conference. Nachman Syrkin, a founder of Poale Zion, labeled it a triumph for the cause, and happily noted that the American Jewish Committee had finally come home to Eretz Yisroel. Only the failure to invite Jewish labor groups marred the occasion. For Weizmann, triumph was complete, and he declared that "everybody present was much nearer to real Zionism than any of us ever suspected." He admitted that a "clumsy phraseology" had been used, but only to make it easier for the Americans to come into the work. Arthur Ruppin glowingly described all of the speeches as "completely Zionistic in spirit and very enthusiastic."[36] The non-Zionist participants also interpreted the meeting as a triumph, this time of reason over emotion. The executive vice president of the Joint Distribution Committee, David Brown, concluded that the Zionists had given up the idea of a Jewish state once and for all, while Marshall described the gathering as "successful beyond my anticipation."[37]

* Cf. the Christian view in T. S. Eliot's view in *Murder in the Cathedral:* "The last temptation is the greatest treason; to do the right deed for the wrong reason."

Obviously, Weizmann's "clumsy phraseology" had been more than just that. The non-Zionist position remained consistent: They did not oppose the development of a Jewish culture and settlement in Palestine, and in fact encouraged it, but they objected strenuously to the idea of a separate political state for the Jews. The Zionists, however, had from the beginning always sought a state. Theodore Herzl had entitled his manifesto *The Jewish State,* and the declared aim of every major Zionist pronouncement had been political independence. The Zionists and the authors of the Balfour Declaration had agreed that ultimately there would be a Jewish commonwealth in Palestine, but the wording had been deliberately chosen so as not to antagonize non-Zionists. The fact that the mandate did not specifically mention political Zionism or a state was at best semantic camouflage, since it included the earlier declaration verbatim, with its implied promise of eventual autonomy. For Weizmann to stand before the Americans in 1924 and nod agreement when Marshall declared that no one had any intention of establishing a state, can only be interpreted as a deliberate distortion and misrepresentation of all past Zionist history and ideology. For him to agree to the primacy of Palestine, to the near dismissal of political Zionism, to the granting of enormous power to non-Zionists, to an emphasis on private investment separated from donations—all of this would appear as a complete conversion to the Brandeisian program he had so vehemently denounced less than three years before. Brandeis, moreover, had never been willing to give the non-Zionists control over policy, while Weizmann's proposal gave each side 50 per cent of the votes. With the bulk of the money coming from the non-Zionists, obviously their influence would be dominant.

The problem, as Weizmann undoubtedly realized, lay in the refusal of the majority of American Jews to adopt the purist program he had advocated in 1921. ZOA members, as we have seen, turned the Brandeis/Mack group out not so much because they disagreed with the economic principles of the Pittsburgh program, but because of political maladroitness and lack of communication on the part of the leadership. Having capitalized on his pronounced Jewishness, Weizmann claimed that the opposition thought and acted like non-Jews, and denounced their program as assimilationist and anti-Zionist. Yet he soon came to understand that in substance, if not in form, the Brandeis proposals were the only ones that could interest the wealthier American Jews. He continued to denounce Brandeis, and even in 1948 when he wrote his memoirs, refused to admit that he had taken over the Justice's program practically *in toto*. As for the ideological Zionists who insisted that he cling to his earlier stance, he denounced them as naïfs who did not recognize that "the difference between [the non-Zionists] and the Zionists was not only political, it was also social."[38] Still, next to the Balfour Declaration, the enlarged Jewish Agency must rank as Chaim Weizmann's greatest achievement. By appealing to the sentiment of the upper-class Jews, by urging that work for Palestine would satisfy traditional Jewish commandments of charity, he secured the co-operation and the money of an essential group in the Jewish community. He had much more difficulty handling his own followers, who had to be diverted and smooth-talked lest they undo his diplomatic missions to the *yahudim*.

III

In the end, it took five years of meetings and proposals and compromises before the "pact of glory" could be signed. Marshall and Weizmann named the two committees necessary to implement the conference resolutions, and by the end of the year the Palestine Economic Corporation, headed by Marshall, Warburg, Samuel Untermyer, Morris Wertheim, and Bernard Flexner, issued a prospectus and began selling three million dollars' worth of stock. Both sides had a much harder job selling Zionists and non-Zionists on the idea that collaboration on Palestinian work would not constitute a betrayal of principle.[39] Then, from a totally unexpected quarter, a crisis developed that almost wiped out three years of work and nearly killed off any prospect for an enlarged Agency.

As an immediate result of the first non-Zionist conference, officials of the Joint Distribution Committee and the Keren Hayesod met to plan a joint appeal, with certain amounts earmarked for Palestinian work. But the JDC from the start had been staffed by people opposed to Zionism, and David Brown, who directed the JDC's programs, in particular objected to any notion of a Jewish state. From his point of view, work in Palestine rested upon the Zionists, while his organization had millions of Jews in Europe to look after. Moreover, in 1924 and 1925 he had a major problem which, in his mind, far outweighed the need to support chimerical plans for a Palestinian homeland.

A disastrous series of crop failures in Russia, beginning in 1921, had resulted in mass starvation, with tens of thousands of Jews leaving the land to look for bread and work in the cities. At first the JDC had directed its assistance through the American Relief Administration, headed by Secretary of Commerce Herbert Hoover. But where the Hoover task force limited itself to relief and food distribution, the JDC began to explore the possibility of massive resettlement of Jewish refugees in the Crimea. In July 1924, the JDC created a new operating agency to handle its work in Russia, the American Jewish Joint Agricultural Corporation, known as the Agro-Joint, and for the next five years spent six million dollars in settling and retraining Russian Jews.

The idea of creating large-scale Jewish settlements in the empty reaches of the Soviet Union appealed particularly to Julius Rosenwald, who personally underwrote much of the cost. The Chicago millionaire and head of Sears, Roebuck had no use for Palestine, which he considered a barren desert. "I shall not lift a finger to advance the immigration of Jews to Palestine," he declared, "for Palestine has nothing to offer them. The soil is too poor to support them. Nor is Palestine a field for either manufacture or industry. The Jews never went to Palestine of their own choice. They were simply lured to go there by all sorts of promises; and they went; and when the bait will be withdrawn, they will certainly refuse to settle there."[40] In 1928 he took the lead in creating the American Society for Jewish Farm Settlement in Russia, with a capitalization of eight million dollars of which he gave five million dollars. Between the efforts of the Agro-Joint and Rosenwald's Society, the American relief officials ultimately colonized over two hundred thouand Jews on some three million acres of relatively fertile farmland in the Soviet Union.

Weizmann, in an effort to keep peace with the non-Zionists, agreed not to interfere with their scheme, since it had the backing of Herbert

Lehman and Louis Marshall. But he could not keep his followers quiet. Nahum Sokolow began complaining as early as 1922, when the JDC poured large sums into the Hoover mission, that the money could better help Jews if it went to Palestine, but his pleas fell on deaf ears in JDC offices. Stephen Wise complained that Weizmann had betrayed the movement by his approval of the Crimea plan, and felt that the non-Zionists had proved that they had never really meant to support the Yishuv.[41] Given the scarcity of Zionist resources in the mid-twenties, it is little wonder that they clamored for the JDC to divert funds from the Soviet project to Eretz Yisroel. Even Felix Warburg's donation of fifty thousand dollars to the Keren Hayesod, meant to show his continuing devotion to the homeland, failed to convince them that the non-Zionists had little commitment or true feeling for Palestine.

In order to forestall some of the Zionist ire, Marshall decided that at least 1.5 million dollars of the funds to be raised by the JDC in 1926 should go to Palestinian projects. There had, after all, been a second non-Zionist conference earlier in 1925, and while it lacked the spirit of the first gathering, the participants had still decided to continue planning for the Agency. The Fourteenth Congress, at Vienna, also approved an Agency resolution, although Marshall objected to a three-year limit the Zionists had placed on its activities. So the New York lawyer advised David Brown not only of the division of funds, but also suggested that the Agro-Joint publicity on the Crimea project be kept at a very low key, "both for strategic reasons and because of moral obligations." But Brown and his colleagues, who were responsible for daily operations as well as fund raising, decided that perhaps it was the information on Palestine that should be kept quiet, since they believed that Palestinian work detracted from general relief in Europe, which they considered their prime responsibility. In the circular letter announcing the new campaign, Brown deleted all reference to any money going for Palestinian work, and emphasized plans in the Crimea. He had done this, he explained to Marshall, since a number of contributors who supported the JDC's work had not yet been reconciled to work in Palestine.[42]

The Zionists exploded. They withdrew from the United Jewish Campaign and established a separate drive, the United Palestine

Appeal, in October 1925. Marshall worked at a frenzied pace trying to avert the split. He publicly announced his plans for 1.5 million dollars to go to Palestine; privately he tried to explain away the problem as one of psychology. Palestine would always have a claim on Jews, but the Crimea project was a *mitzvah* [good deed], and not an expression of faith, to which Abba Hillel Silver responded that, after all the words, it meant quite simply putting Palestine in second place, something the Zionists would not agree to. At an organizational conference of the new drive in late November, Marshall tried once again to make peace, but only precipitated a bitter debate. At one point, Eliezar Kaplan, the Palestinian labor leader, suggested that "all peace maneuvers cease so that both sides could stop the war."[43]

Needless to say, negotiations on the Agency came to a halt, much to Weizmann's chagrin. He had been in Europe during the fall crisis, and thus unable to mediate between the Marshall group and the more militant Zionists. At the ZOA convention in June 1926, nearly all of the debates focused on money problems, with charges that the JDC had consistently short-changed the needs of Palestine, despite great contributions by Zionist workers to its campaigns.* On Zionist platforms around the country, orators began to attack the *shtadlanim* with a vigor not seen since the congress fight a decade earlier. Weizmann began to fear that the Marshall group no longer wanted to join in the great work ahead, and as he usually did when dissident groups within the ZOA criticized his leadership, he began to suspect dark plots being hatched against him in Washington. "Brandeisism is raising its head again," he moaned, "and the old arguments which we have fought in Cleveland are being smuggled into a back door into the program of American Zionism."[44] On the non-Zionist side, Marshall and Felix Warburg felt personally embittered by the attack launched against them, and refused to contribute to the 1926 Keren

---

* In the first ten years of its existence (1916–26), the JDC raised 60 million dollars, of which 7 million dollars, or about 12 per cent, had gone to Palestine. Brown insisted that the JDC distributed on the basis of need, not of ideology, and therefore Palestine had gotten all help to which it had been entitled. In comparison, the Zionists sent over 20 million dollars to the Yishuv in that decade, and also contributed heavily to the wartime relief campaigns.

Hayesod campaign. Warburg called attention to a speech by Stephen Wise in which the outspoken rabbi said he would give "one thousand Warburgs for one Bialik [the great Hebrew poet]. Warburg gives out of his surplus, while Bialik gives out of his soul." As the financier sardonically noted, "some diplomatic agent from Palestine to the non-Zionist Jews is badly needed."[45]

That diplomatic agent had to be Weizmann, who during much of this controversy had been recuperating from severe physical exhaustion at a Swiss sanitarium. Unable to act, he watched helplessly while his efforts to unite Zionist and non-Zionist came apart at the seams. He wrote bitter letters to both sides, accusing them of reneging on their promises to him, and one of these missives led Louis Marshall to unburden himself of several years of pent-up grievances and emotions. Of all the non-Zionist leaders, Marshall had been most open to Weizmann's appeal to help in the rebuilding of Palestine, and had done his best to convince other members of the German-Jewish aristocracy to join in this work. But Marshall also was the leader of this group, and to those not part of it, he symbolized both its best and its worst qualities. Thus, when the Joint Distribution Committee sent millions to resettle Jews in Godforsaken Russia but neglected deliberately to aid in the rebuilding of the sacred land of Israel, the Zionists had poured out their wrath upon Marshall's head. In eleven pages of catharsis, Marshall repeated instance after instance where the Zionists had falsely accused him of subverting their work, of being indifferent to Palestine, of being opposed to things Jewish. Nonetheless, he still remained committed to the rebuilding of the land of their fathers, and if Weizmann would come to America, they would make one last attempt to create a working agency.[46]

Weizmann took up the offer, and arrived in the United States toward the end of 1926. He immediately announced that political Zionism had no place in the discussions. "Neither you nor I will dictate to those on the hills of Palestine what political form their life will assume." Over the next five months he lobbied constantly, and holding out the olive branch, criticized his overzealous Zionist supporters for being too suspicious of the *yahudim*. He even unbent enough to go to Washington to meet with Justice Brandeis. The two men discussed a commission of experts who might be sent to Palestine to survey needs and determine the most efficient and effective way that money raised in the different funds could be used.[47] Marshall and Weizmann finally came to terms, and as a prelude to establishing the enlarged Agency, announced that a Survey Commission, to be headed by Lee Frankel, would be sent to the Holy Land. Nonpartisan in makeup, its findings would determine the practicability of their plan. Then on March 22, 1927, the Zionists and non-Zionists signed an agreement at the Hotel Biltmore in New York. "I am not a Zionist and never have been one," Marshall declared afterward. "I have always felt that I am something better than Zionist or non-Zionist; I am a Jew. I can stand on that platform. . . . The time has come when we should forget everything but the fact that this problem of Palestine is a Jewish problem."[48] That summer, the Fifteenth Congress, meeting once again in Basle, approved the agreement.

The Frankel Commission completed its work rapidly, and delivered its report within a year. The experts spoke glowingly of the land's potential, but Zionists were outraged by the total lack of commitment evident in the document. The idea of Palestine as a Jewish homeland did not even receive a passing reference, and the strongest language used referred to "the land of our origin." At an Actions Comité meeting, several members who had supported Weizmann in his negotiations now began to have second thoughts about the loyalty of their new partners. But at a third nonpartisan conference in New York in October 1928, the participants voted overwhelmingly to proceed with the founding of an enlarged Jewish Agency.

According to the pact, the Agency would have a council of 220 members, divided evenly between Zionists and non-Zionists. Of the 110 non-Zionist seats, the Americans would receive at least 40 per cent, or 44. The Zionist seats would be distributed along the same proportions as in the Congress, which meant that the ZOA would have only 10 or 11, a ratio unacceptable even to the non-Zionists, who realized the trouble this might cause. But that was a detail that could be worked out,* and in the summer of 1929, Chaim Weizmann and Louis Marshall traveled to Zurich, where the final agreement would be ratified by the Sixteenth Congress.

* The Congress awarded the ZOA 18 seats and 36 alternates.

An emotional affair, the Congress marked the culmination of nearly a decade's work by Weizmann, and with the exception of the militant Revisionists, all of the Congress parties voted overwhelmingly to endorse the "pact of glory." Weizmann, re-elected president of the WZO, then introduced his guest, simply and directly, as "Mr. Louis Marshall," and the delegates gave Marshall a standing ovation. It was a touching tribute to a man they knew did not agree with much of their philosophy, but whose devotion to the welfare of his people matched or exceeded their own. He had worked all of his life to protect and defend Jews, both in Europe and the United States; he had argued for Jewish rights at the peace tables and had provided food and succor for the victims of the war. Now, in the crowning hour of his career, he would share the direction of a new agency that would rebuild Eretz Yisroel. The delegates to the Sixteenth Congress adjourned on August 10 in a mood of exhilaration and high hopes, more optimistic than they had been since the war. That day, the founding session of the new Jewish Agency convened.

On August 23, Arabs stormed into the streets of Jerusalem. Hebron, and Safed, and before they had spent their fury, 133 Jews lay dead and 400 more injured. On September 11, Louis Marshall died from complications following an emergency operation. And on October 29, 16.4 million shares changed hands on the New York Stock Exchange, climaxing a five-day selling spree in which the value of American equities declined 32 billion dollars, and the Great Depression came to the *goldenah medinah*.

IV

Despite the apparent warmth with which the Congress received the Agency, there were some who did not care for it at all. The Reform leaders in Germany opposed it, as did some ideological purists in the Zionist camp. Chaim Arlosoroff, the Palestinian labor leader and theoretician, warned against any compromise of belief for the sake of the plan, and insisted that despite the denials of the non-Zionists, Diaspora nationalism remained one of the Zionist articles of faith. The starting point of the movement still lay in the idea that "we are sons of an essentially solid, if scattered and torn, Jewish nation, which we want to organize for unified political and cultural action." If the Zionists had been willing to concede this central and controlling principle, a Jewish Agency "could have been secured thirty years ago."[49]

But with the approval of the Zionist Congress, the Jewish Agency had become a reality, and it had benefits and liabilities, not all of which its promoters had foreseen. On the negative side, the differing business methods, which had caused part of the fight at Cleveland, soon became a sore point between the Zionists and non-Zionists. Felix Warburg, who took over the leadership of the non-Zionists after Marshall's death, had much less tolerance for ideological differences than had Marshall; Warburg also had a lot less tact and, unfortunately, a much thinner skin. He took the ideological attacks on the Agency personally, and for many years refused to speak to Stephen Wise. He expected that once he struck a bargain with Weizmann, that agreement would be as binding as he expected his business deals to be, and never comprehended that Weizmann not only had to compromise between the Zionists and the non-Zionists, but between Zionists and Zionists as well. The Zionist inability to understand simple rules of business procedure continuously irked him, and in desperation he once defined what he saw as the real difference between the two groups. "A Zionist," he declared, "considers a loan an asset, while a non-Zionist considers it a liability."[50] The great financial sums that the Zionists expected failed to materialize, and many of Weizmann's backers who had worked vigorously for the Agency, like Arthur Ruppin, now complained bitterly that the Agency failed to meet the needs of the Yishuv. Marshall's assurances to Weizmann that Zionist financial troubles would be over ran aground on the shoals of an international depression, which saw the purses of the *yahudim* shrink alongside those of the *yidden*. In the four years before the Agency pact, Keren Hayesod contributions averaged a little over two million dollars yearly; in the next four years, the fund brought in little more than half of that, and in 1932–33, received less than seven hundred thousand dollars. Certainly this could not be blamed on the Agency, and undoubtedly the sums would have been even smaller without the contributions of the non-Zionists.[51]

The Agency also failed to attract the non-Zionists into a deeper involvement. On the whole, with the exception of some of the leaders, they did not support the work of the Agency as the Zionists did. Hardly any of the leaders wanted to serve on the Executive, which had offices in London and Jerusalem. Instead, they sent representatives, good, solid men, but who lacked the authority of their Zionist counterparts, such as Weizmann or David Ben-Gurion. The fifty-fifty principle soon proved irrelevant, since the non-Zionists had difficulty securing volunteers to serve on the Agency council. In the end, control reverted to the Zionists, and the Agency ultimately ceased to stand for a union between the two groups.[52]

Certainly the claims that the Agency had made all Jews into Zionists did not hold water. Shmaryahu Levin's insistence that in the Agency agreement all Jews now turned eastward and away from assimilation seemed ludicrous to the *yahudim*.[53] The Agency did, however, make work for the homeland palatable to many of those who had been repelled by Zionist ideology, and a number of prominent Jews did join the Council, including Léon Blum, the French socialist, Lord Melchett, a leader of British industry, and financiers such as Felix Warburg. It brought into the work that type of person who, if a Zionist, had previously identified with the Brandeis/Mack groups—assimilated, well-to-do, and insistent upon a practical and efficient administration.[54] And the Agency also made it possible for American Reform Judaism to gracefully abandon its extreme anti-Zionist attitude and join in the rebuilding of Palestine.

This *rapprochement* had gotten off to a rocky start in 1920 when the Central Conference of American Rabbis overwhelmingly defeated a resolution applauding the mandate and urging aid to help the ZOA in its Palestinian reconstruction work. Two years later, however, an invitation to join the Palestine Development Council elicited a counterproposal that if the Council would reorganize to give non-Zionists half of the seats, then the CCAR would be glad to participate; and in 1924, Reform leaders attended the nonpartisan conference.[55] Undoubtedly the presence of one of America's most distinguished lay Jews, Louis Marshall, helped soften some Reform hostility, and Marshall consistently proclaimed that he saw no incongruity between Reform Judaism and work in Palestine. "If there

is, then so much the worse for Reform Judaism," he publicly declared; "indifference to Palestine on the part of any Jew to me spells
inconsistency with the spirit of Judaism."[56] By the end of the decade,
the outward hostility had gone. In 1928, Hebrew Union College
awarded an honorary doctorate to Chaim Weizmann, and the following year the seminary's president, the noted scholar Julian Morgenstern, presided over a veritable love feast at the annual ZOA
convention. To the cheering Zionists, Morgenstern announced: "Zionists and non-Zionists, and even anti-Zionists, have in general not
been nearly as far apart as they have themselves generally imagined."[57]

Palestine, the ancient and the modern, Herzl's Altneuland, became the common ground on which Zionists, non-Zionists, and
even some anti-Zionists could stand; even the Reverend Dr. Philipson no longer dismissed Palestine as a historical relic.[58] The differences between factions now often seemed to revolve around semantic
problems. Mordecai Kaplan, the Zionist theoretician and founder
of the Palestine-centered Reconstruction movement, defined Zionists
as those who felt a Jewish Palestine fulfilled a spiritual need and
served as a cultural center; non-Zionists, on the other hand, were
those for whom Palestine held no relevance to their inner spiritual
makeup. But under this definition, nearly everyone could be defined
as a Zionist, and especially someone like Louis Marshall. Palestine
was no longer a possibility but an actuality, and men like Marshall,
by deliberately blunting philosophical edges and ignoring semantic
definitions, took long steps toward unifying American Jewry.

But the most amazing aspect of the entire episode is that Chaim
Weizmann, in creating the Jewish Agency as the prime vehicle for
Palestinian work, enacted the very program that Louis Brandeis had
proposed a decade earlier, and that Weizmann at that time had so
bitterly denounced.[59] By 1929, many of those who had supported
Weizmann at Cleveland were speaking of the need for private investment and the development of small business. In his speeches,
Weizmann stopped talking about political Zionism or Diaspora nationalism or *gegenwartsarbeit,* and spoke almost entirely about the
need to develop the land and to build up the economy.[60] Shortly
after the third nonpartisan conference had approved the final Agency

agreement, Benjamin V. Cohen, Julius Simon, Leo Wolman, and Horace Kallen issued a statement that the Brandeis plan, defeated in 1921, now stood triumphant, a judgment that the great Zionist historian Adolph Böhm concurred in.[61] So practical, so Palestine-oriented had Zionism become that Dr. Abraham Coralnik, one of the few purists still in the ZOA administration, lamented: "The new generation that grew up in America in the last few years never did learn the alphabet of Zionism. And since the older generation is forgetting it, there are no teachers to teach them."[62] With the continued acceptance of the Brandeisian program came a growing demand for the return of the old leadership.

CHAPTER NINE

HOLLOW VICTORY

For some people defeat, especially in a fight involving deeply cherished beliefs, leads to despair; for others, who take comfort in the faith that right will ultimately prevail, a sense of serenity overcomes the bitterness. In the months following their ouster at the 1921 convention, the various members of the Mack administration took heart from the words and example of Louis D. Brandeis. Throughout the 1920s, they sustained and renewed their interest in Zionism, and each, in his own way, worked to further the cause. Some co-operated in a marginal manner with the Lipsky regime, while others rallied around the Palestine Development Council. They kept open their lines of communication to different Zionist factions, and with few exceptions, showed little bitterness or hostility to the Eastern Europeans, and many who had voted against them soon came over to their side. As the decade wore on, they saw one after another of their policies vindicated, while Chaim Weizmann, whom they all distrusted, espoused the very programs he had once excoriated. In the end, those who had expelled the Americanized leadership at Cleveland in 1921 called them back, but by then, the whole nature of American Zionism had been greatly transformed.

I

In the months following the debacle at Cleveland, the deposed leaders took their cue from the silent leader, whom Alvin Johnson once described as a "serenely implacable democrat." The veteran of numerous reform fights, Brandeis knew that defeat, while temporarily painful, need not be final. He had suffered setbacks in his earlier battles against the New England transportation monopoly and other trusts, ultimately to see his policies triumph. In a letter that summed up his credo of reform, he wrote: "Remember that progress is necessarily slow; that remedies are necessarily tentative; that because of varying conditions there must be much and constant enquiry into facts . . . and much experimentation; and that always and everywhere the intellectual, moral and spiritual development of those concerned will remain an essential—and the main factor—in real betterment."[1] Within a few days after their mass resignation from office, his followers gathered to plan their next moves, and Brandeis set the mood in calm and deliberate tones.

They had not resigned from Zionism, he reminded them, and they still believed in the goal of a Jewish homeland in Palestine. "We are from now on to free ourselves from all entanglements in order that we may the sooner accomplish that end. By making our efforts simple and direct, we can work to attain that end with the least possible embarrassment. We shall, of course, remain members of the Zionist Organization of America. But we are supporters of an administration whose policies and principles have been repudiated. Those represented by the new administration we believe to be wrong. The differences between us are fundamental. As long as the new officers pursue policies and methods which we deem to be wrong we cannot share in their work. The responsibility is theirs. . . . Because our differences are fundamental, we must content ourselves with being merely members of the Zionist Organization."[2]

The Brandeis group, however, had limited options on how they could best serve the cause. Despite the fine rhetoric of remaining "humble soldiers in the ranks," these were men accustomed to the exercise of power, to leading rather than following. They would have been welcomed back to the ZOA immediately, and even in the emotional period following the schism, the Lipsky regime would have had to make room for some of them on the Administrative and Executive committees. But this would have meant acquiescence in those policies they had sworn to boycott. They might have carried their fight to the Twelfth Congress, which met at Carlsbad in August, and have attempted to impress upon the delegates the dangers inherent in Weizmann's program. In fact, Julius Simon did launch such an attack on the Weizmann leadership at the Congress, and when he deplored the loss of Brandeis to the Zionist movement, a large number of delegates rose in a prolonged ovation for the Justice. But while the breach in the American movement dominated much of the discussion at the Congress, Weizmann easily controlled the assembly. Many of the Europeans still resented Brandeis' handling of the London Conference, while the differences between the two economic programs mystified many of those present. Nahum Goldmann, in a brilliant defense of Weizmann, correctly pointed out that the Zionist movement owed its strength and character to its mass base, but then inaccurately labeled the Brandeis proposals as a reversion to the old colonization schemes of Baron de Rothschild. He warned the Congress against putting all of its emphasis on Palestinian work, and ignoring *gegenwartsarbeit,* lest it deteriorate into just another settlement society.[3]

In the end, the Brandeisists decided to create one or more corporations that would work for the economic development of Palestine and Palestinian institutions. The Palestine Endowment Funds, organized in 1922 under Julian Mack's direction, utilized charitable donations for a variety of purposes. One of its first, and largest, funds went to the support of Hebrew University in Jerusalem; in 1935, at David Ben-Gurion's request, PEF provided the funds to purchase land near Akaba on the Red Sea, now the site of the important Israeli port of Eilat.[4]

A more ambitious scheme led to the establishment of the Palestine Development Council, which would be the investment counterpart of the donation-oriented PEF. Discussion of an investment corporation had begun in 1920, and as part of the growing *rapprochement* between the Zionists and the American Jewish Committee, Judge Mack and Louis Marshall had held preliminary discussions on coordinating investment work. The ZOA leadership recognized that the wealthy members of the German-Jewish community would have a key role to play in the economic rebuilding of the homeland. Although work on the PDC continued after the Cleveland convention, with Mack now out of power and Weizmann actively soliciting Marshall's goodwill, efforts to enlist the support of the *yahudim* came to naught.

In creating the PDC, the Brandeis group tried to blend social idealism with economic realism, a reflection of their progressive view of enlightened business. As Julian Mack explained it, the PDC would fund enterprises of a strictly business nature, but "the members of this group have a definite social vision which in their judgment should permeate all of the activities. They believe that in especially a small country like Palestine, emphasis had to be on co-operative work, whether in production, consumption or furnishing of credit. They therefore feel it their duty to stimulate the creation of, and to strengthen the existing co-operative societies and credit unions in Palestine."[5] The goal of the PDC, therefore, involved socioeconomic work, with limited dividends to the investors. They hoped to prove that by offering opportunities for sound investment, reasonable returns, and social benefits, numerous investors, both small and large, would co-operate in the building of the land.

Despite much time and effort, the PDC never achieved the results hoped for by its creators. Working outside of the Zionist organization, without the benefit of its propaganda apparatus or infrastructure, by which it could have reached masses of people, it was doomed to depend upon a few large donors. Its promoters totally misjudged the willingness of small businessmen to put their money into Palestinian projects, especially without the assurances that would have accompanied the participation of the Marshall/Warburg group.[6] The PDC in fact tried several times to form a partnership with the Joint Distribution Committee, hoping to create a business bridge between the wealthy *yahudim* and the smaller entrepreneurs of the newly prosperous Russian community. But as Yonathan Shapiro points out, the small businessmen were overawed by the German-Jewish millionaires. When Sol Rosenblum, the PDC treasurer, began negotiations with the JDC on a possible joint project, Judge Mack worriedly wrote that Rosenblum "seems completely captivated by these people. . . . His complete trust in them made me and makes me apprehensive."[7]

Even when projects came along that met PDC criteria, its members found they lacked the resources to undertake them alone. The Rutenberg Hydroelectric Development scheme clearly illustrated the limitations of the PDC. Pinhas Rutenberg, a Russian-born electrical engineer, had settled in Palestine in 1919, and was known to American Zionists for the work he had done during the war, when he lived in the United States. Rutenberg had drafted plans to harness the upper waters of the Jordan and Yarmukh rivers for hydroelectric power, and despite Arab opposition, the British had granted him a concession in 1921. He had immediately turned to the Brandeis group to seek financing, and the PDC quickly grasped the importance of the scheme for Palestinian development. Morris Rothenberg, a member of the Lipsky administration, proposed that financing the Rutenberg company might form a first step in restoring peace in Zionist ranks. A few months later, Vladimir Jabotinsky, hoping to exploit this sentiment, proposed that the PDC undertake to raise funds for Rutenberg, and then appoint a board of trustees that would include ZOA representatives. The regular Zionists, in turn, would put their propaganda forces at the disposal of the promoters, and the Keren Hayesod would also participate.[8] Since the Zionists had, for the most part, been extremely critical of the PDC, Mack and his associates, especially Julius Simon, reacted with more than a fair degree of skepticism to this unexpected offer of co-operation. Jabotinsky's insistence on pushing what he saw as a potentially unifying enterprise led to a meeting with Simon to explore the problems involved, but it soon became clear that, despite the obvious benefits of the Rutenberg Development, the PDC feared any involvement with the ZOA. Finally, Judge Mack informed Rutenberg that the Council, while appreciating the importance of the hydroelectric plant, felt that "all different sections of American Jewry, which ought to participate in your scheme, can be effectively reached only if subscriptions are taken, not through any one organization, but from as many quarters as possible."[9] The PDC, in fact, felt unable to handle the project alone, and feared undertaking a responsibility it knew it could not meet. As Robert Szold and Julius Simon admitted, the Council had not gained very much ground in the German-Jewish circles,[10] and without large investors, it had to limit its activities to small or moderately-sized projects; yet unless it could successfully underwrite large enterprises, like the Rutenberg proposal, it would never attract either the big financiers or enough small businessmen to be really successful.

Because the names of the Americanized leaders still had great value, some members of the ZOA who understood Brandeis' economic program hoped to use financial investment as a bridge between the two groups. In 1924, after the first nonpartisan conference voted to establish an investment corporation, Bernard Flexner, whose position in the Joint Distribution Committee and personal friendship with Justice Brandeis gave him entrée to both camps, suggested a merger of the JDC's Palestine Committee and the Palestine Development Council, forming a new association in which all parties could be represented. Julius Simon, Benjamin V. Cohen, and Judge Mack welcomed this offer, seeing it as the opening they needed to secure the involvement and investment of the wealthier Jews. But Brandeis and Jacob deHaas opposed the merger, and although all of the other members of the PDC wanted to go along, out of respect for Brandeis' wishes, they delayed negotiations for two years.[11] Brandeis' obstinacy on this proposal can partially be explained by personal pique at the exclusion of PDC members from earlier planning conferences; but he also bridled at the cavalier manner in which the ZOA had dismissed a plan developed for joint co-operation by deHaas. The former secretary proposed that a membership organization, a Palestine Development League, could be established as an adjunct to the PDC, with dues-paying members eligible to invest on a very small scale in different enterprises. The Lipsky regime immediately branded the proposal as a bid to create an alternative Zionist organization in the United States, one that would take members away from the ZOA, and Lipsky publicly warned American Zionists not to have any traffic with the proposed League. DeHaas, who for better or worse had Brandeis' ear, evidently convinced the Justice to give him some time to launch the League, and this necessitated scrapping any co-operative work for the moment.[12] It was not the first time that deHaas' personal feuds had precluded peace within Zionist ranks; of all the members of the ousted administration, he most allowed his dislike of the Lipsky regime to distort his judgment.

In the end, merger took place with the creation of the Palestine Economic Corporation, headed by Bernard Flexner, with Marshall and Herbert Lehman as the two vice presidents, and several Brandeisists, including Mack, on the executive committee. The men of great wealth could now be reached, although their investments proved to be much less than everyone had anticipated. The PEC proved to be the type of enterprise Brandeis had originally envisioned, and it contributed a great deal to the development of co-operative businesses as well as private ventures in Palestine. The PDC, without access either to the men of great wealth or to the apparatus of the ZOA, was doomed to failure. Yet it would be a mistake to see its efforts at raising capital from small investors as a preoccupation with building up Palestine through private enterprise. Time after time the Brandeis group stressed that it did not want to re-create in the homeland the conditions they fought against in the United States. In the Pittsburgh program and *Zeeland* memorandum, in Mack's letter explaining the PDC's purposes, they made it quite clear that economic development in Palestine would have to follow co-operative lines, without becoming necessarily socialist. But to finance that development, money would be needed, and with the great fortunes closed to them, the only resources they could turn to consisted of small businessmen. Unfortunately, the presence of Marshall and Warburg in the Weizmann camp and the creation of the Jewish Agency undermined their efforts in that direction. Yet if they had had a free hand at the start, it is likely that the agency they would have created would have, in the end, turned out to be very much like the Palestine Economic Corporation.

II

In the years following the Cleveland split, endeavors to make peace surfaced constantly, but all faltered due to the pride and stubbornness of both sides. Numerous rank-and-file Zionists petitioned Brandeis to leave the bench and return to active leadership of the movement. His response, always polite but firm, was that he could do more for Zionism as a Supreme Court Justice than as an officer of the organization.[13] When the Keren Hayesod delegation came to the United States in 1922, Vladimir Jabotinsky, who would soon break with the WZO over its "soft" Palestine policy and would then establish the militant Revisionist movement, made it his special mission to make peace among the dissidents. He appealed to Judge Mack's reason: How could they remain out of the organization when they all worked toward the same goal, a Palestinian homeland? "The logic of the situation seems to point in the one and only direction—namely that such an arrangement [of co-operation] must be carried out." Local feuds could not be allowed to interfere with the work for Palestine. To the Executive, Jabotinsky admitted that in any other circumstances, the dissenters should be read out of the party if they refused to follow Zionist policy. But the schism, even after a year, still undermined Zionist morale. While Keren Hayesod collections had not yet suffered, if the schism continued, great damage would be done to the cause. Peace was not only desirable, but in the long run necessary.[14]

But peace there would not be, although in retrospect we can see that a majority on both sides wanted it badly. Weizmann, Ussischkin, and Lipsky distrusted Mack and Brandeis as much as the ousted Americans suspected them, while personal pride and stubbornness nursed deep-seated rancors. As the Zionists became more involved in the task of creating the Agency, however, they neglected those problems of organization and membership that afflicted the ZOA and that resulted in steadily declining rosters and revenues. As it grew clear that the Lipsky regime could not cope with these difficulties, disaffection in the ZOA increased. Several of the leaders who had resigned in 1921 slowly drifted back into affiliation with some of the administrative committees, disillusioned at the failure of the Palestine Development Council, while a number of former Lipsky supporters made their peace with the Mack group.[15] In Hadassah, where the Brandeisists had never really lost control, the National Board's insistence upon Palestinian work and what they saw as the real desiderata of Zionism proved constant thorns in the side of the administration throughout the 1920s.

The women's Zionist group had practically split apart during the Keren Hayesod fight, since the women had husbands on both sides of the controversy. Henrietta Szold, who had gone to Palestine to supervise Hadassah work there, wrote of her sadness over the loss of Brandeis to the movement, and worried how to keep alive the organization she had founded. Her friends in America wanted her to come home, but Brandeis, when he learned of this, quickly told them that under no circumstances should Miss Szold be recalled. The most important ingredient in the rebuilding of the homeland was "character," and Henrietta Szold, no matter what office she held or what work she did, could make a very great contribution just by being there. He told Rose Jacobs that she would have to assume part of the burden of leadership, and by this decision, he guaranteed the future of Hadassah.[16] By insisting that new women come forward, that new talent be developed, he prevented Hadassah from becoming a manifestation of one person. Henrietta Szold would be given another quarter century in which to serve the cause, but in those years she would be able to rely on an organization that had a rationale and a drive that reflected her own philosophy and commitment but did not depend on her personally.

The establishment of the Keren Hayesod, however, posed a direct threat to Hadassah's main work, the development of health services in Palestine. Under the 1918 reorganization plan, Hadassah became part of the ZOA, and its funds technically went into the ZOA coffers, but with the understanding that all Hadassah-raised monies applied to their medical programs. The new arrangement would have Hadassah collections go into the Keren Hayesod, and that fund would underwrite medical work in Palestine. But the women's organization had no assurances that all of its money would go to medical work, or that it would have any control over those programs. In effect, Hadassah would be reduced to a charity-collecting agency. Miss Szold immediately saw the danger and warned that "every consideration must be waived in favor of immediate efficient and vigorous practical work in Palestine. The Keren Hayesod seems to offer no guarantees of immediacy, or efficiency, or vigor." When Louis Lipsky requested the Hadassah Central Committee to notify its chapters that they should co-operate with other Zionist groups in the KH campaign, seven members refused.[17]

Lipsky's next move was indeed foolhardy, and earned him the enmity of the women Zionists that would last until he was forced from office in 1930. Under the Mack administration, Hadassah had been permitted a semi-autonomous status, despite the technicality that its members had the same status and responsibility as other ZOA members. The Brandeis group understood the potential in the organization and recognized the genius and drive of Henrietta Szold. With Lipsky now in charge, a power struggle inevitably developed. He saw the women as adherents of the despised Brandeis position, while they mistrusted his proposed reorganization that would deprive them of their power and purpose. In the face of the Committee's refusal to co-operate with the KH, Lipsky invoked the charter rules as to the subservience of Hadassah to the ZOA and requested the seven women to resign. They refused, claiming they had been elected by the local chapters, and only the local chapters could dismiss them. In an effort to reach some sort of accommodation, Hadassah requested the new administration to consider a petition that would relieve the organization of all financial obligations except that of medical work; the new Executive Committee, smarting over this affront by women, refused even to discuss it. Given the situation, it would have been better for them to have reached an agreement. In the previous three years, Hadassah membership had been climbing steadily, while ZOA rosters had drastically shrunk. In the summer of 1921, one out of every three members on ZOA rolls belonged to Hadassah.

Hadassah balked at the proposed financial arrangement whereby the KH would support the medical work, with all Hadassah funds turned into the general coffers. The women recognized that they would lose control of their own projects, since they had no guarantees that the money they raised would be applied to medical projects. When Hadassah requested an adjustment of their status, Lipsky jumped to the conclusion that the Brandeisists had put them up to it. But even the pro-Lipsky forces within Hadassah did not want to lose what they saw as their own special role, and faced with such massive opposition, the ZOA finally had to grant Hadassah a semi-automous status, with control over its own collections and guaranteed representation at ZOA conventions and at world congresses. In turn, the total raised by the women would be credited against the four hundred thousand dollars budgeted for medical work by the KH. Basically, the women had formalized the arrangement they had enjoyed under the Mack regime.

The reasons for Lipsky's hostility and Hadassah's victory are not hard to find. The women cared very little for *gegenwartsarbeit,* or cultural work in the Diaspora. They had a mission to bring healing to the inhabitants of the Holy Land, and they recognized and understood the importance of that work in the rebuilding of the homeland. Miss Szold, in very Brandeisian tones, had given them the word: "Be true to the past of Hadassah. . . . I say that the Hadassah rule of action in the past may be summed up in these words: organization, specialization, constancy, and a sense of responsibility for an ideal."[18] Only by choosing one thing, and then doing it well, could they hope to be successful. The insistence on practical work, on fiscal responsibility and on the exclusion of political considerations all smacked of the hated Brandeisian program, and the surprising vigor of the women in defending their organization led Lipsky to suspect (incorrectly) that the Brandeis/Mack group had engineered the whole thing.

As the 1920s wore on, the Hadassah formula seemed to be working, while the ZOA apparently could do nothing right. By 1927, the women's organization had over 34,000 members, while the ZOA had less than 22,000. Four years later, Hadassah had added another 10,000 women to its rolls, while the regular organization slipped down to 13,500. Throughout the decade, periodic attempts to reach a *modus vivendi* between the two groups foundered upon the resoluteness and independence of Hadassah and the administrative incompetence of the Lipskyites. In 1926, for example, Hadassah agreed to co-operate in the United Palestine Appeal. Henrietta Szold and several other Hadassah officials joined the UPA committee, headed by Stephen Wise, who agreed to lead the campaign as a sign of support for the Yishuv. The working arrangement called for all monies raised by Hadassah to go to the UPA campaign, which would then remit them for the medical work in Palestine.

The presence of Wise in the UPA, along with Abba Hillel Silver and several other Brandeisists, indicated that many of them felt that further alienation from the regular organization might eventually prove detrimental to their cause. With the establishment of the Palestine Economic Corporation, they had achieved their goal of creating a sound fiscal agent for Palestinian development, while negotiations over the Jewish Agency would shortly bring in the non-Zionists and their wealth. As to the ZOA program, Lipsky had practically ceased talking about anything other than raising funds for Palestine. His one effort at *gegenwartsarbeit*, the creation of a special cultural association, had been a dismal failure.[19] In an editorial in the *New Palestine*, the administration admitted that for all practical purposes, Zionism in the United States consisted of work for the Yishuv. Maurice Samuel, Lipsky's right-hand man, even went so far as to claim that no real differences existed between Zionists and non-Zionists; they all supported Palestine.[20] The growing chaos and loss of purpose within the ZOA could be seen in the impatience and frustration of some of the Eastern European leaders. Emanuel Neumann, who had been one of the young Turks opposing Brandeis as early as 1918, now admitted that the only hope for Zionist success in the future lay in the return of those who could provide the "non-Zionist qualities" so desperately needed—"efficiency, administrative gifts, financial and economic ability, experience in affairs of state."[21]

This lack of "non-Zionist qualities," as Neumann sardonically labeled them, led to a further estrangement of Hadassah when it discovered that the administrative costs of running the UPA campaign ate up a disproportionate share of the proceeds. Hadassah, which had a minimal paid staff, had always prided itself on the fact that 100 per cent of all monies collected for Palestine went to Palestine, with all overhead expenses paid for out of membership dues. When the UPA had to resort to a bank loan to cover part of its scheduled remittances in 1927, Mrs. Irma Lindheim, Hadassah's president, exploded in anger, and the National Board refused to co-sign the note. In a statement seething with indignation, Mrs. Lindheim declared that Hadassah had never worked that way and never would; sound Zionist principles demanded that the organization should pay its expenses out of its income. She added insult to injury when she sadly noted that the ZOA, then $140,000 in debt, had ceased to stand for any real commitment or ideal, and had become just another money-raising group. If the ZOA wanted Hadassah to continue its affiliation, there would have to be another renegotiation of the 1921 status agreement. Either the ZOA reorganized itself with a strong Hadassah representation, or the women's group would seek full independence. In an effort to avert still another crisis, Lipsky agreed to a joint committee with representatives of his administration, the Brandeis/Mack faction, and Hadassah.[22] But the committee never got off the ground, for 1927 marked the beginning of the end for the Lipsky regime, as a variety of groups began clamoring for the return of the Brandeis leadership.

III

Although their failure to develop the Palestine Development Council led several of the former leaders back into some of the ZOA committees, none of them had come to terms with the Lipsky administration. Stephen Wise, even though he agreed to chair the Palestine appeal and went to the Fourteenth Congress as a member of the American delegation, continued to demand the ouster of

Lipsky. After a tour of Palestine in 1926, Horace Kallen angrily blamed the Executive for the needless suffering he saw there, and concluded that "we are as right as we were in Cleveland in 1921."[23] But some of the Brandeis/Mack group refused to have anything to do with the current administration. Robert Szold, one of the youngest and most talented of the faction, refused a direct appeal from Lipsky to take over part of the Palestine financial program, and nearly fifty years later could still vigorously and emotionally denounce the bumbling incompetence of the ZOA leadership in the 1920s. And although Brandeis understood why some of his supporters worked on ZOA committees, he insisted that there could be no compromise with "Lipsky or any of his ilk."[24]

Brandeis' antipathy toward Lipsky went far beyond resentment over the loss of power; indeed, in no other area of his voluminous correspondence can we find such hostility. Zionism had originally appealed to him because of what he saw as its nobility and idealism, and part of the synthesis of Zionism with Americanism had been the emphasis on moral uplift and on sacrifice. While he did not trust Weizmann or believe in his policies, Brandeis did meet with the WZO leader several times after 1921, and on occasion sent written approval of some particular action. He did this because he recognized Weizmann's deep commitment to Zionism, and he saw him devoting his entire life to the movement at a great personal sacrifice. In New York, on the other hand, he saw a group of men drawing salaries while they ran the ZOA into the ground, mismanaged its finances, and incurred a debt of over $140,000. When Charles Cowen visited the Justice to draw out some of his views on the state of Zionist affairs, Cowen got more than he bargained for. "For five minutes," Brandeis wrote, "I spoke to him impressively and torrentially of the shame to the Jewish people which had come from this self-seeking, incompetent and dishonest administration, which had prostituted a great cause; which, enjoying fat salaries in New York, had let school teachers in Palestine starve with six months of salaries in arrears; which had defied the teachings of the prophets that had sustained and maintained the Jewish People throughout the centuries." When Cowen feebly asked what should be done, Brandeis, whom Franklin Roosevelt called "Isaiah," answered: "Only the teachings of the prophets; return to truth, put an end to the lying. Turn out those who have obtained money under false pretenses and misappropriated that which they secured."[25]

Brandeis' ire at the mismanagement of funds—a charge that would later be confirmed by a special auditing committee—was matched by a growing concern among the rank and file over the continued decline of the ZOA. On the eve of the 1927 convention, despair and frustration highlighted the mood in the Zionist camp. Emanuel Neumann, Israel Goldberg, and several others who had once backed Louis Lipsky now prepared to fight him, and urgent messages went out to members of the Brandeis/Mack faction soliciting their support in the battle. At the convention itself, Lipsky admitted that the financial affairs of the organization were in terrible shape and its members disheartened.[26] If the Brandeisists had been willing to establish a coalition regime, they could have taken control then, but they refused to join in partnership with Lipsky. When Chaim Weizmann sent a special message in support of the administration, the delegates had no choice but to re-elect Lipsky, and in the ensuing debate, he managed to have Neumann, Goldberg, and Bernard Rosenblatt excluded from the Executive Committee. The nomination of Julian Mack and Stephen Wise as part of the Congress delegation, however, led many of those present to hope that the Brandeis group would soon join them in a bid to take over the organization.

The Lipsky administration had relied primarily on the Eastern European masses for its strength, and had come to power by denouncing the alleged lack of Jewish feeling in the Americanized leadership. Moreover, following Weizmann's lead, they had derided the Pittsburgh program and the *Zeeland* memorandum as examples of the non-Jewish approach to Zionism, and had promised that they would emphasize non-Palestinian work, especially cultural programs in the Diaspora, as well as the rebuilding of the homeland. Yet in order to attract the non-Zionists to the Agency plan, Weizmann had to downplay every aspect of Zionism except Palestinian reconstruction, and his lieutenants in the United States followed his cue. By 1927—ideologically, at least—the Brandeis program had won out. Yonathan Shapiro, moreover, has provided a fascinating analysis of the social and cultural evolution of the Eastern Europeans.

Just as they had looked previously to the Americanized leadership to legitimatize their interest in Zionism, now they appealed to them again to provide a prestige for the organization that the Lipsky administration totally lacked.[27]

The prosperity of the war and postwar years had been good to many of the immigrant groups,[28] and numerous Jews had moved out of the sweatshops and tenements into more middle-class jobs and surroundings. They no longer identified with Chaim Weizmann, whose strength rested on his European Jewish characteristics, or with his alter ego in America, Louis Lipsky. Shmuel Margoshes, a featured writer in the Yiddish press, explained how Weizmann no longer fit their needs: "Dr. Weizmann is only a president and a guest in the United States. And even though it is rumored that he converses with kings and prime ministers and that prominent 'goyim' respect him, he is nonetheless a foreigner in this land and does not even occupy a salon on Fifth Avenue. As for Lipsky, he is just a journalist. If at least he would write in the *Times,* instead of choosing to write in the *New Palestine!* I ask you, can one see in him a person who can confer prestige on others?"[29] A few of the Yiddish intellectuals, such as Abraham Coralnik and Abe Goldberg, continued to cling to the older version of a Zionism that would not only rebuild a homeland, but would also rejuvenate Judaism in the Diaspora; Mordecai Kaplan, at the same time, began to fashion Reconstructionist Judaism, which emphasizes Palestine. But most Zionists gradually adopted the demand that the movement fit into the needs of an Americanizing Jewish community.

The logic of the Zionist situation in the 1920s demanded an exclusive emphasis on Palestine. In part, such work attracted the rich, assimilated Jews, who wanted nothing to do with the idea of Jewish nationalism in the Diaspora; but as the East Siders moved uptown, they too lost interest in a concept that might impair their new-found status. Moreover, they now began to transpose their recently acquired American values onto Palestine. S. M. Melamed, who at one time had condemned Brandeis because the American jurist would not have been at ease in a Palestinian colony, now demanded that American civilization be implanted in the homeland. The policies of Weizmann and Lipsky, he now believed, would lead to the re-creation of an inferior

"Jewish ghetto culture" in Palestine. By 1930, he would declare that the Brandeisian approach had been correct all along, and that the European intellectuals, including himself, had been wrong. Even Maurice Samuel, Lipsky's closest associate, argued that Zionism had reached the point where it could discard nationalistic ideology and concentrate on practical projects in Eretz Yisroel.[30]

The combination of unrest and dissatisfaction among the rank and file, the proposed transfer of real power to the Jewish Agency, the financial chaos in the organization, the obvious triumph of a Palestinian-centered program, and the demand for a more prestigious leadership could only be resolved in one way: the return of the Brandeis group. Lipsky tried to head off the demand by inducing some of the Brandeisists to join the Finance Committee, and even declared at the convention that a more businesslike approach would be adopted for both the ZOA's internal affairs and for work in Palestine. But the time for compromise, if ever there had been one, had passed. Although Brandeis professed that his advanced age (he was now over seventy) prevented him from assuming the leadership, the campaign to recapture the Zionist Organization of America bore all the marks of his earlier battles for civic reform: exposure of the crooks, organization of the citizenry, and ultimate control of the political apparatus. When the Lipskyites saw that their earlier concessions had not stilled the criticism or placated their foes, they too adopted a hard line, charging the opposition with fomenting rebellion and disunity. At a time when the Zionists could ill afford such dissension, they practically split into two camps.

By the fall of 1927, UPA collections had fallen so far behind that the ZOA could not send its normal remittances to Palestine for October and November, despite the fact that the organization had taken a considerable loan against anticipated revenues. Mizrachi, which had always balked at close co-operation with the regular Zionists, finally pulled out of the joint campaign completely, charging that the Keren Hayesod had not lived up to its pledges to support religious institutions in Palestine. Henrietta Szold returned to the Holy Land as a member of the Zionist Executive, with the portfolio for health and education, and soon began sending bitter letters home to Hadassah over how the ZOA had failed the Yishuv; without promised funds, schools had to be closed, a step she considered fatal for the future of the homeland.[31] Finally, at two secret meetings on November 5 and December 17, the opposition decided on its course.

Credit that the two meetings even took place belonged to Jacob de-Haas, who worked incessantly throughout the fall of 1927, rounding up support and eliciting Brandeis' reluctant agreement to operate more openly. The chief had no desire to leave the sanctuary of the Court and enter battle, but he finally allowed that he would at least have to meet with his backers and provide them with moral support in their struggle. But his main commitment was to the Supreme Court where he and Oliver Wendell Holmes fought a rear-guard battle to protect civil liberties and liberal reform from the onslaught of the Babbitts. "You know my exigent limitations," he told deHaas. "I hope none of the group will come under any misapprehensions as to the limits and character of my limitations."[32] At the two meetings, they adopted a three-point program: first, creation of pro-Palestine sentiment through propaganda; second, raising funds without inter-ference from outside (i.e., European) leaders; and third, the proper expenditure of funds and promotion of private ventures in Palestine.

The latter two points reflected the ongoing consensus of the Bran-deisists regarding necessary economic policy and the independence of the American organization, but the first represented an acknowl-edgment that fund raising required the creation of a *stimmung* (feel-ing) that only propaganda could achieve.[33] Although the Keren Hayesod had not succeeded nearly as well as Weizmann had hoped, the Brandeis group recognized that its potential for collections far ex-ceeded the older methods they had utilized when in power. What Professor Shapiro has called "the machinery of jazz," with its attend-ant publicity and rallies and exaltation of large donors, did seem to work. Moreover, by conceding the need for publicity and propaganda, the Brandeisists took that one step toward the Eastern Europeans that gave an appearance of compromise. By accepting the KH, they removed the last ideological barrier between the Americanized leader-ship and their former antagonists, and reduced the issue to who could better lead the American Zionist movement.

The first step in the campaign involved the withdrawal of those who had joined the Lipsky administration, and in a series of well-

publicized resignations, Stephen Wise gave up the chairmanship of
the United Palestine Appeal, while lesser figures departed from the
various committees. Samuel Rosensohn and Lawrence Berenson justified their retirement from the Administrative Committee with a
stinging attack on the Lipsky regime, released on the same day that
Chaim Weizmann arrived in the country to begin a fund-raising campaign. "We are moved to this action," they declared, "by the continuing serious condition of Zionist affairs, and the low state to which
the Zionist movement has fallen is due directly to mismanagement by
and the incompetence of the leadership both here and in London. It
is no longer possible for us to co-operate or be associated with that
leadership. The remedy cannot be secured by co-operation with such
leadership, but only through a new leadership capable of rehabilitat-
ing the Zionist movement, and reawakening the moral forces of Zionism."[34]

A few days later, Hadassah threw its potent forces into the balance with an unusual public attack by Mrs. Irma Lindheim upon
Lipsky's leadership. The ZOA president angrily demanded that the
National Board repudiate her for words that could only prove detrimental to Zionism in general and to the UPA campaign in particular.
Instead, the Board gave Mrs. Lindheim an overwhelming vote of
confidence, and to be sure that the men understood its intentions,
passed an additional resolution declaring it had no faith at all in Lipsky. At the end of the meeting, Mrs. Lindheim archly noted that
"there are those who probably believe that Mr. Lipsky is not just a
propaganda leader. I don't believe that he is any more than that."[35]

With their resignations from the ZOA administration and Hadassah's repudiation of Lipsky, the Brandeisists now moved into the
open. They called for a special conference in Washington to reorganize the American movement and to secure new leaders, "so
as to put an end to the present demoralization and restore confidence and idealism." The sponsors of the call included many of
those who had served prior to 1921—Israel Brodie, Jacob deHaas,
Felix Frankfurter, Harry Friedenwald, A. H. Fromenson, Julian
Mack, and Robert Szold—as well as a number of younger men
who had recently joined the cause, including Rabbi Herbert Parzen.
Prior to the conference, the National Board of Hadassah adopted a

reform program that clearly reflected the Brandeisian demands. They called for a nonsalaried executive committee of seven members, each of whom would head a specific department, and who would work to restore confidence in the ZOA through a conservative and balanced fiscal policy. Zionist ideals should be stimulated, and "the American organization shall emphasize the economic aspects of the Palestine program and shall establish a body to initiate, advise and encourage the creation of public and private undertakings in Palestine." When the conference met, it drafted its own statement that embodied all of the Hadassah demands.[36]

The leaders of the meeting, realizing that a number of issues cut across party lines, took care to avoid resolutions dealing with the Jewish Agency, Russian colonization, and the world leadership. Rather, on Brandeis' direction, they decided to attack what they saw as the weakest link in the chain, Louis Lipsky's personal mismanagement of Zionist affairs, and here they felt they had a very strong case.* Faced with growing evidence of financial misfeasance in the ZOA, Weizmann had been forced to name a committee of judges to investigate the organization's affairs. Of the four members all but one belonged to the UPA leadership, and could be considered neutral, if not friendly, toward Lipsky. Their findings indicated that Lipsky had indeed misused the organization's credit, both in the endorsement of loans by members of his administration, and in guaranteeing a loan of $180,000 to the foundering American Zion Commonwealth, a settlement society headed by some of his backers. Moreover, trust funds earmarked for Palestinian uses had been handled poorly, and in some cases misapplied. In all, the committee concluded that although they believed no lasting harm had been done to the ZOA's credit, "no one

---

* Stephen Wise, although supporting the Brandeis program, felt uncomfortable about the attack on Lipsky, and in his resignation had specifically mentioned his dissatisfaction with Weizmann and the Agency. More than any of his colleagues, Rabbi Wise could identify with the masses, and may have felt that Lipsky's devotion to the cause balanced his lack of financial judgment. As to differences with the WZO, Judge Mack noted that the conference chose to limit its discussions to American problems. "Dr. Wise feels differently; he feels it is his duty to speak out his mind on all oppressions. Even those in our group who agree with him on other points, differ with him as to the duty, or as to the wisdom of talking to them at this time."[37]

responsible for the irregularities pointed out should be continued as an officer or a member of any committee of the ZOA."[38] The momentum clearly belonged to the Brandeis group, and as the convention approached, it appeared likely that they would easily carry the day.

Yet when the Zionists met in convention at the end of June, they voted to sustain Lipsky by a vote of 398 to 159, and re-elected him to another term as president, despite the disclosures of financial mishandling, despite the Hadassah attack, and despite the availability of the Americanized leadership. This strange turn of events resulted from several unexpected developments which completely stalled the opposition drive.

In the first place, Lipsky found greater backing than he had anticipated from Chaim Weizmann and the non-Zionist supporters of the Jewish Agency. To Weizmann, it all narrowed down to the fancied manipulations of the evil genius of his opponent: "It is all instigated by old Brandeis who, hidden behind his judicial robes, is capable of the vilest intrigues and tricks worthy of the lowest type of American politician." The point of the attack, as he saw it, involved not the ZOA or even the world organization; rather, his opponents had set sight on the Agency itself, and Weizmann neurotically complained to all and sundry about this despicable attack on his soon-to-be-consummated creation.[39] His non-Zionist allies also wanted Lipsky to remain in office, since they expected he would prove more co-operative in the Agency than the independent Brandeisists. Shortly after Wise resigned from the UPA, Felix Warburg announced a gift of fifty thousand dollars to the campaign, and privately explained that he had done it to bolster up the Lipsky regime. The non-Zionists still controlled the money, and they exerted their influence among the *nouveaux riches* Eastern European businessmen in Lipsky's behalf. The alleged irregularities of ZOA finance evidently disturbed the bankers less than the fact that a number of Lipsky's opponents, including Wise and deHaas, opposed the Agency.[40]

Another unexpected development consisted of a short-lived but momentarily powerful surge of Jewish nationalism among the Yiddish intellectuals. Not all of them shared Baruch Zuckerman's contention that the whole fight boiled down to a question of personalities.[41] To those who believed that a true Jewish and Zionist ideology had triumphed at Cleveland in 1921, the gradual erosion of that commitment proved very painful. In 1928, they realized that given a choice between Lipsky and the more acculturated leaders, their only hope lay in Lipsky, who understood and respected their ideas. The speeches at the convention were rife with charges that the opposition fought, not just against Lipsky and Weizmann, but against Judaism itself. Maurice Samuel spoke of an inevitable conflict between logical and biological Zionists, between those who supported the cause through reasoned analysis and those who felt its rightness in their hearts. Only the latter could be trusted, and even if they took an occasional wrong turn, their Jewish instincts would eventually lead them back to the right path. Two of the most militant of the Yiddish intellectuals, Abraham Coralnik and Abe Goldberg, both defended Lipsky on similar grounds, arguing that he stood for idealism and ideology, next to which problems of administration shrank to insignificance. Goldberg called Zionism "the saving remnant" of the Jewish people, which had to be sustained through faith, not by a balance sheet. The anti-Semitism of the 1920s led Jews, along with other ethnic minorities, to withdraw into a defensive clannishness that condemned outsiders; within these bounds, the claim to be a "real Jew" carried weight.[42]

Lipsky, of course, had not been idle during this period, and he utilized the pages of the *New Palestine* to deride his foes. He attacked Hadassah in general, and Irma Lindheim in particular, as abdicating the principles of Henrietta Szold, "who recognized the proper role of women within the ranks of the ZOA." (Miss Szold, on hearing of this, declared that she did not consider it unwomanly to take part in American or world Zionist affairs.) The Board's insistence on autonomy he condemned as part of a pro-Brandeis plot to sabotage the ZOA administration and the UPA drive.[43] And, although it is difficult to secure precise information, it appears likely that Lipsky took some steps to insure that his backers would dominate the convention. The credentials committee, which he appointed, disallowed a number of delegates who opposed the administration, and approved some questionable seatings that backed him. ZOA rules, for example, called for convention delegates to be apportioned on the basis of

paid-up membership as of the first of each year. The due date for
Hadassah renewals, however, fell several weeks later, a fact that had
never been taken into consideration when allotting delegates. For the
1928 convention, the credentials committee invoked this technicality
for the first time, and disallowed almost one hundred Hadassah delegates who would have certainly supported the anti-Lipsky group.[44] In
contrast, Lipsky sent out a letter to all ZOA chapters asking them to
report both their paid and unpaid membership lists, and then allotted
representatives on the basis of the total. It was later charged that in a
number of cases local delegations had been increased by counting
donors to the UPA as part of the membership. One of the planks, as
a matter of fact, of both the Hadassah and Washington conference
programs called for a strict definition of Zionist membership, limiting
it only to men and women who paid the shekel tax and supported the
Basle program.[45] These steps, together with the strength he had in
the various locals, guaranteed Lipsky control over the convention.

What may have proved the most damaging to the Brandeis group
was nothing that Weizmann or the non-Zionists or the Yiddish intellectuals or even Lipsky did to them, but rather their own inability to
provide candidates acceptable to the convention. Had Brandeis or
Stephen Wise or Judge Mack agreed to head the ticket, it is possible
that the latent dissatisfaction in all areas of the ZOA would have surfaced and carried the Brandeisists into power. But the Justice had
been reluctant even to get involved in the preconvention maneuvering, while none of the other "names" could be prevailed upon to step
forward. Brandeis tried to induce Harry Friedenwald, now almost
sixty-five, a lesser light in the group who had been president of the
Federation of American Zionists two decades earlier, to accept the
leadership, promising that he would only have to serve in a titular
capacity, but the Baltimore ophthalmologist refused. At times it
seemed that the Brandeis/Mack group wanted to depose Louis Lipsky
more than they really wanted to take over control of the foundering
Zionist organization, and this lack of a sufficient commitment to devote full time to the cause hurt them again in 1928, as it had seven
years earlier. The story that Julian Mack had jumped to his feet during one of the Washington meetings to declare that he would never
accept the ZOA presidency did the Brandeisists great harm, and

made Lipsky and his associates look even more devoted by comparison. Only Stephen Wise seemed to sense what this attitude meant, and he argued that amateurs such as Mack, Brandeis, and himself could not exercise more than token influence "in a movement in which all the real leaders are, using the term in the best sense, professionals—that is to say, people giving their full time, strength, and energy to the movement." At the convention, the Brandeisists could not put forward a single "name" around which to rally, and the intellectuals who might have been willing to defect for the sake of securing prestige for the movement had no one offered to them. Given the Jewish chauvinism rampant at the convention, the "Nordics," as one speaker termed them, appeared vacillating and uncommitted, and under these circumstances, charges of poor management meant very little.[46]

IV

It would have been a mistake, after the vote at Pittsburgh, to have dismissed the opposition as completely as Chaim Arlosoroff, the brilliant Palestinian labor leader, did. "The so-called opposition group is in reality no coherent group at all," he declared. "It is a sort of *omnium gatherum* of the various opposing tendencies, current and countercurrent. This opposition consists of adherents to the Agency policy, of opponents to the Agency policy, of Revisionists,* of

* The Revisionist party had been founded in 1925 by Vladimir Jabotinsky to fight for a revision of the Zionist Executive's conciliatory attitude toward Great Britain's whittling down of the Balfour promise, and to urge greater effort in the settling of Palestine. Harking back to Herzl's emphasis on politics, Jabotinsky declared that the Zionist policy should be to "buy acres, build houses, but never to forget politics; ninety percent of Zionism may consist of tangible colonization, and only ten percent of politics, but that ten percent is the precondition of success and the ultimate guarantee of survival." During the late 1920s and 1930s, Revisionism became the focal point of much of the dissatisfaction with the Weizmann regime and with opposition to British policy. But its relatively right-wing stand on economic development, as well as the authoritarian policies of Jabotinsky himself, antagonized many of the labor groups. After the death of Jabotinsky in 1940, the Revisionist

Brandeis followers and of people who fought against Brandeis for many years. Their united aim is opposition."[48] For while Brandeis served as a focus of some of the discontent, the various developments within the ZOA and in the American Jewish community dictated that just as positions on ideology had altered, so now ideas about leadership would change. The Brandeisists would have to bide their time, analyzing what had gone wrong in their strategy, but the opposition to Lipsky would not die down.

Yet for over a year after the attack had failed to unseat him, Louis Lipsky seemed firmly in control of Zionist affairs. The imminent establishment of the Jewish Agency marked the high water mark of Weizmann's administration in the 1920s, and Lipsky, as his American lieutenant, benefited from the negotiations with the wealthy non-Zionists, who temporarily provided a sense of prestige to the movement. The convention's overwhelming vote of confidence, however, misled him as to the real depth of his support. He believed that a large majority of Hadassah's members really backed his administration, in contrast to the Brandeis-oriented National Board, and he determined to rid himself of this nuisance once and for all. When he learned that a coterie of disaffected women planned to nominate a pro-Lipsky slate at the Hadassah convention, he decided to throw his influence into the fight.

A tense, charged atmosphere marked Hadassah's 1928 meeting, with accusations of ZOA chicanery alternating with denunciations of the Brandeisist leaders. Shortly after the opening session, Lipsky made a surprise entrance into the hall, dramatically touching off a ten-minute demonstration among his followers that grew so raucous the chairwoman had to order the room cleared of everyone except delegates and reporters. The ZOA president professed that he had come to make peace, declaring that he would not be "responsible for the reintroduction into the movement of the spirit of rancor, which has been brought into the movement during the past year." The peacemaker then launched into a bitter denunciation of the

party declined, although it still remains one of the smaller groups within the Zionist spectrum. In the United States Revisionism never took a strong hold, although some of the Brandeis group, including Jacob deHaas, embraced it.[47]

National Board and especially of Hadassah's president, Mrs. Irma Lindheim, for their opposition to him. "The people who are responsible for this are cheap. The Zionist movement has gone through two years of hell, and now when reinforcements [i.e., the Agency non-Zionists] are in the offing, we must endeavor to restore the spirit of amity and harmony which seems to have fled from our midst." The only way to secure unity again, he implied, would be to elect the slate pledged to his support headed by Mrs. Archibald Silverman.

The object of his attack, Irma Lindheim, did not attend the convention. Her husband, one of the Brandeisists who had worked with the ZOA, had died only a few months before, and the shock of his unexpected passing, as well as the toll of leading Hadassah, had brought her to the edge of physical collapse. On doctor's orders, she had gone abroad for a rest, but she sent a letter to the convention, and one of her colleagues on the Board now rose to read it in response to Lipsky's attack. "Why was it treason for us to ask that the Zionist Organization live up to the standards we impose upon ourselves?" she asked. "Was it wrong for us to reject a dual standard? Why was it wrong that we asked for the same type of good government as members in good standing of the Zionist Organization as we do as members in good standing of Hadassah? Why was it wrong for us to desire and work for a new leadership in the Zionist movement when we honestly believed that the present leadership was inadequate to meet the needs of Palestine? Why was it wrong for us as members of a democratic organization to inform our constituency of the facts in time for them to examine into their truth before the convention? Why should a Zionist public not protest against a political machine that crushes out the energies of those whose only desire is to work for Palestine?"

By the end of the letter many of the delegates were openly weeping, and Lipsky's dramatic appearance now looked like a cheap and shoddy trick. Mrs. Silverman hastily withdrew her candidacy, averring that she had never wanted to hold office. The convention overwhelmingly re-elected Mrs. Lindheim as well as her supporters on the National Board, and adopted a reform program highly critical of the Lipsky regime. Instead of taming the ladies, Lipsky had earned their continuing enmity. Moreover, within a year he had to agree to a re-

organization plan that cut Hadassah's affiliation fee to the ZOA
by 50 per cent, while increasing their delegate strength to the congresses.[49]

Despite Lipsky's apparent control and the widespread publicity
surrounding the creation of the Agency, a number of analyses of the
ZOA during late 1928 and early 1929 indicated a steady deteriora-
tion of the organization. At the 1929 convention, the treasurer reported that membership had slipped to 18,000, the lowest since the
prewar years, while the deficit, despite a special life-membership
campaign, had climbed to $146,000. UPA collections were running
nearly $500,000 behind schedule, and it had to borrow money each
month in order to meet the Palestinian budget.[50] Within the administration itself, internecine welfare had broken out, with Meyer Weisgal heading one group of Lipsky functionaries and Max Rubinow another. Lesser officials worried constantly over what would happen to
their influence—and their jobs—once the Agency plan went into effect. Then in March, Chaim Arlosoroff released a forty-eight-page
analysis of the ZOA in which he predicted "a complete breakdown,
political, moral and organizational, of the [American] Zionist movement as soon as the organization of the extended Jewish Agency
will begin to function." He accused the Lipsky regime of devoting
too much of its time to politicking and infighting, and of making no
real effort to come to grips with basic problems. The ZOA, he argued,
had never really presented a viable Zionist program to American
Jewry; rather, it spent all of its time trying to raise money.[51]

As the tempo of criticism increased, Lipsky turned once again to
the intellectual purists, hoping to rally the cultural enthusiasts to his
side. He devoted a special supplement of the *New Palestine* to articles demanding adherence to true Zionist feeling. Rabbi Mordecai
Kaplan argued that the ZOA should devote itself to promoting Zionistic ideals in the American Jewish community through social and
cultural work, and that only when that had been done could they legitimate their efforts in Palestine. At the 1929 convention, Coralnik
and Abraham Goldberg endorsed Kaplan's position, and practically
demanded that only those with a full devotion to Zionism, both in
gegenwartsarbeit and in Palestinian work, should remain in the
movement. But such efforts proved futile, since this argument no
longer appealed to more than a small minority of American Zionists.

With the signing of the Agency pact that summer, the Zionists turned over the responsibility for fund raising to the non-Zionists, and the Lipsky bureaucracy openly wondered just what it was now supposed to do.[52]

The Brandeis group, however, also found itself stymied. Its members continued to complain about the Lipsky administration, while erstwhile supporters indicated that they only awaited leadership. Nearly all of them opposed the Agency, although only Stephen Wise carried the fight into the open. The rest followed Brandeis' cue that they focus on domestic incompetence rather than world politics.[53] But this silence on the Agency, as well as their failure to put forward an acceptable alternative to Lipsky, crippled them for more than a year. The membership would not accept nonleadership, even at the recommendation of those who could confer prestige, as an alternative to an earnest, even if bumbling, administration.

Then on August 23, Arab mobs rioted in Palestine, leaving 125 Jews dead, and the crisis jolted American Jewry into action. Numerous groups seconded the Zionist call for a full implementation of the Balfour Declaration and protection of Jewish rights in Palestine. A number of prominent non-Zionists, including Julius Rosenwald, Herbert Lehman, Samuel Untermyer, and Adolph Ochs, publicly proclaimed their support of the Yishuv, and contributed generously to a Palestine Emergency Fund, which soon raised $2.1 million to aid the riot victims.[54] But while Jews around the world called for Britain to live up to its obligations, Chaim Weizmann, the president of the World Zionist Organization, proved unable to influence his British friends at all, and eventually His Majesty's Government issued a White Paper temporarily stopping all immigration into Palestine. Felix Warburg, who took over the Jewish Agency after Louis Marshall's death, resigned in protest over British policy, and this non-Zionist became the symbol of Jewish protest against limitations on Palestinian settlement. Lipsky, like Weizmann, appeared impotent; he carried no influence in the American Government, with his alleged non-Zionist colleagues, and very little even within the movement.

In the fall of 1929, American Zionism was literally coming apart at the seams. Its membership dwindled, its revenues shrank while debts piled up, and its leadership seemed totally incapable of leading.

Had Louis Brandeis tried to create a more advantageous situation in which to re-enter the Zionist arena he could not have done so, yet the gravity of the situation, the real possibility of the ZOA collapsing completely, make charges of opportunism seem inappropriate. It is a measure of the seriousness with which American Jews viewed the crisis of 1929 that Brandeis acted himself, not through an intermediary, and although he limited himself to pledges of support, this personal commitment provided the key necessary to bring his supporters back to power in the movement.

Without a base in the Zionist Organization, Brandeis and his followers felt helpless in responding to the crisis induced by the riots and their aftermath. They would not work through Lipsky, so they decided to feel out Warburg and the other non-Zionists. In earlier days, Warburg had more or less followed the lead of Weizmann and Marshall in dealing with the Brandeisists, preferring to manipulate the more tractable Lipsky administration. But in the crisis, Lipsky had nothing to offer compared to Brandeis' name and influence, and when Bernard Flexner approached the banker on the possibility of co-operation, Warburg jumped at the chance. It was indicative of the changed circumstances in American Jewry that Warburg suggested that Brandeis should leave the bench and assume the leadership, not only of the Zionist movement, but of the American Jewish Committee as well. This far Brandeis would not go, but he agreed to participate in a conference on economic aid for Palestine, going so far as to indicate his willingness to give a talk at the meeting, his first public pronouncement on Zionism in over eight years.[55]

Although original plans did not call for publicity about the meeting, the Brandeisists, who arranged the conference details, carefully leaked the news that not only would the Justice attend and speak to the gathering, but that it had been convened at his request. When the participants met on November 24, 1929, they sealed the final *rapprochement* between the Brandeisian Zionists and the *yahudim* whom they had fought against so bitterly in the Congress fight over a decade before. Besides Felix Warburg, who cosponsored the affair, Cyrus Adler, Lee K. Frankel, Abram Simon, and James Marshall represented the older German community, while a number of *nouveaux riches* Eastern Europeans also attended, basking in the unfamiliar glow of prestige and wealth surrounding them. The speeches dealt only with Palestine and the courage and character of Jewish settlers there. Brandeis publicly declared his faith that Jewish intelligence and fortitude would triumph in Palestine, and reaffirmed his belief in the inevitability of a strong Jewish homeland there. "The road," he said, "is economic and the opportunity is open." In the end, the conferees agreed to establish a committee to investigate the best means of providing aid for economic development, but the plans had to be scrapped when the full extent of the great depression became known.[56]

The main import of the conference lay not in its plans but in the apparent return of Brandeis to an active role in Zionist affairs. Rabbi Louis I. Newman wrote a eulogistic article in which he rhapsodized on "The Return of the Pilot." The *Jewish Tribune* rejoiced that the conference had brought back "a great leader to public participation in the tasks of rebuilding a Jewish homeland," a sentiment echoed throughout the Jewish press. Even the *New Palestine* praised the Justice and printed his speech in full.[57] The press also noted the conspicuous absence of the Lipskyites from the gathering. Just as they had excluded the Brandeisists from the earlier nonpartisan conferences, so now they in turn suffered isolation. It was, however, much more than a mere childish revenge; by exposing Lipsky's lack of standing in the Jewish community, they undermined what little support he had left within the ZOA. To the intellectuals caught between the desire for ideological purity on the one hand and social prestige for the movement on the other, only one choice now remained. Even Weizmann realized that Lipsky could no longer be sustained, and when the ZOA president tried to exert some influence in Agency matters, he met with no encouragement from either Weizmann or Felix Warburg, both of whom had extolled his virtues only months before.

V

The coalition of the Brandeisists and the non-Zionists led by Warburg upset some of the more ideological Zionists who now feared a total abandonment of *gegenwartsarbeit*. But to the rank and file, the union seemed the answer to all that ailed the ZOA. By bringing the Brandeis group back to power, they would secure a prestigious and proven leadership, while the rich *yahudim* would underwrite work in Palestine. For all but a handful of ideologues, the question no longer appeared whether Brandeis would take over the organization, but when. Even Chaim Weizmann evidently now wanted the aging jurist back in the ranks. In early 1930, twelve members of the Administrative Committee met with Jacob deHaas and informed him that the Lipsky regime stood paralyzed by internal dissension, and they wanted to know what had to be done to get Brandeis back. The answer came a few weeks later from Rabbi Louis I. Newman, who outlined a series of alternatives available to the incumbent administration; the only viable one, however, would be for it to resign and turn the organization over to a new alignment headed by Mack and Brandeis. "The catch-phrases of the last ten years have spelled tragedy and disaster. The hour calls for calm, self-sacrificing statesmanship. We must turn a new page in American Zionism. We must set our house in order. American Zionism must not destroy itself, for our failure will be Jewry's failure and we will rightly be accused of having deserted our world-enjoined duties to Palestine."[58] A committee headed by David Frieberger, an Eastern European lawyer and businessman, and consisting of three other ZOA committeemen, began meeting with the Brandeisists to explore specifics, and almost immediately ran into the stone wall of Brandeis' overriding antipathy toward Lipsky. There could be no compromise, nor indeed any sort of arrangement, unless Lipsky went. For the Eastern Europeans, surrender on this point meant more than merely repudiating the Lipsky regime; it implied a full and open confession that for the past nine years they had been blindly pursuing a wrong policy. They pleaded with deHaas to make Brandeis understand that they could not turn Lipsky out in the cold. "Frieberger has been pleading with me for humanism," deHaas wrote to the chief, "that somehow, somewhere, something be done for Lipsky. There is no longer any discussion as to his ability, as to his leadership, but a good deal about bread and butter and face saving." Only one thing could induce them to agree to this demand, if Brandeis himself assumed the leadership.[59]

On May 22, negotiations took a more concrete turn with the release of a memorandum signed by Brandeis, Julian Mack, Robert Szold, and Jacob deHaas, and delivered to the Frieberger committee. The document demanded a complete reorganization of the ZOA in areas of leadership, management, personnel, and finance. To achieve this, a group of nine neutrals should be given control of the ZOA at the convention for a period of six months renewable for two additional years; no one who had recently been an executive officer or closely affiliated with the Lipsky regime could serve; no member of the new administration would receive a salary; and the new administration would have *carte blanche* in its policies and activities. The main purpose of the ZOA, according to the memorandum, revolved around economic work in Palestine, and the four signers reaffirmed their belief in the program first enunciated nearly ten years earlier in the *Zeeland* statement. The new administration would, before anything else, have to put the organization's house in order and begin reducing the crippling debt. The whole tone of this dry, semi-legalistic document indicated that the Brandeis group meant business. They knew that the ZOA stood on the verge of collapse, and they believed they knew how to save it. But they would not engage in politicking or behind-the-scenes deals, and said so: "If the Administration plan is adopted it must be by the act of others than the members of our group. We shall not put forth any propaganda to secure its adoption by the Convention, or to influence the action of the Convention with respect to the continuance of the present method of control, management or personnel." Of Brandeis' own involvement, or that of Mack, Wise, and the others, the memorandum said not a word.[60]

The ZOA Administrative Committee pondered the document and finally decided to submit it to the convention without comment. The debate in the Jewish press, however, more than compensated for the official silence. The ideologues in the Jewish press attacked it vehemently and vowed that the Zionists would never give up a democratic organization for a dictatorship. S. M. Margoshes called the statement a bitter disappointment. "Imagine that the Zionists in America are insane enough and irresponsible enough to accept such conditions—what are they to receive in return? They receive

an indefinite, vague and highly complicated promise that when everyone shall have acted as 'good boys,' then—then what? . . . Not the
slightest hint at a guarantee that Justice Brandeis himself, in person,
will assume the Zionist leadership in America." Jacob Fishman
echoed the sentiments of many people that the memorandum had
really promised nothing except a complicated administrative plan.
"And what does the Brandeis group promise in exchange for the
dictatorship it demands? Absolutely nothing. It will try to find people
who will endeavor to balance the budget. And in the eventuality that
its attempts should fail it reserves the privilege of returning the administration to us on some fine day."[61] Even journals that supported
the Brandeis plan had reservations. A Detroit columnist argued that if
Lipsky, who was anathema to the Brandeisists, had to go, then certainly Jacob deHaas, whom the Lipskyites detested with an equal fervor, should be kept out of any new administration. The most accurate
analysis, however, declared that although the proposal would not gen-
erate much enthusiasm, the Zionists would accept it "chiefly out of
weariness with the present order of affairs."[62]

As the Zionists gathered in Cleveland at the end of June, the same
site where nine years earlier they had ousted the Americanized leadership, few would have been foolish enough to predict what the
outcome would be. They all knew that the organization's troubles
had worsened. In the first five months of the year, only eleven
thousand persons had renewed their membership. Financial troubles, complicated by the general economic depression, had reached
the point where the ZOA had to suspend publication of its Yiddish
periodical, *Dos Yiddishe Folk,* and even the future of the *New Palestine* seemed in doubt. In the Agency, Felix Warburg had confirmed
some of the worst fears of the culturalists, deliberately downplaying
any references to Jewish nationalism or Zionist philosophy. Only
a few weeks before the convention, Abraham Goldberg, one of
Lipsky's staunchest supporters and a champion of Diaspora work,
openly admitted that American Jews had lost all faith and confidence
in the ZOA. Neither side had a majority, and although the Brandeisists probably had greater support, a number of delegates opposed
to Lipsky also had instructions to vote against the memorandum.
And just before the convention opened, Stephen Wise issued a state-

ment to the Associated Press declaring that "in the things that matter most, morally and politically, [the ZOA] is bankrupt." The charges, which no one denied, nonetheless caused a furor because Wise had aired "internal problems" before the Gentiles; undoubtedly, had the members of the American Jewish Committee been present, they would have understood. Zionism in America had come to a sad state.

Unknown to most of the delegates, negotiations had already begun between the Lipsky and Brandeis factions. The unyielding stand of the chief had given way under pressure from Mack and Wise, and the generally unfavorable reception accorded the May 22 memorandum also influenced events. Wise in particular had been upset by the assault on Lipsky, since he considered the real culprit to be Chaim Weizmann. Of all the members of the Brandeis group, Wise had worked most closely with the ZOA during the 1920s, and had grown to respect Lipsky and his colleagues for their wholehearted devotion to the cause, even while continuing to disagree with their policy. If Brandeis, whom Wise thought could still save Zionism and Palestine, would not leave the bench, he had no right to discard those who had given all of themselves to the cause.[63] Moreover, he and Emanuel Neumann shared a deep distrust of the Jewish Agency, a feeling they conveyed to Mack. If they should force Lipsky and his supporters out, they would have no allies except Warburg and the Agency non-Zionists. While good relations had to be maintained there, a gulf of large dimensions still separated them. Common sense, a little compassion, and a close reading of the political conditions dictated a more conciliatory attitude.

Once word got out that negotiations had begun, the tension in the hall, already high, rose to the breaking point. The delegates paid no attention to the numerous committee reports designed to occupy their time, and waited impatiently for word of agreement. At four-thirty, Lipsky came onstage to inform them that a compromise had not been reached, and the convention recessed until the evening. The delegates gathered in the hot and humid auditorium as early as eight o'clock; at nine-thirty Lipsky pleaded in vain with them to go back to their rooms and wait until the next day, but they would not move. Finally, at ten-thirty, several members of the Administrative

Committee came out to report that agreement would not be reached that night. Then, to calm their fears, Robert Szold read a letter that Brandeis had written to the convention. "I appreciate the generous suggestion which many of you have made that I should again assume the official responsibility of leadership in the ZOA," he began, and then reiterated his full and complete faith in Zionism as the best means of preserving the spiritual legacies of Israel. But "added years make it impossible for me to assume now the official responsibilities of leadership as I did prior to 1921, but I am ready now as then to serve the cause. Necessarily the service to be rendered must be limited in scope to advising from time to time when requested on questions of major policy. Such service I am now rendering through Mr. Warburg to the Jewish Agency. Such service I can render also to the ZOA. In my opinion it will be far more effective if rendered to an administration framed on the general lines of the memorandum of May 22, 1930." Szold added that Brandeis had promised to support any administration, even one that rejected the memorandum. The delegates sat stunned. Some rejoiced that a compromise could be reached and unity restored; others had not believed that Brandeis would urge so radical an overhaul unless he himself would leave the bench to head the organization. One reporter argued that had he wanted to, Lipsky at that moment could have swept the convention to his side; if he had, it would have meant disaster for the ZOA. By now both sides were seeking an arrangement that would not only save face, but actually rally all the forces together.

This they did the following day, and Rabbi James Heller presented the six-point compromise to the delegates. In essence, it consisted of an eighteen-member administrative committee, consisting of twelve people named by the Brandeis/Mack group and six by Lipsky which would have full power to run the organization for at least eighteen months. In addition the National Executive Committee would be split between the two sides, and representation on the Jewish Agency would be secured for the Brandeisists. When Heller finished, Lipsky stepped forward and urged the convention to accept; then, turning to deHaas, he clasped his hand as a symbol of unity in the ranks. The delegates, who had seemingly been waiting years for this moment, burst out cheering and then sang "Hatikvah" ("The Hope"), the Zionist anthem.

Lipsky, in addition to himself, named James Heller, William H. Lewis, Morris Rothenberg, Abraham Goldberg, and Nelson Ruthenberg—all of whom had been his staunch supporters—to the new Administrative Committee. The Brandeisists named some obvious choices—Julian Mack, Stephen Wise, Jacob deHaas, Rose Jacobs, and Robert Szold—as well as some lesser-known figures, Israel Brodie, Abraham Tulin, Louis Newman, and Samuel Rosensohn. But they also named Abba Hillel Silver, Emanuel Neumann, and Nathan Ratnoff, all of whom had been closely associated with the Lipsky regime. Ratnoff had been chairman of a major committee, but evidently neither he nor Neumann had been actively involved in the warfare, and Neumann especially had made his peace earlier with the Justice. Silver, however, had been suspected by several of the Brandeisists of actually trying to defeat them and to sustain Lipsky. It would seem that both sides, although committed to certain personalities, tried to get people who could work for unity. The committee's choice of an Executive reflected this desire for harmony. It named Mack as honorary chairman and Lipsky as honorary vice chairman; Robert Szold became chairman with Abba Hillel Silver as vice chairman. There was no doubt where the power resided, for Lipsky introduced Robert Szold to the convention as "a gentleman who presents the authority of Mr. Justice Brandeis."[64]

VI

The aftermath of the Cleveland convention saw an unaccustomed glow of amity and good feeling among American Zionists. Brandeis' retraction of his ultimatum and his offer of support to any administration brought hosannas from the Jewish press. Weizmann personally thanked Brandeis for his "generous attitude" and predicted "future harmony so necessary at this critical stage of our common endeavors."[65] Only a few discordant notes marred the otherwise euphoric atmosphere. Fred Kisch, chairman of the Palestine Executive, bemoaned the new influence of Jacob deHaas, whom he considered a liar and a lunatic, and worried about the Brandeis claim for a seat on the Executive. He urged Weizmann to fill any vacancies with Europeans, since "further Americanization means emasculation. They are working on a deliberate policy to take the Zionism out of Zion."[66]

The new Szold administration settled in quickly to its work. Brandeis urged an immediate accounting of the books to determine just how bad finances really were, and, as he expected, examiners found nearly $30,000 worth of hidden debts beyond the $150,000 previously acknowledged. At the first meeting of the Executive Committee, they agreed to emphasize the program in Palestine, but recognized that the organization had to build up its membership and secure a better understanding by the public of just what Zionism meant. The various bureaus of the ZOA all turned their attentions to economic work, and the *New Palestine* began carrying a number of articles on economics and developmental work in the Yishuv.[67] With vigor and confidence, the Brandeisists took over the reins, certain that they could recapture the public imagination as they had done fifteen years earlier, sure that the policies they had advocated for so long had now been vindicated.

Yet circumstances had changed considerably since the Brandeisists had left office in 1921. The economic depression that struck late in 1929 was growing worse, and it particularly hurt the small businessmen who provided the bulk of Zionist funds. It would be extremely difficult to raise any money for Palestine over the next few years, and most of it would have to come from the wealthy non-Zionists headed by Warburg. If the *yahudim* had now been won over to Palestinianism, they still opposed Jewish nationalism. It would be an extremely difficult task for any Zionist administration to walk an independent line that upheld nationalistic principles yet did not alienate the non-Zionist moneymen.

Not only had the ZOA lost the members and financial resources it had earlier, it had also lost the influence and prestige in world affairs it had enjoyed from 1914 to 1921. The WZO, firmly under the control of the Europeans, considered American Jewry good for only one thing—money—and even there it had not been doing well lately. When Great Britain adopted a policy of appeasement toward the Arabs, the Zionists had no friends in power as they had had earlier. Brandeis did have some connections in London, but none could help him as Woodrow Wilson had during the peace negotiations. It would be several years before the American Zionists could again exert a potent influence in world affairs.

The Brandeisists had assumed all along that everything wrong with the ZOA could be corrected by replacing the Lipsky regime, and failed to realize that more than poor administration plagued the movement. By 1930 the dream of a homeland in Palestine had been partially realized as tens of thousands of Jews poured into the country and began to build a viable Jewish society. The support of the Yishuv became a touchstone of faith among all Jews, Zionists and non-Zionists alike. But as the older generation of immigrants became assimilated, they lost interest in the cultural and nationalistic aspects of Zionism, and their children, born in the United States, had no interest at all. Aside from Palestine, Zionism really had very little to offer American Jews, and thanks in part to the Weizmann policies, it had, as he admitted, reduced the movement to little more than a fund-raising operation.[68] The Brandeis group had been the first to emphasize Palestinian work, but they had always kept it in the perspective of an over-all Zionist philosophy, and during their years in exile had lamented the total loss of intellectual and cultural development (which they meant in terms much different than that of Margoshes or Melamed). They now hoped to change this situation by developing an economic program that would involve American Jews in much more than simple charity. The proposals for investment schemes aimed not at capitalistic exploitation, but at involvement in a sense that simple donation drives would never provide. Unfortunately, the Brandeisists found that the great depression had cut the financial ground from under their feet at the same time that foreign affairs forced a radical rethinking of Zionist policy. They might well have pondered whether, in recapturing the Zionist organization, they had not scored a hollow victory.

CHAPTER TEN

IMPENDING CATASTROPHE

The hope that had attended the return of the Brandeisists to active leadership in American Zionism soon withered in the realization that a miraculous revival of the movement would not happen overnight. The growing economic depression in the United States undermined the new Zionist administration's plans for growth, and foreign developments soon added crises of such unbelievable magnitude that not only Zionists, but men of goodwill all over the world, found themselves reduced to a state of near-helplessness. The Arab riots of 1929 led His Majesty's Government not only to an investigation of the disturbances, but to a full-scale re-evaluation of its policies in Palestine and the Middle East. With the publication of the Passfield white paper in October 1930, the British embarked on a policy of repudiating their pledges made to the Jews in the Balfour Declaration and the Mandate, and despite Zionist objections, Britain practically closed the doors of Palestine to Jewish immigration in 1939. This betrayal of the Mandate would have dealt a severe blow to Zionism in any circumstances, but the rise of Adolf Hitler and his proposed "final solution" to the Jewish problem meant that hundreds of thousands of European Jews who might have immigrated to Palestine would now be condemned to the gas chambers of Auschwitz and the other death camps.

American Jews—and most of the world, for that matter—at first could not believe that the madmen in Germany really meant what they said. But as the Nazi cancer spread, the paralysis of will that gripped the Western democracies frustrated efforts by American Jews to stop Hitler and save their brethren in Europe. Even the apparent friendliness of Franklin D. Roosevelt proved of limited value. The President, despite his avowed sympathy for the Zionist cause and his open repugnance of fascism, found his options severely limited by domestic politics, the national mood of isolation, and later by the need to help Great Britain in its fight for survival. But the crises did galvanize the Zionist movement in America, and membership increased to nearly six hundred thousand—almost one out of every eight American Jews—on the eve of the Second World War. More importantly, the events of the thirties led to an entirely new philosophy in American Zionism, one that for the first time openly and boldly called for the creation of a Jewish state in Palestine.

I

Although the United States had suffered periodic recessions in the past, the depression touched off by the stock market collapse in November 1929 proved to be the longest and most severe economic crisis in the nation's history. The index of manufacturing production, which hit an all-time high of 127 in June 1929, stood at 58 three years later, while American corporations, which had earned over $3 billion in profits before the crash, reported a loss in operations of that same amount in 1932. While all of the economic indicators plunged downward, the real tragedy of the depression could be found in its impact on human lives. Average weekly income shrank from $24.77 to $16.21, and 4 out of every 5 families lived on less than $3,000 a year. By the winter of 1932, 12 million people were unemployed—2 out of every 7 adults—while millions more could be classified as "underemployed," eking out a marginal existence in part-time jobs or working irregularly as factories reduced their labor forces. In the coal fields of West Virginia and Kentucky, evicted families huddled in tents in the midst of winter, while in Los Angeles, people whose gas and electricity had been cut off cooked over wood fires in their backyards. A Philadelphia storekeeper told a reporter of one family he was sustaining on credit: "Eleven children in that house. They've got no shoes, no pants. In the house, no chairs. My God, you go in there, you cry, that's all." When a city government advertised for a hundred men to shovel snow at $.50 an hour, over a thousand showed up, many of them wearing homburgs or chesterfield coats, ironic reminders of their former prosperity. On the outskirts of every city, makeshift shacks of cardboard and scrap metal—dubbed "Hoovervilles"—housed hundreds and thousands of the homeless, the hungry, and the unemployed. In a nation that had boasted that the era of eternal prosperity had dawned and where every family could expect two chickens in every pot, millions now suffered the constant pangs of hunger. In Chicago, fifty men brawled over a barrel of garbage, while in every city dump across the nation, men, women, and children could be found scouring the scraps for half-eaten food or partially rotted vegetables.[1]

Depressions show little prejudice, and American Jews underwent their share of the misery and privation of the 1930s, as sales in retail trades, in which many Jews were employed, dropped from $8.1 billion to only $4.2 billion a year. The well-organized philanthropic federations helped alleviate the worst suffering, as wealthy Jews gave generously to aid their less-fortunate brethren. But it was a bad time to take over a foundering organization with a large debt, or try to raise money for Palestine. Even those with a passionate concern for the Yishuv felt that domestic needs came first. For many people, working desperately to hang onto their homes or to keep a child in school or simply trying to survive, Zionism became a luxury they could no longer afford. In 1930, despite the joint efforts of the Zionists and the Joint Distribution Committee, the Allied Jewish Campaign took in less than a third of its $6 million goal, and sent little more than $800,000 to Palestine. The small merchants and manual laborers constituting the bulk of ZOA membership had second thoughts about sending in $6.00 for their dues. In 1933, that sum could easily feed a family of four for a week. In the first year after the coalition administration took over, ZOA membership dropped to 13,000, and even Hadassah's rosters slipped to less than 32,000.[2]

It is obvious that no group of leaders could have given American Zionism the impetus needed to break out of its doldrums. The primary issues in American Jewish life in the early 1930s were not Jewish nationalism or Palestine, but the same concerns that dominated non-Jewish circles: the economic problems of the United States. The Brandeisist plans for expansion and growth stalled, not for lack of ability or enthusiasm, but because the ZOA had no resources, no members, and no organization. Instead of growth, they had to turn to the glamorless and thankless tasks of retrenchment and regroupment. They inherited a treasury with only $8.00 in it, and had to borrow $20,000 just to pay overhead expenses for their first three months in office; of $100,000 pledged at the convention to reduce the debt, less than a third was paid in. With constant prodding from Brandeis, Szold set out to put Zionist affairs in order.

From the outset it seemed a hopeless task, and in the two years that the coalition committee headed the organization, it had all it could do just to keep the ZOA alive. At the end of that time, the movement had slipped to its lowest point in three decades. Membership dropped to 8,800 despite a dues reduction to $3.00. The *New Palestine* temporarily disappeared, replaced by an irregular four-page news sheet. Hadassah also suffered heavy losses in membership (from 35,000 to 20,500 in two years), but nonetheless felt itself in better shape than the ZOA. Although Hadassah continued to subscribe to Brandeisian principles and to maintain close relations with Robert Szold and his colleagues, the women demanded and secured full independence as well as 50 per cent representation in American delegations to the congresses. About the only positive note Szold could point to was a $20,000 reduction in the deficit achieved through rigorous cost-cutting and a special fund drive, a not insignificant feat considering the circumstances.[3]

The failure of the Brandeisists to secure instant rejuvenation brought a perverse satisfaction to their old antagonists. "Of course I always knew that the so-called Brandeis people would prove a wash-out," crowed Weizmann. "They have neither the capacity for work nor the necessary devotion. They are time-servers, and they ought never to have been allowed to get hold of the machine which they will run to death." As to their chief, "Brandeis is old, and remains enshrined in Washington like an ikon and waits for the worshippers to come and kneel before him. He is not in a position to do any-thing or to inspire anybody in such difficult times."[4] When Louis Lipsky returned from the 1931 Congress, where his hero Weizmann had been voted out of office, he publicly denounced the new regime as a total failure, one with neither ability nor talent for leadership, and which had been unable to keep its promises to the membership. At a speech in Cleveland he called for unity; but unity, he declared, "cannot be based on the fixed desire to dominate on the part of the so-called 'Brandeis/Mack group,' which is merely a trade name used by a group of mediocre men."[5]

Friction between the Szold group and the Lipskyites had been present from the start. The new regime had immediately dropped all references to Diaspora work, and the pages of the *New Palestine* carried little except articles on economic programs, news of Palestine, and appeals for money. In early 1931, over Lipsky's objections, the National Executive Committee adopted a statement of economic prin-ciples that emphasized the development of opportunities for small businesses and investments.[6] At first, the Brandeisists ignored Lipsky, considering the Cleveland decision to implement their proposal a direct repudiation of the former administration. Most of the six members he had appointed to the coalition carefully avoided such in-fighting, content to work with their former antagonists for the good of the organization. In fact, over a year went by before casual readers of the Zionist press would have realized that Lipsky had been trading bitter accusations with some of the Brandeisists. Then a spate of articles appeared in which the former ZOA president denounced the Szold regime for betraying the cause in its mad hunger for power. Stephen Wise, who sarcastically noted that the "outs" seemed rather hungry themselves, delineated the attitude of his colleagues: "The Brandeis/Mack group is not a faction nor a division in American Zionism. It is a body of men and women which has sought to bring a certain mood and spirit into the Zionist Movement. If that spirit be unwelcome, it will be prepared to turn over the leadership to whatever group the Convention may call upon for leadership."[7] The dispute had actually come to a head after the Seventeenth Congress at Basle the preceding July, where a majority of the American delegation had actively worked for the successful ouster of Chaim Weizmann from the presidency of the World Zionist Organization. In order to understand that, however, it is necessary to first examine the growing estrangement of the mandatory power and the Zionists.

II

The Arab riots of 1929 culminated the decade-long efforts of would-be Muslim leaders, especially Haj Amin Hussaini, the so-called Grand Mufti of Jerusalem, to create a political issue with which to confront Great Britain. Individually, few Arabs had real grounds for complaint against the Jewish settlers: Hadassah facilities gave them modern medical treatment, both preventive and curative, for the first time; Zionist schools accepted non-Jewish children, while Arab scholars taught at Hebrew University; agricultural experts hired by the Yishuv provided extension services to Arab farmers, many of whom had never heard of chemical fertilizers or crop rotation; public works and economic investments raised the standard of living for Arabs proportionately more than for Jews. Throughout the one hundred years of Jewish settlement in Palestine, there have been countless stories of personal goodwill and friendship between individual Jews and Arabs. After the reunification of Jerusalem in 1967, Arab residents of the city sought out Jews who had been their neighbors before war had divided them in 1948, and almost before the fighting had stopped, Arabs queued up at the Hadassah hospital, many of them clutching their old, pre-1948 medical cards, and asking for specific doctors.[8] Undoubtedly some Jewish officials lacked tact, and the purchase of large blocs of land from absentee owners worked some hardships on the *fellaheen*. But more often than not, the leaders of the Yishuv went out of their way to tread carefully in dealing with their Semitic cousins. Hadassah, with its limited resources, did not have to care for non-Jews, but did. When more than a handful of Arab peasants were dispossessed by land purchases, the Jewish National Fund frequently arranged for them to take up residence on other sites of at least equal quality, also purchased through Zionist funds. The various Jewish labor unions insisted that Arab workers receive the same pay as Jewish laborers, a policy still enforced in Israel today, even regarding those living in so-called occupied territories. And then there were men like Judah Magnes, chancellor of Hebrew University, and the philosopher Martin Buber, who spent years trying to develop a binational state in which Jews and Arabs would be equal partners.[9]

But despite the fact that individual Arabs enjoyed good relations with the Jewish settlers, and Arab workers and peasants benefited immensely from the influx of Jewish immigrants and capital and technical expertise, on the whole the arrival of large numbers of Occidentals affronted rising Arab nationalism. The introduction of Western culture and techniques highlighted the backwardness and poverty of the Arabs. Had the number of immigrants been very small, and had Jews been willing to disperse into an Arab-dominated society and forever remain a small minority, then perhaps the seemingly inevitable conflict between the two peoples might have been averted. But the Jews came in substantial numbers, and they had no intention of trading one ghetto existence for another. While the Zionists claimed never to have enough money for the tasks confronting them, by Arab standards they brought fantastic wealth and succeeded all too well. The obvious success of the Yishuv, which stirred the pride and admiration of Jews in the rest of the world, aroused envy and dissatisfaction among the Arabs, a malaise that Arab leaders exploited in their fight to win control of the land not only from the Jews, but from the imperial master of them both, the British.*

* The problem of Arab-Jewish relations in Palestine deserves far more attention than can be provided here. In the political context of the sixties and seventies, a number of leftist critics have labeled the Jewish settlers as "imperialists" and "colonialists," and have attacked them for "exploiting" the indigenous Arab population. Equally as incorrect is the interpretation that if the Arabs had let the Yishuv expand peacefully, then the material prosperity now enjoyed by Israel would have

By 1929, this festering resentment had been stirred up several times in short-lived but violent outbursts against the Jews, and they in turn quickly saw the Arabs as the new cossacks responsible for this latest round of *pogroms*. Zionist extremists adopted the same abusive language as the mufti and his rabble-rousers, and described the Arab rioters as "the scum from Hebron, pederasts from Nablus, bastards, hooligans and gangsters from Jaffa," all congregating in that "murderers' den," the Mosque of Omar. Admittedly the Jews had a good deal of provocation. Palestinian Arab newspapers ran as regular features the vilest anti-Semitic lies reprinted from European hate-sheets. A common story claimed that Jews were distributing poisoned sweets, chocolates, and dried figs in the markets to kill Arab children.[11]

The British, caught in a cross fire of conflicting ambitions, at first had tried to placate the Arabs. Sir Herbert Samuel, the Jewish High Commissioner of Palestine in the early 1920s, adopted an unusually tough approach to the Yishuv in order to prove to the Arabs that His Majesty's Government intended to be even-handed and firm. Winston Churchill, while Colonial Secretary, attempted to mollify the Arabs while at the same time sustaining the wartime pledges made to the Jews. In the White Paper of 1922, he declared that the Balfour Declaration had never meant the imposition of a Jewish nationality upon Palestine as a whole, but rather that Jews should have a legally secured and internationally recognized right to develop a viable community in their ancient homeland. They would not be allowed unlimited entry, but rather the rate of Jewish immigration

---

been shared with the Arabs. Both views ignore the dynamics of history. The Jews sought neither an empire nor to exploit the Arabs, while the awakening Arab spirit could hardly allow a large, non-Muslim population to expand in its midst. Moreover, the Arabs did share in the prosperity and health improvements brought to the Holy Land by the Zionists; the enormous growth of the Arab population in Palestine, far larger than that of the Yishuv, was a direct response of Arabs moving there to take advantage of the new economic opportunities created by the Jews. The tragedy is that Palestine could have absorbed both Jew and Arab; the present population of Israel is far larger than any of the experts in the 1930s ever predicted could be established in the Holy Land. But both sides were caught in what some scholars would call historical imperatives, neither of which allowed much room for the other.[10]

would be determined by the "economic absorptive capacity of the country."[12] Churchill also broke off all of the land east of the river Jordan and established a provisional government there under Emir Abdullah, head of the Hashemite family, a temporary arrangement formalized in 1928. Although the Zionists considered the Churchill White Paper a whittling down of the Balfour Declaration, they had little choice but to accept its provisions.

During the 1920s the British attempted to play off not only Arab against Jew, but the Arabs against the French, whom they saw as imperial rivals in the Middle East. Gradually it became clear that the British would not be able to appease the Arabs so long as they allowed open immigration of Jews into Palestine and continued to support the growth of a Jewish homeland there. While a number of British statesmen insisted that the word of His Majesty's Government could not be broken, the dictates of foreign policy do not always allow room for consistency. Imperial security and the sheer number of Arabs as compared to Jews led to the gradual reorientation of British policy around the concept of an Arab-dominated Middle East under English tutelage. This approach had always appealed to many of the Foreign Service careerists, who had considered the wartime pledges a mistake, and the field experiences of British administrators reinforced this view. Zionist pioneers and English civil servants, according to Norman Bentwich, the attorney general of Palestine during this period, "spoke a different language, and temperamentally were incompatible. The Jews were a new element in the record of British Overseas administration; a people who regarded themselves as at least the equals of the ruling class. Whether or not they were born in the country, they did not behave like 'natives.' The Arabs obeyed the order of the British officer, the Jews argued. They and the English were as two chosen peoples, each feeling they had a mission and not comprehending the ideals of the other." Moreover, the wartime assumptions about the universal solidarity of the Jewish people and their international influence turned out to be false. The World Zionist Organization did not speak for all the Jews, and even the enlarged Agency, while it may have been more representative, could not control world Jewry. Instead of a Jewish Palestine as the bulwark of Britain's Middle East empire, Whitehall now viewed the Yishuv as a useful—but not terribly important—tool to prevent the too-rapid extension of self-government to the Arabs.[13]

This new view surfaced after the 1929 riots when Lord Passfield (Sidney Webb), the Colonial Secretary in the Labour Government, appointed a commission to investigate the disturbances. Sir Walter Shaw, a career official in the Colonial Office, and representatives of the three major political parties spent nearly two months in Palestine, and they issued their report in March 1930. Although the Shaw report put the responsibility for the bloodshed directly on the Arabs, it declared that the root cause of the trouble lay in Arab animosity toward the Jews, with Arab fears and disappointments growing out of what they saw as Britain's failure to honor alleged promises made to them during the war. Most of the Arab witnesses before the commission testified to their apprehension that the large numbers of Jewish immigrants would soon reduce the indigenous population to a perpetual second-class status. The new Jewish immigrants especially upset the Arabs, since they had the backing of a wealthy international organization, and had greater energy and initiative than the older "religious" Jews. The Shaw Commission recommended that Great Britain clearly define its future policy toward Palestine and its inhabitants, and that it be made clear that the World Zionist Organization, despite the special position assigned to it by the Mandate, did not "share in any degree in the government of Palestine." Shaw also suggested a complete re-examination of immigration rules to prevent further "excessive immigration" by Jews into the Holy Land.

The Arabs received the Shaw report with joy, since Passfield immediately suspended all further immigration until Sir John Hope-Simpson, who arrived in Palestine in May 1930, could complete the investigations recommended by Shaw. The Jews, who had all along feared that the Shaw Commission would exceed its original mandate to deal only with the riots, were outraged. At the Zionist Congress in 1931, Nahum Sokolow quoted an old Jew in Kishinev: "God protect me from commissions—from *pogroms* I can protect myself."[14] But the Zionists had still not heard the worst. Hope-Simpson, a retired careerist in the India service, spent most of his two months in Palestine listening to Arab complaints. From the start, he considered the land predominantly agricultural and discounted any industrial potential. Working from that assumption, he determined that not only had all the arable land been occupied, but it had been overoccupied, thus causing the extreme poverty of the *fellaheen*. He recommended an immediate cessation of all further immigration until economic conditions stabilized, and then possibly there might be room for perhaps another twenty thousand families. Hope-Simpson paid no attention to Jewish agricultural experts whose estimates of arable land differed from his, or their arguments that Jewish enterprise had benefited the Arabs.

The Colonial Office released Hope-Simpson's report on October 21, 1930, and on the same day Lord Passfield issued a White Paper clearly attempting to redefine the Balfour Declaration and the Mandate so as to arrest further development of the Yishuv. Instead of a promise to the Jews, the Mandate lay down obligations on the Crown to promulgate equally the growth of Jewish and Arab communities and to maintain the balance between them. Echoing Hope-Simpson in finding that no further arable land remained in Palestine, and that all of the Zionist agencies had pursued policies inimicable to Arab rights, Passfield limited all further land purchases by the Jews, and suspended immigration as long as any unemployment remained in Palestine.[15]

The White Paper took the Zionists completely by surprise, since for the first time His Majesty's Government had not consulted with the World Zionist Organization or the Jewish Agency about Palestinian policy. Weizmann, Felix Warburg, and Lord Melchett all resigned from the Agency Executive in protest,[16] while in Parliament David Lloyd George and all the surviving members of the wartime government denounced Passfield for his betrayal of Britain's sacred promise to the Jews. A crushed Chaim Weizmann considered the White Paper a personal betrayal, and in a moment of despair uttered words that would haunt him for years to come: "Never can there be a Jewish State. . . . The fogs have vanished. I see clearly now, and I no longer believe in the Jewish State. It can never be. . . . To speak now of a Jewish State is simply dangerous. I do not believe in the Jewish State." When American Zionists, now headed by the Brandeisists, criticized him for his passive attitude, he turned on them angrily, charging that they had done nothing. "They have made no contributions to the situation," he cried. "They have not given us a single idea of what they want to demand. I have not seen a single helpful statement coming from America."[17]

Actually, American Jews had done quite a bit in stirring up public opinion. The American Jewish Committee issued a strong statement denouncing the White Paper, and the ZOA branded the document as a repudiation of the Balfour Declaration, practically accusing Webb of lying in his efforts to explain away the past. In Madison Square Garden, twenty-five thousand people—with another twenty-five thousand outside—heard a roster of famous Jews, Zionist and non-Zionist, pillory the British Government.[18] Stephen Wise began compiling a list of statements by earlier governments and statesmen proving that the Balfour Declaration and the Mandate specifically promised Palestine to the Jews, and when his health gave way under the strain, Jacob deHaas completed the work; the title they chose, *The Great Betrayal,* reflected the tenor of their arguments. Rabbi Wise also took the White Paper as a personal affront. "No Jew I know has more truly the right to feel betrayed," he wrote, "because personally I gave myself to the limit to the British during the war. No one knows of the services, big and little, that I rendered the British Government. . . . I have never known such disillusion and betrayal. We may get concessions, but evidently we are in for equivocation rather than British truth-speaking."[19] On a more scholarly level, Felix Frankfurter delineated Albion's perfidy in a detailed legal brief published in the influential establishment journal *Foreign Affairs.*[20]

And although Weizmann did not know it, his old nemesis had already begun exploiting his contacts in England. While Weizmann led the public battle against Passfield, Louis Brandeis contacted his old friend and admirer, the great political theorist, Harold J. Laski. Brandeis, together with Frankfurter and Ben Flexner (who were then in London), began pressing Laski shortly after the Shaw report to get them information about Passfield's intentions. In late November, Brandeis suddenly had an entrée to the Labour Government. Prime Minister Ramsay MacDonald, under increasing attack both in the press and Parliament, called in Laski, a Labourite, to help establish a *modus vivendi* between the government and the Zionists. Laski's brilliant correspondence with Oliver Wendell Holmes gives us a clue to Brandeis obstinacy regarding His Majesty's Government living up to its promises. Laski believed in politics as an art of compromise, and found the American jurist's intransigence disturbing. In the Englishmen's view, a bit more flexibility on the part of Brandeis and his alter ego, Frankfurter, might have moved things along more smoothly.[21]

But Brandeis' private obstinacy, coupled with public outcry, gave Chaim Weizmann the leverage he needed in his negotiations with the government, and on February 13, 1931, MacDonald released a letter purporting to "remove certain misconceptions and misunderstandings" with regard to British policy in Palestine and to serve "as an authoritative interpretation of the White Paper." In essence, MacDonald repudiated the anti-Zionist passages of the Passfield statement and praised Jewish reconstructive efforts in Palestine. The Prime Minister also promised that the facilitation of Jewish immigrants and the encouragement of Jewish settlement on the land remained a positive obligation of the mandatory power. The only restrictions would be the ability of the land to absorb the people. Weizmann immediately issued a statement that MacDonald's letter had restored the basis for fruitful co-operation between the Zionists and the Crown.

Weizmann later claimed that the MacDonald letter made possible the great gains in Palestine during the 1930s, and at least one historian has termed it Weizmann's "last major political success for years." In the long run, however, the spirit behind the Passfield paper became dominant, and an even more infamous White Paper sealed the gates of Palestine to those fleeing the Nazi holocaust. In 1931 memories of the war, as well as a pervading sense of honor among the British people, proved too strong for those who wished to reorient imperial policy, but in less than a decade, the latter would have their way.

In the short run, the Passfield paper proved Weizmann's undoing, even though he had done so much to secure its reversal. He had become too closely identified with Great Britain, and what had formerly been his chief asset, his close ties to the government, now became his greatest liability, as many Zionists considered him incapable of standing up to the mandatory power. Shortly after the Shaw report, one American leader summed up the feeling that Weizmann "because of what the British Government had done for him, was the one man in the world who could not represent us in dealing with that government."[22] Weizmann's lament that he no longer believed in the possibility of a Jewish state alarmed many Zionists, and even after the MacDonald letter, he continued to disparage the importance of a Jewish majority in Palestine. "The Jewish State was never an aim in itself," he explained, "it was only a means for a purpose. In the Basle Program, nothing is said about a Jewish State, nor in the Balfour Declaration."[23] While such statements may have been technically correct, their spirit alarmed the more militant Zionists, especially the Revisionist group led by war hero Vladimir Jabotinsky, who demanded a return to Herzlian principles, full and immediate implementation of the Mandate, and the creation of an autonomous, self-governing Jewish commonwealth on both sides of the Jordan.[24]

Not only the extreme Revisionists opposed Weizmann; a number of moderate Zionists also rejected his "minimalist" approach, and believed that a stronger stand by the organization would be the only way to force Great Britain to honor its pledges. At an Agency meeting in 1931, when Weizmann reiterated his belief that no Jewish state could be developed in Palestine, the non-Zionists cheered.* In effect, they now saw all Palestinian work as simply a humanitarian, philanthropic endeavor.[25]

---

* By 1931, many Zionists had also become openly critical of the Jewish Agency, and especially of Felix Warburg, although his protest against the Passfield paper had done much to redeem his honor, if not his image, in Zionist circles. The Agency, and the Zionists, sorely missed Louis Marshall's tact and understanding, and they found Warburg arrogant and domineering. They soon got the impression that the non-Zionists considered themselves the senior partner in the Agency, and Warburg gratuitously drew up a reorganization plan for the Zionists without even consulting them. In a petition presented to Prime Minister MacDonald during his visit to the United States in late 1929, Warburg crossed out nine out of ten references to a Jewish national home. He also maintained that any person not belonging to the ZOA was, by definition, a non-Zionist, and should not be sent any more nationalistic propaganda.

The Brandeisists, now back in power in the United States, considered this view unacceptable. They had always been willing to work with the non-Zionists in economic development, but despite Weizmann's criticisms, they too held deep commitments to Palestine as a symbol of Jewish regeneration, a tie between prophetic Israel of the past and Jewish redemption in the present. During the 1920s, many of them had moved away from their earlier stances against a Jewish state, and especially after the rising anti-Semitism of the 1920s, had come to believe that there had to be some place, controlled by Jews, where other Jews could always find a refuge. Thus they opposed Weizmann's "minimalist" approach, and while they did not agree with all of the revisionist arguments, they too supported demands for full implementation of the Mandate and unhindered opportunities for Jewish development in Palestine. Although they were willing to work with Warburg and the Agency, they too feared that unless the non-Zionists could be checked, Palestine might turn into "a province of the Joint Distribution Committee." And undoubtedly some of them still harbored resentment against what they considered Weizmann's treacherous behavior in 1921, although few were as vehement in their demands for Weizmann's ouster as Stephen Wise.[26]

Even a number of Weizmann's former supporters also questioned whether the time had not come for him to step down. The Eastern Europeans, who had been the heart of his support, had serious misgivings about the Agency. And in the United States, Emanuel Neumann led the call for his retirement. "American Zionists have for years supported Dr. Weizmann," wrote Neumann. "We have followed him with an almost childlike acquiescence. The time seems to have come to ask ourselves openly and frankly: 'Where are we bound and whither are we being led?' The moment is approaching when Dr. Weizmann will have to choose—if indeed he has not already made his choice. On the one hand lies the long and difficult road to Zion. . . . On the other the alluring but slippery path of hasty improvisation and diurnal compromise. It leads to something which is not Zionism, not even Achad-Ha-Amism. It is a neo-Zionism. Its true name is defection."[27] How ironic that in only a decade Chaim

Weizmann, the Jew from Motele, should be accused of lacking a true Jewish feeling for Zion.

At the Seventeenth Congress in Basle in July 1931, Weizmann, bitterly resentful over the mounting wave of attacks, of speeches and articles denouncing him as a traitor, had to step down. His support even among the General Zionists (the middle-of-the-roaders) had slipped to less than a third of the delegates. His statement on Jewish aims in Palestine had aroused great indignation, and the Congress refused to accept his explanations. The American delegation played a central role in forcing his removal, and also had the satisfaction of seeing the Congress endorse a resolution creating a private capital association for Palestinian work.[28] But a few of the Americans, notably Louis Lipsky, supported Weizmann, and came home to the United States furious at the attack on their idol. Thus in the fall of 1931, the tensions between the Szold and Lipsky groups in the ZOA erupted once again into the open.

Lipsky's attacks on the new administration bore little fruit, since the Zionists recognized their peevish quality. The Brandeisists, after all, had been campaigning against Weizmann's policies for more than ten years, and it would have been strange indeed for them to have gone to Basle to support him. About the only real trouble Lipsky did cause came at the ZOA convention in November, when his friends threatened to withdraw unless they received five more seats on the Administrative Committee, a ploy that immediately drew Hadassah's wrath. Adroit maneuvering by Robert Szold and Emanuel Neumann, however, managed to placate both groups, and the delegates readily re-elected Szold to lead the coalition for another year.[29]

Between 1930 and 1932 the ZOA operated under an administrative board dominated by the Brandeisists. During those years, membership slipped considerably and Zionist activities had to be cut to the bone, events directly reflecting the dire economic conditions of the country as a whole. At the annual convention in 1932, when Szold declined to stand for another term, the organization returned to the older form of an elected presidency, and chose Morris Rothenberg, a New York attorney closely associated with Lipsky and Weizmann, and who had collaborated in the creation of the expanded Agency. Some commentators have suggested that this meant a return of the Lipsky-ites to power, but a closer look at American Zionism in the early 1930s indicates that the old ideological differences that had separated the two factions for more than a decade no longer existed. Lipsky and some of the Brandeisists continued to quarrel for the next ten years, bitterly blaming each other for the sad state of Zionist affairs. But the election of Rothenberg marked a return to unity in the ZOA. The governing council included Lipsky and two of his associates, together with three Brandeisists, Stephen Wise, Jacob deHaas, and Judith Epstein of Hadassah. Rothenberg, who two years earlier had been considered Lipsky's man, could now be accepted by all factions. And Lipsky, in 1936, would lead the opposition to Roth-enberg receiving a fifth term, backing his former foe, Stephen S. Wise, a pillar of the Brandeisists!

As we have previously seen, nearly all segments of American Zionism—and of American Jewry—had come around to support the primacy of practical work in Palestine. The transformation of the membership base, from recent immigrants to partially acculturated Americans, a development unnoticed during the 1920s, made many of the slogans prevalent in 1921 obsolete. Although Weizmann's statements after the Passfield paper stirred up some of the old controversies about Jewish nationalism, most Zionists considered the creation of a Jewish state the inevitable end product of long-term evolutionary development in Palestine. Why bother fighting over it now, when if all went well, ultimately it would happen anyway? Louis Marshall's old attitude that the Jews in Palestine would determine their own future now prevailed, even among non-Zionists. Lipsky, whose devotion to the cause was unquestioned, lacked the temperament and the administrative ability that the ZOA needed in the early 1930s, and the reorganization that Robert Szold had effected in his two years in office made it possible for the ZOA to respond to the new crisis on the horizon. Although few people realized it at the time, unity had been restored in American Zionism, and just in time; for across the ocean, the German madness was about to erupt, plunging the world into a horrible devastating war once again, and nearly destroying the Jewish people.

III

There has been so much written about the Third Reich, of its evil geniuses and the devastation they wrought, that it would be impossible to even attempt a summary.[30] There had been a long tradition of anti-Semitism in Europe, and whenever nationalistic emotions had been stirred up, the Jews had always been among the first to suffer. Despite all the hopes of emancipation, despite a century of enlightened promises, between 1933 and 1945 Adolf Hitler and his henchmen were able to focus an entire nation's irrational hatred and general fears upon the Jews, and then with the active and approving support of other European nations, ruthlessly and efficiently butchered six million human beings for no other reason than that they were Jewish. At the Nuremberg trials in 1945, Justice Robert H. Jackson charged that "history . . . does not record a crime ever perpetrated against so many victims or one ever carried out with such calculated cruelty." As for the Jews, Elie Weisel, dwelling in that strange twilight zone between truth and fiction, has drawn us an awesome portrait of a people who had found their God wanting, yet died praising His holy name.[31]

In the early years of Hitler's rise, few people took him seriously. After all, the man obviously was crazy, and only the most rabid anti-Semite applauded his Jew-baiting demagoguery. Even Charlie Chaplin's later caricature of him in *The Great Dictator* could not convey the sense of burlesque that he generated himself. A study of editorial attitudes toward Nazism in America's most prestigious and influential newspapers found a range of response varying from concern to disbelief that anyone in his right mind would pay this raving lunatic the slightest bit of attention. Although Jewish writers could not ignore any anti-Semitic leader who received such widespread publicity, the Jewish press also vacillated in its evaluation of this new Germanic mood.[32]

This failure to respond constructively represented more than mere incredulity. At first German Jews also failed to show any marked concern over Hitler. Very few Jews emigrated from Germany in the early years of the Nazi menace; in fact, German refugees did not use up that country's quota for American visas before 1938. With a depression at home, American Jewish organizations hesitated to push for a more open policy that could conceivably add to domestic relief problems. Martin Rosenblueth, a German Zionist who tried to warn Jewish and non-Jewish leaders in Europe that Hitler constituted a real menace, found that almost no one put any stock in his reports. In England, a Cabinet member told him that such overreacting would only harm the Jewish cause.[33]

There were a few who did sense potential danger in Hitler; throughout the early 1930s Rabbi Stephen S. Wise led a lonely crusade to convince not only American Jewry that the Nazis represented a real threat to their existence, but also to convince his fellow Americans that democracy itself stood in mortal danger. Wise first sensed the Nazi threat as early as 1931, when Felix Frankfurter sent him papers about Hitler's Bavarian escapades and the street riots fomented by the Brown Shirts.[34]

At the beginning of 1933, a wave of anti-Semitic incidents swept around the world. The ancient blood accusation received new currency in Germany, border guards shot unarmed Jewish youth in Hungary, and even in far-off China a gang of Russian thugs shot the mayor of the Jewish community in Harbin. Authorities closed a medical school in Warsaw after anti-Jewish student riots, a sailor leaped overboard in London Harbor after being mercilessly Jew-baited by his crewmates, and in the Prussian Diet, Nazis demanded the enactment of a *numerus clausus* limiting Jewish lawyers to one for each one hundred Gentile attorneys. On the eve of Hitler's assuming dictatorial powers at the invitation of the aging von Hindenburg, Wise feared another St. Batholomew's Day massacre, and lamented the sense of impotence he felt in being unable to awaken his fellow Jews to the danger. "One can only hope and pray that our people, and indeed all peoples, may be spared the horror that threatens."[35] The riots that erupted in Berlin and other German cities that month, and the Nazi call for a boycott of all Jewish stores, finally led the American Jewish Committee and B'nai Brith to approach the State Department and request that American representatives in Germany protest the rising tide of anti-Semitism there.

In order to present a united front in American Jewry, the Committee and the B'nai Brith leaders invited Wise, as president of the American Jewish Congress, to meet with them and plan a joint strategy. The conference committee fell apart almost immediately over an issue that harked back almost twenty years. The Committee and B'nai Brith still operated under the *shtadlan* mentality and wanted to work quietly behind the scenes. Wise, to their horror, planned a huge demonstration at Madison Square Garden, to be addressed by both Jews and non-Jews, protesting anti-Semitism in Germany. "Jews must utter what is in their hearts," he declared in calling for a public outcry against Hitler. "The time for caution and prudence is past. We must speak up like men. How can we ask our Christian friends to lift their voices in protest against the wrongs suffered by Jews if we keep silent?" He warned that "what is happening in Germany today may happen tomorrow in any other land on earth unless it is challenged and rebuked. It is not the German Jews who are being attacked. It is the Jews."[36]

The *shtadlanim* brought immense pressure on Wise, demanding that he keep silent and call off the planned rally. If the protest meeting took place, he was warned, the blood of the Jews of Germany would be on his head. They used their influence to keep the governor and mayor of New York from speaking at the Garden rally. But Wise believed that the Germans would only stop if they believed that the world was indeed watching—and caring—about events inside the Reich. When the German embassy twice contacted Wise and offered moderation in Nazi policies if the meeting was called off, Wise knew that he had been correct. Moreover, he received encouragement from the one man in the country whose judgment he trusted implicitly, Louis Brandeis, who told him to "go ahead and make the protest good as you can."[37]

On March 27, the day of the demonstration, the front page of the New York *Times* carried news that the State Department had informed Rabbi Wise and Dr. Cyrus Adler of the American Jewish Committee that "mistreatment of the Jews in Germany had virtually ceased," and that the Hitler Government had assured American representatives that all anti-Jewish incidents would stop and law and order would be maintained. The announcement, which some people thought had been timed to deflate the Garden rally, failed to appease Wise. Over twenty-two thousand people packed the inside of the hall, while another thirty thousand or more jammed the streets outside. Speakers included former governor Alfred E. Smith, Bishops William T. Manning and Francis J. McConnell, Senator Robert F. Wagner of New York, and Wise's close friend, the Reverend John Haynes Holmes. As chairman of the meeting, Wise pointed out that the Jews asked for no special privileges, but only for equal rights. He warned that Hitler hated the Jews, not for religious or even racial reasons, but because he opposed democracy. "He knows that we Jews, after centuries of fire, have come to believe with all our hearts in the sacredness and in the perpetuity of democratic institutions and the democratic ideal."[38]

Wise had agonized over the decision to go ahead with the rally, and finally decided that to be silent would have been unconscionable. Yet he still worried if he had done the right thing. "I am going through days and nights of hell," he confided to Julian Mack, "for I am mindful of our awful responsibility. But if you had seen the documents that we have seen, you would know that you would have had to choose between virtual silence—and silence is acquiescence—or supporting this tremendous protest. No matter what the Hitlerites do now, it will be nothing more than the overt commission of acts that would have been covertly performed, protest or no protest."[39] The following Saturday, the Nazis launched their boycott against Jewish merchants, and claimed that "atrocity propaganda" by American Jews had caused it. But Wise and other Jewish leaders had reason to believe that only the American protests had prevented the Nazis from turning the boycott into a full-scale *pogrom*. Over the next few months, Wise commuted to Washington regularly, speaking with State Department officials and trying to mitigate the effects of the boycott. When the Nazis held a public burning of books written by Jews, the American Jewish Congress sponsored a series of protest marches on the same day, and then kept up a constant stream of criticism against the Hitler regime.

Despite the fact that the Nazis had instigated numerous anti-Jewish measures, and while growing numbers of German refugees documented the horrendous conditions they had left behind, opposition to Wise's policy of public protest continued. A longtime colleague, Rabbi William Rosenau of Baltimore, pleaded with him to stop, and charged Wise with being responsible for the deaths of German Jews. The American Jewish Committee claimed that Wise's publicity-seeking tactics caused more harm than good. Many Jews, especially among the *yahudim,* could not bring themselves to believe that Germany, the land of Goethe and Heine, the birthplace of Reform Judaism, could do these things. And there were those who, while admitting the possibility of danger, worried that their acts might aggravate the situation.

Not all of the opposition came from the "supercautious" Jews, as Brandeis termed them. Part of Hitler's appeal lay in his vow to destroy the socialist menace, and in the 1930s, nothing scared conservative businessmen more than that specter. Few people swallowed Hitler's charges that the Jews masterminded a worldwide communist conspiracy, but many otherwise intelligent men believed that such a conspiracy did in fact exist. Edmund A. Walsh of the Georgetown University School of Foreign Service wrote that he opposed the Nazi persecution of Jews and hoped that "the offensive and wholly reprehensible practices of Jewish communists in Germany shall not be visited on innocent Jews." But, he added, nothing should be done to oppose the German suppression of the communists. A memorandum in the files of the ultraconservative National Civic Federation, dated October 10, 1933, noted: "If the world is to find Hitler a conservative force fighting against a revolutionary war, it may forgive him his anti-Jewish insanities and offer a prayer for his success."[40]

In the minds of some of the more conservative Jews, Stephen Wise's outspoken liberalism damned him as much as his forthright denunciation of Hitler, and they took pains to disassociate themselves from Wise in the minds of the Gentiles. Ralph Montgomery Easley, a onetime civic reformer and now the reactionary secretary of the Civic Federation, reported on a conversation he had with Morris Waldman, his counterpart on the American Jewish Committee, who "is not only a very able man but a true and loyal American. With him it is 'America first and the Jews second' while with the Rabbi Wise-Untermyer crowd it is 'The Jews first and to hell with everybody else!' I found from my talk with Mr. Waldman that they will greatly appreciate any effort on our part to help make clear to the American people the fundamental difference between the American Jewish Committee and the American Jewish Congress. . . . The Rabbi Wise crowd is practically advocating a superstate and his virulent speeches not only at Geneva but in this country and Europe during the last two years point to the dangerous idea that is in his mind and that of his radical followers."[41]

Wise found at least one group willing to pay heed to his warnings, although not always as rapidly as he wanted it to. Unfortunately, it seemed that only a crisis could galvanize American Zionism into action, and the Nazi menace once perceived became the *force majeure* behind Zionist growth and policy in the 1930s. A touchstone of American Zionist philosophy had been that a Jewish home in Palestine would serve as a refuge, not for American Jews but for those fleeing persecution in Europe. Brandeis had articulated this belief when the first signs of a changing immigration policy had been detected, although until 1933 the expectation had been that Jews would be fleeing Russia and Eastern Europe, not Germany. Indeed Brandeis, even before Wise, had come to the conclusion that the only salvation for German Jewry lay in emigration. The thought struck many as absurd, impossible. Wise wrote: "I really felt as though I had been struck a blow between the eyes to hear two distinguished German Jews, one of whom is about as Jewish-looking as Hitler, speak in these terms. Again and again they said, *'nur heraus'* ['only emigration']. I confess to you that when Brandeis said that two months ago, I could hardly believe my ears; and I could hardly believe that he was sane. A people to migrate! But again, as wisdom and prescience are made clear, if only that consummation could be effected!"[42]

Morris Rothenberg saw the situation as "a new day in the history of the movement" and called for a rededication to the cause. Although he pledged that the Zionists would help German refugees as much as they could, he told the 1933 convention "that a fundamental solution of the aggravated condition of Jewish homelessness had to be sought, and that Palestine offered the most promising hope in that direction." The ZOA called on Great Britain to allow a maximum number of German refugees into Palestine and vowed to go to the League of Nations to open the gates.[43] A number of resolutions passed the convention calling for strong and direct action, yet as the Zionists themselves recognized, the movement, faced with the greatest crisis in Jewish history, had reached the nadir of its strength and influence. In the United States less than forty thousand members belonged to the various Zionist groups out of four million Jews, and comparable figures held true in the European countries as well. Despite the MacDonald letter, British policy in Palestine no longer posited large-scale Jewish immigration and development. And while few would talk about it, the movement had to act with restraint, for the Nazis held over a half million German Jews as hostages, and in order to secure their release, some contacts with German authorities had to be maintained.[44]

The renewal of American Zionism got under way slowly, retarded by the same forces that had opposed Rabbi Wise's anti-Nazi activities. In 1935, the ZOA sponsored a national roll call to get 250,000 registered sympathizers to contribute $1.00 each; less than 20,000 responded. A special extension fund with a goal of $100,000 brought in $13,500. In that same year, the Joint Distribution Committee pulled out of the United Jewish Appeal, fearing that the Zionists would hamper fund-raising endeavors. Yet growth did come, and after the low point of 1932, ZOA membership climbed steadily upward for the next fifteen years. It became increasingly difficult for American Jews to remain indifferent either to the plight of German refugees or to the needs of Palestine. Harry Simonhoff described the reaction of Miami Jewry: "Of course, the victims of Nazi savagery must be helped to leave their harsh, step-father land. . . . What about this thing called Zionism? There might be something to the idea of a Jewish state in Palestine. If it is a matter of money, then here is a check."[45] But as long as the ZOA could do little more than urge the mandatory power to open the doors of Palestine, it lacked that practical program that had been the lever to its phenomenal growth twenty years earlier.

Hadassah, on the other hand, found its key in the most humane and appealing project imaginable: Youth Aliyah, the rescue and resettlement of Jewish boys and girls from the Nazi horror. The movement to bring German Jewish youth to Palestine had begun on a small scale in 1933. Two years later Henrietta Szold recommended it to Hadassah, and in a moving letter described a visit to the *kvutzot* (settlements) where the refugee children had been placed: "I was gripped by the thought of the children—children whom we have lost during the course of generations. I thought of the children who were brought by the Tribunal of the Inquisition to the Isle of St. Thomas; I thought of the children of Russia who were snatched from their parents and brought up in convents; I thought of Edgar Mortara in Italy, and I thought of the crimes that we are committing on our own children—that we have not gathered the funds that Palestine needs to solve the most important problem next to the immigration problem—the problem of the Jewish child. But when I saw the young boys and girls, I said to myself, 'We are making good, where the others have sinned. We alone atone for our crime.' And I went on saying to myself, 'That is Zionism in its truest realization.' "[46]

At its 1935 convention Hadassah formally undertook to sponsor Youth Aliyah (literally, the "going up of the children"), and set about it in the now standard Hadassah manner. A national Youth Aliyah Committee co-ordinated efforts, while individual chapters set up similar committees for local functions. As usual, Hadassah paid all overhead costs out of dues, so that every penny collected at numerous teas and luncheons went to the cause. Women across the land subscribed to *minyanim,* in which ten Hadassah members pledged "to redeem a child," each one donating $18 a year for two years. Symbolically, the Hebrew letters for the number "18" spell *chai,* meaning "life"; practically, it cost $360 to support a child in Palestine during the two years of training and resettlement. In that first year, Hadassah agreed to raise $30,000, and to make sure that they achieved this, they assigned quotas to each chapter based on a goal of $50,000. In the first ten months of the campaign, Hadassah women, assisted by Eddie Cantor, brought in $125,000.[47]

It would be hard to find a project conceived out of greater

compassion or executed in so generous a manner. From its inception until the founding of the State of Israel, Youth Aliyah trained 50,000 youth, 20,000 of them orphans rescued from the death camps after the war. Youth Aliyah is still going strong, and in more than 35 years of its existence has gathered, absorbed, educated, and rehabilitated more than 135,000 children from 80 countries. And while the women were saving children, the men turned to politics.

IV

Although Louis Brandeis, Stephen Wise, Julian Mack, Felix Frankfurter, as well as other members of the Americanized leadership had been Wilsonian Democrats, American Jewry as a whole had not developed a cohesive, bloc-voting mentality in the 1920s. Those who went into commerce and the professions often became Republicans, like Louis Marshall, while others who worked with their hands voted Democratic. Few, if any, political issues in the 1920s roused Jewish self-consciousness; even the Johnson Immigration Act of 1924, although passed by a Republican Congress, had adherents in both parties, and a number of upper-class Jews did not weep overly long at its implications. But Jews, like other groups, were affected by the social and demographic changes that took place in the decade preceding the depression. A nation that for over three centuries had been predominantly rural in character suddenly found that half of its people lived in cities, and as Samuel Lubell pointed out, the increasing urbanization of America created the great power base that the Democrats utilized to seize and hold political control after 1932.[48] And no ethnic group has had its fortunes so closely linked with the cities as have American Jews. In 1936, out of 4,770,000 Jews in the United States, 78 per cent of them lived in the 14 largest cities, with 2,000,000 concentrated in New York City alone. Moreover, 68 per cent of American Jewry lived in the crucial electoral states of New York, Pennsylvania, Illinois, Massachusetts, New Jersey, and Ohio, the very heartland of Democratic strength.

For Franklin D. Roosevelt, who had grown to political maturity in New York State politics, the Jewish vote constituted a factor that he, as *homo politicus,* could hardly ignore. Both he and his wife Eleanor had originally shared the genteel anti-Semitism common to their class, but their native compassion and open-mindedness soon led them to shed such prejudices. Both of them got to know the social reformers in New York, many of whom, like Belle and Henry Moskowitz, opened up a side of life the Roosevelts had never guessed existed. By the time Franklin became President, he had surrounded himself with a body of advisers that, although far from being predominantly Jewish, included more Jews than had ever before had access to a President of the United States. Bernard M. Baruch, Benjamin V. Cohen, Felix Frankfurter, Sidney Hillman, Herbert H. Lehman, David Lilienthal, Isador Lubin, Henry Morgenthau, Jr., David Niles, Anna Rosenberg, and Samuel I. Rosenman all either held top-level jobs in the Roosevelt administration or had regular entrée into the White House. Louis Brandeis, whom the President affectionately called "Isaiah," once again had direct access to the chief of state, and became a focal point around which many of the younger New Dealers congregated.

Jews began to receive more judicial and administrative appointments and to appear in greater numbers in Congress. Ten Jews took seats in the Seventy-fifth Congress, and three of them held important committee chairmanships in the House of Representatives: Sol Bloom led the Foreign Affairs Committee, Samuel Dickstein presided over Immigration and Naturalization, and Emanuel Celler of Brooklyn began his long tenure as head of the House Judiciary Committee. Although Jews seemed more powerful than they really were, there is no doubt that Franklin Roosevelt sparked a love affair on the part of many Jews with the Democratic Party that has lasted to this day. In part, the economic program of the New Deal appealed to Jewish laborers and small businessmen, while the social proposals found a ready echo among teachers and community workers. But Roosevelt's personality, his indefinable charisma, the attraction that this patrician Hudson manor lord generated among the poor and the ethnics in America, struck its most responsive chord in the Jewish community. In each of his four campaigns, Roosevelt's plurality in Jewish wards mounted steadily, and in 1944 often topped 90 per cent. In several Brooklyn precincts that year, even the persons serving as Republican poll watchers voted for "that man" in the White House.[49]

Not everyone rejoiced over this new prominence of Jews in politics; many saw it as an embarrassment, a calling of attention to Jews that would inevitably lead to trouble. Indeed, European fascism spawned several domestic hate groups that seemed to thrive in the turbulence of the depression decade, and who all shared a common hatred of the Jews. Anti-Semites flocked into William Dudley Pelley's Silver Shirts, who claimed to represent "the cream, the head and flower of our Protestant Christian manhood." There was "but one issue in the United States," Pelley declared in 1934, "and that is the forcible removal of the Jew from office." Gerald Winrod, a fundamentalist evangelist who blamed the "international Jew" for "the scourge of international communism," achieved a wide following in the Midwest, while the German-American Bund packed Madison Square Garden for its Nazi-style rallies. In New York, teen-age gangs roamed the streets and subways assaulting Jews; they would often insult a Jewish girl, provoking her escort to a fight, and then mercilessly beat him up. Father Coughlin, the spellbinding radio preacher whose audience reached upwards of 30 million, gradually dropped his emphasis on social justice and began berating Jews on the air. He had once promised that he would "never change my philosophy that the New Deal is Christ's Deal," but he and many others now attacked the "Jew Deal," run by Felix Frankfurter "and his happy little hot dogs." George W. Christians and his white-shirted Crusaders for Economic Liberty, Harry A. Jung and the American Vigilantes, Elizabeth Dilling, George D. Deatherage, and others all claimed to be fighting for the basic values of a free America against the Jew-dominated Roosevelt administration.[50] It was in the extremist groups openly aping the Nazis that the anti-Semitism of the 1930s found its most sensational expression.

But ethnic prejudices in the United States have always surfaced during periods of societal ferment, and the two decades between the wars found many nervous Americans seeking some simplistic explanation for the complex social changes they saw all around them. The old stereotype of the "Jew banker" out to dominate the world might be dismissed by those sophisticated enough to see its absurdity; but as Hitler proved, by providing a scapegoat, rationality could be ignored. Unfortunately, the prominence of Jewish theorists and politicians in the Communist Party, both in the Soviet Union and the United States, stirred up the fears of many who ignored the baser forms of anti-Jewishness. One opinion poll indicated that four out of every ten Americans believed anti-Jewish hostility stemmed from legitimate reasons, the characteristics of the Jews themselves, and another survey found Jews ranked second only to Italians as the group considered to be the worst citizens.[51]

The fear of fascism at home and abroad made the importance of a Palestinian refuge even more pressing, and Zionist leaders had little hesitation in trying to influence the Chief Executive in behalf of their cause. Felix Frankfurter, who enjoyed a particularly close relationship with Roosevelt, became one of the first to alert the President not only to the dangers of fascism, but to the need to keep Palestine's doors open. "The significance of Hitlerism far transcends ferocious anti-Semitism or fanatical racism," Frankfurter told him. "The attack against the Jews is merely an index to the gospel of force and materialism that explains the present rulers of Germany." Even before the general public realized the extent of the refugee problem resulting from Nazi depredations, the Harvard law professor began transmitting copies of news items and reports on the refugee situation to the President. When Frankfurter visited Palestine in 1934, he wrote rhapsodic letters to his friend in the White House about what the Jews had done to transform the land.[52]

Roosevelt spent nearly all of his first term absorbed by domestic events and policies, and while he is frequently given credit for recognizing as early as 1933 and 1934 the international menace posed by Hitler, he had little choice but to focus his energies on pulling the nation out of the depression. He did respond to Frankfurter's enthusiasm over Palestine by inviting other Jewish leaders to the White House, but this also facilitated his efforts to improve his political position in the Jewish community. He learned a little about Zionism not only from Frankfurter, but also from another old friend, Julian Mack, with whom he had often collaborated on Harvard affairs.[53] Still further prodding came from Stephen Wise, who after an earlier disagreement with Roosevelt during the latter's tenure as governor of New York became one of his most ardent admirers and champions, and even took to the campaign trail in 1936 in support of the President's re-election. Wise's enthusiasm stemmed from the White House's intervention with the British in 1936 over Palestinian immigration policy.

The Nazi terror by then had sparked a massive emigration from Germany, and to a lesser extent, from surrounding countries as well. With American quotas discouraging refugees from coming here, many turned their eyes to Palestine, and from 1933 to 1935, 134,000 persons legally entered Palestine, far beyond what Lord Passfield and the Colonial Office had considered the limit of the country's capacity. Like an oasis, the Yishuv prospered amid a worldwide depression, and the new immigrants created jobs and industries that increased the land's capacity to absorb even more people. Palestinian exports and imports rose 50 per cent in those two years, and the Yishuv swelled to 400,000 people; Tel Aviv, founded in 1909 on sand dunes north of Jaffa, grew to a bustling modern city of 135,000, while 160 Jewish agricultural settlements dotted the countryside. Immigration would have increased even more dramatically had the British Government not imposed restrictions. Despite the MacDonald letter, the Colonial Office placed severe limits on the number and types of persons who could enter the country, and never gave the Jewish Agency anywhere near the number of visas requested.

There is no doubt that the Arabs had benefited from this Zionist-generated prosperity, and they now shared in the highest standard of living in the eastern Mediterranean basin. But while they easily outnumbered the Jews (the Arab population practically doubled between 1917 and 1940, to nearly 1.2 million, as Arabs flocked to take advantage of new economic opportunities in the Holy Land), Arab leaders began to express fears of becoming a minority subservient to the Jews. In April 1936 isolated attacks on individual Jews suddenly escalated into widespread rioting. The

Arab Higher Committee, led by the mufti, declared a six-month general strike and encouraged private guerrilla bands to launch attacks on Jewish settlements. Because of a lack of co-ordination among the rival Arab gangs, the assaults were easily beaten back, but an ominous note appeared in the support given the Higher Committee by neighboring Arab countries, and links established between the mufti and the Nazis. The Germans had already recognized that in the event of war, the Middle East would be a strategic theater, and inciting the Arabs against the British might be the key to success there. His Majesty's Government reacted more firmly in 1936 than it had in the past, and the arrival of twenty thousand additional troops led the Arabs to call off the general strike. But to keep things quiet, the British decided to halt further immigration and appointed still another Royal Commission to study the Palestine problem.[54]

Stephen Wise was in Europe when he heard this news, and hurried to London where he joined Chaim Weizmann, David Ben-Gurion, Felix Frankfurter, and Moshe Shertok in attempting to negotiate with the Crown. The futility of their efforts came through in a letter Wise penned to Brandeis, reporting on the talks: "It seems now as if nothing could avert suspension [of immigration]; announcement may be postponed for a time but that is all."[55] When he returned to the United States, however, he requested an interview with the President, who, to Wise's pleasant surprise, appeared to be informed about the situation in the Holy Land.[56] But he also discovered that Roosevelt had been in touch with German banker Max Warburg, who had advised him that the United States could do nothing about the problems in Germany. If Max Warburg said that nothing could be done, then what could Roosevelt do? Wise, whose heart was breaking over what he had seen and heard in Europe, poured out his emotions to Roosevelt, and Wise's great persuasive talents evidently touched the President deeply. Roosevelt promised to consult with Cordell Hull, and later had the Secretary of State inform the British Government that the United States "would regard suspension of immigration as a breach of the Mandate." The British Prime Minister, Stanley Baldwin, decided that by a small gesture he could temporarily placate both the Zionists and their new-found friend, the president of the United States. The day before the scheduled suspension, the British Government announced that until the Royal Commission submitted its report, there would be no change in Palestinan immigration policy.[57]

The Zionists were ecstatic. Brandeis wrote to Rabbi Wise that "you have performed a marvellous feat—nothing more important for us has happened since the Mandate," and predicted that Roosevelt's actions would set a precedent for the future.[58] If pressure on the British could be maintained from Washington, then the troubles of the Yishuv would be over. Roosevelt had also shown his friendliness to the Zionists by directing the State Department to loosen some of its red tape and facilitate the issuance of visas to those people eligible to enter the United States under the quota system.[59]

The Zionists rejoiced prematurely. Roosevelt did intervene in 1936, but American rights in the Holy Land had been circumscribed and defined by the Anglo-American Convention of 1924. In an election year, the President could chance a *coup de théâtre* with nothing to lose. If Britain had said "No," he had at least tried; the British, by merely granting a delay in their final determination, had sacrificed nothing, won Roosevelt's gratitude, and gave the President still another card to play in his bid for reelection. The real political limits on Roosevelt's flexibility would severely cripple his capacity to help at precisely the time when the Jewish people, more than in any other period of their long history, desperately needed a friend in power. But even beyond that, the results of the Peel Commission showed that the Palestine problem was no longer amenable to any simple solution.

By all accounts, the Royal Commission headed by Viscount Peel was the ablest and most distinguished of all the investigatory bodies to visit the Holy Land. It conducted full and comprehensive hearings from November 1936 through January 1937, and its report, issued in July 1937, presented a lucid and critical analysis of the dilemma facing the Crown. The British had won Palestine from the Turks as a prize of war, and could have done almost anything they wanted with it. In fact, had His Majesty's Government immediately drawn up boundaries and established a Jewish state, the Arabs, after initial opposition, would probably have been reconciled to it within a decade or two. The Commisson found that Jewish immigration had benefited the entire country, including the Arab population, and it praised Jewish initiative and endeavors. "The Arab charge that the Jews have obtained too large a proportion of good land cannot be maintained," the Commission noted. "Much of the land had been sand dunes or swamps and uncultivated when purchased. Though today, in the light of experience gained by Jewish energy and enterprise, the Arabs may denounce the vendors and regret the alienation of the land, there was at the time of the earlier sales little evidence that the owners possessed either the resources or the training needed to develop the land."

The Commission concluded that Great Britain had assumed irreconcilable obligations in its promises to the Jews on one side and to the Arabs on the other, and that while it would make numerous recommendations on how to mitigate some of the friction, the troubles lay too deep for mere palliatives. The only solution it saw involved radical surgery, dividing the land into two sovereign states. The Arabs would have Transjordan and most of Palestine, including Samaria and the Negev. Great Britain would retain a mandate for the area around Jerusalem and Bethlehem, with a corridor to the sea, and enclaves at Akaba, Tiberias, Acre, and Haifa. The Jewish state would comprise all of the Galilee, the Jezreel Valley, and the coastal plain as far south as Ashdod near Gaza, a total of 1,554 square miles. Although Peel and his associates felt that partition presented the only viable solution, they feared that it would not satisfy the demands of Arab nationalists, nor "give the Jews the full freedom they desire to build up their National Home in their own way."[60]

The Arabs almost immediately rejected the plan, and a pan-Arab conference in Syria in September resolved that every Arab had a sacred duty to preserve Palestine as an Arab country. F. I. Shalat, president of the Arab National League, declared that "the Arabs do not oppose giving the Jews rights to live and own land in Arab territory, but they cannot agree to partition it."[61] Rioting broke out in the Holy Land again, and it took British forces eighteen months to quell the guerrilla rebellion; five members of the Arab

Higher Committee landed in prison, but the mufti escaped to an asylum provided by Adolf Hitler.

The Jews received the Peel Report and split into several factions over its conclusions. All agreed that the Commission had been thorough and fair, and had received testimony from any and all parties who wished to present it, even the Americans.[62] But the Commission had practically ignored the Jewish Agency, treating it only as a paper creation, a fact that the non-Zionists deeply resented.* At the Fifth Agency Council meeting in August 1937, the American non-Zionists blasted the whole partition plan as a violation of the Balfour Declaration and of the Mandate, a position they stuck to until the establishment of Israel in 1948.[64] Equally vehement were a number of American Zionists. Brandeis wrote Szold that the Commission had gone beyond its instructions in recom-

---

* After all the fanfare surrounding its creation, the Jewish Agency had quickly deteriorated, at least in the United States, into an unrecognized arm of the American Jewish Committee and the Joint Distribution Committee. By the time the Eighteenth Congress met in 1933, non-Zionists had been able to fill only half the seats to which they were entitled on the Council, and the Zionists were urging a redistribution of seats, cutting the non-Zionists back from 50 per cent to less than 20 per cent. Stephen Wise at this time commented: "Of the Agency I will not speak, because one should not speak ill of the dead." The problem was that although many groups had informal and loose ties to the Agency, no one group had responsibility and authority to name people, conduct business, etc. Everything ran out of the hip pockets of Felix Warburg and Cyrus Adler. In 1934, David Werner Senator, Maurice Karpf, and others began agitation for an American branch of the Agency that would fill this administrative void, and eventually they succeeded in their plans. But just as the Zionists took full control of the enlarged Agency within a few years and made it subservient to the WZO, so in the United States the American branch also came under Zionist control; but here, instead of being dominated by the ZOA, it became the primary Zionist umbrella group in the country, eventually eclipsing the ZOA. During the 1930s the ZOA and the non-Zionists fought numerous battles over control of Palestinian policy. Typical was the example during the 1936 riots, when Felix Warburg refused to free money for the Yishuv to buy arms, although Britain had approved the purchase of defensive weapons. Warburg refused to budge, arguing that weapons were not legitimate for the type of Jewish settlement he supported in Palestine. Eventually, Ben-Gurion appealed to Stephen Wise as President of the ZOA, and Wise secured more than $15,000 in a special gift from Justice Brandeis.[63]

mending partition, and that the scheme should be fought. Louis Lipsky and Stephen Wise derided the report and accused Great Britain of "the greatest betrayal of a most sacred trust."[65]

But at the Twentieth Zionist Congress that summer in Zurich, which had preceded the Agency meeting, Chaim Weizmann, again president of the WZO, urged the delegates to accept the principle of partition. He did not like the proposed boundaries, and admitted that the scheme could be easily criticized, but he saw partition as a lesser evil. Of the six million Jews in Europe, perhaps a third of them could be relocated in Palestine. The Zionist divisions on this question did not follow party lines. Many of Weizmann's supporters among the Labor and General Zionists opposed him, while some of his former antagonists backed him. The exclusion of Jerusalem upset many, and Berl Katznelson, a Labor Party leader, declared that a Jewish state without its most holy city was like a body without a head. Rabbi Wise led the American opposition to partition, and in a dramatic speech, declared that there were some things a people could not do. What kind of Jewish state would it be where nearly half the population and three fourths of the land were Arab?

But in back of everyone's mind lay the plight of German Jewry. Where would they go? Great Britain had made it abundantly clear that it had no intention of living up to the original terms of the Mandate, and the League of Nations had already been exposed as a powerless debating society. Various experts had estimated that at least 100,000 immigrants could be brought in annually, and by intensive cultivation of the land, a stable population of at least 2.5 million could be achieved. Most importantly, if partition could be implemented quickly enough, Jewish officials, not the British, would control immigration. Despite many misgivings, the Congress voted 300 to 158 in support of a vaguely worded resolution that, while demanding full implementation of the Mandate, offered to explore in principle the idea of partition.[66]

The Colonial Office, despite Arab rejection of the Peel report, decided to proceed on the basis of minute Zionist interest, and appointed still another commission, this one headed by Sir Charles Woodhead, to explore alternative forms of dividing the land. The

Woodhead report, issued in November 1938, set forth three basic plans, none of which proved acceptable either to Arab or Jew. In essence, the Commission decided that no Jewish state could be devised that would include only a handful of Arabs and still be big enough to absorb new Jewish immigration. A few weeks later, the government issued a white paper which, after two commission studies, turned down the whole idea of partition as politically, administratively, and financially impossible. Only true understanding between Arab and Jew could bring peace in Palestine, and to achieve that end, the Crown had decided to hold a conference in London at which both sides could explore the situation together.[67] This nonsolution bewildered the Jews, for by the beginning of 1939 the refugee problem had reached a critical stage, with the victims of Nazi persecution denied asylum anywhere and signs of war filling the air.

V

The Anschluss in March 1938, in which Germany took over neighboring Austria, added another two hundred thousand Jews to those already in danger from Nazi depredations, and put even more pressure on Jewish leaders in the West to find a solution for the problem. Former League of Nations commissioner James G. MacDonald had been urging the nations of the world since 1933 to liberalize their immigration policies, but to no avail. Several Jewish attempts to secure larger quotas, or special considerations for victims of Nazi persecution, only served to highlight the depth of feeling against further migration into this country. And as it became clearer to officials in the Roosevelt administration that Great Britain would be America's first line of defense against Germany in case of war, their prime concern focused on how to help Britain, and not on forcing her to open up Palestine.

Acutely aware of political realities which limited his options in foreign policy, Roosevelt tried to help in small ways, by speeding up visa processing or extending the allowable length of stay in the

United States for certain groups. But even as he called for State
Department co-operation, career officers in the service, many of
them blatantly anti-Semitic, tried to reduce or even block further
immigration to these shores. The general attitude of Secretary of
State Hull, despite his Jewish-born wife, was not helpful. He had
too legalistic a mind, and tended to accept the counsel of career
officers that the Jewish problem constituted an internal German
matter, one in which we could not legitimately interfere. Emanuel
Celler, who represented an almost all-Jewish constituency in Brooklyn, charged that the Department had no real desire to help, that
it had a "heartbeat muffled in protocol."[68] During these years, it
should be noted, the other nations of the world also did their best
to ignore the problem. The only exceptions could be found in the
isolated programs created to provide homes for children. Nearly all
of the Western European nations established centers that received
over thirteen thousand youth from Germany and Austria before the
war.

It came as quite a surprise, considering the general apathy toward
the problem as well as the political situation, when Roosevelt, at
an impromptu press conference in Warm Springs on March 25,
1938, announced that he had decided to call an international conference on the refugee crisis. The President recognized the considerable risks involved. European countries bordering Germany already had their hands full of unwanted displaced persons and could
hardly be expected to welcome a move by a country that had
made practically no effort to absorb the refugees. Domestically,
unemployment had risen again, so Roosevelt had to make clear
that he did not propose a relaxation of the quota system. The call
to the twenty-nine nations involved suggested creating a special
committee "for the purpose of facilitating the emigration from Germany and presumably Austria of political refugees," but "no country would be expected to receive greater number of emigrants than
is permitted by its existing legislation." The remedies, if any could
be agreed upon, would be borne through private funds.

Despite Roosevelt's hope that the isolationists would not make
the conference a partisan issue, antagonism soon manifested itself.
Representative Thomas A. Jenkins of Ohio attacked the President

for having gone "on a visionary excursion into the warm fields of altruism. He forgets the cold winds of poverty and penury that are sweeping over the 'one third' of our people who are ill clothed, ill housed and ill fed." When Representative Samuel Dickstein introduced legislation that would allow borrowing from future quotas to permit entry of increased immigration in 1938 and 1939, the restrictionists immediately suspected that the devious Roosevelt planned to throw open America's doors to tens of thousands of penniless Jews.[69]

The President's announcement sent Jewish hopes soaring. A number of organizations that had been fighting with each other, including the American Jewish Committee and the American Jewish Congress, temporarily buried their differences and requested a joint interview with the President, but Roosevelt's secretary, sensitive to charges of excessive Jewish influence on the Administration, insisted that they meet with the State Department.[70] For the next several weeks a variety of Jewish groups and Christian societies concerned with the refugee problem bombarded the White House and State Department with messages of congratulations and advice; even Vladimir Jabotinsky wanted to send over a delegation of Polish Jews to thank Roosevelt personally, a suggestion the Department recoiled from in horror.[71] Indeed the overwhelming response by the Jewish community placed the Department in an embarrassing position. Rumor had it that the President had come up with this whole cockeyed scheme at the insistence of Rabbi Wise, and a day hardly passed without some Jewish group wanting the Department to convey through diplomatic channels resolutions damning the British or demanding open immigration into Palestine, requests that the Department politely but firmly turned down. Field officers at the consulates reported themselves besieged by applicants for visas, and the Department constantly had to repeat that the President had specifically noted he would not request any increase in the quotas. Consular officials neglected to point out, however, that they had made the application process so cumbersome and difficult that out of 153,774 places available in 1937, only 27,000 had been filled. When one Jewish group called for utilization of the unfilled quotas to aid refugees, presidential secretary

Marvin McIntyre sent the petition to Undersecretary of State Sumner Welles with a note: "Personally I do not see much necessity for any reply except that a more or less courteous but stereotyped answer signed by me may head off insistence in the future for a specific reply. What do you think?" Welles agreed, since the Department preferred to "head off insistence" than come to grips with real, but difficult, problems.[72]

The American delegation to the conference, scheduled for mid-July at Évian-les-Bains in France, included three Jews: Henry Morgenthau, Jr., Secretary of the Treasury; presidential adviser Bernard M. Baruch; and Rabbi Stephen Wise, the only one of the three actively involved in anti-Nazi and Zionist activities. From the start, the delegates had difficulty determining their objectives and authority, since the Administration did not want to commit itself to any specific plans beforehand. Roosevelt had had a fair degree of success in this type of arrangement early in the New Deal, taking representatives of disparate viewpoints and locking them in a room until they came up with an acceptable compromise arrangement. But the issues involved here were much too complex, and even after James G. MacDonald had been selected as chairman, the group never really resolved the problem of authority. In fact, the White House ignored the delegation after one meeting, and the President's Advisory Committee on Political Refugees, as it became known, bogged down in administrative fights with the State Department over visa lists.[73]

As the opening date of the conference approached, Zionist groups stepped up their demands that Palestine become the major topic for discussion, a development that greatly upset the British. In a series of secret notes to Roosevelt, Great Britain threatened a boycott of the meeting unless discussions focused only on refugees and not on those threatened with future persecutions; Palestine, under no circumstances, should be on the agenda. It is likely that Roosevelt had hoped that Palestine might prove the key to the refugee problem, but in the face of British insistence, he could do little but accede to their request. When American Jewish leaders suggested that Chaim Weizmann testify at the conference, the State Department replied that the British considered Weizmann's appearance undesirable, and American representatives received instructions to keep Weizmann away from the meeting.[74]

Once the Zionists recognized that the conference would seek alternatives to Palestine, they lost all interest in the proceedings. They assumed that the countries really did not want the Jews themselves, and that without the alternative of Palestine, the delegates would make handsome speeches and token gestures but accomplish nothing. The nine days of meetings at Évian-les-Bains from July 6 to 15 fully justified these dire predictions. Aside from creating a permanent Inter-Governmental Committee on Refugees, headed by Earl Winterton, chairman of the British delegation to the conference, the gathering did absolutely nothing. A few countries, notably the Dominican Republic and Australia, offered to take additional refugees, but even had these new quotas been fully utilized, it would have been but a drop in the bucket.[75] Ira Hirschmann, a New York department store official in Évian as an observer, walked out damning the conference as "a façade behind which the civilized countries could hide their inability to act." Zionist representatives, as Henry Feingold notes, adopted the attitude of a beleaguered world Jewry surrounded by a murderous world community.

Despite the explicit announcement that Palestine would not be used to solve the refugee problem, Arab reaction to the Roosevelt proposal and to the conference itself upset the State Department. The American consul general in Jerusalem, George Wadsworth, informed the Department that the Arab press unanimously protested the meeting, and saw Roosevelt's annual messages to the ZOA as proof that the United States opposed Arab nationalist aspirations. Bartley Crum, who later served on the 1946 Anglo-American Commission of Inquiry, reported that he saw a secret file that indicated each time a promise was made to American Jewry regarding Palestine, the State Department promptly sent messages to Arab rulers discounting it and reassuring them that the United States would do nothing to change the situation in Palestine.[76] History seemed to be repeating itself as a President apparently friendly to Zionist plans found his policies thwarted by State Department careerists opposed to Jewish intrusions in international affairs.

In October 1938, the refugee situation took a dramatic turn for the worse. Reinhard Heydrich, chief of the German Security Police, seized thousands of Polish Jews living in Germany and dumped them in the no-man's-land near the Polish border town of Sbonszyn. One of the deportees had a seventeen-year-old son living in Paris, and the youth, Herschel Grynszpan, crazed with grief, shot Ernst von Rath, a junior officer in the German embassy. The Nazi hierarchy, led by Josef Goebbels, seized on the incident to spark the infamous *Kristall-nacht,* or "Night of the Broken Glass," on November 9–10, in which rampaging Nazi gangs destroyed Jewish homes, businesses, and synagogues in every city and town in Germany. "The wrecking, looting and burning continued all day," reported one correspondent. "Huge but mostly silent crowds looked on and the police confined themselves to regulating traffic and making wholesale arrests of Jews 'for their own protection.' "⁷⁷

Roosevelt's Jewish contacts besieged him to help alleviate this distress. Stephen Wise, Felix Frankfurter, and others pleaded with the President to get the British to open up Palestine. The aging Louis Brandeis made one of his rare appearances at the White House to plead the Jewish case personally, and later reminded the Chief Executive to demand that the British do the right thing.⁷⁸ A delegation of Zionist leaders, Louis Lipsky, Stephen Wise, and Solomon Goldman, together with B'nai Brith president Henry Monsky, called on Cordell Hull to remind him that under the Anglo-American Convention of 1924, Great Britain had agreed to make no modifications in the Mandate without the consent of the United States. While admitting that the main purpose of the treaty had been to safeguard commercial interests, the Jewish spokesmen believed it could also be interpreted to give the United States a voice in immigration matters.

The State Department recognized that the furor over the *Kristall-nacht* might force the United States into some kind of retaliatory gesture. Departmental staff came up with a "moderate" proposal that might placate public opinion without necessitating any major policy changes: a presidential order allowing six-month extensions of temporary visas. The President quickly accepted the suggestion. But hopes that more would be done were soon dispelled. Samuel I. Rosenman, part of the White House inner circle and a prominent member of the American Jewish Committee, declared, "I do not believe it either *desirable* or *practicable* to recommend any change in the quota provisions of our immigration law." Regarding American powers over Palestinian affairs, Roosevelt himself conceded that the Anglo-American Convention left him powerless to act in the matter.[79] The letters, the petitions, the pleas had all been in vain. Even worse, the very moderation of the American reaction confirmed Hitler's prediction that the Western democracies would do nothing to save the Jews. Goebbels levied an "atonement fine" of a billion reichsmarks against German Jewry for the destruction it had caused in the rioting, and by December further steps had been taken to confiscate all Jewish assets. The Third Reich took a significant stride down the road toward the "final solution," and as with so many other events on that road to war and destruction, a firm and united stand by the free world might well have prevented it.

In this atmosphere Neville Chamberlain convened the Round Table Conference at St. James Palace in London on February 7, 1939. The ferocity of the *Kristallnacht* and the nonresponse it had evoked assured Hitler, and the Jews, that nothing stood in the way of the total destruction of European Jewry. For those who could read the signs, all-out war on the Continent lay just ahead. Both Hitler and Benito Mussolini openly supported Arab plans, while the Soviet Union and Communist groups following the party line also backed the Arab cause. The Zionists felt themselves totally isolated, and few believed the St. James Conference would prove of much value. The three American representatives from the ZOA—Stephen Wise, Louis Lipsky, and Robert Szold—lapsed into despair even before they sailed. The White House had turned down their request for a special audience with Roosevelt, and Wise sadly prophesied: "We know we are going to be bamboozled. I know that England is going to fool us to the top of her bent. But what can we do about it? If we poor Jews withdraw from the conference with the Arab kings, the world will say we are afraid to meet with them. We have got to take our chance, though it is a rotten chance."[80]

The Zionists had from the start been divided over whether they should attend. The Actions Comité had split evenly on the question and left the final decision to the Executive. Weizmann and Ben-

Gurion finally decided to participate after Malcolm MacDonald, the Colonial Secretary, assured them that His Majesty's Government still felt bound by the Balfour Declaration. Despite the general gloom, few people within the movement believed that Britain would wash its hands entirely of the Yishuv. Yet as the conference wore on, that is exactly what happened. The Arabs showed no signs of willingness either to recognize a special Jewish position in the Holy Land or even to discuss the possibility of a binational state. MacDonald stressed several times that Jews would have to seek Arab permission for further immigration, until Weizmann finally retorted that the British were not in Palestine by Arab consent. After five weeks of fruitless talks, the Conference dispersed on March 17 without having reached agreement on a single item.[81]

The Zionists now braced for the worst, for it had become obvious during the course of the meeting that Great Britain considered its promises to the Arabs of more importance than either the Balfour Declaration or the Mandate. Sixteen million Arabs had to be appeased, lest they turn on the British and endanger the Middle Eastern nexus between the home isles and the Pacific part of the Empire. Just as Chamberlain had sacrificed Czechoslovakia at Munich for the sake of "peace in our time," so he now prepared to offer up the Yishuv in the hope of maintaining good relations with the Arab world. In both cases, his hopes proved futile.

During March and April 1939, Zionist leaders launched a massive effort to avert the impending catastrophe. In the United States, Jewish spokesmen bombarded the White House with pleas that Roosevelt intercede. Justice Brandeis appealed to Roosevelt at least four times between March 6 and May 10 for the United States to prevent Britain from closing Palestine.[82] Friendly Christians also petitioned the President to help the Zionist cause. William L. Green, president of the American Federation of Labor (which had close ties to the labor movement in Palestine), transmitted an urgent cable he had received from Goldie Meyerson (later Golda Meir) explaining how desperate a situation the Jews faced.[83] The siege of letters prompted Roosevelt, who believed that a major shift in policy would be a mistake for the British, to have the State Department inform the Crown that the United States hoped no drastic changes would be implemented. In Europe, Chaim Weizmann flew from Palestine to London for an interview with Neville Chamberlain, but accomplished nothing. "The Prime Minister of England sat before me like a marble statue; his expressionless eyes were fixed on me, but he said never a word. . . . I got no response. He was bent on appeasement of the Arabs and nothing could change his course."[84] The gravity of the problem spurred Brandeis to appeal directly to the British Government, and while he was assured that any opinion he had on the Palestine question would receive "respectful and earnest attention," His Majesty's Government hoped he would discount rumors and defer any final judgment until it could issue an authoritative statement.[85]

That day came on May 17, when the Chamberlain Government promulgated the last major White Paper on Palestine. It set forth the basic plan that had been rejected by the Jews at the St. James Conference: an independent state to be created within ten years; seventy-five thousand immigrants to be admitted over the next five years; after March 1, 1944, no further Jewish immigration without Arab permission; and Jewish settlement would be restricted to specified areas.[86] In Parliament the government came under heavy attack. Herbert Morrison declared he would have more respect for Malcolm MacDonald, who tried to defend the document, "if he had frankly admitted that the Jews were to be sacrificed to the incompetence of the government." Morrison called the White Paper "dishonourable to our good name," and speaker after speaker rang changes on this theme. In the final vote, the Chamberlain Government secured approval only by appealing to party discipline, and even then over one hundred members of the majority abstained.[87] The Jews, needless to say, protested even more desperately. David Ben-Gurion declared, "The greatest betrayal perpetrated by the government of a civilized people in our generation has been formulated and explained with the artistry of experts at the game of trickery and pretended righteousness." In the United States, Stephen Wise and Solomon Goldman echoed this charge of further betrayal by a country whose word they had once considered sacred and inviolate. Goldman, now president of the ZOA, practically accused the British of adopting an official policy of anti-Semitism.[88] But the anguish felt by millions of Jews all over the world found expression in Louis Brandeis' simple question: "Where will a poor Jew go now?"

Over the summer of 1939, the Zionists began planning how they would fight the White Paper, and two schools of thought emerged. Chaim Weizmann still expected to co-operate with the British, cajoling them and hoping for a change of policy in the future. For him, the destiny of the Yishuv would always be tied to Britain. A new and growing sentiment favored the militant policy of David Ben-Gurion, who had come to see the possibility of armed conflict with the mandatory power. He favored an increase in the "Aliyah Bet," the illegal immigration that had begun around 1936. "For us the White Paper does not exist," he declared, and in a cable to Chamberlain he warned that the Yishuv stood ready to make the supreme sacrifice rather than submit to the terms of the White Paper.

In the United States, those non-Zionists associated with the Jewish Agency tended to follow Weizmann's lead, and although discouraged by the latest shift in British policy, believed that only by working within the system could they achieve future success. Within the ZOA, however, sentiment tended to favor Ben-Gurion's tougher approach. In a memorandum outlining suggested Zionist policy, Robert Szold called for a firm and uncompromising stand on the principles enunciated in the Balfour Declaration and the Mandate, and a refusal to accede to or co-operate in any diminution of the homeland. Such an attitude disturbed the non-Zionists, whose concern about possible violence soon led some of them to warn that unless the Zionists toned down their rhetoric, they would resign.[89]

The whole debate terminated with breathtaking suddenness. On August 24, the Nazi-Soviet Pact stunned the world. With the Russians now pacified, Hitler turned east, and on September 1, 1939, launched his offensive against Poland. The war Chamberlain had hoped to avert had come, and the Jews, whom the civilized nations of the world had tried to ignore, would now fall victim to a crime whose magnitude and cruelty is still incomprehensible. For the Jews, the feared hour had come. For Zionism, however, a new beginning was at hand.

A NEW BEGINNING

The mood in the United States after September 1939 differed significantly from what it had been a quarter century earlier. The outbreak of a world war in 1914 had caught the American public, and indeed most of the world, unawares, and although different groups held strong feelings for one side or the other, the majority of citizens had considered the fracas strictly a European affair; they fully endorsed Woodrow Wilson's call for neutrality in thought and in deed. Gradually a strong pro-Allied sentiment developed, but right up to the eve of American entry in April 1917, large numbers of people, especially in the Midwest, backed the German cause. In 1939, in contrast, only the most obtuse persons could have ignored the long train of events that led to war. While isolated pockets of Germanophiles and Nazi sympathizers existed, public opinion favored the French and British against the Axis; in March 1940 one poll reported that 85 per cent backed the Allies.

Yet at the same time, an overwhelming majority of Americans did not want this country to get involved in the war. Pacifists, isolationists, and a variety of anti-British or pro-German ethnic groups all had their own reasons for wanting the United States to avoid involvement. The signing of the Nazi-Soviet pact added those who followed the party line to those insisting that American boys were not going to get killed "over there." Conservative Republicans had their own special justification for opposing American entanglement, since they feared that Franklin Roosevelt would seize upon the war powers to do away with the Constitution (a document, they claimed, he had already seriously undermined). Publisher Frank Gannett told a New York Young Republicans gathering: "If we do get in, everything is gone. We would have a dictatorship more complete than in Italy or Germany or Russia. We would go down to ruin with the rest."[1]

Confidence that the Allies would easily defeat Hitler's goose-stepping martinets accounted for part of the isolationist mood. Why should we have to fight if the British and French could do the job themselves? During the winter of 1939–40, events in Europe seemed to justify this attitude. The Wehrmacht, after overrunning Poland, had stalled on the Western Front, and many people agreed with Senator Borah's derision of the "phony war." But in April 1940, the *sitzkrieg* suddenly turned into *blitzkrieg*, as lightning-fast Panzer divisions sliced through the Low Countries and took the supposedly impregnable Maginot Line from the rear. The British Expeditionary Force managed to rescue most of its men in the debacle at Dunkirk, but left all of its arms and heavy equipment on the beach. The British people braced for the onslaught, while the Luftwaffe tried bombing them into submission.

The surrender of France on June 22 led the Roosevelt administration to ask Congress for authority to beef up America's own defensive forces. Moreover, through the destroyer-bases deal and the Lend Lease program, Roosevelt over the next fifteen months managed to get sorely needed supplies to a beleaguered Britain, now led by the dauntless Winston Churchill. Isolationists would oppose these and every other measure they saw as a presidential plot to get us into war, but in the summer of 1940 American opinion definitely shifted in favor of sustained aid to Great Britain. While approving support, however, most Americans still opposed direct involvement in the war. In his unprecedented bid for a third term, Roosevelt responded to isolationist charges by promising that we would not be sucked into the fight: "I have said this before, but I shall say it again and again and again. Your boys are not going to be sent into any foreign wars." Yet in his victory, Roosevelt correctly read a mandate that this country's overseas policy should somehow stop fascist aggression.[2]

During this period, American Jews found themselves caught between their loyalty and sympathy for their persecuted brethren in Europe, and their awareness of the isolationist mood of the country. Unlike the First World War, when the community had been split in support of opposing belligerents, every Jew in the United States detested Hitler and wanted everything possible done to stop the Nazis. Once again, American Jewry had become "the last pillar of strength for Israel," and the menace of Hitler even led the competing fund-raising groups to join together in the United Jewish Appeal, which raised millions for refugee relief. In a report on the mood he had found in America, David Werner Senator, a member of the Agency Executive, wrote: "American Jews are fully conscious of the great responsibility the world situation has thrown upon them. They have made an extraordinary financial effort, by far the greatest ever made in the history of American and world Jewry in general to cope with a unique situation."[3]

The huge increase in funds, however, hid and perhaps assuaged the deeper anxieties of the community. Could American Jews ask the country to go to war to save European Jewry? Wouldn't the isolationists cry, "See, the Jews are dragging us into the war! The Jews want American boys to die for them!"? Many feared that all the old charges of dual loyalties would be dragged up, unleashing a wave of anti-Semitism in this country akin to that which now terrorized Europe. As if to confirm this worry, Charles A. Lindbergh, the golden hero of the twenties, publicly warned that if the United States went to war, the Jews would be the first to suffer. To those who believed that safety lay in maintaining a low profile, the prominent role played by a number of Jews, especially radio and film personalities and officials, in the Fight for Freedom and other interventionist groups only reinforced the chance of a *pogrom*.[4]

This split between concern for Hitler's victims and fear of reprisals affected to some extent the Zionists as well. Moshe Shertok believed the movement in America had not responded well to the Nazi threat, while Eliahu Golomb wrote: "The American Jew thinks of himself first and foremost as an American citizen. This is a fact, whether we like it or not. When the Jew—and the Zionist—goes to vote in American elections, it is not the candidate's attitude to Zionism which will determine his choice. . . . Loyalty to America is now the supreme watchword." When David Ben-Gurion arrived in the United States in late 1940, he discussed Jewish and Zionist problems with many of the country's leading Jews. In one interview, after the Palestinian leader had made an impassioned plea for American aid to Britain and to the Yishuv, the other man nodded his agreement, but said that he could do nothing publicly. Ben-Gurion then asked him, "Which are you first, a Jew or an American?" The answer: "A Jew. We are a minority here. If I stand up and demand American aid for Britain, people will say after the war that dirty Jews got us into it, that it was a Jewish war, that it was for their sakes that our sons died in battle." Ben-Gurion reported that he had found this attitude prevalent in all the Zionist groups with whom he spoke.[5] Surface appearances, however, can be misleading, and while normal Jewish fears had been exacerbated by the Nazi menace, they still reflected the general dichotomy in American thought. As public opinion in favor of aid to Great Britain increased, so did Jewish opinion for it; at the same time, a stronger and more militant Zionist movement emerged in the United States.

Membership in the ZOA had increased steadily during the 1930s, and by 1941 stood at 46,000. Hadassah's membership had tripled in the decade to 80,000, and the various smaller groups counted an additional 55,000 members. Contributions to the Keren Hayesod and the Jewish National Fund in 1940 totaled almost $4 million, Hadassah support added another $1.3 million, and the United Jewish Appeal allotted several million more. Most importantly, within the Jewish community organized anti-Zionism had practically disappeared. After the failure of the Évian conference, even previously hostile or neutral groups like B'nai Brith and the American Jewish Committee endorsed Zionist demands for open immigration to Palestine and supported the building of the Yishuv. If nothing else, Adolf Hitler had convinced American Jewry that a national home in

Palestine was an absolute necessity. Even Reform leaders changed their minds, and in 1935 the Central Conference of American Rabbis dropped its official opposition to the movement and declared Zionism a matter of personal conscience.[6]

The old slogan of "Men! Money! Discipline!" suddenly came alive once more, as Zionist organizers began talking to the community of the need to support the cause, of giving to help their brethren, of publicly endorsing a Jewish Palestine. As this happened, the ZOA took on a more and more Brandeisian outlook. Some of the old purists once again complained of the lack of understanding and true Zionist sentiment, that Jews only joined in times of crisis, but most people recognized that the situation called not for ideology but for action.[7] At the Pittsburgh convention in 1940, Robert Szold engineered the election of an Executive Committee fully committed to a strong and militant policy, although the choice of Washington philanthropist and businessman Edmund Kaufmann proved a disappointment. Brandeis, who had retired from the Supreme Court in 1939 at the age of eighty-two after a heart attack, now gave what strength he had to almost constant consultations with the Zionist leadership.[8]

The 1940 convention marked the beginning of an increasingly aggressive and nationalistic policy on the part of American Zionists, a trend that burst into full bloom at the Biltmore conference in 1942. For Emanuel Neumann, it concluded the end of a long period of subservience to the "Weizmann-Histadrut" leadership, but it also denoted the passing of an outmoded fiction among American Jews. Well into the 1930s, the ZOA leadership, both Lipskyites and Brandeisists, eschewed the idea of a Jewish state in Palestine. As long as the Jews had a place to go, as long as Great Britain seemed intent on fulfilling the Balfour Declaration, American Jews gave little thought to the ultimate form of a Jewish homeland. Felix Frankfurter, in his important statement in *Foreign Affairs,* had gone to great effort to define a homeland as different from a state. "The authoritative Jewish demand," he wrote, "is not for a Jewish state; it does not ask the right to govern others. Jews desire only the opportunity of national development within their ancestral land."[9] For all intents and purposes, the homeland could continue to be a Crown colony forever.

When Great Britain, in whom the Zionists had put so much trust, reneged on its promises and then closed the door to further immigration at the precise moment when Hitler's refugees needed a homeland most, American Zionists realized that only a country controlled by the Jews themselves would meet the needs not only of Zionism but of Judaism itself. It is doubtful whether a strong Zionist nationalism could have appealed to American Jewry before Hitler; but with the Holocaust, an independent Jewish state became the *sine qua non* of the Zionist movement. Despite opposition from some Jews who still feared the old bugaboo of divided loyalty, the ZOA finally came to grips with the essential meaning of Jewish redemption.

In 1940 and 1941, the ZOA embarked on several undertakings designed not only to bring unity to American Jewry, but to spread the Zionist message to non-Jews as well. Julian Mack and the Reverend Charles Edward Russell had created a Pro-Palestine Federation of America in 1930, which had enlisted a number of Christian clergymen in support of the Zionist program. Another Christian group, the American Palestine Committee, created in 1932, had counted senators, congressmen, and other dignitaries among its sponsors. But for the most part, Zionists had not done much missionary work in the greater community during the 1930s, despite the obvious willingness of Christian friends to support Zionist demands during the recurrent crises precipitated either by Hitler or the British. Emanuel Neumann charged that "we Zionists have isolated ourselves from the vital currents of American life and American thought. We have withdrawn into our shell." To come out of that shell, Brandeis encouraged Neumann to reactivate the American Palestine Committee in April 1941. Neumann's genius soon turned what had been a defunct propaganda piece into an impressive group of men and women who reached into areas hitherto untouched by Zionism. From the outset, it had an illustrious membership including sixty-eight senators, two hundred congressmen, and numerous academics, clergy, and leaders in many walks of life. The ZOA spent over seventy thousand dollars annually during the war years "to crystallize the sympathy of Christian America for our cause, that it may be of service as the opportunity arises. Sympathy is like any other force; it is effective only when properly channeled."[10]

Unity within the Zionist movement again proved to be a difficult task to achieve. At the Twenty-first Congress in August 1939, the World Zionist Organization had created an Emergency Committee for Zionist Affairs to help co-ordinate the efforts of the movement and avoid some of the confusion that had marked Zionist proceedings during the First World War. Relations between the Emergency Committee and the ZOA seemed friendly enough, especially with men like Emanuel Neumann directing the Committee's business. But at the 1940 convention, Solomon Goldman, although a member of the Emergency Committee, declared that the ZOA could not continue to remain subservient to a body deriving its authority from a foreign group, namely the Agency Executive; he demanded that a new interparty committee be created that would give the ZOA a dominant voice. Through this move, Goldman hoped to establish clearly the independence of the ZOA, not so much from the world movement but from Weizmann's leadership, and immediately Louis Lipsky, now a failing figure in Zionist circles, leaped to the defense of the Committee and indirectly of Weizmann.[11]

The Szold-dominated leadership undoubtedly considered Weizmann much too passive a leader at this stage, one whose devotion to Great Britain clearly clouded his judgment. The American Zionists had already begun supporting the militant Palestinians headed by David Ben-Gurion, and in a series of articles in the *New Palestine,* they hammered away at the need for a strong and independent stand by American Zionists.[12] The issue of the Emergency Committee had not been solved when the Japanese launched a surprise attack on Pearl Harbor on December 7, 1941, and once again changed the conditions under which the Zionists had to operate.

The entry of the United States into the war against the Axis removed the last restraints on American Jews in calling for the defeat of Hitler. The Emergency Committee, in a call to action, declared: "Fellow Zionists! Assume the responsibility which world events impose upon you. Take up the challenge. Impress your communities with the urgency of the matter. . . . If we stand up now as men and women, as Americans and as Jews, we can make certain that the Star of David will be carried to the inevitable victory of the Allied cause, along with the banner of our Republic and the flags of the free peoples of the world."[13] The mood in the Jewish community now changed from uncertainty to confidence, as Jews realized they no longer stood alone in their fight against Hitler. The Emergency Committee for Zionist Affairs managed to put aside most of its internal squabbling, and in fact as well as name became the spokesman for American Zionism.

To those who questioned how the Zionists could support the British, the country that had closed the doors of Palestine, Zionists pointed out that they could hardly back Germany in the war. They quoted Ben-Gurion's dictum that they would fight the war as if there were no White Paper, and they would fight the white paper as if there were no war. First Hitler had to be defeated, and that required aid to Britain; but Palestine had to be supported and strengthened so that the Jews, at the end of the fighting, could demand full control of their homeland. "Palestine as a Jewish State," wrote Ben-Gurion, "is the only possible solution to postwar Jewish misery, and we are determined to achieve it."[14] Although some Jews pointed to Winston Churchill's endorsement of Zionist aims as the sign of a new attitude, British treachery in the 1930s left few Zionists willing to trust His Majesty's Government again.

The catastrophe that had overtaken European Jewry, and the threat to the Yishuv posed by German forces in the Mideast, finally overcame much of the factionalism that had plagued American Zionism in the 1930s, and erased much of its caution as well. Not only did the various groups within the ZOA agree to co-operate, but the Mizrachi, which had boycotted the organization since 1918, consented to return to the fold. In order to secure a common platform on which they could all stand, the Emergency Committee called a special meeting at the Biltmore Hotel in New York in early May 1942. The 586 American delegates, as well as 67 foreign leaders, represented every known faction in the movement. Rabbi Stephen S. Wise, who forty-five years earlier had been a founding member of the Federation of American Zionists, gaveled the conference to order. "We are met together in order that all American Zionists, irrespective of party affiliation, place the sacred cause of Zionism above party sectarianism," he declared. Their goal would be nothing less than "the freedom of Jews in all lands and the final establishment under the Victory Peace Conference of a free Jewish Commonwealth in Palestine."

The delegates sat in somber silence as a weary and visibly distraught Chaim Weizmann told them of the horrors being inflicted upon European Jewry, and he predicted that 25 per cent of them would not survive the war. Sadly, he admitted that the British had not kept their word in Palestine; had the spirit of the Mandate been upheld, tens of thousands of Jews might have been saved. But the old man's devotion to Britain could not be quenched, and he still grieved over the death of his son Michael, an RAF pilot, only three months before. He pleaded with the delegates not to make this a Jewish war against Britain, but to fight alongside the brave English people in their battle against Hitler's tyranny. The audience, obviously moved by their aging leader, applauded him at length. But in the momentum of the conference, leadership passed to a new and more vigorous group, led by the militant David Ben-Gurion, chairman of the Jewish Agency Executive, and by Rabbi Abba Hillel Silver, who would over the next six years make American Jewry the strongest ally the Yishuv had in its fight for independence.

(Many of the old leaders, of course, stayed on. Stephen Wise would continue to play an important role as a spokesman for the cause. Emanuel Neumann, Robert Szold, Israel Goldstein, Louis Levinthal, and many of the younger Brandeisists would lead the movement in the crucial decade ahead. But Brandeis himself had died six months earlier. Jacob deHaas had died five years before. Julian Mack was in poor health and would be dead within a year. Felix Frankfurter had gone onto the Supreme Court and no longer took an active role in Zionist affairs. Louis Lipsky and his group faded from sight, brought out periodically to denote unity in the movement. Among the Europeans, Weizmann would still serve as the voice and conscience of the movement, but little else. Menahem Ussischkin had just died, and many of the European leaders—too many—would not survive the war. During these years, the Palestinians whom Amos Elon has termed "the founders" came to full control of world Zionism and of Palestine.)

Ben-Gurion had just returned to the United States, and he took a tough, noncompromising stand. After the war, the Mandate had to go,

with responsibility for Palestine and its development turned over
to the Jewish people. He brought the assembly to its feet with his
ringing affirmation that "A Jewish Palestine will arise. It will redeem
forever our sufferings and do justice to our national genius. It will
be the pride of every Jew in the Diaspora, and command the respect
of every people on earth." In the meantime, he demanded that the
British turn over to the Jewish Agency complete control of immigration, so that at least some remnants of European Jewry could be
saved.

Abba Hillel Silver, rabbi at the prestigious Temple in Cleveland,
Ohio, epitomized the new toughness in American Zionism when he
launched into an impassioned attack on those "Bourbon mentalities"
who still opposed the movement. There could be only one solution
to the Jewish problem, a Jewish state in Palestine, and he called for
a full-scale effort to achieve that end. As to those who still counseled
caution, he read a letter that the great Irish patriot, Daniel O'Connell,
had written in 1829 to Isaac Leon Goldsmith, a champion of Jewish
emancipation in England: "Nothing is to be obtained by delay, at
least, in politics. You must, to a certain extent, force your claims on
Parliament. You cannot be worse, remember, even by failure, and
you ought to be better by experiment. I once more repeat: Do not
confide in any liberality but that which you yourself will arouse into
action and compel into operation."

The Declaration adopted by the Biltmore conference clearly indicated the new mood of American Zionism in its rejection of British
policy. "The Conference demands that the gates of Palestine be
opened; that the Jewish Agency be vested with control of immigration into Palestine and with the necessary authority for upbuilding
the country, including the development of uncultivated lands; and
that Palestine be established as a Jewish Commonwealth integrated
in the structure of the new democratic world. Then and only then
will the age-old wrong to the Jewish people be righted."

In an emotional final session, the delegates unanimously adopted
the Biltmore Declaration, as it became known, and the various
factions publicly made peace with one another. Stephen Wise, who
had bitterly opposed Chaim Weizmann for over twenty years, embraced him on the platform and gave him one of his most treasured

possessions, a ring that had belonged to Theodore Herzl. He called on Weizmann to wear that ring when, at the end of the war, he would once again plead the cause of the Jewish people at the peace conference.[15] Even as Hitler's henchmen implemented their final solution, Zionism set forward on the road that would see the creation of a Jewish state in Palestine almost six years to the day after the Biltmore conference. In that struggle, American Zionists would play a crucial role.

Indeed, American Zionism had come a long way since Zvi Falk Halevi had despaired of ever interesting American Jews in the redemption of Eretz Yisroel. Thanks to the genius of Louis Brandeis, the essential contradictions between Herzlian Zionism and loyalty to the United States had not only been resolved, but the synthesis had helped make Zionism a legitimate part not only of the Jewish experience in America, but also of that general humanitarian impulse that marked progressive and liberal reform in this century. The Brandeisian argument that by becoming Zionists American Jews would be both better Jews and better Americans indelibly molded the Zionist movement here in the activist, efficient, and practical image that has marked so much of American life. The forces that shaped it have been both Jewish and American, and its subsequent difficulties and success have been the result of that unique mixture.

For the success that the Americanization of the movement achieved was not without its costs. To make Zionism acceptable to acculturated Jews, the Brandeisists discarded much of the neomessianic mood that appealed to the Eastern European immigrants. The lack of a Jewish heart, of *Yiddishkeit,* upset the Eastern Europeans, and led to charges that Zionism had been intellectually sterilized. By emphasizing the need for Palestine as a refuge, by focusing on practical work there, the Brandeisists deliberately downplayed the nationalistic ideology upon which European Zionism thrived. To have done otherwise would have condemned Zionism in America to the perpetual status of an ethnic fringe group, which immigrants in the process of acculturation would have shed along with their strange clothing and Old World customs.

In the end, despite the bitterness engendered by this clash of the two Zionist philosophies, a new and typically American Zionism emerged that combined the emphasis on practical work with a true love of Zion and of Palestine. The American impatience with theorizing made a Zionism based on abstract ideology inappropriate at the American scene. Yet a Palestinianism without understanding of the role of the Holy Land in Jewish life would have been mere colonization, a cheap form of philanthropy. The Brandeisists taught the Eastern Europeans how to rebuild Zion utilizing American techniques, and to frame their faith in terms acceptable to the political and social demands of this society, and laid down as a cardinal rule the idea that only by being American could Zionism succeed in this country. In turn, the eastern Europeans taught that Zionism had to be something more than men, money, and discipline, that it had to involve the heart as well as the mind. In a larger sense, this same Hegelian process took place between the Zionist Organization of America and the World Zionist Organization.

The Biltmore conference marked a clear cleavage between an old and a new Zionism in America. Once again, the changing developments in American society made it not only possible, but in fact necessary, for the Zionists to adopt new ideas and stratagems. Before the rise of Hitler, American Jews, while acknowledging a kinship with their European brethren, did not tend to identify overly much with the concept of a *Klal Yisrael,* of a Jewish people. Not only the non-Zionist *yahudim,* but the Americanized leadership also resented the implications of a Jewish state. There had to be a refuge, a place where Jews could live and develop freely, but one that, to a large extent, would not affect American Jewry too much. The Americans would help the Yishuv to help itself, but did not expect, nor indeed want, the homeland to have an impact here. In this sense, charges that the Americanized leadership had a debilitating effect on the non-Palestinian aspects of Zionism are true.

The shock of British perfidy and of Nazi savagery snapped this cord, and the general revulsion at the horrors inflicted upon European Jewry made the larger society more amenable to the idea that American Jews could and should take a greater interest and responsibility for Jewish affairs overseas. The melding of American and European thought had already set the stage for a greater acceptance of Jewish nationalism, and events in the 1930s allowed these seeds to blossom. American Jews had always assumed that anti-Semitism had more or less been tamed in "civilized" countries like Great Britain, Germany, and the United States. Its resurgence in the 1930s shocked them into an awareness that perhaps Herzl had been right after all, that only the guarantee of a truly Jewish state could provide the safety valve in the event of future *pogroms*. Not all of the six million souls who perished in the Holocaust could have been saved, but tens, perhaps hundreds, of thousands of them could have been absorbed into Palestine. The cry of "Never Again" did not originate in the 1960s; its meaning had already become clear before the *Kristallnacht*. Yet without the understanding and approval of the broader Gentile society, even this tragedy might not have spurred American Zionism into the fateful steps taken in 1942.

Before Biltmore, American Zionists saw Palestine as a refuge; after Biltmore they fought for a state, and have sustained the continuing growth and development of that state since 1948. In many ways, the quarter century between the two extraordinary conferences, one at the Hotel Marseilles and the other at the Biltmore, were the apprentice years of American Zionism. Now, firmly committed to the goal of a *Jewish* state, they utilized the *American* techniques of organization, fund raising, and political lobbying to serve as partners in the creation of Israel. Though they did not know it then, the struggle to create Israel would be even more difficult than they assumed, the devastation wrought by the war even more extensive than anyone could have imagined, and the success they sought would come sooner than they hoped. But from Biltmore on, Zionism in America assumed its burdens with an air of confidence that reflected both the American creed of achievement and that Jewish optimism summed up in the old Herzlian dictum: If you will it, it is no dream.

KEY TO MANUSCRIPT CITATIONS

Berlin Office Files

Records of the Central Zionist Office in Berlin (1911–20), Record Group Z3, Central Zionist Archives, Jerusalem

Bliss MSS

Tasker Howard Bliss Papers, Manuscript Division, Library of Congress, Washington, D.C.

Brandeis MSS

Louis Dembitz Brandeis Papers, University of Louisville Law Library, Louisville, Kentucky

Brodie MSS

Israel Benjamin Brodie Papers, Record Group A251, Central Zionist Archives, Jerusalem

Cologne Office Files

Records of the Central Zionist Office in Cologne (1905–11), Record Group Z2, Central Zionist Archives, Jerusalem

Copenhagen Office Files

Records of the Copenhagen Office of the Zionist Organization (1914–20), Record Group L6, Central Zionist Archives, Jerusalem

deHaas MSS

Jacob deHaas Papers, Zionist Archives and Library, New York, New York

Flexner MSS

Bernard Flexner Papers, Zionist Archives and Library, New York, New York

Foreign Office Records   Records of H.M.G. Foreign Office, Public Records Office, London

Frankfurter MSS   Felix Frankfurter Papers, Harvard Law School Library, Cambridge, Massachusetts

Frankfurter MSS (CZA)   Felix Frankfurter Papers, Record Group A264, Central Zionist Archives, Jerusalem

Friedenwald MSS   Harry Friedenwald Papers, Record Group A82, Central Zionist Archives, Jerusalem

Friedlaender MSS   Israel Friedlaender Papers, Library of the Jewish Theological Seminary of America, New York, New York

Gottheil MSS   Richard James Horatio Gottheil Papers, Record Group A38, Central Zionist Archives, Jerusalem

Jabotinsky MSS   Vladimir Jabotinsky Papers, Jabotinsky Institute, Tel Aviv

Karger MSS   Gus Karger Papers, American Jewish Archives, Cincinnati, Ohio

London Office Files   Records of the Zionist Organization/the Jewish Agency for Palestine, Central Office in London (1917–55), Record Group Z4, Central Zionist Archives, Jerusalem

Mack MSS   Julian William Mack Papers, Zionist Archives and Library, New York, New York

Magnes MSS   Judah Leon Magnes Papers, Central Archives for the History of the Jewish People, Hebrew University, Jerusalem

Marshall MSS   Louis Marshall Papers, American Jewish Archives, Cincinnati, Ohio

Morgenthau MSS   Henry Morgenthau, Sr., Papers, Manuscript Division, Library of Congress, Washington, D.C.

Non-Zionist Section Files Records of the Zionist Executive/Jewish Agency, Section for the Organization of Non-Zionists, Record Group S29, Central Zionist Archives, Jerusalem

Richards MSS Bernard Gerson Richards Papers, Jewish Information Bureau, New York, New York

Roosevelt MSS Franklin Delano Roosevelt Papers, Franklin D. Roosevelt Library, Hyde Park, New York

Schiff MSS Jacob Henry Schiff Papers, American Jewish Archives, Cincinnati, Ohio

Sokolow MSS Nahum Sokolow Papers, Record Group A18, Central Zionist Archives, Jerusalem

Silver MSS Aba Hillel Silver Papers, Archives of The Temple, Cleveland, Ohio

H. Szold MSS Henrietta Szold Papers, Record Group A125, Central Zionist Archives, Jerusalem

R. Szold MSS Robert Szold Papers, Zionist Archives and Library, New York, New York

State Department Records Records of the United States Department of State, Record Group 59, The National Archives, Washington, D.C.

Vienna Office Files Records of the Central Zionist Office in Vienna (1897–1905), Record Group Z1, Central Zionist Archives, Jerusalem

Warburg MSS Felix Warburg Papers, American Jewish Archives, Cincinnati, Ohio

Weizmann MSS Chaim Weizmann Papers, Library of the Weizmann Institute, Rehovoth, Israel

Wilson MSS Woodrow Wilson Papers, Manuscript Division, Library of Congress, Washington, D.C.

Wise MSS   Stephen Samuel Wise Papers, American Jew-
                      ish Historical Society, Waltham, Massachu-
                      setts

Wise MSS (AJA)   Stephen Samuel Wise Papers, American Jew-
                      ish Archives, Cincinnati, Ohio

NOTES TO CHAPTER ONE

"If I Forget Thee, O Jerusalem"

NOTES TO PAGES 6–13

1. Abraham S. Halkin, ed., *Zion in Jewish Literature* (New York, 1961), *passim.*
2. Amos 9:14–15; Gen. 13:14–15; Jer. 46:27; Daniel 12:1; Zech. 8:7–8.
3. Abba Hillel Silver, *A History of Messianic Speculation in Israel* (New York, 1927), pp. 154–55.
4. Salo Baron, "Newer Approaches to Jewish Emancipation," *Diogenes* 29 (Spring 1960):56–81.
5. Mark Zborowski and Elizabeth Herzog, *Life Is With People* (New York, 1962), passim.
6. For a much different interpretation of the Enlightenment and anti-Semitism, see Arthur Hertzberg, *The French Enlightenment and the Jews* (New York, 1968).
7. Robert Alter, "Emancipation, Enlightenment and All That," *Commentary* 33 (February 1972):62–68.
8. Mordechai M. Kaplan, *A New Zionism* (New York, 1955), pp. 58–59.
9. Joseph L. Blau, *Modern Varieties of Judaism* (New York, 1966), p. 40.
10. Ibid.
11. Walter Laqueur, *A History of Zionism* (New York, 1972), p. 20.
12. Ben Halpern, *The Idea of the Jewish State* (Cambridge, Mass., 1961), p. 10.
13. Israel Cohen, *The Progress of Zionism* (London, 1943, 6th rev. ed.), p. 4.
14. Quoted in Richard J. H. Gottheil, *Zionism* (Philadelphia, 1914), p. 40.

15. Arthur Hertzberg, ed., *The Zionist Idea* (Garden City, N.Y., 1959), pp. 103–4.

16. Laqueur, *History of Zionism*, p. 53.

17. Ibid., p. 71.

18. Gottheil, *Zionism*, p. 66; Hertzberg, *Zionist Idea*, pp. 195–96.

19. Halpern, *Idea of Jewish State*, p. 63.

20. Hertzberg, *Zionist Idea*, p. 169.

21. Chaim Weizmann, *Trial and Error* (New York, 1949), p. 11.

22. Quoted in Simcha Kling, *Nachum Sokolow, Servant of His People* (New York, 1960), p. 69; see also Halpern, *Idea of Jewish State*, p. 15. An example of how the Zionists looked beyond the goals of the Hoveve Zion can be found in a letter written by Chaim Weizmann when he was only eleven years old: "How lofty and elevated the idea which inspired our brethren the sons of Israel to establish the Hoveve Zion Society. Because of this we can rescue our exiled, oppressed brethren who are scattered in all corners of the world and have no place where to put up their tents . . . and this may become the *Beginning of Redemption.*" This grand view was typical, not of Hibbat Zion, but of the later Zionist movement. Chaim Weizmann to Shlomo Tsvi Sokolovsky (Summer 1885), in *The Letters and Papers of Chaim Weizmann* (London, 1968–), 1:36.

23. The manifesto of the Biluim can be found in Nahum Sokolow, *History of Zionism, 1600–1918* (2 vols.; New York, 1969 ed.), 2:332–33.

24. Samuel Kurland, *Biluim: Pioneers of Zionist Colonization* (New York, 1943), p. 26.

25. Laqueur, *Zionism*, p. 76.

26. Jacob R. Marcus, "Zionism and the American Jew," *The American Scholar*, 2 (May 1933):279.

27. Theodore Herzl, *The Jewish State*, Jacob deHaas (New York, 1904), p. 4.

28. Ibid., p. 15.

29. Halpern, *Idea of Jewish State*, p. 101.

30. Weizmann, *Trial and Error*, p. 43.

31. Hertzberg, *Zionist Idea*, pp. 47–48.

32. *Diaries of Theodore Herzl*, ed. and tr. Marvin Lowenthal (New York, 1956), p. 96, entry for February 10, 1896.

33. In 1900, Max Nordau declared: "The colonies are wholly without significance for the redemption of the Jewish people." Quoted in Leonard Stein, *The Balfour Declaration* (New York, 1961), pp. 62–63.

34. Herzl to Baron de Hirsch (July 5, 1895), in *Herzl Diaries,* p. 26.

35. Ibid., Introduction, p. xxv.

36. Joseph Adler, *The Herzl Paradox* (New York, 1962), p. 124.

37. Rufus Learsi (pseud. Israel Goldberg), *Fulfillment: The Epic Story of Zionism* (Cleveland, 1951), p. 90.

38. Gottheil, *Zionism,* pp. 93–94.

39. Neville Barbour, *Palestine: Star or Crescent?* (New York, 1947), p. 48.

40. Max Isidore Bodenheimer, *Prelude to Israel,* ed. H. H. Bodenheimer and tr. I. Cohen (London, 1963), p. 89.

41. Sir Clement Hill to L. J. Greenberg, August 14, 1903, in Gottheil, *Zionism,* pp. 122–24.

42. Simcha Kling, *The Mighty Warrior: The Life Story of Menachem Ussischkin* (New York, 1965), p. 40.

43. December 14, 1903, in the *Maccabean* 6 (January 1904):39–40. At the end of the Congress, Herzl wrote in his diary: "Although originally simply a partisan of a Jewish state—anywhere—I later grasped the standard of Zion, and have myself become one of the Lovers of Zion. Palestine is the only land where our people can find peace."

44. Halpern, *Idea of Jewish State,* pp. 154–55.

45. Mark Twain, *The Innocents Abroad, or The New Pilgrims' Progress* (2 vols.; New York, 1906 ed.), 2:392–93.

46. Halpern, *Idea of Jewish State,* p. 108.

47. See Arthur Ruppin, *Memoirs, Diaries, Letters,* ed. A. Bein and tr. K. Gershon (New York, 1972), passim.

48. Raphael Patai, *Tents of Jacob: The Diaspora—Yesterday and To-day* (Englewood Cliffs, N.J., 1971), p. 46.

49. Gottheil, *Zionism,* pp. 22–23.

50. Ibid., pp. 103–4; Halpern, *Idea of Jewish State,* p. 144.

51. Learsi, *Fulfillment,* p. 82; Laqueur, *History of Zionism,* p. 96.

52. Quoted in Alter, "Emancipation . . . ," p. 62.

53. Entry (November 10, 1895), *Herzl Diaries,* p. 73.

54. Gottheil, *Zionism,* pp. 101, 102. Gabriel Riesser, one of the most persistent advocates of emancipation, suggested that any Jew who preferred a nonexistent state to Germany ought to be shut away as obviously insane. Of his own feelings there could be no doubt: "Whoever disputes my claim to the German fatherland disputes my right to my thoughts and feelings, to the language I speak, the air I breathe. He

deprives me of my very right to existence and therefore I must defend myself against him as I would against a murderer." He believed that a mystic bond existed between Jews and Germany. *"Einen Vater in den Hohen, eine Mutter haben wir, Gott ibn aller Wesen Vater, Deutschland unsere Mutter hier."* (We have one Father in heaven and one Mother—God the father of all beings, Germany our mother on earth.) Laqueur, *History of Zionism,* p. 8.

55. Bernard Hourwich, *My First Eighty Years* (Chicago, 1939), p. 240.

56. Weizmann, *Trial and Error,* p .115.

57. Ibid., p. 47.

58. Melech Epstein, *Jewish Labor in the United States . . . 1882–1952* (2 vols.; New York, 1950), 1:305–6; see also Henry J. Tobias, *The Jewish Bund from Its Origins to 1905* (Stanford, Cal., 1972).

59. Quoted in Yonathan Shapiro, *Leadership of the American Zionist Organization, 1897–1930* (Urbana, Ill., 1971), p. 16.

60. Gershon Winer, *The Founding Fathers of Israel* (New York, 1971), p. 216.

61. *The Jewish Question and the Socialist Jewish State* (1898), quoted in Marie Syrkin, *Nachman Syrkin: Socialist Zionist* (New York, 1961), p. 54; see also Syrkin's *Essays on Socialist Zionism* (New York, 1935).

62. Adler, *Herzl Paradox,* pp. 31–34.

63. Syrkin, *Nachman Syrkin,* p. 73. The disdain was returned by the Fraction. Weizmann wrote his fiancée: "Thank God, the Jewish movement has until now been free of socialist megalomania. Now this too has appeared. I live in the hope that this filth will not spread. . . . However, all kinds of pestilence start from very little." Weizmann to Vera Khatzman (June 25, 1901) in *Weizmann Letters,* 1:137.

64. "The Wrong Way," in *Ten Essays on Zionism and Judaism,* tr. Leon Simon (London, 1922), p. 15.

65. "Summa Summarum," ibid., p. 132.

66. See "The Jewish State and the Jewish Problem" (1897) and "Pinsker and Political Zionism" (1902), both ibid.

67. Weizmann, *Trial and Error,* pp. 68–69.

68. See, for example, Bodenheimer, *Prelude to Israel,* p. 285.

69. "The Mission of Israel and Its Nationhood" (1901), quoted in Winer, *Founding Fathers of Israel,* pp. 230–31.

70. "What Kind of Life Should We Create in Eretz Yisroel?" (1922), in Hertzberg, *Idea of Zionism,* p. 549.

71. Patai, *Tents of Jacob,* p. 132.

72. Learsi, *Fulfillment,* p. 123. In the end, the reality of the State of Israel brought most of Agudat Israel into the religious bloc, and one of the leaders of Agudat Israel in Palestine, Isaac Meir Levin, became a member of a coalition Cabinet headed by a socialist.

73. Halpern, *Idea of a Jewish State,* p. 85; Gottheil, *Zionism,* pp. 176–78.

74. Ibid., p. 154.

75. Quoted in Stein, *The Balfour Declaration,* pp. 59–60.

NOTES TO CHAPTER TWO

The Goldenah Medinah

NOTES TO PAGES 45–48

1. Max J. Kohler, "Some Early American Zionist Projects," *Publications of the American Jewish Historical Society* 8 (1900):84–85 (hereafter cited as *PAJHS*).

2. Noah's full address is printed in *PAJHS* 21 (1913):230–52.

3. Milton Plesur, "The American Press and Jewish Restoration During the Nineteenth Century" in Isidore S. Meyer, ed., *Early History of Zionism in America* (New York, 1958), pp. 60–61.

4. Kohler, "Early Zionist Projects," p. 86; Hyman Grinstein, *The Rise of the Jewish Community of New York, 1654–1860* (Philadelphia, 1945), pp. 455–56.

5. Kohler, "Early Zionist Projects," pp. 81–82; see also Abraham J. Karp, "The Zionism of Warder Cresson" in Meyer, ed., *Early History of Zionism*.

6. Ha-Pisgah (May 8, 1891), quoted in Marnin Feinstein, *American Zionism, 1884–1904* (New York, 1965), pp. 60–61. The Reverend J. M. Haldeman predicted the success of the Zionist movement on his interpretation of Jeremiah 13:3, "And the word of the Lord came unto me the second time." New York *Times* (December 16, 1901). For general historical interest by Americans in Palestine, see "America and the Holy Land: A Colloquium," *American Jewish Historical Quarterly* 62 (September 1972): 3–62 (hereafter cited as *AJHQ*).

7. Maxine S. Seller, "Isaac Leeser's Views on the Restoration of a Jewish Palestine," ibid. 58 (September 1968):118–35.

8. Moshe Davis, "Jewish Religious Life and Institutions in America (a Historical Study)" in Louis Finkelstein, ed., *The Jews: Their History, Culture and Religion* (2 vols.; New York, 1955), 2:510; Grinstein, *Rise of Jewish Community*, p. 19.

9. Arthur Zeiger, "Emma Lazarus and Pre-Herzlian Zionism" in Meyer, *Early History of Zionism*, p. 91.

10. Learsi, *Fulfillment*, p. 37.

11. Emma Lazarus to Editor, *American Hebrew* (May 9, 1883), quoted in Philip Cowen, *Memories of an American Jew* (New York, 1932), pp. 337–38.

12. Nathan Glazer, *American Judaism* (Chicago, 1957), pp. 16–17; for a dissenting view, see Stanley F. Chyet, "The Political Rights of the Jews in the United States: 1776–1840," *American Jewish Archives* 10 (April 1958):14–75.

13. Address to Hebrew Congregation of Newport, R.I., August 17, 1790, in John C. Fitzpatrick, ed., *The Writings of George Washington* (39 vols; Washington, 1931–44), 31:93–94.

14. See Donovan Fitzpatrick and Paul Saphire, *Navy Maverick: Uriah Phillips Levy* (Garden City, N.Y., 1963).

15. Allan Tarshish, "The Board of Delegates of American Israelites (1859–1878)," *PAJHS* 49 (September, 1959):22.

16. Weyl, *Jews in American Politics*, p. 59.

17. The story of the German-Jewish immigrants, with numerous anecdotes, can be found in Stephen Birmingham, *Our Crowd* (New York, 1967).

18. Nathan Glazer, "Social Characteristics of American Jews, 1694–1935," in Finkelstein, *The Jews*, 2:1701. A contemporary study by the Union of American Hebrew Congregations yielded similar results. As Ben Halpern points out, however, these figures can be distorted to mean that all Jews were rich and successful, whereas only an elite did so well. Most German-Jewish immigrants remained small businessmen. Even so, few immigrant groups produced so successful an elite so quickly.

19. Milton Doroshkin, *Yiddish in America* (Rutherford, N.J., 1969), p. 58.

20. Moses Rischin, *The Promised City: New York's Jews, 1870–1914* (Cambridge, Mass., 1962), p. 33.

21. Not all inspectors were antagonistic; most were merely overwhelmed by the number of people they had to process. For the kindness often shown, see Cowen, *Memories of an American Jew*, Chap. 7.

22. Quoted in John Higham, *Strangers in the Land: Patterns of American Nativism, 1860–1925* (New York, 1963 ed.), p. 67.

23. See Leon Stein, *The Triangle Fire* (Philadelphia, 1962).

24. Jacob Riis, *How the Other Half Lives* (New York, 1890), pp. 106–7. For a much more sympathetic view of Jewish life on the East Side, see Hutchins Hapgood, *The Spirit of the Ghetto* (New York, 1902).

25. Weyl, *Jew in American Politics*, p. 79; see also Rufus Learsi [pseud. Israel Goldberg], *The Jews in America: A History* (Cleveland and New York, 1954), p. 128.

26. See Max Vanger, "Memoirs of a Russian Immigrant," *AJHQ* 63 (September 1973):57–58.

27. Quoted in Robert Silverberg, *If I Forget Thee, O Jerusalem* (New York, 1970), p. 53.

28. Ande Manners, *Poor Cousins* (New York, 1972), p. 82.

29. Ibid., p. 67.

30. Augustus A. Levey to Hermann Makower, secretary for German Central Committee for Russian Refugees (July 21, 1882), quoted in Zosa Szajkowski, "The Attitude of American Jews to East European Immigration (1881–1893)," *PAJHS* 40 (1950):242. See also Esther L. Panitz, "The Polarity of American Jewish Attitudes Toward Immigration (1870–1891)," *AJHQ* 53 (December 1963):99–130.

31. Laqueur, *History of Zionism*, p. 57. In 1911 an immigration commission again reported the obvious: "Jews are emigrating, not because it is impossible for them to find sufficient earnings in Russia, but because the Government deprives them of the most elemental conditions of life and property. . . . Let but the *pogroms* cease, and the emigration of the Jews will immediately and considerably diminish."

32. Manners, *Poor Cousins*, p. 97.

33. The proceedings of the conference have been translated in Sefton D. Temkin, *The New World of Reform* (London, 1971), which also contains a very useful introduction.

34. W. Gunther Plaut, ed., *The Growth of Reform Judaism: American and European Sources to 1948* (New York, 1965), pp. 31–41 contain the Pittsburgh Platform and related documents. See also Gershon Greenberg, "The Significance of America in David Einhorn's Conception of History," *AJHQ* 63 (December 1973):160–84, and "Samuel Hirsch's American Judaism," Ibid. 62 (June 1973):362–81.

35. Glazer, *American Judaism*, p. 55.

36. John Higham, "American Anti-Semitism Historically Reconsidered" in Charles Herbert Stember et al., *Jews in the Mind of America* (New York, 1966), p. 244.

37. Weyl, *Jew in American Politics*, p. 66; Arthur Mann, *Yankee Reformers in an Urban Age* (New York, 1966 ed.), p. 53.

38. Higham, *Strangers in the Land*, pp. 26–27.
(September 1971):71; Rischin, *Promised City*, p. 262; Memorandum,

39. Stephen Steinberg, "How Jewish Quotas Began," *Commentary* 52 "Situation of the Jews in America," June 1907, in the Records of the

Zionistische Centralbureau, Cologne, Record Group Z2, Central Zionist Archives, Jerusalem, Israel (hereafter cited as Cologne Office).

40. E. J. Kuh, "The Social Disability of the Jew," *Atlantic Monthly* 101 (April 1908):433.

41. Richard Hofstadter, *The Age of Reform: From Bryan to F.D.R.* (New York, 1955), pp. 77–82; for an opposing view, however, see Walter T. K. Nugent, *The Tolerant Populists* (Chicago, 1963). Oscar Handlin, "American Views of the Jew at the Opening of the Twentieth Century," *PAJHS* 40 (1950):327. In general, one should avoid exaggerating Populist anti-Semitism, which was but a minor note in their revolt against industrialism.

42. Learsi, *Jews in America*, p. 175; Handlin, "American Views," p. 325.

43. J. L. Talmon, "European History—Seedbed of the Holocaust," *Midstream* 19 (May 1973):3–25.

44. Higham, "Anti-Semitism Reconsidered," p. 247.

45. Ben Halpern, *The American Jew: A Zionist Analysis* (New York, 1956), pp. 31–32. See also Ellis Rivkind, "A Decisive Pattern in American Jewish History," *Essays in American Jewish History* (Cincinnati, 1958), pp. 43–58.

46. Joseph Buchler, "The Struggle for Unity: Attempts at Union in American Jewish Life, 1654–1868," *American Jewish Archives* 1 (June 1949):21–46.

47. Bernard G. Richards, *Organizing American Jewry* (New York, 1947), pp. 3–15; Tarshish, "The Board of Delegates," pp. 16–32.

48. Abraham G. Duker, "Structure of the Jewish Community" in Oscar I. Janowsky, ed., *The American Jew: A Composite Portrait* (New York, 1942), p. 157; Zosa Szajkowski, "The Alliance Israelite Universelle in the United States, 1860–1949," *PAJHS* 39 (1950): 389–443.

49. Selma Stern, *The Court Jew* (tr. by Ralph Weimen, Philadelphia, 1950), ch. 7; see also Zborowski and Herzog, *Life is with People*, pp. 234–36.

50. Cyrus Adler, ed., *The Voice of America on Kishineff* (Philadelphia, 1904), pp. ix–xi; Philip Ernest Schoenberg, "The American Reaction to the Kishinev Pogrom of 1903," *AJHQ* 63 (March 1974): 262–83; Adler and Margolith, *With Firmness in the Right*, p. 276.

51. Morton Rosenstock, *Louis Marshall, Defender of Jewish Rights* (Detroit, 1965), p. 23.

52. Learsi, *Jews in America*, p. 213.

53. For the Committee's organization and early activities, see Naomi W. Cohen, *Not Free to Desist: The American Jewish Committee, 1906–1966* (Philadelphia, 1972), Chaps. 1–4.

54. Arthur A. Goren, *New York Jews and the Quest for Community: The Kehillah Experiment, 1908–1922* (New York, 1970), p. 29.

55. *The Two Hundred and Fiftieth Anniversary of the Settlement of The Jews in the United States* (New York, 1906), p. 105.

56. Joel S. Geffen, "Whither: To Palestine or to America in the Pages of the Russian Hebrew Press, *Ha-Melitz* and *Ha-Yom* (1880–1890)," *AJHQ* 59 (December 1969):179–200.

57. Higham, "Anti-Semitism Reconsidered," pp. 249–50.

58. Louis Marshall to editor *American Israelite* (August 23, 1926) in the Papers of Louis Marshall, American Jewish Archives at Hebrew Union College, Cincinnati, Ohio (hereafter cited as Marshall MSS).

59. Ephraim Morris Wagner, "The Village Boy," unpublished memoir in YIVO Institute for Jewish Research, quoted in Joseph Brandes, "Liberty's Fruit: Acculturation in the New Eden," paper delivered at the 1971 meeting of the American Historical Association.

60. Manners, *Poor Cousins,* pp. 49–50.

61. Steinberg, "How Jewish Quotas Began," p. 68.

62. *Ha-Melitz* 25 (January 25, 1885):116, quoted in Joel S. Geffen, "Jewish Agricultural Colonies as Reported in the Pages of the Russian Hebrew Press," *AJHQ* 60 (June 1971):324.

NOTES TO CHAPTER THREE

Zionism Comes to America

NOTES TO PAGES 82–90

1. *Ha-Maggid* (February 28, 1884), quoted in Feinstein, *American Zionism*, pp. 24–25.
2. Hyman B. Grinstein, "The Memoirs and Scrapbooks of the Late Dr. Joseph Isaac Bluestone of New York City," *PAJHS* 35 (1939):54.
3. Shlomo Noble, "Pre-Herzlian Zionism in America as Reflected in the Yiddish Press" in Meyer, *Early History of Zionism*, p. 39.
4. Alexander Levin, *Vision: A Biography of Harry Friedenwald* (Philadelphia, 1964), p. 143. The concept of dignity is theologically and philosophically developed by J. B. Soloveitchik in "The Lonely Man of Faith," *Tradition* 7 (Summer 1965):5–67.
5. Feinstein, *American Zionism*, p. 55.
6. Hourwich, *My First Eighty Years*, p. 231.
7. Maxwell Whiteman, "Zionism Comes to Philadelphia" in Meyer, *Early History of Zionism*, p. 193.
8. Joseph Tabachnik, "American Jewish Reaction to the First Zionist Congress," *Herzl Year Book* 5 (1963):62–63.
9. Feinstein, *American Zionism*, pp. 102–4.
10. Ibid., Ch. 7; Herbert Parzen, "The Federation of American Zionists (1897–1914)" in Meyer, *Early History of Zionism*, pp. 246–47.
11. Samuel Halperin, *The Political World of American Zionism* (Detroit, 1961), p. 10.
12. New York *Times* (June 19, 1899).
13. Hertzberg, *The Zionist Idea*, pp. 499–500; an idea of Gottheil's continuous efforts to promote Zionism can be seen by examining his diary, manuscript in American Jewish Historical Society.

14. New York *Times* (February 5, 1899); cf. speech by his father, reported ibid. (September 25, 1899).

15. Stephen S. Wise to Theodore Herzl (November 28, 1899), in Carl Herman Voss, ed., *Stephen S. Wise: Servant of the People* (Philadelphia, 1969), p. 13.

16. Julius Haber, *The Odyssey of an American Zionist* (New York, 1956), pp. 37–39; Lewis N. Dembitz, "The Future of Zionism," *The Maccabean* 6 (August 1904):83–84.

17. New York *Times,* June 11, 1900.

18. Feinstein, *American Zionism,* p. 19; Joseph P. Sternstein, "Reform Judaism and Zionism," *Herzl Year Book* 5 (1963):12. Philipson's comment reflected the attitude expressed in David Einhorn's prayerbook, *Olat Tamid.*

19. Mann, *Yankee Reformers in an Urban Age,* pp. 57–62.

20. Zeiger, "Emma Lazarus," p. 96; Feinstein, *American Zionism,* p. 19.

21. Silverberg, *If I Forget Thee,* p. 57.

22. Goren, *New York Jews and the Quest for Community,* p. 14; Shapiro, *Leadership of the American Zionist Movement,* p. 33; Horace M. Kallen, *Zionism and World Politics* (Garden City, N.Y., 1921), p. 132.

23. Blau, *Modern Varieties of Judaism,* p. 127; CCAR *Yearbook* 1 (1890):19, 25–31; see also Melvin Weinman, "The Attitude of Isaac Mayer Wise toward Zionism and Palestine," *American Jewish Archives* 3 (January 1951):3–23.

24. *UAHC Proceedings* 5 (1898):40–41; CCAR *Yearbook* 7 (1897): 12, 51; New York *Times* September 10, 1897; Tabachnik, "Reaction to the First Congress," p. 59.

25. CCAR *Yearbook* 9 (1899):174; Naomi Weiner, "Reform Judaism in American and Zionism, 1897–1922," masters essay, Columbia University (1949), pp. 23, 26. While Zionism was the main issue, the three professors were also involved in a power struggle to drive Kohler out of the seminary.

26. Abraham Goldberg, "American Zionism up to the Brandeis Era" in Joseph Shalom Shubow, ed., *The Brandeis Avukah Annual of 1932* (New York, 1932), p. 549.

27. CCAR *Yearbook* 11 (1901):31.

28. Ibid. 17 (1907):31; Herschel Levin, "The Other Side of the Coin," *Herzl Year Book* 5 (1963):40.

29. Norman T. Mendell, "Glimpses into the Life of a Famous Rabbi and

Zionist: Max Heller," rabbinic thesis, Hebrew Union College (1965); "Memoirs of Abba Hillel Silver," typescript in Silver MSS; interview with Jacob Rader Marcus (October 26, 1971).

30. Cyrus Adler, *I Have Considered the Days* (Philadelphia, 1941), pp. 231–33.

31. Jacob Schiff to Solomon Schechter (September 22, 1907 and August 8, 1907) in Cyrus Adler, *Jacob Schiff: His Life and Letters* (2 vols.; Garden City, N.Y., 1928), 1:167–68, 165.

32. Louis Marshall to Jacob Schiff (October 2, 1908) in Charles Reznikoff, ed., *Louis Marshall, Champion of Liberty: Selected Papers and Addresses* (2 vols.; Philadelphia, 1957), 2:704.

33. Bernard A. Rosenblatt, *Two Generations of Zionism* (New York, 1967), pp. 40–41.

34. Weizmann, *Trial and Error,* p. 75.

35. Stephen S. Wise to Jacob deHaas (October 26, 1898), quoted in Feinstein, *American Zionism,* pp. 160–61.

36. Grinstein, "Memoirs . . . of Dr. Bluestone," p. 57.

37. Haber, *Odyssey of an American Zionist,* p. 72.

38. *The Hebrew Standard* (July 22, 1904), cited in Wiener, "Reform Judaism and Zionism," p. 7.

39. *Maccabean* 7 (July 1904):40.

40. See Herbert Parzen, "Conservative Judaism and Zionism, 1896–1922," *Jewish Social Studies* 23 (October 1961):235–64.

41. C. Bezalel Sherman, "The Beginnings of Labor Zionism in the United States" in Meyer, *Early History of Zionism,* pp. 275–77.

42. Bernard H. Bloom, "Yiddish-Speaking Socialists in America, 1892–1905," *American Jewish Archives* 12 (April 1960):61.

43. "Fifty Years of American Zionism, 1897–1947: A Documentary Record," *Palestine Yearbook* 3 (1947–48):399–401; A. Kretchmar-Isreeli, "The Poal-Zion Movement," in *The Jewish Communal Register of New York* (New York, 1918), pp. 1374–83. In practice this meant hiring only Jewish workers to till the fields of Palestine, a practice later cited as a cause of Arab resentment against the Jews.

44. Ellis Rivkin, "A Decisive Pattern in American Jewish History" in *Essays in American Jewish History* (Cincinnati, 1958), pp. 45–47; Epstein, *Jewish Labor in the United States* 2:7.

45. Stephen S. Wise, *Challenging Years* (New York, 1949), p. 34; Wiener, "Reform Judaism . . . and Zionism," p. 19.

46. Henrietta Szold to Affiliated Societies (September 28, 1910), Cologne Office Records, Z2/375.

47. Richard Gottheil to Theodore Herzl (March 28, 1899), quoted in Feinstein, *American Zionism*, pp. 142–43.

48. Horwich, *My First Eighty Years*, p. 231; Judah L. Magnes to Johan Kreminetzsky (May 17, 1905), Vienna Office Records, Z1/407.

49. Bernard A. Rosenblatt Interview in Oral History Project, Institute for Contemporary Jewry, Hebrew University, Jerusalem.

50. Jacob deHaas, "Brandeis in Zionism," *The Menorah Journal* 14 (February 1928):136.

51. Judah Magnes to David Wolffsohn (October 9, 1907); Friedenwald and Magnes to Societies (May 28, 1908); both in Cologne Office Records, Z2/377.

52. Henrietta Szold to Solomon Schechter (November 10, 1910) in Marvin Lowenthal, *Henrietta Szold: Life and Letters* (New York, 1942), p. 74.

53. Editorial in *Maccabean* 1 (December 1901):126.

54. Parzen, "The Federation of American Zionists," pp. 250–52.

55. "Proceedings of the Fifth Annual Convention," *Maccabean* 2 (June 1902):331.

56. Richard Gottheil to Actions Comité (May 18, 1900), quoted in Feinstein, *American Zionism*, p. 224.

57. Richard Gottheil to Theodore Herzl (July 6, 1899); Jacob deHaas to Actions Comité (September 10, 1902 and May 29, 1903); all in Vienna Office Records, Z1/407.

58. Stephen Wise to Richard Gottheil (April 21, 1904) in Voss, *Servant of the People*, pp. 21–22.

59. Richard Gottheil to Actions Comité (February 6, 1904), Vienna Office Records, Z1/407. This complaint of lack of information would also crop up periodically; see Judah Magnes to Actions Comité (June 13, 1905), Vienna Office Records, Z1/407 and Actions Comité to Louis Lipsky (October 16, 1911), Berlin Office Records, Z3/754.

60. Jacob deHaas to Oscar Marmorek (November 18, 1904); Harry Friedenwald to Actions Comité (March 8 and 28, 1905); all in Vienna Office Records, Z1/407; Harry Friedenwald to David Wolffsohn (November 4, 1908), Cologne Office Records, Z2/377.

61. Feinstein, *American Zionism*, pp. 235–37.

62. Actions Comité to Max Shulman (Knights of Zion) (December 13, 1912), Berlin Office Records, Z3/932; Joseph Jaison to Zionistische Centralbureau (October 13, 1908), Cologne Office Records, Z2/377.

63. Plesur, "American Press and Restoration," p. 136; *Maccabean* 6 (January 1904):41–43.

64. Arthur P. Dudden, "The Single Tax Zionism of Joseph Fels," *PAJHS* 46 (June 1957):478–79; "Reminiscences of Bernard Gershon Richards," Oral History Research Office, Columbia University, p. 141.

65. Copy of speech in Cologne Office Records, Z2/377; Bernhard Felsenthal, "Israel's Mission," *Maccabean* 4 (March 1903):135.

66. New York *Times* (January 6, 1902, June 11, 1900); *Maccabean* 5 (July 1903):51, and 6 (July 1904):27–29; Cologne Office Records, Z2/377.

67. Adolph Böhm, *Die Zionistische Bewegung* (2 vols.; Berlin, 1935), 1:637.

NOTES TO CHAPTER FOUR

"Men! Money! Discipline!"

NOTES TO PAGES 117–121

1. Rosenblatt, *Two Generations of Zionism*, p. 47.
2. "Seventeenth Annual Convention of the Federation of American Zionists," *Maccabean* 24 (July 1914):17–38.
3. Arthur Ruppin to Henry Morgenthau (August 12, 1914); Morgenthau to Jacob Schiff (cable) (August 28, 1914), Morgenthau MSS, Box 4.
4. DeHaas, "Brandeis in Zionism," p. 135.
5. In addition to Brandeis, the Provisional Committee consisted of Joseph Barondess of New York; Harry Friedenwald of Baltimore (president of the FAZ); Elias Wolf Lewin-Epstein of New York (long-time representative of the Carmel wineries in Palestine); Nathan Kaplan of Chicago (president of the Knights of Zion); Louis Lipsky of New York (executive secretary of the FAZ); Rabbi Judah L. Magnes of New York (a member of the American Jewish Committee and of the New York *Kehillah*); Rabbi Stephen S. Wise of the Free Synagogue in New York; Henrietta Szold, honorary secretary of the FAZ and president of Hadassah. In addition, the Mizrachi and Poale Zion were each asked to designate a member. The religious Zionists chose Rabbi Meyer Berlin, while the Labor Zionists named Nachman Syrkin.
6. Of all the Dembitz family, only Frederika's younger brother Lewis reverted to a strict Orthodox Judaism, a development regarded by most of the family as eccentric. A brilliant lawyer and scholar, it was Lewis who inspired his nephew to pursue the study of law, and young Louis Brandeis changed his middle name from "David" to "Dembitz" in honor of his uncle. The older Dembitz wrote several standard legal texts and played a prominent role in Republican politics in Kentucky; in 1860 he was one of three men to place Abraham Lincoln's name in nomination at the Republican National Convention. Dembitz also

earned a reputation as a student of Jewish culture, and when the Jewish Publication Society undertook a new English translation of the Scriptures, they turned to him to do the books of *Exodus* and *Leviticus*. A founding member of the FAZ, he wrote frequently for the *Maccabean* and was elected honorary vice president of the Federation in 1903. Dembitz never sought leadership, however, and one historian has characterized him as a *Gefuhlszionist,* a Zionist of feeling but not of action (Böhm, *Die Zionistische Bewegung* 1:638). Although young Louis knew that his uncle held religious notions different from the rest of the family, he evidently never discussed Zionism with him, and in later years seemingly forgot that Lewis Dembitz had been a Zionist.

7. *Reminiscences of Frederika Dembitz Brandeis,* tr. Alice Goldmark Brandeis (privately printed, 1943), pp. 8, 32–34; *The American Hebrew* (December 2, 1910).

8. Barbara M. Solomon, *Pioneers in Progress: A History of the Associated Jewish Philanthropies of Boston* (Boston, 1956), pp. 59, 176; Richards, Oral History Memoir; Jacob deHaas, *Louis D. Brandeis: A Biographical Sketch* (New York, 1929), p. 51.

9. The literature on Brandeis' career is voluminous. The best biography is Alpheus T. Mason, *Brandeis: A Free Man's Life* (New York, 1946), which can be supplemented by Melvin I. Urofsky, *A Mind of One Piece: Brandeis and American Reform* (New York, 1971), in which the bibliographical essay provides notes for further reading. Much of his work can be traced in Melvin I. Urofsky and David W. Levy, eds., *Letters of Louis D. Brandeis* (4 vols. to date; Albany, N.Y., 1971–). See also Brandeis' *Business—A Profession* (Boston, 1914) and *Other People's Money* (New York, 1914).

10. Isa. 3:14–15. Milton R. Konvitz, "Louis D. Brandeis" in Simon Noveck, ed., *Great Jewish Personalities in Modern Times* (New York, 1960), p. 300.

11. DeHaas, *Brandeis,* pp. 51–52; *The American Hebrew* (December 2, 1910); Brandeis to Bernard G. Richards (February 2, 1911 and April 26, 1912), Richards MSS.

12. Rosenblatt, *Two Generations of Zionism,* p. 56; Boston *Jewish Advocate* (April 4, 1913); Solomon Goldman, ed., *Brandeis on Zionism* (Washington, 1942), p. 37.

13. See, for example, Brandeis to Julius Meyer (April 17, 1913) and to Louis Lipsky (July 23, 1913 and February 2, 1914), Brandeis MSS, Z1–2 and LtB. While declining leadership in the Federation, he promised Sokolow that he would work on establishing a million-dollar investment corporation to help develop Palestinian agriculture and industry. The American Palestine Corporation, as it was called, never got

off the ground, since neither the FAZ nor the AC could provide Brandeis with the facts he wanted. Brandeis to Nahum Sokolow (August 1, 1913), ibid., Z1–2; Louis Lipsky to Zionistische Centralbureau (May 21, 1914), Berlin Office Records, Z3/757.

14. The question of why Brandeis became a Zionist continues to fascinate historians, and a number of hypotheses have been put forward. Ben Halpern, "Brandeis' Way to Zionism," *Midstream* 17 (October 1971):3–13, argues that a sense of blood kinship, derived from strong familial ties, led the Boston attorney to seek roots among his own people, while Yonathan Shapiro in "American Jews in Politics: The Case of Louis D. Brandeis," *AJHQ* 55 (December 1965):199–211 charges that Brandeis embraced Zionism in a bid to further his political ambitions after failing to receive a position in Wilson's Cabinet. Of all the theories, this is most debatable, and I have argued its fallacies in other places. Shapiro's book on American Zionism is sociological in approach, arguing that Brandeis and his associates were "marginal men," i.e., excluded from the full fruits of their talents by discrimination, who were forced to turn inward to lead their own kind. Stuart M. Geller, "Why Did Louis D. Brandeis Choose Zionism?," *AJHQ* 62 (June 1973):383–400, argues that Brandeis' economic philosophy provides the key. David Ben-Gurion told the Justice's granddaughter that it was a simple case of justice: he joined the movement to secure freedom for his people; she related the incident to me in an interview in July 1969. There is a story, probably apocryphal, that when Brandeis read about the First Congress and Herzl's ideas, he told his wife that there was a cause to which he could give his life (Wise, *Challenging Years*, p. 185); since that was in 1897, and Brandeis paid no further attention to Zionism for over a decade, there seems little base to the tale.

15. "What Loyalty Demands" (November 28, 1905); Boston *Jewish Advocate* (December 9, 1910). Interestingly enough, Brandeis' reiteration of his 1905 statement appeared in the context of an interview headlined as supporting Zionism.

16. Michael M. Hammer and Samuel Stickles, "An Interview with Louis D. Brandeis," *The Invincible Ideal* 1 (June 1915):7.

17. *Menorah Journal* 1 (January 1915):4; *Maccabean* 23 (July 1915):34; Boston *American* (July 4, 1915).

18. DeHaas, *Brandeis,* p. 163; Baltimore *American* (September 16, 1914).

19. Louis D. Brandeis, *The Jewish Problem, and How to Solve It* (New York, 1915), p. 12. This pamphlet, originally a speech to Reform rabbis, represents the best single presentation of Brandeis' Zionist philosophy, and with the exception of some of Mordecai Kaplan's writings, the most developed ideological statement of American Zionism.

20. Brandeis to Jacob H. Kaplan (February 10, 1916), Brandeis MSS, NMF 80–1. The speech, entitled "True Americanism," can be found in *Brandeis on Zionism*, pp. 3–11.

21. *Menorah Journal* 1 (January 1915):13–19.

22. "Why I Am a Zionist," speech to the Free Synagogue in New York (October 25, 1914), later reprinted in *Opinion* 17 (September 1947):12–15; Brandeis to V. H. Kriegshaber (September 20, 1913), Brandeis MSS, Z1–2; Boston *American* (July 3, 1915).

23. Norman Podhoretz, "Now, instant Zionism," New York *Times Magazine*, February 3, 1974, explores this theme.

24. Brandeis to Alfred Brandeis (January 7, 1912), Brandeis MSS, M3–3; Brandeis to Jacob Billikopf (January 25, 1915), ibid., Z7–1; Boston *Post* (September 28, 1914).

25. Quoted in Shlomo Bardin, *Self-Fulfillment through Zionism* (New York, 1943), p. 97.

26. Between 1914 and 1928 alone, he gave $450,000 to Zionism, channeled mainly through deHaas or the Palestine Economic Corporation set up after 1921. At his death, he left half of his $3 million estate to Zionist agencies.

27. Brandeis to Louis E. Kirstein (September 10, 1915), Brandeis MSS, Z7–3; Konvitz, "Brandeis," pp. 312 ff.

28. Shmaryahu Levin to Actions Comité (October 6, 1915), Brandeis MSS, Z22–1.

29. Harry Barnard, *The Forging of an American Jew: the Life and Times of Judge Julian W. Mack* (New York, 1974), passim. Thanks to the courtesy of the Herzl Press and Professor Marie Syrkin, its director, I was able to read this book in galleys.

30. Horace M. Kallen, *Of Them That Say They Are Jews* (New York, 1954), p. 137; American Jewish Committee, Executive Committee meeting (May 9, 1915), quoted in Moses Rischin, "The Early Attitude of the American Jewish Committee to Zionism (1906–1922)," *PAJHS* 49 (1959):192.

31. Stephen Wise to Louis Marshall (January 5, 1906) in Justine Wise Polier and James Waterman Wise, eds., *The Personal Letters of Stephen S. Wise* (Boston, 1956), p. 80.

32. Leonard J. Mervis, "The Social Justice Movement and the American Reform Rabbi," *American Jewish Archives* 7 (June 1955):171–230, especially 171–80.

33. Wise to Louise Waterman Wise (1900), *Personal Letters*, p. 56.

34. *The Autobiography of Nahum Goldman: Sixty Years of Jewish Life* (New York, 1969), p. 124.

35. Wise to James W. Wise (1925), *Personal Letters,* pp. 201–2; Wise to Brandeis (November 18, 1914), Brandeis MSS, Z6–2; Wise to Horace Kallen (November 4, 1915) in Voss, *Servant of the People,* p. 67.

36. Wise, "Zionism, Religion and Americanism," *Maccabean* 28 (June 1916):125–26; Boston *Journal* (June 28, 1915); Louis Lipsky, *A Gallery of Zionist Profiles* (New York, 1956), p. 149.

37. Felix Frankfurter with Harlan B. Phillips, *Felix Frankfurter Reminisces* (New York, 1960), p. 290; author's interview with Louis E. Levinthal (December 22, 1972).

38. Brandeis to Chaim Weizmann (January 5, 1919), London Office Records, Z4/16046; Brandeis to Charles Cowen (April 6, 1916), Brandeis MSS, Z11–2; *Felix Frankfurter Reminisces,* pp. 181–82.

39. See Lawrence A. Cremin, *The Transformation of the School* (New York, 1961), Part One, passim.

40. Lowenthal, *Szold: Life and Letters,* p. 53; notes for speech to Twentieth Congress, Zurich (August 1937), H. Szold MSS (Personal), A125/13.

41. Lowenthal, *Szold: Life and Letters,* pp. 67–68.

42. Ibid., pp. 76–77.

43. Statement on death of Louis D. Brandeis (October 6, 1941), H. Szold MSS (Personal), A125/55.

44. The full story of Hadassah can be traced in Donald H. Miller, "A History of Hadassah, 1912–1935," doctoral dissertation, New York University (1968), and in Marlin Levin, *Balm in Gilead* (New York, 1973). I also profited immensely from interviews with Rose Halprin and Charlotte Jacobson on March 23, 1973.

45. Midge Decter, "The Legacy of Henrietta Szold," *Commentary* 30 (December 1960):480–88.

46. Brandeis, *The Jewish Problem,* p. 16; Brandeis to Louis Lipsky (December 31, 1914), Brandeis MSS, Z1–4; Brandeis to Horace Kallen (February 23, 1915), ibid., Z3–1; Brandeis to Lipsky (December 8, 1920), deHaas MSS.

47. Brandeis to Alec H. H. Fingerhut (February 13, 1915) and to Ezekial Leavitt (July 8, 1915), Brandeis MSS, Z7–2; Brandeis to Lydia Littman (December 2, 1914), ibid., Z1–2; Eugene Meyer, Jr., to Felix Frankfurter (December 12, 1915), ibid., Z10–2.

48. Brandeis to David deSola Pool (March 2, 1915), ibid., Z7–1.

49. Brandeis to Jews of Chelsea, Massachusetts (June 22, 1915), ibid., ScB–2; Brandeis to Abraham Alpert (March 19, 1915), ibid., Z12–1.

50. Brandeis to Rabbi Morris Lazaron (November 17, 1915), ibid., Z8–1.

51. *The Jewish Monitor* (July 1, 1915).

52. Shapiro, *Leadership of the American Zionist Movement*, passim; Learsi, *Fulfillment*, pp. 148–49; Halpern, *American Jew*, pp. 27–28; Oscar I. Janowsky, *The Jews and Minority Rights, 1898–1919* (New York, 1933), pp. 161–62.

53. Bloom, "Yiddish Speaking Socialists," passim; Brandeis to Julian Mack (October 26, 1915), R. Szold MSS.

54. See Victor R. Greene, "Slavic American Nationalism, 1870–1918," in Anna Cienciala, ed., *American Contributions to the Seventh International Congress of Slavists* (The Hague, 1973), 197–215.

55. Abe Goldberg to Brandeis (March 31, 1916), cited in Shapiro, *Leadership*, p. 155.

56. Mordecai Soltes, *The Yiddish Press: An Americanizing Agency* (New York, 1950 ed.), p. 18.

57. *Maccabean* 25 (August 1914):42.

58. Chaim Weizmann to Brandeis, (April 25, 1918), Foreign Office Records, 371/3395.

59. Louis Lipsky to Zionistische Centralbureau (July 23, 1914), Berlin Office Records, Z3/757; speech by Henrietta Szold to Actions Comité (October 15, 1941), H. Szold MSS (Personal), A125/55.

60. Boston *Herald* (June 28, 1915); Philadelphia *Public Ledger* (September 15, 1914); Brandeis to Bernie F. Green (January 28, 1915), Brandeis MSS, NMF 66–1; Brandeis to Abraham B. Cohen (February 13, 1915), ibid., Z7–1.

61. Louis Kirstein to Henry Morgenthau (November 26, 1917), Magnes MSS, F3/L92.

62. Ibid. (June 28, 1915); Brandeis to Alfred Brandeis (November 27, 1914), Brandeis MSS, M4–1; Brandeis and Lipsky to Zionists (June 1, 1915), ibid., Z7–2.

63. Brandeis to Edward Bromberg (March 19, 1915), ibid., NMF 66–1; Baltimore *Jewish Comment* (September 24, 1915).

64. Horace Kallen to Stephen Wise (December 3, 1914), Wise MSS (AJA).

65. This theme is explored in detail in the various essays in Jerry Israel, ed., *Building the Organizational Society: Essays on Associational Activities in Modern America* (New York, 1972), and its broader applications can be seen in Robert Wiebe, *The Search for Order, 1877–1920* (New York, 1967).

66. *Zionist Profiles*, pp. 157–58.

67. Brandeis to Morris L. Avner (March 29, 1916) and to Jacob de-

Haas (January 25, 1915), Brandeis MSS, Z16–2. This passion for facts had characterized his career as a reformer, and would be a hallmark of his work on the Supreme Court as well.

68.   Robert Kesselman to Brandeis (March 29, 1916), ibid., Z14–1.

69.   Brandeis to Benjamin Perlstein (March 30, 1915), ibid., Z3–2; circular letters, Brandeis and S. Levin to Zionists (March 8, 1915, July 9, 1915, and October 15, 1915), Berlin Office Files, Z3/757.

70.   Brandeis to Benjamin Perlstein (June 2, 1915), Brandeis MSS, Z3–2.

71.   Brandeis to Nathan Kaplan (December 6, 1915), ibid., Z3–1.

72.   See Brandeis to Meyer Berlin (April 25, 1915 and June 15, 1915), ibid., Z12–3.

73.   S. Levin and L. Lipsky to Brandeis (August 20, 1914), ibid.; Judah L. Magnes to Chaim Weizmann, Berlin Office Files, Z3/758; minutes of Provisional Executive Committee (March 27, 1915), Magnes MSS, SP/205.

74.   Weizmann to Brandeis and Levin (October 18, 1914), quoted in Weizmann, *Trial and Error,* p. 165.

75.   Memorandum, Jacob deHaas to Brandeis (October 6, 1914), Brandeis MSS, Z6–1; Judah Magnes to Chaim Weizmann (October 4, 1914); Provisional Executive Committee to Zionistische Centralbureau (November 2, 1914); S. Levin, N. Straus, and J. Magnes to same (November 28, 1914), all in Berlin Office Files, Z3/758; ibid.; Leo Motzkin to Copenhagen Office (November 28, 1914), Copenhagen Office Files, L6/12(1).

76.   Nahum Sokolow to Provisional Committee (November 17, 1914), Berlin Office Files, Z3/757; Chaim Weizmann to Horace Kallen (January 24, 1915), deHaas MSS.

77.   Brandeis to Arthur Hantke (March 19, 1915), Berlin Office Files, Zs/757; Benjamin Perlstein to Copenhagen Office (June 22, 1915), Copenhagen Office Files, L6/12(1); Brandeis to Henry Morgenthau (October 22, 1914), Morgenthau MSS, Box 4; Brandeis to Actions Comité (September 15, 1915), Berlin Office Files, Z3/759; Brandeis to Actions Comité (January 23, 1916), Copenhagen Office Files, L6/12(9).

NOTES TO CHAPTER FIVE

The Congress Fight

1. CCAR *Yearbook* 27 (1917):132–33.
2. Brandeis to Louis Lipsky (October 5, 1914), Brandeis MSS, Z1–4.
3. Cincinnati *Times-Star* (October 10 and 13, 1914).
4. Brandeis to Horace Kallen (February 10 and 23, 1915); Kallen to Brandeis (February 21, 1915), Brandeis MSS, Z3–1.
5. Brandeis to Samuel M. Fechheimer (February 23, 1915), ibid., Z2–4.
6. See, for example, David Philipson to Jacob deHaas (August 9, 1915) in Boston *Jewish Advocate* (August 13, 1915); Philipson, "Zionism and Americanism," *American Israelite* (December 16, 1915); Samuel Schulman, "Back to Palestine," *National Sunday Magazine* (November 14, 1915); Schulman, "Why American Jews Consider Zionism Undesirable," *Outlook* 112 (January 5, 1916):40–42; Boston *Morning Globe* (March 6, 1916).
7. New York *Sun* (April 27, 1915).
8. Stephen Wise to Horace Kallen (October 27, 1915), Wise MSS (AJA), Box 947.
9. David Philipson, *My Life As an American Jew* (Cincinnati, 1941), passim.
10. Brandeis to Louis Marshall (August 31, 1914), Marshall MSS.
11. The American Jewish Committee appropriated $25,000 from its Emergency Fund, while Jacob Schiff and the Provisional Committee each contributed $12,500.
12. Stephen Wise to Henry Morgenthau (October 27, 1914), Morgenthau MSS, Box 9; Wise to Horace Kallen (October 27, 1914), Wise MSS (AJA), Box 947; Alvin S. Roth, "Backgrounds and Origins of the American Jewish Congress," rabbinic thesis, Hebrew Union College (1953), pp. 130–31. The Roth thesis has very little analysis but con-

tains an extraordinary amount of documentation regarding the Congress fight.

13. Horace Kallen to Stephen Wise (December 3, 1914), Wise MSS (AJA), Box 947.

14. See, for example, Brandeis to Judah L. Magnes (March 13, 1915), Brandeis MSS, Z5–1 (July 8, 1915), ibid., Z10–4 (September 8 and 16, 1915), Magnes MSS, SP/215; Brandeis to Felix Warburg (November 19, 1915), Brandeis MSS, Z10–4; Nathan Straus to Brandeis (September 14, 1915), ibid. See also Zosa Szajkowski, "Private and Organized American Jewish Overseas Relief (1914–1938)," *AJHQ* 57 (September 1967):52–106, and subsequent articles by him over the next two years in the same journal.

15. Brandeis to Office Committee (October 27, 1915), Brandeis MSS, Z8–2; Shapiro, *Zionist Leadership*, pp. 78–79.

16. Brandeis to Julian W. Mack (December 2, 1915), Brandeis MSS, Z8–2; Brandeis to Joseph Barondess (March 24, 1916), ibid., Z16–2; Stephen Wise to Brandeis (March 23, 1917), ibid., Z22–1.

17. *Maccabean* 28 (June 1916):2.

18. Brandeis to Louis Marshall (August 31, 1914), Marshall MSS.

19. Bernard G. Richards, "Where the Congress Idea Originated," *Congress Bi-Weekly* 10 (April 9, 1943):11; among the backers of this early congress was David Philipson, who in 1916 violently opposed the Zionist-led proposal.

20. Syrkin, *Nachman Syrkin,* p. 167.

21. Rischin, "Early Attitude of the A.J.C.," p. 190; Louis Lipsky to Zionistische Centralbureau (November 20, 1913), Centralbureau to Lipsky (December 18, 1913), Berlin Office Files, Z3/756.

22. Jacob Schiff to Bernard Richards (January 31, 1916), Brandeis MSS, Z5–1; Nathan Schachner, *The Price of Liberty* (New York, 1948), p. 65; see also Goren, *New York Jews and Community,* p. 221.

23. Adler, *Jacob Schiff* 2:297–98.

24. Abraham L. Sachar, *Sufferance Is the Badge* (New York, 1939), p. 510.

25. Goren, *New York Jews and Community,* p. 220; Rosenstock, *Louis Marshall,* p. 273; see also Louis Marshall to Judah Magnes (October 10, 1908) in Reznikoff, *Louis Marshall: Selected Papers* 1:33–34.

26. Louis Marshall to Cyrus Sulzberger (June 14, 1902), quoted in Doroshkin, *Yiddish in America,* p. 131; Marshall to William D. Guthrie (April 7, 1924) in Rosenstock, *Louis Marshall,* p. 35.

27. Kallen, *Zionism and World Politics,* pp. 143–44; see also Kallen to Brandeis (January 5, 1916), Brandeis MSS, Z3–1.

28. Louis Marshall to Brandeis (August 31, 1914), Marshall MSS.

29. *American Hebrew* (September 11, 1914); *American Israelite*, quoted in Boston *Jewish Advocate* (January 8, 1915); Roth, "Origins of Congress," pp. 134–35. From overseas Chaim Weizmann warned that Jews had to be ready with their demands and programs before the war ended, or they would not be heard at the peace table. Weizmann to Judah Magnes (September 8, 1914), Weizmann MSS.

30. Louis Marshall to Solomon Schechter (February 19, 1915) in Reznikoff, *Louis Marshall: Selected Papers* 2:506.

31. Interview with Bernard G. Richards (September 7, 1967); Reminiscences of Bernard G. Richards, Columbia Oral History Office.

32. Judah Magnes to Brandeis (June 30, 1915), Magnes MSS, SP/215; Magnes to Chaim Weizmann, (September 2, 1915), Weizmann MSS; Norman Bentwich, *For Zion's Sake: A Biography of Judah L. Magnes* (Philadelphia, 1954), p. 72.

33. Shapiro, *Zionist Leadership,* pp. 89–91; Richard Gottheil to Brandeis (May 6, 1915), Brandeis MSS, Z6–1.

34. Moses Rischin, "The American Jewish Committee and Zionism, 1906–1922," *Herzl Year Book* 5 (1963):65–81; Cyrus Adler to Harry Friedenwald (August 4, 1915), and Julian W. Mack to Brandeis (August 20, 1915), Brandeis MSS, Z11–1.

35. Louis Marshall to Adolph Kraus (June 12, 1915) in Reznikoff, *Louis Marshall: Selected Papers* 2:509; Adler, *Jacob Schiff,* 2:296–97.

36. Boston *Jewish Advocate* (July 9, 1915); Stephen Wise to Henry Morgenthau (August 23, 1915), Morgenthau MSS, Box 9.

37. New York *Times* (June 21, 1915).

38. Boston *Evening Transcript* (June 28, 1915); Harry Schneiderman to Brandeis (July 2, 1915), Brandeis MSS, Z11–1.

39. Felix Frankfurter, "Memorandum of meeting . . . between Louis D. Brandeis and Cyrus Adler" (July 12, 1915), ibid., Z11–1.

40. Cyrus Adler to Brandeis (July 21 and 28, 1915, August 3, 1915); Brandeis to Adler (July 28 and August 10, 1915). The entire correspondence, together with other documents, was issued as *The Jewish Congress versus the American Jewish Committee* by the Congress Organizing Committee.

41. Levin, *Vision,* p. 230.

42. See, for example, Adler to Henry Morgenthau (July 30, 1915), Morgenthau MSS, Box 4.

43. *Jewish Comment* (September 7, 1915); Boston *Post* (October 4, 1915); Brandeis to Stephen Wise (August 26, 1915), Brandeis MSS, Z11–1; Roth, "Origins of Congress," pp. 193–96.

44. Horace Kallen to Brandeis (October 20, 1915), Brandeis MSS, Z3–1; Julian Mack to Brandeis (November 25, 1915), ibid., Z11–1; Harry Friedenwald to Brandeis (November 25, 1915), ibid., Z11–2; Stephen Wise to Henry Morgenthau (November 6, 1915), Morgenthau MSS, Box 9.

45. Brandeis to Horace Kallen (November 29, 1915), Brandeis MSS, Z3–1.

46. Brandeis to Bernard Richards (November 16, 1915), ibid., Z11–1.

47. Brandeis to Louis Lipsky (December 4, 1915), ibid., Z1–4.

48. Brandeis to Lipsky (December 28, 1915); Lipsky to Brandeis (January 3, 1916), ibid.

49. The speech is in deHaas, *Brandeis,* pp. 218–31.

50. Louis Marshall to Harry Cutler (February 11, 1916), Marshall MSS.

51. Louis Marshall to Brandeis (February 14, 1916), ibid.; Jacob Schiff to Brandeis (February 29, 1916), Schiff MSS.

52. Louis Marshall to Bernard Richards (March 16, 1916) and to J. Walter Freiberg (March 18, 1916), Marshall MSS; *American Hebrew* (March 3, 1916).

53. Quoted in Samuel Caplan, "In the Beginning," *Congress Bi-Weekly* 35 (May 6, 1968):6.

54. *American Israelite* (June 8, 1916).

55. Rabbi Horace J. Wolf, "The Passing of Benevolent Feudalism," *American Hebrew* (March 3, 1916); Shapiro, *Zionist Leadership,* pp. 84–86.

56. Harry Friedenwald to Louis Marshall (June 12, 1916) in Levin, *Vision,* pp. 230–31. The Zionists, naturally, were delighted with the resignation, which received wide publicity. See letters to Friedenwald from Stephen Wise (June 16, 1916) and from Brandeis (June 14, 1916) in Friedenwald MSS, A182/20.

57. Jacob Schiff to Brandeis (February 29, 1916), Schiff MSS.

58. See, for example, Rabbi S. Pereira Mendes to Brandeis (May 15, 1916), Brandeis MSS, Z16–2; Lipsky, *Thirty Years of American Zionism* (New York, 1927), p. 55.

59. A verbatim transcript of the proceedings can be found in the *American Hebrew* (July 21, 1916); most of the details are also in the New York *Times* (July 17, 1916).

60. "Out of Place," New York *Times* (July 18, 1916). The editorial evoked a bitter denunication of the paper and its allies from the *Warheit* (July 20, 1916), which accused the *yahudim* of conspiring to put Brandeis in such an embarrassing position.

61. Henry L. Levenson to Brandeis (January 28, 1916), Brandeis MSS, NMF 72–1; Richard Gottheil to Brandeis (February 4 and 11, 1916), ibid., Z6–1; Horace Kallen to Stephen Wise (March 16, 1916), Wise MSS (AJA), Box 947; Wise to Louise Wise ([late] January 1916), in Polier and Wise, *Personal Letters,* p. 153.

62. Brandeis to Hugo Pam (July 21, 1916), Brandeis MSS, Z16–3.

63. Urofsky, *Mind of One Piece,* Chaps. 2, 6.

64. Shapiro, *Zionist Leadership,* p. 96.

65. Janowksy, *Jews and Minority Rights,* p. 179; Roth, "Origins of Congress," p. 361.

66. Louis Marshall to Brandeis (July 24, 1916) in Reznikoff, *Louis Marshall: Selected Papers* 2:517–18.

67. Shapiro, *Zionist Leadership,* p. 97.

68. Horace Kallen to Stephen Wise (October 31, 1916), Wise MSS (AJA), Box 947.

69. Jacob deHaas to Copenhagen Bureau (December 26, 1916), Copenhagen Office Files, L6/12(7).

NOTES TO CHAPTER SIX

War and Peace

NOTES TO PAGES 196–199

1. Arthur Ruppin to Henry Morgenthau (January 5, 1916) and Morgenthau to Louis Marshall (February 23, 1915), Morgenthau MSS; Frank E. Manuel, *The Realities of American-Palestine Relations* (Washington, 1949), p. 127.

2. Louis Lipsky to Federations, n.d. (fall 1914), Gottheil MSS, A138/15(2); Judah L. Magnes, "Our Duty in the Present Crisis," speech in New York (September 13, 1914), Magnes MSS, SP/201.

3. Stephen Wise to Henry Morgenthau (October 26, 1914), Morgenthau MSS, Box 9; *Menorah Journal* 1 (January 1915):18. See similar statements by Wise and Jacob deHaas, quoted in Joseph Rappaport, "Jewish Immigrants and World War I: A Study of American Yiddish Press Reactions," doctoral dissertation, Columbia University (1951), pp. 132–34.

4. Judah Magnes to Chaim Weizmann (January 28, 1915), Sokolow MSS, A18/20.

5. Magnes to Brandeis (November 30, 1914), Magnes MSS, SP/202; Harry Friedenwald also cautioned Gottheil in a letter of December 1, 1914 Friedenwald MSS, A182/29.

6. Magnes to Brandeis (September 2, 1915), Weizmann MSS; Bentwich, *For Zion's Sake,* pp. 68–69; Zosa Szajkowski, *Jews, Wars and Communism* (New York, 1972), ch. 6; Louis Marshall to Richard Gottheil (May 31, 1917), Gottheil MSS, A138/17.

7. Stephen Wise to Horace Kallen (April 21, 1915), Wise MSS (AJA), Box 947.

8. Brandeis to Felix Warburg (December 31, 1914), Brandeis MSS, NMF 66–1; Brandeis to Lord Eustace Percy (June 26, 1916), Weizmann MSS.

9. Jabotinsky, "Sippin Yamai," quoted in Oskar K. Rabinowicz, *50 Years of Zionism: A Historical Analysis of Dr. Weizmann's "Trial and Error"* (London, 1952), p. 70.

10. *Jewish Daily News* (August 12, 1914), quoted in Rosenstock, *Louis Marshall*, p. 102; *Forwards* (August 14, 1914) and *Litertur un Labor* (December 1914), quoted in Rappaport, "Jewish Immigrants and World War I," pp. 75, 98; Szajkowski, *Jews, Wars and Communism*, pp. 3–10.

11. Stein, *Balfour Declaration*, pp. 203, 208, 215–16; Israel Zangwill to Richard Gottheil (January 20, 1915), Gottheil MSS, A138/14; Roth, "Origins of Congress Movement," p. 88. A small group of Yiddish journalists was pro-Allied, including Abraham Coralnik and A. Tcherikower, both Zionists, and both of whom wrote for *Der Tag*. They saw German victory as merely reinforcing the Jew-hatred already extant among the Turks.

12. Christopher Sykes, *Two Studies in Virtue* (New York, 1953), pp. 178–79.

13. Abe Goldberg to Brandeis (February 29, 1916), Brandeis MSS, Z16–2; Henry Morgenthau to Stephen Wise (August 3, 1915, December 1 and 6, 1915), Morgenthau MSS, Box 9.

14. *Dos Yiddishe Folk* (October 15, 1915), quoted in Rappaport, "Jewish Immigrants and World War I," p. 123; Syrkin, *Nachman Syrkin*, pp. 162–63.

15. Szajkowski, *Jews, Wars and Communism*, ch. 7; Joseph Rappaport, "Zionism as a Factor in Allied Central Power Controversy (1914–1918)" in Meyer, *Early History of Zionism*, pp. 311–13.

16. Szajkowski, *Jews, Wars and Communism*, p. 209; for pro-war Jewish socialist thought, see ch. 12.

17. Lipsky, *Profiles*, p. 42; Stein, *Balfour Declaration*, pp. 3, 33–34; Nahum Sokolow devoted much of his two-volume *History of Zionism* to examples of British friendliness, all of which culminated in the Declaration.

18. Sykes, *Two Studies in Virtue*, p. 171; Rabinowicz, *50 Years of Zionism*, p. 67; Chaim Weizmann to Israel Zangwill (October 18, 1914), quoted in Stein, *Balfour Declaration*, pp. 126–27.

19. R. H. S. Crossman, "Gentile Zionism and the Balfour Declaration," *Commentary* 33 (June 1962):487–94. The deep interest of high British officials in expanding imperial interest in Palestine is explored in depth in Isaiah Friedman, *The Question of Palestine, 1914–1918* (New York, 1973).

20. British ambassador in Petrograd to Russian Minister of Foreign Affairs (March 13, 1916) in Stephen Wise and Jacob deHaas, *The Great Betrayal* (New York, 1930), pp. 28–29.

21. Edwin S. Montagu, "The anti-Semitism of the Present Government" (August 23, 1917); see also his memorandum "Zionism" (October 9, 1917), both in Foreign Office Records, 371/ 3083; Memorandum by M. P. A. Hanky (October 17, 1917), ibid.; Chaim Weizmann to Secretary of State (October 24, 1917), ibid., 371/3054; Weizmann, *Trial and Error*, p. 154; Isaiah Berlin, *Chaim Weizmann* (New York, 1958), pp. 10–11.

22. Earl Graham to Lord Hardinge (September 24, 1917), Foreign Office Records, 371/3083; Manuel, *American-Palestine Relations*, p. 164.

23. DeHaas, "Brandeis in Zionism," p. 144; William Jennings Bryan to Henry Morgenthau, cable (April 27, 1915), Morgenthau MSS, Box 4; Brandeis to Morgenthau (June 25, 1915), ibid.; Brandeis to Benjamin Perlstein (February 16, 1915), Brandeis MSS, Z3–2.

24. Josephus Daniels to Brandeis (March 9, 1915), ibid., Z2–1; Manuel, *American-Palestine Relations*, pp. 138–39.

25. Ben Halpern believes that Weizmann deliberately did not keep the Provisional Committee informed, since he felt that its members did not back his pro-British maneuverings. He knew the problems involved in American neutrality and was aware that many American Jews were reportedly pro-German. ("Brandeis and the Origins of the Balfour Declaration," MS, Zionist Archives and Library, New York.) However, although the PC did not know all the details of Weizmann's negotiations, the leaders had some idea of what he was about. Horace M. Kallen had extensive contacts among the British intelligentsia, and served as a conduit for some of their ideas to Brandeis. In 1915, Alfred Zimmern was in the United States as a visiting professor at the University of Wisconsin, and he kept Kallen in touch with the British embassy. After he had returned to England, Zimmern continued to act as a contact for Kallen with Weizmann and other European Zionists.

26. Brandeis to Chaim Weizmann (December 8, 1915), Weizmann MSS; Stephen Wise to Edward M. House (January 29, 1917), in Voss, *Servant of the People*, p. 74; Manuel, *American-Palestine Relations*, p. 167. It seems that Wilson never held a particularly high opinion of Lansing's ability, and this, in fact, led to Lansing's appointment, since he supposedly would not interfere with the President being his own Secretary of State. Arthur S. Link, *Wilson: The Struggle for Neutrality, 1914–1915* (Princeton, 1960), pp. 427–28.

27. Weizmann to Brandeis, (April 8, 1917), Weizmann MSS; Stephen Wise to Jacob deHaas (April 9, 1917), deHaas MSS; Wise to Harry Friedenwald (April 9, 1917), Friedenwald MSS, A182/20.

28. Sir Mark Sykes to Arthur James Balfour (April 8, 1917), Weizmann MSS; Sykes to Ronald Graham (April 15, 1917), Foreign Office Records, 371/3052; Sykes, *Two Studies in Virtue*, pp. 195–201; Jules Cambon to Nahum Sokolow (June 14, 1917), quoted in Fannie Fern Andrews, *The Holy Land under the Mandate* (2 vols.; Boston, 1931), 1:332. Sokolow also received an audience with Pope Benedict XV on May 8, 1917, in which the Pontiff praised Zionist efforts and promised that if they secured a homeland, "We shall be good neighbors." This constituted a total turnabout from Herzl's interview with Pius X in 1904, when the Pope said: "We cannot prevent the Jews from going to Jerusalem but we could never sanction it. . . . The Jews have not recognized our Lord; therefore we cannot recognize the Jewish people."

29. Brandeis repeated this view to Sir Eric Drummond, who reported it to Balfour on April 24, 1917. Foreign Office Records, 371/3053.

30. Weizmann, *Trial and Error*, p. 193; Silverberg, *If I Forget Thee*, pp. 76–77.

31. Ronald Graham to Lord Hardinge (April 23, 1917), Foreign Office Records, 371/3052; James de Rothschild to Brandeis, cable (April 25, 1917), Brandeis MSS, Z22–2; Weizmann, Rothschild, and Joseph Cowen to Provisional Committee (April 30, 1917), ibid., Z22–1; Stein, *Balfour Declaration*, p. 426.

32. Memorandum of meeting (May 6, 1917), deHaas MSS.

33. Brandeis to Weizmann (May 6, 1917), Brandeis MSS, Z22–2; Brandeis to James de Rothschild (May 15, 1917), ibid., Brandeis to Norman Hapgood (May 14, 1917), Weizmann MSS.

34. Jacob A. Rubin, *Partners in State Building: American Jewry and Israel* (New York, 1969), p. 56; Herbert Parzan, "Brandeis and the Balfour Declaration," *Herzl Year Book* 5 (1963):328; Halpern, "Brandeis and Origins of the Balfour Declaration."

35. British idealism cannot, of course, be dismissed. There was definitely a great deal of philo–Semitism among members of the wartime Government, and one commentator has called the Balfour Declaration "the last altruistic act of a British Government." However, a very recent book by Isaiah Friedman, which extensively utilizes recently-opened Foreign Office materials, demonstrates conclusively that whatever else may have been their intentions, the men who approved the Balfour Declaration very much had imperial interests in mind. Isaiah Friedman, *The Question of Palestine, 1914–1918*, passim.

36. Abram Elkus to Brandeis (October 25, 1916), State Department Records (all citations in this chapter are to microfilm reel 79–353); Zionbureau Copenhagen to Brandeis (July 26 and August 8, 1916), Jacob deHaas to Victor Jacobson (August 1, 1916), Copenhagen Office Files, L6/85; Weizmann, *Trial and Error*, pp. 196–99; *Felix Frankfurter Reminisces*, p. 151; William Yale, "Ambassador Henry Morgenthau's Special Mission of 1917," *World Politics* 1 (April 1948):308–20. Zionist interference, as he saw it, had aborted his mission, and Morgenthau became an avowed anti-Zionist after the war.

37. Brandeis to Robert Lansing (June 2, 1917), State Department Records; Stein, *Balfour Declaration*, pp. 597–98; Wise, *Challenging Years*, p. 189. Josephus Daniels recalled that Wilson had a real commitment to the Balfour Declaration and that the President saw it not only as the rebirth of the Jewish people, "but the birth also of new ideals, of new ethical values, of new conceptions of social justice which shall spring as a blessing for all mankind from that land and that people." The phrasing could hardly have been more Brandeisian. Josephus Daniels, *The Wilson Era: Years of War and After, 1917–1923* (Chapel Hill, 1946), pp. 219–20.

38. Selig Adler believes House was anti-Semitic and two-faced, promising the Zionists one thing, then working against them. "The Palestine Question in the Wilson Era," *Jewish Social Studies* 10 (October 1948): 303–34. Richard Ned Lebow concurs that House was not as pro-Zionist as he made himself out to be to Wise and Brandeis. "Woodrow Wilson and the Balfour Declaration," *The Journal of Modern History* 40 (December 1968):501–23.

39. Minutes of War Cabinet Meeting (September 3, 1917), Foreign Office Records, 371/3083; Manuel, *American-Palestine Relations*, pp. 167–68; E. M. House to Sir Eric Drummond for Lord Robert Cecil (September 10, 1917), Foreign Office Records, 371/3083.

40. Weizmann to Harry Sachar (September 18, 1917), Weizmann MSS; Weizmann to Brandeis, two cables, (September 19, 1917), Brandeis MSS, Z22–2; Weizmann to Jacob deHaas and E. W. Lewin-Epstein (September 20, 1917), deHaas MSS; Brandeis to E. M. House (September 24, 1917), House MSS; Brandeis to Weizmann (September 26, 1917), Weizmann MSS.

41. Stein, *Balfour Declaration*, pp. 507–8; Arthur Balfour to E. M. House (October 6, 1917), Foreign Office Records, 371/3083.

42. Weizmann to Brandeis (October 7 and 10, 1917), Weizmann MSS; Stephen S. Wise, "The Balfour Declaration: Its Significance in the U.S.A." in Paul Goodman, ed., *The Jewish National Home* (London, 1943), p. 42.

43. Manuel, *American-Palestine Relations,* p. 169; Sir William Wiseman to Sir Eric Drummond (October 16, 1917), and Weizmann to Sir Ronald Clark (October 21, 1917), Foreign Office Records, 371/3083. Professor Lebow suggests that Wilson changed his mind because of the form of representation: The first time it was an informal request for his opinion; the second request was for approval of a document sent through official channels. "Wilson and the Balfour Delcaration," p. 521.

44. Norman Bentwich, "Chaim Weizmann," in Noveck, *Great Jewish Personalities,* p. 282.

45. Rappaport, "Zionism as a Factor," p. 297; Maurice Simon, ed., *Speeches, Articles and Letters of Israel Zangwill* (London, 1937), p. 331.

46. Jacob deHaas to Weizmann (December 13, 1917), Weizmann MSS; Charles Israel Goldblatt, "The Impact of the Balfour Declaration in America," *AJHQ* 57 (June 1968):476–80; *Dos Yiddishe Folk* (November 9, 1917), quoted in Rappaport, "Jewish Immigrants and World War I," p. 330.

47. CCAR *Yearbook* 28 (1918):133–34 and 30 (1920):141. For further debate with the Reform movement, see CCAR *Yearbook* 27 (1917):95, 132–39, 201–2, and UAHC *Proceedings* 9 (1916–20): 8479, 8489, 8520; David Philipson, *My Life as an American Jew* (Cincinnati, 1941), pp. 265–67, 276–77.

48. Shapiro, *Zionist Leadership,* pp. 254–55; Wiener, "Reform Judaism and Zionism," pp. 16, 42; see also Max Senior to Louis Marshall (September 30, 1918), Marshall MSS.

49. Louis Marshall to Jacob Schiff (November 14, 1917) in Reznikoff, *Marshall: Selected Papers* 2:710–11; Julian Mack to Schiff (November 26, 1917), Brandeis MSS, Z22–1.

50. The United Synagogue of America, the Conservative alliance, wanted to endorse the Declaration in 1918, but Adler, who was then president, stood opposed. To avoid a break, Israel Friedlaender, a fervent Zionist, managed to soften the wording of the resolution, but the overwhelming Zionist sentiment of the body led Adler to resign. Herbert Parzen, "Conservative Judaism and Zionism (1896–1922)," *Jewish Social Studies* 23 (October 1961):240–41.

51. Rischin, "Early Attitude of the A.J.C.," pp. 194–95, and "A.J.C. and Zionism," p. 73; Judah Magnes to Harry Schneiderman (April 10, 1918), Magnes MSS, F12/27; Schachner, *Price of Liberty,* pp. 79–80.

52. The full statement by the AJC is in Cohen, *Not Free to Desist,* pp. 109–10. Marshall and Adler had met with Secretary of State Lansing to clear the statement before its announcement; Marshall to Lansing

(April 11 and 16, 1918) and Lansing to Marshall (April 17, 1918), State Department Records.

53. Lansing to American ambassador, London (December 15, 1917), Samuel Edelman to Hugh R. Wilson (November 15, 1917), ibid.

54. Lansing to Woodrow Wilson (December 13, 1917), ibid.; Cecil Spring-Rice to Foreign Office (December 21 and 27, 1917), Foreign Office Records, 371/3054.

55. Woodrow Wilson to Stephen S. Wise (August 31, 1918), New York *Times* (September 5, 1918); Nahum Sokolow to Wilson (September 27, 1918), State Department Records. Letters also came from prominent anti-Zionists such as Rabbi Louis Grossman of the Plum Street Temple in Cincinnati, but these were in a distinct minority.

56. Lipsky, *Profiles*, p. 22; Achad Ha'am, "Introduction," *Ten Essays*, pp. xv–xvii; Kling, *Sokolow*, p. 114.

57. Laqueur, *Zionism*, p. 201.

58. Norman and Helen Bentwich, *Mandate Memories, 1918–1948* (New York, 1965), pp. 25–26.

59. Barbour, *Palestine: Star or Crescent?*, p. 69.

60. Rappaport, "Zionism as a Factor," p. 297.

61. See Robert D. Cuff, *The War Industries Board* (Baltimore, 1973), Chaps. 4–6.

62. Weizmann's comment is quoted in Silverberg, *If I Forget Thee*, p. 82; Manuel, *American-Palestine Relations*, pp. 177–78.

63. Jacob deHaas to Copenhagen Bureau (July 20, 1916), Copenhagen Office Records, L6/12(5); deHaas to Weizmann (December 7, 1917), Weizmann MSS; Robert Lansing to Woodrow Wilson (February 26, 1918), State Department Records; deHaas, "Brandeis in Zionism," p. 144.

64. Andrews, *Holy Land under Mandate* 1:327; Sokolow, Weizmann, and Tschlenow to Brandeis (January 10, 1918), Foreign Office Records, 371/3394; deHaas to Copenhagen Bureau (February 3, 1918), Copenhagen Office Files, L6/12(12); Manuel, *American-Palestine Relations*, p. 175.

65. Brandeis to Weizmann (January 13, 1918), Weizmann MSS.

66. Brandeis to Weizmann (April 5, 1918), ibid.; Nahum Sokolow to Sir Mark Sykes (June 13, 1918), Foreign Office Records, 371/3395.

67. Weizmann to Brandeis (April 25, 1918), ibid.; (June 17, 1918), Weizmann MSS; (October 31, 1918), London Office Files, Z4/244.

68. Weizmann to Nahum Sokolow (July 17, 1918), Sokolow MSS, A18/41.2(5).

69. Aaron Aaronson to Weizmann (September 25, 1918), Foreign Office Records, 371/3395.

70. See, for example, Louis Lipsky to Brandeis (December 30, 1914), Brandeis MSS, Z1–4, and letter to editor from Vladimir Jabotinsky, *Maccabean* 27 (January 1916):9.

71. Weizmann to Horace Kallen (January 24, 1915), Weizmann MSS.

72. Brandeis to Meyer Berlin (April 25 and June 15, 1915), Brandeis MSS, Z12–3; minutes of PC meetings (April 3, 1915), Magnes MSS, SP/206; Rubin, *Partners in State Building*, pp. 50–51.

73. Jacob Schiff to Israel Malten (April 24, 1917), Brandeis MSS, Z22–1; Schiff to Elisha Friedman (October 26, 1917), ibid., *Jewish Chronicle* (April 7, 1917); Adler, *Jacob Schiff* 2:308–15.

74. Louis Marshall to Adolph S. Ochs (March 5, 1919) and to Rabbi Isaac Landman (March 5, 1919), Marshall MSS, Box 1589.

75. Janowsky, *Jews and Minority Rights*, pp. 246–47; Marshall to David Philipson (March 5, 1917) in Reznikoff, *Marshall: Selected Papers* 2: 524; Marshall and Schiff to Cyrus Adler (July 16, 1917); Schiff MSS, Box 460; *Jewish Correspondent* (February 2, 1917).

76. Reznikoff, *Marshall: Selected Papers* 2:526.

77. Cohen, *Not Free to Desist*, p. 112; Schachner, *Price of Liberty*, p. 82.

78. James Parkes, *The Emergence of the Jewish Problem, 1878–1939* (London, 1946), pp. 104–5.

79. Louis Marshall and Julian Mack to Woodrow Wilson, telegram (November 11, 1918); Wilson to Joseph Tumulty (November 13, 1918); Marshall to Wilson (November 16, 1918); and Wilson to Marshall (November 20, 1918), all in Wilson MSS; Adler, *I Have Considered the Days*, pp. 314–15. Later, in the midst of all this bloodshed, Mack and Frankfurter met with one of the American Comissioners to the Peace Conference, and asked him about the chances of securing rights for Jews in Eastern Europe as part of the League of Nations Covenant; the answer was extremely pessimistic. David Hunter Miller, *My Diary at the Conference of Paris* (21 vols.; New York, 1924), 1:217.

80. Paul L. Hanna, *British Policy in Palestine* (Washington, 1942), p. 41.

81. Richard Meinertzhagen, *Middle East Diary, 1917–1956* (London, 1959), p. 51; Harry Friedenwald to Jonas Friedenwald (May 1, 1919), Friedenwald MSS, A182/13(3); memorandum (May 14, 1920), Foreign Office Records, 371/5139; John W. Davis (American ambassador to Gre t Britain) to Robert Lansing (April 22, 1920), State Department Records.

82. Stein, *Balfour Declaration*, p. 595; Wilson statement (March 3, 1919), State Department Records; Bernard Richards Memoir, COHC, p. 89.

83. Morris Jastrow, *Zionism and the Future of Palestine: The Fallacies and Dangers of Political Zionism* (New York, 1919); "Appeal to the Representatives of the United States" (January 1919), Bliss MSS, 249/853; New York *Times* (March 5, 1919); Stephen Wise to Nathan and Lena Straus (March 6, 1919) in Voss, *Servant of the People*, p. 87.

84. Manuel, *American-Palestine Relations*, pp. 219–20; Miller, *My Diary at the Conference of Paris*, 4:263–64.

85. W. L. Westermann to William C. Bullitt (March 27, 1919); Hanna Iskandar El-Khuri, "The Claims of the Jews vs. the Rights of the Palestinians," Bliss MSS, 256/897; W. M. F., "The proposed Jewish state in Palestine" (December 21, 1918), ibid., 249/853. Otis Glazebrook, the American counsel in Jerusalem who had been of much help to the Jews before the war, now had severe doubts about a Jewish state, and his dispatches in the State Department files predicted Arab outbursts and bloodshed if Zionist plans were adopted.

86. See Joseph L. Grabill, *Protestant Diplomacy and the Near East: Missionary Influence on American Policy, 1810–1927* (Minneapolis, 1971).

87. Manuel, American-Palestine Relations, pp. 234–35; New York *Times* (March 5, 1919); *Felix Frankfurter Reminisces*, pp. 155–56.

88. PC to Weizmann and Sokolow (October 26, 1917), Weizmann MSS; memorandum, "Acceptable Political Conditions" (1919), Sokolow MSS, A18/20. The statement of the Zionist delegation to the Peace Conference can be found in United States Department of State, *Papers Relating to the Foreign Relations of the United States: The Paris Peace Conference, 1919* (4 vols.; Washington, 1943), 4:161–65.

89. Bernard Richards to Jacob Schiff (April 3, 1919), Schiff MSS; Janowsky, *Jews and Minority Rights*, p. 307.

90. Frankfurter to Wilson (May 8, 1919), Frankfurter MSS.

91. Frankfurter to Wilson (May 14, 1919), Wilson to Frankfurter (May 16, 1919), ibid. Frankfurter kept Brandeis informed of this exchange, and the Zionists tried to utilize Wilson's second letter as a further statement of American policy.

92. Wilson had also received a lengthy letter from Howard Bliss, president of the American University at Beirut, urging an American commission, because the people of Syria were relying upon his ideals for justice. Wilson may have also promised Arab leaders that no Middle East settlement would be made without consulting them, and the Commission would provide a forum for their views. Harry N. Howard,

"An American Experiment in Peace Making: The King-Crane Commission," *The Moslem World* 32 (1942):124, 130.

93. See correspondence (June through August, 1920) in Urofsky and Levy, *Louis D. Brandeis Letters*, vol. 4.

94. Haber, *Odyssey*, p. 171; Crane-King to Wilson, cable (June 20, 1919), Morgenthau MSS, Box 6; Crane-King to Wilson, cable (July 10, 1919), Wilson MSS; Hanna, *British Policy*, pp. 53–54. The Commission visited 36 major towns, heard delegations from many more, and received almost 1900 petitions.

95. Wilson to Joseph Tumulty (September 1, 1919), Wilson MSS.

96. Felix Frankfurter to Andre Tardieu (January 13, 1920), London Office Files, Z4/16046; Brandeis to Wilson (February 3, 1920); Wilson to Robert Lansing (February 4, 1920), State Department Records; Jacob deHaas to Chaim Weizmann (February 5, 1920), Sokolow MSS, A18/14(5), informed the Europeans of American moves and urged them to pressure their respective governments.

97. Sheldon Whitehouse to Lansing (February 5, 1920): Lansing to Hugh Wallace (February 6, 1920), State Department Records.

98. Wallace to Lansing (February 11, 1920), Frankfurter to Frank Polk (February 18, 1920), Julian Mack to Polk (February 23, 1920), ibid.

99. Throughout this period, the Zionists kept up their pressure on different governments. Stephen Wise and Julian Mack to Woodrow Wilson (October 27, 1920), ibid.; Brandeis to Zionist Organization (April 7, 1920), London Office Files, Z4/287; Brandeis to Arthur Balfour (October 28, 1920), Foreign Office Records 371/5247; Weizmann to Balfour (July 2, 1920), ibid., 371/5036.

100. Hanna, *British Policy*, pp. 18–19.

101. Bentwich, *Mandate Memories*, pp. 25–26.

102. Laqueur, *Zionism*, p. 210; *Maccabean* 31 (January 1918):10–12; *Felix Frankfurter Reminisces*, pp. 155–56.

103. Zeine N. Zeine, *The Emergence of Arab Nationalism* (Beirut, 1966), p. 147; see also the statement of M. Chekri Ganem at the Peace Conference, *Foreign Relations of the United States* 4:1037.

104. Statement of HUC Board of Governors (May 25, 1920), quoted in Naomi Weiner Cohen, "The Reaction of Reform Judaism in America to Political Zionism (1897–1922)," *PAJHS* 40 (1950–51):382; CCAR *Yearbook* 30 (1920):107; Abba Hillel Silver to Max Heller (March 26, 1919), Silver MSS; Louis Marshall to Jacob Schiff (April 24, 1920) and to Bernard Richards (June 1, 1920), Schiff MSS; Richards to Marshall (June 23, 1920), Marshall MSS.

105. See, for example, Stephen Wise to Wilson (May 5, 1920), Wilson MSS.

106. Urofsky, *A Mind of One Piece,* pp. 121–30.

107. In an interview with Jacob deHaas in 1911, Wilson had pledged to help in the restoration of Palestine if he ever got the chance. At the Paris conference, Wilson reminded deHaas of that promise, which he had now kept, and which he felt would be "one of the few things worthwhile that will come out of all this." Halpern, "Brandeis and Balfour Declaration," p. 12.

108. Cecil Spring-Rice to Richard Gottheil (July 23, 1915), reported in Gottheil to Brandeis (July 30, 1915), Brandeis MSS, Z6–1; Stein, *Balfour Declaration,* p. 156; Thomson Gray (American consul in Egypt) to Robert Lansing (April 25, 1918), State Department Records.

NOTES TO CHAPTER SEVEN

Schism!

NOTES TO PAGES 247–252

1. William Howard Taft to Gus Karger (January 31, 1916), Karger MSS; Jacob Schiff to Thomas W. Gregory (February 17, 1916), Schiff MSS.

2. Felix Warburg to Max Senior (January 17, 1919), cited in Shapiro, *American Zionist Leadership,* p. 130; Memorandum of conference at Justice Brandeis' library (November 1, 1917), Mack MSS, File 115, reporting that Schiff said to Brandeis, "Now that we are so close we shall not part again"; Louis Marshall to Cyrus Adler (August 11, 1919), in Reznikoff, *Marshall: Selected Papers* 2:725–26.

3. Jacob deHaas to Zionist Office (November 12, 1919), Berlin Office Files, Z3/764.

4. Marshall to Rabbi Isaac Landman (December 19, 1919) in Reznikoff, *Marshall: Selected Papers* 2:536; see also Parkes, *Emergence of the Jewish Problem,* p. 118.

5. Marshall to unnamed publicist (June 6, 1923) in Reznikoff, *Marshall: Selected Papers* 2:564–65.

6. Julian Mack to Brandeis (March 8, 1920), deHaas MSS; Henry Morgenthau, "Zionism a Surrender, Not a Solution," *World's Work* 42 (July 1921):1–8 (supp.).

7. Shapiro, *American Zionist Leadership,* p. 101; Bernard Richards Memoir, COHC; *Maccabean* 31 (August 1918):246–48.

8. Ibid., 28 (July 1916):161.

9. Brandeis to Mack et al. (January 1, 1920), deHaas MSS; *Jewish Morning Journal* (July 2, 1918), quoted in Shapiro, *American Zionist Leadership,* p. 105.

10. Providence (R.I.) *Journal* (June 30, 1915).

11. Brandeis to Nathan D. Kaplan (November 29, 1915), Brandeis MSS, Z3–1.

12. *Maccabean* 30 (August 1917):311.

13. Minutes of meeting, Provisional Committee (May 25, 1918), de-Haas MSS.

14. *Maccabean* 31 (August 1918):251–52; the text of the new ZOA constitution can be found at pp. 258–60.

15. Meyer Berlin, "The Week in Pittsburgh" and Nachman Syrkin, "The Triumph of Social Democracy," *Maccabean* 31 (August 1918):24–48 and 248–50; Learsi, *Fulfillment*, p. 209.

16. Shapiro, *American Zionist Leadership*, pp. 124–27.

17. Weizmann, *Trial and Error*, p. 241; Weizmann to Brandeis (November 24, 1915); Brandeis to Weizmann (November 29, 1917), Felix Frankfurter to Weizmann (November 2, 1918), all in Weizmann MSS; Weizmann and Sokolow to Brandeis (November 13, 1918), London Office Files, Z4/244.

18. Weizmann, *Trial and Error*, p. 176; Richard H. S. Crossman, *A Nation Reborn* (New York, 1960), pp. 11, 14–15; Speech at Harlem banquet (April 10, 1923) in Chaim Weizmann, *American Addresses* (New York, 1923), p. 21.

19. Laqueur, *Zionism*, p. 472; *Felix Frankfurter Reminisces*, p. 184; Edward Warburg interview, Hebrew University Oral History Collection.

20. Norman Angell, "Weizmann's Approach to the British Mind" in Meyer Weisgal, *Chaim Weizmann* (New York, 1944), pp. 83–84; author's interview with Emanuel Neumann.

21. Jacob deHaas to Weizmann, cable (November 18, 1918), London Office Files, Z4/244; see also memorandum, "Acceptable Political Conditions," n.d. (1918), Sokolow MSS, A18/20.

22. Weizmann to Brandeis (November 29, 1918), Weizmann MSS; Weizmann and A. Aaronson to Brandeis (December 5, 1918), London Office Files, Z4/244.

23. Memorandum of conference, Stephen Wise, Mary Fels, Chaim Weizmann, and Charles Cowan (January 6, 1919), Sokolow MSS, A18/14(5).

24. Report of Rabbi Wise to National Executive Committee (February 1 and 9, 1919), ibid.

25. Felix Frankfurter to Brandeis, two cables (June 2, 1919 and June 6, 1919); Brandeis to Frankfurter (June 9, 1919), State Department Records, reel 79–353; Brandeis to Alice Goldmark Brandeis (June 22, 1919), Brandeis MSS, M3–3; memorandum of meeting between Bran-

deis and Arthur Balfour (June 24, 1919), Wise MSS (AJA), notes on reception for Brandeis by members of the Actions Comité (June 24, 1919), Wise MSS.

26. For Brandeis' personal impressions of his trip, see the series of letters to his wife during July and August 1919 in Brandeis MSS, M4–3, and published in *Letters of Louis D. Brandeis*, Vol. 4.

27. Brandeis to Alice Goldmark Brandeis (July 8 and 10, 1919). Brandeis visited Weizmann's family in Haifa and wrote: "Palestine has won our hearts and souls. It is no wonder that the Jews love her so." Brandeis to Weizmann (July 20, 1919), Weizmann MSS. See also deHaas, *Brandeis*, p. 116; Boston *Post* (June 25, 1923); Robert Szold, *77 Great Russell Street* (privately printed, n.p., n.d.), p. 9.

28. Memorandum from Major General Money, chief administrator, marked "Secret" (July 26, 1919), Sokolow MSS, A18/14(5).

29. Silverberg, *If I Forget Thee*, p. 99; Bentwich, *Mandate Memories*, pp. 51–52; deHaas, *Brandeis*, p. 118.

30. ZOA press release, translating report of Dr. Auerbach in Haifa from *Juedische Rundschau* (June 13, 1919, dated September 12, 1919), Berlin Office Files, Z3/764; Henrietta Szold to her family (September 14, 1920), in Lowenthal, *Szold: Life and Letters*, pp. 146–47.

31. See Samuel Haber, *Efficiency and Uplift: Scientific Management in the Progressive Era* (Chicago, 1964).

32. The Zionists also secured an additional two hundred thousand dollars from the JDC for the Medical Unit. Shapiro, *American Zionist Leadership*, pp. 140–44.

33. DeHaas, *Brandeis*, pp. 119–20.

34. See, for example, deHaas to Brandeis (January 22 and February 21, 1919) and Brandeis to R. D. Kesselman (December 15, 1919), deHaas MSS.

35. Emanuel Neumann, "Causes of the Conflict: A Statement of Facts," *New Maccabean* 1 (June 1, 1921):51.

36. Very little of the tension between American and European leaders surfaced even at the 1919 ZOA convention in Chicago, although there was a great deal of criticism about the Brandeis/Mack regime's "dictatorial" habits, high-handedness, and lack of consultation with its followers. Even critics of the administration, however, such as Emanuel Neumann, did not claim that they wanted to overthrow the Brandeis/Mack group; rather, they wanted to introduce greater democracy into the Zionist movement. The official summary of the convention noted: "Whatever injustices there may have been in the criticism of the [Brandeis/Mack] administration, it was, generally speaking, reducible

to the charge that habits of action created by war conditions had been continued after war conditions had disappeared." Louis Lipsky, "From Words to Deeds: A Review of the Chicago Convention," *Maccabean* 32 (December 1919):322. See also Emanuel Neumann, "Zionist Democracy," ibid., pp. 337–38.

37. Stephen Wise to Brandeis (January 19, 1920), Brandeis MSS, Z27–2; Julian Mack to Jacob deHaas (March 13, 1920), deHaas MSS.

38. Minutes of NEC (February 12, 1920), London Office Files, Z4/16046. Only Emanuel Neumann and Morris Rothenberg questioned the wisdom of the plan, Rothenberg because he felt other American groups should be included to sponsor the corporation, and Neumann because he feared that an independent corporation would undermine the authority of the WZO.

39. Frankfurter to Weizmann (March 8, 1918 and May 22, 1920), Weizmann MSS; Frankfurter and Julian Mack to Weizmann (October 1, 1919), London Office Files, Z4/16046; Frankfurter to Weizmann (May 15, 1920), Sokolow MSS, A18/14(5).

40. Jacob deHaas to Zionistische Centralbureau (January 8, 1920), Berlin Office Files, Z3/764; deHaas to Julian Mack (March 24, 1920), deHaas MSS.

41. ZOA per M. Lowenthal to WZO, London (April 13 and June 8, 1920), London Office Files, Z4/1523.

42. Stephen Wise to Brandeis (June 2, 1920), Brandeis MSS, Z27–2; M. Lazarus to Weizmann (June 9, 1920), Weizmann MSS.

43. Julius Simon, *Certain Days* (Jerusalem, 1971), pp. 98–101; Simon to Benjamin I. Brodie (November 14, 1964), Brodie MSS, A251/259.

44. Bernard Rosenblatt interview, Hebrew University Oral History Collection; Julius Simon to Benjamin I. Brodie (November 14, 1964) and Brodie to Simon (December 8, 1964), Brodie MSS, A251/259.

45. The National Executive Committee, at a special meeting on May 9, and 10, had passed several resolutions concerning the goals of the delegation to the London conference. The NEC wanted the delegation to urge adoption of the Pittsburgh Platform as the basic plan for rebuilding Palestine; request the WZO to urge Great Britain to open immigration immediately; urge the WZO to establish public sanitation and medical work; establish an experimental station; and to get the WZO to adopt a budget system. *New Palestine* 1 (May 14, 1920):1.

46. Julian Mack to Jacob deHaas (June 24, 1920), and deHaas to Mack (June 22 and 23, 1920), deHaas MSS: minutes of meeting of WZO Executive (June 22, 1920), Weizmann MSS. Shortly after the London Conference, Robert Kesselman, the accountant sent over to Palestine by the ZOA, reported that the Zionist Commission was over-

drawn on its account by $30,000, and unless that sum could be made up, and quickly, it might ruin the Anglo-Palestine Bank. Bernard Flexner to Felix Frankfurter (August 19, 1920), Flexner MSS.

47. Shapiro, *American Zionist Leadership*, p. 146.

48. DeHaas, *Brandeis*, pp. 233–34.

49. Author's interview with Emanuel Neumann; Lipsky, *Profiles*, p. 162; Bodenheimer, *Prelude to Israel*, pp. 290–91; Bernard Richards interview, Hebrew University Oral History Collection; Martin Rosenbluth, *Go Forth and Serve* (New York, 1961), p. 190.

50. Frankfurter to Weizmann (July 15, 1920), Weizmann MSS; Simon, *Certain Days*, p. 103; *Statement of Justice Brandeis to the American Delegation to the Zionist Conference at London, July 14, 1920* (New York, 1920).

51. Alexander Sachs to Julian Mack (July 22, 1920), deHaas MSS.

52. Stephen Wise to Julian Mack (August 11, 1920) Mack to Wise (August 13, 1920), Louis Lipsky to Brandeis (August 17, 1920), minutes of NEC (August 29, 1920), all in ibid.

53. Minutes of NEC (September 29–30, 1920), ibid.

54. See daily digest of Yiddish press (October and November 1920), Brandeis MSS, ScB–3.

55. Statement by Benjamin V. Cohen, London *Evening Standard* (November 22, 1920), copy in London Office Files, Z4/820(1); Vladimir Jabotinsky to Weizmann (October 7, 1920), Jabotinsky MSS; Brandeis to Weizmann (November 22, 1920), Weizmann MSS.

56. Buffalo *Courier* (November 25, 1920).

57. F. Lubin to Weizmann (November 29, 1920), Weizmann MSS; S. Dingol, article in *Der Tag* (November 30, 1920), quoted in Shapiro, *American Zionist Leadership*, p. 163.

58. Szold, *77 Great Russell Street*, pp. 4–6.

59. Simon, *Certain Days*, pp. 110–11; the best account of the Reorganization Commission is the essay by Evyatar Friesel, "The Impossible Mediation," *Certain Days*, pp. 141–68. See also *Report of the Re-Organization Commission of the Executive of the Zionist Organization on the Work of the Zionist Organization in Palestine* (New York, 1921); the letter of resignation is in *New Palestine* 1 (May 13, 1921):2.

60. Weizmann, *Trial and Error*, p. 262; Weizmann to Mack (January 6, 1921), Weizmann MSS; *Jewish Morning Journal* (March 14, 1921).

61. *Der Zeit* (March 2, 1921), in daily digest of Yiddish press (March 4, 1921), Brandeis MSS, ScB–3; Louis Robinson to Weizmann (August 19, 1920), Nahum Sokolow to Weizmann (October 3, 1920), Bernard Rosenblatt to Weizmann (February 8, 1921), all in Weizmann MSS.

62. A. Goldberg to Julian Mack (March 26, 1921), quoted in Shapiro, *American Zionist Leadership,* pp. 106–7.

63. Ibid., p. 168; Weizmann, *Trial and Error,* p. 267.

64. Mack to Weizmann (April 1, 1921), Weizmann MSS; Lipsky, *Profiles,* pp. 56–57; Bernard Richards Memoir, COHC; Haber, *Odyssey,* p. 183.

65. "Summary of Conference between Dr. Weizmann and Judge Mack and their associates, April 4–9, 1921," and minutes of NEC (April 9–10, 1921), Weizmann MSS; memorandum, "Negotiations between Dr. Weizmann and the Zionist Organization of America" (May 29, 1921), London Office Files, Z4/303(9).

66. Louis Marshall to Weizmann (April 14, 1921), ibid.; Bernard Rosenblatt to Weizmann (April 15, 1921), Weizmann MSS; Louis Marshall to James H. Becker (March 19, 1923) in Reznikoff, *Marshall: Selected Papers* 2:731.

67. Weizmann, "Address to N.E.C." (April 16, 1921), London Office Files, Z4/303(1).

68. *Jewish Daily News* (April 19, 1921); Weizmann to Zionbureau (April 17, 1921), Weizmann MSS; statement of Keren Hayesod delegation (April 18, 1921) and circular letter, Julian Mack to ZOA members (April 17, 1921) in London Office Files, Z4/303(2); Rosenblatt interview, Hebrew University Oral History Collection.

69. Weizmann received numerous cables from London urging him to reach some agreement; although he and Mack exchanged one more round of letters, they could not get together. Weizmann to Mack (April 24, 1921) and the reply dated the following morning, Weizmann MSS.

70. Lipsky to Mack (April 19, 1921), copy in Magnes MSS, F43/L231; Stephen Wise to Felix Frankfurter (April 18, 1921) in Voss, *Servant of the People,* p. 104. The hardening line can be seen even among lesser figures. Alexander Sachs, one of the administrative secretaries, declared that the Weizmann group could not be trusted, so the leadership should adopt a firm stance and not budge. Sachs to Jacob deHaas (March 9, 1921), Mack MSS, File 114.

71. Memorandum of telephone conversation, Brandeis and Mack (April 15, 1921), Mack MSS, File 119. Brandeis definitely underestimated the force of emotion and counted on logic prevailing. He met with Albert Einstein later in the month and sent him data on the misuse of Zionist monies, assuming this would influence a rational scientist. It did, but not to the extent that he expected. Brandeis to Einstein (April 29, 1921) and to deHaas, same date, ibid.

72. Meyer Weisgal, . . . *So Far: An Autobiography* (Jerusalem, 1971), p. 58; Emanuel Neumann to Weizmann (May 27, 1921), London Office Files, Z4/303(4); Weizmann, speech to New York organizations (May 15, 1921), Weizmann MSS; editorial, *New Maccabean* (May 13, 1921); Boris Goldberg, "The Crisis in American Zionism," *Ha'aretz* (May 2, 1921).

73. *Report of the Proceedings of the 24th Annual Convention of the Zionist Organization of America* (New York, 1921); Mack's speech can be found on pp. 5–12.

74. Bernard Rosenblatt interview, Hebrew University Oral History Collection.

75. *Report of Proceedings,* pp. 119–21. On June 19, Brandeis also sent in his resignation as honorary president of the World Zionist Organization.

76. *American Israelite* (June 16, 1921), cited in Goldblatt, "Impact of Balfour Declaration," p. 489; S. M. Melamed, "L. D. Brandeis and Chaim Weizmann," *Reflex* 2 (May 1928):6; Lipsky, *Profiles,* p. 153.

77. "The Jewish State and the Jewish Problem," *Ten Essays,* p. 44.

78. *Felix Frankfurter Reminisces,* p. 180; Bernard Rosenblatt interview, Hebrew University Oral History Collection; Eisig Silberschlag, "Zionism and Hebraism in America (1897–1921)" in Meyer, *Early History of Zionism,* pp. 336–37.

79. Weizmann to Herbert Samuel (August 8, 1920), Weizmann MSS; Maurice Samuel, *Level Sunlight* (New York, 1953), pp. 30, 47.

NOTES TO CHAPTER EIGHT

The "Pact of Glory"

NOTES TO PAGES 301–307

1. Leonard Dinnerstein, *The Leo Frank Case* (New York, 1968).

2. Rosenstock, *Louis Marshall*, pp. 217, 205.

3. Ibid., p. 43; Steinberg, "How Quotas Began," p. 69; Shapiro, *American Zionist Leadership*, pp. 248–50. In a survey, respondents ranked Eastern European Jews poorly in terms of desirable citizenship traits.

4. Cohen, *Progress of Zionism*, p. 32; Silverberg, *If I Forget Thee*, p. 108.

5. *Autobiography of Nahum Goldmann*, p. 107.

6. Cohen, *Progress of Zionism*, pp. 14–15; Silverberg, *If I Forget Thee*, p. 111; Weizmann, *Trial and Error*, pp. 290–91.

7. Henrietta Szold to her family (June 22, 1921) and to Thomas Seltzer (January 25, 1922) in Lowenthal, *Szold: Life and Letters*, pp. 170–71, 183–84, 202–3; Laqueur, *Zionism*, p. 338; Ruppin, *Memoirs*, p. 199.

8. Bernard Rosenblatt interview, Hebrew University Oral History Collection; William F. Spiegelman, "From Cleveland to Cleveland," *New Palestine* 18 (June 27, 1930):405.

9. "An Unpleasant Task," ibid., 2 (February 24, 1922):113.

10. Jacob deHaas, memorandum, "Review of Z.O.A. Finances" (November 3, 1927), Mack MSS, File 115; Bernard Richards to Weizmann (July 7, 1922), Weizmann MSS; Vladimir Jabotinsky to Zionist Executive (February 13, 1922), Jabotinsky MSS; Louis Lipsky to Joseph Cowen (May 18, 1922), London Office Files, Z4/764.

11. Abraham Tulin to Leonard Stein (June 23, 1922), Weizmann MSS.

12. Lipsky to Zionist Executive (June 15 and November 22, 1921, April 19, 1923), Executive to Lipsky (December 24, 1921, February 7 and December 3, 1922), all in London Office Files.

13. Manuel, *American-Palestine Relations,* pp. 275–76; Zionist delegation to WZO Executive (November 27, 1921), Foreign Office Records, 371/6386.

14. Philipson, *Life as an American Jew,* pp. 299–305.

15. New York *Times* (May 7, 1922).

16. A. E. Southard (consul in Jerusalem) to Secretary of State (May 4 and June 4, 1921); Near Eastern Division to Secretary (July 1, 1921), State Department Records, reel 79–353.

17. Quoted in Irwin Oder, "American Zionism and the Congressional Resolution of 1922 on Palestine," *PAJHS* 45 (1955–56):42.

18. Hanna, *British Policy in Palestine,* p. 65; Manuel, *American-Palestine Relations,* pp. 288–89.

19. Manuel, *American-Palestine Relations,* p. 278.

20. The text of the resolution can be found in Adler and Margolith, *With Firmness in the Right,* p. 84.

21. Manuel, *American-Palestine Relations,* pp. 281–84.

22. Oscar I. Janowsky, "The Rise of the State of Israel" in Finkelstein, *The Jews* 2:693.

23. Spiegelman, "From Cleveland to Cleveland," p. 403.

24. Jabotinsky to Keren Hayesod directors (January 15, 1922), Jabotinsky MSS. Interestingly enough, the Brandeis group also disapproved of these mass drives, since they put such an emphasis on giving, without any thought to commitment. See Stephen Wise to Julian Mack (January 22, 1923) in Voss, *Servant of the People,* p. 119.

25. Weizmann to Fred Kisch (April 3, 1923), Weizmann MSS.

26. Jacob deHaas to Brandeis (March 22, 1923), Brandeis MSS, ScB–3; Arthur Ruppin to Shlomo Kaplansky (February 1, 1924), Weizmann MSS.

27. Weizmann to Joseph Cowan (December 21, 1923), Weizmann MSS.

28. Louis Marshall to Henry Cohen (February 6, 1925) in Reznikoff, *Marshall: Selected Papers* 2:745.

29. Felix Warburg to Louis Marshall (July 12, 1923), Warburg MSS, Box 213.

30. Halperin, *Political World of American Zionism,* p. 119; diary entry for November 14, 1922 in Ruppin, *Memoirs,* p. 201; see also Bentwich, *Mandate Memories,* p. 83.

31. Weizmann, *Trial and Error,* pp. 309–11.

32. The complete text of the Mandate can be found in Raphael Patai, ed., *Encyclopedia of Zionism and Israel* (New York, 1971), 2:757–60.

33. Weizmann to Rabbi A. A. Neumann (February 11, 1924), Weizmann MSS.

34. Weizmann to Actions Comité (February 14, 1924), ibid.

35. A summary of the proceedings, including verbatim transcripts of the more important speeches, can be found in *Zionist Review* 7 (April 1924):supplement, copy ibid.

36. *Der Tag* (February 18, 1924), cited in Sam Z. Chinitz, "The Jewish Agency and the Jewish Community in the United States," masters essay, Columbia University (1959), p. 26; Weizmann to Executive (February 19, 1924) and Ruppin to Executive (February 22, 1924), Weizmann MSS.

37. Chinitz, "Jewish Agency," p. 27; Louis Marshall to Weizmann (February 23, 1924), Weizmann MSS.

38. Weizmann, *Trial and Error,* p. 306.

39. See, for example, Weizmann to Berthold Feiwel (January 15, 1924), Weizmann MSS; Marshall to Henry Cohen (February 16, 1925) in Reznikoff, *Marshall: Selected Papers* 2:746.

40. Allan I. Freehling, "The American Jewish Community's Reaction to the Fluctuating Immigration Policy of the United States Congress," rabbinic thesis, Hebrew Union College-Jewish Institute of Religion (1967), pp. 69–70.

41. Nahum Sokolow to Weizmann (June 23, 1922), Weizmann MSS; Stephen Wise to Harry Friedenwald (October 12, 1925), Friedenwald MSS, A182/20; see also Jacob Billikopf to Max Steur (September 14, 1927), Silver MSS.

42. Chinitz, "The Jewish Agency," pp. 42–44.

43. Ibid., pp. 45–46.

44. Weizmann to Louis Lipsky (March 18, 1926) and to Samuel Untermyer (November 9, 1925), Weizmann MSS.

45. Felix Warburg to Fred Kisch (April 23, 1926) and Louis Marshall to Warburg (April 5, 1926), ibid.; see also Marshall to Emanuel Neumann (December 22, 1925) in Reznikoff, *Marshall: Selected Papers* 2:749.

46. Marshall to Chaim Weizmann (May 28, 1926), Weizmann MSS.

47. Julian Mack to Felix Warburg (December 24, 1926), Mack MSS, File 115.

48. Chinitz, "The Jewish Agency," p. 58.

49. *New Palestine* 17 (March 15, 1929):228.

50. Edward Warburg interview, Hebrew University Oral History Collection; Lee K. Frankel to Felix Warburg (February 6, 1930), Warburg MSS.

51. Ruppin, *Memoirs,* p. 255; Parkes, *Emergence of Jewish Problem,* p. 81.

52. Goldmann, *Autobiography*, pp. 102–3.

53. Syrkin, *Syrkin*, p. 214; *New Palestine* 17 (February 1, 1929):64.

54. E. Neumann, "What of the Agency?," ibid., 10 (January 15, 1926):55–57.

55. CCAR *Yearbook* 30 (1920):107; 32 (1922):24.

56. Rosenstock, *Marshall*, p. 44.

57. Chinitz, "The Jewish Agency," p. 75.

58. *American Israelite* (March 4, 1920).

59. Ben Halpern believes that the program espoused by Weizmann in 1929 was not significantly different from his views of a decade earlier. While this may be so, the rhetoric used by Weizmann certainly differed in 1921 and 1929, and by the end of the decade he had adopted Brandeisian proposals even while continuing to damn Brandeis.

60. Rosenblatt, *Two Generations of Zionism*, pp. 125, 134–35; Laqueur, *Zionism*, p. 470; Weizmann, *Trial and Error*, p. 339.

61. *New Palestine* 17 (January 25, 1929):53; Böhm, *Die Zionistische Bewegung* 2:217, 232, 582.

62. *Der Tag* (June 16, 1929), quoted in Shapiro, *American Zionist Leadership*, p. 197.

NOTES TO CHAPTER NINE

Hollow Victory

NOTES TO PAGES 335–341

1. Brandeis to Robert W. Bruere (February 25, 1922), Frankfurter MSS; see also Urofsky, *A Mind of One Piece,* pp. 151–59.

2. Meeting on June 10, 1921, in deHaas, *Brandeis,* p. 273.

3. *American Hebrew* (September 9, 1921); Learsi, *Fulfillment,* pp. 231–32; Haber, *Odyssey of an American Zionist,* p. 188.

4. Szold, *77 Great Russell Street,* p. 8; Brandeis personally gave more than $750,000 to PEF.

5. Julian Mack to Herbert Lehman (October 7, 1921), Silver MSS.

6. Author's interview with Robert Szold (March 21, 1972); A. H. Silver memoirs, Silver MSS.

7. Shapiro, *American Zionist Leadership,* p. 190.

8. Memorandum (December 4, 1921), Silver MSS; Vladimir Jabotinsky to Pinhas Rutenberg (May 14, 1922), Jabotinsky MSS.

9. Memorandum of private conference between Jabotinsky and Julius Simon (May 26, 1922); Julian Mack to Rutenberg (May 29, 1922), Jabotinsky MSS.

10. Weizmann to Berthold Feiwel (March 12, 1923), Weizmann MSS.

11. Arthur Ruppin to Weizmann (February 28, 1924), ibid.

12. Ruppin to Zionist Executive (January 15, 1924), ibid. The League consisted of local versions of the PDC, and once a minimum amount had been subscribed, that League would be entitled to a seat on the Council. The experiment was a complete failure.

13. See, for example, open letter of N. S. Burstein to Brandeis (July 25, 1921), in *Israel's Messenger* (October 2, 1921), Brandeis MSS, ScB–2; see also Harry Friedenwald to Brandeis (March 16, 1922), Friedenwald MSS, A182/28.

14. Jabotinsky to Mack (March 28, 1922), Jabotinsky MSS; "Negotiations with the Brandeis-Mack Group," memorandum by Jabotinsky (June 13, 1922), London Office Files, Z4/303(12).

15. Rosenblatt, *Two Generations of Zionism*, pp. 102–3; author's interview with Emanuel Neumann.

16. Rose Jacobs, "Justice Brandeis and Hadassah," *New Palestine* 32 (November 14, 1941):17–19.

17. Henrietta Szold to Alice Seligsberg (June 20, 1921), quoted in Donald Herbert Miller, "A History of Hadassah, 1912–1935," doctoral dissertation, New York University (1968), p. 123. The seven women were Ruth Fromenson, Caroline Greenfield, Rose Jacobs, Dora Lefkowitz, Alice Seligsberg, Minnie Sobel, and Bertha Weinheim.

18. Ibid., pp. 140–41. Henrietta Szold and many other women in the leadership, as well as the entire Young Hadassah movement, went in quite strongly for self-education, and since 1948 the regular Hadassah program has been more concerned with educating its members about Israel and Jewish affairs. But in the 1920s the organization stood staunchly opposed to having its money used for anything but health care in Palestine.

19. Shapiro, *American Zionist Leadership*, p. 200.

20. "Pervasive Propaganda," *New Palestine* 10 (January 8, 1926):29; Maurice Samuel, "Fundamentals Regarding the Jewish Agency," ibid., (12 March 1926):246–49. See also "Strengthening the Organization," ibid., (9 April 1926):319.

21. Emanuel Neumann, "What of the Agency?," ibid., (January 15, 1926):56.

22. Miller, "Hadassah," pp. 140–64, passim.

23. Stephen Wise to Brandeis (August 27, 1925), Brandeis MSS, ScB–3; Horace Kallen to Wise (December 16, 1926), Wise MSS (AJA).

24. Robert Szold to Julian Mack (January 6, 1925), Mack MSS, Box 1; author's interview with Robert Szold (March 21, 1972); Brandeis to deHaas (June 5, 1927), deHaas MSS.

25. Brandeis to deHaas (December 24, 1927), Mack MSS, File 96.

26. Norvin Lindheim to Weizmann (June 7, 1927), Weizmann MSS; Robert Szold to Zip Szold (June 22, 1927), Mack MSS, File 115; Stephen Wise to his children (1927), *Personal Letters*, pp. 211–12; "Summary Report of the 30th Annual Convention of the Z.O.A.," *New Palestine* 13 (July 15, 1927):5–24.

27. Shapiro, *American Zionist Leadership*, ch. 8.

28. See, for example, Mario Puzo's fine fictional treatment of this in *The Fortunate Pilgrim* (New York, 1964), which deals with an immigrant Italian community.

29. *The Day* (May 5, 1928), quoted in Shapiro, *American Zionist Leadership,* p. 208.

30. Ibid., pp. 207–12.

31. Weizmann to Louis Lipsky (November 11, 1927), Lipsky to Felix Rosenblueth (December 29, 1927), London Office Files, Z4/3215(1).

32. Brandeis to deHaas (November 2, 1927), deHaas MSS.

33. As David Levy has reminded me, Brandeis knew all about the uses of propaganda, and had utilized it effectively in his earlier reform battles in Massachusetts. The difference is that he had always utilized publicity around specific events, in order to move the public to action. The Europeans, on the other hand, spoke of propaganda as a continuous stream of information designed to raise levels of consciousness, to create *stimmung.* In the fight between the differing wings of American Zionism, the Brandeisists deplored what they considered the aimlessness and futility of merely creating *stimmung,* while the Lipskyites saw it as part of *gegenwartsarbeit,* the development of Jewish culture and feeling in the Diaspora.

34. Samuel J. Rosensohn and Lawrence Berenson to ZOA Administrative Committee (March 19, 1928); Weizmann to Eder, Feiwel, and Rosenblueth (March 21, 1928), Weizmann MSS.

35. New York *Times* (March 31, 1928); Louis Lipsky, "The Zionist Controversy—Hadassah Leaders and Their Methods," *New Palestine* 14 (April 27, 1928):451–53; Miller, "Hadassah," p. 164.

36. Ibid., p. 165.

37. Julian Mack to Abba Hillel Silver (May 7, 1928), Silver MSS.

38. Edward Lazansky, Mitchell May, Grover M. Moscovitz, and Otto A. Rosalsky to Chaim Weizmann (June 1928), Friedenwald MSS, A182/30(1); Robert Szold to Henrietta Szold (July 24, 1928), R. Szold MSS.

39. Weizmann to Blanche Dugdale (April 4, 1928), to Zionist Executive (April 10 and 23, 1928), and to Felix Warburg (March 23, 1928), Weizmann MSS.

40. Shapiro, *American Zionist Leadership,* p. 237. It may seem strange that, if the Jewish Agency embodied so many of the Brandeis group's proposals, so many people like Wise and deHaas opposed it. The original plan put forward by Brandeis in 1920 envisioned bringing in non-Zionists to work with the World Zionist Organization, but with the ultimate power to set policy residing in the Zionist Congress. The

Agency plan gave 50 percent of the seats to non-Zionists, and since they would raise most of the money needed for Palestinian work, they could dominate the Agency and strip the Zionists of all their power.

41. Baruch Zuckerman, "The Split in the Z.O.A.," memorandum (1928), London Office Files, Z4/3215(1).

42. Shapiro, *American Zionist Leadership,* pp. 228–29; "New Zionism for Old: An Interview with Abraham Goldberg," *New Palestine* 14 (February 19, 1928):201, 211; "An Ideal Not a Plan: An Interview with Dr. Abraham Coralnik," ibid. (March 2, 1928):262.

43. Ibid. (June 8, 1928):593–94.

44. Miller, "Hadassah," pp. 172–76.

45. Robert Szold to Henrietta Szold (July 24, 1928), R. Szold MSS; Herbert Solow, "The Vindication of Jewish Idealism," *Menorah Journal* 15 (September 1928):259–70; Zalman Yoffeh, "Peace in American Zionism," ibid. 19 (October 1920):51.

46. Shapiro, *American Zionist Leadership,* pp. 223–25; for commentary on this charge of "Nordicism" see A. H. Fromenson, "The Real Cause of the Zionist Controversy," *Jewish Tribune* (June 22, 1928).

47. For the Revisionist movement, see Joseph B. Schechtman and Yehuda Benari, *History of the Revisionist Movement* (Tel Aviv, 1970), as well as Schechtman's two-volume *The Jabotinsky Story* (New York, 1956, 1961).

48. Chaim Arlosoroff to Weizmann, open letter, (May 1, 1928), London Office Files, Z4/3215(1).

49. Miller, "Hadassah," pp. 176–79.

50. "Summary Report of the 32nd Annual Convention," *New Palestine* 17 (July 19, 1929):11–44.

51. Jacob deHaas to members of ZOA Reorganization Committee (January 31, 1929), Friedenwald MSS, A182/30(1); Chaim Arlosoroff to Felix Rosenblueth (March 1, 1929), London Office Files, Z4/3215(2), later published as a highly controversial pamphlet.

52. Mordecai Kaplan, "Our Zionist Program," *New Palestine* 16 (March 15, 1929):219–20; see also the fuller development of his thought in *Judaism as a Civilization* (New York, 1934); "The Future of the Z.O.A.," *New Palestine* 17 (November 29, 1929):451–52.

53. Morris S. Lazaron to Abba Hillel Silver (October 1, 1928), Silver MSS; Stephen Wise to Nahum Goldmann (July 11, 1928) in Voss, *Servant of the People,* p. 156; Jacob deHaas to Wise (February 1, 1929), Mack MSS, Box 2.

54. Halperin, *Political World of American Zionism,* p. 17.

55. Minutes of meeting among Justice Brandeis, Felix M. Warburg, and Bernard Flexner (September 19, 1929), Frankfurter MSS.

56. New York *Times* (November 25, 1929); *Jewish Tribune* (November 29, 1929).

57. Ibid. (December 20, 1929); see also, for example, *Jewish Guardian* (November 21, 1929) and Detroit *Jewish Chronicle* (December 6, 1929); Louis D. Brandeis, "The Will to a Jewish Palestine," *New Palestine* 17 (November 29, 1929):454–55.

58. Louis I. Newman, "Will American Zionism Destroy Itself?," *Jewish Tribune* (February 21, 1930); for a rebuttal of Newman's charges, see S. M. Margoshes, "Dame Gossip Struts Again," ibid., (February 28, 1930).

59. Jacob deHaas to Brandeis (March 21, 1930), deHaas MSS; statement by Abraham Goldberg, *Jewish Tribune* (April 4, 1930).

60. Brandeis et al. to Nathan Ratnoff et al. (May 22, 1930), reprinted as "Brandeis Defines Terms," *New Palestine* 18 (May 30, 1930):338–39.

61. *The Day* (May 24, 1930) and the *Jewish Morning Journal* (May 25, 1930), both reprinted ibid., pp. 339–40.

62. Detroit *Jewish Chronicle* (June 20, 1930); *Jewish Tribune* (May 30, 1930).

63. Stephen Wise to Lee and Justine Polier (March 20, 1929), Weizmann MSS.

64. Yoffeh, "Peace in American Zionism," pp. 50–62; "The Cleveland Convention," *New Palestine* 19 (July 25, 1930):4–26.

65. See, for example, Detroit *Jewish Chronicle* (July 11, 1930); Cincinnati *Every Friday* (July 11, 1930); *Jewish Layman* (September 1930); Weizmann to Brandeis (July 4, 1930), London Office Files, Z4/3215(2).

66. Fred Kisch to Weizmann (June 10, 1930), Weizmann MSS.

67. Brandeis to Julian Mack (July 5, 1930), Mack MSS, File 93. See, among others, Robert Szold, "An Economic Program," *New Palestine* 19 (September 19, 1930):70–71; Israel Brodie, "Palestine's Economic Future," (October 3, 1930):94–96; Szold, "The Economic Approach," 20 (May 15, 1931):138.

68. Halperin, *Political World of American Zionism*, p. 13.

NOTES TO CHAPTER TEN

Impending Catastrophe

1. William E. Leuchtenburg, *Franklin D. Roosevelt and the New Deal, 1932–1940* (New York, 1963), pp. 1–3; Cabell Phillips, *From the Crash to the Blitz, 1929–1939* (New York, 1969), pp. 34–35.

2. Silverberg, *If I Forget Thee, O Jerusalem*, p. 135; Robert Szold to Brandeis (March 19, 1931), Mack MSS, File 4; "Annual Report of the Z.O.A.," *New Palestine* 21 (November 6, 1931):42–49.

3. "Annual Report of the Z.O.A.," *New Palestine* 22 (July 1932):1; Miller, "Hadassah," pp. 189–90.

4. Weizmann to Felix Warburg (November 28, 1931), Weizmann MSS.

5. New York *Times* (August 14 and September 6, 1931).

6. *New Palestine* 20 (May 1, 1931):118.

7. Stephen S. Wise, "Plain Speaking About Zionism," ibid., 21 (October 2, 1931):20; see also the following issue October 9–16:26–27, 31–33.

8. Author's interview with Mrs. Charlotte Jacobson (March 23, 1973).

9. Barry Silverberg, "Judah L. Magnes and the Idea of a Bi-National State," seminar paper, State University of New York at Albany (December 1972).

10. The classic statement regarding Arab nationalism is George Antonius, *The Arab Awakening* (London, 1938), but Albert Memmi, *The Colonizer and the Colonized* (New York, 1965) does much to explain the intellectual and emotional attitudes of a society in which one group is progressing at the seeming expense of the other.

11. Laqueur, *Zionism*, p. 248.

12. Parliamentary Papers, Cmd. 1700 (1922).

13. Bentwich, *Mandate Memories*, p. 91; Manuel, *American-Palestine Relations*, pp. 301–2.

14. Laqueur, *Zionism*, pp. 490–91.

15. Parliamentary Papers, Cmd. 3692 (1930).

16. See Warburg, "Why I Resigned," *New Palestine* 19 (October 24, 1930):109ff.

17. Chinitz, "Jewish Agency," p. 122; Weizmann to Felix Warburg (November 1930) and to Morris Rothenberg (December 24, 1930), Weizmann MSS.

18. New York *Times* (November 3 and 24, 1930).

19. Stephen S. Wise and Jacob deHaas, *The Great Betrayal* (New York, 1930); Wise to Meyer Weisgal (June 3, 1930), Weizmann MSS.

20. Felix Frankfurter, "The Palestine Situation Revisited," *Foreign Affairs* 9 (April 1931):409–34.

21. Harold J. Laski to Oliver Wendell Holmes, Jr. (June 15, November 22 and 30, and December 27, 1930) in Mark A. DeWolfe Howe, ed., *Holmes-Laski Letters* (2 vols.; Cambridge, Mass., 1953) 2:1261, 1296, 1298–99, 1301–2.

22. Stephen Wise to Meyer Weisgal (June 3, 1930), Weizmann MSS.

23. Chinitz, "Jewish Agency," p. 123.

24. For revisionism, see J. Schechtman and Y. Benari, *History of the Revisionist Movement* (Tel Aviv, 1970), and Schechtman's two-volume biography of Jabotinsky (New York, 1956 and 1961).

25. Joseph Salmark, "A review of the year 5690," Cincinnati *Every Friday* (September 19, 1930); Chinitz, "Jewish Agency," pp. 117–25.

26. See, for example, Stephen Wise to Israel Rosoff (December 17, 1930), Weizmann MSS.

27. Emanuel Neumann, "Whither Bound?," *New Palestine* 19 (September 5, 1930):53.

28. Weizmann to Morris Rothenberg (February 2, 1931), Weizmann MSS; New York *Times* (July 11, 1931).

29. Ibid. (November 9, 1931); Emanuel Neumann to London Executive (November 14, 1931), London Office Files, Z4/1315(3).

30. The most complete bibliography is the Yad Vashem *Guide to Jewish History Under Nazi Impact* in Hebrew, Yiddish, and English (9 vols.; New York, 1960–66); for a survey of some of the recent writing, see Gerd Korman, "The Holocaust in American Historical Writing," *Societas* 2 (Summer 1972):251–70.

31. Among others, see Wiesel's *Legends of Our Times* (New York, 1968) and *The Gates of the Forest* (New York, 1966).

32. Margaret K. Norden, "American Editorial Response to the Rise of Adolf Hitler: A Preliminary Consideration," *AJHQ* 59 (March 1970):290–301.

33. David Brody, "American Jewry, the Refugees, and Immigration Restriction," *PAJHS* 45 (June 1956):222–25; Rosenblueth, *Go Forth and Serve,* p. 256.

34. Stephen Wise to Julian Mack (December 28, 1931) in Voss, *Servant of the People,* pp. 170–71; Stephen Wise, "German Jewry at the Crossroads," *Opinion* (1932), quoted in Randye Kaye, "Stephen S. Wise and the Holocaust," seminar paper, State University of New York at Albany (April 1973).

35. Jacob Rader Marcus, "Zionism and the American Jew," *The American Scholar* 2 (May 1933):286; Stephen Wise to Julian Mack (March 1, 1933) in Voss, *Servant of the People,* p. 179.

36. Moshe Gottlieb, "The First of April Boycott and the Reaction of the American Jewish Community," *AJHQ* 57 (June 1968):527; New York *Times* (March 21, 1923).

37. Kaye, "Wise and the Holocaust"; Justine Wise Polier, "The Middle Years," *Congress Bi-Weekly* 35 (May 6, 1968):9–10; Wise to Brandeis (March 23, 1933) in Voss, *Servant of the People,* pp. 180–81.

38. New York *Times* (March 27 and 28, 1933); Wise, *Challenging Years,* p. 246.

39. Wise to Mack (March 29, 1933) in Voss, *Servant of the People,* p. 182.

40. Quoted in Zosa Szajkowski, "A Note on the American-Jewish Struggle Against Nazism and Communism in the 1930's," *AJHQ* 59 (March 1970):272.

41. Ralph Montgomery Easley to William Phillips (Undersecretary of State) (December 17, 1934), quoted ibid.:274.

42. Wise to Mack (June 7, 1933) in Voss, *Servant of the People,* p. 190.

43. *New Palestine* 23 (April 28, 1933):1; (July 1, 1933):1–20; New York *Times* (April 17, 1933).

44. Laqueur, *Zionism,* pp. 501, 503.

45. Quoted in Halperin, *Political World of American Zionism,* p. 21.

46. *Hadassah Newsletter* (October 1935), quoted in Miller, "Hadassah," p. 318.

47. Ibid., pp. 319–20; Levin, *Balm in Gilead,* ch. 10.

48. Samuel Lubell, *The Future of American Politics,* rev. ed. (New York, 1955), ch. 3.

49. Ibid., p. 220; Henry L. Feingold, *The Politics of Rescue: The Roosevelt Administration and the Holocaust, 1938–1945* (New Brunswick, N.J., 1970), p. 9.

50. Leuchtenburg, *Roosevelt and the New Deal,* pp. 101, 276; Arthur M. Schlesinger, Jr., *The Politics of Upheaval* (Boston, 1960), pp. 78–82.

51. Feingold, *Politics of Rescue*, pp. 8–9; Szajkowski, *Jews, Wars and Communism*.

52. Felix Frankfurter to Franklin D. Roosevelt (October 17, 1933), Roosevelt MSS, PPF/140; James G. MacDonald to Frankfurter (November 20, 1933), enclosed in Frankfurter to Roosevelt (November 23, 1933); also letters of April 14 and 23, 1934, all in Max Freedman, ed., *Roosevelt and Frankfurter, Their Correspondence, 1928–1945* (Boston, 1967), pp. 173–74, 211, 212–13.

53. Julian Mack to Roosevelt (January 30, 1935) and Roosevelt to Mack (February 12, 1935), Roosevelt MSS, PPF/2211; M. Maldwin Fertig, a New York attorney involved in Jewish affairs, at the White House's request arranged an interview among the President and Cyrus Adler and Louis Lipsky. Fertig to Roosevelt (February 7, 1935), ibid., OF/700.

54. Laqueur, *Zionism*, pp. 508–14.

55. Stephen Wise to Brandeis, (July 24, 1936) in Voss, *Servant of the People*, p. 213.

56. Roosevelt had also directed the State Department to provide the ZOA with any news it received about Palestinian events. Wise to Roosevelt, (May 18, 1936); Cordell Hull to Roosevelt (May 28, 1936); Roosevelt to Wise (June 8, 1936), Roosevelt MSS, OF/700.

57. Wise to John Haynes Holmes, (September 1936), in *Personal Letters*, pp. 233–34; Wise to Harry Friedenwald (October 12, 1936), Friedenwald MSS, A182/20.

58. Brandeis to Stephen Wise (September 4, 1936), R. Szold MSS.

59. Sir Herbert Samuel wrote to Felix Warburg of delays in securing visas. Warburg passed it on to New York Governor Herbert Lehman, who sent it to Roosevelt. The President checked with the State Department, and later reported to Lehman that the government had taken steps to ease the backlog. The entire correspondence is in Roosevelt MSS, OF/133.

60. Parliamentary Papers, Cmd. 5479 (1937).

61. New York *Times* (July 9, 1937).

62. See *Memorandum Submitted to the Palestine Royal Commission on American Interests in the Administration of the Palestine Mandate* (New York, 1936) signed by all the major groups in American Zionism: the Zionist Organization of America (per Stephen Wise), Hadassah (Rose Jacobs), Keren Hayesod (Louis Lipsky), the Jewish National Fund (Israel Goldstein), the Palestine Economic Corporation (Bernard Flexner), the American Economic Committee for Palestine (Israel Brodie), and Palestine Endowment Funds (Julian W. Mack).

63. For the group frustration of the non-Zionists, see Chinitz, "Jewish Agency," pp. 160ff. The early agitation for an American branch is noted in Hexter and Berkson to Ben-Gurion (January 19, 1934); memorandum by David Werner Senator, "The Future of the Enlarged Agency" (August 5, 1934); and Samuel Schulman to Cyrus Adler (August 12, 1934), all in Records of the Section for the Organization of Non-Zionists, S29/22, 23, and 81. The dispute over money for arms is in the correspondence among Ben-Gurion, Eliezar Kaplan, and Stephen Wise (August 20, 1936 to May 24, 1937), Mack MSS, File 20.

64. Halpern, *Idea of Jewish State,* p. 207.

65. Brandeis to Robert Szold (July 12, 1937), Mack MSS, File 24; New York *Times* (July 9, 1937).

66. Laqueur, *Zionism,* pp. 518–20. The ZOA Executive Committee voted in September to endorse the Congress resolution.

67. Parliamentary Papers, Cmd. 5634, 5893 (1938).

68. Stephen Wise to Harry Friedenwald (January 24, 1938), Friedenwald MSS, A182/20; Feingold, *Politics of Rescue,* p. 19.

69. Feingold, *Politics of Rescue,* pp. 24–25.

70. M. Maldwin Fertig to Roosevelt (March 25, 1938) and Marvin McIntyre to Fertig (March 31, 1938), Roosevelt MSS, PPF/5029.

71. Solomon Goldman to Cordell Hull (April 24, 1938); Joint Committee for Protection of Minorities to Roosevelt (April 26, 1938); U. S. ambassador in Poland to Secretary of State (April 26, 1938) and reply (April 30, 1938), and Judith Epstein to Cordell Hull (April 27, 1938), all in State Department Records, File 840.48.

72. Sumner Welles to Solomon Goldman (April 30, 1938), Wallace Murray (Chief, Near Eastern Division) to Judith Epstein (May 5, 1938), ibid.; Silverberg, *If I Forget Thee,* p. 161.

73. Feingold, *Politics of Rescue,* pp. 25–26.

74. Mark Wischnitzer, *To Dwell in Safety: The Story of Jewish Migration Since 1800* (Philadelphia, 1948), p. 201; Silverberg, *If I Forget Thee,* p. 162.

75. Rosenblueth, *Go Forth and Serve,* p. 273; Ruppin, *Memoirs,* p. 293; New York *Times* (July 5, 1938).

76. George Wadsworth to Secretary of State (July 11, 1938), State Department Records, 840.48; Manuel, *American-Palestine Relations,* p. 315.

77. New York *Times* (November 11, 1938).

78. Stephen Wise to Roosevelt (October 6, 1938), Roosevelt MSS, PPF/3292; Brandeis to Roosevelt (December 28, 1938), ibid.,

PSF/62; Benjamin V. Cohen to Missy LeHand (October 13, 1938) and Felix Frankfurter to Roosevelt (November 25, 1938) in Freedman, *Roosevelt and Frankfurter,* pp. 463, 466.

79. Feingold, *Politics of Rescue,* p. 42; Silverberg, *If I Forget Thee,* p. 166.

80. Benjamin V. Cohen to Missy LeHand (January 24, 1939), Roosevelt MSS, OF/700; Wise to John Hayne Holmes (January 1939) in *Personal Letters,* pp. 253–54.

81. Laqueur, *Zionism,* pp. 524–27.

82. Brandeis to Roosevelt (March 16, April 17, 1939), Henry Montor to Brandeis (May 8, 1939) and Sumner Welles to Roosevelt (May 11, 1939), all in Roosevelt MSS, PSF/62; Brandeis to Roosevelt (May 4, 1939), ibid., OF/700.

83. Goldie Meyerson to William L. Green, cable (April 21, 1939); Green to Roosevelt (April 25, 1939), ibid.

84. Weizmann, *Trial and Error,* p. 410.

85. R. C. Lindsay to Brandeis (March 6, 1939), Flexner MSS.

86. Parliamentary Papers, Cmd. 6019 (1939).

87. Laqueur, *Zionism,* p. 529; Parkes, *Emergence of the Jewish Problem,* p. 32.

88. Stephen Wise and Solomon Goldman to Roosevelt (May 17, 1939), Roosevelt MSS, PPF/3292; New York *Times* (June 26, 1939).

89. Maurice J. Karpf to Weizmann (July 7, 1939) and to David Werner Senator (August 3, 1939), Records of the Section for Organization of Non-Zionists, S29/99; Robert Szold to Executive (August 3, 1939), R. Szold MSS, 3/19.

NOTES TO EPILOGUES

A New Beginning

NOTES TO PAGES 418–422

1. Mark Lincoln Chadwin, *The Hawks of World War II* (Chapel Hill, N.C., 1968), pp. 8–15.

2. Leuchtenburg, *Roosevelt and the New Deal*, pp. 320–23.

3. David Werner Senator to members of the Agency Executive (April 5, 1940), Records of the Section for Non-Zionists, S29/100.

4. Chadwin, *Hawks*, pp. 210–11; Silverberg, *If I Forget Thee*, p. 181. In a report on the mood of the non-Zionists in the United States, David Werner Senator wrote: "[They] feel that the present situation in Palestine, the struggle with the British government, a certain Jewish attitude toward Arabs as expressed in the terrorist acts, may involve them in responsibilities, tactics and actions with which they cannot identify themselves. On the other hand, there is a very genuine, keen and earnest desire not to do anything which may do harm to the cause of Jewish Palestine at this critical hour." Senator to David Ben-Gurion (June 30, 1939), Records of the Section for Non-Zionists, S29/99.

5. Silverberg, *If I Forget Thee*, pp. 183–84.

6. CCAR *Yearbook* 45 (1935):103.

7. Halperin, *Political World*, pp. 23–24; Maurice Samuel, *Level Sunlight*, p. 60.

8. *New Palestine* 29 (June 23, 1939):10; Robert Szold to Brandeis (July 2, 1940), R. Szold MSS: Brandeis to Bernard Flexner (July 2, 1940), Flexner MSS; author's interview with Louis Levinthal (December 22, 1972).

9. Frankfurter, "Palestine Situation Revisited," *Foreign Affairs*, p. 415.

10. For the activities of the American Palestine Committee, see Halperin, *Political World*, pp. 179–86.

11. Emanuel Neumann to Brandeis (March 19, 1941), R. Szold MSS; Louis Lipsky to Editor, *New Palestine* 31 (July 18, 1941):12; Herbert Parzen, "American Zionism and the Quest for a Jewish State, 1939–43," *Herzl Year Book* 4 (1962):348.

12. Robert Szold, "The Issue Before the Convention," *New Palestine* 31 (July 18, 1941):9; "The Proposed Zionist Commission," ibid. (August 15, 1941):4–5; "The Main Task of the Convention," ibid. (September 5, 1941):4.

13. Halperin, *Political World,* p. 30.

14. David Ben-Gurion, "A Policy that Failed," *New Palestine* 32 (November 28, 1941):8.

15. "Stenographic Report of the Extraordinary Zionist Conference of the American Emergency Committee for Zionist Affairs" (May 9–11, 1942), at the Hotel Biltmore in New York, MS in Zionist Archives and Library, New York.

BIBLIOGRAPHIC ESSAY

Primary sources.

Fortunately for the historian, numerous manuscript collections are available depicting both the institutional developments and personal involvements. The most important collections are the Louis D. Brandeis Papers in the University of Louisville Law School and the Jacob deHaas Papers in the Zionist Archives and Library (ZAL) in New York: both men were inveterate collectors and threw practically nothing out. The records of the Zionist Organization in its early years are for the most part missing, but nearly all of the important memoranda, minutes of meetings, and policy statements between 1914 and 1921 can be found in one or both of these collections. The Chaim Weizmann Papers at the Library of the Weizmann Institute in Rehovot, Israel, are invaluable for the light they shed on American affairs, and naturally include material critical of the Brandeis leadership not available elsewhere. For the later years, the Robert Szold Papers and Julian W. Mack Papers (both ZAL), and two collections of the Stephen S. Wise Papers, one in the American Jewish Historical Society in Waltham, Massachusetts, and the other at the American Jewish Archives in Cincinnati, Ohio, were useful. The Abba Hillel Silver Papers at The Temple in Cleveland, Ohio, deal only marginally with early events, but become indispensable for the years after the Biltmore conference in 1942.

The records of the World Zionist Organization from the time of Herzl have been meticulously kept, and the Central Zionist Archives (CZA) in Jerusalem, Israel is a magnificent storehouse of historic materials. The records of the main Zionist offices in Vienna (1897–1905), Cologne (1905–11), and Berlin (1911–20) all shed light not only on developments in the movement worldwide, but on American relations with the WZO. Of especial significance is record group Z4, the files on the World Zionist Organization/the Jewish Agency for the years after 1917. For the war years, the papers of the Copenhagen office and the Palestine Amt were helpful, and for the later years the Zionist Executive, Section for the Organization of Non-Zionists, should be consulted.

Among individual collections, the Papers of Harry Friedenwald and Richard J. H. Gottheil (CZA) were most helpful for the early years of the Federation of American Zionists. For the years of the Brandeis leadership, the following proved useful: Judah Leon Magnes Papers in the Central Archives for the History of the Jewish People, Hebrew University, Jerusalem; the Israel Friedlaender Papers at the Jewish Theological Seminary in New York; the Felix Frankfurter Papers, some of which can be found in the CZA and the rest at the Law School of Harvard University, Cambridge, Massachusetts; the Bernard Flexner Papers (ZAL); and of especial value, the Nahum Sokolow Papers (CZA). The late Bernard Richards also allowed me to examine his files, then privately held at the Jewish Information Bureau in New York.

Among non-Zionists, the Papers of Louis Marshall, Jacob Schiff, and Felix Warburg at the American Jewish Archives in Cincinnati were indispensable. For the war period, one should also see the Woodrow Wilson, Henry Morgenthau, Sr., and Tasker Howard Bliss Papers, all in the Library of Congress, Washington, D.C.; the records of the United States Department of State in the National Archives, Washington; and the records of the British Foreign Office in the Public Records Office, London. The Franklin Delano Roosevelt Papers at the Roosevelt Library, Hyde Park, New York, contain much information on Zionist affairs and refugee problems in the 1930s. Of marginal interest were the Israel B. Brodie and Henrietta Szold (Private) Papers (CZA) and the Vladimir Jabotinsky Papers at the Jabotinsky Institute, Tel Aviv, Israel.

The files of the *Maccabean* (1901–20), the *New Maccabean* (1921), and the *New Palestine* (1921–42) provide an indispensable guide to attitudes and official positions of the FAZ and the ZOA. Digests of the daily Yiddish press can be found in the Brandeis Papers, and general events can be followed in the pages of the New York *Times.*

General works.

There is, unfortunately, no definitive history of the Zionist movement, although there have been several attempts. One of the earliest, Richard J. H. Gottheil, *Zionism* (Philadelphia: Jewish Publication Society, 1914), was primarily a propaganda work, although it contains interesting material on the early years of the movement. Nahum Sokolow's two-volume *History of Zionism, 1600–1918* (New York: Longmans, Green, 1919) attempted to prove that the Balfour Declaration had been the end product of three centuries of pro-Zionist sentiment in Great Britain. Although now out of date and unavailable in English, Adolph Böhm's *Die Zionistische Bewegung* (2 vols., Berlin: Jüdischer Verlag, 1935) was undoubtedly the best of the earlier works. The recent *History of Zionism* by Walter Laqueur (New York: Holt, Rinehart and Winston, 1972) is disappointing. Two popular studies worth consulting are Israel Cohen, *The Zionist Movement* (New York: ZOA, 1946), which represented the organization's official statement, and Rufus Learsi [pseud. Israel Goldberg], *Fulfillment: The Epic Story of Zionism* (Cleveland: World Publishing Company, 1951), a well-written account that, almost alone in such works, does not neglect the movement in the United States. In a special category there is Ben Halpern's *The Idea of a Jewish State,* 2nd ed. (Cambridge, Mass.: Harvard University Press, 1961), which does a fine job of placing Zionism in its several contexts, and the brilliant Introduction by Arthur Hertzberg to his anthology *The Zionist Idea* (New York: Herzl Press and Doubleday, 1959), the best single piece of intellectual history on Zionism available. The anthology itself provides samples of the most important Zionist writings in a single volume.

There are several histories of Jews and Judaism available, and one of the most useful is Howard Morley Sachar, *The Course of Modern Jewish History* (New York: Delta Books, 1958). For

Jewish life in Europe, the best single volume is Mark Zborowski and Elizabeth Herzog, *Life is with People* (New York: Schochen Books, 1962) which can be supplemented by Lucy S. Dawidowicz, ed., *The Golden Tradition: Jewish Life and Thought in Eastern Europe* (Boston: Beacon Press, 1967). Numerous facets of Jewish life can be explored in the various articles in Louis Finkelstein, ed., *The Jews: Their History, Culture, and Religion* (2 vols.: Harper & Row, New York, 1955), while Raphael Patai, *Tents of Jacob: The Diaspora —Yesterday and Today* (Englewood Cliffs, N.J.: Prentice-Hall, 1971) is unique in its exploration and explication of the *Galut*. For recent religious thought, see Joseph L. Blau, *Modern Varieties of Judaism* (New York: Columbia University Press, 1966), while an interesting economic interpretation is in Ellis Rivkind, *The Shaping of Jewish History* (New York: Charles Scribner's Sons, 1971).

Zionism in the United States has been all but ignored in most studies of the movement, although recently a number of scholars have begun turning their attention to this subject. Marnin Feinstein, *American Zionism, 1884–1904* (New York: Herzl Press, 1965) provides much information but little analysis of the Hoveve Zion; much better is Evyatar Friesel. *Ha-Tnuah Ha-Tzionit Be-Artzot Ha-Brit be-Shanim 1897–1914* (Tel Aviv: Hakibbutz Hameachud, 1970), which unfortunately has still not been translated into English. Isidore S. Meyer, ed., *Early History of Zionism in America* (New York: Theodore Herzl Foundation, 1958) and Raphael Patei, ed., *Studies in the History of Zionism in America: The Herzl Year Book* 5 (1963) both contain illuminating articles on specific people and areas. Although I disagree with some of his arguments, which ignore major political trends in American history, Yonathan Shapiro's *Leadership of the American Zionist Organization, 1897–1930* (Urbana, Ill.: University of Illinois Press, 1971) is the best single analysis of the movement in the United States in those years. Two popular histories that are laden with good anecdotal material are Robert Silverberg, *If I Forget Thee, O Jerusalem* (New York: William Morrow and Co., 1970) and Jacob A. Rubin, *Partners in State Building: American Jewry and Israel* (New York: Diplomatic Press, 1969). Samuel Halperin has done a fine study of *The Political World of American Zionism* (Detroit: Wayne State University

Press, 1961), of which only the early chapters were applicable to this study, and the same is true for Joseph B. Schechtman, *The United States and the Jewish State Movement: The Crucial Decade, 1939–1949* (New York: Thomas Yoseloff, 1966).

Judaism in the United States has been the subject of many works, and here again the reader may choose from a wide range. Jacob Rader Marcus has provided the definitive study for the early years in *The Colonial American Jew: Fourteen Ninety–Two—Seventeen Seventy–Six* (3 vols., Detroit: Wayne State University Press, 1969), while material between the Revolution and the Jacksonian eras can be found in Joseph L. Blau and Salo W. Baron, eds., *The Jews of the United States, 1790–1840: A Documentary History* (3 vols., New York: Columbia University Press, 1963). The best single volume is Oscar Handlin, *Adventure in Freedom: Three Hundred Years of Jewish Life in America* (New York: McGraw-Hill Co., 1954), while the Hebrew Union College *Essays in American Jewish History* (Cincinnati: American Jewish Archives, 1958) has several interesting pieces. Oscar I. Janowsky, ed., *The American Jew: A Composite Portrait* (New York: Harper & Brothers, 1942) is useful for the prewar community, while Nathaniel Weyl, *The Jew in American Politics* (New Rochelle, N.Y.: Arlington House, 1968) casts a critical eye on that subject. For religion, see Nathan Glazer, *American Judaism* (Chicago: University of Chicago Press, 1957); Moshe Davis has provided a first-rate monograph on *The Emergence of Conservative Judaism* (Philadelphia: Jewish Publication Society, 1965), a work that only highlights the absence of comparable works on Orthodox and Reform. Although sorely out of date, David Philipson, *The Reform Movement in Judaism,* 2nd ed. (New York: Macmillan, 1931), is still the most reliable source. For the heart of the debate on shifts in theological issues, as well as the attitude toward Zionism, see the debates in the CCAR *Yearbooks* for 1936–38, while Sefton D. Temkin has written a concise but thorough appraisal of the UAHC in "A Century of Reform Judaism in America," *American Jewish Year Book* (1973), pp. 3–75.

Much of the background for this work is drawn from sources dealing with other aspects of American history, citations for which can be found in the text. Of especial interest, however, is Jerry

Israel, ed., *The Organizational Society* (New York: The Free Press, 1972) and Robert Wiebe, *The Search for Order, 1877–1920* (New York: Hill and Wang, 1967), both of which provide an appropriate context in which to study Zionism. For the most part, though, Jacob Talmon's complaint that the "Jewish component" is missing from most general histories is certainly borne out in American historiography.

Memoirs, biographies, and collected works.

If nothing else, the Zionists have certainly been prolific in the production of their reminiscences. Among the European leaders, Chaim Weizmann's *Trial and Error* (New York: Harper and Brothers, 1949) is not only a personal memoir, but is practically a history of the movement. Much of it, however, is colored by his experiences in factional strife, and this is especially true in his account of the American Zionists. For a useful corrective, see Oskar K. Rabinowicz, *Fifty Years of Zionism: A Historical Analysis of Dr. Weizmann's "Trial and Error"* (London: Robert Anscombe & Co., Ltd., 1952). Weizmann's *Letters and Papers* have begun to appear slowly in a fine letterpress edition (London: Oxford University Press, 1968–), and the reader would also find of interest a series of appreciative essays in Meyer Weisgal, ed., *Chaim Weizmann* (New York: Dial Press, 1944). Other memoirs of European leaders that are useful include Max Isidore Bodenheimer, *Prelude to Israel,* Israel Cohen, tr. (New York and London: Thomas Yoseloff, 1963); Nahum Goldman, *Sixty Years of Jewish Life* (New York: Holt, Rinehart and Winston, 1969); Shmaryahu Levin, *Forward from Exile,* tr. and abridged from the original three volumes by Maurice Samuel (Philadelphia: Jewish Publication Society, 1967); Martin Rosenblueth, *Go Forth and Serve* (New York: Herzl Press, 1961); and Alex Bein, ed., *Arthur Ruppin: Memoirs, Diaries, Letters,* Karen Gershon, tr. (New York: Herzl Press, 1972).

Among American Zionists, the following were most useful: Harlan B. Phillips, ed., *Felix Frankfurter Reminisces* (New York: Reynal & Co., 1960); Julian Haber, *The Odyssey of an American Zionist* (New York: Twayne Publishers, 1956); Bernard Hourwich, *My First Eighty Years* (Chicago: Argus Books, 1939), is especially good on the movement in the Midwest; Louis Lipsky, *Thirty Years of American Zionism* (New York: Nesher Publishing Co., 1927), provides invaluable material on the Federation; Bernard A. Rosenblatt, *Two Generations of Zionism* (New York: Shengold Publishers, 1967); Julius Simon, *Certain Days,* Evyatar Friesel, ed. (Jerusalem: Israel Universities Press, 1971); and Meyer Weisgal, . . . *So Far* (Jerusalem: Weidenfeld and Nicolson, 1971). The best by far is Stephen S. Wise, *Challenging Years* (New York: G. P. Putnam's Sons, 1949). Dr. Emanuel Neumann kindly permitted me to read his memoirs in manuscript, and when they are published in the near future they will prove an indispensable source to historians of American Zionism. The memoirs of Abba Hillel Silver, at The Temple in Cleveland, remained unfinished at the time of his death.

Other autobiographical works that shed light both on Zionism and American Jewish life were: Cyrus Adler, *I Have Considered the Days* (Philadelphia: Jewish Publication Society, 1941); Philip Cowen, *Memories of an American Jew* (New York: International Press, 1932); Adolf Kraus, *Reminiscences and Comments* (Chicago: Privately printed, 1925); Sol Liptzin, *Generation of Decision: Jewish Rejuvenation in America* (New York: Bloch Publishing Co., 1958); David Philipson, *My Life as an American Jew* (Cincinnati: John G. Kidd & Son, 1941), is a remarkable record of a productive life as well as an unchanging anti-Zionism; and Morris Waldman, *Nor by Power* (New York: International Universities Press, 1953), also reflects the old-line American Jewish Committee aversion to Zionism.

A very special type of memoir is the oral history interview. I conducted several of these in the course of research on this book, and the tapes and transcripts of those sessions are now on deposit in the Oral History Collection of the Institute of Contemporary Jewry at the Hebrew University in Jerusalem. These include interviews with Rabbi Israel Goldstein, Mrs. Rose Halprin, Mrs. Charlotte Jacobson, Hon. Louis Levinthal, and Robert Szold. In the same collection I utilized the interviews of George Backer, Bernard G. Richards, Bernard A. Rosenblatt, and Edward Warburg. In addition, there is a much more extensive interview with Bernard G.

Richards on deposit at the Oral History Collection at Columbia University.

While Louis D. Brandeis did not write his memoirs, we do have a wealth of information about him. The most comprehensive biography is Alpheus T. Mason, *Brandeis: A Free Man's Life* (New York: Viking Press, 1946), which may be supplemented by Melvin I. Urofsky, *A Mind of One Piece: Brandeis and American Reform* (New York: Charles Scribner's Sons, 1971). His letters are now available in Melvin I. Urofsky and David W. Levy, eds., *Letters of Louis D. Brandeis* (4 vols. to date; Albany, N.Y.: State University of New York Press, 1971–). Brandeis' family background is portrayed in Frederika Dembitz Brandeis, *Reminiscences,* Alice G. Brandeis, tr. (privately printed, 1943). Jacob deHaas, *Louis D. Brandeis: A Biographical Sketch* (New York: Bloch Publishing Co., 1929), is practically idolatrous, but contains much useful information on Brandeis' Zionist work. Many of his Zionist writings are collected by Solomon Goldman, *Brandeis on Zionism* (Washington: ZOA, 1942).

Unfortunately, only a few other members of the Zionist leadership have been given adequate biographical treatment. Harry Barnard, *The Forging of an American Jew: The Life and Times of Judge Julian Mack* (New York: Herzl Press, 1974), appeared too late for me to utilize. Marvin Lowenthal presents a full and sympathetic portrait of Henrietta Szold in *Henrietta Szold: Life and Letters* (New York: Viking Press, 1942), while Harry Friedenwald receives a similar treatment in Alexander Levin, *Vision* (Philadelphia: Jewish Publication Society, 1964). Norman Bentwich deals sympathetically but not uncritically with the controversial Judah Magnes in *For Zion's Sake: A Biography of Judah L. Magnes* (Philadelphia: Jewish Publication Society, 1954). In a special category is Louis Lipsky, *A Gallery of Zionist Profiles* (New York: Farrar, Straus and Cudahy, 1956), which provides an intimate and often acerbic view of the men Lipsky worked with for over a half century.

Regrettably, there are no good published biographies of Stephen S. Wise, Felix Frankfurter, or Abba Hillel Silver. The defect for Wise is partially compensated for in two volumes of his letters. The one edited by Carl Herman Voss, *Stephen S. Wise: Servant of the People* (Philadelphia: Jewish Publication Society, 1969) has much biographical material, while his children, Justine Wise Polier and James Waterman Wise, in *The Personal Letters of Stephen S. Wise* (Boston: Beacon Press, 1956) provide us with a good portrait of his nonpublic side. In addition, some of his more important speeches are in *As I See It* (New York: Jewish Opinion Publishing Corp., 1944). Frankfurter's connection with Zionism in the 1930s is only partially seen in Max Freedman, *Roosevelt and Frankfurter, Their Correspondence* (Boston: Little, Brown and Co., 1967), while some of Silver's more important speeches are collected in *Vision and Victory* (New York: ZOA, 1949). Among the important non-Zionists, Jacob Schiff has received a worshipful treatment in Cyrus Adler, *Jacob Schiff: His Life and Letters* (2 vols., New York: Doubleday, Page & Co., 1928), while Morton Rosenstock admirably examines *Louis Marshall: Defender of Jewish Rights* (Detroit: Wayne State University Press, 1965). A much more comprehensive portrait of Marshall emerges in Charles Reznikoff, ed., *Louis Marshall, Champion of Liberty: Selected Papers and Addresses* (2 vols., Philadelphia: Jewish Publication Society, 1957). There is still a great need for definitive scholarly biographies of both men.

Among Europeans who were involved in American Zionist affairs, in one way or another, Marie Syrkin gives us an affectionate yet critical portrait of her father in *Nachman Syrkin, Socialist Zionist* (New York: Herzl Press, 1961). Simcha Kling's biographies *Nahum Sokolow: Servant of His People* (New York: Herzl Press, 1960) and *The Mighty Warrior: The Life Story of Menahem Ussischkin* (New York: Jonathan David, 1965) are both superficial. Theodore Herzl, on the other hand, has been exhaustively studied by historians. The definitive biography is Alex Bein, *Theodore Herzl*, Maurice Samuel, tr. (Philadelphia: Jewish Publication Society, 1942), which is far superior to Jacob deHaas's *Theodore Herzl: A Biographical Study* (2 vols., Chicago: The Leonard Co., 1927). Marvin Lowenthal has edited and translated *The Diaries of Theodore Herzl* (New York: Dial Press, 1956), while Joseph Adler, *The Herzl Paradox* (New York: Hadrian Press-Herzl Press, 1962) examined his political, social, and economic theories. Herzl's major works, including *The Jewish State* and *Altneuland,* as well as most of his minor essays, are also readily available in English.

American Jewry and Zionism.

The attitude of Jewish immigrants to the United States is examined by Joel S. Geffen in two articles in the *American Jewish Historical Quarterly* (*AJHQ*) 51 (March 1962):149–67, and 59 (December 1969):179–200. Immigration itself is examined in general by Philip Taylor, *The Distant Magnet: European Emigration to the United States* (New York: Harper & Row, 1971), and for Jews in particular in Mark Wischnitzer, *To Dwell in Safety: The Story of Jewish Migration since 1800* (Philadelphia: Jewish Publication Society, 1948). The reaction of Americans to the immigrants can be seen in John Higham, *Strangers in the Land: Patterns of American Nativism, 1860–1925* (New York: Atheneum, 1963 ed.), and his later thoughts on the subject, "American Anti-Semitism Historically Reconsidered," in C. H. Stember, et al., *Jews in the Minds of America* (New York: Basic Books, 1966), pp. 237–58. A favorable interpretation of American attitudes is Oscar Handlin, "American Views of the Jew at the Opening of the Twentieth Century," *Publications of the American Jewish Historical Society* (*PAJHS*) 40 (1951):323–44, which should be read with Stephen Steinberg, "How Jewish Quotas Began," *Commentary* 52 (September 1971):67–76. For efforts to deal with immigrants, see Edward G. Hartmann, *The Movement to Americanize the Immigrant* (New York: Columbia University Press, 1948); the same subject receives a great deal of attention in Lawrence A. Cremin, *The Transformation of the School* (New York: Alfred Knopf, 1961). Of particular applicability see M. Soltes, *The Yiddish Press: An Americanization Agency* (New York: Teachers College Press, 1950). The changing attitudes of progressives toward acceptance of cultural diversity is marked by Horace Kallen, *Cultural Pluralism and the American Idea* (Philadelphia, 1956).

For Jewish attitudes toward the "new" immigration, a number of studies are available. Originally most scholars stressed the antipathies of the older Sephardic and Germanic communities, such as in

Zosa Szajkowski, "The Attitudes of American Jews to East European Immigrants (1881–1893)," *PAJHS* 40 (1950):221–80, and in Myron Berman, "The Attitude of American Jewry Toward East European Jewish Immigration, 1881–1914," doctoral dissertation, (Columbia University, 1963). This view was questioned by Esther L. Panitz, who in two articles first showed that serious differences existed in the established communities and that the immigrants had many defenders: see *AJHQ* 53 (December 1963):99–130 and 55 (September 1965):57–97. Szajkowski has also revised his earlier estimates in "The *Yahudi* and the Immigrant: A Reappraisal," *AJHQ* 63 (September 1973):13–44.

Two of the most famous contemporary studies of the immigrant Jewish community were Jacob Riis's caustic *How the Other Half Lives* (New York: Charles Scribner's Sons, 1890) and the corrective offered by Hutchins Hapgood, *The Spirit of the Ghetto* (New York: Funk and Wagnalls, 1902), both of which are now available in inexpensive editions. The arrival of the older Jewish communities is explored in Hyman Grinstein, *The Rise of the Jewish Community of New York, 1654–1860* (Philadelphia: Jewish Publication Society, 1945), while Moses Rischin has given us a definitive portrait of the new immigrants in *The Promised City: New York's Jews, 1870–1914* (Cambridge, Mass.: Harvard Unversity Press, 1962). On a more anecdotal, but highly fascinating and informative level, see Stephen Birmingham, *Our Crowd* (New York: Harper & Row, 1967) and Ande Manners, *Poor Cousins* (New York: Coward, McCann & Geoghegan, Inc., 1972). A specialized study is Milton Doroshkin, *Yiddish in America* (Rutherford, N.J.: Fairleigh Dickinson University Press, 1969), and see also Melech Epstein, *Jewish Labor in the United States* (2 vols., New York: Trade Union Sponsoring Committee, 1950). One should also take note of the many useful studies of Jewish communities in some of the smaller American cities.

For efforts to organize American Jewry, begin with Allan Tarshish, "The Board of Delegates of American Israelites (1859–1878)," *PAJHS* 49 (September 1959):16–32, and Zosa Szajkowski, "The Alliance Israelite Universelle in the United States, 1860–1949," *PAJHS* 39 (1950):389–442. Arthur A. Goren, *New York*

Jews and the Quest for Community: The Kehillah Experiment, 1908–1922 (New York: Columbia University Press, 1970), shows how the diverse Jewish groups in the nation's largest Jewish center tried to unite, while Barbara Miller Solomon's *Pioneers in Service* (Boston: Associated Jewish Philanthropies, 1956) explores the successful efforts of Boston's Jewish philanthropies to unite for better service to the community. The most important and influential Jewish group prior to 1916 was, of course, the American Jewish Committee. It has been favored with two good studies, Nathan Schachner, *The Price of Liberty* (New York: American Jewish Committee, 1948), and the more recent Naomi W. Cohen, *Not Free to Desist* (Philadelphia: Jewish Publication Society, 1972). The Committee's anti-Zionism is detailed in Moses Rischin, "The Early Attitude of the American Jewish Committee to Zionism (1906–1922)," *PAJHS* 49 (1959):188–201.

The reaction of Reform Judaism to Zionism is analyzed in Naomi Wiener, "Reform Judaism in America and Zionism, 1897–1922," masters essay (Columbia University, 1949), and Joseph P. Sternstein, "Reform Judaism and Zionism," *Herzl Year Book* 5 (1963): 11–31, although Herschel Levin, "The Other Side of the Coin," ibid., pp. 33–56, cites some early pro-Zionist sentiment in Reform ranks. For changing attitudes as expressed in Reform journals, see Hayyim Tzafun [Jonathan M. Brown]'s prize essay on deposit at the Hebrew Union College library (1967). For Orthodox and Conservative reaction, see Hyman B. Grinstein, "Orthodox Judaism and Early Zionism in America" in Meyer, *Early History of Zionism*, pp. 219–27, and Herbert L. Parzan, "Conservative Judaism and Zionism, 1896–1922," *Jewish Social Studies* 23 (October 1961): 235–64.

A practically contemporaneous evaluation of nineteenth-century Zionist activity in the United States is Max Kohler, "Some Early Zionist Projects," *PAJHS* 8 (1900):75–118, and the same journal carried Hyman Grinstein's edition of Dr. Joseph Isaac Bluestone's fragmentary memoir, which is very useful for the Hoveve Zion, 35 (1939):53–64. For general American connections to Palestine, see Moshe Davis, "American Relationship to Eretz Yisrael in Historical Perspective," *AJHQ* 62 (September 1972):5ff. Other materials related to early Zionism include "Fifty Years of American Zionism, 1897–1947: A Documentary Record," *The Palestine Yearbook* 3 (1947–48):383–430; Herbert L. Parzan, "The Federation of American Zionists (1897–1914)" in Meyer, *Early History of Zionism,* pp. 245–74; and Abraham Goldberg, "American Zionism up to the Brandeis Era" in Joseph Shalom Shubow, ed., *The Brandeis Avukah Annual of 1932,* pp. 549–68. For Labor Zionism see A. Kretchmar-Isreeli, "The Poale-Zion Movement." *Jewish Communal Register of New York* (New York: The Kehillah, 1918), pp. 1374–83, and C. Bezalel Sherman, "The Beginnings of Labor Zionism in the United States" in Meyer, *Early History of Zionism,* pp. 275–88, which should be supplemented by Bernard H. Bloom, "Yiddish-Speaking Socialists in America, 1892–1905," *American Jewish Archives* 12 (April 1960):34–70. Samuel Rosenblatt, *The History of the Mizrachi Movement* (New York: Mizrachi Org., 1951), is very superficial, and is mainly an informational piece issued by the organization.

The Brandeis years.

A number of studies have attempted to determine the roots of Brandeis' involvement in Zionism, but none of them is, to my mind, convincing. Stuart M. Geller, "Why Did Louis D. Brandeis Choose Zionism?," *AJHQ* 62 (June 1973):383–400, finds the answer in economic factors, while Ben Halpern, "Brandeis' Way to Zionism," *Midstream* 17 (October 1971):3–13, believes it to be a form of blood return to the family. A totally unfounded charge is made by Yonathan Shapiro, "American Jews in Politics: The Case of Louis D. Brandeis," *AJHQ* 55 (December 1965):199–211, who alleges that Brandeis turned to Zionism in order to further his political ambitions within the Wilson administration; Shapiro's thesis of marginality, set forth in *Leadership of the American Zionist Movement* cited above is much more convincing. Ezekiel Rabinowitz, *Justice Louis D. Brandeis: The Zionist Chapter of His Life* (New York: Philosophical Library, 1968) offers a good sampling of documents, but no explanation, while the biographies by Mason and deHaas are also silent as to intent. My own guess has been spelled out in *A Mind of One Piece,* Chapter 5, but the reader can find the best guide in Brandeis' Zionism in his own writings. The more important statements are collected in Goldman's *Brandeis on Zionism;* the most important single document is Brandeis' *The Jewish Problem: How to Solve It* (New York: Zionist Essays Publication Committee, 1915), which was kept in print by the ZOA until the founding of the State of Israel.

Hadassah, unfortunately, has not received the scholarly attention that it deserves. Midge Decter, "The Legacy of Henrietta Szold," *Commentary* 30 (December 1960):480–88 is a marvelously appreciative and perceptive interpretation of what Miss Szold meant to American Jewish women, while Rose Jacobs, "Beginnings of Hadassah" in Meyer, *Early History of Zionism,* pp. 228–44, is the recollection of a past president. A new book, Marlin Levin, *Balm in Gilead* (New York: Schocken Books, 1973), is primarily anecdotal, and although almost devoid of analysis, tells a good deal about Hadassah's medical and social work in Palestine and Israel. The only good examination of the structural and political development of the organization is Donald Herbert Miller, "A History of Hadassah, 1912–1935," doctoral dissertation (New York University, 1968). Other Zionist groups have also received very little historical treatment, although Samuel Grand fills in one part of the gap in "A History of Zionist Youth Organizations in the United States from Their Inception to 1940," doctoral dissertation (Columbia University, 1950).

The fight over the Congress is well documented in Alvin S. Roth, "Background and Origin of the American Jewish Congress," rabbinic thesis (Hebrew Union College, 1953). Bernard G. Richards, *Organizing American Jewry* (New York: Jewish Information Bureau, 1947) traces some of the earlier efforts to bring all segments of the community together, while Moses Rischin, "The American Jewish Committee and Zionism, 1906–1922," *Herzl Year Book* 5 (1963): 65–81 looks at the conflict in terms of institutional and organizational prestige. The exchange between Brandeis and Adler was issued as *The Jewish Congress versus the American Jewish Committee* (New York: Congress Organizing Committee, 1915), while several articles on the early and middle years of the Congress appeared in a special issue of the *Congress Bi-Weekly* (May 6, 1968). A useful corrective to the anti-Russian portrait of Louis Marshall that appeared during the Congress fight is Lucy S. Dawidowicz, "Louis Marshall's Yiddish newspaper, *The Jewish World:* A Study in Contrasts," masters thesis (Columbia University, 1961).

For relief service during the war years, the best single source is the monographic study by Zosa Szajkowski, "The Private and Organized American Jewish Overseas Relief, 1914–1938," published in six installments, *AJHQ* (beginning September 1967) 57:52–106, 191–54, 285–352; 58:376–407, 484–506; 59:83–138. Joseph C. Hyman's *Twenty-Five Years of American Relief to Jews Overseas* (New York: Joint Distribution Committee, 1939) is the quarter-century report of the Joint Distribution Committee, and one should also see the annual reports of the JDC and articles in *The American Jewish Yearbook* during this period.

Frank E. Manuel, *The Realities of American-Palestine Relations* (Washington, D.C.: Public Affairs Press, 1949), although covering a much broader spectrum and now out of date, continues to be the best source on that subject for the World War I years. The reaction of Jewish immigrants in America to World War I is detailed in Joseph Rappaport, "Jewish Immigrants and World War I: A Study in Yiddish Press Reaction," doctoral dissertation (Columbia University, 1951), while the same author attempts to place Zionism within the context of a world power struggle in Meyer, *Early History of Zionism,* pp. 297–325. Zosa Szajkowski, *Jews, Wars and Communism* (New York: KTAV Publishing House, 1972), covers many facets of Jewish life during this period.

The standard work on the British promise to Zionism is Leonard Stein's monumental *The Balfour Declaration* (New York: Simon & Schuster, 1961), but a recent work by Isaiah Friedman, *The Question of Palestine, 1914–1918* (New York: Schocken Books, 1973) does much to revise earlier estimates of Weizmann's role, and also pays close attention to British negotiations with the Arabs. Both authors, however, conclude that the architects of the Declaration intended it to mean the creation of a Jewish commonwealth in the Holy Land. The role of American Jews and politicians in the negotiations has occasioned much debate. Herbert Parzan, "Brandeis and the Balfour Declaration," *Herzl Year Book* 5 (1963):309–50, and Ben Halpern, "Brandeis and the Origins of the Balfour Declaration," unpublished paper (ZAL), both accuse the Justice of adopting an indifferent and passive attitude when action was essential, while Selig Adler, "The Palestine Question in the Wilson Era," *Jewish Social Studies* 10 (October 1948):303–34, accuses Secretary of State Lansing and Colonel House of anti-Semitism and duplicity. Richard Ned Lebow, "Woodrow Wilson and the Balfour Declaration," *Journal of Modern History* 40 (December 1968):501–23, suggests that the President did not realize how important affirmation was to the hesitant British Cabinet. For reception of the document in the United States, see Charles Israel Goldblatt, "The Impact of the Balfour Declaration in America," *AJHQ* 57 (June 1968):455–515. The bizarre effort of Henry Morgenthau to negotiate a special peace is delineated in William Yale, "Ambassador Henry Morgenthau's Special Mission of 1917," *World Politics* 1 (April 1949):308–20. Morgenthau's autobiography, *All in a Lifetime* (Garden City: Doubleday, Page & Co., 1922) is worth a brief perusal.

For Zionism at the Peace Conference, a number of works previously cited contain much useful information, especially Reznikoff's book on Marshall and Manuel, *American-Palestine Relations*. Oscar I. Janowsky, *The Jews and Minority Rights, 1898–1919* (New York: Columbia University Press, 1933) has much useful information on the goals of the Jewish delegations at Paris, as does Allan Taylor, *Prelude to Israel: An Analysis of Zionist Diplomacy, 1897–1947* (New York: Philosophical Library, 1959). David Hunter Miller, *My Diary at the Conference of Paris* (21 vols., privately printed, 1924), has nearly all of the relevant documents on Palestine and Jewish matters. An anti-Zionist tract published in an effort to influence the peacemakers was Morris Jastrow, *Zionism and the Future of Palestine: The Fallacies and Dangers of Political Zionism* (New York: The MacMillan Company, 1919), a position strongly attacked in Horace M. Kallen, *Zionism and World Politics* (Garden City: Doubleday, Page & Co., 1921). The early chapters of Irwin Oder's doctoral dissertation deal with the U. S. Government's interpretation of the mandate; "The United States and the Palestine Mandate, 1920–1948: A Study of the Impact of Interest Groups on Foreign Policy" (Columbia University, 1956). In this area, see also Joseph P. O'Grady, ed., *The Immigrant Influence on Wilson's Peace Policies* (Lexington, Ky.: University of Kentucky Press, 1967).

The events leading up to the schism between Brandeis and Weizmann must be pieced together from numerous sources, most of which, unfortunately, are polemical. Weizmann's *Trial and Error*, written a quarter century later, reflected how embittered he remained; Meyer Weisgal's . . . *So Far* and Maurice Samuels, *Level Sunlight* (New York: Alfred A. Knopf, 1953) both reflected their chief's view. Samuel M. Melamed, "L. D. Brandeis and Chaim Weizmann," *The Reflex* 2 (May 1928):1–10 was an all-out attack on Brandeis' alleged shortcomings as a Jew, while Judd Teller, "America's Two Zionist Traditions," *Commentary* 20 (October 1955):343–52 took a similar but more balanced view. The most scholarly examination of these events is unfortunately unpublished, an essay by Esther L. Panitz, "Louis Dembitz Brandeis and the Cleveland Convention" (ZAL). Most of the relevant documents have been assembled in Evyatar Friesel, "Ha-maabek bain Brandeis v'Weizmann," (Mimeo, Beer-Sheva: University of the Negev, n.d.). Some of the friction between the Americans and Europeans is recalled in Robert Szold, *77 Great Russell Street,* a brief memoir of his years at Zionist headquarters and on the Palestine Commission (New York: privately printed, 1967)

The interwar years.

One of the most written-about aspects of Zionism is the development of the Holy Land under British rule. Of especial interest are the following: Maurice Samuel, *Harvest in the Desert* (New York: Alfred A. Knopf, 1944); Norman and Helen Bentwich, *Mandate Memoirs, 1919–1948* (New York: Schocken Books, 1965), which relates Palestinian development to outside events; Paul L. Hanna, *British Policy in Palestine* (Washington, D.C.: American Council on Public Affairs, 1942); Neville Barbour, *Palestine: Star or Crescent* (New York: Odyssey Press, 1947), which pays considerable attention to developing Arab nationalism; and, of course, the massive Fannie Fern Andrews, *The Holy Land Under the Mandate* (2 vols., Boston: Houghton Mifflin Co., 1931). Documents regarding British policy can be found in Jacob C. Hurewitz, *Diplomacy in the Near and Middle East,* Vol. 2: *A Documentary Record* (Princeton: Van Nostrand, 1956), and the official *Documents on British Foreign Policy, 1919–1939* (London: Her Majesty's Stationary Office, 1946–). The reversal of British policy is indicated in Stephen S. Wise and Jacob deHaas, *The Great Betrayal* (New York: Brentano's 1930).

The one major achievement of American Zionists during the 1920s is looked at in Irwin Oder, "American Zionism and the Congressional Resolution of 1922 on Palestine," *PAJHS* 45 (1955):35–47. Weizmann became a regular commuter to the United States in these years, and a good sampling of his message can be found in ,Weizmann, *American Addresses* (New York: Keren Hayesod, 1923). His long-sought unity of Zionists and non-Zionists, and the effects it had, are looked at critically in Sam Z. Chinitz, "The Jewish Agency and the Jewish Community in the United States," masters essay (Columbia University, 1959). Nearly all of the material on American Zionists activities, including the reunification of the movement, came from archival sources and the numerous articles in the *New Palestine.*

The literature on the Holocaust is immense, and for particular areas one should see the *Guide to Jewish History Under Nazi Impact* (9 vols., New York: YIVO Institute for Jewish Research and Yad Vashem, 1960–66); for a brief survey of the impact on American Jewish writing, see Gerd Korman, "The Holocaust in American Historical Writing," *Societas* 2 (Summer 1972):251–70. For background on European anti-Semitism, see James Parkes, *The Emergence of the Jewish Problems, 1878–1939* (London: Oxford University Press, 1939) and the very stimulating article by Jacob L. Talmon, "European History—Seedbed of the Holocaust," *Midstream* 19 (May 1973):3–25.

For particular aspects of the American Jewish struggle against fascism, see the following articles: David Brody, "American Jewry, the Refugees and Immigration Restriction," *PAJHS* 45 (June 1956): 219–47; Moshe Gottlieb, "The First of April Boycott and the Reaction of the American Jewish Community," *AJHQ* 57 (June 1968): 516–56; Margaret K. Norden, "American Editorial Response to the

Rise of Adolf Hitler: A Preliminary Consideration," *AJHQ* 59 (March 1970):290–300, which looks at more than just Jewish papers; and Zosa Szajkowski, "A Note on the American Jewish Struggle Against Nazism and Communism in the 1930's," *AJHQ* 59 (March 1970):272–89.

The wavering policy of the Roosevelt administration toward involvement in the war has been studied by many scholars, but for specific purposes one should see Mark L. Chadwin, *The Hawks of World War II* (Chapel Hill: University of North Carolina Press, 1968), which looks at Jewish involvement in the pro-Allied campaigns. A colloquim edited by Selig Adler looked at American policy toward Palestine in the 1930s, *AJHQ* 62 (September 1972):11–29. Two damning indictments of Roosevelt's policy on refugees are Arthur D. Morse, *While Six Million Died: A Chronicle of American Apathy* (New York: Random House, 1967), and Henry L. Feingold, *The Politics of Rescue: The Roosevelt Administration and the Holocaust, 1938–1945* (New Brunswick, N.J.: Rutgers University Press, 1970).

INDEX